COUNTER-REVOLUTION

COUNTER-REVOLUTION

*The Second Civil War
and its Origins, 1646–8*

ROBERT ASHTON

YALE UNIVERSITY PRESS
NEW HAVEN AND LONDON · 1994

Set in Bembo by Best-set Typesetter Ltd., Hong Kong
Printed and bound in Great Britain by The Bath Press, Avon

Library of Congress Cataloging-in-Publication Data

Ashton, Robert.
    Counter-revolution : the second civil war and its origins, 1646–8
    Robert Ashton.
      p. cm.
    Includes bibliographical references and index.
    ISBN 0–300–06114–5
    1. Great Britain—History—Civil War, 1642–1649.
  2. Counterrevolutionaries—Great Britain—History—17th century.
  I. Title.
    DA415.A79 1994
    941.06′2—dc20   94–19546
                                          CIP

A catalogue record for this book is available from the British Library.

In Memoriam
Brian Patrick Lyndon

CONTENTS

LIST OF ILLUSTRATIONS

The following illustrations are between pages 234 and 235.

PREFACE AND
ACKNOWLEDGEMENTS

This book, the product of research over many years both before and after my retirement from academic life, is very different from the one which I originally planned to write. When working on my earlier and more general study, *The English Civil War*, I became increasingly aware of the abundant scope and the need for a detailed modern study of the years after the end of the First Civil War. What I first contemplated was a very large book in two parts: the first part dealing with the period between the two civil wars and, while doing the utmost to avoid the temptations of hindsight, focussing around the origins of the Second Civil War; and the second part dealing with the second war itself with special attention accorded to the complex problems of strategy, co-ordination, the links between the various risings, and, more particularly, to the even more complex and often intractable questions relating to the relationship between the leaders of these revolts and their mostly obscure followers down to the lowest possible level. In other words, one of the main tasks which I envisaged undertaking in Part II was a large-scale exercise in network analysis and to that end I collected a vast amount of detail relating to the insurgents whose names I encountered in the course of my research. But it has become clear that such a study would require not two parts of a large book, but two large volumes. The materials for a second volume still remain, mostly, though not completely, unused in the enormous card index of participants which I have constructed over the years and it is possible that they may serve as a basis for another book. As it is, this present volume is, except for the penultimate chapter, more or less the originally planned Part I. The other characteristic which it has in common with my original concep-tion is sheer length. Although every draft chapter has been subjected to agonizing cuts, I have always had to bear in mind the fact that, in such a study as this, detail is in effect at a premium. A glance at the chapter subheadings will quickly reveal that a good deal of material relating to the Second Civil War has indeed found its way into the earlier chapters where I found that this was appropriate. However, this apart, the half of the originally planned book which was to have been devoted to this subject has now become a single chapter. Here the main issues of allegiance, co-ordination, insurgent war aims, and recruitment are sketched in, though, in the last case, without the exhaustive exercise in network analysis which a thoroughgoing treatment requires. Thus what was to have been a study of the Second Civil War and its origins has become a study of its origins with a somewhat summary treatment of the outcome in the penultimate chapter. Whether the subject is sufficiently important to justify a large-scale work is for the reader to judge. Needless to say, I am confident that it is.

After this preliminary apologia, it is agreeable to turn to the acknowledgement of help and encouragement which I have received from many sources. During my concluding years at the University of East Anglia, the University granted me two periods of study leave when I engaged both in producing a second edition of my book on the Civil War and in research for the present book. For the second of these periods the Warden and Fellows of All Souls College once again did me the honour of electing me to a Visiting Fellowship during Hilary and Trinity terms 1987–8 as they had done in the 1970s when I was working on an earlier book. The advantages of daily contact with Oxford scholars, added to generous provision of accommodation, the delights of All Souls and the accessibility of the Codrington Library, were great boons for which I am appropriately grateful. Much of my research in Oxford had been done during my earlier tenure of a Visiting Fellowship at All Souls, but there remained a great deal to be done, not only on materials in the Bodleian, but also on the wonderful collection of Clarke Papers and other materials in the library of Worcester College. I had greatly underestimated the volume of this material and am very deeply indebted to the co-operation and invaluable assistance given to me by the then Librarian, Mrs Lesley Le Claire, and her assistant, Mr Laurence Weeks. I would like to pay a warm tribute to both of them for efficient and friendly assistance well beyond the normal course of duty, extending, in Mrs Le Claire's case, to having me as her guest to luncheon in the SCR. Like them, the Librarian and staff of the Codrington Library at All Souls were ever helpful in affording me comfortable and easy access to materials and copying facilities. I would also like to thank the staff at the Bodleian Library as well as at numerous libraries and record offices outside Oxford: at the Public Record Office; the Department of Manuscripts and the North Library of the British Library; the Scottish Record Office; the National Library of Wales; and Dr Williams's Library, this last a new and very agreeable experience occasioned by my need to consult that part of Thomas Juxon's Journal which is not available among the Additional MSS. in the British Library. Since the fragile condition of this manuscript made photocopying out of the question, I had to make a large number of visits to the Library to make extensive transcriptions, but this was amply compensated by the pleasure of working in such a pleasant atmosphere. I would also like to acknowledge my debt to the professionalism and courtesy of Mr Harry Cobb and his colleagues at the House of Lords Record Office; and to Mrs Laetitia Yeandle of the Folger Shakespeare Library in Washington DC, where I spent a few profitable days working on the seventeenth-century Folger Manuscripts.

My debt to archivists in local and county record offices is very great and perhaps especially to four of them. The first is to Miss B.R. Masters, the Deputy Keeper of the Records at the Record Office of the Corporation of London; the second to Mr M.Y. Ashworth of the North Yorkshire Record Office at Northallerton who, in addition to the advice which one has come almost to take for granted from dedicated professional archivists, most generously made available to me his own transcripts from the records of the borough of Scarborough which he is preparing for publication; and to Miss Jean Kennedy and Mr Paul Routledge of the Norfolk and Norwich Record Office. But there are many other local archivists to whom my debt is hardly less great: to archivists of the West Yorkshire Archive Service, and notably Mr W.J. Connor at Leeds and Mr Robert Frost and Ms Caroline Martin at Wakefield; to Mr Peter Walne, county archivist at the Hertford Record Office; to Mrs J.J. Smith at the Essex Record Office at Chelmsford; to Mr Christopher Whittick and Ms Jean Chaudhuri of the East Sussex Record Office at Lewes; to Mrs S. Corke of the Surrey Archive Service in the Guildford Muniment Room; to Mrs M.M. Rowe of the Devon Record Office at Exeter; and to Mr J. Grisenthwaite and Mr D.M. Bowcock of the Cumbria Archive Service at Kendal and Carlisle respectively.

Historians of the politics of these years have necessarily to spend a great deal of time working on the magnificent Thomason collection in the British Library and I am no exception. However, the enormous amount of time which I had to spend on this material in the North Library, and the consequent expense of visits to London, was greatly reduced by the kind co-operation of the administrators of the National Trust at Blickling Hall who, through the good offices of the then UEA Librarian, Dr W.L. Guttsman, made available to me many years ago a large quantity of material which is also in the Thomason collection. The significance of their generosity in terms of saved journeys to London can be gauged by the large number of references in footnotes bearing the designation BHPC., viz. Blickling Hall Pamphlet Collection.

When I retired, I ceased, of course, to be eligible for the generous financial assistance towards travelling and other research expenses which had been accorded to me over the years by the UEA and for which I am properly grateful, as I also am for the accommodation which the

University has allowed me in retirement. For the first two years of my retirement, when travelling and photocopying expenses were at their heaviest, the financial gap was bridged by the Leverhulme Trust, which elected me to an Emeritus Fellowship. I am most grateful for the generous assistance of the Trust and I can only regret that I still had a number of research visits to make and the bulk of the typing still to be done and paid for, when my Emeritus Fellowship expired. I have always been a rather slow worker and my chapters go into innumerable drafts before the final version emerges.

My personal and scholarly debts are too many to be listed in full. When I was working at the Record Offices at Leeds and Wakefield, I enjoyed the generous hospitality of Gordon and Mary Forster as well as Dr Forster's invaluable guidance on local sources. At Oxford I benefited greatly from conversations and discussions with Dr Gerald Aylmer, Dr J.D. Clark, Sir John Habakkuk, Dr Paul Slack and Sir Keith Thomas; outside Oxford with Professor Lord Russell, Dr J.S.A. Adamson, Dr J.S. Morrill and Professor Ian Gentles whose admirable book on the New Model Army I regret not having had to hand earlier; and, at UEA, with my former colleagues Professors A. Hassell Smith and J.R. Jones and Dr Victor Morgan, and my successor, Professor J.C. Davis. I owe a very great debt both to Professor Jones and to Dr Morrill of Selwyn College, Cambridge, who have read drafts of some of these chapters and contributed valuable criticism and suggestions.

It was quite late in the production of this book that I decided that many of its readers would probably welcome the opportunity to put faces to the names of some of its principal characters. I have four great debts to acknowledge in connection with the search for illustrations: to my former pupil Clare Gittings, now education officer at the National Portrait Gallery, who on this occasion reversed roles and educated me; to my son-in-law Geoffrey Fisher of the Courtauld Institute who provided expert guidance on the provenance of some portraits as well as on other matters; to Sheila Lee, picture researcher for Yale University Press; and to Miss Norma Aubertin-Potter of the Codrington Library.

When he first approached me about publishing with Yale and I told him that I had in any case never published two books with the same publisher, Dr Robert Baldock's first reaction was to describe this as promiscuous. His sustained interest, encouragement and, not least, his forbearance have made it likely that my next book (if indeed I write one) will mark an end to this deplorable record of inconstancy. Another who has again displayed the quality of forbearance is my wife who has also helped me check footnotes while still on the word-processor. Mention of the word-processor reminds me of another great debt. When my former colleagues at UEA generously gave me a word-processor as a retirement present, my initial response was a shade ambivalent, compounded of gratitude for their kindness and apprehension bordering on terror at the prospect of having to acquire the necessary skills to put it to proper use. As it is, I now simply do not know what I would do without it. Two of the chapters and the footnotes to most of the others have been processed in this way, though for the production of a typescript of the remainder I am, as in earlier books, deeply indebted to the deciphering skills and professional competence of Mrs Vera Durell. I would also like to acknowledge my debt to the meticulous and sensitive copy-editing, of Mr Malcolm Gerratt and to the unfailing efficiency, consideration and resourcefulness of Candida Brazil at Yale University Press during the final stages of production.

This book is dedicated to the memory of a scholar whose tragic death in a car accident a few years ago robbed seventeenth-century studies of what would certainly have been an important study of Essex in the Second Civil War and perhaps another of that war in general. Brian Lyndon was a young Oxford graduate who went on to teach history at King Edward VI School in Southampton. The fragmentary drafts of what would have been his Southampton doctoral thesis have been put together through the dedication of his former research supervisor Dr Kevin Sharpe and his colleague Dr George Bernard, both of Southampton University. These drafts were very kindly made available to me at their suggestion by Mr M.H. May, senior history master at King Edward VI School. I have made considerable, and I hope worthy, use of them and of other materials which Brian provided for me during his life. I carry what is now a poignant recollection of one summer day in Colchester when my wife and I were conducted by him, an inspired and superbly informed cicerone, around the former fortress town whose siege was so skilfully conducted by Fairfax and so resolutely resisted by Lucas, Lisle, Capel and Goring. As the fragments of his unfinished thesis suggest, Brian would have told the story of that siege with distinction and panache. All that I can offer here are a few observations in the penultimate chapter which themselves owe something to that glorious summer day as well as to numerous lunchtime conversations which now seem a very long time ago.

R.A.

NOTE ON ABBREVIATIONS
AND DATING

The following abbreviations are used in the footnotes. The place of publication is London unless otherwise stated. In the case of Whitelock, *Memorials*, I have cited the dates, as well as page references for entries, since the pagination of my own 1682 edition is defective. All dates are old style, but the year is assumed to begin on 1 January, not 25 March.

Add. MSS.	Additional Manuscripts
A&O.	C.H. Firth and R.S. Rait (eds.), *Acts and Ordinances of the Interregnum 1642–1660* (3 volumes, 1911)
Ashburnham, *Narrative*	*A Narrative by John Ashburnham of his Attendance on King Charles the First* (2 volumes, 1834 edn.)
Ashton, *Civil War*	R. Ashton, *The English Civil War: Conservatism and Revolution 1603–1649* (2nd edn., 1989)
Aylmer, *Interregnum*	G.E. Aylmer (ed.), *The Interregnum: The Quest for Settlement 1646–1660* (1972)
Baillie, *Letters*	D. Laing (ed.), *The Letters and Journals of Robert Baillie A.M.* (3 volumes, Edinburgh, 1841–2)
Bell, *Memorials*	R. Bell, *Memorials of the Civil War: correspondence of the Fairfax family* (2 volumes, 1849)
BHPC.	Blickling Hall Pamphlet Collection
BIHR.	*Bulletin of the Institute of Historical Research*
BL.	British Library
Bodleian	Oxford University, Bodleian Library
Boys Diary	D.E. Underdown (ed.), 'The

Parliamentary Diary of John Boys 1647–8', *BIHR.*, XXXIX (1966)

Burnet, *Lives of the Hamiltons* — G. Burnet, *Memoirs of the Lives and Actions of James and William dukes of Hamilton* (2nd edn., Oxford, 1852)

Cal.CAM. — *Calendar of the Proceedings of the Committee for Advance of Money 1642–1656* (ed. M.A.E. Green) (3 volumes, 1888)

Cal.CC. — *Calendar of the Proceedings of the Committee for Compounding 1643–1660* (ed. M.A.E. Green) (5 volumes, 1889–92)

Cal.SPD. — *Calendar of State Papers Domestic*

Carlyle, *Cromwell* — T. Carlyle, *Oliver Cromwell's Letters and Speeches* (3 volumes, 1857)

Carter, *True Relation* — Matthew Carter, *A true Relation of the Honourable though Unfortunate Expedition of Kent Essex and Colchester in 1648* (1650) (2nd edn., Colchester 1789)

Cary, *Memorials* — H. Cary (ed.), *Memorials of the Great Civil War in England from 1646 to 1652* (2 volumes, 1842)

Charles I in 1646 — J. Bruce (ed.), *Charles I in 1646. Letters of King Charles the First to Queen Henrietta Maria*, Camden Soc., old series, LXIII (1856)

C.J. — *Journal of the House of Commons*

Clarendon, *Rebellion* — W.D. Macray (ed.), *The History of the Rebellion and Civil Wars in England . . . by Edward earl of Clarendon* (6 volumes, Oxford, 1958 edn.)

Clarendon SP. — R. Scrope and T. Monkhouse (eds.), *State Papers collected by Edward earl of Clarendon commencing 1621* (2 volumes, Oxford, 1776–8)

Clarke Papers — C.H. Firth (ed.), *The Clarke Papers. Selections from the Papers of William Clarke secretary to the council of the army 1647–1649*, vols. I and II, Camden Soc., new series, XLIX (1891) and LIV (1894)

CLRO. — Corporation of London Record Office

Codrington — Oxford, All Souls College, Codrington Library

Eng. Hist. Rev.	*English Historical Review*
Evans, *Norwich*	J.T. Evans, *Seventeenth-Century Norwich* (Oxford, 1979)
Everitt, *Kent*	A. Everitt, *The Community of Kent and the Great Rebellion 1640–1660* (Leicester, 1960)
Everitt, *Suffolk*	A. Everitt, *Suffolk and the Great Rebellion* Suffolk Record Society, III (Ipswich, 1960)
Fletcher, *Sussex*	A. Fletcher, *Sussex 1600–1660. A County Community in Peace and War* (Chichester, 1980)
Gardiner, *Civil War*	S.R. Gardiner, *History of the Great Civil War 1642–1649* (4 volumes, 1893)
Gardiner, *Constitutional Documents*	S.R. Gardiner (ed.), *Constitutional Documents of the Puritan Revolution 1625–1660* (1962 edn.)
Hamilton Papers	S.R. Gardiner (ed.), *The Hamilton Papers; Being Selections from Original Letters in the Possession of His Grace the Duke of Hamilton and Brandon . . . 1638–1650*, Camden Soc., new series, XXVII (1880)
Hist.J.	*Historical Journal*
HLRO.	Westminster, House of Lords Record Office
HLRO., MP.	House of Lords Record Office, Main Papers
HMC.	*Historical Manuscripts Commission*
Hughes, *Warwickshire*	A. Hughes, *Politics, Society and Civil War in Warwickshire 1620–1660* (Cambridge, 1987)
JBS.	*Journal of British Studies*
J.Mod.Hist.	*Journal of Modern History*
Jor.	Journal of Court of Common Council
Ketton-Cremer, *Norfolk*	R.W. Ketton-Cremer, *Norfolk in the Civil War* (Norwich, 1985 edn.)
Kingston, *Hertfordshire*	A.K. Kingston, *Hertfordshire During the Great Civil War and the Long Parliament* (1894)
L'Estrange his Vindication	[Roger L'Estrange] *L'Estrange His Vindication to Kent and the Justification of Kent to the World* (1649) (BL., C. 136, f31)

Leveller Manifestoes   D.M. Wolfe (ed.), *Leveller Manifestoes of the Puritan Revolution* (1967 edn.)

Leveller Tracts   W. Haller and G. Davies (eds.), *The Leveller Tracts 1647–1653* (Gloucester, Mass., 1964 edn.)

L.J.   *Journal of the House of Lords*

Ludlow Memoirs   C.H. Firth (ed.), *The Memoirs of Edmund Ludlow* (2 volumes, Oxford, 1894)

MacCormack, Revolutionary Politics   J.R. MacCormack, *Revolutionary Politics in the Long Parliament* (Cambridge, Mass., 1973)

Maseres, *Select Tracts*   F. Maseres (ed.), *Select Tracts relating to the Civil War in England in the Reign of King Charles I* (2 volumes, 1815)

Mayo, *Dorset*   C.H. Mayo (ed.), *The Minute Books of the Dorset Standing Committee 23rd. September 1646 to 8th May 1650* (Exeter, 1902)

Meikle, *Correspondence*   H.W. Meikle (ed.), *Correspondence of the Scots Commissioners in London 1644–1646* (Roxburghe Club, Edinburgh, 1917)

Montereul Correspondence   F.G. Fotheringham (ed.), *The Diplomatic Correspondence of Jean De Montereul and the Brothers De Bellièvre French Ambassadors in England and Scotland 1645–48* (2 volumes, Edinburgh, 1898)

Morrill, *Cheshire*   J.S. Morrill, *Cheshire 1630–1660. County Government and Society During the English Revolution* (1974)

Morrill, *Provinces*   J.S. Morrill (ed.), *The Revolt of the Provinces. Conservatives and Radicals in the English Civil War 1630–1650* (1976)

Naval Documents   J.R. Powell and E.K. Timings (eds.), *Documents relating to the Civil War 1642–1648*, Navy Records Society, volume CV (1963)

Newman, *Royalist Officers*   P.R. Newman, *Royalist Officers in England and Wales 1642–1660. A Biographical Dictionary* (1981)

Nicholas Papers   G.F. Warner (ed.), *The Nicholas Papers. Correspondence of Sir Edward Nicholas Secretary of State. vol. I: 1641–1652*, Camden Soc., new series, XL (1886)

NNRO.	Norwich, Norfolk and Norwich Record Office
NRA.	National Register of Archives
Ormerod, *Tracts*	G. Ormerod (ed.), *Tracts relating to Military Proceedings in Lancashire during the Great Civil War*, Chetham Soc., old series, II (1844)
P&P.	*Past & Present*
Parliamentary History	*The Parliamentary or Constitutional History of England . . . collected by several hands*, volumes IX–XVIII (1751–62)
Phillips, *Wales*	J.R. Phillips, *Memoirs of the Civil War in Wales and the Marches 1642–1649* (2 volumes, 1874)
Politics and People	C. Jones, M. Newitt and S. Roberts (eds.), *Politics and People in Revolutionary England* (Oxford, 1986)
PRO.	Public Record Office
QS.	Quarter Sessions
Rec.CGA.	A.F. Mitchell and J. Christie (eds.), *The Records of the Commissioners of the General Assemblies of the Church of Scotland holden in Edinburgh . . .* , vol. I, 1646–8 (1892); vol. II, 1648–50 (1896)
Rep.	Repertory of the Court of Aldermen
RO.	Record Office
Roberts, *Devon*	S.K. Roberts, *Recovery and Restoration in an English County. Devon Local Administration 1646–1670* (Exeter, 1985)
Rushworth, *Historical Collections*	J. Rushworth (ed.), *Historical Collections of Private Passages of State . . .* , volumes VI and VII (1721)
SP.	State Papers (Domestic)
SRO.	Scottish Record Office
State Trials	W. Cobbett, T.B. Howell et al. (eds.), *A Complete Collection of State Trials and Proceedings for High Treason and other Crimes*, volume IV (1809)
Stevenson, *Government*	D. Stevenson (ed.), *The Government of Scotland under the Covenanters* (Edinburgh, 1982)
Stevenson, *Revolution and Counter-Revolution*	D. Stevenson, *Revolution and Counter-Revolution in Scotland 1644–1651* (1977)
Sydney Papers	R.W. Blencowe (ed.), *Sydney Papers.*

	Consisting of a Journal of the Earl of Leicester and Original Letters of Algernon Sydney (1825)
TRHS.	*Transactions of the Royal Historical Society*
Underdown, *Somerset*	D. Underdown, *Somerset in the Civil War and Interregnum* (Newton Abbot, 1973)
Walker, *Independency*	Clement Walker, *The History of Independency* (1647)
Walker Revised	A.G. Matthews, *Walker Revised. Being a Revision of John Walker's Sufferings of the Clergy during the Grand Rebellion* (Oxford, 1948)
Walker, *Sufferings*	John Walker, *An Attempt towards recovering an Account of the Numbers and Sufferings of the Clergy of the Church of England who were Sequester'd Harass'd &c. in the Grand Rebellion* (1714)
Waller, *Vindication*	*Vindication of the Character and Conduct of Sir William Waller Knight . . . (Written by Himself)* (1793)
Webb, *Herefordshire*	J. Webb, *Memorials of the Civil War between King Charles I and the Parliament of England as it affected Herefordshire and the Adjacent Counties* (2 volumes, 1879)
Welford, *Durham and Northumberland*	R. Welford (ed.), *Records of the Committees for Compounding etc. with Delinquent Royalists in Durham and Northumberland during the Civil War etc. 1643–1660*, Surtees Soc., CXI (1905)
Western Assize Orders	J.S. Cockburn (ed.), *Western Assize Orders 1629–1648. A Calendar*, Camden Soc., 4th series, XVII (1976)
Westminster Assembly Minutes	A.F. Mitchell and J. Struthers (eds.), *Minutes of the Sessions of the Westminster Assembly of Divines (November 1644 to March 1649) . . .* (1874)
Whitelock Diary	R. Spalding (ed.), *The Diary of Bulstrode Whitelock 1605–1675* (Oxford, 1990)
Whitelock, *Memorials*	Bulstrode Whitelock, *Memorials of the English Affairs . . .* (1682)
Woolrych, *Soldiers and Statesmen*	A. Woolrych, *Soldiers and Statesmen: The General Council of the Army and its Debates 1647–1648* (Oxford, 1987)

INTRODUCTION

During the spring and summer of 1648 England was again convulsed by civil war after the two years of very uneasy peace which had followed Charles I's surrender to the Scots in May 1646. This book seeks to examine both the politics of the intervening period between the two wars and the causes and character of the Second Civil War. It asks how far the Second Civil War can be construed simply as a renewal of the conflicts of the first war, fought between much the same antagonists and over much the same issues; or, alternatively, how far the interwar years saw the emergence of new issues which in turn both reflected and generated fundamental changes in the outlook of those who had fought in the first war, not to speak of those who had been indifferent to, or wished a plague on, both warring parties.

It could, of course, be argued that this way of stating the problem unfairly prejudges the issue: that, as will be seen, most of the principal parties involved refused, rightly or wrongly, to see their political attitudes as having been altered by events. In particular those parliamentarians who had gone to war in 1642 for, as they honestly saw it, King and Parliament certainly would reject any ascription of their growing sense of alienation from the parliamentary government over the interwar years to changes of attitude on their own part. No, it was not they but the rest of the world which had changed. Having gone to war in 1642 to preserve what they conceived to be the ancient constitution, they now saw both King and Parliament threatened by alarmingly revolutionary forces thrown up by the First Civil War but not disappearing with its conclusion. Similarly, those whose main reason for their choice of the parliamentary side in 1642 had been their enthusiasm for religious reform – whether the reform of episcopacy or its replacement by a Presbyterian form of church government – watched the excesses of sectaries with no less apprehension and horror. Such wild men had occasioned great alarm as long ago as 1641–2, but now they were not only mounting attacks on everything the conservative and moderate reformers held dear, but were even threatening to seize the initiative and get into the saddle themselves. The metaphor is not inappropriate since the main medium through which sectarian influence was exerted was – or at least was deemed to be – the New Model Army. In turn that army was itself perceived as offering a potent threat to the authority of both parliament and the monarchy itself. What more natural than that, as twin foci of radical and sectarian attack, these two institutions should be drawn closer together, notwithstanding unhappy recent memories of their mutual antagonism and the bloody war between them? At the very least, this was a situation which afforded some scope for rapprochement between royalists and some of their former enemies both during the interwar years and even when war was renewed in 1648.

To understand the above developments it is necessary to appreciate the central significance of the army as a focus of conservative parliamentarian discontents and this is the particular concern of chapter V of this book. It matters not that the army of 1647, which was itself seeking to come to terms with the king, was anything but the radical and sectarian juggernaut of conservative parliamentarian and royalist imagination; nor that it was certainly not yet dominated by the ideas which were increasingly to characterize it in 1648 when it fought the Second Civil War, purged parliament and arranged to bring the king to trial for his life. For it is perceptions rather than realities which matter in this context; or, to put it differently, such perceptions, however misconceived they may have been, are themselves a form of reality which the historian ignores at his peril. Moreover, as is argued in the same chapter and elsewhere, it was their consciousness of the danger that the army and the king might reach agreement which impelled conservative parliamentarians to move more urgently along the road to compromise with the king and his supporters. Thus whether its actions were construed as tending to the destruction of monarchy and subversion of parliament or to the reaching of agreement with the king on terms which were unacceptable to conservative parliamentary Presbyterians, the army became a particular object of conservative disapprobation.

There are a number of other reasons for this. It was the perceived need to keep the army in being to guard against the danger of a resurgence of militant royalism which was mainly responsible for the prolongation of wartime forms and levels of taxation into the interwar years. The importance of this as an additional cause of discontent and alienation is considered in chapter II. The sheer element of cost as well as the political advantages of getting rid of the army explains why its disbandment became a central feature of the parliamentary conservatives' policy early in 1647. An at least equally potent irritant was the survival into peacetime of much of the wartime institutional machinery of parliamentary government. Particularly notable here were the county committees which incurred strong conservative disapproval, partly because of their significance as institutional innovations in contrast to the traditional mechanism of the Commissions of the Peace; partly because of the lowborn origins of many committeemen; and not least because of the connection of the committees with taxation to maintain the army. These and similar major issues are the concern of chapter III. How far the failure of hard-pressed subjects to obtain the redress of such grievances through the medium of petitioning parliament further intensified their sense of alienation and brought them to the brink, and in some cases over the brink, of armed insurrection is a central concern of chapter IV.

There can be no doubt that the factors emphasized above contributed powerfully to the alienation of many conservative parliamentarians from government both at Westminster and in the provinces. This is especially apparent from the latter half of 1647 when such government was increasingly dominated by radical – or at least by Independent as distinct from Presbyterian – elements. (The distinction between the two parliamentary 'parties' is explained in chapter VIII.) What is more problematical, however, and a further question which this book seeks to answer, is whether this alienation was strong and deep enough to align many former parliamentarians firmly alongside their old enemies even to the point of war. Or, to put it in another way, did insurgency in the Second Civil War really amount to much more than a revival of militant cavalierism? If it did amount to more, how far is this reflected in the nature of the insurgent war aims? (These problems are explored in detail in chapters XI and XII.) Was it the world of 1639 or that of 1641 that the insurgents aspired to restore? If the latter, how far was this the product of the royalists' need to attract support from alienated parliamentarians and how far is it ascribable to an increased influence of moderates in the royalist councils? These two possibilities are, of course, by no means mutually exclusive. But what if the alienation of parliamentary conservatives was no more than a negative panic reaction of frightened politicians who found the triumph of the army and its radical Independent allies a more frightening prospect than the victory of the resurgent Cavaliers? If that was the case, was there any need for the latter to make any substantial concessions at all? In some cases that may be true but in others the alienation and shifting alliances of parliamentary conservatives are ascribable to a complex variety of considerations and motives each of which operated with different force as between different persons. As well as the religious affiliations, constitutional scruples and anti-radical fearfulness which have already been mentioned, it is important not to lose sight of less respectable motives such as inordinate greed, frustrated ambition and envy of those former colleagues who had done better out of the parliamentary victory in the

First Civil War. As is demonstrated in chapter XI, such considerations were to play a significant part in some crucially important cases.

What of the role of the king himself? How far did the attitude and initiatives of Charles I contribute towards the reconciliation of former enemies and perhaps to a revival of that moderate royalism whose voice had been hushed since the death of Lord Falkland on the battlefield in 1643? The varied nature of revived royalism is the subject of chapter VI. What areas of former Roundhead support appeared to offer special opportunities for royalist proselytization and what sort of concessions were the king and his adherents prepared to offer as part of a bid for their support? What were the limits of these concessions and did these limits impose serious obstacles to the success of attempts to widen the basis of royalist support? If so, was it a matter of the concessions being too few and insubstantial or of their being made too late? Charles's record in this respect is critically examined in chapter I, which deals with the peace negotiations of 1646–7, and in chapters VIII and IX which examine his relations with the English Presbyterians and the Scots as well as considering the final peace negotiations in the autumn of 1648.

It was indeed these two areas which offered the most promising opportunities for royalist proselytization. In the case of the Scots, the king enjoyed some substantial, though by no means complete, success. During the First Civil War the Scottish kirk and parliament had en-thusiastically embraced the Solemn League and Covenant in 1643 and Scotland had entered the war on the side of the English parliament. Why was it that the Scots who had fought alongside the English Roundheads in the first war should fight against them and for the king in the second war? What opposition, if any, did this reversal of alliances evoke within Scotland and was such opposition sufficiently powerful seriously to impair the efficiency of the Scottish war effort; or, perhaps more correctly, the effort of that part of the Scottish nation which held by the Engagement which some of its leaders had made with the king at Christmas 1647? What concessions did the king have to make to secure their support; or, more significantly, how was it that he was able to secure their support on the basis of such slender concessions? Was the minimal nature of these concessions itself a cause of the disastrous split which meant that the English parliament was faced by an enfeebled and divided Scotland at the time of the invasion of the Scottish army of the Engagement in 1648? These are among the main questions on which chapter IX seeks to shed light.

While the success of the royalist attempts to win over the Scots was at best only partial, their efforts to recruit allies from the ranks of the English parliamentary Presbyterians were not successful even in this limited sense. In their foiled counter-revolution of the high summer of

1647, which is examined from several different angles in a number of the chapters of this book, the English parliamentary Presbyterians, along with their close allies in the City of London, had seemed to be on the verge of throwing in their lot with the king. Why did they fail to do so when things again came to the crunch a year later? Were they exhausted and disillusioned by the ignominious failure of their own bid for power in 1647? Or had this experience taught them a salutary lesson which pointed to the need for greater caution in the future; or, at least that their ends were more likely to be achieved by other means than that of support for the English insurgents and Scottish invaders in the Second Civil War? Was it not indeed a clear demonstration of the wisdom of these more cautious and pacific tactics that the English parliament, whose army had so recently triumphed over both Scottish Engagers and English insurgents, was now prepared to negotiate a peace settlement with the king whose own forces had been so decisively crushed? Why was it that, at the point of the greatest triumph of parliamentary arms in the late summer of 1648, parliament was prepared to go back on its decision of the beginning of the year that no further approaches should be made to the king? In turn, how far is the final failure of these negotiations attributable to similar causes to those which explain the very limited previous success of efforts to create a wider constituency for royalism? Or how far did they fail owing to intervention from outside; by the army which, at the beginning of December 1648, brutally brought the treaty to an end and purged parliament as the prelude to the trial and execution of the king and the establishment of a republic? As part of the examination of the role of the parliamentary Presbyterians, these problems receive detailed consideration in chapter VIII.

Chapter X considers the significance of the earlier outbursts of counter-revolutionary activity before the second war and asks to what extent these early risings paved the way for the more general revolt of 1648. How far is there continuity of personnel between the risings of 1647 and 1648? Are the aims of both and indeed the aims of participants in the different risings in the Second Civil War mutually consistent (the last point is dealt with in chapter XII)? Is there any connection between political conservatism and the revival of enthusiasm for older forms of worship which is the subject of chapter VII? Was the Second Civil War an Anglican as well as a royalist revolt?

This Introduction has indicated some of the central questions on which this book seeks to throw some light even if it does not always succeed in finding conclusive answers. As the chapter titles and sub-headings indicate, the main emphasis is analytical rather than chrono-logical – the period covered is, after all, very short even if also very momentous. However, within each of these analytical divisions, proper attention has been paid to chronology. Whether there emerges from this a unified and comprehensive picture of the totality of developments from the last days of the First Civil War in 1646 to the aftermath of the Second Civil War in the closing weeks of 1648 is for the reader to judge.

I

THE FAILURE OF SETTLEMENT
JUNE 1646–FEBRUARY 1648

... we must necessarily conclude that, as it is contrary to *Conscience* for the two Houses not to contribute their utmost indeavours to restore a firm and happy Peace ... so it is apparent to all the *world* that there is no visible way left to procure this peace, but a speedy Accommodation with His *Majesty*, by sending to him such Propositions as may agree with *Right Reason, Conscience* and *Honour*: And if the Peace of their languishing bleeding *Country* be not a sufficient *Motive*, yet let a tender regard be had to their owne security, in this their tottering condition. Retreat, Retreat *Gentlemen* with speed; you have been at your highest pitch long since, and now in the opinion of all wise men are *declining*; take heed of a *fall*; it will be the most dangerous, one next to that of the bottomlesse Pit. ...

The Case of the King stated (1647), pp. 9–10

What hath the Army to do in settling the peace of the Kingdome which belongs wholly to the parliament ... and of what dangerous consequence will it be even to the overthrowing of the Fundamentall Constitution?

Queries whether the Army ought to insist vpon the Charge against those persons they have accused (1647),
Oxford, Worcester College MSS., 41, fo. 56(b)

The Newcastle Propositions, June 1646–7

On 26 June Charles I met the peace commissioners of England and Scotland at Newcastle, whither he had been taken by the Scottish army, to whom he had surrendered his person at Southwell in Nottinghamshire on 5 May. As Charles had informed his queen in a letter dated two days before this meeting, he could expect no more than surrender terms, in which circumstances he saw his only hope as lying in the employment of delaying tactics and in playing off the victors in the Civil War against one another, even if, as he later admitted, 'any delaying answer from me ... will be taken for a denial, in which case the rebels

will go to all extremities'.[1] The meeting with the commissioners on 26
June had something of the character of the preliminaries at Oxford in
November 1644 in preparation for the Treaty of Uxbridge of the
following January, and indeed of that treaty itself;[2] at least in the matter
of Charles's affected surprise that parliament's commissioners had no
authority to step beyond their instructions, in which circumstances 'a
good honest Trumpeter might have don as much'. So, despite the en-
treaties of the senior parliamentary commissioner, the earl of Pembroke,
that the king's failure to agree to the Anglo-Scottish terms would have
'dangerous consequences . . . to himselfe, his Kingdom & Posterity',
Charles sent an answer which in their view was no answer at all.[3]

Although, as the London Independent Thomas Juxon noted with
relief in his diary entry for 12 June, the Anglo-Scottish propositions
contained no trace of anti-monarchical or republican sentiment,[4] it was
most unlikely that even a defeated king would find himself able to
accept these Newcastle Propositions, as they came to be called. In one
form or another, these were to remain the basis of the Anglo-Scottish
terms for the next eighteen months.[5] Given his religious views, he must
surely draw the line both at taking the Covenant himself and at giving
the royal assent to a bill imposing it on his English subjects (proposition
2); at consenting to the complete abolition of episcopacy (proposition
3); or to the prohibition of the use of the Roman Catholic Mass at court
(proposition 10), since this would effectively prevent the queen from
returning to England as well as being a violation of the terms of the
marriage treaty with France. As to the control of the militia, one of
the issues which had sparked off the First Civil War in 1642, there were
parliamentarians who regarded parliamentary control even for twenty
years (proposition 13) as a wholly inadequate safeguard, even if they
were not prepared to countenance the very minority radical view that
the king had no right whatever to the militia in any circumstances and
ought to be 'brought to exemplary and condign punishment'.[6] But in
any case twenty years was too long a period to be acceptable to Charles.

---

1. *Charles I in 1646*, pp. 50–1, 53.
2. See Ashton, *Civil War*, pp. 236–7.
3. Bodleian, Carte MSS. 80, fos. 479–80; BL., Add. MSS., 31,116, fos. 280–80(b); *C.J.*,
    IV, 642. See also *Charles I in 1646*, pp. 55, 56–7.
4. BL., Add. MSS., 25,465, fo. 77.
5. The Newcastle Propositions and the king's first reply are printed in Gardiner, *Consti-
    tutional Documents*, pp. 290–308. They were not formally presented until 13 July. For
    an interesting comment on the Propositions by a French diplomat, Bellièvre, see
    Montereul Correspondence, I, 263–4.
6. *Cal.SPD. 1645–7*, pp. 451–2. Montereul, the French ambassador to the Scots, writing
    in late September, informed Cardinal Mazarin that his conversations in London with
    the Scottish commissioners and English parliamentary Presbyterians gave grounds for
    believing that the period might be reduced to ten years (*Montereul Correspondence*, I,
    281).

Only slightly less objectionable, from the king's point of view, were the propositions prohibiting peers who had been created since May 1642 (when Lord Keeper Lyttleton had absconded with the Great Seal to the king at York) from sitting in the House of Lords (proposition 14); and pronouncing all royal acts made under the Great Seal since that time null and void, while demanding royal recognition of parliamentary acts made under what Charles regarded as a counterfeit Great Seal (proposition 19). Perhaps the most difficult of all for Charles to stomach, however, was the long proposition dealing with his wartime adherents (proposition 16), and more especially that part of it which excluded fifty-seven of them from pardon, including Princes Rupert and Maurice, Sir Edward Hyde, Sir Marmaduke Langdale, and the Scottish Lords Huntly and Montrose.

So the king played for time, hoping especially that he would ultimately receive an invitation to treat at London and that in the meantime there might be a growth of revulsion against parliament and a revival of enthusiasm for him which would strengthen his bargaining position.[7] To secure such an invitation was for the next two years to be a principal royal objective, but one which was firmly resisted by the English parliamentarians, who rightly feared the dangers of tumult and disorder which the king's presence in the capital might provoke. Their fears were not shared by the Scots, who were, however, no less anxious to avoid taking Charles back to Scotland, where he might serve as a similar rallying point for the followers of Montrose, who had been defeated but not completely crushed in September 1645.[8] Accordingly the Scottish Commissioners in London formally proposed on 20 October that Charles be invited to London – or, at least, to one of his houses near London – to treat, but their proposal was ignored by the English parliament.[9]

Religion was the issue which might seem to offer Charles most scope for manoeuvre and for playing off his English against his Scottish

7. See BL., Add. MSS., 38,847, fo. 34; Cal.SPD. 1645–7, p. 498; L.J., VIII, 627–8; Hamilton Papers, p. 110; Charles I in 1646, p. 75; Gardiner, Constitutional Documents, pp. 306–9. According to Montereul, the duke of Hamilton advised the king to this effect at the end of July (Montereul Correspondence, I, 232).

8. In early April, before the king had even left Oxford, there were precautions against disturbances in London in the event of Charles's coming there (Bodleian, Carte MSS., 80, fos. 736–7). The arguments in favour of the king going to London but not to Scotland were eloquently put by the Scottish Lord Chancellor, the earl of Loudoun, at a conference in the Painted Chamber on 6 October (Several speeches spoken by John, earl of Loudoun (Edinburgh, 1646), pp. 23–5). For arguments that it was against the king's interests to go to London, see Montereul Correspondence, I, 253, 275–6. Montereul had reported in May that the Scots did not want the king to go to London (ibid., I, 205; but see also ibid., pp. 293–4).

9. Some papers given in by the Commissioners (Edinburgh, 1646), pp. 23–5.

ex-enemies, not to speak of the various English dissident religious groups, and notably the Presbyterians against the Independents. It was not that Charles was prepared to adopt his queen's cynical – or at best totally uncomprehending – recommendation that he should opt for a Presbyterian ecclesiastical settlement in order to bring the Scots over to his side and to profit by setting the English Presbyterians and Independents at one another's throats.[10] On this issue he would no doubt have completely agreed with the views of his former minister Edward Hyde, as expressed in a letter of 14 August 1646 to Sir John Berkley. Hyde argued that

> ye stratagem of yielding to them [viz. the Propositions], to make the Quarrell ye more popular, and to divide ye Presbyterians & Independents is soe farr aboue my Politiques yt I am confident a generall horror and infidelity will attend he that submitts to them.[11]

While Charles's sincerity on religious issues is not in doubt, it is not true that he disapproved of a Presbyterian ecclesiastical settlement simply on account of his concern to preserve episcopacy, the beauty of holiness, and, indeed, as much as possible – however little this might be – of the Caroline church. He was no less concerned with what he saw as the political significance of Presbyterianism as removing 'the dependence of the Church from the Crown'.[12] Nor had he altered his views in the slightest by the end of the year, as several of his letters written in December make abundantly clear. In one of these he reflected bitterly that 'this damned Covenant is the product of Rebellion and breathes nothing but treason'.[13] Given Henrietta Maria's disinclination to regard distinctions between different brands of Protestant heresy as a matter of importance, it is hardly surprising that Charles was particularly concerned to emphasize the political connotations of Presbyterianism in his letters to his wife, who would be likely to lend more credence to such matters than she would to purely religious arguments. In one of a stream of such letters between February and December 1646, first from Oxford, and later, following his giving himself up to the Scots in May, from Newcastle, he rams home the

10. For Charles's disagreement with the queen's views on this matter, see *Charles I in 1646*, pp. 16–17, 19, 21–3, 26–7, 29–30, 62, 70, 74–5, 79–83. On the distinction between religious and political Presbyterians and Independents, see Ashton, *Civil War*, pp. 241–6.
11. Bodleian, Clarendon MSS., 28, fos. 178(b)–9.
12. *Clarendon SP.*, II, 242–4 (Charles I to Lords Jermyn and Culpepper and John Ashburnham, 22 July 1646). For similar views in a letter of 12 August to the same, see ibid., pp. 247–8.
13. Ibid., II, 313–14.

point that Presbyterianism 'never came into any country but by rebellion'.[14] While his observation in a letter of 19 February that he 'put little or no difference between setting up the Presbyterian government, or submitting to the Church of Rome' was far more likely to irritate than to convince her, she might be more responsive to the points made in his next surviving letter of 3 March, leading up to the conclusion that 'the nature of Presbyterian government is to steal or force the crown from the king's head. For their chief maxim is . . . that all kings must submit to Christ's kingdom, of which they are the sole governors.'[15] Be this as it may, those closest to the queen were at pains to emphasize, as Sir Robert Murray observed in a letter to the duke of Hamilton in December, that 'she hath done her utmost to have satisfaction giuen to the Scotts'.[16]

But the queen's insistence that the king should be prepared to make concessions on religion did not betoken a willingness for him to agree to the Propositions in general. On 12 August Sir Robert Murray reported that she had rebuked the French ambassador for his observation 'that there was no way left for the King but to signe the propositions'.[17] One of the reasons why she favoured making concessions on religion was probably that she feared that Charles might seek to balance his immovability on this front with a readiness to make concessions on other matters, and notably on the control of the militia. In a letter of 30 November from Newcastle Charles did his best to reassure her on this point, explaining that, in his view, 'unless religion be preserved, the militia will not be much useful to the crown'.[18] Henrietta seems to have been unconvinced, and her letter written early in December from Paris complained that Charles's willingness to concede control of the militia to parliament – even if only for ten as distinct from the twenty years postulated in the thirteenth proposition – was jeopardizing both his and her safety, and sacrificing a crucial right of sovereignty on account of his concern to save episcopacy and avoid a Presbyterian settlement. As a consequence, she concluded despairingly,

. . . nous [ne] verrons jamais une fin a nos malheurs. Car tant que le Parl[ament] durera, vous n'estes point Roy. Et pour moy, je ne

14. *Charles I in 1646*, p. 27.
15. For these two letters, see ibid., pp. 18–23. For similar points made in other letters, see ibid., pp. 41–2, 57–8, 62, 65, 71, 73, 79–83. See also *Montereul Correspondence*, I, 318–19.
16. *Hamilton Papers*, p. 139. For Scottish and other pressure on the queen to this end, see *Montereul Correspondence*, I, 213, 321, 333–4.
17. *Hamilton Papers*, p. 108.
18. *Charles I in 1646*, p. 79.

remettray pas le pied en Ang[leterre]. Et avec le biais que vous avez accordé la Milice, vous vous esté coupé la gorge. Car leur ayant donné ce pouvoir, vous ne pouves plus rien refuser, pas mesme ma vie s'ils vous la demandent; mais je ne me mettray pas entre leur mains. J'oserois dire que si vous eussies suivi nos avis, que vos affaires seroient dans un autre estat qu'ils ne sont.[19]

If it was Charles's aim to divide his English and Scottish former enemies by a policy of temporizing and equivocation, he was miscalculating and his policies in fact had the reverse effect.[20] At a conference between the two English Houses of Parliament on 13 August the earl of Pembroke was at pains to commend the Scottish commissioners at Newcastle for their efforts to persuade the king of the need to accept the Propositions.[21] Indeed, the Scottish Lord Chancellor, the earl of Loudoun, with astonishing prescience, urged upon the king the awful consequences of refusing to accept the Propositions *in toto*, in even more emphatic terms than those which Pembroke had employed at the initial meeting of the Anglo-Scottish commissioners with Charles on 26 June. Pointing to the alarming growth of anti-monarchical sentiment in England, Loudoun stressed that this would surely be exacerbated by a royal refusal to co-operate, which could only result in a settlement being reached without his participation. On the other hand, Charles's acquiescence to the terms, even though 'they are higher [viz. more severe] in some things . . . than we do approve of', ought in itself to provide a firm basis for a revival of royal popularity and a decline of the influence of those who wished ill to the monarch. Loudoun was the brother of the marquess of Argyll, Scottish Covenanter *par excellence*, but Charles was to receive similar advice from the moderate earl of Lanark, who urged him to accept the Propositions, not because they were just, but 'out of an opinion of their fitness in relation to your present condition, which is more threatening now than ever'.[22]

But Charles continued to play his waiting game, bent on exploiting differences both between his English and Scottish subjects, and, within each of his two kingdoms, between Presbyterians and Independents in England,[23] and, in Scotland, between Hamiltonians, Argyll high kirk men, and the 'neutrals', as Charles described them, whose principal

---

19.   Ibid., pp. 95–7.
20.   Anglo-Scottish agreement was not, however, manifested over the issue of the disposal of the king's person. On this, see below, pp. 311–3.
21.   BL., Add. MSS., 31,116, fos. 280(b)–1.
22.   For Loudoun, see *Several speeches spoken by John Campbell earl of Loudoun* (Edinburgh, 1646), pp. 28–30; Bodleian, Carte MSS., 80, fos. 488–9. For Lanark, who was the brother of the duke of Hamilton, see Burnet, *Lives of the Hamiltons*, pp. 392–3.
23.   See *Charles I in 1646*, pp. 6, 9–10, 11.

figures were Callander and Dunfermline.[24] In a letter of 21 September
to the duke of Hamilton, Sir Robert Murray mentions the alarming
possibility that Charles might reach agreement with the English Independents, to whom he might offer full toleration in return for what
Murray described as 'moderated episcopacy',[25] and in November the
London Independent Thomas Juxon wrote in his diary of a willingness
on the part of the Independents to accommodate the king on religious
matters.[26] With the aid of hindsight such suggestions might seem like
an anticipation of the developments following the army's seizure of
the king on 4 June 1647, when for a few months Charles would toy
with the Independent-backed army's peace terms, the Heads of the Proposals, playing them off against parliament's Newcastle – or, as they later
came to be called, Hampton Court – Propositions. It is particularly in
the context of this royal double-game that one is reminded of the
appropriateness of Macaulay's celebrated description of Charles's 'incurable propensity to dark and crooked ways'. 'The king is driven from
one to another desperate cause', confided Thomas Juxon to his Journal
as early as 31 July, 'and always the loser', concluding that 'no prince ever
used such dissimulation'.[27] But it availed him nothing. Charles might
contemplate the advantages of an agreement with the Independents, but
in an undated paper for the parliamentary committee at Newcastle,
which survives in a copy made by Lanark, he emphasized that one
advantage of a Presbyterian religious settlement for a trial period of three
years, even if accompanied by the survival of episcopacy only in a very
attenuated form, would be 'the present putting down [of] all sectaries
and Independents'.[28] Even more striking is a royal letter to Lanark on 4
December 1646, with which the king enclosed a copy of a draft paper
on the Newcastle Propositions which he had resolved to send to London:

> . . . wherein you will find a clause in favour of the Independents, to wit,
> the forbearance I give to those who have scruples of conscience; and

---

24. On this, see Charles's letter of 17 June to the queen (*Charles I in 1646*, pp. 48–9). On
    Charles and the Scottish factions, see Stevenson, *Revolution and Counter-Revolution*,
    pp. 71–2. For interesting comment on the king's relations with Loudoun and the
    Hamiltons, see *Montereul Correspondence*, I, 199–200, 203–4.
25. *Hamilton Papers*, p. 115.
26. London, Dr Williams's Library, MS. 24.50 (Thomas Juxon's Journal), fo. 93.
27. BL., Add. MSS., 25,465, fos. 82–2(b). In a much later entry on 19 December Juxon
    remarks that Charles 'had hoped ere now to have brought us to blowes', by encour-
    aging the Scots to make impossible demands (Dr Williams's Library, MS. 24.50,
    fo. 96(b)).
28. Burnet, *Lives of the Hamiltons*, pp. 369–70. Bellièvre observed that 'les modiffications
    [sic] qu'il [viz. Charles] avoit aposées pour la conservation des euesques destruisoit le
    presbitère qu'il faisoit semblant d'accorder' (*Montereul Correspondence*, I, 284–5). For
    some earlier comments on the same subject by Montereul's secretary, see ibid., I, 210.

indeed I did it purposely, to make what I sent relish the better with that kind of people. But if my native subjects will so countenance the answer, that I may be sure they will stick to me in what concerns my temporal power, I will not only expunge that clause, but likewise make what declarations I shall be desired against the Independents.[29]

Such a declaration would doubtless go down well with both English and Scottish Presbyterians. The Scottish Commissioners in England, in a communication of 12 August to the English parliament, went out of their way to emphasize that nothing could be further from the intention of the Scots than 'to make use of their Army . . . to any ends other than those expressed in the Covenant'.[30] But percipient Englishmen were not unaware that such an assurance did not completely rule out the possibility of a military intervention by that part of the Scottish army which was still in England, if Charles were to make the concessions to the Scots which were urged upon him by the queen. Nevertheless, however eager the commissioners of the General Assembly of the Scottish kirk might be to see the establishment of high Presbyterian uniformity in England, they were equally aware of the dangers arising from a disunity between allies which the king would be quick to exploit. Hence on 16 December they issued a statesmanlike warning against any interpretation of the Solemn League and Covenant which would 'presse the defence of the Kings Authoritie and of Religion, to engage us in those wayes that would tend to the ruine of both'. In short, 'the want of full satisfaction in the much desired work of [religious] uniformity' should not be the ground or occasion of Anglo-Scottish disunity. The Scottish Engagement with the king was still more than a year away.[31]

Consistent with this, a committee of the Scottish Estates voted on 16 December that the government of that realm would have to be settled without the agreement of the king unless he consented to the Newcastle Propositions.[32] In a letter from Newcastle at the beginning of the New Year, Charles pronounced to his queen, with an air of finality which he may have hoped would convince even her, that 'it is now cleare that the

29. Burnet, *Lives of the Hamiltons*, p. 381.
30. Bodleian, Carte MSS., 80, fos. 488–8(b). On the possibility of Scottish military support for the king, given his acquiescence on religion, see also *Montereul Correspondence*, I, 213, 274, 288, 294, 296–7, 310–13, 342.
31. *A Solemne and Seasonable Warning . . . for holding fast the League and Covenant . . .* (1646, 16 December), BL., E.419(34), p. 3. For the Engagement, see below, pp. 324–6. In November Thomas Juxon's diary expresses some apprehension about the danger of such a Scottish military intervention (Dr Williams's Library, MS. 24.50, fos. 93–93(b)).
32. On these events, see Stevenson, *Revolution and Counter-Revolution*, pp. 76–8.

demands concerning Religion are distructive as well to my Crowne as conscience'.[33] He had a few more futile and unavailing meetings with the Scottish Commissioners in England,[34] but the ultimate failure of the tortuous policies he had hitherto pursued was to be signalized by the Anglo-Scottish agreement for the settlement of the debt of the English parliament to the Scots, the withdrawal of their army from England in February 1647, and their handing over of the king to the English parliament to live in comfortable but irksome duress at Holdenby House in Northamptonshire.[35]

In a letter to the duke of Hamilton on 24 January Sir Robert Murray had confidently asserted that Charles would never concede at Holdenby what he had refused at Newcastle.[36] A similarly depressing view of the prospects is to be found in a letter from Captain Silas Titus to his friend Colonel Cox in Hertfordshire. Titus, who was soon to be completely won over by the king, had been sent north with the duty of escorting Charles from Newcastle to Holdenby. While hoping that 'the iournie may defeat bad mens hopes and good mens feares', he admitted that, if the king's comportment and expressions were anything to go by, 'there is as little hope of Compliance Now as euer'.[37] However, while Charles's third reply to the Newcastle Propositions on 12 May conceded nothing more than what he had been prepared to grant before leaving Newcastle,[38] there can be no doubt that the departure of the Scots had opened up new possibilities of settlement. Charles emphasized somewhat disingenuously to parliament that the fact that he was not prepared to capitulate completely over the Propositions should inspire confidence rather than mistrust, since he could, after all, have conceded all without the slightest intention of keeping to his undertaking.[39] Parliament should therefore be prepared to accept his concessions in the spirit in which he had made them; and especially his willingness to

33. *Clarendon SP.*, II, 324.
34. Bodleian, Carte MSS., 80, fos. 527, 531–2; *Hamilton Papers*, pp. 145–6; *Montereul Correspondence*, I, 433–4.
35. See Gardiner, *Civil War*, III, 180–2, 184–5, 188–91.
36. *Hamilton Papers*, p. 147.
37. Hertford, Hertfordshire R.O., MSS. 70057. For Titus's later defection to the king and complicity in his attempt to escape, see P. Gregg, *King Charles I* (1981), p. 421; C. Carlton, *Charles I: The Personal Monarch* (1983), pp. 329–30, 344.
38. Rather than a direct reply this was more a response to suggestions emanating from the earls of Warwick, Holland, Manchester and Northumberland which had originally been transmitted from the queen through Bellièvre in January. The essence of the proposals is contained in a memorandum from Bellièvre to Mazarin, printed in Gardiner, *Constitutional Documents*, pp. 309–11. On this incident, see Gardiner, *Civil War*, III, 213–14. For Charles's answer in May, see Gardiner, *Constitutional Documents*, pp. 311–16; *L.J.*, IX, 193–4.
39. Gardiner, *Constitutional Documents*, pp. 311–12.

concede a Presbyterian ecclesiastical settlement, except for himself and his household, for a trial period of three years, following which period the form of the ultimate settlement was to be recommended to King and Parliament by the Westminster Assembly of Divines and twenty divines of Charles's nomination. The significance of this proposal, which Charles had already indicated his readiness to make in a letter to the queen on 30 November 1646,[40] may be judged from his observations in a letter of 5 December that such a trial period for a Presbyterian settlement would be 'but a temporary permission to continue that unlawful possession (which for the present I cannot help) so as to lay the ground for a perfect recovery';[41] in fact, *reculer pour mieux sauter*.

Charles's private asseveration of 5 December 1646 may serve as an apt comment on the worth of the concessions which he was to offer five months later: that, based on opportunism in a desperate situation, there were no grounds for assuming that he would keep to his undertaking if things improved for him. As for his position on the other main Propositions, he asked for a respite on the demand that he take the Covenant until he had time to consult his chaplains, a facility which had hitherto been denied him. He was willing to agree to the proposed restrictions on Catholic recusants and to those relating to Sabbath observance, the suppression of religious (viz. Laudian) innovations and the discouragement of clerical pluralism and non-residence. He offered to concede control of the militia to parliament for ten years – as distinct from the twenty years stipulated in the thirteenth proposition; and to recognize parliament's acts under what he regarded as a counterfeit great seal. He would not, however, concede that his own acts under the real Great Seal from May 1642 should be null and void.[42]

Notwithstanding a report from William White to Lord Fairfax on 16 May that the king's latest answer had not given any satisfaction,[43] the deadlock appeared to have been broken, and both the Scottish commissioners and the English Presbyterian party which dominated parliament seemed well disposed to the king's offer. But this hopeful rapprochement of May 1647 was to be dramatically aborted by Cornet Joyce's spectacular coup on 4 June, abducting Charles from Holdenby House. However, while this may have been a blow to the peace hopes of the Scots and the English parliamentary Presbyterians, to Charles it offered new opportunities of playing off those whom he still regarded as his enemies against one another. From here on, our discussion of the quest

40.   *Charles I in 1646*, p. 80.
41.   Ibid., p. 83.
42.   *Propositions from the Parliament to the King for Peace. His Majesty's Answers to both of them in order* (May 1647), BL., E.390(4).
43.   Bell, *Memorials*, I, 342.

for settlement will have to take account not only of the peace proposals of parliament and the Scots (the Newcastle, or, later, Hampton Court Propositions), but also of the evolution and reception of the alternative terms which were to be presented to Charles on 1 August by the army, the so-called Heads of the Proposals.

Alternative quests for settlement from June to September 1647

The causes of the abduction of Charles I from Holdenby House on 4 June 1647 by a troop of soldiers led by a very junior officer will probably always remain one of the great unsolved mysteries of history.[44] How far Cornet Joyce was acting with the connivance, or under the instructions, of the army commanders, and how far independently (surely most unlikely), or as part of a radical movement led by the newly elected agitators in the army – the agents of a sort of soldiers' soviet as Professor Woolrych evocatively puts it – will never admit of a certain answer. The firm denial by Lord General Fairfax of any personal responsibility for Joyce's coup[45] is accepted even by the vehemently anti-New Model politician and former General, Sir William Waller, although his account certainly does not absolve Cromwell and Ireton of responsibility.[46] The king himself was later to insist that Joyce 'could not venture to . . . bring mee away but that he had the councell of greater persons'.[47] One thing that is certain is that, however innocent they may have been of original involvement, the army commanders came quickly to realize that the coup had not only enormously strengthened their hand in their current disputes with parliament about arrears of pay, Irish service and terms of disbandment, but had also

44. The best modern account is in Woolrych, *Soldiers and Statesmen*, pp. 106–15.
45. *A Letter from his Excellency Sir Thomas Fairfax* (6 June 1647), BL., E.391(7), no pagination; *Another Letter from his Excellency Sir Thomas Fairfax* (8 June 1647), BL., E.392(11), pp. 6–7; *Parliamentary History*, XV, 414–15. A later memoir attributed to Fairfax repeats his denial of responsibility for the coup (West Yorkshire Archives, Leeds City RO., Bacon Frank MSS., BF/13/7, pp. 182–3). On Fairfax's role, see J. Wilson, *Fairfax* (New York, 1985), pp. 105–10.
46. Waller, *Vindication*, pp. 138–9. For similar views as to Cromwell's complicity, see *The Machivilian Cromwellist* (1648), BL., E.422(12), p. 4; Walker, *Independency*, p. 7; *A Word to Lieut. General Cromwell and his Privy Council* (30 December 1647), BL., E.421(20), p. 49. For Presbyterian accounts less inclined to exculpate Fairfax, see, e.g., *The Army Anatomized* (4 December 1647), BL., E.419(6), pp. 9–10; *Hinc Illae Lacrimae or the Impietie of Impunity* (23 December 1647), BL., E.421(6), pp. 10–11.
47. *Clarke Papers*, I, 124. For a similar view in a royalist pamphlet, see *The Case of the King Stated* (1647), BHPC, p. 6.

transformed the general situation by giving to the army the potentiality of becoming a quasi-independent agency in the quest for settlement with the king.

From the first the coup was defended as a necessary preemptive strike: as in Joyce's alleged reply when Charles asked him why indeed he should go with him from Holdenby:

> That a Plot . . . contrived by some Members of both Houses, to over-throw the Laws of the Kingdom, and a Design to convey his Person to an Army newly to be raised for that Purpose were the Causes of their undertaking this Employment. . . .[48]

There were, it was later argued, four distinct but connected elements in this counter-revolutionary design: the seizure of the artillery train at Oxford, which was ordered by the parliamentary commissioners for Irish affairs on 31 May; the removal of the king from Holdenby, which was thwarted by Joyce's *coup*; the recruitment of a counter-revolutionary force in London; and, finally, a Scottish invasion.[49] 'If they had the King, I mean Hollis and Stapleton', John Rushworth, the secretary of the army council, informed Ferdinando Lord Fairfax on 9 June, 'the Scots in particular had come in to have crushed this army'.[50]

Needless to say, the leading parliamentary Presbyterians poured scorn on what they regarded as a feeble army excuse to justify the seizure of the king in order to give the army the edge in its disputes with parliament. Sir William Waller, for instance, described the notion of a Presbyterian and Scottish plot as 'mere fiction and poetry'.[51] The king's own version of events seems to have varied according to the different recipients of the information and Charles's calculation as to which version would serve to his greatest advantage. Both the earl of Dunfermline on the day after the *coup* and a certain Mr Reymes, with whom Charles lodged at Newmarket on being brought there by the soldiers,

48. *Parliamentary History*, XV, 47. See also *New propositions from the Armie propounded by Cornet Joyce* (17 July 1647), BL., E.399(5), no pagination; *A Copy of the Paper delivered by Cornet Joyce* (June 1647), BL., E.391(10), no pagination. Here the danger of a second war is emphasized. See also *A true impartiall Narration concerning the Armies preservation of the King* (June 1647), BL., E.393(1), esp. pp. 2–9, where the coup is presented as being designed to prevent the king from being secretly conveyed away from Holdenby. Such a counter-revolutionary design on Charles was also emphasized by Fairfax. See *A Copy of the Warrant from his Excellency Sir Thomas Fairfax* (8 June 1647), BL., E.392(11), pp. 4–5.
49. For full details, see below, pp. 379–84.
50. Bell, *Memorials*, I, 353.
51. Waller, *Vindication*, p. 137. For a modern view which is also sceptical about the dangers of a second war and the raising of a counter-revolutionary force, see M.A. Kishlansky, *The Rise of the New Model Army* (Cambridge, 1979), pp. 231, 341 note 80. The threat was, however, treated as very real by Gardiner, *Civil War*, III, 273–4.

affirmed that the king had told them that he had gone unwillingly from Holdenby; according to Reymes Charles had told him that 'rather then be carried by neck and heeles . . . I went along'.[52] On the other hand, once Fairfax had got over his initial horror at Joyce's effrontery, he was prepared to avow to parliament on 6 June that Charles had not only given his consent to the move, but had expressed strong disapproval of the idea of a return to Holdenby, when the General had suggested this as the proper course of action.[53] Even if we accept that the king was at first reluctant to go with Joyce, there can be little doubt that, once with the army, he experienced more considerate treatment than had previously been the case. This is attested by his letter to the earl of Lanark from Caversham on 12 July, stressing 'that I am now at much more freedom than I was at Holmby: for my friends have free acess to me, my chaplains wait upon me . . . and I have free intelligence with my wife and any body else whom I please, all which was flatly denied me before [viz. at Holdenby]'.[54] Although, as Clarendon and others emphasize, there was some deterioration in the army's treatment of the king in the course of the late summer and early autumn, Charles's letter in answer to the proposals delivered by the Scottish commissioners to him at Hampton Court on 22 October, only two weeks before he absconded to the Isle of Wight, still points up both his willingness to leave Holdenby and the continued improvement in his treatment by the army compared with what he had experienced before 4 June.[55]

52. *A true Copy of his Maiesties Message sent to . . . Parliament* (8 June 1647), BL., E.391(8); *A Narration of several passages betwixt His Majesty and Master B. Reymes* (17 June 1647), BL., E.392(31), pp. 3–4. For corroboratory statements, see *Clarke Papers,* I, 124–5; 'Memoirs of Sir John Berkley' in Maseres, *Select Tracts,* I, 359–60.
53. *A Letter from his Excellency Sir Thomas Fairfax (6 June 1647),* BL., E.391(7). See also *A true impartiall Narration* (June 1647), BL., E.393(1), pp. 6–8; *The Kings Majesties last Declaration To the Lord Montague and the rest of the Commissioners* (June 1647), BL., E.396(14), no pagination; *An Extract of certain Papers of Intelligence* (June 1647), BL., E.393(15), p. 3; *Another Letter from His Excellency* (June 1647), BL., E.392(11), pp. 3–5; *Papers of the Desires of the Souldiers* (June 1647), BL., E.392(5), no pagination; a letter from R. Rushton of 9 June in *New Propositions from the Souldiery* (10 June 1647), BL., E.392(12), no pagination; *A letter from a Gentleman to his Father* (3 July 1647), BL., E.396(13), pp. 5–6; *A Vindication of His Majesty and the Army* (July 1647), BL., E.396(5), pp. 3–4; *Parliamentary History,* XV, 414–16; West Yorkshire Archives, Leeds City R.O., Bacon Frank MSS., BF 13/7, pp. 182–3.
54. Burnet, *Lives of the Hamiltons,* p. 402. For confirming statements of the improvement in the king's condition, see *Two Declarations, the first from Newmarket* (June 1647), BL., E.393(31), p. 6; *A Speedy Hue and Crie* (August 1647), BL., E.401(20), pp. 1–2; *HMC., 5th Report,* part i, p. 179.
55. *Clarendon SP.,* II, 381–2. On Charles's access to his children and his chaplains see Clarendon, *Rebellion,* IV, 228, 236–8, 250–3; *Clarke Papers,* I, 140–1; Bell, *Memorials,* I, 365; *Ludlow Memoirs,* I, 152; *Two Letters from His Excellency* (8 July 1647), BL., E.397(15), pp. 3, 6–7; also E.398(2), no pagination. For Clarendon's general observations on the army's treatment of the king, see Clarendon, *Rebellion,* IV, 228–32, 250–1, 256–7.

The army's seizure of the king significantly increased the number of options open to Charles. He could share in the horror of the English Presbyterians and the Scots at the army's unconstitutional *coup*; or he could throw in his lot with the army and its Independent allies; or he could stand aloof and play his ex-enemies off against one another. In fact he got the worst of all these worlds and increased his reputation for inconsistency and duplicity by attempting them all in turn and, on occasions, simultaneously. As early as 8 June the unnamed writer of a letter from Cambridge describes the king's attitude as 'politique and subtle, to lay hold upon any thing for his owne advantage, either to comply with the Army, or [the Parliamentary and Scottish?] Commissioners [or] to be against either, as he sees it worke for his ends'.[56] The radical Independent politician Edmund Ludlow tells how, after 4 June, the king 'began to promise to himself that his condition was altered for the better, and to look upon the Independent interest as more consisting with Episcopacy than the Presbyterian, for that it could subsist under any form, which the other could not do . . . being fully perswaded how naturally his power would revive upon his restitution to the throne, and how easy it would be for him to break through all such promises and engagements upon pretence that he was under a force'.[57] That might have been a sensible policy if it had been consistently pursued, but it was not. It is therefore hardly surprising that, as Charles's adviser Sir John Berkley reports, the army came to suspect the king of double-dealing: that he 'bent all his thoughts to make an absolute Breach between the Army and the Parliament'.[58] Nor were all the ex-Cavaliers on whom Charles drew for advice as judicious and circumspect as Berkley. John Ashburnham in particular seems to have urged the king to continue to play his ill-conceived double game.[59] 'The Kings party carry themselves very high and insolent', observed John Rushworth to Lord Fairfax on 6 July, 'as conceiving the army acts their game; whereas they have little cause to think it'. Rushworth went on to say that if only Charles were willing to grant what the army deemed necessary for national security, such as the settling of the control of the militia in trustworthy hands, he might entertain reasonable hopes of being restored to his just rights; but only then.[60]

56. BL., E.392(11), p. 8.
57. *Ludlow Memoirs*, I, 151; see also p. 154.
58. Maseres, *Select Tracts*, I, 360.
59. See Berkley's criticism, ibid., especially pp. 367–9. For Ashburnham's own account, see Ashburnham, *Narrative*, II, 44–6, 88–100. According to Montereul, the French ambassador at Edinburgh, writing in early August, 'il [Charles] a l'interest d'enretenir toujours ces deux partis en quelque sort d'egalité afin qu'ils s'affablissent entre eux' (*Montereul Correspondence*, II, 214–15).
60. Bell, *Memorials*, I, 365.

On 22 June Charles informed the parliamentary commissioners at Newmarket that he would be happy to come to Richmond as a prelude to negotiating with parliament on the basis of the Newcastle Propositions. There had been a parliamentary demand to Fairfax on 15 June that he should hand over the king, and indeed it was reported on 23 June that the General had agreed that Charles should take up residence at Richmond Palace.[61] But that very same day saw the appearance of a formidable Remonstrance from the army, taking strong exception to the proposal that the king should reside only eight miles from London, when the army had been commanded to keep to a distance of forty miles from the capital. Not surprisingly, this proposal had revived some of those fears of the soldiers which had been a prime cause of the *coup* of 4 June at Holdenby. For at Richmond the king would have been within dangerously easy reach of those in London who were already enlisting troops to serve their counter-revolutionary designs.[62]

The king did not go to Richmond, but in the following month the army's fears were revived by a London petition of 21 July that he be brought to London to treat;[63] a demand which was intensified after the counter-revolutionary coup of 26 July in London which afforded Charles still further opportunities for intrigue.[64] However, while the incident did cause delay in the army's pursuit of alternative peace proposals,[65] the immediate danger of a counter-revolutionary triumph was short-lived, and Charles had again to come to terms with the fact that, following its occupation of London on 6 August, the army had

61. *C.J.*, V, 210–11; *The Resolutions of the Army concerning the King's Majesties going to Richmond* (23 July 1647), BL., E.393(34); Cary, *Memorials*, I, 254; *Montereul Correspondence*, II, 176–7.

62. *Parliamentary History*, XVI, 14; *Several Heads of a Declaration Sent from the Army . . . the 23 of June* (1647), BL., E.393(21).

63. *C.J.*, V, 254; *A Petition from the City of London, 21 July 1647* (1647), BL., E.399(35), pp. 1–6. For further statements to this effect both in the petition and in the City's Solemn Engagement of 21 July, see Rushworth, *Historical Collections*, VI, 638, 639; *L.J.*, IX, 352–3; *HMC., 6th. Report*, p. 190; CLRO., Jor. 40, fos. 241–1(b), 242. See also *C.J.*, V, 259, 260; *Several Orders and Votes of both Houses* (1647), BL., E.400(34), pp. 1–2; *A Declaration of the Lords and Commons . . . for the King's Majesties speedy coming to London* (1647), BL., 669, f11.(55); *A Remonstrance and Declaration of the young men and Apprentices* (31 July 1647), BL., E.400(31), pp. 5–6.

64. *C.J.*, V, 262, 264; *A Declaration* (31 July 1647), BL., 669, f11(55).

65. See the declaration of Fairfax and the Council of War of 2 August, *Parliamentary History*, XVI, 210–12; BL., E.401(4). For a well-argued case that these proposals originated not with the army but with a group of Independent peers, including Lords Northumberland, Saye and Sele and Wharton, see J.S.A. Adamson, 'The English Nobility and the Projected Settlement of 1647', *Hist.J.*, XXX (1987), 567–602. For our purposes, it is sufficient that the army's support was essential to their success. For a view disagreeing with Dr Adamson, see M.A. Kishlansky, 'Saye What?', *Hist.J.*, XXXIII (1990), 917–37.

reasserted its dominant position, even if parliament, and especially the House of Commons, was slow to recognize this.[66]

In restoring in early August the fugitive Independent and other MPs to the parliament from which they had fled in face of the disturbances of 26 July, the New Model Army was acting as the restorer of the integrity of parliament and the opponent of high Presbyterian counter-revolution and its potential links with resurgent Cavalierism. In doing so it was also giving the lie to the widely circulating rumours that it might itself take the lead in the revival of royalism and the forcible restoration of the king on terms acceptable both to him and it.[67] That such fears were greatly exaggerated in no way detracts from the eagerness of the army grandees to reach an understanding with Charles and to formulate the army's and its Independent allies' own peace terms, which, given the king's approval, might be submitted for parliament's consideration as an alternative to the Newcastle Propositions. Such terms had been in process of formulation before the turbulent days of late July, and preliminary articles had been presented for the king's consideration as early as 19 June, at which time also, it will be recalled, parliament was about to try to get the king to Richmond for negotiations on the basis of the Newcastle Propositions. The army's terms were very different, even if somewhat indefinite at this early date. The king was to be restored to 'Crowne and dignity'; the church was to be left '*in statu quo prius*' – before *when*? one might ask – and the king should act as 'umpire' in the current disputes between parliament and the army, for the soldiers 'will haue noe other judge between them then his Majestie'. How far the possibility of such a reconciliation with parliament was from reality may be gauged from the fact that among the articles was the provision that Charles should dissolve parliament and issue writs for a new election by 1 August.[68] This, of course, did not materialize, but there had been at least one major triumph for the army on 2 July when parliament reluctantly accepted its insistence 'not to propose any Place for his Majesty's Residence nearer *London* than they will allow the quarters of the Army to be'.[69]

In a well-known passage in his Memoirs Sir John Berkley tells how Commissary General Henry Ireton on one occasion bluntly told the

---

66. For the July coup in London and its aftermath, see below, pp. 182–8, 349–55.
67. On the notion of the New Model Army as a potentially counter-revolutionary force, see below, pp. 165–70.
68. 'Certain Independent Articles presented by the Army' (19 June 1647), BL., E.393(11). Draft in Thomason's hand.
69. *Parliamentary History*, XVI, 38; L.J., IX, 299–300, 309. See also *A Manifesto from Sir Thomas Fairfax and the Army . . . 27 June 1647*, BL., E.394(15), no pagination; *The Propositions of his Excellency Sir Thomas Fairfax and the rest of the Officers* (27 June 1647), BL., E.394(19), p. 3.

king: 'Sir, you have an intention to be the Arbitrator between the Parliament and us [viz. the army], and we mean to be it between your Majesty and the Parliament'.[70] There is a very real sense in which this accurately sums up the role of the army grandees, now that the army, since its Solemn Engagement on Newmarket Heath on 5 June, the day after the seizure of the king at Holdenby, was increasingly assuming a quasi-independent political stance.[71] As one observer put it, 'the Armies ayme is not to goe against this Parliament by closing with the King without Them . . . but first to make termes with the Parliament in behalfe of the *King, Themselves*, and the *Kingdome*'.[72] In a letter to the Speaker of the House of Commons in early July Fairfax indignantly denied that he and his army colleagues were engaging in underhand dealings with the king and acting as unwitting agents of Charles's design to intensify the mutual antagonism between army and parliament. They had nothing to be ashamed of, he protested, since all their addresses to the king had been made with the object of bringing about his con-currence with parliament in the establishment of a lasting peace.[73] But the General's protest fell on deaf ears. To the Presbyterian majority in the House of Commons and to other conservative parliamentarians it was bad enough for the army to be playing any part whatsoever in the peacemaking process. It was even worse when the alarmingly democratic developments within the army were taken into account: the election of 'agitators' to sit on the army council which had been created the previous month. In such circumstances 'what can be ex-pected but Anarchy and Confusion?'[74] Such suspicions were confirmed by Fairfax's order of 18 July, associating twelve elected agitators with twelve senior officers in the business of perfecting the army's peace proposals.[75]

What chance was there that these proposals might become the basis of a permanent settlement? Sir John Berkley, the former royalist governor of Exeter who had made the acquaintance of several high-ranking officers in the New Model Army at the time of his surrender of Exeter in April 1646, seems to have come to favour the option of royal negotiation with some of the army grandees rather than with the less

70. Maseres, *Select Tracts*, I, 360.
71. The Solemn Engagement is printed in *Leveller Manifestoes*, pp. 146–51. See also the army's Declaration of 14 June, printed in *Leveller Tracts*, pp. 52–63.
72. *A Letter from a Gentleman to his Father* (July 1647), BL., E.396(13), p. 3. Italics in original.
73. *Two Letters from His Excellency* (July 1647), BL., E.397(15), E.398(2).
74. 'Queries whether the Army ought to insist vpon their Charge against those persons they have accused' (1647), Oxford, Worcester College Library, Worcester College [viz. Clarke] MSS., 41, fos. 56(b)–7.
75. *Clarke Papers*, I, 216–17.

radical but more inflexible parliamentary Presbyterians.[76] Both this inclination and his own cautious and diplomatic temper made him a particularly happy choice by the queen as her envoy from France to advise Charles about a settlement. However, in his judicious and revealing account of his mission, Berkley tells how Charles's indecision and his attempt to play off parliament against the army proved to be his undoing. The king, he tells us, was unhappy about the peace terms approved by the army, the so-called Heads of the Proposals, when, through Berkley's agency, he obtained a preliminary view of these at Woburn about a week before they were officially submitted to him on 1 August.[77] If Berkley's account is to be credited, he himself injected a much-needed note of realism into the proceedings by urging upon a very grudging Charles the view that there would in fact have been real grounds for suspicion if the terms had been less severe, given the army's strong position vis-à-vis the king. But Charles was unconvinced and continued to object: more specifically to the facts that the Heads of the Proposals excepted seven of his principal followers from pardon; that his adherents in the war would be disqualified from serving as MPs; and that while, in sharp contrast to the Newcastle Propositions, nothing was objected against episcopacy, nothing was urged positively to affirm its desirability as a form of ecclesiastical government.

The king, whose views were soon to be reinforced by the far less realistic counsels of Ashburnham, was convinced that he should stick out for better terms despite Berkley's sensible advice that the army's current terms, which had already been significantly modified in his favour, offered him at least as much as he could reasonably expect. If Edmund Ludlow is to be believed, the king's optimism was partly based on the calculation that 'the Independent party had infinite obligations to him, for not consenting to the propositions sent to him at Newcastle, which would have totally ruined them'.[78] It was shared by the writer of a royalist newsletter at the beginning of August, who reported that a final settlement was imminent, that the king would yield no essential interest, and that the army's condition was desperate.[79] With the army about to occupy London, its condition was in fact anything but desperate, and it may be that the counter-revolutionary events in London in late July had gone to the writer's, as to the king's, head.[80] Certainly on

76. For Berkley's account of his mission, see Maseres, *Select Tracts*, I, especially pp. 355–73.
77. The Heads of the Proposals are printed in Gardiner, *Constitutional Documents*, pp. 316–26; the Newcastle Propositions, in ibid., pp. 290–306.
78. *Ludlow Memoirs*, I, 156.
79. Bodleian, Clarendon MSS., 30, fo. 24.
80. On these events, see below, pp. 182–8.

or around 28 July Charles had thrown away what seems to have been a golden opportunity of settlement presented to him by the army grandees, insisting, according to Berkley, that '*You cannot be without me. You will fall to ruin if I do not sustain you*'; a remark at which no-one was more astonished than Berkley himself, who asked the king if he had some secret source of strength unknown to him.[81] It is just possible that Charles, who had met the Scottish commissioner Lauderdale on 22 July, had a Scottish card up his sleeve, hoping to engineer a Scottish military intervention on his behalf. But any such hopes rested on the illusory assumption that the king's conditions would be as acceptable to the Scottish parliament as they were to the more accommodating Lauderdale. The royal Engagement with the Scots was only a few months away, but its time had certainly not yet come,[82] in which circumstances, in his confrontation with the senior army officers in late July, Charles was resorting to the emptiest of bluffs. However, even in late September Ashburnham informed Bellièvre, the French ambassador, that there were still ample grounds for optimism since the army commanders were convinced that their own security depended on the king's restoration.[83]

On the earlier occasion at least, Charles seems to have had second thoughts, for on 3 August, with the army's occupation of London now virtually inevitable, he wrote a conciliatory letter to Fairfax. In it he not only remarked on the courteous and considerate way in which he had been treated by the army, but was also at pains to disclaim any personal responsibility for the counter-revolutionary coup of 26 July in London, even though some ex-Cavaliers had been deeply involved in it. Charles's letter also commends the army's peace terms, about which he had been so scornful only a few days earlier. He expressed his pleasure that these did not insist on the abolition either of episcopacy or of his negative voice in parliament; nor on the prohibition of the use of the Book of Common Prayer, the disabling of non-Puritan clergymen and the forcing of the Covenant on all. He also welcomed the army's concern for the restoration of his royal rights and authority, and of his family 'to safety, honour and freedom'. Some of these terms – especially on religious matters – point a clear contrast to the more rigid and unyielding Newcastle Propositions (or Hampton Court Propositions, as we should now describe them). What more, it may be asked, could the king desire? Well, some things apparently, for there were still some

81. Maseres, *Select Tracts*, I, 368–9. Italics as in text.
82. On this, see Gardiner, *Civil War*, III, 334–5; Stevenson, *Revolution and Counter-Revolution*, pp. 90–1. For the Engagement, see below, pp. 321–6.
83. *Montereul Correspondence*, II, 267. For the vacuous comment that it was Fairfax not Charles who missed his opportunity on this occasion, see *A true account and character of the times* (August 1647), BL., E.401(13), p. 7.

unspecified matters to which he could not in conscience consent. Nevertheless, he was now concerned to stress that he saw in the Heads of the Proposals, 'notwithstanding the desires of liberty and freedom in conscience . . . a willingness to . . . conform to a settled Government',[84] and his opinion seems to have been shared by other royalist sources.[85]

Writing to Sir Richard Leveson at the end of August, the royalist William Smith remarked that of the two alternative sets of proposals, the Heads of the Proposals offered much more than the Newcastle Propositions. Although the king's consent on all matters was not to be expected, a little compromise on both sides and a royal reply 'agreeable to the sense of the army' ought to clinch the matter.[86] Indeed, before the end of the month preliminary agreement had been reached on a number of points, including – doubtless to the horror of the parliamentary Presbyterians – liberty of conscience for all; arrangements for the adjournment and subsequent dissolution of parliament and elections to its successor; the continuation of bishops '*in statu quo prius*', and their restoration 'to their indubitable rights' (whatever these might be); the banishment of some former Cavaliers; the relief of Ireland; and the replacement of Fairfax's soldiers at the Tower by City militiamen.[87] In the meantime, on 27 August, parliament had yielded to Scottish pressure to submit again to the king an only marginally altered version of the Newcastle Propositions.[88] According to Major Robert Huntingdon's account, he was sent by Ireton to urge the king to concentrate on the Heads of the Proposals and not worry about parliament's renewed approach, to which it had agreed only to placate the Scots.[89] At any rate, when the king formally received parliament's and the Scots' Propositions, he remarked that they were in substance much the same as the all too familiar Newcastle Propositions, and that he found the army's terms, which Ashburnham was to describe as 'the best of all the Evells offered

84. *Clarendon SP.*, II, 373–4. See also *The Kings Majesties Declaration and Profession* (August 1647), BL., E.401(23); *The Kings Gracious Majesties Most Gracious Message . . . To . . . Sir Thomas Fairfax* (August 1647), BL., E.401(19); *Parliamentary History*, XVI, 205. For a Londoner's scepticism about the King's claim not to be involved in the London coup, see Thomas Juxon's Journal, Dr Williams's Library, MS. 24.50, fos. 116–16(b).
85. Bodleian, Clarendon MSS., 30, fos. 30, 35; *Two Declarations* (15 August 1647), BL., E.402(15), no pagination.
86. *HMC., 5th. Report (Duke of Sutherland's MSS.)*, pp. 172–3, wrongly calendared as 31 [*sic*] April.
87. BL., E.405(11); Bell, *Memorials*, I, 394–6.
88. *Propositions Agreed upon By Both Houses of Parliament* (August 1647), BL., E.404(36), pp. 1–4; *The Proceeding of both Houses of Parliament touching the Kings coming to London* (27 August 1647), BL., E.405(25), pp. 4–6. The Propositions were to be presented to the king on 7 September (*C.J.*, V, 288; *L.J.*, IX, 413). On the tactical significance of this move, see Adamson, *Hist.J.*, art. cit., pp. 582–3.
89. *Parliamentary History*, XVII, 367.

to Him',[90] a far better foundation for a lasting peace. Indeed, to add insult to injury, Charles even suggested that parliament would do well to take the Heads of the Proposals into its serious consideration as a far more suitable basis for a personal treaty.[91] Not surprisingly, on 21 September both Houses declared that the king's reply of a week earlier was in effect 'a denyall of all the Propositions presented to Him from both Kingdomes'.[92]

In the meantime the army did its best to press home its apparent advantage in terms of the king's preference for its peace proposals. On 16 September Fairfax summoned the General Council of the Army to a meeting at Putney. This debated, among other things, the *desiderata* of a just settlement and issued a declaration for presentation to the parliamentary commissioners with the army, who in turn were to submit it to both Houses. In it the Council announced that, following the settlement of peace and the security of the realm, the next priority was the restoration of the king and royal family 'without diminution of their personall Rights or further limitation to the exercise of the Royall power, &c.'.[93]

In a letter of 28 September William Langley described the king's rejection of parliament's propositions and his declared preference for those of the army as simply another royal attempt to foster division between the two.[94] Charles was in fact juggling rather maladroitly with three balls in the air: the parliamentary and Scottish Newcastle (Hampton Court) Propositions; the army's Heads of the Proposals; and, finally, despite the fact that the former were a Scottish no less than an English parliamentary initiative, the possibility of a Scottish military intervention on his behalf. His hopes in connection with this third option were almost certainly confirmed as result of a visit from the Scottish Commissioners on 22 October. The commissioners assured him that the Scots had no intention of insisting that he take the Covenant himself, and that in the event of the failure of the current

90. Ashburnham, *Narrative*, II, 98. Sir John Maynard's sharp criticism of Ashburnham's role and capability in a letter written probably in early August reflects conservative Presbyterian fears of a rapprochement between king and army. (HLRO., Braye MSS., 96, fos. 238–9. This source is a copy of the Commonplace Book of John Browne, of which the original is in the Beinecke Library, Yale University.)
91. *His Majesties Answer to the Propositions . . .* (September 1647), BL., E.407(3), E.407(8), E.407(13); *A Letter from Hampton Court Containing the Substance of His Majesties most Gracious Answer* (September 1647), BL., E.407(2), pp. 1–6; *Papers of the Treatie* (18 September 1647), BL., E.407(34).
92. *The Resolutions of both Houses of Parliament* (September 1647), BL., E.407(6), p. 6.
93. *A Declaration from His Excellency Sir Thomas Fairfax and the General Council of the Army* (18 September 1647), BL., E.407(38), no foliation. See also *The Intentions of the Army* (21 September 1647), BL., E.408(16), passim.
94. *HMC., 5th. Report, part i*, p. 179.

parliamentary peace initiative, they would be prepared to intervene with military force to assist him to recover his throne.[95] It seems likely that such hopes, which were ultimately to come to fruition in Charles's Engagement with the Scots at Christmas, tempered his enthusiasm for a quick settlement on the basis of the army's terms, notwithstanding his declared preference for the Heads of the Proposals in his reply to parliament's peace initiative. Although John Ashburnham is not the most reliable of witnesses and one whose propensity to exaggerate his own contribution to events needs always to be borne in mind, the plan which he describes as the product of his own devising, and from which his colleagues Sir John Berkley and William Legge, who had previously agreed to it, withdrew immediately before the king's flight to the Isle of Wight, might well have appealed to Charles. This was for the king to arrange to meet the Scottish commissioners, who were currently visiting him at Hampton Court, at the Lord Mayor's house in London on the following day. The commissioners would then declare their approbation of the king's last reply to parliament's peace propositions. This in turn would win over the Presbyterians in the City 'over whom they [viz. the Scots] had then a strange influence'. With their backing the king would make a like offer to the House of Lords, and, if necess-ary, 'come in person to the House and . . . give them all other imagin-able Contentment'. If this plan failed, Ashburnham would at least be better placed, with the king in London and not at Hampton Court, to carry him overseas. However, the plan did not even get as far as the first stage, since the Scottish Commissioners, following some initial enthusiasm, later judged that it would not find ready acceptance with the Scottish parliament.[96]

Whether the army's peace initiative would have survived the king's equivocation is a question whose significance is entirely counter-factual, since Charles's abscondence from Hampton Court on 11 November put an abrupt end to what could have been the most promising attempt at settlement since the end of the war. Nevertheless, there can be no doubt that for some time the army grandees had been under some pressure from radical elements to abandon their approach to the king. According to the radical Independent Edmund Ludlow, many in the army com-plained to the agitators 'against the intimacy of Sir John Barkley [sic] and Mr. Ashburnham with the chief officers of the army, affirming that the doors of Cromwell and Ireton were open to them when they were shut to those of the army'.[97] Indeed, in this anti-settlement agitation, the

---

95. On this, see Gardiner, *Civil War*, IV, 1.
96. Ashburnham, *Narrative*, II, 103–7.
97. *Ludlow Memoirs*, I, 165. Complaints to this effect were apparently made in parliament by, e.g., Thomas Scot, the radical Independent MP (*HMC., 5th. Report, part i*, p. 173).

'agitators', the elected representatives of the soldiers, were especially prominent. One of the most damaging charges against the army grandees was that they were cynically disregarding the firm undertaking in the army's momentous Declaration of 14 June not to restore the king before the people's rights had been unshakeably established.[98]

The question of the constitutional position of both the king and the House of Lords was to be the subject of a celebrated debate in the Council of the Army in Putney church on 1 November. There the arguments against the negative voice of the King and Lords were fiercely advanced by agitators such as Everard and Sexby and challenged by Ireton and Cromwell, who defended the royal veto and the Upper House as constitutionally appropriate, at least until such time as a divine dispensation should unequivocally demonstrate that Charles was, as Sexby evocatively put it, the irredeemable Babylon which the army grandees had mistakenly tried to heal.[99] A royalist letter of intelligence on 4 November was certainly premature in stating that Cromwell had already yielded to radical pressure and been won over against the king.[100] A more optimistic – from the royalist point of view – diagnosis had been made, admittedly much earlier on 27 September, by William Smith. Smith argued that, caught between the opposition to army peacemaking from both parliamentary conservatives and Scots on the one hand and the army agitators and the radical wing of the parliamentary Independents on the other, the army grandees would be driven into total dependence upon the king. However, Smith went on to stress that, if this did not happen, the king's prospects would be black indeed, for the only peace option left to him would then be parliament's Hampton Court Propositions which were totally unacceptable to him.[101] On 16 October the Commons had voted to submit these once more for the king's approval within ten days, though they had still not been submitted by that time.[102]

98. See *The Case of the Armie Truly Stated* in *Leveller Manifestoes*, pp. 203–4. For the undertaking in the Declaration of 14 June, see *Leveller Tracts*, p. 61. For other attacks on attempts at settlement with the king, see Francis White, *The Copy of a Letter Sent to His Excellency Sir Thomas Fairfax* (1647), pp. 4, 8–10 (pagination corrected from the original), BHPC.; *A Copy of a Letter Sent by the Agents of several regiments* (11 November 1647), p. 2, BHPC.; *A Call to All the Soldiers of the Armie* (29 October 1647), BL., E.412(10), part i, pp. 6–7, part ii, pp. 5–6. For a comment on the agitators' suspicions about Cromwell's and the grandees' relations with the king, see *HMC., 5th. Report, part i*, p. 179.

99. For the debate, see A.S.P. Woodhouse (ed.), *Puritanism and Liberty* (1966 edn.), pp. 95–124, and especially pp. 102–7.

100. O. Ogle and W.H. Bliss (eds.), *Calendar of Clarendon State Papers preserved in the Bodleian Library* (Oxford, 1872), I, 398.

101. *HMC., 5th. Report, part i*, p. 173.

102. *C.J.*, V, 335–6.

Smith's prognostication might conceivably have been different if he had been aware either of Charles's hopes of what in a few months was to become the party of the Engagement in Scotland; or of the intrigues of the ex-Cavalier Sir Lewis Dyve with his fellow prisoner in the Tower, the Leveller John Lilburne. Ever sanguine, Dyve hoped either to bring the Levellers, and through them the army agitators, over to the king's cause, or, if this failed, to use them to foster irreconcilable divisions among the king's former enemies, both parliament and the army.[103] The first of Dyve's intentions was completely unrealistic, but the second is perfectly consistent with Smith's verdict on how Cromwell and his colleagues might be driven, by the opposition of extremists, into the arms of the king. Certainly they were increasingly coming under attack from both conservatives and radicals. On 22 September one of their opponents, the irrepressible radical Henry Marten, who later was to describe Cromwell as 'king-ridden',[104] had attempted to get a vote through the House of Commons that no more addresses should be made to the king. The vote was not carried and on 24 September the House voted for a further approach to be made to the king.[105] That another Vote of No Addresses was to be passed at the beginning of the next year was to be due less to radical pressure from Marten and his like than to the conversion of Cromwell, Ireton and others who had been the advocates of rapprochement with the king in the summer and autumn of 1647 to the view that all such approaches were futile. That certainly was not a position which they had reached by the beginning of November, and to explain how they came to it will involve the examination of a disastrously worsening situation largely precipitated by Charles's incurable propensity for intrigue and chronic inability to come to terms with reality.

From the king's flight from Hampton Court to the Declaration on the Vote of No Addresses, November 1647–February 1648

The abscondence of Charles I from Hampton Court on 11 November 1647 may have been a necessary, but it was not a sufficient cause of the changed attitude of Cromwell and the army grandees towards negotiations with the king, as manifested by their cold response to his renewed

103. On this, see P. Gregg, *Freeborn John* (1961), pp. 197–205.
104. Cary, *Memorials*, I, 354–5.
105. *C.J.*, V, 312, 314; *Boys Diary*, p. 149. On Marten's measure, see Gardiner, *Civil War*, III, 366–8.

approaches to them from the Isle of Wight. While it is undeniable that the king's flight could have done nothing but worsen his position vis-à-vis the army leaders, it was only one factor behind their change of attitude to him which was due to more complex causes. Both the great Victorian historian of the period and the most recent historian of the army's role in contemporary politics are at one in seeing the fading of hopes of settlement as being very much in progress before 11 November. 'The most disquieting feature of the week's debate [viz. in the Army Council], from 1 to 6 November', writes Professor Woolrych, 'was the growing animus against the king, which threatened the whole basis of a moderate settlement'.[106] Cromwell's and Ireton's insistence at Putney on 1 November on the need to maintain a monarchical constitution was made very much on the defensive. It involved, in Cromwell's case at least, an admission of his willingness to abandon monarchy if God demonstrated that this was His will. Increasingly the king's defenders in the army were becoming preoccupied by the need to counter arguments that he must be brought to account by emphasizing that this was a matter for parliament and not for the army to decide.[107] For the most powerful and emotive of arguments against further negotiations with the king had become emphasis on his war guilt.[108] And that apart, was it not a flagrant defiance of the clear verdict of the God of Battles to negotiate with the king for an indemnity for those to whom He had given decisive victory? And what was the point of all the blood which had been shed if the leaders of the army which had vanquished him were prepared to restore most of his powers including his negative voice? Having won the war, the generals seemed now to be casting aside most of the liberties for which it had been fought. They had, in the words of one of their critics, moved from king-catching to king-courting. Why should victorious soldiers who had fought for the right need pardon or indemnity? What had they done to be pardoned for or indemnified against? So argued the radical pamphlet *An Alarum to the Headquarters* which appeared on 9 November and occasioned a great deal of embarrassment among those against whom its forthright arguments were directed.[109]

---

106. Woolrych, *Soldiers and Statesmen*, p. 262; cf. Gardiner, *Civil War*, IV, 8–9. For an interesting comment by Bellièvre, who however confuses Rainsborough with Desborough, see *Montereul Correspondence*, II, 304–5.

107. See Woodhouse (ed.), *Puritanism and Liberty*, especially pp. 96–7, 103–7, 110–12, 114–15, 120. See also Woolrych, *Soldiers and Statesmen*, pp. 267–8.

108. See especially the contributions of Sexby, Bishop and Wildman to the debate at Putney on 1 November (Woodhouse (ed.), op. cit., pp. 102–3, 107, 108). For Harrison's views (not at Putney), see Woolrych, op. cit., p. 267.

109. *The Coppy of a dangerous paper published called an Alarum to the Headquarters* (1647), BL., E.420(5), pp. 11–19.

If a combination of the clearly connected factors of growing opposition within the army and the king's unwillingness to agree to what in the circumstances were very reasonable terms had put the main proponents of a settlement, Cromwell and Ireton, into a very awkward position, the real importance to them of Charles's precipitate flight from Hampton Court may well have been that it got them off the hook. This is among the main pieces of circumstantial evidence in favour of the likelihood that the king's flight was engineered by Cromwell who deliberately alarmed him by tales of planned attempts on his life by Levellers and others. This view was later to be given credence by the royalist newswriter *Mercurius Pragmaticus*, who, in the following month, reported that the Levellers were petitioning Fairfax to exculpate them from the charge that they had planned to kill the king, which in fact had simply been put about as a stratagem to drive him from Hampton Court.[110] Indeed, the very ease with which Charles's escape had been managed might be regarded as a further argument in favour of this view of events. In a self-exculpatory letter to Speaker Lenthall, Colonel Whalley, who had been in charge of security at Hampton Court, emphasized the very loose terms on which, in accordance with the instructions which he had received, the king had been held there: 'I cannot term it an escape, because he never was in custody as a prisoner'. Moreover, Whalley mentions a letter which he had received from Lieutenant General Cromwell, intimating 'some murderous designe, or at least fear of it, against his Majesty'. This he had shown to the king, while assuring him of his diligence in protecting him against any such danger.[111]

Whalley was not the only person to go in for self-exculpation about this incident. John Ashburnham, who had played a crucial part in

110.   *Mercurius Pragmaticus, no. 14* (14/21 December 1647), BL., E.421(1), no pagination.
111.   *Colonel Whaleyes* [sic] *Relation concerning His Majesties going from Hampton Court* (1647), BL., E.420(5), pp. 4–8. See also *A more full Relation of . . . His Majesties departure . . . by Colonel Whaley* [sic] (22 November 1647), BL., E.416(23), pp. 1–6. For the letter from E.R. warning Charles, see *A Letter which His Majestie left on the table* (1647), BL., E.420(5), pp. 19–20. For statements that the king absconded because he felt himself to be in danger, see *A Letter written by John Ashburnham Esquire* (1647), BL., E.420(5), pp. 9–11; *The Copy of a Letter from Mr. Ashburnham to a Friend* (1648), especially pp. 1–3, Oxford, Codrington pamphlet collection; Clarendon, *Rebellion*, IV, 261–2. For Charles's corroboration of these reasons for his flight, see L.J., IX, 519–20; *His Majesties Most Gracious Declaration Left by him on his Table* (11 November 1647), BL., E.413(15), especially pp. 6–7; *His Majesties most Gracious Declaration from the Isle of Wight* (November 1647), BL., E.416(33), pp. 3–7; *Another Gracious Message from the Kings most Excellent Majesty* (November 1647), BL., E.417(7), pp. 5–6; *A Letter from Colonel Hammond to the Speaker of the Lords House* (1647), BL., E.417(10), pp. 5–6. For a radical Independent view that the king's flight was urged by Cromwell, see *Ludlow Memoirs*, I, 168–9, 171–2. For the views of a Presbyterian to the same effect, see *The Army Anatomized* (December 1647), BL., E.419(6), pp. 36–7.

Charles's escape, certainly felt no need to justify the withdrawal of his parole to Colonel Whalley shortly before the event, and later insisted that it was clear that by so doing he had also disengaged the king.[112] If this is true, it makes Whalley's responsibility for the king's escape so much the greater. But the heavy charge which Ashburnham ultimately had to face from his fellow Cavaliers was that, as the person most influential in persuading Charles to abscond to the Isle of Wight, he bore a terrible responsibility for the subsequent deterioration of relations culminating in the abandonment of attempts at negotiation, the presentation by parliament of hard-and-fast terms in the form of the Four Bills in December, and, following the king's refusal to give the royal assent to these, the Vote of No Addresses at the beginning of 1648. There were indeed royalists who argued that Ashburnham had been corrupted – or, at best, duped – by the Machiavellian Cromwell into instigating Charles's flight from Hampton Court.[113] Needless to say, he not only denied the charge indignantly, but confidently asserted that the events leading up to the Vote of No Addresses would have taken place even if Charles had never left Hampton Court.[114] There is a sense in which this is true, even if the reality is once again rather more complex. Just as the rumours of a plot to assassinate him provided Charles and his advisers with an excuse for a flight which had already been planned before these things came to light, so did his flight strengthen the arguments of both army and parliament for a tougher line with the king, a policy towards which the army at least was probably already moving before 11 November.

This was soon to be abundantly clear to almost everybody but the king. In a declaration which he left in his chamber at Hampton Court Charles was at pains to emphasize that his primary aim was still 'the setling of a safe and well-grounded Peace', which would satisfy all parties: 'the Presbyterians, Independents, Army, those who have adhered to me, and even the Scots'. The army's arrears of pay should be met, and there should be an Act of Oblivion and provision for a generous measure of religious toleration.[115] This last point, like Charles's previous observation approving the army's suggestion that there should shortly be an end to the existing parliament,[116] may have been designed to set the army and its parliamentary Presbyterian opponents at one

112. *A Letter written by John Ashburnham Esquire* (1647), BL., E.420(5), pp. 9–11.
113. Clarendon's scepticism about such allegations about Ashburnham (they also applied to a lesser extent to Berkley) is the more convincing in view of the rather low opinion which he had of him anyway (Clarendon, *Rebellion*, IV, 268–73).
114. Ashburnham, *Narrative*, II, 130; *The Copy of A Letter from Mr Ashburnham . . .* (1648), p. 3, Oxford, Codrington pamphlet collection.
115. *His Majesties Most Gracious Declaration . . .* (1647), BL., E.413(15), pp. 3–5; T. May, *A Breviary of the History of the Parliament of England* (1813 edn.), in Maseres, *Select Tracts*, I, 106.
116. See above, p. 22.

another's throats. In a letter of 16 November to the Speaker of the House of Lords Charles paid scant attention to the changed situation brought about by his flight to the Isle of Wight.[117] Propounding details of the sort of settlement he would find acceptable, he emphasized that he was prepared to yield to some of the Hampton Court Propositions, but not to others, or at least not without substantial modification. Three significant concessions, however, were parliamentary control of the militia for his own lifetime, but for no longer, since that would deprive the Crown, as distinct from himself, of an inalienable right; parliamentary nomination of his councillors; and a revocation of his wartime declarations against the parliament. He also undertook to give parliament satisfaction in the matter of Ireland. As to religion, he would countenance the continuation of the Presbyterian settlement established by parliament in 1645–6 for a trial period of three years, though with some provision for tender consciences, including his own. After the three years a permanent settlement should be made by King and Parliament acting on the recommendation of the Westminster Assembly of Divines and twenty additional divines nominated by himself. But while Charles was prepared to recommend the association of 'presbyters' with bishops in diocesan government and emphasized the need for a preaching episcopate, his religious concessions were less substantial than they at first seemed in that he declared that a total and permanent abolition of episcopacy would be repugnant to his conscience and a violation of his coronation oath. No less unacceptable to him would be the permanent alienation of episcopal lands which would both be sacrilege and subvert the pious intentions of the original donors. Moreover, it would probably militate against the interests of lay lessees of such lands who often enjoyed more favourable terms than they would get from secular landlords, even though it had been the firm intention of archiepiscopal economic reformers from Bancroft to Laud to maximize revenues by diminishing, or even entirely removing, this advantage.

Although such concessions as he was prepared to make would have been unimaginable a year or two earlier, Charles had no grounds for believing that they would be acceptable to parliament now. It is true that, in a letter of 19 November to the earl of Lanark, he protested that he had gone out of his way 'to placate all interests with all possible equality (without wronging my conscience)', and that some of his concessions would certainly displease many of his former adherents.[118]

117. *His Majesties Gracious Message and Propositions* (19 November 1647), BL., E.416(10)́, pp. 4–8, also E.416(11). The king's letter, read in the House of Lords on 18 November, is also fully reported in *The Perfect Weekly Account no. 47* (17/23 November 1647), BL., E.416(27), no pagination.

118. Burnet, *Lives of the Hamiltons*, p. 413.

But they cut no ice with parliament. Even before his flight the House of Commons had voted on 6 November, on completion of the latest version of the Propositions to be sent to the king, that it was his constitutional duty to give his assent to bills presented to him by the Houses. If parliament chose to present the propositions in the form of bills – as it was shortly to do in the case of four of them – the king's duty was to accept these without pressing the sort of amendments which he now did from the Isle of Wight.[119] But that was unthinkable. As a royalist pamphlet which appeared on 12 November before the king's escape had become widely known put it, it would involve Charles's relinquishment of his God-given authority, as a result of which 'Tyranny would be incorporated into our very Constitution and Government, and our slavery would be both grievous . . . and remedilesse, being tyed to it by Act of Parliament'.[120]

So Charles reverted to his alternative option: a renewal of the lapsed negotiations with the army. On 26 November he wrote to Fairfax informing him that he was sending Sir John Berkley to discuss this matter. In his letter he took pains to stress that the disorders associated with the agitators in the army, and which had – or so he alleged – driven him from Hampton Court, could only issue in confusion and anarchy if no settlement were reached. Fairfax chose to play the king's communication with a very dead bat, protesting that Charles's request for a personal treaty was not a matter for him or the army council but for parliament. Recognizing that there was nothing more to be said or done, Berkley left the council at the army headquarters at Windsor and returned to the Isle of Wight.[121]

Fairfax's reply is a clear indication of the total failure of Charles's strategy of playing off the army's terms against parliament's. Indeed, far from consenting to a personal treaty in response to the king's approach of 16 November, parliament was preparing a new approach insisting that he give unqualified assent to four propositions, which were now to take the form of bills, as a condition of negotiation on the remainder. That Charles no longer had any alternative proposals from the army to fall back on was something for which he had only his own duplicity and vacillation of the summer and autumn to thank. There remained the Scottish option. On 19 November Charles wrote to Lanark asking him to assure his fellow commissioners that the king's move to the Isle of Wight had in no way altered his intentions from what they had been

119. *C.J.*, V, 352; see Gardiner, *Civil War*, IV, 9.
120. *The Rev-view* [sic] *of the Propositions Presented To His Majesty* (12 November 1647), BL., E.414(7), especially pp. 3–4.
121. BL., Egerton MSS., 2618, fo. 21; *The King's last Message and Declaration* (4 December 1647), BL., E.419(7), pp. 1–4; Maseres, *Select Tracts*, I, 383–4.

when they had last met him at Hampton Court.[122] At about the same time a royalist newsletter stressed the contrast between the Scottish insistence on full negotiations on all matters – a personal treaty – and the English parliament's disinclination to a personal treaty 'untill His Majesty have granted them all *that He intends to Treate with them about*'.[123] One possibility of which the king was certainly very conscious was that, if the English parliament remained adamant about a personal treaty, which the Scottish commissioners again requested on 23 November,[124] this might provide the occasion for a Scottish military intervention on his behalf: the catch for which he had earlier been angling at Hampton Court.

It was only a matter of a few weeks before such a Scottish Engagement with Charles would be concluded, but first the English parliament had to demonstrate its unwillingness to respond to the king's request for a personal treaty and his offer to make substantial concessions.[125] Its only response in fact was the constitutional transmutation of four of the Hampton Court Propositions into bills, royal assent to which was to be the condition of negotiations taking place on the remainder. By 14 December the bills had passed through both Houses and a committee had been nominated to carry them down to the king in the Isle of Wight.[126] Parliament disregarded four successive protests from the Scottish commissioners between 14 and 20 December, refusing to respond either to their request to inspect the bills or to their insistence that a personal treaty ought to precede the drafting and presentation of bills.[127] On Christmas Eve the earl of Denbigh informed the Speaker of the Upper House that the four bills had that day been submitted to the king, who had promised an answer within a few days.[128] Even if parliament had abolished Christmas, the king had not.

122. Burnet, *Lives of the Hamiltons*, p. 413.
123. *Mercurius Elencticus Number 4* (19/29 November 1647), BL., E.417(9), pp. 28–9. Italics in text. See also Clement Spelman, 'Reasons why we should Admitt the King to a Personall Treaty', Bodleian, Tanner MSS., 58, fos. 1–2(b).
124. Bodleian, Tanner MSS., 58, fo. 593. For details about the role of the Scots, see below, pp. 323–6.
125. *His Majesties Reasons Given to both Houses for a Personall Treaty* . . . (28 November 1647), BL., E.417(12), pp. 3–8. For a similar later approach, see *His Majesties Most Gracious Message to His Two Houses* . . . (6 December 1647), BL., E.419(11), pp. 3–6, also reproduced on 9 December in *The Kingdomes Weekly Intelligencer, number 238* (7/14 December 1647), BL., E.419(24), pp. 761–2.
126. *The Perfect Weekly Account* (8/15 December 1647), BL., E.419(28), no pagination; Gardiner, *Civil War*, IV, 36–7. For a good succinct account of the content and significance of the bills, see ibid., IV, 31–2. For the text of the bills and the accompanying propositions, see Gardiner, *Constitutional Documents*, pp. 335–47. For some interesting comments by Bellièvre, see *Montereul Correspondence*, II, 331–2, 339–40, 348–9, 355.
127. *C.J.*, V, 385, 386; *L.J.*, IX, 582–4, 605; *Parliamentary History*, XVI, 430–73; *Cal.SPD. 1645–7*, pp. 582–3.
128. *Cal.SPD. 1645–7*, p. 582 (*The Kingdom's Weekly Post*, no. 1).

It was the first and fourth bills which probably presented the most difficulty for the king. Certainly the other two were unpalatable in that they involved Charles in the distasteful business of eating his own words by revoking his wartime declarations against parliament and making void the titles of honour which he had granted since Lord Keeper Lyttleton had carried off the Great Seal to him at York on 20 May 1642. But the first and fourth bills aimed mortal blows at the heart of the royal prerogative. The first bill gave parliament complete control over the militia and the navy for twenty years, with no provision that control should revert automatically – viz. without specific parliamentary approval – to the Crown thereafter. Here was one major issue over which war had originally broken out in 1642, and parliament was intent on making certain that the fruits of its victory would not be squandered. The fourth bill transferred from the king to parliament itself the prerogative of adjourning parliament to a specific time and place. The non-party MP Clement Walker criticizes the bill as designed to secure the hegemony of the parliamentary Independents and their allies in the army by facilitating what would virtually amount to a purge of MPs of a contrary opinion through adjournment to a place near to army headquarters, where opponents of the Independents 'shall neither sitt with accommodation nor safety'.[129] But this appears to postulate an Independent majority in parliament in order for such an adjournment to be carried out in the first place. Moreover, Walker's verdict needs to be tempered by careful consideration of the measure in the light of the events of the past few months, and more particularly those of 26 July and their aftermath. For to many – and not exclusively Independent – MPs the need for parliament to be able to move nearer to the protection of the army was a corollary of its need to move out of danger of coercion by royalist and other counter-revolutionary elements, such as had been spectacularly manifested in London and Westminster during the previous July.

Would Charles's assent to the Four Bills have amounted to, as one royalist put it, 'an Actuall Abdication of his Kingdome and . . . surrender of his Crowne'?[130] Charles himself was to argue on 18 January 1648 that the bills left nothing else worth negotiating about, and that it was outrageous to expect him 'to grant beforehand the most considerable part of the . . . subject matter'.[131] On the contrary, however, there were some crucially important considerations among the Additional Propositions which would be open to negotiation if only Charles would give

---

129. Walker, *Independency*, p. 42. On the bills in general, see ibid., pp. 41–2, 48.
130. Bodleian, MSS., dep. C.168, no. 43 (Nalson MSS., XV, 43), fos. 99(b)–100.
131. *The Kings Declaration To All His Subjects* (February 1648), BL., E.426(5), p. 2.

his assent to the bills. Among these was the proposed restoration of parliamentarians whom the king had deprived of office or other benefits for supporting parliament in the war; the matter of an Act of Indemnity or Oblivion; the abolition of the Court of Wards; royal *ex post facto* approbation of the wartime treaties between parliament and the Scots; the satisfaction of the army's arrears of pay out of the sale of episcopal lands; the abolition of episcopacy and the establishment of a Presbyterian ecclesiastical polity; the treatment of former Cavaliers, including the exception of some of them from hope of pardon; and provision for tender consciences, that toleration which was so execrated by English and Scottish Presbyterians alike. These were hardly trivial matters, though it could be argued that a diminution of the king's bargaining power in respect of them would have been a probable consequence of any previous assent to the Four Bills.

In explaining, in his formal communication to the Speaker of the House of Lords on 28 December, why he must withhold that assent, Charles objected both to the questionable mode of parliament's approach and to the substance of the bills.[132] He lost no opportunity of emphasizing that on both these things his Scottish subjects had made their own objections known to him.[133] What he did not specify was his own most cogent reason for refusing his assent: the Engagement which he had made with the Scottish commissioners on the eve of his receiving the Four Bills. This now offered him the distinct likelihood of a Scottish military intervention on his behalf.[134] For the time being, however, the Scottish strategy was to continue to press for a personal treaty without prior conditions, leaving the extreme measures envisaged in the Engagement in reserve to be employed as a consequence of the English parliament's continued refusal of their demands.

Clarendon observes how, 'upon the [king's] refusal to pass these bills, every man's mouth was opened against him with the utmost sauciness and license'.[135] Hostile reaction both inside and outside parliament

132.   The king's answer is printed in Gardiner, *Constitutional Documents*, pp. 353–6. See also, *L.J.*, IX, 621; *Cal.SPD. 1645–7*, p. 583; *His Majesties Declaration and Resolution*, 28 December 1647 (5 January 1648), BL., E.422(6), pp. 2–4; *The Kingdomes Weekly Intelligencer*, no. 241, for 31 December 1647 (27 December/4 January 1647–8), BL., E.421(30), pp. 789–90; *The Kingdomes Weekly Post* (29 December/5 January 1647–8), BL., E.422(1), pp. 6–7.

133.   In a letter of 28 December, the same day as his formal refusal of assent to the Four Bills, *Cal.SPD. 1645–7*, pp. 582–3, viz. *Perfect Occurrences*, no. 53; see also, *A Declaration of the Estates of the Kingdome of Scotland*, 28 December 1647 (6 January 1648), BL., E.422(6), p. 5; *The Kingdomes Weekly Intelligencer*, number 241 (27 December/4 January 1647–8), BL., E.421(30), p. 787; *The Perfect Weekly Account number 1* (28 December/5 January 1647–8), BL., E.421(33), no pagination.

134.   On the Engagement, see below, pp. 321–6.

135.   Clarendon, *Rebellion*, IV, 281.

ranged between proposing his impeachment for high treason and settling peace without him.[136] One pamphleteer, incensed by the incessant Scottish harping on the need for a personal treaty, pronounced that he failed to see why, 'if the Parliament have made war without the king . . . they may not make peace without him'.[137] And this is precisely what was done through the Vote of No Addresses. The Vote passed the House of Commons on 3 January 1648 by a very comfortable margin but had a much rougher passage in the Lords, who did not pass it until 17 January.[138] In the meantime on 9 January Fairfax and the Army Council had agreed a forthright declaration in favour of the Vote.[139] If Clement Walker is to be believed, it was this, together with Fairfax's garrisoning of the Mews and Whitehall, that finally tipped the scales in the Lords in favour of the Vote.[140]

To royalists the Vote of No Addresses was significant as the first official parliamentary admission of a long-cherished, but hitherto tacit, anti-monarchical objective.[141] Moreover, parliament's Declaration on the Vote, which appeared in February, provided some additional grist to the royalist propaganda mill.[142] In what was in a sense a new version of

136. For some reactions, see Walker, *Independency*, pp. 42–3; W.C. Abbott (ed.), *The Writings and Speeches of Oliver Cromwell* (1937–47), I, 576; *Boys Diary*, pp. 155–6; *Mercurius Elencticus Number 6* (29 December/5 January 1647–8), BL., E.421(6), p. 48.
137. *England's Condition Considered and Bewailed* (18 January 1648), BL., E.423(6), p. 15.
138. On the passage of the Vote, see Gardiner, *Civil War*, IV, 50–4. For contemporary reports on its progress in the Lords, see *The Kingdomes Weekly Intelligencer*, no. 142. (4/11 January 1648), BL., E.422(18), p. 798; *Heads of the Chiefe Passages in Parliament* (12/19 January 1648), BL., E.423(11), p. 12. The Vote is printed in Gardiner, *Constitutional Documents*, p. 356.
139. *A Declaration from Sir Thomas Fairfax and the generall Councel* (11 January 1648), BL., E.422(21), pp. 3–7, E.422(22), pp. 1–5. For a later declaration from the Hampshire Grand Jury to a similar effect, see *The humble and thankful Acknowledgement and Declaration of the County of Southampton* (24 January 1648), BL., 669, f.11(120); *The Kingdomes Weekly Post* (19/26 January 1648), BL., E.423(25), pp. 28–9. For scornful royalist comment on the Hampshire declaration, see *Mercurius Pragmaticus*, no. 4 (27 January/3 February 1648), BL., E.425(12), p. 27. For other local expressions of support for the Vote, see *The Humble Petition . . . of the Town of Taunton* (9 February 1648), BL., E.427(21), pp. 3–7; 'The Grand Inquest at the Assizes held at Chard', *HMC., 13th. Report, Portland MSS.*, I, 448; *The Kingdomes Weekly Post* (9/15 February 1648), pp. 49–50.
140. Walker, *Independency*, p. 45. For other criticisms of the army council's declaration from various points of view, see 'Consideration upon occasion of the Late Declaration of the Army', Bodleian, MSS., dep. C.168, no. 43 (Nalson MSS., XV, 43), fos. 97–103; *Memorials of Denzil Lord Holles*, Maseres, *Select Tracts*, I, 304–5.
141. For examples, see *Mercurius Elencticus, no. 12* (12 January 1648), BL., E.422(25), p. 46; *Mercurius Pragmaticus, no. 17* (4/11 January 1648), BL., E.422(17), no pagination; ibid., no. 18 (11/18 January 1648), E.423(2), no pagination. Italics in texts. See also *An Allarme to the City of London* (29 August 1648), BL., E.461(19), p. 7; Clarendon, *Rebellion*, IV, 283–6.
142. The Declaration was dated 5 February. It is printed in *Parliamentary History*, XVIII, 2–24. For the king's answer, see ibid., pp. 31–43.

the Grand Remonstrance of 1641 now brought right up to date, all the familiar arguments about royal misgovernment were dragged out again; not forgetting the absurd innuendo about the circumstances attending the death of James I. As more than one observer remarked, here was a deliberate design to tarnish the image of the king so as to make the ultimate extirpation of monarchy the easier to accomplish.[143]

The declared object of the Declaration on the Vote of No Addresses was 'to un-deceive the people', though one royalist commentator saw it as being 'to preserve that little *Esteeme* they have left'.[144] Royalist replies to it, including the king's own poignant and moving appeal,[145] vary in character from the crude abuse of newsletters to the more impressive denunciation in a pamphlet published on 17 February which varies such intemperate abuse with reasoned argument. Taking a leaf out of the book of the most able royalist apologists in 1642–3 by frankly admitting that not every royal action could be justified,[146] owing to the faults of the king's ministers, the author made an eloquent appeal for the king to be given the opportunity to reply to the Declaration and for his reply to be afforded equivalent publicity. He countered the Declaration's charge that it was the king who had been the obstacle to a just settlement by citing Charles's own offers of November and December as exhibiting a willingness to 'sacrifice all his owne power and greatnesse . . . to the peace and preservation of his people'. The pamphlet makes an impassioned appeal for a personal treaty and pleads for parliament not to 'expose us to the hazard of another bloody war'.[147]

Just how inviolable was the Vote of No Addresses? As Clement Walker gleefully points out, there seems to have been one rule for the generality and another for the army grandees. Certainly Cromwell and his colleagues were not above disregarding the Vote, at least in their exploratory feelers made through persons close to the king such as the

143. Walker, *Independency*, pp. 45–9. See also *An Allarme to the City of London* (29 August 1648), BL., E.461(19), p. 7.

144. *Mercurius Elencticus*, no. 11 [sic], (2/9 February 1648), BL., E.426(12), p. 81. Italics in original. For other royalist attacks on the Declaration, see *Mercurius Bellicus*, no. 4 (14/20 February 1648), BL., E.428(4), defective pagination; *Mercurius Pragmaticus*, no. 23 (15/22 February 1648), BL., E.428(9), no pagination; *A New Magna Charta* (17 February 1648), BL., E.427(15), p. 2; *Great Britans* [sic] *Vote or God save King Charles* (27 March 1648), Codrington, pamphlet coll., pp. 28–32.

145. *The Kings Declaration to All His Subjects, 18 January* (February 1648), BL., E.426(5); *Parliamentary History*, XVIII, 27–43. On the king's reply and the growth of sympathy for his cause, see below, pp. 213–14.

146. On this, see Ashton, *Civil War*, pp. 177–8, and idem, 'From Cavalier to Roundhead Tyranny 1642–9', in J.S. Morrill (ed.), *Reactions to the English Civil War 1642–1649* (1982), pp. 188–9.

147. *An Antidote Against An Infectious Aire* (17 February 1648), BL., E.427(18), no pagination.

earl of Southampton and Captain Silas Titus, the former parliamentarian officer but now a trusted confidant of Charles.[148] Nor were such approaches confined to the army. In February and early March 1648 the English correspondent of the earl of Lanark reported that parliament was about to make a new approach to the king.[149] Although in this case he seems to have simply been retailing current rumour, parliament was to make more definite approaches in April and August, the first involving a dispensing with the Vote and the second its rescission.[150] What is at first especially surprising, however, is not so much that the Vote was ultimately rescinded and another treaty with the king agreed upon, as that this event took place in August near to the conclusion of a second civil war in which the forces which had tried to restore the king to power by military might were decisively crushed. If parliament believed that there was no case for a personal treaty in January, why should it sanction one in August when the hopes of militant Cavaliers and their Scottish allies lay in ruins? Since this is a question whose answer is closely bound up with much of the material of the later chapters of this book, it is more appropriately dealt with in that context.[151] Here it must suffice to observe that among the main reasons for the defeat of the royalist insurgents and their Scottish allies in the Second Civil War was their failure to obtain the active support of that parliamentary group which had appeared to be their most likely potential ally: those parliamentary Presbyterians who had been the most enthusiastic advocates of a settlement with the king even if on terms which proved to be unacceptable to him. It will be argued later that the decision to treat with the king in the Isle of Wight in the autumn of 1648 was in one sense a government pay-off for Presbyterian quiescence during the Second Civil War. But the paradox is that, while it was the parliamentary Presbyterians who were the most prominent agitators for the rescinding of the Vote of No Addresses and the reopening of negotiations with Charles I, it was also their – no less than the king's – intransigence which inhibited the successful conclusion of these negotiations. It is true that the treaty was brought to an abrupt end at the beginning of December by the intervention of an irate army, fearful that its recent gains on the battlefield were being put in jeopardy by the

---

148. Walker, *Independency*, pp. 49–50.
149. *Hamilton Papers*, pp. 149–50. See also, *HMC., 11th. Report, Appendix, part 6 (MSS. of the Duke of Hamilton)*, p. 117; SRO., GD/406/1/2227.
150. On the resolution of 28 April, see *C.J.*, V, 547; Rushworth, *Historical Collections*, VII, 1074. The resolution dispensing with the Vote passed without a division, following the defeat of the procedural motion that it be not put by 146 votes to 101.
151. See below, pp. 294–5, 479.

politicians. But even if the army had not purged parliament and brought the king from the Isle of Wight to stand trial, there are scant grounds for assuming that these negotiations would have been attended with any greater success than those which have formed the subject of the present chapter.

II

DISILLUSIONMENT AND ALIENATION: I. NO PEACE DIVIDEND

... the common sort of people thought we should have had a golden Age ... they expected *England* to have become a second Paradise. ... But ... the remedy of these pretenders to Reformation is ... worse than the disease: the two Houses have filled the Kingdom with Serpents, bloodthirstie Souldiers, extorting Committees, Sequestrators, Exisemen, all the Rogues and scumme of the Kingdom have they set on work to torment and vex the people, to rob them, and to eat the bread out of their mouthes. ...

> The Declaration of many thousands of
> the City of Canterbury, or County of Kent
> (5 January 1648), BL., E.421(23), pp. 3–4

The sour fruits of victory

The failure to reach a settlement with the king, which was the subject of the last chapter, was one of the main reasons why the unprecedented burdens borne by the English people during the First Civil War were continued beyond the end of hostilities. Others were prolonged uncertainty about the line which the Scots would take both before and after their withdrawal from England in February 1647 and the fear of a revival of militant royalism. However, there is an element of circularity about this observation, in that the need to keep a large army under arms to guard against these dangers was itself contributing to their intensification by swelling the discontents on which they fed and making both alienation from the victorious parliamentary regime and the revival of Cavalierism the more likely. It was greatly to be hoped, petitioned the Deputy Lieutenants, Justices of the Peace and other inhabitants of Essex on 13 March 1647, that their shire, which had been the most enthusiastic parliamentarian county during the war, should 'now that God hath blest us out of the hands of our Enemies . . . not be eaten up, enslaved and destroyed by an Army raised for our defence'.[1]

The closing years of the First Civil War had abounded with complaints against ruinously high taxation and exactions more oppressive than those of Egyptian taskmasters.[2] But, groaned complainants from the north of England in November 1647, these wartime burdens 'were but molehills to the numerous pressures which now we are crushed under': oppressive taxes, free quarter, rape and pillage, which were the more intolerable since they were exacted and committed by 'an useless and insaturate Souldiery'.[3] 'Observe', declared the indignant anti-Independent MP Clement Walker, 'that when the War was at the highest, the *monthly tax* came but to 54 000 l. . . . But now this Army hath 60 000 l a month and 20 000 l a month more *pretended for Ireland'*. 'What', queried rhetorically another anti-Independent in December 1647, 'has occasioned all the Taxes upon the Kingdom but their Armies?' – armies, moreover, whose original raison d'être had been removed with the end of the war.[4]

Needless to say, complaints against the army elicited howls of righteous indignation from the soldiers and their Independent allies in parliament. The latter's claims that the disbandment of the army, which was a main plank in the parliamentary Presbyterian platform in 1647, would solve nothing since parliament would then need to raise another force, so that 'the taking away the Army will not take away the military charge from you',[5] cut little ice since the unpopularity of the army cannot be construed solely in terms of the financial burden on the community, though this is the main emphasis of the present chapter.[6] There is certainly more than a grain of truth in the assertion of one Independent pamphleteer that Holles, Stapleton, Prynne and other Presbyterian politicians were co-ordinating a none too scrupulous propaganda campaign to put suspicions about the army into the minds of simple folk.[7] Similarly, that stalwart champion of the army, the chaplain Hugh Peter, insisted forcefully on the perils that would attend disbandment, 'not seeing a suitable power to stand betwixt honest men

1. *The humble Petition of the Deputy Lieutenants, Iustices of the Peace and Commons of the County of Essex* (March 1647), BL., 669, f.10 (102). See also another Essex petition in April (*The Humble Petition of the Inhabitants of the County of Essex* (April 1647), BL., E.383(24), pp. 6–8: *A new found stratagem* (April 1647), BHPC., pp. 3–4).
2. For an example from Dorset on 17 June 1646, see Bodleian, Tanner MSS., 59, fo. 345.
3. *A Remonstrance of the Northern Association* (15 November 1647), BL., E.414(12), especially pp. 4–5, 7–8.
4. Walker, *Independency*, p. 38; *A Word to Lieut. General Cromwell and his Privy Councel* (December 1647), BL., E.421(20), p. 23.
5. *A new found stratagem* (April 1647), BHPC., pp. 4–14.
6. For other reasons for the army's unpopularity, see below, pp. 159–65.
7. *A Vindication of the Armies Proceedings* (July 1647), BL., E.395(6), pp. 2–3.

and their dangers'. Certainly there was more than a smattering of truth in Peter's contention that the army was being made the scapegoat for all the evils of the kingdom.[8] Indeed, Holles and the Presbyterians seemed to be on to a very good thing when they made disbandment the centre-piece of their programme in the spring of 1647. As a letter from Bucking-hamshire written on 28 June by one who clearly supported that programme maintained, the soldiers might protest that wherever they came, 'the Countrey petitions them to redresse their Grievances, and not to disband till they are redressed: whereas it is very well known that there was a Petition prepared in this County to have the Army disbanded'.[9] Even radical and sophisticated pro-army sources had to admit, as did the famous radical tract *The Case of the Army Truly Stated*, which was presented by the army 'agitators' to Lord General Fairfax on 18 October 1647, that 'The love and affection of the people to the Armie . . . is decayed, cooled and neere lost'; and 'the people say that their resolutions not to disband were because they live idly on the peoples labours'.[10]

The unpopularity of the army and the unpopularity of wartime taxation carried over into a period of peace were of course clearly connected. The fact that for a variety of reasons, many of which are dealt with in a later chapter,[11] the army was increasingly unpopular made the weight of taxation necessary to maintain it the more bitterly resented, and conversely, the weight of that taxation contributed to the growing unpopularity of the army. The connection between the two things is beyond dispute, even in the matter of forms of taxation other than monthly and weekly assessments and free quarter where the con-nection with military need is unmistakable.[12] One does not have to go to the extremes of a royalist newsletter of November 1647, which argued that not only the monthly and weekly assessments but also the Excise were wholly consumed by the army[13] in order to concede that point. Even in the case of the Excise, where the connection with

8. Hugh Peter, 'A Word to the Army', *Harleian Miscellany* (1810), VI, especially pp. 66–8. For some examples of criticism of the army, see [William Prynne], *IX Queries* (June 1647), BL., E.394(1), passim; *A Religious Retreat sounded to a Religious Army* (August 1647), BL., E.404(34), passim: *The Army Anatomized* (December 1647), BL., E.419(6), passim; [Nathaniel Ward], *To the High and Honourable Parliament of England . . . The humble Petitions, serious suggestions* (May 1648), BHPC., especially pp. 21–9; *The humble Desires of the Loyall hearted, wel-affected Freemen of the City of London* (June 1648), BL., 669, f12(39); *A Speedy Cure to Open the Eyes of the Blinde, and the Eares of the Deafe Citizens of London* (August 1648), BL., E.456(28), especially p. 7.
9. *Two Letters Written out of Lancashire and Buckinghamshire* (July 1647), BL., E.397(24), p. 5.
10. *Leveller Manifestoes*, pp. 205–7.
11. See below, pp. 159–65.
12. For an eloquent statement to this effect, see [Nathaniel Ward], *To the High and Honourable Parliament . . .* (May 1648), BHPC., p. 21.
13. *Mercurius Melancholicus* (1 November 1647), BL., E.412(3), pp. 53–4.

military expenditure is not so intimate as in that of the assessments, it is significant to find that as much as £600,000, half the expected yield of the Excise voted in an ordinance of 24 December 1647, was to be devoted to satisfying the arrears of pay of the army and its supernumerary forces.[14]

However, not every petition complaining about the burden of taxation was unmindful of the necessity of attending to the army's needs. Of the petitions from Essex, Surrey, Sussex and Kent in the spring and summer of 1648, all asking for a personal treaty with the king and a reduction of taxes, only the last, a prelude to Kentish insurgency in the Second Civil War, fails to make even cursory mention of the nation's debt to the army and the just grievances of the soldiers in the matter of unpaid wages.[15]

The novel, and indeed unprecedented, characteristic of the taxes was one of the main factors making for their greater unpopularity and that of the army for which they were raised. Criticism of 'such new toles & taxations as the nation was never acquainted with'[16] became part of the stock-in-trade not only of resurgent Cavalierism but also of conservative Presbyterians with a strong political interest in denigrating the army. As to the first, a Remonstrance of 27 November 1647 purporting to come from the inhabitants of the Isle of Wight, Guernsey and Jersey chose to see 'unusuall taxations . . . never heard of before in this Nation' as an important element in a sinister design to impose arbitrary government on England and to 'support a needlesse Army for the upholding of their greatnesse'.[17] The notorious non-parliamentary levies of Charles I's personal rule in the 1630s were as nothing compared with these innovations, argued royalist apologists,[18] and they were not alone in this. The little finger of the rulers of wartime and post-war England, argued

14. *A&O.*, I, 1049: *Severall Ordinances of the Lords and Commons* (24 December 1647), BL., E.421(9), p. 4; *The Moderate Intelligencer* (16/23 December 1647), BL., E.421(7), no pagination.
15. On Essex, Rushworth, *Historical Collections*, VII, 1101–2. On Surrey, *L.J.*, X, 260–1; *Parliamentary History*, XVII, 139–40; BL., 669, f12(26). On Sussex, *The humble Petition of the Knights, Gentry, Clergie and Commonalty of the County of Sussex* (7 June 1648), BL., 669, f12(42): *The Answer of the Lords and Commons . . . to the Petition . . . of the County of Sussex* (9 June 1648), BL., 669, f12(45); *L.J.*, X, 315–16; *HMC, 7th. Report (House of Lords MSS.)*, p. 30; Lewes, East Sussex R.O., MSS. SM. 147, DM. 263–75 (copies of the petition circulating for signature in Pevensey rape). On Kent, *Cal.SPD. 1648–9*, p. 63; *The humble Petition of the Knights, Gentry, Clergy and Commonalty of the County of Kent* (11 May 1648), BL., E.441(25), pp. 2–3.
16. Edward Symmons, *A Vindication of King Charles* (1647), BL., E.414(16), p. 53. See also *The Case of the King Stated* (1647), BHPC., pp. 19–20; D. Jenkins, *Lex Terrae* (1647), BHPC., p. 16; *A New Magna Charta* (February 1648), BL., E.427(15), p. 3.
17. *The Remonstrance of the Inhabitants of the Three Isles* (November 1647), BL., E.417(5), p. 5.
18. See e.g. *Mercurius Pragmaticus Number 23* (15/22 February 1648), BL., E.428(9), no pagination; *Mercurius Melancholicus* (12/19 February 1648), BL., E.437(23), p. 150.

the Presbyterian leader Denzil Holles, 'has been heavier than the loins of Monarchy. What was all that, in comparison of Free quarter, Excise, and even the 100 000 l [assessment] a month, which they say they must have for the maintenance of the Army? Those oppressions were but flea-bitings to these. At the worst, one may say, we were then chastised with Whips, but now with Scorpions.'[19]

Aware of how the novelty and weight of these taxes, and especially the monthly assessment, was contributing to the unpopularity of the army and no less concerned with how, for want of adequate returns from the assessment, 'the poore Souldier . . . is compelled to grind the faces of the poore', Lord General Fairfax and the Army Council on 7 October 1647 had urged on the government the desirability of attempting to anaesthetize the taxpayer by employing more traditional modes of raising the money. Thus *it may bee most contenting and effectuall too: To passe it by way of the High-Sheriffe, &c. As it used to be in the Case of Subsidies, the Name and power of Committees being so unpleasant to the people, and the High Sheriffe being so responsall [sic] both for his Estate and power in the County'.*[20] One is reminded of how Clement Walker, though no friend to Fairfax and the army, was to seek a remedy for the tangled and oppressive fiscal innovations of the time – he counted eighteen different ways of raising money, many of them completely new – in a reversion to tradition: in his case to a revived course of the Exchequer, 'the exactest and best known way of account'.[21] But it was apparently not recalled by Fairfax and his advisers that the Crown's employment of sheriffs in the levying of Ship Money had certainly not succeeded in making either the levy or the office in question popular. Walker's recommendation was clearly connected with his suspicion about malversation and mismanagement of the new taxes. In his view the Excise alone, if properly managed, would have yielded sufficient to pay for the war.[22]

Complaints against the tax burden were thus grist to the mills of a wide variety of enemies of the army and their Independent allies in parliament: from out-and-out Cavaliers, to conservative parliamentary Presbyterians and non-aligned MPs. On 12 November 1647 *Mercurius Rusticus* inveighed against the excessive cost of paying for a voracious army: especially in Excise, free quarter and the monthly assessment, the latter 'a Tax of no less then 60 000 l. each moneth which will swallow up all the money, & consume the trade of the Kingdom to support them in their idleness, mutinies and rebellion against the Parliament'. The

19. 'Memoirs of Denzil Lord Holles', Maseres, *Select Tracts*, I, 307.
20. *Proposalls From . . . Sir Thomas Fairfax And The Counsell of his Army* (October 1647), BL., E.411(5), pp. 3–5. Italics in text.
21. C. Walker, 'The Mystery of the Two Juntoes . . .', Maseres, *Select Tracts*, I, 339–42.
22. Ibid., pp. 340–1.

army's principles, he complained – confusing the army in general with its more radical members, whose voices had admittedly been very much in evidence in recent weeks – believed the supreme power to be in the people. But when had the people ever consented to the exorbitant new military establishment and the resultant crippling burden of new taxes and free quarter?[23]

While this last complaint makes it abundantly clear that it can be very misleading to consider individual taxes in complete isolation from one another, some account of the peculiarities and particular burdens imposed by the more important of them will be in order if this qualification is borne constantly in mind. The remainder of this chapter is therefore devoted to a discussion of what were the three most burdensome and unpopular levies: the monthly assessment, the taking of free quarter, and the Excise.

The army and assessments

With the above proviso in mind it will be appropriate to begin with a complaint from the closing months of the first war whose substance is that the unpopularity of the monthly assessment needs to be seen in the context of a multiplicity of burdens heaped on the taxpayer. On 14 March 1646 the county committee of Yorkshire claimed that the Yorkshire taxpayers' lot was rendered intolerable by this multiplicity of charges among which they singled out for special mention the monthly assessment and free quartering by the Scottish army. Indeed, the committeemen claimed that they themselves had had to pledge their estates to provide pay for the soldiers, not to speak of a debt of £3,000 which they had contracted for purchase of clothing for them. The county's quota of £7,000 in monthly assessment was, they groaned, 'a burthen too heavie for it to beare', which occasioned a plea for relief via the decentralization of both the Excise and the composition fees paid by delinquents. An additional burden, and positively the last straw, was the assessment for the British forces in Ireland, from which the committee pleaded – vainly – the county should be exempt in view of its burdens, sufferings and services. As the summer wore on, the complaints from Yorkshire, which never lost anything in the manner of their relation, swelled in a doleful crescendo with the intimation of 19 June that if no relief came, the county would surely perish under the weight both of quartering the Scots and of a monthly assessment of about £140,000. Even more dramatic was the complaint of 26 June 'that if releife come

23. *Mercurius Rusticus* (12 November 1647), BL., E.414(5), especially pp. 4, 6.

not presently, it will be too late to thinke vpon vs when we are perished . . . for wee are brought to soe lowe an ebb, that a very few dayes will now serue to stopp our breath and quit you of our further Clamour'.[24]

Such complaints did not cease with the end and the aftermath of the first Civil War. A pamphlet published at the beginning of 1648 complained bitterly that, far from disbanding in compliance with parliament's orders of the previous year, the army had forced parliament 'to pass a new Establishment of forty thousand pounds a moneth for their future pay to be levyed on the Kingdom (who now expect ease from all such Taxes) besides the Excise and all other publick payments . . .'. The pamphlet demanded the lifting of the monthly assessment of £60,000 for maintenance of the idle army and the limiting of such levies to the cost of the force for Ireland and of such very few other soldiers as were really needed at home.[25]

The burden of free quarter is considered later in this chapter,[26] but it is here germane to point out that the insistence on the inability to raise weekly or monthly assessment money or other taxes on account of having to bear the charges of free quarter might sometimes conceal an element of double counting; certainly in areas where, as in the West Riding of Yorkshire in the summer and autumn of 1646, the county committee allowed individual taxpayers to present tickets for money due to them for free-quartering soldiers in lieu of so much of their contributions to the monthly assessment.[27] Moreover, as a circular letter sent out to county committees on 4 December 1646 emphasized, there was an obvious connection between the allowing of assessments to fall into arrears and the need for soldiers to take free quarter in view of the consequential lack of funds to pay them.[28]

One factor which helped to increase the discontent felt in many areas, of which Yorkshire was only the most vociferous, was the belief that they were being made to bear an unfair share of the national burden and that others were getting off very lightly by comparison. On 1 August

24. Bodleian, Tanner MSS., 59, fos. 75, 351–1(b), 366–6(b); Tanner MSS., 60 fos. 556–6(b). For similar, if less dramatic, complaints from other counties in 1646, see Tanner MSS., 59, fo. 345 (Dorset); Tanner MSS., 59, fo. 230 (Cheshire). *Western Assize Orders*, p. 252 (Widcombe, Somerset); Tanner MSS., 59, fo. 537 (Durham). For further complaints from Yorkshire in 1647, see Bodleian, Tanner MSS., 58, fos. 21, 22(b)–3.
25. *The Petition of Right of the Free-holders and Free-men of the Kingdom of England* (January 1648), BL., E.422(9), pp. 14, 20. For a similar complaint see *The earnest and passionate Petition of divers thousands* . . . (February 1648), BL., E.425(10), pp. 1–3.
26. See below, pp. 57–70.
27. PRO., SP. 28/249, 250, no piece references.
28. Bodleian, Tanner MSS., 59, fo. 606. The point was also made emphatically in a letter of 20 June 1648 from Speaker Lenthall to the Surrey committee (Surrey RO., Guildford Muniment Room, MS. 111/10/7).

1646 Philip Mainwaring wrote to Roger Wilbraham complaining at the heavy burden of assessment on their county of Cheshire as compared with formerly royalist counties such as Worcestershire 'that were reduced [viz. to the obedience of parliament] but as yesterday'.[29] On 27 December 1647 the borough of Great Yarmouth complained to its MP, the influential Independent politician Miles Corbet, that its rating of £138. 12s. towards the monthly assessment was excessive, and that 'the Towne . . . allwaies have [sic] beene much overcharged far beyond other places'.[30] Again in Norfolk, the mayor of Norwich, the county and regional capital, came under fire from his counterpart in King's Lynn in August 1646 on account of the adverse effect on the rest of the county of the substantial arrears of monthly assessment money which were due from Norwich. However, second city of the kingdom though it was, Norwich regarded its own share of the burden – one ninth of that of the county as a whole – as excessive and was currently – against the advice of one of its MPs, Thomas Atkins – appealing to parliament for mitigation.[31] As a final example we may cite the petition that was being organized in Devon in February 1648, whose subscribers, it was hoped, would run into thousands. This too complained of the disproportionate burden borne by the county towards the assessment for the army in Ireland as well as the ordinary monthly assessment: more, it was claimed, than the whole of Wales and much more than other English counties of comparable size and wealth.[32]

For assessment collections to be in arrears appears to have been very much the rule rather than the exception. The most striking case of all, that of the City of London, is treated elsewhere on account of its importance in connection with London's own political position and its relations with the army and parliament.[33] The outbreak of a second war in the spring and summer of 1648 was to make such delays even more reprehensible in the eyes of the government, as Speaker Lenthall informed the local authorities in Surrey on 20 June. The army being 'now in continuall Action', county assessment commissioners ought to meet at least once a month, and weekly within their respective divisions in order to keep a close eye on both collectors and defaulters.[34] On 4 August the Devon committee protested to the Speaker that the county

---

29. Bodleian, Tanner MSS., 59, fo. 446.
30. NNRO., Great Yarmouth Assembly Book 1642–1662, fo. 115.
31. BL., Add. MSS., 22,620, fos. 74, 76, 82, 84, 88, 90(b)–1. For a further complaint from Lynn in October, see Add. MSS., 19,399, fo. 36.
32. Exeter, Devon RO., QS. Records, box 55 (the petition has been filed with QS. material for the previous year); S.K. Roberts, *Devon*, p. 10.
33. See below, pp. 179, 180, 188–9, 194–5, 196.
34. Surrey RO., Guildford Muniment Room, MS. 111/10/7. For general letters from the Speaker to the counties to similar effect, see Rushworth, *Historical Collections*, VII, 1154, 1213.

assessment commissioners and collectors had been diligent and that the arrears were nothing like so large as he believed. But this did not stop them from emphasizing that they saw little benefit from the levy which they claimed to have collected so dutifully and assiduously. It was all very well for the Speaker to make much of the claim that the army was now very much on active service, for, so far as Devon was concerned, what mattered was that the commander of the armed forces in the south-west, Sir Hardress Waller, had been ordered to move his forces out of the county, which 'wilbe the hazard of the totall Losse of the West'. To denude the county of proper military protection was, they implied, poor reward for their assiduity in the matter of the assessment. For once parliament responded favourably, and on 7 August, recognizing the county's vulnerability especially from the insurgent fleet, the offending order was rescinded, and a further order was given that Waller's brigade, now finally anchored in Devon, should be paid out of the assessment money from that county, and, if it should prove necessary, from adjacent counties also.[35]

Many localities were burdened with additional levies, not all of them as properly authorized as the monthly assessment or the assessment for the British army in Ireland. During the First Civil War some army commanders had levied illegal assessments on the areas where their troops were quartered and the practice was sometimes continued after the end of the war.[36] On 17 November 1647 Lord General Fairfax offered the taxpayers of North Wales his full protection if they refused to contribute to such extra-parliamentary levies and promised that he would bring those responsible for exacting them to a strict account, not least because such demands rendered taxpayers less capable of paying their contributions to the legitimate monthly assessment for the army's needs.[37] However, during the Second Civil War in 1648, Wales, an important field of conflict, was not exempted from additional levies, though of a less unofficial and illegal sort. As an additional charge towards the defence of parliamentarian South Wales against the revolts of Colonels Poyer and Powell and Major General Laugharne, the parliamentary Commissioners for South Wales initiated an additional small monthly assessment on all the counties of south and central Wales, ranging from £192. 9s. for Monmouthshire to £23. 2s. 7d. for Radnorshire and £10. 2s. 6d. for

35. Bodleian, Tanner MSS., 57, fo. 173; Rushworth, *Historical Collections*, VII, 1218.
36. See, e.g., C. Holmes, *The Eastern Association in the English civil war* (Cambridge, 1974), p. 142. For complaints from Yorkshire and Northumberland in this respect against the Scots in 1646, see Bodleian, Tanner MSS., 59, fos. 206, 294, 351, 366–6(b), 387–7(b); Tanner MSS., 60, fo. 556.
37. *A Declaration to the Knights, Esquires and Gentlemen of North Wales* (1 November 1647), BL., E.412(18), pp. 3–4.

the town of Haverfordwest.[38] Similarly a parliamentary ordinance of 21 August empowered the recently created association of the five counties of North Wales to raise an additional tax of £1,000 per month on the counties as a whole in face of the disturbances there, and especially of the revolt in Anglesey.[39]

If the weight of the monthly assessments and other levies was a real grievance, the treatment of those who either could not or would not pay their contributions undoubtedly exacerbated discontent. While, like the Poll Tax in our own time, there may have been some resentment against tax-resisters on the part of those who dutifully paid the sums rated on them, the sanctions employed against such defaulters almost certainly served on balance to intensify resentment against the taxes. Defaulters were sometimes imprisoned,[40] but things did not normally go so far as this and the usual sanction employed against them was distraint of their property and livestock.[41] Recourse to distraint in cases of default was regularized by a parliamentary ordinance of 12 October 1647, which made defaulters who had not paid in the taxes due from them within ten days of the date of the ordinance automatically subject to distraint.[42] Often enough it was not simply the fact of distraint but the circumstances accompanying it which were particularly important in swelling the volume of discontent. The records of the parliamentary Indemnity Committee from the time of its creation in May 1647 to the end of the period covered in this book contain as many as twelve cases in which the committee was petitioned to stay lawsuits brought by the victims of such distraint against those responsible for putting it into effect.[43] Such a case was that of Miles Hill of Weobley in Herefordshire, whose petition was considered by the Indemnity Committee on 3 December 1647. The suit which Hill wished to be stayed turned on the circumstances and allegedly fatal consequences of his attempt, in obedience to an order from the Gloucestershire county committee, to distrain on the goods of one Francis Smith, for defaulting on his monthly assessment contribution. Smith claimed – and Hill denied – that his mother had died as a result of a blow administered by

---

38. Bodleian, Tanner MSS., 57, fos. 181–1(b).
39. A&O., I, 1183–5: L.J., X, 447–8.
40. For a reference to complaints in the London Court of Common Council against the imprisonment of citizens who had defaulted on their contributions, see Bodleian, Clarendon MSS., 29, fo. 72(b).
41. For the case of an inhabitant of Newcastle-under-Lyme who was imprisoned for resisting distraint and in 1648 brought a lawsuit against the responsible officer, see PRO., SP. 24/2, fo. 164.
42. A&O., I, 1025–6; An Ordinance of . . . Parliament For Bringing in the Arrears of the Assessments (12 October 1647), BL., E.410(21), pp. 1–6.
43. On this, see R. Ashton, 'The Problem of Indemnity 1647–1648', in Politics and People, p. 130.

Hill on this occasion.[44] In the circumstances it is hardly surprising that some of the lawsuits brought against distrainers were for actions such as trespass, illegal entry and assault.[45]

When personal goods or livestock were distrained for non-payment of taxes, the normal practice was for them to be sold off, any surplus over and above the tax due being repaid to the defaulter. At least one such person, however, indignantly refused the offer of reimbursement made to him, probably some time in 1648, by the tax-collector of St Albans and proceeded to sue the latter instead.[46] Not even those who purchased such distrained goods were always free from litigation by defaulters and recourse to writs of *replevin* to regain control of property was not unknown.[47]

Things might have been even worse if it had not been for the fact, so deplored by Speaker Lenthall in his circular letter of August 1648 and his letter to the Surrey authorities of June,[48] that it required constant vigilance to keep collectors and assessors up to the mark. Indeed, some of them may not have been simply lazy or inefficient but also themselves susceptible to popular currents of feeling against the weight of taxation. It was, for instance, not only taxpayers who responded to the notorious outbursts of Colonel Edward King from the chair at the Lincolnshire Sessions of the Peace at Sleaford and Folkingham in 1646–7. Thomas Cook, a collector and assessor in the Lincolnshire village of Rowston, responded by refusing to go ahead with the business of assessment, for which offence he was fined, imprisoned and his goods distrained.[49]

But the opposite extreme of over-assessment and over-collection was probably far more common, especially when assessors and collectors were under intolerable pressure from the soldiers, whose wages were dependent upon efficient collection of the taxes. This applied even more strongly when the military were themselves involved in the business of collection. Late in 1648 Major Thomas Blayne, who had been in charge of troops collecting assessment money in Herefordshire, had a lot of explaining to do, having to disclose why the account which he now presented 'in a strickt sence may not in every perticuler come vp to the right rule'. Blayne had, in fact, been incapable of restraining his men from helping themselves to what they clearly regarded as their

---

44. PRO., SP. 24/1, fo. 102.
45. There is an example in PRO., SP. 24/1, fo. 48.
46. PRO., SP. 24/3, fos. 159, 165. The suit was stayed by the Indemnity Committee on 18 January 1649.
47. There is an example in PRO., SP. 24/3, fo. 153.
48. See above, p. 49.
49. Edward King, *A discovery . . . of the arbitrary, tyrannicall and illegal actions* (1647), BHPC., pp. 23–5. For a similar case of imprisonment of a collector in the City of London in 1648, see *C.J.*, VI, 99.

just due out of the proceeds. 'The vyolence of which souldyers', he pleaded, 'is well knowne to divers of the [Assessment] Commissioners, therefore he hopes that himself & his small estate shall not againe suffer for what he could not then resist'.[50]

For all their unpopularity, the weekly and monthly assessments do not seem to have occasioned the mass outbursts of mob violence which characterized public reaction to the Excise.[51] Sometimes the distraint of goods for non-payment met with violent resistance from the defaulters, and there is a case in Herefordshire in 1648 of such a defaulter not only resorting to a lawsuit against distraint, but also taking violent action to regain possession of the items which had been distrained.[52] Colonel King's astonishing provocation from his position of authority on the bench in Lincolnshire in 1646–7, seems, if the complaints of the county committee on 2 April 1647 are to be credited, to have engendered violent resistance to the assessment in Lincolnshire earlier that year, in which some collectors were wounded. But the most damaging effect of King's outspoken pronouncement was the virtual campaign of civil disobedience and strikes against tax payments which they initiated.[53] Yet even this seems to have been an isolated instance, whose closest parallel is the prolonged foot-dragging over assessment arrears in the City of London.[54] The attempt of the royalist insurgents, holed up in Colchester during the Second Civil War, to capitalize on such discontent by appealing in July 1648 for a national strike against payment of assessment and Excise money seems to have fallen upon deaf ears.[55]

Any attempts to lighten the burden of taxes were mere palliatives so long as the army remained in being or at least was not spectacularly reduced in size. Only disbandment could produce a substantial improvement, and to Denzil Holles and his conservative Presbyterian associates the risks attendant on disbandment seemed less than those of keeping the army at its current strength: in terms both of the continued popular disaffection at the undiminished tax burden and of the army's alliance with the parliamentary opponents of the Presbyterians. On 4 March 1647 the House of Lords, in tune, no doubt, with the Presbyterian strategy in parliament, voted against a motion being put to continue the monthly assessment for the army, though the

50. PRO., SP. 28/229, no piece reference.
51. See below, pp. 75–9.
52. PRO., SP. 24/3, fo. 161(b).
53. Bodleian, Tanner MSS., 58, fo. 39.
54. See below, pp. 179, 180, 188–9, 194–5.
55. *The Remonstrance and Declaration of the Knights, Esquires, Gentlemen and Freeholders in Colchester* (July 1648), BL., E.451(11), p. 8; also Oxford, Worcester College pamphlet collection, BB 8.7 (17.7), p. 8.

impact of this vote was lessened by the formal protestation of as many as eleven of the peers against it.[56] If the parliamentary Presbyterians had succeeded in their twin plans of disbandment and tax-reduction, their popularity would unquestionably have soared and facilitated the implementation of their conservative political and religious programme of a restored but strictly limited monarchy and a strict Presbyterian religious settlement. The Second Civil War might well have been avoided.

But they did not succeed, and such reforms as were achieved were little more than cosmetic. Certainly the drastic reorganization of the assessment in December 1647 and January 1648 was unlikely to assuage discontent since it resulted, if anything, in greater, not reduced, fiscal burdens. The immediate origins of the reform lay in the Army Council's Humble Recommendation to parliament of 5 December. Granted that parliament could not yet afford large-scale disbandment – at least if the soldiers' arrears of pay, or a significant portion of them, were to be paid – it had no choice, argued the Representation, but to keep the soldiers under arms. But if the evils of free quarter were to be reduced to a minimum, assessment would have to be made to yield more, so as to give the soldiers the wherewithal to pay for their quarters. Parliament must face up to this awkward fact and provide for such an increased yield, even budgeting for a surplus of £10,000 a month. The increase was to be only for a limited time, for while some of this surplus should go towards the payment of soldiers in Ireland, it was hoped that the greater part of it could be used to build up a capital fund towards the discharge of the soldiers' arrears of pay, thus facilitating their progressive demobilization. With the consequent reduction of the wages bill there would be a progressive increase in the capital fund for payment of arrears, thus facilitating further disbandment. Ultimately it ought to be possible either to reduce the burden of the monthly assessment or to provide increased sums for the Irish service.[57] Less popular, however, was the suggestion that extensive powers should be conferred upon the General in the actual levying of the tax. Great emphasis was laid on the disgraceful dilatoriness of the City of London, as reflected in the shocking level of its assessment arrears and the disastrous effect this had had in terms of the burden of free quarter laid on the home counties. Thus it was suggested that the soldiers should be paid out of the assessment due from the counties where they were stationed, a practice which had worked with fair success in wartime Warwickshire, but

56. *Parliamentary History*, XV, 330–1.
57. *An Humble Representation from Sir Thomas Fairfax* ... (8 December 1647), BL., E.419(16), pp. 1–25, and especially pp. 10–23; *L.J.*, X, 556–63; especially pp. 559–62. See also *The Kingdomes Weekly Intelligencer, Number 238* (1 December 1647), BL., E.419(24), pp. 757–60.

was hardly likely to command the approval of English countrymen in peacetime.[58]

Although parliament's response was less thoroughgoing than Fairfax and the army had hoped it would be, an ordinance of 24 December 1647 laid down that those counties which had paid six of their nine months' arrears of assessment by the following 15 January should not only be excused payment for the other three months but also be exempt from free quarter, with the exception of individuals whose assessment contributions were in arrears.[59] Letters to collectors in east Sussex from the committee at Lewes on 30 December, following earlier instructions to that committee from the Speaker of the House of Commons, made it clear that, provided the conditions of the ordinance were fulfilled, only individual defaulters would be subject to quartering.[60] However, counties such as Devon and Cornwall which did not pay up the stipulated arrears by 15 January did not enjoy any such general exemption. Conscious perhaps of the unfairness of penalizing dutiful taxpayers for the sins of individual defaulters, Sir Hardress Waller, Commander-in-Chief of the forces in these parts, ordered on 14 March 1648 that all such defaulters should suffer an additional penalization. This was to take the form of having a 'more than ordinary Number of Soldiers sent unto them as the only Obstructors of the present Ease of those Counties'.[61] More equitable, it would seem, was an order of 12 June to the parliamentary committee for the army to the effect that, as in the case above from east Sussex, only those individuals who had not paid up their assessments should have *any* soldiers quartered on them.[62]

The last few cases have highlighted the inverse relationship between the assessment and the exaction of free quarter, where the latter is seen very much as a *pis aller* and the inevitable consequence of and penalty for the failure to make adequate arrangements for getting in the former. While this is clearly an important aspect of the connection between the two, it will become clear that in practice things were not quite so straightforward when we turn our attention to a detailed examination of the problem of free quarter itself.

58.   For a complaint against it, see *The Petition of Right of the Freeholders and Free-men of the Kingdom of England* (January 1648), BL., E.422(9), pp. 14–15. For collection by the military in wartime Warwickshire, see Hughes, *Warwickshire*, pp. 184–8, and 'Militancy and Localism in Warwickshire Politics and Westminster Politics 1643–1647', *TRHS.*, 5th. ser. XXXI (1981), 54–5.
59.   *A&O.*, I, 1048–9; *C.J.*, V, 396; *Several Ordinances of the Lords and Commons* (24 December 1647), BL., E.421(9), pp. 1–3. Another ordinance of the same date ordered the appointment of a General Receiver of Assessments in each county to receive the assessment money from the collectors and transmit it to Treasurers at Wars (*A&O.*, I, 1054: *Several Ordinances . . .* (December 1647), BL., E.421(9), p. 15).
60.   BL., Add. MSS., 33,058, fos. 75–5(b), 77, 78.
61.   Rushworth, *Historical Collections*, VII, 1027–8.
62.   Ibid., p. 1147; *C.J.*, V, 595.

The burden of free quarter[63]

According to a petition from the inhabitants of Essex in April 1647 demanding the disbandment of the army, the burden of free quarter was 'like to equall all precedent charges, and to surmount the worst and heaviest of our former taxes'.[64] 'Did inforced Loan [*sic*], privy Seals and Monopolies', protested another complainant, 'grinde the Subject, and have not inforced Assessments and free-quarter grated them as small?'[65]

There were those who saw forcing the army to have recourse to free quarter by allowing assessment arrears to pile up as a nefarious stratagem on the part of the army's Presbyterian opponents to make it odious in the eyes of the people.[66] But even Lord General Fairfax himself had to admit, in a letter of 24 September 1647 in response to complaints from Sussex about the insolence of Colonel Rich's officers in the county, that the bad behaviour which was often associated with quartering was all too likely to provoke disorder and tumults; not least since people's understandable hopes that peace would bring some relief from wartime burdens had been so sadly disappointed.[67] In that same month there were reports of violent clashes on the issue between soldiers and townspeople in King's Lynn, whose mayor was later ruefully to observe that 'where soldiers are and no money to pay them, the cry of the inhabitants must needs be great'.[68] Earlier that year in June the misbehaviour of soldiers quartered in Deptford, Greenwich and Lee had helped to provoke the Kent committee to the prophetic utterance that swollen discontent at the abuses of free quartering 'may be a meanes to make this County the seat of a new Warre'.[69] The royalist newswriter *Mercurius Melancholicus* in his news-sheet for the week before Christmas 1647 rejoiced in the discomfiture of some soldiers in Cheshire, where 'the Cheshire ladds, not able any longer to endure the insolence of the Free-quarterers, fell upon 'em and utterly routed millions [*sic*] of Egyptian vermine',[70] while around the same time, in

63. My former research student, Mrs Anne Oestmann, is working on a study of free quarter in the 1620s and 1640s. The present section, however, is based entirely on my personal research on the subject.
64. The petition is printed in *Letters from Saffron Walden* (April 1647), BL., E.383(24), pp. 6–8; also in *A new found Stratagem* (April 1647), BHPC., pp. 3–4.
65. [Nathaniel Ward], *To the high and honourable Parliament* . . . (May 1648), BHPC., p. 17.
66. See, e.g., *The Declaration of the Armie under His Excellency Sir Thomas Fairfax* (May 1647), BL., E.390(20), pp. 1–2; *A Perfect and True Copy of the Severall Grievances of the Army* (May 1647), BL., E.390(3), no pagination; 'The Case of the Armie Truly Stated' (October 1647), in *Leveller Manifestoes*, pp. 206–7; L.J., IX, 558; *Fruitfull England Like to Become a Barren Wilderness* (October 1648), BL., E.467(36), pp. 5–6.
67. *Cal.SPD. 1645–7*, pp. 572–3; Oxford, Worcester College, Clarke MSS., 66, fo. 16.
68. *Cal.SPD. 1645–7*, p. 600 (*Perfect Occurrences*): Bell, *Memorials*, I, 325.
69. Bodleian, Tanner MSS., 58, fos. 181, 182, 211; C.J., V, 215.
70. *Mercurius Melancholicus* (18/25 December 1647), BL., E.421(10), p. 99.

the neighbouring county of Lancashire, the former Cavalier gentleman William Blundell of Crosby Hall, with the aid of a few servants and neighbours, succeeded in preventing three troopers from withdrawing their mounts from his stables until they had agreed to pay their quartering charges in full.[71] More seriously, in a description of the armed resistance of north Yorkshiremen to the free quartering of some of Lambert's soldiers in September 1647, the ominous word 'clubmen' was employed.[72]

Something is said elsewhere in another context about the hardships experienced by northerners in respect of the exaction of free quarter by the Scottish army during the First Civil War and in the post-war months before the departure of the Scots in February 1647.[73] But it was not only the Scots from whose attentions they suffered. On 17 July 1646 the Yorkshire committee complained of the attitude of English soldiers from Nottinghamshire and the counties of the Northern Association who 'growe discontented and high in their deportment towardes those from whome they were wont to receive their enterteinment'.[74] On 12 October and 9 December 1647, at meetings of Major General Lambert's Council of War, two death sentences were passed on soldiers for offences in quarters, and although one – a case of murder – was later remitted by Lambert's order, the other, a case of theft in quarters, was carried out, and the offender was hanged on 23 November. On 9 December another soldier was sentenced to a week's imprisonment on bread and water for divers misdemeanours committed at Sir Henry Vaughan's house in Whitewell, where he had been quartered. His offences included 'being discontented at his diet, strikeing and abuseing the maid servant . . . thrusting the Lady Vaughan against the dresser table and hurting her and killing her hens'. On the following 28 January four troopers were ordered to give satisfaction to their hosts for misdemeanours in quarters as well as to be imprisoned for six days, though the quartermaster charged with them was acquitted.[75] In his new comprehensive orders at the end of 1647 for the regulating of billeting of soldiers under his command, Lambert devised arrangements for the decentralization of machinery for hearing complaints, though with provision for referral of divers cases to the Council of War and for

71. M. Blundell (ed.), *Cavalier: Letters of William Blundell to His Friends 1620–1698* (1933), pp. 26–7.
72. *A Fight in the North at the Dales in Richmondshire* (September 1647), BL., E.407(45), no pagination.
73. See below, pp. 305–9.
74. Bodleian, Tanner MSS., 59, fo. 399.
75. West Yorkshire Archive Service, Wakefield R.O., MSS. C.469/1, 2, no foliation (Minute Books of Council of War . . . at Ripon, Knaresborough, York and Pontefract).

punishment of negligent officers who had not responded adequately to just complaints.[76]

A general account of the abuses of free quarter which is all the more credible on account of its moderate tone, its insistence on the gratitude owed to the army by the nation and its disavowal of any desire to see wholesale demobilization, makes the telling point that 'how obedient soever Souldiers are, when they are united in a body, and under the discipline of war, . . . yet they may, and probably will, be guilty of many insolencies when they are out of the sight of their Commanders, especially in the houses of poore Countrey people, who neither have the spirit to oppose nor the wit to persuade'. More than that, with free quartering, even 'the best of our Gentry and their wives are looked on but as Hosts and Hostesses, subject unto the insolency and imperiousnesse of the Common Souldiers . . .' who indeed were sometimes guilty of 'inveigling of the Daughters of many Gentlemen of ranke and quality to the great discomfort of their Parents and their owne sad ruine'.[77] This general complaint is instanced by the particular grievances of the inhabitants of Hertfordshire. Along with those of Buckinghamshire and Middlesex, these petitioned parliament on 7 December 1647 for relief from 'the intolerable Burden of Free Quarter', under which not only were the poor eaten out of house and home, but 'the best of us [are] forced to be Soldiers Servants in our own Families, a Burden every way unsufferable to Free People'.[78]

Buckinghamshire, it seems, and especially the districts on the Berkshire border near Windsor, saw gross over-quartering with as many as forty soldiers quartered in some houses (whose size is, however, not specified). It seems also to have been overcrowding which was especially responsible for the discontent both of the local inhabitants and of the soldiers of Colonel Rainsborough's regiment in the villages around Abingdon in Berkshire. Here the soldiers were quartered so thick that the inhabitants were unable to find sufficient food for them and the soldiers exacted money from them instead at the rate of half-a-crown a day for each man. The district was also the scene of mutinous violence in which an ensign and a sergeant-major were lucky to escape with their lives.[79]

The line between proper soldiers and marauding irregulars was not always easy to draw. During the summer of 1647 Somerset, which

76. *Against the Disorders of the Soldiers* (30 December 1647), BL., E.421(31), pp. 10–13.
77. *The Supplication and Proposalls of the Subjects of this miserable Kingdome, languishing . . . under the burden of Free Quarter &c* (November 1647), BL., E.412(15), especially pp. 4–5.
78. *L.J.*, IX, 564.
79. On Buckinghamshire, see ibid., pp. 564–5; on the Abingdon district, Cary, *Memorials*, I, 221–2.

had already suffered grievously from Goring's retreating Cavaliers after his defeat at Langport two years earlier, was plagued by a regiment of foot and several troops of horse, supposedly in transit for Ireland, 'which . . . Free Quarter at their Pleasure upon us, until they can have Money given them'. Their curses coupled with their vilification of Roundheads suggested to the Somerset Grand Jury that many of them were in fact ex-Cavaliers.[80] But at least they were more or less identifiable as being under a particular command, unlike the bands of demobilized soldiers, both Roundheads and Cavaliers, which a news-letter of February 1648 describes as free quartering forcibly under pretext that they were soldiers of Fairfax's army and burgling the premises when their unwilling hosts had retired to bed.[81] Charges of theft and burglary in quarters were sometimes brought against regular soldiers also, though the parliamentary Indemnity Committee stayed two such lawsuits on the grounds that the accused had made forcible entries in the line of duty.[82]

Free quarter was denounced by a wide variety of opponents of the army and its Independent allies: by, for instance, the conservative non-party MP, Clement Walker, who saw it as a device to render the soldiers 'the less craving for their pay';[83] and by the Presbyterian Colonel Edward King, because it afforded to his enemies on the Lincolnshire committee the opportunity to retain assessment collections in their own hands.[84] It is often difficult to decide who suffered more: the soldiers whose pay was often months in arrears or the civilians on whom whey were, in consequence, forced to quarter freely. At Plymouth in 1647, where both soldiers and civilians were seriously short of bread, 'the complaints of the Poore are most lamentable' and violence from both the latter and 'the enraged and halfe starved soldier, was hourly expected'.[85] In fairness to the army it needs to be emphasized that in

80.   L.J., IX, 172. For similar complaints from Devon and Oxfordshire, see ibid., pp. 171, 179; C.J., V, 161–2.
81.   The Kingdoms Weekly Account (20/28 February 1648), BL., E.429(16), p. 53.
82.   PRO., SP. 24/2, fos. 118(b)–19, 175–5(b); SP. 24/3, fos. 22(b), 58–8(b), 63, 162–2(b). In one case in pursuit of a Cavalier fugitive and in the other for compulsory quartering.
83.   C. Walker, 'The Mystery of the Two Juntoes . . .', in Maseres, Select Tracts, I, 340.
84.   Edward King, A discovery . . . (1647), BHPC., p. 14. For similar allegations about the connection between misappropriation of funds and recourse to free quarter, see [A. Wilbee], Prima Pars de Comparatis Comparandis (July 1647), BL., E.396(11), pp. 4–5: The Case of the King Stated (1647), BHPC., p. 19. The first treatise is by an Independent; the second by a royalist.
85.   In Plymouth the Governor, Colonel Ralph Weldon, ultimately had to appropriate money from local Customs, Excise and other tax sources to pay the quartering debts of his men. These revenues were made good by an order of the House of Commons on 23 May 1648 (Bodleian, Tanner MSS., 57, fo. 554; Tanner MSS., 58, fo. 209; Cary, Memorials, I, 294–5, C.J., V, 571; Rushworth, Historical Collections, VII, 1132).

general it was by no means unaware of or unresponsive to the hardships endured by civilians through free quarter.[86] Conscious that the chief culprits were assessment dodgers, notably, but by no means exclusively, in the City of London, there is, in the circumstances, not the least contradiction between the soldiers' awareness of the hardships inflicted by free quarter and the use of it as a form of pressure to expedite the collection of assessment arrears, as for example in London in August 1647 and December 1648.[87]

While this is by far the commonest occasion of the employment of free quarter as a form of pressure on communities, there are also examples of its being used for ends which are totally unrelated to the failure to provide soldiers with the pay which would enable them to discharge their quarters. While England in the 1640s affords no such notorious examples as were to be supplied four decades later by Louis XIV's dragonnades to coerce the French Huguenots into religious conformity, there were some significant, if far less spectacular, cases.[88] On 19 July 1647, exactly a week before London was to be convulsed by counter-revolutionary disorders, the Army Council proposed to the parliamentary commissioners for the army that if the control of the City of London militia were to be put into the hands of persons in whom the army could trust, as distinct from the current Presbyterian-dominated Militia Committee, the soldiers might move 'to larger quarters in severall parts for ease of the Country', a move from which Londoners would certainly benefit by the easing of prices in nearby districts from which they drew their food supplies.[89] More striking still is the incident complained of by the mayor of Rochester on 21 May 1648, that the Kent county committee had sent for an infantry regiment to be quartered in that city with the object of stifling the organization there of a petition to parliament by 'fyninge & plundering the petitioners'.[90] Although horrified reaction to the rumour was temporarily quietened

---

86. See the celebrated petition of the soldiers in March 1647, Bodleian, Tanner MSS., 58, fos. 13–13(b); *Parliamentary History*, XV, 342–4. For another example, see *The humble Representation of the Soldiers of the Northern Association* (July 1647), BL., E.399(7), p. 3; *Proposals from . . . Sir Thomas Fairfax And the Councell of his Army* (7 October 1647), BL., E.411(5), pp. 1–4.

87. See below, pp. 188, 194–6. For an example from Dorset in February 1647, see Mayo, *Dorset*, p. 352.

88. Scotland offers a somewhat nearer parallel in the quartering of soldiers in the summer of 1648 on opponents of the Engagement to bring about the restoration of the king's authority in England. Baillie claims, with some exaggeration, that the faithful suffered greater losses from this than they had from Montrose (Baillie, *Letters*, III, 47–8). But these, of course, were exactions by royalists, not their opponents.

89. CLRO., Jor. 40, fos. 237(b)–8. For a detailed treatment of these events, see below, pp. 180–82.

90. Bodleian, Tanner MSS., 57, fo. 93; *A Letter from Rochester in Kent* (22 May 1648), BL., E.443(26).

by an assurance that the order would not be put into effect, it acquired a notoriety which was significantly to fan the flames of Kentish insurgency in the Second Civil War.

Royalists and conservative parliamentary opponents of the army were deaf to arguments stressing the connection between free quarter and unpaid taxes. As the newswriter *Mercurius Rusticus* complained, with palpable exaggeration in December 1647:

> The whole Souldiery . . . are now wholly devoted to idleness, epicurism, ease and avarice, refusing to work, or return to their callings, living upon free quarter, and the labour of others, and instead of disbanding to ease the Country of their burthens, they dayly recruit . . . to double the number they were this spring, listing all that come without exception though formerly Cavaleers and Officers in the Kings Army and husbandmens servants and plowboys, who now refuse to work, when they may live idle and have free quarter and pay without labor or danger.[91]

Free quarter, argued another anti-army writer at around the same time, was part of the heavy price paid by Englishmen for the army's disobedience to parliament in refusing to disband – he says nothing of the taxdodgers' disobedience to parliament. The continued resistance of an army increasingly dependent on free quarter and deeply resentful of a parliament which failed to provide its arrears of pay, he saw simply as part of a sinister Cromwellian design – Lord General Fairfax is seen as no more than a cipher – whereby Oliver and his Independent associates sought to achieve complete hegemony.[92]

But even in cases where sufficient taxes were collected to facilitate at least piecemeal disbandment, the results were often, to say the least of it, in no way commensurate with the efforts and sacrifices of collectors and taxpayers; as is clear from some complaints from the JPs of Denbighshire in September and of Devonshire in November 1647. In the latter case, the major of a troop of horse to be disbanded appears to have distributed to his men one month's pay out of the monthly assessment, the condition of disbandment, but neglected to disband the troop, which continued to live on forced contributions and free quarter, 'to the great Greivance, oppression and Terror of the County'.[93] Devonshire's sense

91. *Mercurius Rusticus* (December 1647), BL., E.419(19), pp. 3–4. See also *A New Magna Charta* (February 1648), BL., E.427(15), p. 6.
92. *A Word to Lieut. General Cromwel and his Privy Councel* (December 1647), BL., E.421(20), pp. 12–14, 26. For this view of Fairfax, see ibid., p. 6.
93. On Denbighshire, Bodleian, Tanner MSS., 58, fo. 520. On Devon, Exeter, Devon RO., QS. Order Book 8 (1640–1651), no foliation: *The Copy of a Letter to . . . Sir Thomas Fairfax . . . by the Justices . . . and County Committee of Devonshire* (November 1647), BL., E.413(12), pp. 2–6. An anti-Cromwellian pamphlet accused Cromwell himself of similar deceits over the receipt of funds and subsequent failure to disband (*The Machivilian Cromwellist* (January 1648), BL., E.422(12), pp. 8–10).

of grievance may have been exacerbated by the feeling, strongly expressed in the county petition of February 1648, that the county bore a disproportionate share of quartering burdens, although complaints to this effect from other counties are also not hard to find.[94] On 1 November 1646 an account purporting to be a petition pleaded that even if the hated practice could not be done away with, Fairfax should try as far as possible to restrict it to 'such parts of the Kingdome as have least tasted the calamities of this lingering war and are still fresh and full both of stock and money and consequently better able to beare the burden'. It suggests that households might be permitted to compound for free quarter at the rates of 6d. a day for infantrymen and 2s. for cavalrymen. In addition, every effort should be made to quarter soldiers in market towns, 'where there are many Innes and victualing houses which would be glad of such guests, and many a poore honest man who willingly would turne victualer vpon such occasion'.[95]

One licensed innkeeper, Thomas Gerrison of Derby, would certainly not have been prepared to endorse this optimistic view of the profitability of quartering troops in his establishment. In May 1648 Gerrison petitioned the Derbyshire county committee, telling of how the debts which he had incurred during the past three years, when his premises had been requisitioned for the quartering of soldiers and their horses, had landed him in gaol, since the proceeds did not make up for the potential income he had lost for taking civilian guests; quite apart from the loss of his timbers taken to repair bulwarks and 'his Stables & barnes . . . pulled in peeces by the troopers'.[96]

An abuse which was serious and common enough to prompt specific action by both Lord General Fairfax and by Major General Lambert, who commanded in the north, was the practice of both cavalry and dragoon officers of exacting up to twice as much provender for their horses as the official regulations allowed.[97] In addition Lambert seems to have determined to try, as far as possible, to equalize the quartering burden between districts even though the effect of this policy might, of course, be simply to transfer discontent from one district to another, as

94. For Devon, see Exeter, Devon R.O., QS., Box 55; no piece reference, but the piece is wrongly included with the QS. material for 1647. For other counties see Bodleian, Tanner MSS., 57, fos. 378–8(b) (Yorkshire 1648); Tanner MSS., 59, fos. 446 (Cheshire 1646), 418 (Monmouthshire 1646).

95. *The supplication and Proposalls of the Subjects of this miserable Kingdome* (1 November 1647), BL., E.412(15), pp. 6–7.

96. PRO., SP. 28/226, no foliation. The committee ordered that Gerrison be paid £20 of the £67. 14s. 6d. which he claimed for quartering charges, repairs and servants' wages.

97. For Fairfax's orders of 20 November 1647, see Oxford, Worcester College pamphlets, Aa, 1.19 (134); for Lambert's, BL., E.421(31), pp. 1–9. The latter piece is misleadingly titled *A Letter Concerning the Countries resolution in Relation to the Scots* and is dated 30 December 1647.

had happened in Gloucestershire in the early autumn of 1647.[98] The same occurred in Middlesex in the summer of that year, when the Council of War decided to spread the burden of quartering to places much nearer to London such as Harrow, Hayes and Harlington.[99] According to Thomas Juxon, a Londoner friendly to the army, it was this that first 'made ye Citizens sensible of free Quarter & . . . Interrupted y^m at there country howses . . . In soe much y^t now ther was a Generall Complaint and the mouthes of very maney wer opened'.[100]

As in modern wartime practice, influential persons often succeeded in obtaining exemption from the worst quartering burdens or at least having only superior officers quartered in their houses.[101] However, the exalted status of the parliamentarian peer, the earl of Lincoln, did not prevent soldiers from being quartered in Tattershall Castle with resultant great damage to the building, nor did it enable him to get rid of them promptly in July 1648, despite the efforts of the House of Lords on his behalf. It is interesting to find the earl being appointed by the Upper House on 6 October to a committee charged with preparing an ordinance to exempt peers from having soldiers quartered on them.[102]

One of the incidents of free quartering which was made much of by anti-army propagandists was the soldiers' 'most abusive, insolent and proud refusal of the moderate and wholesom dyet in poor and mean mens houses'.[103] There had been many such complaints against the Scottish soldiers before their departure in February 1647,[104] but in this, as in so much else, the Scots were by no means the only offenders. Among the numerous misdemeanours for which a foot soldier was locked up for a week on bread and water by the Council of War of the Army sitting at York on 9 December 1647 – 'to get him a better stomack' as one account puts it – was 'being discontented at his diet in quarters'.[105] In the wholesale reorganization of the distribution of quartering which was made by Major General Lambert and his Council

98.   Oxford, Worcester College MSS., 66, fo. 17.
99.   *Three Letters from His Excellency Sir Thomas Fairfax* . . . (June 1647), BL., E.394(11), p. 2.
100. London, Dr Williams's Library, MS. 24. 50, fo. 119(b). These factors making for higher quartering charges are specifically mentioned in the Middlesex and Buckinghamshire petitions of December 1647 (*L.J.*, IX, 564–5; *C.J.*, V, 375–6).
101. For actual cases of such exemption, see *HMC., Tollemache MSS.* (1979), I, 24; Oxford, Worcester College MSS., 66, fo. 15(b); (August 1647), BL., E.402(16), pp. 2–3. For a later radical objection to such practices, see C. Hill (ed.), Winstanley, *The Law of Freedom and Other Writings* (Harmondsworth, 1973), p. 281.
102. *L.J.*, X, 487, 531; *C.J.*, VI, 18; Rushworth, *Historical Collections*, VII, 1257.
103. *The Army Anatomized* (December 1647), BL., E.419(6), p. 6.
104. See Bodleian, Carte MSS., 80, fo. 471; Cary, *Memorials*, I, 67, 69; and below, p. 305.
105. West Yorkshire Archive Service, Wakefield R.O., MS.C. 469(1), no foliation; also BL., E.420(2), p. 6.

of War at the end of the year, it was specifically decreed that all soldiers 'shall be content with such dyet as those with whom they quarter usually afford themselves and their families'.[106]

How long did those who had soldiers freely quartered upon them have to wait for satisfaction of the debts due to them? One problem in dealing with this question is the very vagueness of some of these arrangements. The proceedings of two officers in Buckinghamshire in 1646 are a good case in point. Not only did they not pay for their quarters in several places where their hosts, as one of them claimed, rather implausibly, 'would take no money of mee for it'. In other places in the county one of them was unable to remember whether he had paid or not.[107] In the same county, whose inhabitants, along with those of nearby Oxfordshire, petitioned the House of Commons in September 1647 asking for an end to free quarter, the quartering debts to some persons contracted in 1644 were repaid in 1646, but others of the same year had to wait until 1648 and 1649, and this is true of many of the quartering debts contracted in 1646. Villagers in the neighbouring county of Bedfordshire seem to have done better, a period of between one and five months being the apparent norm for waiting for repayment at least of such quartering debts as have been recorded as having been contracted in 1646–7.[108] One legal action brought by a householder of Linton in Cambridgeshire against a constable in connection with a quartering debt contracted in 1646 and still unsatisfied in 1648 was stayed by the action of the Indemnity Committee in June of the latter year.[109] Finally there is the harrowing case of Christopher Miller, a poor, helpless, lame man whose wife and children were wholly dependent on him. Miller petitioned the county committee of Warwickshire on 16 January 1647, pleading that he was in danger of landing in prison on account of the debts, amounting to nearly £60, which he had contracted on account of the free quartering of soldiers on him.[110]

It is sometimes difficult to determine whether the communities complaining against the exaction of free quarter in 1648 ought rightfully to have been exempt, having honoured the terms of the ordinance of 24 December by paying up six of their nine months' assessment arrears by 15 January.[111] Some certainly had done so and were justly indignant

106. *A Declaration of the Northerne Army* (5 January 1648), BL., E.421(31), p. 8.
107. PRO., SP. 28/221, no piece reference.
108. PRO., SP. 28/219, 221, no piece references. For the petitions to the House of Commons, see *C.J.*, V, 301; *The Copie of Three Petitions* (September 1647), BL., E.407(29), pp. 1–4.
109. PRO., SP. 24/2, fos. 131, 146(b).
110. PRO., SP. 28/248, no piece reference.
111. See above, p. 56.

because free quarter continued to be exacted.[112] In other cases it is difficult to be sure either way,[113] while in still others such as the West Country garrisons of Dartmouth, Exmouth and Pendennis, if a declaration of 14 March by Sir Hardress Waller, the Commander in Chief in Devon and Cornwall, is to be believed, the appropriate amount of assessment arrears had still not been paid over.[114]

Exeter presents a most notable example of backwardness both in paying assessment arrears and resisting the consequent free quartering, though the case is perhaps not quite so simple as this statement suggests. On 9 May 1648 the mayor of the city, who had originally asked for the garrison to be reinforced, refused to countenance the quartering of a number of companies of Sir Hardress Waller's infantry regiments there.[115] In a letter to Lord General Fairfax describing this and subsequent incidents Waller maintained that 'the Town was put into such a Rage by the ill Carriage of the Magistrates that it is even a Miracle how we escaped Cutting of Throats'. He does not seem to have been exaggerating. Relations between the city and the garrison had been bad for some considerable time, and back in February Exeter had petitioned for an easing of the burden of free quarter.[116] According to the testimony of Waller and his principal subordinate officer, Lieutenant-Colonel Edward Salmon, the obduracy of the mayor and

112.   E.g. Radnorshire and Herefordshire (*Two Letters read in the House of Commons on Monday January 24, 1647* (viz. 1648), (1648), BL., E.423(20), p. 5); Rochester (*A Letter from the Mayor and Aldermen of the City of Rochester* (January 1648), BL., E.423(17), pp. 2–3); parts of Devon (Bodleian, Tanner MSS., 57, fo. 93); Nottinghamshire (Tanner MSS., 57, fo. 263, see also fo. 352). For more general complaints, see a Remonstrance from early in 1648 (BL., Stowe MSS., 361, fos. 100–100(b)); a conservative Presbyterian petition of 3 February, heard in the House of Commons on 22 April 1648 (*The earnest and passionate Petition of divers thousands . . .* (February 1648), BL., E.425(10), p. 2); and a more extended complaint in the same month (*A publike Declaration and Solemne Protestation . . . against the illegal Intollerable . . . Grievance of Free Quarter* (February 1648), BL., E.426(3), especially pp. 4–5).
113.   For Essex, see *The Humble Petition and Desires of the Grand Jury at the last Assizes holden at Chelmsford on the 22 of March* 1647 (viz. 1648), Oxford, Codrington, pamphlet collections; *The Petition and desires of the loyall and true hearted Knights Esquires Gentlemen and Free-holders . . . of Essex* (April 1648), BL., E.434(22), pp. 2–3, 5–6. For Hull and other parts of Yorkshire, *The Copy of a Letter from Major-Generall Lambert's Quarters at York* (January 1648), BL., E.424(11), p. 5; Rushworth, *Historical Collections*, VII, 1020–1. The latter is a complaint about free billet as distinct from free quarter; for parts of Devon, Bodleian, MSS. Dep C. 158, no. 75 (Nalson MSS., vii, no. 75); *C.J.*, V, 541, 549; Rushworth, *Historical Collections*, VII, 1067; Whitelock, *Memorials*, p. 301 (22 April 1648).
114.   Rushworth, *Historical Collections*, VII, 1027–8.
115.   Exeter, Devon R.O., Act Book of the Exeter Common Council no. 9, 1647–1655, fos. 13(b), 14; *HMC., Report on the Records of the City of Exeter* (1916), p. 212. The mayor did, however, indicate his readiness to comply with any parliamentary order requiring the city to accept the soldiers.
116.   Exeter, Devon R.O., Act Book of the Exeter Common Council, no. 9, 1647–1655, fo. 8; QS. Box 55, no piece reference (the petition).

aldermen was encouraged by the presence of the local MP, Samuel Clarke, despite the fact that, being behind in its assessment, the city was liable to free quartering according to the terms of the ordinance of the previous 24 December. Clarke's role in the incident can be explained in terms of his own political standpoint, if the testimony of some soldiers is to be credited. To one of them he protested 'That . . . the Army had done no Service for the Parliament', while accusing a captain of having been 'one of them that would have pulled the Parliament out by the Ears'. Endeavouring to compromise, Lieutenant-Colonel Salmon had offered to quarter his men in churches and outhouses, but the church of which he was reluctantly given the key proved insufficient to house half of them.[117] Ultimately they had to be quartered in sheds, a churchyard and a church porch and other open places. Nor did the mayor offer any assurance that his authority would be used to quell any disorders against the soldiers arising out of their quartering. He seems, if anything, to have been the ultimate victor, since, although the soldiers were forcibly quartered in Exeter, it was only for a short time, and on 23 May the House of Commons ordered the removal of the soldiers from the city.[118]

Since Exeter had clearly not complied with the terms of the December ordinance in the provision of assessment arrears, the above case cannot be regarded, like many others, as an instance of a coach and horses having been driven through this ordinance. But even if its provisions were dutifully observed, there were still loopholes to be exploited. One of these related to the permitting of quartering for two nights, even in places whose assessment arrears had been dutifully paid over in accordance with the terms of the December ordinance. In a petition of 3 July 1648 the Hampshire Grand Jury complained that 'very many who pretend themselves to be soldiers under pretext that they are . . . permitted to make quarter for one night onely . . . come sucessively [sic] one Company after another so that your Peticioners . . . are forced so soone as one Company is gone to provide for the entertainment of a second . . .'.[119] Small wonder perhaps that the inhabitants of Surrey had showed such unwillingness in May to allow soldiers from outside to enter their county. This seems to have prompted a warning from the Derby House Committee to Fairfax to see to it that such soldiers as were sent there should 'carry themselves inoffensively for the people of the County, and to their owne quartering that they may bee in safety'.[120]

117. According to Waller's account the church was even smaller, not holding even a third of the men (Bodleian, Tanner MSS., 57, fo. 128(b)).
118. L.J., X, 269–72. For a lengthy account of the incident by Waller, see Bodleian, Tanner MSS., fos. 124, 127–9(b).
119. Bodleian, MSS., dep. C. 175, no. 119 (Nalson MSS., XXII, no. 119).
120. Clarke Papers, II, 20.

The last few examples have taken us into the period of the Second Civil War, during which, of course, Cavalier as well as Roundhead soldiers were exacting free quarter. In a declaration in March the Scottish soldiers who were soon to constitute the army of the Engagement expressed a determination, which is hardly surprising in view of the hardships which they had experienced in 1645–6, not to go in England 'again to lie upon Free Quarter but will have . . . constant Pay'.[121] But while the English royalists and their new Scottish allies were quick to denounce free quarter as one of the most oppressive features of the English parliamentary regime, from which a royalist victory would bring relief to the much-enduring Englishmen, they were in fact forced to have recourse to it themselves, as were their opponents.[122] On 2 May the Yorkshire committee, conscious of the threat to the county following the fall of Berwick and Carlisle to the insurgents, urgently requested reinforcements to be sent to Yorkshire, but, hardly less urgently, stressed the importance of funds being sent with them to ensure that they were properly paid and would not have to resort to the free quarter which had so impoverished Yorkshire people during the First Civil War. In October, however, the same committee was protesting that Colonel Rainsborough's forces, sent up to lay siege to Pontefract Castle now in royalist hands, were arriving 'without . . . Monies to pay their Quarters', and the Derby House Committee for once responded promptly to their plea by earmarking assessment collections for their pay.[123]

There were still further troubles in Devon in June over the quartering of Waller's troops,[124] while in the following month, Sir Anthony Weldon, the chairman of the Kent county committee, suggested that the ultimate cost of the quartering of soldiers raised to put down the rebellion there ought to be borne out of the compounding fines and the proceeds of the sale of the sequestered estates of the royalist

121. For the Scots, see Rushworth, *Historical Collections*, VII, 1041, and below, pp. 305–9. For an English denunciation of Scottish free quartering and plunder in the north, see *The Moderate Intelligencer Number 182* (7/14 September 1648), BL., E.463(16), defective pagination.

122. For royalist denunciations of free quarter, see *The Declaration of Sir Marmaduke Langdale* (June 1648), BL., E.446(17), p. 7; F.H.S. Sunderland, *Marmaduke Lord Langdale* (1926), p. 113; *The Declaration of his Highnesse Prince Charles* (July 1648), BL., E.457(14), pp. 2–3; E.456(11), p. 5; 669 f12(95); *The Declaration of the Sea Commanders and Marriners* (August 1648), BL., E.457(6), pp. 3–4; *The Declaration of the Gentlemen and others now in Armes in the County of Hereford* (August 1647), BL. 669, f13(4); Webb, *Herefordshire*, II, 423. For a complaint against the free quarter (among other charges) exacted by the royalist commander of Scarborough Castle, see Northallerton, North Yorkshire R.O., Scarborough Corporation Minute Book, fo., 163(b). I am indebted to the kindness of Mr M.Y. Ashcroft for this reference.

123. Bodleian, Tanner MSS., 57, fos. 29, 109–9(b), 365, 378–8(b).

124. *HMC., 13th Rep., Appendix I; Portland MSS.*, I (1891), 466.

activists.[125] A slightly different expedient at the expense of delinquents and papists who had not compounded recommended itself to the county committee of Lancashire, another county wracked by civil war as well as, in this case, by foreign invasion, and where free quarter taken by both sides figured very prominently. The committee warned the government that if its recommendations were not adopted, the Roundhead soldiers were likely to take matters into their own hands, to the detriment of, amongst others, those delinquents who had already compounded and were therefore entitled to expect parliamentary protection.[126] A contemporary historian of the county, moreover, provides details of shocking quartering abuses to which some of its inhabitants were subjected. Following Cromwell's defeat of the Scots at Preston on 17 August, the district around Kirkham was apparently plagued by 'the most theevish Companies that ever the Country was pestered with'. This was a Durham regiment which quartered there and subjected the district to violence and plunder, 'stealing whatever they could conveniently carry away', notwithstanding the fact that the parish had already laid out £1,000 for three days' quartering. Relief came only with Cromwell's return to gather up detachments to march into Yorkshire.[127]

A letter from the army headquarters at St Albans on 29 September tells an all too familiar story.

His Excellency [Fairfax] takes all the Care he can to satisfie the Country that undergoes the great Burthen of free Quarter, Complaints coming daily concerning the same: and that which adds to Afflictions, that the Soldiers are not paid, whereby to enable Them to discharge their Quarters: some Regiments having not one Penny Pay these eighteen weeks past, and none having had above one Months Pay in all that time, except the two Regiments which were in Kent, and the Soldiers begin to be much discontented that the Fault should be imputed unto them, for not satisfying for what they have in Provisions, whereas they have been so ill paid, it is very much feared, if some speedy Course be not taken herein, neither the Country nor the Soldier will with Patience long undergo the same.[128]

On 6 November another letter from St Albans reported that 'the cry of free-quarter was so great in the ears of the Souldiers that it was feared it would occasion some distemper in them'.[129] In the circumstances it is

125. Bodleian, MSS., dep. C.158, no. 47 (Nalson MSS., VII, no. 47).
126. Bodleian, Tanner MSS., 57, fo. 171.
127. [Edward Robinson], *A Discourse of the Warr in Lancashire* (ed. W. Beaumont) (Chetham Soc. XLIII (1864), 67–8).
128. Rushworth, *Historical Collections*, VII, 1279.
129. Whitelock, *Memorials*, p. 342 (6 November 1648).

hardly surprising that some local authorities were prepared to go to great lengths to avoid free quartering. In September 1648 the borough of Great Yarmouth borrowed £900 on its own account to provide money to enable the soldiers billeted there to pay for their quarters. An ad hoc assessment was raised for this purpose in October and right into November there was a series of hand-to-mouth expedients, including the levying of a local rate to be used either to provide soldiers' wages so as to enable them to pay for their quarters, or to repay those on whom free quartering had been inflicted during the two weeks following the soldiers' first entry into the town in September.[130]

Thus free quarter not only enjoyed a new lease of life during the Second Civil War but survived it as it had the First.[131] Among the aims of the new republican regime as outlined in a declaration of 22 March 1649 was the abolition of free quarter and easing of tax burdens, aims that would earlier have been regarded as mutually incompatible – or at least, unless accompanied by large-scale demobilization. They were clearly incompatible now, for it was only following a parliamentary vote for a further £90,000 in the monthly assessments for the army on 7 April that the House of Commons ordered the parliamentary Committee for the Army to draw up an ordinance for the permanent abolition of free quarter.[132] The problem of how far this was successful falls outside the scope of this book.

Fiscal innovation: the Excise

Despite the stress laid by radicals such as Winstanley on the heavy burden of free quarter on poorer people, one tax which was certainly more widespread in its application and probably more regressive in its incidence was the Excise. Certainly an even more potent reason for its unpopularity than its character as a 'Dutch' innovation was, as one royalist pamphlet published in November 1647 put it, that it fell especially on 'all Commodities that are used for the life of

130. NNRO., Great Yarmouth Assembly Book 1642–1662, fos., 129(b), 132, 133, 133(b), 134(b). *The Moderate Intelligencer* for 8 September emphasizes Yarmouth's prolonged resistance to receiving troops (*The Moderate Intelligencer*, number 182 (7/ 14 September 1648), BL., E.463(16), defective pagination).

131. For evidence of its exaction in 1649, see Oxford, Worcester College pamphlets, AA 8.3 (109): Whitelock, *Memorials* (1 February, 19 March, 30 April), pp. 371, 380(b), 384(b).

132. *A Declaration of the Parliament of England* (22 March 1649), BHPC., p. 26; *C.J.*, VI, 182. For the passing of the ordinance and subsequent orders regarding its implementation, see *C.J.*, VI, 198, 206, 207, 208, 214, 270; Whitelock, *Memorials*, pp. 399 (20 July), 400 (29 July).

man'.[133] Royalists were naturally prepared to derive the utmost benefit from the unpopularity of the tax, to see that this rubbed off on the government which imposed it (even though the king had raised a similar tax during the war) and to contrast it with the exaggerated burdens of the levies of the 1630s.[134] If the implication was not clear, the point was made explicitly by another royalist pamphlet in 1648. It was that a return to the old royal order would surely bring about a return to older and better ways. 'Then no mans house would be broken up, nor his goods taken from him. . . . No Excise, nor Taxes ever heard of more.'[135] And such royalist complaints were echoed by those of conservative parliamentarians and men of no party, all eager to blame what they saw as the exorbitant level of taxation on the hated New Model Army. The impact of the Excise was insidious, argued one such London pamphlet of June 1648, 'so cunningly contrived as . . . we find the sad effects of it at second hand, both in the impoverishing those customers we deale withall in Country Townes, and in the Dearth of all manner of Victuals'.[136]

Such complaints abounded in conservative circles and it would be surprising if they did not find at least equally violent expression in Leveller and other radical pamphlets.[137] Certainly few would be found to go along with what most would have considered a perverse counter-argument from an anti-Leveller source that the Excise was in fact the least grievous of all taxes, 'because every man is in a sort his owne assessor, it being . . . in his owne power by his frugallity to reduce it to as small a summe as he please'; a view which does not simply ignore, but positively denies the fact that Excise was especially profitable to the government precisely because it fell on the necessities of life.[138] Indeed, when in the summer of 1647 parliament had modified the Excise,

---

133. Edward Symmons, *A Vindication of King Charles* (November 1647), BL., E.414(16), p. 53; see also pp. 109–11.
134. *The Mistake of the Times* (July 1647), BL., E.399(18), p. 3; *England's Dust and Ashes raked up* (August 1648), BL., E.459(10), pp. 25–8, 88.
135. *A Letter to Alderman Warner . . .* (1648), BL., E.435(27), p. 2.
136. *The necessity of the speedy calling a Common Hall* (June 1648), BL., E.449(10), p. 3. For other attacks on Excise from conservative quarters, see e.g., *A New Magna Charta* (February 1648), BL., E.427(15), p. 6: *A Remonstrance of the Kings Majesties loyall Subjects within the City of London* (August 1648), BL., E.462(6), p. 2; 'Memoirs of Denzil Lord Holles', in Maseres, *Select Tracts*, I, 292.
137. See, e.g., *A Call to All the Souldiers of the Armie* (October 1647), BL., E.412(10), p. 2; 'The Case of the Army Truly Stated' (October 1647), in *Leveller Manifestoes*, p. 213; 'The mournful cryes of many thousand poor Tradesmen', ibid., pp. 275–6; and the Leveller petition of January 1648, ibid., p. 270; *A New Engagement or Manifesto* (August 1648), BL., 669, f12(99), item ii, no pagination; *The Bloody Project* (August 1648), in *Leveller Tracts*, p. 138: *The Humble Petition of divers well-affected Citizens . . . of London* (31 August 1648), BL., 669, f12(106).
138. *A Declaration of Some Proceedings of Lt. Col. John Lilburn And his Associates* (February 1648), *Leveller Tracts*, pp. 123–4.

removing it from meat and salt, it quickly found it necessary to make it clear in an ordinance of 28 August that no amount of violent agitation for the extension of this remission to other commodities would be of any avail to those attempting to emulate the butchers who had been among the most prominent and vociferous opponents of the tax. Hardly less prominent were the brewers, who had the greater cause for complaint in that, at the same time as the Excise was removed from meat and salt, it was doubled on strong beer; a commodity which, the brewers complained, was much in demand by the poor, 'who necessarily make Use of it in their Families, as the cheapest Food . . . with which and Bread they can well discharge the hardest of Labour'. Not entirely consistent with this, however, was the brewers' further contention that, unlike the practice in the Low Countries, the tax was levied on them rather than at the point of sale, and that, since the demand for beer was by no means inelastic, they were unable to pass on its incidence.[139]

The failure of the London brewers to persuade parliament to remove the excise on beer was followed by a number of private suits by brewers against Excise officials, messengers and constables distraining goods for non-payment of the tax, and sometimes resorting to violence in pursuit of this end. Such officials sometimes had to have recourse to the parliamentary Indemnity Committee to rescue themselves from the consequences of such prosecution.[140] Of all tax collectors, the Excise commissioners and their underlings seem to have incurred by far the greatest odium: 'such a covey of Cormorants as was never seen in a Commonwealth' was the verdict of the royalist newswriter *Mercurius Melancholicus* in November 1647.[141] Quite apart from their unpopularity as administrators of a hated and burdensome tax, it was widely believed that they feathered their own nests out of the proceedings, 'being now so well fledg'd with borrowed feathers that they need not feare to flie abroad'.[142] At best gross mismanagement and at worst flagrant peculation are implied by critics ranging from royalists to radicals. One of the former argues that the Excise alone, if properly managed, ought to be sufficient to pay for all the charges of the army, as it did in the United Provinces.[143]

139. For these developments, see *L.J.*, IX, 402–3, 411–12: *An Ordinance and Declaration For Re-establishing the Duty of Excise* (August 1647), BL., E.404(37); *A&O.*, I, 1004–7.

140. The records of the Indemnity committee (PRO., SP. 24/1–3, passim) afford numerous examples. For particular cases of violence to a London brewer and a Derby butcher see SP. 24/1, fos. 52(b), 57, 90(b), 105(b); SP. 24/2, fo. 47.

141. *Mercurius Melancholicus* (1 November 1647), BL., E.412(13), pp. 53–4. See also *Mercurius Rusticus* (12 November 1647), BL., E.414(5), p. 4.

142. *Queries to be considered of on the King's much wished and hoped for arrival* (June 1647), BL., 669, f11(33).

143. *The Case of the king stated* (1647), BHPC., p. 20.

Obviously the most appropriate body to investigate such charges would be the parliamentary Committee for Examining the Accounts of the Kingdom, but its records give the impression that, for a long time at least, it was more concerned to restrain the keenness of its sub-committees in the counties to expose Excise frauds and peculation than to encourage them to undertake any such rigorous examination. There can be no doubt that, as the disappointed Sussex Accounts sub-committee informed the Speaker of the House of Commons on 31 August 1646, thoroughgoing examination of the proceedings of the Excise Commissioners and their local agents would have been very popular in the country, nor was Sussex the only county where attempts were made in high places to warn off the Accounts sub-committee from proceeding with such investigations. The same thing occurred in Herefordshire in September.[144] Complaints of peculation by Excise men remained common, and few probably credited the assertion of the Excise ordinance on 28 August 1647 that the cost of collecting the tax rarely rose above two shillings in the pound, as opposed to half of the gross receipts as claimed by some critics.[145] On 25 September 1648 the House of Lords decided to give a hearing to an individual who offered to prove that the state was prejudiced in £50,000 per annum by the ill management of the Excise. It is not specified whether his charges included dishonesty as well as bad management.[146]

The Excise was also unpopular on account of its centralized appropriation, which meant that the localities where it was raised, however great their need, found it difficult to pinpoint any tangible benefit coming to them from it. During the First Civil War there had been several requests for the decentralization of the appropriations of both the royalist and the parliamentary Excise,[147] and similar recommendations were made in May 1647 in a petition from the Grand Inquest of Devon, and in June 1648 in a strongly localist

144. For the Accounts Committee, see below, pp. 100–103; and D.H. Pennington, 'The Accounts of the Kingdom 1642–1649', in F.J. Fisher (ed.), *Essays in the Economic and Social History of Tudor and Stuart England* (Cambridge, 1961), pp. 182–203. On Sussex, Bodleian, Tanner MSS., 59, fo. 521; on Herefordshire, PRO., SP. 28/253(A) (Letter Book of Committee for Taking Accounts, 1646–9), fo. 17(b).

145. *An Ordinance and Declaration for the establishing the Duty of Excize* (28 August 1647), BL., E.404(37), pp. 6–7; *A&O.*, I, 1006. Excise officers were paid on a poundage basis on their receipts (see E. Hughes, *Studies in Administration and Finance 1558–1625* (Philadelphia, reprint 1980), p. 126.

146. *L.J.*, X, 511.

147. For the request from Oxford apropos of the royal Excise in 1644, see BL., Add. MSS., 18,980, fo. 32. For requests concerning the parliamentary Excise in 1643, 1645 and 1646, see Bodleian, Tanner MSS., 62, fo. 469 (Ely); Tanner MSS., 59, fos. 195–5(b) (Yorkshire); ibid., fo. 345 (Dorset).

and anti-army paper circulating amongst the freemen of the City of London.[148]

Resistance to the tax ranged from individual refusals to pay to frightening acts of mob violence. On Tuesday 24 August 1647, the same day on which the London brewers' petition was read in the House of Commons, eight of them were called to the bar of the Lower House and asked if they had paid the Excise due from them. All pleaded that 'If they could receive what was owing to them, they would [pay]'. The House was not impressed by this excuse, and the brewers were ordered to pay by the coming Friday on pain of attachment of their persons and property. Indeed, the House expressed suspicion that there was 'something worse . . . in it than the bare Non-payment of the Money'.[149] Recent experience had no doubt led MPs to a realization that, if not checked, such refusals were likely to get completely out of hand.

The classic case of this happening is Lincolnshire, where Colonel Edward King's inflammatory outburst against, inter alia, the Excise and assessments, from the chair at the Folkingham Sessions of the Peace had caused widespread refusal to pay, and on 4 December 1646 complaint had been made in the House of Commons about this.[150] When King was in consequence called before the parliamentary Excise committee, he was unrepentant, arguing that it was in no way improper for him to have invited charges to be brought against Excise officers since they had 'oppressed and poled the people'. King's anti-Excise activities continued into the new year, and on 6 January 1647 the Excise sub-commissioners in Spalding wrote to their counterparts in Boston imparting to them the contents of a letter from King – how had they got hold of it? – informing an acquaintance in Spalding that 'he had routed the Excise-men cleane and hoped the Countrey men would looke for theire money againe from them'. On 11 January at the Sleaford Quarter Sessions King launched another vitriolic attack on those who were bleeding the county white, including the Excise men among their number.[151]

While in Lincolnshire we encounter the astonishing spectacle of the chairman of Quarter Sessions inciting refusal to pay taxes and urging the presentation of Excise men by the Grand Jury for their extortions, in other counties it was the tax refusers who appeared in the dock. At the Hertfordshire Sessions of the Peace on 6 March 1647 an Excise officer deposed that in the previous month one William Wilkinson of Ware had abused and threatened him, and that Thomas Moulson, a Hertford

148.   For Devon, L.J., IX, 171; for London, The humble Desires of the Loyall hearted, wel-affected Freemen of the City of London (June 1648), BL., 669, f12(39), no pagination.
149.   C.J., V, 283.
150.   BL., Add., 31,116, fo. 291(b) (Whitacre's diary).
151.   Bodleian, Tanner MSS., 59, fos. 638, 668.

butcher – the Excise had not yet been taken off meat – 'came to Ware . . . to Raile at me and the proceedings of the Excise & tould me I had vndone him & I must not thinke to goe free nor the Commissioners themselves, for they might as well have Robbd him of his money as to take it for Excise'. At the same sessions another informant deposed that when he had asked Jonas Addison why he had ceased to butcher pigs, the latter replied that he would 'never kill none to pay excise for yᵉ Committees att Hertford to sitt & drink . . .'.[152]

While it is clear that most refusals to pay Excise reflect simply the unpopularity of the tax, there were occasions on which such refusal was a means of applying pressure to the government for quite different reasons. Such were the decisions of some London Presbyterians, recorded in Thomas Juxon's diary for 13 April 1646, not to pay Excise until parliament had resolved to act on a hitherto disregarded petition about their religious grievances,[153] and, more than two years later, in 1648, the Engagement of the Grand Jury and other inhabitants of Essex in May 1648 not to pay Excise or other taxes until the various demands of their petition had been acceded to.[154] But such cases were emphatically the exception rather than the rule, and more usually the Excise was a cause rather than just the occasion of anti-Excise activities, even if it was sometimes only one of a number of causes: as in the cases of the riots at Canterbury at Christmas 1647 and in Norwich in April 1648,[155] though the troubles in the former city were no doubt exacerbated by the fact that the mayor was himself an Excise officer as well as being, if one report is to be believed, 'a man of a rough and unkind nature'.[156]

The point at which refusal to pay Excise would merge into violent anti-Excise tumults was often difficult to predict. Parliamentary ordinances concerning the Excise, such as those of 22 February and 28 August 1647, show great concern about attacks on Excise collectors and urge local authorities such as mayors, sheriffs and JPs, if necessary aided by the army, to maintain civil order and put down such disturbances.[157] Sometimes, however, the soldiers were to be found on the other side; as participants in the disturbances rather than assisting in their

152. Hertford, Hertfordshire RO., QS. Roll 7, nos. 151, 152. For other examples of resistance to payment of Excise early in 1647 in Somerset and Gloucestershire, see *Western Assize Orders*, p. 254; Bodleian, Clarendon MSS., 29, fo. 146.
153. BL. Add. MSS., 25,465, fo. 68(b).
154. *The Ingagement and Declaration of the Grand Jury, Freeholders and other Inhabitants of the County of Essex* (May 1648), BL., E.443(9), E.443(13), not paginated.
155. *The Declaration of many thousands of the City of Canterbury and County of Kent* (5 January 1648), BL., E.421(23), pp. 3–4, 7; NNRO., Norwich Corporation Records, 12(c)(i), deps. 252, 264, 271.
156. *A Letter from a Gentleman in Kent* (15 June 1648), BL., E.448(34), pp. 2–3.
157. *A&O.*, I, 916–20, 1004–7; *An Ordinance . . . for the establishing the Duty of Excise* (28 August 1647), BL., E.403(37), pp. 3–7; *L.J.*, IX, 411–12.

suppression, as seems to have been the case in Cheshire in the summer of 1646.[158] This was no isolated instance and in June 1647 the government showed great concern to enlist the firm support of the Commander-in-Chief and his subordinates not only in prohibiting and punishing such behaviour by the soldiers but also in assisting civil authorities in suppressing such tumults.[159] That Fairfax's co-operation was forthcoming was, of course, no assurance that it was completely successful in achieving either of these aims.

The army was even sometimes requested to afford its assistance and protection to those collecting the duty.[160] On 19 October it was given a strong self-interest in doing so, when the House of Commons having adjourned into a Committee of the Whole to consider the matter of assigning specific funds for the soldiers' pay, fixed on the Excise and ordered that Fairfax should employ some of his soldiers to assist in its collection.[161] But that military escorts for Excisemen were no infallible safeguard against violence was to be demonstrated on New Year's Eve at Chippenham in Wiltshire, where Excise collectors and their escorting soldiers were attacked by rioters, from here and neighbouring parts, including, so it was said, the adjoining counties of Gloucestershire and Hampshire.[162]

Sporadic disturbances against Excise mark the whole of the inter-war period and continue into the time of the Second Civil War. Even more spectacular than the incidents so far mentioned were the anti-Excise disturbances at Norwich in December 1646, of which we have vivid and colourful accounts in letters from the Norwich sub-commissioners for Excise to the Excise Commissioners in London. The riots, which predate by several months the lifting of Excise from meat, seem to have been occasioned by the arrest of one of four butchers who had refused to pay the tax, and the resultant surge of angry butchers from the market-place to release him from the sheriff's custody. The messenger, in whose hands the defaulting butcher was to be conveyed out of the city, had his sword taken from him and was beaten within an inch of his life, as were the city officers accompanying him. With some difficulty, the sheriff assuaged the tumult but on the following Monday another crowd, armed with clubs and staves, endeavoured to intimidate the magistrates whose response seems to have been an injudicious mixture

158. HMC., 13th. Report. Appendix, Portland MSS., I, 390.
159. Whitelock, Memorials, p. 259 (28 June); A Proclamation from His Excellency Sir Thomas Fairfax (July 1647), BL., E.396(23), pp. 3–4; For a sceptical interpretation of his order, see 'Memoirs of Denzil Lord Holles', in Maseres, Select Tracts, I, 292.
160. For an example from Dorset in November 1646, see Mayo, Dorset, p. 55.
161. 'Perfect Occurrences', no. 42, Cal.SPD. 1645–7, pp. 601–2.
162. A Declaration Concerning His Majesties Royall Person (5 January 1648), BL. E.422(6), pp. 1–2; D. Underdown, Revel, Riot and Rebellion . . . 1603–1660 (Oxford, 1985), p. 216.

of toughness and cajolery, and before the crowd withdrew there was an attempt to break into the Excise house. Ultimately the four defaulting butchers were made to enter into bonds to appear before the parliamentary Excise committee on 19 January 1647, but the troubles were not yet over. The incidents foreshadow the even more violent and general Norwich riots of April 1648 and, though in the latter case the causes are manifold and much more complex,[163] there is one striking parallel in an incident of 17 December 1646, when 'one Holland, a poore butcher . . . rode about the Citty, Crieing . . . Arme, Arme, Arme: if you intend to saue your lives & estates'. For a time things got badly out of control and the local Excise authorities reported that they were 'threatned to bee chopt in peeces'. On 28 December, eleven days after their first letter, they reported that the local butchers were still refusing to co-operate, 'but giue revileing language to them whom we send to take notice what [beasts] they kill', and that a municipal officer had been assaulted in the street by a butcher who, failing to wrench his cane from him, 'tooke vpp the Jaw of a beast . . . and hit him on the head with it'. On 8 January 1647 the sub-commissioners reported that no Excise had been paid by the butchers since the troubles had begun in Norwich in the second week of December. To make matters worse, disaffection had spread to the nearby country districts as well as from the butchers to the brewers.[164] On 4 March Thomas Atkins, MP for Norwich and a native of that city as well as being a senior London alderman, warned the Mayor of Norwich about the strong inclination of many MPs to blame the local magistrates for not showing appropriate firmness to the troublemakers.[165] Finally, in the much more violent disturbances which again broke out in Norwich more than a year later, on 24 April 1648, the local Excise office and officers were again among the foci of the rioters' unruly attentions.[166]

Probably even more alarming to the government were the anti-Excise disturbances in London. Doubtless the royalist Sir Edward Nicholas, in exile in France, was delighted to get news, in a letter of 18 February 1647, of riots in Smithfield resulting in the burning down of the Excise office and the destruction of the records housed there. The continued refusal of the Smithfield butchers to purchase beasts was in fact a protest against the imprisonment of some of the rioters in Newgate while awaiting trial. In his diary Thomas Juxon reports that following these disturbances 'by the Buchers and the rascally Crew', a new Excise house was to be built and to be

---

163. On this, see below, pp. 369–70, 373–4.
164. Bodleian, Tanner MSS., 59, fos. 610, 623, 649.
165. BL., Add. MSS., 22,620, fo. 56.
166. NNRO., Norwich Corporation Records, 12(c)(i), deps. 252, 264, 271. For these incidents, see below, pp. 369–75.

deliberately designed as a dwelling house in order that those guilty of future attacks on it would be liable to the capital charge of felony.[167]

Nicholas the royalist obviously rejoiced in the event, but a pamphleteer from the opposite end of the political spectrum, admittedly in retrospect, in October 1648, derived no less satisfaction from it. 'Parliament . . .', he observed, 'never met with their match . . . untill they began to vex the Butchers of *London*, because the Butchers scorned to be enslaved . . . so that neither the Lord Mayor, Sheriffs, nor trained bands . . . could appease them, untill they had both burned the Excise House, terrified the Par[iament] and fought themselves free, like brave fellowes, from paying any more Excise'. Violence, in a word, had paid off, 'for is there any sort . . . of men, yea Souldiers themselves . . . more desperate, bloody and dangerous than Butchers are, their hands being for the most part in blood whereas Souldiers will rest many weeks and months without shedding of blood and . . . as they are most perfect in knocking down and beating out the brains, and letting of blood, so are they most skilfull in drawing all away, cleaving asunder, hanging up, quartering, drawing . . . and . . . dispersing of everything in its own due order . . . as it becommeth wise, able and discreet men'.[168] Even if the immediate result of these and other riots was the policing measures envisaged in the ordinance of 22 February,[169] there can be little doubt that they also played their part in bringing about the ultimate removal of the Excise from meat.

The anti-Excise violence in London was to achieve a dangerous notoriety as an example to be emulated. Giving evidence before the Hertfordshire Quarter Sessions on 6 March 1647, a local Excise officer deposed that one George Wilkinson of Ware had 'threatened that he and others would beate me out of ye Countrii [*sic*] very shortly & that the excize howse was burnt downe at London & they would burne the howse where I lived . . . & that they that set the Excise first on foote were Roges & Rascales'.[170] Unlike this case, there were other places besides Norwich and London where anti-Excise behaviour moved beyond threats to violent action: at Leeds in Yorkshire in January 1647, where the assault on local Excise officers seems to have been the work of a few wild ex-Cavaliers rather than local butchers or brewers;[171] at Frome and Somerton in Somerset and Great Torrington in Devon early

167. *Nicholas Papers*, p. 75; Dr Williams's Library, MS. 24.50, fos. 102–2(b). See also Bodleian, Clarendon MSS., 29, fo. 146.
168. *Fruitfull England like To Become A Barren Wilderness* (October 1648), BL., E.467(36), pp. 10–11.
169. *A&O.*, I, 916–20.
170. Hertford, Hertfordshire RO., QS. Roll 7, no. 151.
171. Bodleian, Tanner MSS., 59, fo. 663.

in 1648;[172] while closer parallels to the London riots are to be found in Worcestershire and neighbouring Shropshire, in the assault and looting of the Excise houses at Worcester in January and Market Drayton in May 1648, the latter allegedly by a crowd of women – perhaps a 'skimmity' of sorts.[173]

Needless to say, the insurgents in the Second Civil War numbered the Excise prominently among the grievances of the realm which would be removed as a result of their triumph,[174] and while the burden of taxation may have helped to swell their numbers, it was deplored by many more who themselves would probably have been all too ready to acquiesce in a royalist victory. Among these were probably those citizens of London who had risen in July 1647 and most of whom were not to stir again in 1648, but who, as a pamphlet circulating during that summer emphasized, detested 'that most accursed and hellish imposition of Excise' which it saw as the major cause of the Second Civil War.[175] It is, of course, a gross oversimplification to see insurgents rising in arms simply or even mainly because of such grievances. Men may engage more or less readily in minor disturbances but are unlikely to go to war simply because they conceive themselves to be overtaxed. Nevertheless, it is undeniable that the matters dealt with in this chapter provided potent reasons for popular discontent and for alienation from the regime at Westminster. When coupled with a multiplicity of other grievances with which they had much in common, and not least a deep mistrust of

172. *Western Assize Orders*, pp. 276, 279–80; Exeter, Devon R.O., QS. Order Book, VIII, 1640–1645, no foliation.
173. *The Kingdomes Weekly Post . . . Number 5* (26 January/2 February 1648) (entry for 29 January), BL., E.425(5), pp. 35–6; *A Letter to a Member of the House of Commons* (1 February 1648), BL., E.425(20), pp. 3–5; *The Kingdomes Weekly Post Number 6* (2/ 9 February 1648) (entry for 7 February), BL., E.426(13), pp. 47–8; *Mercurius Pragmaticus Number 23* (15/22 February 1648), BL., E.428(9), no pagination. Among other things, some tobacco distrained for non-payment of Excise was looted from the Worcester Excise House to the discomfiture of a local sub-commissioner for Excise who was being sued for distraining it (PRO., SP. 24/2, fo. 12).
174. See, e.g., (i) in South Wales, *Colonell Powell and Coll. Poyer's Letters . . . With their Declarations* (1648), Codrington pamphlet coll., p. 5; (ii) in Kent, *To the Lords and Commons . . . the humble Petition of the Knights, Gentry, Clergy and Commonalty of the County of Kent* (May 1648), BL., E.441(25), p. 3; 669, f12(28), no pagination; (iii) in the north, *The Declaration of Sir Marmaduke Langdale* (June 1648), BL., E.466(17), p. 7; F.H.S. Sunderland, *Marmaduke Lord Langdale* (1926), p. 113; (iv) in Essex, *The Remonstrance and Declaration of the Knights, Esquires, Gentlemen and Freeholders in Colchester* (6 July 1647), BL., E.451(11), p. 7; (v) in Herefordshire, *The Declaration of the Gentlemen and others now in Arms in the County of Hereford* (August 1648), BL., 669, f13(4), no pagination; (vi) by the insurgent mariners, *Naval Documents*, p. 354; also BL., 669, f12(69), no pagination; *The Declaration of his Highnesse Prince Charles* (July 1648), Codrington pamphlet coll., pp. 2–3, BL., 669, f12(95), no pagination; BL., E.456(11), p. 5; E.457(14), p. 3; *Parliamentary History*, XVII, 344; *The Declaration of the Sea Commanders and Mariners with Prince Charles* (August 1648), BL., E.457(6), p. 5.
175. *The necessity of the speedy calling a Common Hell* (June 1648), BL., E.449(10), p. 3.

novelty and innovation which had earlier fuelled much of the opposition to Charles I and now worked to the detriment of the parliamentary regime, they afforded scope for the development of a community of interest between militant royalists and conservative but alienated parliamentarians. In the final resort this may even have induced a minority of the latter to throw in their lot with the former in their bloody and desperate renewal of civil war in 1648. The chapter which follows is concerned with some of those other grievances in which the dislike of conservative Englishmen for innovation and novelty bulked no less large.

III

DISILLUSIONMENT AND ALIENATION: II. REVOLUTIONARY ILLEGALITY

To preserve our Ancient and Fundamentall Lawes, to purchase our just Liberties, To conserve the Kings known Rights, were our solemne Protestations. All these being like *Sampsons* cords broken, I believe my selfe disengaged: The Reformation desired is extirpation endeavoured; In stead of Petition [*sic*], as Subjects ought, we command as Rebels use; The preservation of our Ancient and Fundamentall Lawes is out-lawed by new Votes, and illegall Ordinances; The purchase of our just Liberties is turn'd into unjust licentiousnesse; And the conservation of the Kings known Rights is overturn'd by unknown wrongs.

A Letter of an Independent to his Honoured Friend in LONDON (27 November 1647), BL., E.393(16), pp. 1–2

And thus we may see how this body of men, who cry out against arbitrary government in a prince, can, even to blood, remorselessly execute it by themselves.

Sir Philip Warwick, *Memoirs of the Reign of King Charles I* (1702) (Edinburgh, 1813 edn.), p. 184

Fundamental law set at nought

Before 1640 the fundamental law, as exemplified by Magna Carta and the Petition of Right of 1628, had been frequently cited as the safeguard against what some deemed the aggrandisement of the power of the king at the expense of that of the subject, although, in the months between the calling of the Long Parliament and the outbreak of the First Civil War, Charles I was prepared to take a leaf out of his opponents' book and charge them with misusing fundamental law to justify their illegal infringements of his prerogative.[1] The parliamentary triumph in the First Civil War gave further scope for such charges.

---

1. See, e.g., *A Collection of severall speeches messages and answers (1642)*, BHPC., pp. 13, 29. Clarendon, *Rebellion*, II, 69, 138; *His Majesties Answer to a Book Entituled The Declaration or Remonstrance of the Lords and Commons (1642)*, BHPC., p. 8.

In practice, one royalist newswriter observed in January 1648, law was whatever those in power chose to make it. Far from Justice being blindfold, there was one law for the victors and another for the vanquished. It was, insisted another, precisely because the king stood up for his own and his subjects' rights according to the fundamental law of the land that parliament had imprisoned him in the first place.[2]

During the 1620s Magna Carta had been considered the most important statement of the fundamental law, some of whose principles had been reaffirmed in the Petition of Right of 1628. But, as one royalist was to argue after the war, it was the Roundheads not the Cavaliers who needed to have these principles brought home to them, for parliament 'have ravish'd *Magna Carta*, which they are sworn to maintaine, taken away our birth right and transgressed all the lawes of heaven and earth'.[3] There were indeed some parliamentary Presbyterians, of whom William Prynne in his *The Soveraigne Powers of Parliament* was the most eminent, who claimed that 'the Parliament is above the Lawes . . . yea *Magna Carta* itself'.[4]

An appropriate point at which to begin our examination of how Magna Carta and the Petition of Right developed from being weapons used against the excesses of royal arbitrary rule to becoming part of the royalist armoury against the excessive powers exercised by the victors in the First Civil War is the practices complained of in the Petition of Right in 1628. Arbitrary taxation has already been dealt with in the previous chapter.[5] Other practices considered in the Petition of Right were arbitrary imprisonment and the enforcement of martial law, and, as in the 1620s, the later 1640s see an abundance of complaints against both. Nor were royalists the only complainants. Conservative parliamentarians such as Colonel Edward King and Clement Walker were eloquent in their denunciation of arbitrary imprisonment by parliamentary committees, and especially by county committees.[6] Similarly, the

---

2. *Mercurius Elencticus Number 10* (26 January/2 February 1648) BL., E.425(7), pp. 70, 74–5; *Mercurius Pragmaticus Number 18* (11/18 January 1648), E.423(1), no pagination.
3. James Howell, *A Letter to the Earle of Pembrooke* (1647), BHPC., p. 11.
4. For a persuasive explanation of Prynne's view see W. Lamont, *Marginal Prynne 1600– 1669* (1963), pp. 93–102. For an attack on this view and assertion 'that there is a fundamentall Law . . . against which the Parliament cannot act', see *Plain Truth without Feare or Flattery* (1647), Oxford, Worcester College pamphlet coll., p. 15. For a more balanced and profound view than either of these, by another eminent Presbyterian lawyer, Sir John Maynard, see below, pp. 115–16.
5. See above, pp. 43–80. For a comparison of arbitrary taxes in the 1630s with those in the 1640s, see Nathaniel Ward, *To the high and honourable Parliament of England . . . the humble petitions, serious suggestions* (2 May 1648), BHPC., p. 17; see also p. 25.
6. Bodleian, Tanner MSS., 59, fos. 668(b)–9; Walker, *Independency*, pp. 62–3. King's denunciation was made in his charge to the Grand Jury at the Lincolnshire Sessions of the Peace at Sleaford on 11 January 1647.

arbitrary imprisonment by parliamentary commissions, such as that appointed for the investigation of Oxford University in 1647–8, was declared to be contrary to the liberty of the subject.[7] In place of the agitation against imprisonment by the Privy Council, which had been a feature of the 1620s, the later 1640s saw protests against imprisonment by the House of Lords and other bodies from a number of very articulate victims of such action, as politically variegated as the Levellers Richard Overton and John Lilburne, the royalist ex-judge David Jenkins, the parliamentary Presbyterian lawyer Sir John Maynard, and the London aldermen imprisoned for their role in the counter-revolutionary disturbances in the metropolis in July 1647.[8] A pamphlet of January 1648, significantly entitled *The Petition of Right of the Free-holders and Free-men of. . . England*, singles out for condemnation the continued persistence of arbitrary imprisonment and the ineffectiveness of writs of habeas corpus, the issue on which the famous Five Knights' Case of 1627, which had been so important to the genesis of the original Petition of Right, had turned.[9] Here again the post-war government could be charged with a similar disregard for the rights of the subject. In the previous July Lord General Fairfax and his Council of War had been at pains to stress the need for cases pending to be brought speedily to trial and for the accused to be released on bail when this proved impossible.[10]

As it was to turn out, the army in this matter proved to be less white than driven snow, and the most appropriate epilogue to this brief treatment of the issue of arbitrary imprisonment relates to one of the most spectacular cases of which the army itself was the culprit. In a spirited letter to the Lord General on 3 January 1649 the irrepressible William Prynne, who had been incarcerated since Pride's Purge on 6 December, demanded to know what sort of a prisoner he was. He had been held prisoner 'against the Priviledges of Parliament, the Liberty of the Subject, the Lawes and Statutes of the Realm, & all rules of Justice, Conscience & Right'. Was he a prisoner of peace or of war? he asked,

---

7. Bodleian, Bodley MSS., 338, fo. 81.
8. *Leveller Manifestoes*, pp. 136, 166–7; D. Jenkins, *Lex Terrae* (1647), BHPC., pp. 18–19; *The Royall Quarrell . . . by Sir John Maynard* (9 February 1648), BL., E.426(11), pp. 3–4; *The Lawes Subversion; or Sir John Maynard's Case truly Stated* (6 March 1648), E.431(2), pp. 5–6; *Parliamentary History*, XVII, 349–56 (Maynard's speech of 29 July 1648 against the imprisonment of Lilburne). On the aldermen, *L.J.*, X, 231–2; Rushworth, *Historical Collections*, VII, 1070: *The Humble Petition of the Worshipful Thomas Adams, John Langham and James Bunce, Aldermen* (25 April 1648), Oxford, Worcester College, pamphlet coll., pp. 3–8. For Maynard and Jenkins, see below, pp. 109–16.
9. BL., E.422(9), pp. 7–8.
10. *The Proposal Delivered to . . . the Commissioners of Parliament residing with the Army . . .* (18 July 1647), BL., E.399(10), p. 5.

pointing out that it could be argued that in Pride's Purge the army had, in fact, waged war on parliament.[11]

In a remonstrance against free quarter sometime early in 1648 it was complained that soldiers were claiming to be exempt from trial at common law '& are to be tryed for any capitall offence or other misdemeanor . . . according to Marshall Law, as is vsed in armyes in ye tyme of warre'.[12] As in the case of arbitrary imprisonment, here is another close parallel with the conditions which had produced the Petition of Right in 1628. As Conrad Russell has convincingly argued, in the later 1620s it had been feared that emergency taxation and emergency measures such as forced billeting and martial law might too easily be drawn into regular custom and become permanent features of English life in peacetime as well as during war.[13] The events at the end and following the end of the First Civil War seemed again to be bearing out this gloomy prognostication.[14] For the time being it was more the trial of soldiers by martial rather than common law for what were civilian offences which caused especial alarm rather than the possible extension of the martial law to the civilian population. Certainly most military commanders would favour commissions of martial law as a necessary means both of maintaining military discipline and of protecting the civilian population against the wilder excesses of the soldiery.[15] On 28 July 1648, Sir Henry Cholmely wrote to Speaker Lenthall requesting the right to exercise martial law in his command, without which 'I shall not be able to keepe the souldiers in yt order yt boath ye Committee . . . and all ye Kingdome will expect'. He chose to illustrate his point by telling how he would have hanged two troopers who had murdered two civilians, a father and his son, at Wakefield, 'but not having power of martiall law, I durst not'.[16] In the following month Lord Admiral Warwick, with some difficulty and to the ridicule of royalist observers, obtained a parliamentary ordinance enabling him to exercise martial law at sea as a safeguard against the disaffection of some mariners who might easily join those of their fellows who had already deserted to the Prince of Wales.[17] The most eminent of the latter, the

11. BL., Egerton MSS., 2618, fo. 31.
12. BL., Stowe MSS., 361, fos. 100–100(b).
13. See C. Russell, *Parliaments and English Politics 1621–1629* (Oxford, 1979), pp. 323–89.
14. The ordinance of 3 April 1646 establishing a court martial to try Cavaliers returning to London without permission was still in being at the end of the war (*A&O.*, I, 842–5).
15. On these excesses, see below, pp. 159–62.
16. Bodleian, MS., dep. C.158, no. 93 (Nalson collection, VII, 93): *HMC., 13th. Report, Appendix, Portland MSS.*, I, 491–2.
17. *L.J.*, X, 414, 435, 446, 449; Rushworth, *Historical Collections*, VII, 1214, 1236; *A&O.*, I, 1185: *Naval Documents*, pp. 361–2: *The Kingdomes Weekly Intelligencer Number 274* (22/29 August 1648), BL., E.461(14), p. 1058; *The Sea-men's Answer* (4 October 1648), E.465(27), pp. 23–4.

displaced Vice-Admiral, Sir William Batten, described this commission of martial law as 'the most ridiculous piece of Tyrannie that ever was hard in the World', and another royalist as being 'against the *Custom* of the Sea and the *grain* of all Sea-men'.[18]

Of course, by the time of Cholmely's and Warwick's requests, the Second Civil War had long since begun. Nevertheless, apprehensions about martial law had long preceded its outbreak. The so-called *Petition of Right of the Free-holders and Free-men of . . . England* of January 1648, which has already been cited as protesting against that other *bête noire* of the real Petition of Right of 1628, arbitrary imprisonment, also demanded the revocation of all Commissions of Martial Law, and that offences by soldiers should be tried according to normal legal processes in Quarter Sessions, Assizes or other appropriate courts of common law.[19] Insurgents in the Second Civil War naturally did their utmost to foster similar and even more serious apprehensions. The declaration in August 1648 by the Herefordshire royalists under Sir Henry Lingen complained among other things that the parliament 'have laid a foundation for the future of a new *Militia*, to over-awe and inslave us to the Law-martiall for ever'.[20] That parliament almost certainly entertained no such intentions is not so much to the point as is the plausibility of the charge and its power to alarm countrymen. Nor could there be any doubt that the Commission of Martial Law granted to the Kentish MP and county committeeman Sir Michael Livesay on 14 August 1648 to punish spies coming ashore from the Prince of Wales's ships would be implemented with the maximum severity and probably not be interpreted narrowly.[21] Ominously, in a debate in the House of Commons on 10 October on a petition demanding swift justice on delinquents, the Independent MP, Colonel White, proposed that an ordinance be forthwith passed to try all of them by martial law.[22] This had been a regular feature of the treatment of many prisoners during the second war,[23] but, with the parliamentary victory, there had been some revulsion against the practice and White's proposal seemed

18. *Mercurius Pragmaticus number 22* (22/29 August 1648), BL., E.461(17), no pagination.
19. BL., E.422(9), p. 20.
20. *The Declaration of the Gentlemen and others now in Armes in the Countie of Hereford* . . . (22 August 1648), BL., 669, f 13(4); Webb, *Herefordshire*, II, 423.
21. *C.J.*, V, 670.
22. *Parliamentary History*, XVIII, 34.
23. For its general authorization, *C.J.*, V, 642; Rushworth, *Historical Collections*, VII, 1198–9. For its application (i) in Wales, *C.J.*, V, 679; Rushworth, *Historical Collections*, VII, 1121, 1131–2; *The Moderate Number 7* (22/29 August 1648), BL., E.461(16), sig. G2ᵛ; (ii) in Kent and Essex, *C.J.*, V, 589; Rushworth, *Historical Collections*, VII, 1161; Whitelock, *Memorials*, p. 310; (iii) at Woodcroft House in Northamptonshire, *L.J.*, X, 313–14: F. Peck (ed.), *Desiderata Curiosa* (1735), pp. 43–4; (iv) at Chester, *L.J.*, X, 388; *C.J.*, V, 641; Rushworth, *Historical Collections*, VII, 1170; (v) at Oxford, *C.J.*, V, 659; (vi) in Yorkshire, *C.J.*, VI, 43.

counter-productive even to some of his Independent colleagues. According to the royalist newswriter *Mercurius Pragmaticus* the parliamentary committee which framed the ordinance for a court martial in August to try the Londoners accused of plotting to betray London to the Scots was packed with violent opponents of the monarchy. The plot itself he pooh-poohed as a 'whimsey', but went on to forecast correctly that ' 'tis *ten to one* but they will hang a few to make the world beleeve the *Juggle* is a *reality*'.[24] In a Remonstrance of early July the insurgents in Colchester roundly condemned the exercise of martial law, under which two of them were soon to be shot to death and others grievously to suffer following the fall of that town. Martial law, it declared, was an abomination, since 'the Courts of Justice are open and sitting at Westminster', and its exercise was of course seen as a firm step in the subversion of English justice and along the road to tyranny.[25]

During, and indeed before, the years of Charles I's personal rule in the 1630s, there had been many complaints against the administration by the Privy Council and the prerogative courts of oaths such as the notorious *ex officio* oath whereby individuals were forced to incriminate themselves on interrogatories being submitted to them. The Grand Remonstrance of November 1641 had condemned such practices, but they proved too convenient to be abandoned once the former complainants were themselves in the saddle, and there are numerous complaints of them not only by radicals such as the Levellers,[26] but also by conservative MPs, such as the Presbyterian lawyer Sir John Maynard and the non-party man Clement Walker. Maynard himself had been at the sharp end of the process, while Walker's eloquent denunciation of it as contrary to both Magna Carta and the Petition of Right was made as part of his attack on the parliamentary Committee of Examinations, chaired by the notorious Independent and later regicide, Miles Corbet, under which Maynard had suffered.[27] As a Somerset man, Walker might have found examples nearer home, for John Pyne, the chairman of the

24. *Mercurius Pragmaticus Number 22* (22/29 August 1648), BL., E.461(17), sig. Dd. On the London plot and the use of court martials see *C.J.*, V, 680; *The discovery of a great plot in the City* (August 1648), BL., E.460(25), pp. 1–3; *The Moderate Number 7* (22/29 August 1648), E.461(16), sig. G2ᵛ; *The Kingdomes Weekly Intelligencer Number 274* (22/29 August 1648), E.461(14), pp. 1060, 1061.

25. *The Remonstrance and Declaration of The Knights, Esquires, Gentlemen and Freeholders in Colchester* (6 July 1648), BL., E.451(11), p. 4, also Oxford, Worcester College pamphlet collection.

26. *Leveller Manifestoes*, pp. 121, 136.

27. *The Lawes Subversion: or Sir John Maynard's Case* (6 March 1648), BL., E.431(2), pp. 5–7; Walker, *Independency*, p. 28. For a denunciation of interrogatories as contrary to the Petition of Right, see [A. Wilbee], *Prima Pars de Comparatis Comparandis* (July 1647), E.396(11), p. 5. For Maynard's stand, see below, pp. 115–16.

Somerset county committee, acquired an unsavoury reputation for employing similar practices.[28]

It was not only survivals or adaptations of the dubious procedures which had occasioned complaints under Charles I's Personal Rule which continued to be grievances after 1646. There were also some questionable legislative and administrative innovations of which the most dubious were the Indemnity Ordinances of 21 May and 7 June 1647, giving legal protection to both soldiers and civilians for acts done under orders in the service of the parliament.[29] As one complainant put it in January 1648, the ordinances ran 'contrary to the expres Letter of *Magna Charta We will deny, We will deferr right and justice to no man*'. Not only did individual plaintiffs have to travel to Westminster, 'there to dance attendance upon Committees of Indempnity . . . for many weeks and moneths'. The Committee even reversed some judgments already given in the courts. The Indemnity Ordinances, continued the same critic, 'were only made to free those who acted for the Parliament from unjust suits and vexations . . . and not exempt any from legal prosecution for . . . unjust, malicious and oppressive actions and abuses of their trust and power'.[30] But it was not only in the relatively small number of cases where this happened that the Committee was violating Magna Carta. Many cases were by no means straightforward and many plaintiffs whose suits were stayed or discontinued felt as strong a sense of grievance at the violation of their legal rights as had the defendants who had been genuinely aggrieved at being sued for acting under orders. Clement Walker's verdict on the matter – 'Oh prodigious acts, and of greater Tyranny than any King ever durst venture upon!' – has found a modern and less intemperate echo in Dr Morrill's observation: 'No King had ever claimed such wide powers to set aside the law'.[31] At best, the indemnity regulations afford a notable manifestation of the doctrine that necessity knows no law.

In 1646 a parliamentary apologist felt it necessary to challenge allegations that the people 'are in a worse case in respect of Liberty then formerly, by paralleiling Committees with the Star-Chamber and Taxes with Ship-money'. His argument turned on the distinction between ends and means. The end of parliament's burdens and regulations was 'our preservation, not our burthen, as the other [viz. royalist] Courts

---

28. Underdown, *Somerset*, p. 136.
29. *A&O.*, I, 936–8, 953–4. On this whole subject, see R. Ashton, 'The Problem of Indemnity, 1647–8', in *Politics and People*, pp. 117–40.
30. *The Petition of Right of the Free-holders and Freemen of the Kingdom of England* (8 January 1648), BL., E.422(9), pp. 8–9, 18.
31. C. Walker, 'The Mystery of the two Juntoes . . .', in Maseres, *Select Tracts*, II, 336; Morrill, *Provinces*, p. 76.

were';[32] a distinction which is always part of the stock-in-trade of unpopular and arbitrary government and one which was met with spirited royalist rebuttal.[33] Such excuses were seen by some as a clear sign that Parliament was losing its grip. As one royalist pamphleteer claimed in 1647, 'the people begin to grow extream weary of their Physitians, they find the remedy to be far worse then their former disease'; not least because it involved the ravishing of the principles of Magna Carta by a parliament which, in proper constitutional terms, was no real parliament at all, since it lacked both a head and many of its elected members.[34] The name of parliament had become as odious to the people, asserted another royalist writer in November 1647, as Star Chamber and High Commission had been in the 1630s, and they longed for it to meet the same fate.[35]

Accordingly it was to become a commonplace of royalist criticisms of the parliamentary regime to contrast the current oppressions of government with those of Charles's Personal Rule, very much to the detriment of the former.[36] It could, of course, be argued that this is just what one might expect diehard royalists to argue, but such views were by no means confined to them. Smarting under the burden of what they regarded as unfair and inequitable taxes, the inhabitants of Hertfordshire in their petition to parliament on 7 December 1647 gave vent to a *cri de cœur* to the effect that 'we are now subject to greater Bondage than when we first engaged for Freedom'.[37] This notion of having jumped from the royal frying pan into the parliamentary fire is echoed throughout the whole political spectrum, from conservative parliamentary Presbyterians like Sir John Maynard and Denzil Holles[38] to radicals including both Leveller politicians[39] and newly politicized soldiers and their radical Independent allies.[40] Presbyterians even argued that the

---

32. [Edward Bowles], *Manifest Truths* (1646), BHPC., p. 51.
33. See, e.g., *The Mistake of the Times* (July 1647), BL., E.399(18), pp. 2–3; Edward Symmons, *A Vindication of King Charles* (November 1647), E.414(16), pp. 53–4.
34. James Howell, *A Letter to the Earle of Pembrooke* (1647), BHPC., pp. 10–11. For a similar argument, see *A Parallel of Government . . .* (August 1647), BL., E.400(41), pp. 7, 10.
35. Symmons, *A Vindication of King Charles*, Preface, sig. b.
36. See, e.g., ibid., pp. 109–11; Bodleian, Bodley MSS., dep. C.158, no. 43 (Nalson MSS., XV, no. 43); *Mercurius Melancholicus* (12/19 February 1648), BL., E.437(23), p. 150; *Mercurius Pragmaticus Number 12* (15/22 February 1648), E.428(9), no pagination.
37. *L.J.*, IX, 564.
38. See, e.g. [Sir John Maynard], 'A Spech [*sic*] in answer to Mr. Martyn' (January 1648), BL., E.422(32), no foliation (Thomason's transcript); 'Memorial of Denzil Lord Holles', in Maseres, *Select Tracts*, I, 307; Edward King, *A Discovery of the arbitrary, tyrannicall and illegal action . . .* (1646), BHPC., pp. 1–2.
39 *Leveller Manifestoes*, pp. 119–22.
40. *A Second Apologie of all the private Souldiers . . .* (3 May 1647), BL., E.385(18), pp. 5–6 (on the authorship and provenance of this, see Woolrych, *Soldiers and Statesmen,*

army's projected impeachment of the eleven Presbyterian MPs in the summer of 1647 was, if anything, an even more shocking violation of parliamentary privilege than Charles's attempted arrest of the Five Members in January 1642.[41] Their opponents, of course, thought differently. Emphasizing 'the Tyranicall and oppressive Courses that some under Colour of Parliamentary authority have exercised', the army and its Independent allies, themselves about to seek rapprochement with Charles I, asserted that if the king were to be restored to power with the backing of Holles's Presbyterian clique, 'wee shall be tenn times more slaves than ever we were'.[42] But memories were short and Charles was beginning to symbolize a return to legality and to a normality whose more unpleasant features were rapidly becoming forgotten.

Committee tyranny

Among the most potent factors making for discontent against Charles I's Personal Rule had been resentment at the increasing impingement of central power on local affairs, often at the expense of the influence of the local magistracy, and, even when not, using that magistracy for ends with which it was totally out of sympathy.[43] To many gentlemen who in 1642 had reluctantly gone to war for, as they had put it, King and Parliament, the main objective had been to restore the equilibrium between the central government and the localities. But the fact that, for example, the Kentish insurgents in the Second Civil War went to war in 1648 with 'For God, King Charles and Kent' as their battle cry suggests that their aims of 1642 had been frustrated; worse, that the whips of the royal Solomon had been replaced by the scorpions of the parliamentary Rehoboam. To make matters still worse, the traditional apparatus of local and county government had been replaced by county committees which both were an agency for the imposing of unprecedented burdens on the subject and, to a greater or lesser degree, involved the replacement of the traditional governing class in the counties by more obscure and less prestigious individuals; a development which, it was argued, made the county committees even

pp. 57–9); *A Call to All the Souldiers of the Armie* (29 October 1647), E.412(10), p. 2; 'The Case of the Armie Truly Stated' (15 October 1647), in *Leveller Manifestoes*, p. 206; *A new found stratagem* (April 1647), BHPC., p. 5.

41. [William Prynne], *IX Queries* (June 1647), BL., E.394(1), pp. 6–7: *The Lawfulnesse of the Late Passages of the Army* (June 1647), BL., E.394(12), p. 13. For specific denials of Prynne's parallel, see *Vox Militaris* (August 1647), BL., E.401(24), pp. 14–15; *Reasons why the House of Commons ought . . . to suspend the Members charged by the Army* (July 1647), BL., E.396(1), especially p. 13.

42. Oxford, Worcester College, Clarke MSS., 41, fos. 59–9(b).

43. For a summary of these developments, see Ashton, *Civil War*, pp. 42–69.

more responsive to, and less inclined to offer resistance to, central initiatives.

This is to put it too simply. County committees were by no means always the obedient and exemplary executants of the policies of central government.[44] Even though they might seem to be just this to many hard-pressed countrymen, there are notable examples of county committees pleading with the central government on behalf of the inhabitants of their counties in matters such as the burden of taxes and free quarter[45] and the violence and plunder of unruly soldiers.[46] But, as in the case of the Lieutenancy in earlier decades,[47] there can be little doubt that provincials were more conscious of the committees' role as agencies of central government and its fiscal and other demands. Nor are there wanting cases of committees going far beyond the scope of the demands of central government, and in doing so, some of their resultant unpopularity rubbed off on to the parliament rather than vice versa. Among cases of such abuse of power and grossest cruelty is the action of the Oxfordshire committee in February 1646 in nailing a woman's tongue to a signpost 'whilst Three Companies might march by',[48] and the murder of the Dean of Wells, namesake and nephew of the great Elizabethan Sir Walter Raleigh, when in the custody of the Somerset committee's marshal. The dominant figure on the Somerset committee was its chairman, the formidable and irascible John Pyne, whose tyrannical behaviour became a byword, whether or not he was frequently drunk when taking the chair, as his countryman Clement Walker alleged. Certainly as tension rose throughout England in the course of 1648, feeling against Pyne and his committee rose with it, and it was said that the committee's officers went 'in fear of martyrdom by stoning'. When one of the committee's soldiers killed a royalist in a brawl, he was tried, condemned and executed through the verdict of a jury which, com-

44. A good example is the Kent committee, on which see Everitt, *Kent*, passim.
45. For examples, (i) from Cornwall, in November 1646, see *HMC., 6th. Rep. Appendix (House of Lords Cal. 1646)*, p. 140; *C.J.*, IV, 728; (ii) from Durham and Northumberland in May and July, Dorset in June and Monmouthshire in July 1646, Bodleian, Tanner MSS., 59, fos. 225, 345, 387–7(b), 418; (iii) from Kent in June 1647 and Warwickshire in February 1648, Tanner MSS., 58, fos. 181, 211, 719; (iv) from Nottinghamshire in August and September 1648, Tanner MSS., 57, fos. 263, 265, 266; (v) from Yorkshire on several occasions between the spring of 1646 and the autumn of 1648, Tanner MSS., 57, fos. 378–8(b); Tanner MSS., 59, fos. 75, 168–8(b), 195–5(b), 216–16(b), 218–18(b), 266, 290, 294, 351–1(b), 366–6(b); Tanner MSS., 60, fos. 415–15(b).
46. For examples see *C.J.*, IV, 728; *HMC., 6th. Report Appendix (House of Lords Cal. 1646)*, p. 140.
47. On this, see Ashton, *Civil War*, pp. 59–60, 270; K. Sharpe, *The Personal Role of Charles I* (1992), pp. 30–31, 494–506, 542–4.
48. *C.J.*, IV, 435.

mitteemen said, would be prepared to do the same to anyone who had fought for parliament in the war.[49]

One of Pyne's and the Somerset committee's most notable opponents William Prynne alleged in January 1648 that his denunciation of its practices had brought spiteful retribution on his own local associates and dependants, including his chaplain, complaints which echo those of Colonel King against the Lincolnshire committee more than a year earlier.[50] Another opponent was William Strode, who, like Prynne, was both a Somerset man and a Presbyterian MP (Pyne was an Independent). On 22 March 1648 one Colonel William Gallop gave evidence before the Somerset committee that, at some time during the previous year, Strode had not only pronounced on the desirability of using a counter-revolutionary force to bring about the disbandment of the New Model Army without arrears of pay, but had also castigated all committeemen, and especially those of Somerset, as rogues. 'As for Pyne . . .', he is reported to have said, 'we shall have him hanged and then what will become of the rest, the country will rise and knock them all in [sic] head as soone as their guard is gone'.[51] Normally such strong and vocal criticism of committees brought swift retribution, at least on those who carried less clout than Prynne and Strode; as is shown by the action taken by the committee of neighbouring Dorset against a parson in October 1646 and another offender in February 1648, for abusive words against the committee.[52]

The dominance of John Pyne in Somerset was paralleled by that of Sir Anthony Weldon in Kent, where the county committee was no less unpopular, even though it was not consistently compliant with the wishes of the central government. A royalist newsletter of mid-January 1647 refers – perhaps a trifle over-optimistically – to 'a great Combustion . . . about an appeale to the Parliament against the iniustice & oppressions of the Kentish Committee', adding, however, that the matter was unlikely to come to a public hearing.[53] The committee's letter to the House of Commons on 9 October 1647 complaining of the multitude of lawsuits being brought against it may have prompted the House to order a review of the provisions of the Indemnity

---

49. On the misdeeds of the Somerset committee, see Underdown, *Somerset*, pp. 135–7, 147–8. For a contemporary account by the Somerset MP, Clement Walker, see 'The Mystery of the Two Juntoes . . .', in Maseres, *Select Tracts*, I, 338–9.
50. Bodleian, Tanner MSS., 58, fos. 687–7(b); Cary, *Memorials*, I, 368–75: *Cal.SPD. 1648–9*, pp. 4, 12–13; Edward King, *A discovery of the arbitrary, tyrannicall and illegal actions* . . . (21 December 1646), BHPC., especially pp. 6–7, 10–11, 22–7. On King, see below, pp. 92–3.
51. *HMC., 13th. Rep., Appendix, Portland MSS.*, I, 447–8. On Strode and the Somerset committee, see Underdown, *Somerset*, pp. 125, 141–2.
52. Mayo, *Dorset*, pp. 19, 342.
53. Bodleian, Clarendon MSS., 29, fo. 72.

Ordinance of the previous May. It is perhaps significant that Kent was the one concession which was ultimately made, in an ordinance of April 1648, in the direction of the decentralization of the hearing of indemnity cases, which had previously been very widely canvassed.[54] Professor Everitt has concluded that royalism, though a factor in Kentish participation in the Second Civil War, was 'comparatively feeble', and Professor Fletcher draws similar conclusions about Sussex.[55] However it was in Kent not Sussex that a full-scale revolt took place, and there can be no doubt that it was there, as contemporaries complained, and Everitt's analysis confirms, 'a plaine *Committee-war*, without the least premeditate [*sic*] designe or plot against the *Parliament*'.[56]

While Somerset and Kent were notorious cases where the behaviour of the committeemen was particularly obnoxious, they were by no means unique. In December 1646 the pertinacious Colonel Edward King was defending himself before a parliamentary committee to which charges against him had been preferred by the Lincolnshire committee. In the previous October, from the chair at the Lincolnshire Sessions of the Peace at Folkingham, King had delivered a charge to the Grand Jury which was an astonishing *tour de force*, and immediately made him a figure of national renown. As well as urging the Grand Jury to present the usual range of malefactors, King took especial pains to emphasize the offences of the local committeemen, and not least their issue of warrants contrary to the law and to parliamentary ordinances. The committee was denounced for having 'oppressed and tyrannized over the people, wasted the treasure of the County and consumed the estates of Delinquents . . . letting them to the Owners and Malignants [and] abusing the Honor of Parliament'. The Grand Jury, he had insisted, should present offenders 'without respect of Persons', for 'Justice is painted blind that she might not distinguish of persons'.[57]

After thus distinguishing himself and causing disciplinary proceedings to be initiated against him in the House of Commons, it is both astonishing and not a little mystifying to find King again occupying the chair at the Lincolnshire Sessions of the Peace held at Sleaford on 11 January 1647. Although on this occasion the more ordinary run-of-the-

54. *C.J.*, V, 341; *A&O.*, I, 1119–20; R. Ashton, 'The Problem of Indemnity 1647–8', in *Politics and People*, pp. 120–1.
55. Everitt, *Kent*, p. 185; Fletcher, *Sussex*, pp. 272–4.
56. *A Letter from a Gentleman in Kent* (15 June 1648), BL., E.448(34), pp. 8, 10, 12–13. Italics in original. For a less entertaining and much wordier attack on the Kent committee, see *A Brief Narration of some Arbitrary Proceedings of the Committee chosen for the County of Kent* (August 1648), Codrington pamphlet collection, also BL., E.459(12).
57. For King's charge to the Folkingham sessions in October 1646 and his petition to the House of Commons and answer to the charges brought against him, see Edward King, *A discovery of the arbitrary, tyrannicall and illegal actions* (1646), BHPC., passim.

mill malefactors – including perjurers, extortioners, disturbers of the peace, rogues and vagabonds, gypsies, drunkards and barretors – loom rather larger among those specified by him to the Grand Jury as suitable subjects for presentment, the county governors, committeemen, were once again not exempt from his denunciation. This time he laid great stress on the evils of arbitrary imprisonment, while his urging the Jury to present not just Catholic recusants but sectaries also – King was a Presbyterian – could not have pleased his radical enemies on the committee.[58] According to a report a few days later from some of his other enemies among the local Excise men, he had recently suggested in a letter which had somehow fallen into the hands of one of them that the committeemen were courting a similar fate to that which had befallen Empson and Dudley.[59]

In the last chapter it was shown how one of the consequences of King's actions was a virtual tax-strike in Lincolnshire,[60] which in turn produced a plaintive protest from the Lincolnshire committee to the parliamentary commissioners about King's 'false calumnies and malitious slaunders' in which he represented them 'instead of Patriottes [as] Oppressors of our County'.[61] Indeed, committeemen everywhere had good cause for anxiety about the adverse publicity which this and other cases were getting. Demands for the abolition of county committees were beginning to come in and not only from the obviously interested parties. Such a demand was, for example, included in a pious orthodox Presbyterian *Representation . . . of the well-affected Freemen and Covenant-engaged Citizens of London* on 19 December 1646, and in a petition to parliament from some military officers on 22 March 1647.[62]

For a time at least such proposals seem to have been quite seriously entertained. Writing to the Cardiganshire Sub-Committee of Accounts on 15 April the central Accounts Committee at Cornhill in London sympathized with its difficulties arising out of the obstructionism of the county committee to its attempts to scrutinize local accounts. Nothing could be done, the Cornhill committee admitted, holding out one small ray of hope, 'till the standing Committee of each Countie be dissolved, for which purpose there is an ordinance now in the house'.[63] And indeed at a conference between the two Houses, the earl of Manchester, Speaker of the Upper House, had given as its opinion that the realm would benefit from the abolition of county committees, whose mis-

58. Bodleian, Tanner MSS., 59, fos. 668–9(b).
59. Ibid., fo. 638.
60. See above, p. 53.
61. Bodleian, Tanner MSS., 58, fo. 39.
62. *Parliamentary History*, XV, 230, 338, 341; *The Petition of Colonels, Lieutenant-Colonells [sic], Majors and other Officers* (March 1647), BL., E.382(4), pp. 4, 8.
63. P.R.O., SP. 28/253(A) (Letter Book of the Committee for Taking the Accounts of the Kingdom 1646–9), fos. 49–9(b).

deeds had brought odium on parliament. Such committees might be for 'the benefit of some private Persons', but they were 'without any considerable Advantage to the State'.[64] However, the committees were neither abolished nor regulated along the lines suggested in a number of proposals in 1647.[65]

Manchester's comments about private benefits pinpoint a principal reason for popular suspicions about the practices of committeemen. Not only were they locally identified with the raising of unpopular taxes. According to critics such as Clement Walker they 'levy one tax three or four times over, and continue their levies after the Ordinance expires'.[66] In addition there were suspicions that some of the public money going through their hands stuck to their fingers in the process. On 13 January 1647 an information was filed at a meeting of the Wiltshire committee against one Nicholas Barrye, who 'did speake wordes against the Authority of Parliament and this Committee, rayleing and Cursing them, sayeing they tooke the 5th. parte of his Estate and put it vpp in theire owne purses', and that if he had his way, they would be summarily dismissed from office.[67] In that part of their general petition of 1 July 1647 which deals with the abuses of county committees, the City fathers of London voiced misgivings 'that much of the publique Money hath beene imployed to private ends'.[68] In May 1648 the manifesto of those who were to become the insurgents in Kent accused the Kent committee of, *inter alia*, 'increasing the taxes of the county above due proportion, only for maintaining their own private luxury and pride'.[69] Rumours abounded in the county that the committee had 'erected to themselves a *Seraglio* at *Knoll* [viz. Knole], and after at *Ailesford*; maintaining their . . . princely Oeconomie at the said charges of the County; living at the height of pride and luxury, till in the terror of their owne consciences they broke up,

64. *C.J.*, V, 142–3.
65. E.g. *The Last Propositions proposed by . . . Sir Thomas Fairfax* (15 June 1647), BL., E.393(4), article VIII; *Parliamentary History*, XV, 468; *Two Letters written out of Lancashire and Buckinghamshire* (12 July 1647), BL., E.397(24), p. 6; *Leveller Tracts*, p. 62.
66. C. Walker, 'The Mystery of the Two Juntoes', in Maseres, *Select Tracts*, I, 338. For similar allegations of overassessment by the Lincolnshire committee, see Edward King, *A discovery of the arbitrary tyrannical and illegall actions* (1646), BHPC., pp. 20–3; Bodleian, Tanner MSS., 59, fos. 668–8(b).
67. BL., Add. MSS., 22,084, fo. 127(b).
68. CLRO., Jor. 40, fo. 231(b); *The humble Petition of the Lord Mayor, Aldermen and Commons of the City of London* (2 July 1647), BL., E.396(15), p. 2. For similar allegations, see [A. Wilbee], *Prima pars de Comparatis Comparandis* (July 1647), E.396(11), pp. 4–5; *A Letter sent from several Agitators* (14 December 1647), BHPC., p. 7.
69. *The Manifesto of the County of Kent* (May 1648), BL., 669, f12(33): *The Declaration and Resolutions of the Knights, Gentry and Free-holders of the County of Kent . . .* (29 May 1648), BL., E.445(10), p. 3; Carter, *True Relation*, p. 25.

when the *Devill* himself came to appear amongst them . . . as a *Commit-tee-man*'.[70] Sceptics might have doubts about the diabolical apparition but the rumours of gross extravagance and misappropriation of funds were less easily dealt with. It was precisely to investigate such matters that the Committee for taking the Accounts of the Kingdom had been created in 1644.[71] As to self-improvement and self-examination by the committees themselves, there is little evidence of it. It is uncertain how much credence should be given to the apparent good intentions of the Dorset committee, which on 18 April 1647 invited information about malpractice in its service and promised restitution to injured parties and punishment of offenders.[72] Significantly, the later minutes of the committee provide no examples of anyone acting on this information.

Committee malpractices, murmured conservative gentlemen, were only what was to be expected since the new county governors were recruited from men of such social standing as would never have penetrated the county magistracy before the war; 'men not born to it', as the earl of Denbigh had described them in the days of his losing battle with the committee at Coventry in 1643–4. Such complaints were to be heard from all over the country. In Warwickshire there were outcries against committeemen 'of inconsiderable fortunes, [and] others of little or no estate and strangers in our county'.[73] Much the same is true of Somerset, where Pyne's increased control of the committee led to social dilution of its membership, though less rapidly than in Warwickshire; while in Kent under Weldon a similar process occurred.[74] Here the committee core came to consist of what one critic describes as 'men of weak fortunes, weaker wits and yet lesse merit', as well as of 'obscure parentage and education'.[75] As in East Anglia,[76] élite county gentry predominated on the Sussex county committee. However, the social composition of the committees of the Sussex rapes, and especially in the west of the county, was heavily diluted by 'men of sordid condicon' drawn both from townsmen and from parish rather than county gen-try.[77] Similarly, in Dorset, according to a declaration of 1648, many committeemen were drawn from 'the taile of the gentry, men of ruinous fortunes and despicable estates, whose insatiate desires . . .

70. *A Letter from a Gentleman in Kent* (15 June 1648), BL., E.448(34), p. 2.
71. On the Committee for Accounts, see below, pp. 100–103.
72. Mayo, *Dorset*, p. 236.
73. Hughes, *Warwickshire*, pp. 223, 234; see also ibid., pp. 169, 179–80.
74. Underdown, *Somerset*, pp. 124–6; Everitt, *Kent*, pp. 143–4, 151–2, 185.
75. BL., E.448(34), pp. 1–2.
76. On East Anglia, see R.W. Ketton-Cremer, *Norfolk in the Civil War* (Norwich, 1985 edn.), pp. 172, 204–5; Everitt, *Suffolk*, pp. 15–16, 25, 26–7.
77. Bodleian, Tanner MSS., 60, fo. 254 (a statement by the Sussex clubmen in September 1645). For the Sussex committees, see Fletcher, *Sussex*, pp. 325–7.

prompts them to . . . stripping us to repayre themselves'.[78] In Lincoln-shire a succession of political squabbles had reduced and diluted the pool of gentry able or willing to serve as committeemen;[79] while in neigh-bouring Nottinghamshire only four members of the county committee were men of county gentry status, including the formidable Colonel Hutchinson, Governor of Nottingham Castle, and Francis Pierrepoint, the third son of the royalist earl of Kingston.[80] Finally in Wales sub-stantial county gentry had always been in short supply and in any case most of them were royalists.[81]

In the eyes of many conservatively inclined persons such social inadequacy and religious heterodoxy were closely connected. A Presby-terian pamphleteer in December 1647 complained bitterly about what he saw as a Jesuitical willingness of sectaries and Independents to take the Covenant in order to qualify for membership of county committees and other magisterial bodies, on which, once seated, they would not hesitate to do all in their power – in flat contradiction of both the letter and the spirit of the Covenant – 'for the propagation of their . . . diabolicall and accursed *Liberty of Conscience*'.[82] The Kent committee, according to one of its critics, was just such a notorious patron of sectaries and Independents.[83] Many committees also made other enemies than Presbyterians by the part they played in the extrusion of parsons who were not deemed to conform to the new religious ortho-doxy, but who were often popular local figures, which could not always be said for their replacements.[84]

If religious Presbyterians and Independents differed on much, they at least had in common a strict sabbatarianism and a refusal to countenance the traditional celebration of Christmas time. These factors are dealt with elsewhere,[85] but it is appropriate to notice here that the part played by committees in enforcing these restrictions did their popularity no good at all. It was the role of the Kent committees in forbidding the celebration of 'that Darling of rude and licentious persons called Christ-mas' in 1647 and its subsequent brutal repression of the demonstrations and tumults which its action had occasioned that was to lead almost

78. *The Declaration of the County of Dorset* (June 1648), BL., E.447(26), especially pp. 4–5.
79. On this, see, C. Holmes, 'Colonel King and Lincolnshire Politics, 1642–1646', *Hist.J.*, XVI (1973), 451–84.
80. A.C. Wood, *Nottinghamshire in the Civil War* (Oxford, 1937), pp. 124–34.
81. On this, see A.H. Dodd, *Studies in Stuart Wales* (Cardiff, 1971), pp. 110–76.
82. *Hinc Illae Lacrimae, Or the Impietie of Impunity* (23 December 1647), BL., E.421(6), pp. 19–20.
83. BL., E.448(34), p. 13.
84. For discontent and disturbances in Devon and Dorset about such cases, see Bodleian, Walker MSS., c.4, fos. 207, 208, 212; Walker, *Sufferings*, pp. 327–8; Mayo, *Dorset*, pp. 370–1. On this whole subject, see below, pp. 246–65.
85. See below, pp. 234–41.

inexorably to Kentish insurgency in the Second Civil War. Nothing could be more eloquent of that committee's unpopularity and consequent vulnerability than its correspondence with the Speaker of the House of Commons early in January 1648 describing the Canterbury tumult and begging not to have the number of soldiers at its command reduced. The committee also strove unsuccessfully to persuade parliament to opt for more summary methods of justice on the rioters than the proposed Commission of Oyer and Terminer, and it did so for the reason that no local jury could be trusted to convict the offenders owing to what it described as 'the general and strong Malignity of the distemper in these places'.[86] Its prognostication was correct, for out of the failure of the Grand Jury to find a true bill against the accused, and parliament's subsequent order on 15 May that the committee 'proceed to the further Examination of the Riot',[87] arose the famous Kent petition, while out of the committee's desperate attempt to suppress this, came Kentish participation in the Second Civil War.[88]

The Canterbury Christmas riots were one of a number of cases of mob violence against county committees before the coming of the Second Civil War, which itself was regarded by many Kentish insurgents as being fought primarily against the county committee not parliament. There are a number of other, if less spectacular, cases, among them the murder of a trooper in the service of the Somerset committee in the summer of 1646, and in the following autumn an affray at Blandford in Dorset arising out of the Dorset committee's attempt to administer the negative oath to 'divers ill-affected and dangerous persons'. The more serious disturbances in Glamorgan in June 1647 were directed mostly against the county committee, and the same is true of the incident at Kendal on 11 August, when the Mayor and members of the Westmorland committee were hauled out of the council chamber by a number of armed rowdies and imprisoned for a while in the house of 'a known Malignant'. The mob which sacked the Excise House at Worcester in January 1648 had other objects for their disapproval besides the hated Excise men if one account is to be believed, which tells of their crying 'downe with the Committee and for God and King Charles'.[89]

86. Bodleian, Tanner MSS., 57, fos. 60–60(b); Tanner MSS., 58, fos. 645, 653, 672–3(b). For the riot, see below, pp. 359–61. For royalist condemnation of the 'Plundring Committee' and its action against 'the gallant Men of Kent', see *Mercurius Pragmaticus no. 29* (28 December 1647), BL., E.421(29), sig. Q2ᵛ; also E.448(34), pp. 2–4.
87. *C.J.*, V, 534, 559; Rushworth, *Historical Collections*, VII, 1113.
88. For the Kent petition and its aftermath, see below, pp. 144–8.
89. For the disturbances (i) in Somerset, see *Western Assize Orders*, 241; (ii) in Dorset, Mayo, *Dorset*, p. 80; (iii) in Glamorgan, *A Full Relation of the whole Proceedings of the Late Rising and Commotion in Wales* (June 1647), BL., E.396(9), pp. 6–10, and below, pp. 341–6; (iv) in Westmorland, *L.J.*, X, 42–3 (information given to the House of Lords

The account of the Excise riot at Worcester mentions the fact that the rioters were assisted by soldiers quartered in that city, and there are indeed a number of startling cases of soldiers, especially in the provincial armies and not the New Model, taking violent action against county committeemen.[90] However, it was not so much against the general oppressions of committees that the soldiers acted, as on account of the hardships which the military endured because their pay was often months in arrears, for which they, rightly or wrongly, held the committeemen responsible. On 8 October 1647 the committees of all three Yorkshire Ridings reported that soldiers had seized the persons of some of them and had not released them until the Lord Mayor and aldermen of York had undertaken to provide some twenty-four days' pay for them, which some of the committeemen had had to engage themselves to see repaid.[91] The soldiers had had ample precedent for their action. Back in July 1646 some Cheshire Deputy Lieutenants had reported apprehensively on the insolence of soldiers quartered at Alderley and Peover for want of pay.[92] But the storm really broke a year later, when the body of Cheshire Deputy Lieutenants, who were a county committee in all but name, wrote to Speaker Lenthall with an astonishing tale to tell. Enraged by the continued failure to cough up their arrears of pay,

> the soldiers . . . have the boldness and impudence to seize our persons . . . and to draw and enforce us to Chester, like rogues and thieves, in base and disgraceful manner, and to bring us openly through all the streets (there being no street free from the infection of the plague . . .) and throwing us all, being in number of fifteen persons, into one little room, part of the common gaol, where was neither bread nor provision of meat or drink, nor any accommodation for nature, but publicly, like beasts amongst ourselves; our friends denied [forbidden] to come to us; and . . . we were threatened by some of them shouting to hang us, and others to cut our throats or destroy us, and cast us into infected houses.

Although their conditions of imprisonment admittedly improved later, the unfortunate magistrates were convinced that the barbarity

six months later on 11 February 1648). The incident is also dealt with in two letters of 1 November 1647 and 24 January 1648 from another victim of the disturbance, the parson Henry Massy, to Lord Wharton (Bodleian Rawlinson Letters, 52, nos. 36, 40). For a more detailed account of the incident, see below, p. 364; (v) at Worcester, *A Letter to a Member of the House of Commons* (February 1648), BL., E.425(20), pp. 3–6.

90. On this development in general, see J.S. Morrill, 'Mutiny and Discontent in English Provincial Armies 1645–47', *P&P.*, 56 (1972), especially 61–71.
91. PRO., SP. 28/249, no piece reference.
92. Bodleian, Tanner MSS., 59, fos. 426, 436.

with which they had been treated was in no small measure due to the fact that among their captors were ex-Cavalier soldiers and former Irish rebels. In any case, like the committeemen later in Yorkshire, they had to provide more than £4,000 for satisfaction of soldiers' arrears as the condition of obtaining their freedom, and although the bonds on which some of the money was raised fell due and were about to be sued in November, the magistrates had still not been reimbursed by the central government.[93] In the circumstances it was small wonder that the committee of the neighbouring county of Lancashire begged the Speaker on 18 August that £20,000 be sent up for soldiers' arrears, 'otherwise we are afraid we cannot possibly keepe them in a peaceable Condicion ourselves'.[94]

Startling as these cases are, they are not isolated instances. During the same summer of 1647 the Leicestershire committeemen were marched up and down the county by angry and unpaid soldiers, 'in what disgracefull manner they can, remoueing our quarters about foure or fiue miles a day'.[95] The tale told by the sheriff of Dorset to the Speaker on 8 July is hardly less harrowing. Hungry, unpaid and mutinous soldiers had marched from their garrisons to Dorchester, where they 'very rudely seized on some of the gentlemen of the committee, forcing them out of the chamber, telling them they would carry them to the army their masters', which was avoided only by the sheriff's assurance that he would engage himself to provide their pay; 'but', he added, 'which way to get money to make good my promise, God knows'. The lack of local support of which the sheriff complained was probably at least as much due to the fact that the victims of the mutinous soldiers' violence were county committeemen as to the inability of potential supporters to act effectively for want of arms.[96] In the adjacent county of Devon, the committee reported on 4 September a similar violent intrusion by mutinous soldiers from the Plymouth garrison. As usual the soldiers' behaviour had been occasioned by mountainous arrears of pay, and it is ironical that the committee at Plymouth had been in process of considering how to levy £8,000 for this purpose, when they had been so rudely interrupted. As they observed, 'the Souldiery are apt to take infection each from other, and to spread it the more'.[97] General alarm at the violence of the soldiers may have been not untinged with a certain ambivalence insofar as it was directed against county committees, the *bêtes noires* of so many countrymen.

93. Tanner MSS., 58, fos. 429, 432, 590: Cary, *Memorials*, I, 277–82.
94. Tanner MSS., 58, fo. 469.
95. Ibid., fo. 329.
96. Cary, *Memorials*, I, 295–7.
97. Tanner MSS., 58, fo. 507.

Committees to control committees

The Committee for Taking the Accounts of the Kingdom which met at Cornhill in London and its sub-committees in the counties had been created in February 1644 as a means of control through the scrutiny of the accounts of all through whose hands public money passed.[98] Prominent among these were of course county committeemen, some of whom, as has already been seen, had incurred suspicions of helping themselves to public money.[99] On 30 July 1646 one of the Sub-committees for Accounts in Sussex had complained to its parent committee at Cornhill that 'there is such an Antipathy between the Committee for Sequestracions & vs that there is no way . . . unattempted by them that may render . . . our accions odious or hinder our proceedings'.[100] Beyond all doubt the county committees were the main obstructors of the operations of the Accounts sub-committees. By 1647 such obstructions had become so widespread that the Cornhill committee was impelled to catalogue their main features as a means of indicating to parliament that the intention of enforcing the public liability of its local agencies was likely to be totally frustrated.[101] Among the obstructionist tactics specified in this certificate, which probably dates from March 1647, were the disregard of warrants from Accounts sub-committees to provide documents for scrutiny;[102] the forcible interruption of their meetings;[103] the victimization of the more active and diligent members of the Accounts sub-committees by wrongly sequestering or imprisoning them;[104] or unduly over-assessing them towards payment of taxes;[105] all part of organized campaigns to persuade Accounts sub-committeemen that they would be well advised not to

98. On the whole subject see D.H. Pennington, 'The Accounts of the Kingdom 1642–1649', in F.J. Fisher (ed.), *Essays in the Economic and Social History of Tudor and Stuart England* (Cambridge, 1961), pp. 182–203.
99. See above, pp. 94–5; and see also William Strode's observation in a letter of 27 August 1646, contrasting his own willingness to submit to the strictest scrutiny of his accounts with the dislike of some of the members of the Somerset committee for the procedure (PRO., SP. 28/256, no piece reference).
100. SP. 28/256, no piece reference, dated 30 July 1646. See also the remarks (above, p. 93) about the complaint of the Cardiganshire sub-committee of Accounts of the obstruction to its activities by the county committee.
101. Bodleian, Tanner MSS., 59, fo. 680. For accounts of committee and other obstructions, see Underdown, *Somerset*, pp. 141–2; Everitt, *Kent*, pp. 181–3; Fletcher, *Sussex*, pp. 334–6, and Hughes, *Warwickshire*, pp. 244–6, 249.
102. For examples (i) from Sussex, see Fletcher, *Sussex*, p. 335; PRO., SP. 28/253(A), fos. 43(b), 44; (ii) from Somerset, SP. 28/253A, fo. 49(b); (iii) from Coventry, SP., 28/253(A), fo. 15(b).
103. For an example from Somerset, see Underdown, *Somerset*, p. 141.
104. For examples (i) from Leicestershire, see 'The Scottish Dove' (5/12 August 1646) printed in *Montereul Correspondence*, II, Appendix, 592; (ii) from Sussex, see Fletcher, *Sussex*, p. 335.
105. For an example from Coventry, see PRO., SP. 28/235(A), fos. 50(b), 51(b).

take their investigations too seriously. Potential witnesses were terrorized into not giving incriminating evidence to the Accounts sub-committees, who were also sometimes refused access to garrisons and other places which it was necessary for them to enter if they were to conduct their investigations properly. Finally, in some cases when the sub-committee had imprisoned recalcitrant persons who had refused to submit their accounts for scrutiny, the latter were quickly freed by orders of county committees,[106] and, in one case in Leicestershire, subsequently sued the Accounts sub-committeemen for wrongful arrest.[107] If such obstructions continued, the Cornhill committee protested, the whole work of investigating accounts might just as well be discontinued. The obstructions obviously continued, since the committee delivered a similar complaint in November 1647, also protesting that the salaries and expenses of its officers were heavily in arrears.[108]

A number of county historians have contended that the members of Accounts sub-committees were often tactless, officious and over-punctilious in their behaviour and demeanour.[109] A careful study both of the Order Books and other records of the Cornhill committee in the Public Record Office, along with records relating to county committees and other local bodies, suggests that the charge has some substance. However, it is also significant that the Cornhill committee was quick to urge restraint on its over-zealous sub-committees; as in the case of the Montgomeryshire sub-committee's relentless persecution of one local accountant in 1646, which had occasioned 'many Clamors against you both here and elce where of your hard dealings towards him'. The sub-committee had been technically correct but disastrously tactless in its dealings.[110] This was probably even truer of the Buckinghamshire sub-committee's dealings in 1646 with a local sequestrator, who, as the Cornhill committee reminded it, 'hath suffered very much by the enemy both in person and estate';[111] and of the Coventry sub-

---

106. For an example from Coventry, see ibid., fos. 50(b)–1.
107. The case of Colonel Hacker, who sued the sub-committee, was instrumental in bringing the Accounts committees within the purview and protection of the Indemnity ordinance (PRO., SP. 24/1, fos. 18, 176; SP. 24/2, fo. 17; C.J., V, 492; L.J., X, 572; Rushworth, *Historical Collections*, VII, 1023; HLRO., MP., 31/10/1648).
108. HLRO., MP., [20]/11/1647; C.J., V, 364.
109. See Hughes, *Warwickshire*, pp. 242–6; Everitt, *Kent*, p. 183; Fletcher, *Sussex*, p. 336.
110. PRO., SP. 28/253(A), fos. 12(b), 13, 14, 15, 17, 19(b), 42(b), 46; SP. 28/256, no piece reference, dated [1646?].
111. SP. 28/253(A), fo. 46(b). The sequestrator was a Mr Russell, who had had to pay £300 during the First Civil War to rescue himself from imprisonment in plague-infected Wallingford, where he had been carried by order of Sir George Penruddock, the rents of whose sequestered lands in Wycombe he had been responsible for collecting and against whom he was barred from taking legal action, because Penruddock could claim the protection of the surrender articles of Oxford. For a letter on Russell's behalf, see SP. 28/200, no foliation.

committee's rather incautious and over-zealous pressing charges against influential members of the county committee at Coventry in 1647.[112]

On the other hand, the behaviour of local Accounts committees by no means invariably fits the above rather officious stereotype. On 30 January 1647 the Shropshire sub-committee for Accounts offered excuses to the Cornhill committee for imperfections in the accounts of one Captain Farrington which they had scrutinized, pleading the special circumstances of a county which had been under royalist domination for most of the war. In such circumstances, they emphasized, 'how can it be expected they would bring in their accomptes in a right method, having inough to doe to keepe their Throtes from beinge Cutt'.[113]

The disclosures of the obstacles raised by county committees to the investigation of their affairs were obviously so much grist to the mill of their conservative critics, such as William Prynne and Colonel Edward King whose radical Independent adversaries controlled the committees of Somerset and Lincolnshire respectively. The politically conservative affiliation of the Accounts Committee is well brought out in a reported speech in the House of Commons early in 1648, which was almost certainly made by the Presbyterian MP, Sir John Maynard. In it Maynard developed, *inter alia*, a swingeing attack on the malpractices of parliamentary committees in general and county committees in particular. But the Accounts committees he specifically, and significantly, excepted from his strictures.[114] By contrast, the conservative, if non-party, MP Clement Walker was more sceptical. No-one hated county committees more than he did, but he expressed serious doubts about the value of the Accounts Committee's activities on the grounds that the members of its local sub-committees 'were nominated by those Members that ought to give Accompts, and it must needs be suspicious for an Accomptant to choose the persons before whom he shall accompt'.[115] But this was a highly questionable generalization as to membership, for the mode of nomination varied from county to county. In any case, if county committees had in fact nominated the members of Accounts sub-committees one can only conclude, in the light of subsequent events, that this was done with astonishing lack of foresight. There are in fact relatively few instances of Accounts sub-committeemen being in the pocket of the county committees. One such rare case is that of Derbyshire. Here a complaint in 1646 alleges that, of the twelve members of the Accounts sub-committee, as many as ten were creatures of Sir John Gell, the dominating figure on the

112. PRO., SP. 28/253(A), fos. 51, 51(b).
113. PRO., SP. 28/257, no piece reference (dated 30 January 1647).
114. 'A Spech [*sic*] in answer to Mr. Martyn' (transcript in Thomason's hand) (January 1648), BL., E.422(32), no foliation.
115. 'The Mystery of the Two Juntoes...', in Maseres, *Select Tracts*, I, 342–3.

county committee. Moreover, on 16 February 1647 when the Cornhill committee informed its Derbyshire sub-committee that it was planning reform of abuses and obstacles to proper investigation of accounts, it went on to cite numerous complaints which it had received that 'those Accomptants who have any relacon vnto you, either as frends or favoretts, you deny or refuse to receive any charge against them'.[116]

Notwithstanding the undisguised contempt of some royalists for the Accounts Committees' activities,[117] they were a useful source of propaganda material. Thus the Glamorgan insurgents in the abortive revolt of June and July 1647 alleged not only that the county committee refused to render its accounts, but also that, 'if any presumed to speake in the behalf of the oppressed Countrey, they were presently made Delinquents'.[118] Indeed, on 20 November 1647 the House of Commons decided to investigate the charge that in some counties royalist malignants had got on to some sub-committees of Accounts, where they were using their influence to harass well-affected county committeemen and other local authorities.[119] Be this as it may, and according to one account five of the sub-committee for Derbyshire were royalists,[120] it is not true that county committees objected to the Accounts Committees chiefly on this account or even because they always had something to conceal. Outraged *amour propre* was often an important determinant of their attitude; as is the case of the Kent committee's objections in June 1646 to the Accounts sub-committee's claim that the arrears of revenue collectors in the county should be paid to them and not to the county committee, as well as in other cases where right was not so clearly on the side of the latter.[121]

Of course, such institutions as the Accounts Committees, and, to a lesser extent, the Assessment Commission,[122] were themselves even newer creations than the county committees, however useful they might prove to be as organs of conservative policies. But to parliamentary conservatives and Cavaliers alike the thing most desired was an end to county committees and the return of what one royalist described as 'the ancient and happy government of Justices of Peace in their severall Counties'.[123] The abolition of county committees and the return of the

116.   PRO., SP. 28/332, pt. iv, p. 686; SP. 28/253(A), fo. 41(b).
117.   E.g. *Mercurius Pragmaticus number 11* (23/30 November 1647), BL., E.417(20), no pagination.
118.   *The Heads of the Present Grievances of the County of Glamorgan* (1 July 1647), BL., E.396(3), p. 2.
119.   *C.J.*, V, 364.
120.   PRO., SP. 28/332, pt. iv, p. 686.
121.   PRO., SP. 28/234, no piece reference (dated 26 June 1646).
122.   On the Assessment Commission in Somerset, see Underdown, *Somerset*, pp. 142–3.
123.   *A true account and character of the times* (August 1647), BL., E.401(13), p. 2. For similar views by a parliamentary Presbyterian, see 'Memoirs of Denzil Lord Holles', in

ancient system of local government had ranked high in the expectations of many moderates and conservatives.[124] The second was to be fulfilled but not the first and the Commissions of the Peace and county committees were to exist in often very uncomfortable juxtaposition during the post-war years.

The mechanism for the re-creation (where it had lapsed) and renewal of the Commission of the Peace was for local MPs, following consultation with Justices of Assizes, to recommend the names of suitable candidates to the Commissioners of the Great Seal, who then had the power to nominate JPs.[125] These were obviously precautions against the dangers of infiltration of the Commissions of the Peace by ex-Cavaliers, especially since élite county gentry were not only willing but eager to serve as JPs.[126] On 1 May 1648 the House of Commons stressed the need to impress on MPs in each county the need to 'be as careful to present honest Men to the Commissions of the Great Seal, to serve in all Parts for Justices of the Peace'.[127] In December 1647 a royalist newswriter had been especially scathing about the insertion of a provision in one of the four bills about to be presented to the king that no-one who had borne arms for the king could serve as a JP. This, he observed, would result in the Commissions of the Peace being staffed by bumpkins totally subservient to the government at Westminster.[128] The point is, of course, overdone, but while it is legitimate to point a contrast between the social standing of JPs and of many members of the county committees, it needs to be borne in mind that Commissions of the Peace were being remodelled for political reasons, and in a way which softened this contrast. On 3 February 1648, for instance, the pro-Presbyterian 'earnest and passionate petition of divers thousands' complained about 'the late illegal sudden putting of divers honest Knights and . . . Gentlemen . . . out of the *Commissions of the Peace* in *Buckinghamshire* and other *Counties* before their last Quarter Sessions . . . by Mr. *Speakers* meere arbitrary power'.[129]

For all that, some conflict of interest and policy between county

Maseres, *Select Tracts*, I, 265–6; and by a conservative, non-party man, C. Walker, 'The Mystery of the Two Juntoes', ibid., I, 338–9.

124. See the emphasis on sheriffs, JPs etc. in the peace proposals of the Presbyterians in May 1647. Committees are not mentioned (*Propositions from the Parliament to the King for Peace* . . . (May 1647) (BL., E.390(4), pp. 7–8).
125. For the procedure in practice in Kent, see BL., Add. MSS., 13,399, fo. 45; in the south-west, *C.J.*, V, 534.
126. On the infiltration of the Commissions of the Peace by royalists, see below, pp. 219–21.
127. Rushworth, *Historical Collections*, VII, 1091.
128. *Mercurius Pragmaticus number 22* (7/14 December 1647), BL., E.419(22), sig. N2–N2ᵛ. For similar comments about the Hampshire Commission of the Peace, see *Mercurius Melancholicus* (12/19 February 1648), BL., E.437(23), p. 148.
129. BL., E.425(10), pp. 3–4.

committees and the newly constituted Commissions of the Peace was only to be expected. Professor Underdown shows how in Somerset Pyne was unable – at first at least – to pack the Commissions of the Peace with his own radical supporters quite in the way he had packed the county committee. Some of his allies did in fact get on to the Commission, but so did some of his conservative enemies, such as Prynne and Strode, and even one ex-Cavalier. Pyne ultimately succeeded in 1648 in getting rid of Prynne and other conservative JPs who had done their best to expose the illegal actions and irregularities of the county committees, but while this did tighten his hold on county government, it also cut both ways, providing further propaganda material to be used by the likes of Prynne and Strode to demonstrate Pyne's and the committee's iniquity.[130] In the adjacent county of Wiltshire, there is evidence of at least one clash between the county committee and the JPs, though the complaint of the former to the Speaker on 28 June 1647 contains only three signatures. The committeemen were incensed at what may in many parts of the country have reflected a crucial difference between committees and the JPs: the slackness of the latter about affording assistance to an intruded parson who had been deprived of his tithes and subjected to a variety of other forms of harassment by his extruded predecessor and his local following.[131]

However, it needs to be emphasized that there are many counties where no such notable clash of interests is discernible. This seems to be true, for example, of Devon, where the county committee had in any case never exercised very tight control; and of Sussex and Kent, where there was overlapping membership of county committees and the Commissions of the Peace. In Kent in particular Weldon's committee exercised great influence over both the selection of JPs and their activities when appointed.[132]

County committees and the Second Civil War

With the advent of the Second Civil War committeemen were faced with the danger of more general violence against them than in any of the sporadic outbursts they had previously encountered. The Kent committee which had tried unsuccessfully to suppress the May petition and, it was rumoured, threatened to hang two petitioners in every parish, now found the boot emphatically on the other foot, and, as a letter from Chatham on 23 May reported, 'the Committee know not

130. Underdown, *Somerset*, p. 149.
131. Bodleian, Tanner MSS., 58, fo. 283.
132. Roberts, *Devon*, pp. 13–14, 16; Fletcher, *Sussex*, pp. 342–3; Everitt, *Kent*, p. 135.

what to doe, nor where to sit for safety'.[133] It was reported on 4 April that the Welsh insurgents in Pembrokeshire had taken some of the county committee prisoner, a report which is not necessarily contradicted by that of Captain Thomas Wogan on 13 May that many committeemen had sided with the insurgents and had joined with Colonel Poyer in Pembroke Castle.[134]

But the most striking cases of hostage-taking came from Essex, and began with the insurgents carrying off members of the county committee from Chelmsford and imprisoning them in Colchester Castle.[135] Writing to the Speaker and the Derby House Committee in July, Sir Thomas Honeywood declared that the insurgents in Colchester Castle were using their prisoners as – to use a phrase suggested by a more recent war – human shields by exposing them to unnecessary danger, while another account suggests that they were in danger of having their throats cut.[136] But the Roundhead response was hardly less savage. It was seriously proposed in the House of Commons on 15 June that Lady Capel and Lady Norwich, the wives of two royalist commanders in Colchester, should be sent to the besieging army under Fairfax to be exposed to similar dangers. When one MP objected to this barbaric proposal, pointing out that 'the Lady Capel was great with Child and near her *Time*', it was reported that John Gurdon, an Independent and MP for Ipswich, 'pressed for it the more eagerly as if he had taken the General for a Man Midwife'. The ultimate solution of taking other hostages, among them Capel's eldest son, and sending them instead was only somewhat less outrageous.[137] The committee hostages were eventually released by the insurgents immediately prior to the surrender of Colchester, and on 29 August a local diarist reports that he 'met my Cosin Arthur Bar who with ye rest of the Committee were delivered out of Colchester'. Another of the released committeemen, of whom the most important was Sir William Masham, was one Sampson Sheffield. Sheffield had formerly been a servant of Charles I and had been discharged by him for disloyalty. Just as Charles's father three decades earlier had discharged Sir Anthony Weldon, later to be chairman of

133. Bodleian, Tanner MSS., 57, fo. 93; *Sad Newes out of Kent* . . . (24 May 1648), BL., E.443(41), p. 3. On the Kent petition, see below, pp. 144–8.
134. Rushworth, *Historical Collections*, VII, 1049; Bodleian, Tanner MSS., 57, fo. 62.
135. *C.J.*, V, 589, 601, 629,635; *L.J.*, X, 402; Rushworth, *Historical Collections*, VII, 1151, 1153, 1183, 1204; Chelmsford, Essex R.O., D/DQ.S. 518 (Clopton's Diary), fo. 39, *A Message to the Lord General Concerning the surrendering of the town of Colchester (1648)* (Landon coll. Essex R.O.), p. 2: Oxford, Worcester College, Clarke MSS., 114, fos. 54, 55.
136. *HMC., 13th Rep. App., I., Portland MSS* (1891), I, 470, 480; Rushworth, *Historical Collections*, VII, 1221. For a denial that the committeemen were deliberately exposed in Colchester, see Carter, *True Relation*, pp. 144–5.
137. *C.J.*, V, 611; Rushworth, *Historical Collections*, VII, 1165; *Parliamentary History*, XVII, 236–7; *Hamilton Papers*, p. 216; *HMC., 13th. Rep. App. I* (1891), I, 470.

the Kent Committee, on account of his authorship of a scurrilous anti-Scottish lampoon, so had Sheffield fallen foul of the son because of his refusal to serve against parliament in the First Civil War. Like Weldon, he took his revenge by active participation on the side of the king's enemies and indeed, following Charles's execution, he was to ask for a grant out of the late king's estate.[138]

The Westmorland committeemen who, it will be remembered, had been on the receiving end of anti-committee violence in August 1647,[139] were a year later to be among the chief objects of the now ascendant Cavaliers in that county, as Francis Higginson, the fugitive parson from Kirkby Lonsdale, informed Lord Wharton in a letter of 25 August 1648. It is interesting to observe that some orders for levying contributions, which were issued by the royalist commander in these parts, Sir Philip Musgrave, and local insurgent commissioners four days before Higginson's letter was written, stipulated 'that the assessments be made according to the old wonted course and not according to any new precedent by the usurped power of the Committee'.[140]

The abolition of the county committees figured prominently among the war aims which were a feature of a number of insurgent manifestoes in the Second Civil War. For example, the Kentish manifesto in late May is directed almost entirely at the oppression of the Kent committee, while 'the Arbitrary and uncontrolled power of the Committee and Governors of the said Citie and County' figured very prominently among the grievances of the Herefordshire insurgents under Sir Henry Lingen.[141] But even more eloquent of the general dislike of the county committees as a motive force of the insurgents is its prominence in revolts which have no strong county base, such as that of the duke of Buckingham and the earls of Holland and Peterborough.[142] The declaration of 8 July by the mariners who had deserted with their ships to the Prince of Wales would be an even more striking example, were

---

138. Chelmsford, Essex R.O., D/D. QS. 18, fo. 51(b); *HMC., 13th. Rep. App. I*, 508. Masham had earlier been exchanged for Ashburnham.
139. See above, p. 97.
140. Bodleian, Carte MSS., 103, fo. 167(b); *HMC., 12th. Rep. App. pt.vii (Le Fleming MSS)*, pp. 19–20.
141. *The Manifesto of the County of Kent* (May 1648), BL., 669, f. 12(33); *The Declaration and Resolution of the Knights, Gentry and Free-holders of the County of Kent* (29 May 1648), BL., E.445(10), pp. 1–4; Carter, *True Relation*, pp. 23–6; *The Declaration of the Gentlemen and others now in Armes in the County of Hereford . . .* (22 August 1648), BL., 669, f. 13(4), no pagination; Webb, *Herefordshire*, II, 423.
142. *L.J.*, X, 367–8; *The Declaration of the Duke of Buckingham and the Earles of Holland and Peterborough* (6 July 1648), BL., E.451(33), pp. 1–2; *Parliamentary History*, XVII, 289. The point was again stressed by the duke in his address to the magistrates at St Neots in Huntingdonshire on 9 July, before the final rout at that town (*A Great Victory Obtained by Colonell Scroope against the Duke of Buckingham* (12 July 1648), BL., E.452(15), p. 1).

it not for the close relationship established between them and the Kentish rebels whose programme they adopted.[143]

With the parliamentary victory in the Second Civil War, the survival of the county committees whose abolition had been so earnestly sought by so many insurgents was assured. For many of them the last, if not entirely unexpected, straw was the order of the House of Commons in November 1648 that an ordinance should be drawn up preventing delinquents who had not been discharged by parliament from moving more than five miles from their places of residence, so that 'they will not act any thing prejudicial to the Parliament'.[144] In counties such as Kent and Somerset with strong and overwhelmingly radical committees, there was no reason why such regulations could not be put into effect with the maximum discomfort for those who had gambled and lost in the Second Civil War. Indeed, in February 1649 the Kent committee was to be given the additional power of compounding with delinquents, a power hitherto vested solely in the Committee for Compounding in London.[145] This motion had been put in the House of Commons by the radical Independent MP and county committeeman Sir Michael Livesay, whom the Kentish rebel Sir Thomas Peyton had earlier described as 'a man I have the happins [sic] neuer to be intimately acquainted with, & the honour to have received from him many disobliging actes since these late troubles'. Peyton's hopes for a moderate composition were now confounded since the parliamentary order had in effect given to Livesay the power of 'gratifying his own preiudices against any not in his favor'.[146]

The triumph of the committees was not quite universal, however. In most counties their real or imagined iniquities had been a major cause of the Second Civil War. In the isle of Anglesey, which had been a main seat of the revolt in North Wales, the creation of a county committee was to be its consequence; or at least this was what was desired in a petition late in 1648 from the local Roundheads. The petition complained that no serious action had been taken against the defeated Cavaliers who, far from being punished for their delinquency, were still strongly represented on the local magistracy. What was urgently required, the petitioners went on, was the creation of a county committee – Anglesey had not had one previously – to take these vital matters in hand. But the Derby House Committee, to whom

---

143. *A Declaration of the officers and . . . Seamen abord HIS MAJESTIES ships* (8 July 1648), BL., 669, f. 12(69), no pagination; *Naval Documents*, p. 354. See also *The Declaration of the Sea Commanders and Marriners in the Royall Navy and Fleet* (2 August 1648), BL., E.457(6), p. 5.
144. *C.J.*, VI, 72.
145. *C.J.*, VI, 146.
146. BL., Add. MSS., 44,846, fos. 39(b), 48.

their petition was addressed, was unconvinced by their arguments. So Anglesey, recently recaptured from the royalist insurgents, remained under military rule.[147]

Champions of legality: two case studies

The opposition to what came to be seen as the tyranny and illegality of the parliamentary regime was shared by persons of very diverse political persuasions ranging from royalists to Levellers. The two case studies in the final section of this chapter are designed in particular to point up the opportunities which this afforded for the coming together of moderate royalists and conservative parliamentarians.

During the second half of 1647 and the whole of 1648 the reputation of the Welsh former judge David Jenkins as a constitutional royalist and unyielding opponent of what he regarded as revolutionary illegality was second to none. 'The Ship *Royall*', declared a royalist admirer, 'cannot sinke so long as it hath so able a Steeresman as renowned Iudge *Jenkins*, whose stout heart scornes to stoope an inch to the tyrannie of the Rebels'.[148] His repeated assertions that, as Gardiner puts it, 'the rule of the law was inseparable from the rule of the King'[149] brought him into continuous conflict with the regime, long imprisonment and ultimately a charge of high treason in 1648.

Jenkins's case against the parliament was the more telling in that he was no ordinary swashbuckling Cavalier, but a former judge, who, as he explained in the preface to his treatise on the law of the land addressed to members of the Inns of Court and to lawyers in general, had won his constitutional spurs in the 1630s as an opponent of Ship Money, monopolies and the excesses of the bishops. Whether, as he suggested, his constitutional scruples were shared by most royalists is, of course, quite another matter.[150] The claim of the county committee at Usk that Jenkins's countrymen, the Glamorgan insurgents of June and July 1647, had been crucially influenced by him, even though he was at that time incarcerated in the Tower,[151] if at first sight implausible, perhaps derives

---

147. Aberystwyth, National Library of Wales, Llanfair and Brynodol MSS., P505. See also A.H. Dodd, *Studies in Stuart Wales* (Cardiff, 1971), pp. 142–3.
148. *Mercurius Bellicus: or an Allarum to all Rebels number 4* (14/20 February 1648), BL., E.428(4), no pagination.
149. Gardiner, *Civil War*, III, 309. See, for example, Jenkins's spirited statement to an army colonel when being carted off to prison at Wallingford in October 1648 (*The Declaration of David Jenkins* (16 October 1648), BL., E.467(31), p. 2).
150. D. Jenkins, *Lex Terrae* (1647), BHPC., pp. 1–2, 19.
151. *A Letter from the Committee at Usk* (1647), BL., E.394(5), p. 2; Phillips, *Wales*, II, 341. See a similar claim in a letter of 21 June from Bussy Mansell and others (Bodleian, Tanner MSS., 58, fo. 218).

some support from the fact that both Jenkins and the insurgents had applauded the army's abduction of the king from Holdenby on 4 June. Jenkins indeed had viewed the army as a possible saviour to bring about the restoration of the king and the rule of law. With the negotiations over the Heads of the Proposals still to come,[152] this was not an altogether extravagant idea. Who were the guilty parties, he asked rhetorically, 'they who imprison the king, or they who free him from prison?' How dare the parliament complain of the army's disobedience in refusing to disband and abducting the king, when they themselves had set the example by even greater disobedience against their king? The realm had far more to hope from this 'just, faithfull and honourable' army than from parliament. Jenkins dangled before Fairfax his glorious opportunity to earn the gratitude of 'this present Age and all posteritie' as the restorer of monarchy, the law and permanent peace.[153] It was, as he was to argue elsewhere, not only their pay which the impoverished soldiers would have to gain from taking such action, but peace of mind and that assurance which would come from knowing they were doing right and from the knowledge that the king could give them greater assurance of indemnity against past illegal acts than current parliamentary Indemnity Ordinances could ever offer.[154] Jenkins was apparently prepared to consort with almost anyone, whether the Lord General or the Leveller John Lilburne, who might do his case good.[155] But Fairfax at least, though anxious to reach agreement with the king, was not prepared to risk everything and anticipate the role of Monck thirteen years later.

The popular attention which Jenkins was to attract on the occasion of his numerous rather theatrical appearances before parliament and the courts in 1648 was to become a source of great embarrassment to the government.

> When force of Armes could not one jot prevaile,
> To make resistance 'gainst the Dragons taile,

152. On these, see above, pp. 24–7.
153. D. Jenkins, *An Apology for the Army* (1647), BHPC., pp. 2, 8, 10; cf. the more orthodox defence of the army's abduction of the king as designed to forestall a plan to put him at the head of an invading Scottish army (*A true impartiall Narration* . . . (7 June 1647), BL., E.393(1), passim; *A Vindication of His Majesty and the Army* (July 1647), E.396(5), pp. 5–6). Jenkins seems to have retained a good opinion of the army, repeating it when he was being conveyed as prisoner to Wallingford Castle in October 1648 (*The Declaration of David Jenkins* (16 October 1648), E.467(31), p. 2).
154. D. Jenkins, *The Armies Indempnity* (24 May 1647), BHPC., passim. On the army commanders' alleged consultations with Jenkins about the possibility of obtaining the royal consent to a bill of indemnity, see Walker, *Independency*, p. 6. This may be an attempt by Walker to discredit both parties.
155. For Jenkins's alleged consultations with Lilburne in the Tower, see *Leveller Tracts*, p. 105.

> That Giant monster call'd a multitude,
> Then (like *Gamaliel*) in the gap did stand
> Iudge *Jenkins*; he with law and Eloquence,
> Hammer'd the sencelesse people into sence
> Of all illegal ills which they have done
> Against the King in this rebellion.[156]

During the spring and summer of 1647 Jenkins had frequently crossed pens with the eminent parliamentarian theorist Henry Parker. To the modern historian of ideas, Jenkins is no match for his opponent, lacking his dialectical skill and subtlety and penetration of argument. But the ex-judge's stubborn refusal to budge one inch from his central position about the inadmissibility of the constitutional self-sufficiency of a parliament lacking both a head and a sufficiency of members, counted for more in terms of general esteem than the formidable dialectical qualities of his opponent.[157]

Jenkins had been interrogated by the Committee of Examinations of the House of Commons, to whose authority and procedures he took exception on the grounds that the House of Commons was not a Court of Record and therefore had 'no power to try any offence'. From here he went on to denounce what he deemed to be the Long Parliament's outrageous usurpation of the royal power. In particular the fact that parliament had been summoned by the authority of the king's writ could not be used to justify its citing that authority as its grounds for acts which were patently derogatory to the royal power and against the king's wishes.[158]

On 11 January 1648 the royalist newswriter *Mercurius Pragmaticus* notes with disapproval the coming trial in the King's Bench of 'that old heart of Oake, gallant Judge *Jenkins*', along with the Cavalier activists, Sir Lewis Dyve and Sir John Stawell.[159] However, in his entry for 14 January, another royalist newswriter, *Mercurius Elencticus*, reports a significant change, in that Jenkins's impeachment by the Commons before

---

156. *Vpon Iudge Ienkin and his Plea* (14 February 1648), Codrington pamphlet coll., pp. 6–7.
157. D. Jenkins, *The Cordiall of Judge Jenkins* (1647), BHPC., pp. 9–10, *Lex Terrae* (1647), BHPC., p. 8, 11; *The Armies Indempnity* (1647), BHPC., p. 3. For Parker's point by point rebuttal of Jenkins's *Cordiall*, see H. Parker, *The Cordial of Mr David Jenkins . . . Answered* (1647); BHPC., especially p. 16; also his earlier *An Answer to the Poysonous Sedicious Paper of Mr David Jenkins* (12 May 1647), BL., E.386(14), passim.
158. D. Jenkins, *The Cordiall of Judge Jenkins*, especially pp. 4–9; also *Lex Terrae*, p. 6. Elsewhere Jenkins was at pains to point out the mutual inconsistency of the Triennial Act and the Act for a Perpetual Parliament, both of 1641 (D. Jenkins, *A Discourse touching the Inconvenience of a Long Continued Parliament* (1647), BHPC., passim).
159. *Mercurius Pragmaticus, number 18* (11/18 January 1648), BL., E.423(2), no pagination. See also *The heads of the Chiefe Passages in Parliament, no. 2* (12/19 January 1648), E.423(11), p. 12; *The Kingdomes Weekly Intelligencer, no. 243* (14 January 1648), E.423(7), p. 806.

the Lords was to be substituted for trial in the King's Bench. Clement Walker ascribed the change of plan to Jenkins's legal eminence which meant that 'the Solicitor [General] durst not venture upon him' in an ordinary trial in the King's Bench.[160] However, far from quailing before the majesty of the law, Jenkins saw the charges as affording him the opportunity of fearlessly denouncing the illegality both of the regime which had brought them against him and the measures such as the Covenant and the Negative Oath by which parliamentary opposition to the king was justified.[161]

> Tis not by Law that thou a Prisoner art,
> But for thy taking Law and Justice part.'[162]

On 15 February and again on the following day Jenkins appeared before the Chancery bar to answer a quite different suit against him in the matter of an orphan's money which had been put in his trust before the war. He appeared under protest, and the two papers he submitted in his defence characteristically challenge not the matter in dispute before the court, but the legality of the jurisdiction of all existing courts of law under what he regarded as an illegal regime. Parliament having 'broken the true Great Seal, their own was a counterfeit . . . the Court, no Court'.[163] A vivid and deeply shocked account of his first appearance before Chancery on 15 February was given in the official newsletter *The Kingdomes Weekly Post*, telling not only of his defiance of the Court but of the speech to the people outside on his way back to Newgate prison; again to the effect that 'the Judges had no power to try him, the King being absent'.[164]

In the meantime arrangements went forward for his impeachment for high treason 'to purge his law querks through the tryall of both Houses'.[165] Brought before the House of Commons on 21 February, he gave a characteristically contumacious and unyielding display. Refusing to kneel before the bar of the House, he 'abused the House and spoke against the power of Parliament', an act which earned him a fine of £1,000 for contempt. Charged with his acts when a judge in con-

---

160. *Mercurius Elencticus* (12/19 January 1648), BL., E.423(10), p. 56; Walker, *Independency*, pp. 44–5.

161. [D. Jenkins?], *A Looking Glasse for the Parliament* (1648), Codrington pamphlet coll., especially pp. 6–48.

162. *Vpon Iudge Jenkins and his Plea*, Codrington pamphlet coll., p. 4.

163. *The Moderate Intelligencer, Number 152* (10/17 February 1648), BL., E.427(19), p. 1169; HMC., *7th. Report (H. of Lords Cal. 1647–8)*, p. 11.

164. *The Kingdomes Weekly Post, Number 7* (9/15 February 1648), BL., E.427(8), p. 56. For Jenkins's own plea, see *Judge Jenkins' plea* (February 1648), E.427(12) (16).

165. *A Perfect Summarie of the Chiefe Passages in Parliament, Number 1* (February 1648), BL., E.428(1), p. 4; *The Kingdomes Weekly Post, Number 8* (16/22 February 1648), E.428(13), p. 58; *The Kingdomes Weekly Account* (22/28 February 1648), E.429(16), p. 56.

demning 'severall innocent persons to suffer death for their affections to the Parliament' as well as with publishing allegedly treasonous books and pamphlets against parliament,[166] he was vigorously to assert his constitutional credentials by claiming the benefit of Magna Carta and the Petition of Right, and that, far from being guilty of treason himself, it was parliament which had behaved treasonably by imprisoning the king, counterfeiting the Great Seal and altering religion.[167] Jenkins had clearly been a great embarrassment to the government and a dispatch from a supporter in England to a Scottish royalist was emphatic that 'they intend speeding to Condemne and Execute him', going on to make an observation that the pertinacious Welshman would have appreciated: that 'by the Example who wilbee safe[?]'[168]

But the prosecution was postponed and Jenkins was ultimately to escape with his life. In October 1648 he was removed from Newgate to Wallingford Castle in accordance with an order of the previous August. 'Taffie the Welch Judge to be removed to Wallingford', stated a hostile newsletter, adding sarcastically, 'and will his Clyents come so far to him for his Royall advice?'[169] They underestimated him. Not only did he lecture the colonel in charge of the troop of horse conducting him to Wallingford about the king's rights and the law, but he also dispatched a letter from his new prison to Charles I, which was intercepted en route, advising the king to take a moderate and reasonable line in the treaty negotiations in the Isle of Wight in hope that the treaty would be transferred from there to Westminster.[170] Although in November Jenkins was one of seven prime delinquents who were specifically exempted from any possibility of pardon,[171] he lived to see the end of the regime he hated and the restoration of the monarchy in 1660.

What brought the views of the royalist ex-judge Jenkins and the parliamentary Presbyterian, Sir John Maynard, himself an eminent lawyer, closer together was a shared antipathy to forms of revolutionary illegality which was also to give them both some rapport with the Leveller John Lilburne, who, like them, had been the victim of arbitrary imprisonment. Indeed, on 29 July 1648 Maynard made in the House of

166. *C.J.*, V, 469–70; *L.J.*, X, 72, 79; *The Kingdomes Weekly Account, Number 7* (16/23 February 1648), BL., E.428(16), no pagination; *The Kingdomes Weekly Post, Number 8*, pp. 63–4; *The Triall of Judge Jenkins* (22 February 1648), BL., E.428(14), passim.
167. *Judge Jenkins' Remonstrance to the Lords and Commons* (February 1648), BHPC., passim.
168. SRO., GD/406/1/2458.
169. *C.J.*, V, 679–80; *The Moderate, Number 7* (22/29 August 1648), BL., E.461(16), sig. G2. See also *The Kingdomes Weekly Intelligencer, Number 274* (22/29 August 1648), E.461(14), p. 1060. For a more sympathetic account in a royalist newsletter, see *Mercurius Pragmaticus, Number 22* (22/29 August 1648), E.461(17), sig. Dd.
170. *The Declaration of David Jenkins* (16 October 1648), BL., E.467(31), pp. 2–6.
171. *L.J.*, X, 600; Rushworth, *Historical Collections*, VII, 1013, 1021–2, 1062, llll.

Commons, to which he had been restored only the previous month following his suspension as one of the eleven Presbyterian members impeached by the army,[172] a characteristically generous speech in praise of Lilburne's services to the realm and the injustices which he had suffered; injustices of which Maynard himself had his own personal experience.[173]

Like the royalist Jenkins and the Leveller Lilburne, Maynard created a constitutional stir by his objections to the House of Lords passing judgement on him contrary to the celebrated clause in Magna Carta securing a man's right to trial by his peers. On 27 January 1648 the charges against him and several others were completed in the House of Commons to be sent up to the Lords. He was charged with having plotted in 1647 'to ruin and destroy the king, Parliament and Kingdom' around the time of the counter-revolutionary coup in London in late July, and that he and the others had planned to initiate a second civil war at that time.[174] Called before the Lords on 4 February, he refused to kneel before the bar of the House or acknowledge its jurisdiction over him, which, he claimed, was contrary to Magna Carta. Fined £500 for contumacy, he was sent back to the Tower.[175] The Upper House at this time was dominated by the Independent clique led by Northumberland, Wharton and Saye and Sele, but Maynard's defiance was applauded not only by their Presbyterian opponents, but also by royalists, one of whom writing to Scotland rejoices that 'Sir John Maynard made the Lords merry; denyed theire right of Judicature; refused to kneele; but in a complement (as hee said) hee bowd as low as a Bishopp to the Altar'.[176] On 14 February Maynard made a more public protest to the House of Lords,[177] in which he turned his legal expertise – he was one of the most eminent lawyers of his day – to very good account. His argument that it was legally improper to proceed against him by articles

172. *L.J.*, X, 307–8. According to the most prominent of the eleven, Denzil Holles, Oliver Cromwell had confessed that although he himself had nothing against Maynard, he 'must be put in amongst the rest, only because he was a busy man against him and his faction' (*Memoirs of Denzil Lord Holles*, in Maseres, *Select Tracts*, I, 256–7).

173. A version of Maynard's speech is printed in *Parliamentary History*, XVII, 349–56. On Maynard's association with Lilburne, see MacCormack, *Revolutionary Politics*, pp. 234, 257, 280; P. Gregg, *Freeborn John* (1961), pp. 197–8, 245, 329, 358. This speech is naturally by no means entirely uncritical of Lilburne.

174. *L.J.*, X, 13–14; *The Kingdomes Weekly Intelligencer* (25 January/1 February 1648), BL., E.424(10), pp. 821–2. The other accused included seven peers. For the July coup, see below, pp. 182–8, 349–55.

175. *Several Votes and Orders of the House of Peers Against Sir John Maynard* (February 1648), Codrington pamphlet coll., also BL., E.425(20), pp. 1–4; *The Kingdomes Weekly Post, Number 6* (2/9 February 1648), E.426(13), pp. 45, 46; *L.J.*, X, 25; Gardiner, *Civil War*, IV, 55.

176. SRO., GD/406/1/2209.

177. *Cal.SPD. 1648–9*, pp. 16–17.

rather than by bill was a neat way of hoisting the parliament, which had so recently passed the Vote of No Addresses, with its own constitutional petard. For a bill to be law needed the royal assent, which in the view of parliament's vote against addresses to the king was ruled out.[178] The argument must have afforded real satisfaction to Maynard, who had himself been one of the most eloquent opponents of the Vote of No Addresses in the Lower House.[179]

Five days before sending his Letter and Protest to the Parliament Maynard had published his pamphlet *The Royall Quarrell.* Here he developed a lengthy and measured attack against the vicious abuses to which the nation was being subjected: the arbitrary proceedings of parliamentary committees; the disregard of Magna Carta, the Petition of Right and the fundamental law; and the arbitrary imprisonment other than by due process of which he and others had been victims. He denounced what he saw as a long-standing plot against him and his associates by their enemies in the army and their Independent allies in parliament, whereby he and the ten other Presbyterian MPs had been attacked in the previous summer and through whom he was now being brought to trial by the House of Lords, which anyway had no legal jurisdiction over a commoner. The treatise concludes with an impassioned appeal to readers to take up Maynard's cause and demand he be given a proper legal trial. Above all, Englishmen must not 'suffer . . . your lawes to become useless; and your selves to be made the worst of slaves . . . at the pleasure of a few Tyrants'.[180]

An even more eloquent appeal for support emphasizing the disastrous consequences if his trial by the Lords were to become a precedent was made, either by Maynard or on his behalf, in early March.[181] The substance of the argument is conveyed in the title, *The Lawes Subversion.* The author asks rhetorically '. . . are not our Lawes subverted and turned into arbitrary Decrees . . . every day rising and . . . withering like Mushromes, and are we not governed by those who conceive themselves absolved from all Lawes or Rules of Government?'[182] Maynard had, the author claimed, been arrested under a warrant in which no cause of arrest was expressed – shades of the Five Knights' case of 1627! – and subjected by the infamous Examinations Committee to the illegal procedure of examination upon interrogatories without any

178. There is a copy of Maynard's Letter and Protest printed in *The Kingdomes Weekly Post, Number 8* (16/22 February 1648), BL., E.428(13), pp. 58–9.
179. Clarendon, *Rebellion,* IV, 284–5.
180. *The Royall Quarrell* by Sir John Maynard (9 February 1648), BL., E.426(11). For a savage attack on this, see *The Kingdomes Weekly Account . . .* (20/28 February 1648), BL., E.429(16), p. 55.
181. *The Lawes Subversion: or Sir John Maynards Case truly stated* (9 March 1648), BL., E.431(2).
182. Ibid., p. 3.

specification of the charges of which he was accused. This was surely astonishing behaviour by 'this Parliament that hath deemed the Starre-Chamber and the Councell Tables names worthy to be cursed'.[183] Not only had Maynard been imprisoned without cause shown, contrary to Magna Carta. He was also imprisoned during pleasure, in which circumstances he could have no more efficacious recourse to habeas corpus than the five knights had had in 1627.[184] The author expresses distaste for the view expressed by some – among them the Presbyterian William Prynne – that parliament was above the law and above Magna Carta, the supreme expression of the fundamental law. For

> ... this great Charter hath a double consideration, either as it is in part a Statute Law ... to be altered, repealed or confirmed, or as it is a Declaration of the common Law, or of common reason and equity and thus it is not prostrate at the feet of Parliaments will.

In matters such as imprisonment parliament was 'oblieged to proceed in every puntilio [sic] without the least aberration otherwise they do not put the Law in Execution, but execute their lawlesse wills'.[185] Maynard's case was one in which all these principles had been violated and was therefore of vital importance to the legal rights and freedoms of all.[186]

Sir John Maynard is almost certainly the MP who, in a debate in January, denounced an anti-monarchical speech by Henry Marten, whom he described as a Catiline both in terms of his seditious views and his debauched private life. This speech is a staunch defence of monarchical institutions and expresses deep regret that parliament, led and dominated by the army, was losing a golden opportunity of restoring and reforming the monarchy and in so doing creating the most perfect monarchical constitution in the world.[187] As both this and the comparison of views between Maynard and Jenkins – except in attitudes to the army – demonstrate, there was considerable scope for common action between conservative parliamentarians and moderate royalists.

---

183. Ibid., pp. 4–7.
184. Ibid., pp. 8–12.
185. Ibid., pp. 13–14.
186. Ibid., pp. 15–37.
187. 'A Spech [sic] in answer to Mr. Martyn', (January 1648), BL., E.422(32), passim. MS. copy in Thomason's hand.

IV
PETITIONS AND POLITICS

... it is now grown to a Custom for all Sorts of People to intermeddle
in Affairs of State, and vent their own Sense and Humour under the
Notion of a Petition ...

> Report of a Speech in the House of Commons,
> 10 October 1648, *Parliamentary History*, XVIII, 32

Modi operandi

Most of the grievances dealt with in the two previous chapters found
proper constitutional expression in petitions to parliament for remedy.
This chapter is not concerned with the very numerous petitions of
private individuals for private ends, but with corporate petitions, and
more especially those of a strongly conservative nature. In the case of
provincial petitions, Dr Morrill has emphasized the advantages of giving
these the authentic stamp of county approval conferred by grand juries
at one of the four sessions of the peace or by grand inquests at one of
the six assizes held every year.[1] As examples of such petitions we may
cite the Devon and Somerset petitions of May 1647 about grievances
such as the Excise, free quarter and the depredations of soldiers, and the
conservative petitions from Essex, Kent and Surrey in the spring and
summer of 1648.[2] On the other hand, the petition initiated at the
Somerset grand inquest in October 1648 was anything but conservative.
Unlike the earlier petitions from Essex, Kent and Surrey, far from
requesting parliament to initiate a treaty with the king, it was concerned
to put an end to the treaty currently in progress in the Isle of Wight, as
well as to demand the punishment of those responsible for two civil

---

1. J.S. Morrill, *The Cheshire Grand Jury 1625–1649*, University of Leicester, Dept. of
   English Local History. Occasional Papers, 3rd. ser., I (1976), 6.
2. On the Devon petition of May 1647, see *L.J.*, IX, 171–2; on the Essex petition of 1648
   see below, pp. 141–4; on the Kent petition, pp. 144–8; on the Surrey petition, pp.
   148–53.

wars from the king downwards.[3] In this case the influence of the radical Independent assize judge Serjeant John Wylde may have been crucial. Presiding at the Somerset assizes the previous month, Wylde would probably not have been above giving an encouraging prod in the direction of formulating such a petition which would have been meat and drink both to him and his political ally, the Somerset county boss John Pyne. As an MP himself, even if not for Somerset, Wylde would be in a position to present the petition to parliament. Another example, though without the same political overtones, is the petition from the Hertfordshire Grand Inquest which came before parliament on 26 September 1648 through one of the assize judges who had ridden circuit there and was adding his own weight to the representations of local inhabitants about the crushing and inequitable burden of taxation.[4]

But many provincial petitions did not have the stamp of grand jury or grand inquest approval. On 6 April 1647 the House of Commons discountenanced an anti-army petition from Essex on the grounds that it had been 'first . . . contrived in *London* and sent down privately into Essex to get Hands unto it'. Framed by (presumably) Presbyterian MPs, the petition had been sent to Joseph Hall, the High Constable of Essex, at his home in Little Bardfield for signatures to be collected at every parish church in the county in time for a rendezvous scheduled for 8 April, when the subscribed copies were to be taken to Westminster. The House of Commons took exception to this manner of proceeding and the knights of the shire for Essex and for Norfolk and Suffolk, where similar petitions were reportedly being organized, were told to warn the organizers to desist, since parliament had its own plans to dispose of the army.[5]

The above allegations raise the question of how many of such petitions originated in the counties whose names they bore and how many in Westminster as political weapons in the struggle between competing factions in parliament. Although the source is not entirely reliable, two royalist newsletters of the second half of January and mid-February mention a number of anti-army petitions circulating in the eastern counties under the direction of MPs at Westminster and notably Denzil Holles and his Presbyterian associates.[6] The convenience of such petitions for Holles's designs is not in doubt, but that is hardly proof

3. *Parliamentary History*, XVIII, 31–2. See also Underdown, *Somerset*, p. 151.
4. HLRO., MP., 26/9/1648; *L.J.*, X, 512.
5. *C.J.*, V, 134; Rushworth, *Historical Collections*, VI, 449; *The humble Petition of the Deputy Lieutenants Justices of the Peace and Commons of the County of Essex* (13 March 1647), BL., 669, f10(102); *A full Vindication of the Army* (12 October 1647), BL., E.410(18), p. 23; *Letters from Saffron Walden* (3 April 1647), BL., E.383(24), p. 8.
6. Bodleian, Clarendon MSS., 29, fo. 72(b); *Nicholas Papers*, pp. 74–5.

that they had metropolitan rather than provincial origins. While they may have done, it is also possible that Holles and his associates were responding to pressures from the country rather than scheming to initiate such pressures. It did not need an MP to demonstrate the disadvantages of what the Essex petition described as 'a great and unsupportable Army quartered upon us', though the petition's additional emphasis on the likelihood of an army 'designe to have an awing influence on the proceedings of Parliament' is perhaps more suggestive of promptings from Westminster. So is the description of some in authority in the army as 'Men of erroneous Judgements and opposite to the Government of the Parliament'.[7]

Even where Holles and his colleagues were not responsible for the initiation of such petitions, there can be no doubt that they were grist to their political mill. When the boot was on the other foot, however, and their parliamentary opponents set about organizing – or, alternatively, simply encouraging – such petitions in the provinces, Holles's disapproval knew no bounds. There is a somewhat mysterious letter of 27 March 1647, around the time, that is, of the furore in parliament about the soldiers' famous petition to their general. It was written by three members of the Wiltshire county committee and its recipient was Denzil Holles himself. Enclosed with the letter was a copy of a printed petition, 'earnestly prosecuted by some in this County which endeavor To gett handes therevnto', and 'Of dangerous Consequence . . . if not suppressed'. But what is of particular interest in the present context is the writers' statement that 'the same Peticon is on ffoote in many partes of this Kingdome', though whether this refers to a national petition for which subscriptions were being sought in Wiltshire or to a large number of similar petitions based on a national model is uncertain, since the copy has not survived.[8]

But MPs at Westminster had other roles in respect of petitions than to provoke or sometimes initiate them. When a petition was brought up to Westminster, the delegation of petitioners was often met outside the parliament house by their MP, who then presented the petition, sometimes accompanied by a handful of petitioners, who then withdrew while the House decided on the appropriate course of action. MPs might also offer advice to petitioners on the most opportune occasion for and suitable tone of their petitions. For instance, on 24 August 1646 Thomas Atkins, MP for Norwich, advised the mayor of that city that this was emphatically no fit time to present a petition offering excuses about the city's monthly assessment being so heavily in arrears. It was better to rely on Atkins, the man on the spot, 'to do what I cann

7. BL., 669, f10(102).
8. Bodleian, Tanner MSS., 58, fo. 14.

to spare the payment of it, & if not, then to present the petition which is against my minde'.[9]

It would be unwise to be categorical about the reasons why some petitions were submitted through grand inquests and grand juries and some were not. Certainly some petitions would not commend themselves to such bodies. Cases in point are probably the petitions from inhabitants of Buckinghamshire, Oxfordshire and Hertfordshire in September 1647, at least in their concern for the abolition of tithes, if not for their less controversial aim of relief from free quarter. On the other hand, although the petition against free quarter from Buckinghamshire and Hertfordshire in December contained no such radical demands, it certainly did not emanate from either the grand jury or the grand inquest in these counties. Nor did the more radical petition from Buckinghamshire of 9 March 1648, although, in this case, while the petitioners' warm approval of the Vote of No Addresses and parliament's Declaration on that Vote might find abundant support in a parliament in which the Independents were now a much stronger force, this may not have been forthcoming from conservative gentlemen on local grand juries and grand inquests.[10]

The rabidly anti-Independent MP Clement Walker alleged that the above September petitions were 'all penned by the enraged party of the Houses and Army and sent abroad by Agitators to get subscriptions'. The strategy here envisaged is a sort of radical mirror-image of that which we have already described in the cases of conservative petitions devised by Holles and the parliamentary Presbyterians, the ultimate objective in this case, however, being Independent hegemony in parliament and the country, 'and', adds Walker hyperbolically, 'to destroy Monarchy it self'.[11] If they did nothing else, such allegations helped to fuel the engines of counter-revolution.

Of the organization of the conservative petitions, especially those of 1648, something has already been said about the Essex petition, while those of Kent, Surrey and Sussex are treated in detail below.[12] The

---

9. BL., Add. MSS., 22,620, fo. 76.
10. On the September petitions, *The Copie of Three Petitions* (September 1647), BL., E.407(29), pp. 1–6. On the December petitions, *C.J.*, V, 368, 375–6; *L.J.*, IX, 556, 564–5; *The Perfect Weekly Account* (30 November/8 December 1647), BL., E.419(17), no pagination (entry for 6 December). On the Buckinghamshire petition of March 1648, Rushworth, *Historical Collections*, VII, 1022; *The humble Petition . . . of many Inhabitants of the County of BUCKINGHAM* (8 March 1648), BL., E.432(12), pp. 3–8.
11. Walker, *Independency*, pp. 32–3. Italics in original. Walker confuses the Hertfordshire with the Buckinghamshire petition. See also his comments on the attempts of Pyne and other county bosses to whip up support for radical petitions approving (*inter alia*) the Vote of No Addresses (ibid., p. 61).
12. See below, pp. 141–53; and (for Essex) above, pp. 118, 119.

Devon petition of February 1648 was an abortive effort and was never presented to parliament. It seems not to have emanated from either grand jury or grand inquest, and though it was doubtless intended to present it to assizes in the following month, it never got there.[13] Subscriptions were to be organized through the parish constables who were required to see to it that the petition was read in their parish churches. The subscribed copies were to be returned before the next assize, where it was to be adopted, presumably by the grand inquest. The surviving record in the Exeter archive contains the signatures (no-one made his mark) of 113 persons for four Devon parishes, and included the incumbents of each. The researches of Dr Steven Roberts reveal that the petition circulated in at least thirty-two parishes, mostly in the north-west of the county, and that very different proportions of the estimated adult male population, varying between almost a half and around eleven per cent, subscribed in each. The main object of the petition was to protest against the inequitable burden of taxation in Devon, as compared with other counties, and it has already been noted in that context.[14]

Similar information is available about the organization of the Sussex petition which was presented to parliament on 7 June 1648. The petition had been drafted at a meeting at Lewes at the end of May and among its organizers were a number of conservative and neutralist gentry. In all it seems to have attracted around 10,000 persons with, as Professor Fletcher observes, a wide spread in terms both of their geographical location and political sympathies: old Cavaliers, neutralists, former parliamentarians, militia captains, and even a few of the more moderate county committeemen.[15] In the East Sussex Record Office at Lewes there are signed copies of this petition which circulated in the rape of Pevensey at the end of May and beginning of June.[16] Within that rape the process of subscription had to be completed by 3 June, and petitioners in each parish were asked to nominate gentlemen to attend a rendezvous at East Grinstead on the following Tuesday, along with other nominated petitioners from other parts of the county, to take the petition up to Westminster.

---

13. The petition and accompanying documents are in Exeter, Devon R.O., QS. box 55. See also Roberts, *Devon*, pp. 10–11.
14. See above, p. 50, 62–3.
15. Fletcher, *Sussex*, pp. 291–2.
16. The petition and related documents are available in Lewes, East Sussex R.O., SM 147, DM 263–75. The copy of the petition and signatures from all parts of the county (viz. not just Pevensey rape) is available in ibid., A 4788 and HLRO., parchment collection, box 11. Unlike the copies circulating for Pevensey rape, this makes no distinction between different parishes. I am indebted to Mr C. Whittick of the East Sussex Record Office for his kind assistance with these materials.

Signatures were to be obtained in two ways. The petition was to be read out in church by parsons after their sermons, or by another responsible person if the parson was unwilling. Alternatively, those not present or not choosing to subscribe on that occasion were asked to attend at Uckfield at an appointed time if they wished to subscribe. The record is incomplete even for those 28 parishes within Pevensey rape (the only rape in which the records clearly distinguish between parishes) for which evidence has survived, since some of the documents have been badly damaged. However, in all but two of these parishes a total number of petitioners is given, and, assuming these figures are correct, there were at least 1,322 petitioners in the 28 parishes, the names of 944 of whom are available either through their signatures or from the 302 cases where their names are written beside their marks. There were in all six parishes in which all the names of the petitioners which we have are attested by their signatures, and eleven in which half or more of the names we have are of persons who made their marks. Whether in fact illiterates were likely to be especially docile and more easily chivvied by their betters into acquiescence in the petition, or, indeed, whether many of those who signed their names were any more than nominally literate are questions to which no firm answer can be given. But it was clearly not just the élite or even the moderately prosperous who supported this petition, whose main aim was to persuade parliament to treat with the king.

Our next example is an urban petition, though one which never reached parliament; a petition organized on behalf of the very conservative mayor of Norwich, John Utting, in late April 1648. Utting was in trouble for having connived at the election of an ex-Cavalier alderman contrary to parliamentary ordinance, and a messenger had been sent to convey him under guard to Westminster. According to one account the mayor called a meeting of the Court of Aldermen for 22 April in order to draw up a petition testifying to his good behaviour and asking that he should not be sent up to Westminster to answer the charges against him. The petition was to circulate around the city and ultimately petitioning and tumultuous rioting become inextricably entangled.[17] In a letter of 4 May written several days after the riots had been quelled, Christopher Barret, the newly appointed deputy mayor, was at pains to identify the organizers of the petition with the ringleaders of the ensuing tumult.[18] The occasion resulted in another petition of a very different sort recounting the damage and disorder of the tumult and asking for strong remedies for the abuses which had precipitated the trouble.[19] While this

17. On the Norwich tumult or 'great blow', see below, pp. 369–75.
18. Bodleian, Tanner MSS., 57, fo. 35.
19. *L.J.*, X, 246; *C.J.*, V, 553; Rushworth, *Historical Collections*, VII, 1105.

latter met with a favourable response in parliament, it is the earlier
abortive petition in favour of Mayor Utting that is of particular interest
here, even though it got no further than Norwich. This interest lies in
the abundance of information provided by depositions made by persons
many of whom were later accused of riotous behaviour.

Signatures were solicited in people's homes, churches, taverns, alehouses, in the streets, in the market-place, and, in one case, in a barber's
shop. Wherever possible, signatories were persuaded to find others
to sign. One man told of how he had been persuaded to sign in the
market-place, whence he had been taken to Mayor Utting's house and
offered a cup of sack. While there, he had noticed a pile of copies of the
petition lying on a table. Although there may well have been cases of
individuals signing under duress, the depositions not surprisingly offer
little evidence, and some positive disclaimers, of the use of violence in
the obtaining of hands. Naturally collectors of signatures were anxious
to dissociate their activity from the subsequent rioting, active participation in which was to become a hanging matter. The nearest thing to
incitements to violence recorded in the depositions relates not to the
coercion of signatories but to the objects of the petitioners' displeasure;
they were deemed responsible for the attempt to carry off the mayor
to London. One Thomas Rogerson deposed that he had been asked
by Thomas Toly, a butcher, to sign the petition, and 'that Toly said he
would hamstring some of those that shall carry Mr Mayor away,
and . . . would have Captain Ashwell [viz. the sheriff] hanged upon the
Castle Hill'. It was not, however, such objects of popular displeasure
who ultimately suffered this fate, but several of those who, fired by the
popular enthusiasm generated by the petition, and doubtless also by
liberal potions of strong drink, committed acts of violence in the tumult
which followed.[20]

Moving from the second to the first city of England, not only do
the petitions from the City of London greatly outnumber those from
any other municipality, but there were some, both critics and friends,
who saw them as exercising a great influence on provincial petitioning.
As to the official City petitions, the author of one hostile pamphlet of
June 1648 forecast that when the army returned from its campaigns in
the Second Civil War, 'they would make that Popish Common Counsell know sorrow for their saucy Petition'. He does not specify which
petition he refers to, but only that it had provided a disastrous precedent
for and influence upon the petitioners of Essex, Kent and Surrey, whose
petitions had been the prelude to the renewal of civil war.[21]

20. NNRO., Norwich Corporation Records, 12(c)(1), depositions numbers 35, 59, 109,
     111–12, 122, 154–7, 159, 196, 207, 256.
21. *Take a warning before it is too late: or Notice to the City of London* (1648 [June]), BL.,
     E.445(39), p. 4.

In procedural terms the petitions associated with the City of London fall into three broad categories, the first of which is petitions directly emanating from Common Council or one of its committees. Examples are the petition of 8 June 1647 asking for a treaty with the king to be arranged as well as associating the City with the need to satisfy the arrears of pay of the army which had abducted Charles from Holdenby only four days earlier;[22] and the petition of 6 July asking for a renewal of the ordinance of 11 June giving the City Militia Committee the right to raise horses, where the Common Council was responding to a petition from that committee.[23] The second category is where the Common Council acted as a sort of forwarding agency, giving the stamp of its approval to other petitions which it forwarded to parliament often accompanied by its own. Examples are the contentious petition of 'well affected citizens' at the end of May 1648, recommending a personal treaty with the king, the union of metropolitan militias, the reinstatement of the deposed Vice-Admiral Batten, and – most contentious of all – the advisability of dealing with the Kentish rebels 'by way of Accommodation and not by Engagement in Blood';[24] the petition of some officers of the London trained bands on 4 July for a union of the metropolitan militias;[25] and an apparently innocuous petition from some 'well affected' citizens in August, recommending in vague terms the unexceptionable case for unity and an end to discord in both city and kingdom.[26]

Our third and final category is where petitions *to* the Common Council served as a basis for official petitions *from* it to parliament.[27] Good examples are provided by the official City petitions during 1646 and early 1647 which have their origins in other petitions submitted to the Common Council by high Presbyterians often in association with

22. CLRO., Jor. 40, fos. 218(b), 219; *L.J.*, IX, 251–2; *The humble Petition of the Lord Mayor, Aldermen and Commons* . . . (8 June 1647), BL., E.391(6), pp. 1–6; *Parliamentary History*, XV, 420–3.
23. CLRO., Jor. 40, fos. 233–3(b).
24. CLRO., Jor. 40, fos. 278(b)–9, 280; *L.J.*, X, 294, 295–6; *C.J.*, V, 581; *HMC., 7th. Rep. (House of Lords Cal. 1648)*, p. 28; *Two Petitions to . . . the Lords and Commons* (June 1648), BL., E.445(24), pp. 1–5; *Parliamentary History*, XVII, 194–7. The petition was presented to parliament on 1 June.
25. CLRO., Jor. 40, fos. 283, 284(b)–5; *C.J.*, V, 624; Rushworth, *Historical Collections*, VII, 1176; *Two Petitions Presented To . . . the Lords and Commons* (4 July 1648), BL., E.451(4), pp. 1–5.
26. CLRO., Jor. 40, fos. 295(b)–6(b); *L.J.*, X, 476; *C.J.*, V, 694; *Three Petitions* (31 August 1648), BL., E.461(23), pp. 1–10. The petition was passed on to the House of Commons on 31 August.
27. It must not be assumed, however, that a petition to Common Council to endeavour to persuade parliament to take action on a particular matter necessarily implies that it would do so by petitioning. An uncertain case in point is *The humble Petition of divers Citizens* . . . (17 June 1647), BL., 669, f11(24).

Sion College.[28] Another case is the official City petition to parliament approved by Common Council on 26 June 1647 which drew its substance from a petition of 'many peaceable Citizens' who had hoped that it would be brought before Common Hall, the body consisting of City liverymen, whose functions some were anxious to extend.[29] Rather than do this, Common Council incorporated the petitioners' request for a settlement with the king, the suppression of county committees, the better observance of the Covenant and the institution of a national day of humiliation into an official City petition, which, moreover, added requests for an Act of Oblivion to be passed and for ex-Cavaliers to be evicted from London.[30] A final example is the City's petition to parliament on 8 August 1648, citing a petition to Common Council from the governing body of the city Weavers' Company, who were disturbed by what they saw as alarmingly democratic tendencies within the lower reaches of the company in opposition to the traditional oligarchical modes of electing company officers. Common Council's petition in turn asked for a parliamentary declaration against 'such irregular and tumultuous Innovations', and a parliamentary committee was set up on 9 August to consider the matter.[31]

Petitioning no remedy?

During the period of the Presbyterian ascendancy at Westminster down to the beginning of August 1647 there can be no doubt that preferential parliamentary treatment was accorded to petitioners whose requests harmonized with – or, at the very least, did not contradict – the aims of the dominant faction. By contrast, radical petitions, such as the famous March petition of the soldiers to their General was mistakenly assumed to be, got very short shrift, sometimes being not only rejected but also burnt by the common hangman.[32] Why, soldiers and radicals

---

28. See below, pp. 133–5.
29. On Common Hall, see V. Pearl, *London and the Origins of the Puritan Revolution* (1961), pp. 50–3; R. Ashton, *The City and the Court 1603–1643* (Cambridge, 1979), p. 10. See below, p. 154–5.
30. For the citizens' petition to Common Council, CLRO., Jor. 40, fo. 230(b); *The humble Petition of many peaceable Citizens* (25 June 1647), BL., E.394(17), pp. 2–8. For the official City petition, Jor. 40, fos. 231(b)–2(b); *L.J.*, IX, 310–11; *The humble Petition of the Lord Major [sic], Aldermen and Commons . . .* (2 July 1647), BL., E.396(15), pp. 1–9.
31. *L.J.*, X, 427, 428, 429; *C.J.*, V, 664.
32. An example is the fate of the 500 petitioners from Hertfordshire and Buckinghamshire on behalf of Lilburne and other imprisoned radicals in January 1647, 'who did not find that faire accesse unto the Parliament that they expected', and of the six representatives they left behind, who returned home unsatisfied (*The humble Petition of the Inhabitants*

complained, was parliament so partial in its treatment of petitioners?[33] They inevitably concluded 'that [as] there is little good to be hoped for from such Parliaments as need to be Petitioned; so there is none at all to be expected from those that burn such Petitions as these'.[34] There was some force in the argument of the Leveller Richard Overton that 'if they will not give us leave to use our *tongues and our pens* to present . . . our grievances, we must . . . make use of our *hands and swords* for the *defence* . . . of our lives, our Lawes and our Liberties . . .'.[35] The reference to swords perhaps suggests violent action through the army, and consciousness of this danger may well have influenced Holles and his associates, impetuous though some of them were, to urge anti-army petitioners, such as those from Essex, to exercise restraint. It may even have suggested arguments for turning down some of these petitions in the interest of creating an appearance of equitable parliamentary dealing with different sorts of petition. This would further strengthen their position in their constitutionally justifiable claim that, as one of them was to put it later in 1647, parliament was the sole judge of the propriety and appropriateness of petitions, and would add still further force to their condemnation of the view expressed by Overton and others that 'what you cannot have by Petition, you will force by Power . . . *Vi & Armis*'.[36] But such restraint, if indeed it was exercised, was quite insuf-

   of Buckingham-shire and Hartfordshire (February 1647), BL., 669, f10(95); *Clarke Papers*, I, 92–3). For the imprisonment of some radical petitioners in May and the order that their petitions be burnt by the common hangman, see *C.J.*, V, 162, 179–80; *Gold tried in the fire* (June 1647), BL., E.392(19), sig. A2; *The poore Wise-man's Admonition unto all the plaine People of London* (June 1647), E.392(4), pp. 2, 6; [A. Wilbee], *Plaine Truth without Feare or Flattery* (1647), Oxford, Worcester College pamphlet coll., pp. 14–15, 20; *A Copy of that Letter . . .* (12 July 1647), E.398(7), pp. 1–3; *Clarke Papers*, I, 92–3. On the soldiers' March petition and its immediate aftermath, *Parliamentary History*, XV, 343–5; *Cal.SPD. 1645–7*, pp. 543–4; *L.J.*, IX, 115; *C.J.*, V, 132; Cary, *Memorials*, I, 185; BL., 669, f9(14); BL., Add. MSS., 31,116, fo. 306; and Woolrych, *Soldiers and Statesmen*, especially pp. 31, 36–40, 43–4, 55–6; M.A. Kishlansky, *The Rise of the New Model Army* (Cambridge 1979), pp. 189–91, 201–2.

33.   See, e.g., *Letters from Saffron Walden* (3 April 1647), BL., E.383(24), pp. 1–5, 9–14; *The Vindication of the Officers of the Army* (27 April 1647), E.385(19), no pagination; *Parliamentary History*, XV, 353–4, 357; *A new found stratagem* (April 1647), BHPC., pp. 4–14; *A Second Apologie of all the private Souldiers* (May 1647), BL., E.385(18), p. 7; *Divers Papers from the Army* (15 May 1647), E.388(18), pp. 3–4, 7; *The Declaration of the Armie* (16 May 1647), E.390(26), pp. 3–6, 9–10. See also the later pamphlet *A full Vindication of the Armie* (12 October 1647), E.410(18), pp. 4, 5–6, 13, 20.

34.   BL., E.392(19), sig. A2; E.392(4), p. 6.

35.   'An Appeale from the degenerative Representative Body of the Commons of England' (July 1647), in *Leveller Manifestoes*, pp. 171–3. Italics in original. For a very cogently argued anti-Presbyterian attack on the denial of the right to petition, see [A. Wilbee], *Plaine truth without Feare or Flattery* (1647), Oxford, Worcester College pamphlet coll., pp. 14–15, 20; also *A short discourse of the power of Parliament* (20 July 1647), BL., E.399(34), pp. 5–6.

36.   *A Word to Mr. Peters and two Words for the Parliament and Kingdom* (9 November 1647), BL., E.413(7), pp. 14–15.

ficient to quiet the doubts about parliamentary double standards in the matter of petitions.[37]

Nevertheless, there was every likelihood that petitions of a more conservative nature would be subjected to similarly rough treatment if Holles's opponents ever got control of parliament. As Holles himself pointedly emphasizes in his Memoirs:

> They will have a liberty of petitioning: which is to make way for schismatical, seditious Petitions; for if any Petition stick at their *Diana*, none so fierce to punish. Who, more than they, [were] against the Petitions from *London* and the Counties, for disbanding of the Army, and complaining of their factious ways? . . . Yet the world must think that they would have it free for all to Petition.[38]

Although the pot was here abusing the kettle, Holles's charges have substance. Following the quelling of the London counter-revolution of 26 July by the army's occupation of London on 6 August, the City Common Council was, on 18 and 21 August, ordered to deliver up records relating to two counter-revolutionary petitions of 26 and 27 July for scrutiny by the parliamentary Committee of Examinations with a view to taking action against those responsible.[39]

The heightening of tension in 1648 sees further determined action to suppress petitions even before they were fully subscribed, let alone reached parliament. A Leveller petition canvassed in Kent and London was aborted by government action in January, its principal organizers, including Lilburne and Wildman, imprisoned and the petitioners sharply reminded that 'a Petition is to set forth your grievances, and not to give a rule to the Legislative Power . . .'.[40] But during the coming

---

37. For scepticism about such doubts, see [W. Prynne], *IX Queries* . . . (June 1647), BL., E.394(1), pp. 5–6, where they are regarded as an excuse for extremist actions such as the army's attack on the eleven members. Their rejection of petitions and petitioning figures prominently among the charges against the eleven. See *Parliamentary History*, XVI, 75–9. The MPs against whom such charges were particularly levelled were Denzil Holles, Sir Philip Stapleton, and the Recorder of London, John Glyn. For their answers to these, see ibid., pp. 123–4, and for the answers of others (as well as Holles) to charges relating to the soldiers' March petition and the Declaration of Dislike of 30 March, see ibid., pp. 126–30. See also *A grave and learned Speech . . . by Denzil Holles, Esq.* (2 July 1647), BL., E.399(14), p. 4. For a similar derogatory description of the soldiers' petition of March as seditious, see *The Army Anatomized* (4 December 1647), E.419(6), pp. 7–8.
38. Maseres, *Select Tracts*, I, 292.
39. CLRO., Jor. 40, fos. 253(b), 254. For a later complaint against the alleged imprisonment of three citizens for trying to get signatures to a pro-Presbyterian petition, see *Hinc Illae Lacrimae* . . . (23 December 1647), BL., E.421(6), pp. 8–9 (corrected pagination).
40. *C.J.*, V, 438; BL., Stowe MSS., 189, fo. 39; *Leveller Tracts*, p. 118. The petition is printed in *Leveller Manifestoes*, pp. 263–72, and *Leveller Tracts*, pp. 106–15.

spring and summer it was the more conservative petitioners, such as those from Kent and Surrey in May, who found cause to complain at their treatment.[41] Indeed, in June the men of Dorset, influenced, as they claimed, not simply by the distance of their county from Westminster, but also by the sorry fate of petitioners in other counties such as Kent and Surrey, disdained to offer a petition as a means of achieving their ends: a conservative political and religious settlement, with the divines of the Westminster 'sent home to their lectures', and government by known laws and 'men of visible eastates'. Instead they issued an aggressive Declaration whose peremptory tone was, however, belied by their own subsequent quiescence.[42]

One recourse which was not open to the frustrated conservative petitioners of 1648 and had been widely employed by their radical predecessors of the previous year was the remarkable expedient of petitioning the Lord General and army council to take up the demands for which parliament had shown such scant sympathy or even positive hostility. Seen alongside the radical developments in the army in 1647, this was an expedient calculated to set parliamentary Presbyterian teeth on edge. Its dangerously radical potentialities emerge clearly from a circular, probably datable to July 1647 and designed to be sent to civilian petitioners who had already petitioned the General and the army council asking for the army's aid in 'the recovery and establishment of your native liberties'. No less alarming, it was suggested that petitioners should themselves elect civilian 'agitators' who, along with the soldiers' elected agitators, should attend the Council of War and discuss infringements of their liberties and possible measures for relief. Both the tone and the substance of the document suggest a device of the radical agitators in the army rather than of Fairfax and his council. However, it would seem to underline the worst fears of conservative politicians about the implications of civilian petitions to the army, to which subject we must now turn.[43]

Petitioning the army

Denzil Holles and the parliamentary Presbyterians have been justly criticized for overreacting to the soldiers' petition to their General in March 1647 for the redress of purely soldierly grievances. However, the petitions of some officers on 23 May, protesting against the imputation

---

41. On the Kent and Surrey petitions, see below, pp. 144–53.
42. *The Declaration of the County of Dorset* (June 1648), BL., E.447(26), pp. 1–6.
43. *HMC., 13th. Rep., Portland MSS.*, I, 432–3.

of disloyalty, and more especially the soldiers' petition of 29 May against piecemeal disbandment were perhaps less innocuous.[44] A letter of 25 May to some 'agitators' in the army reveals that the latter petition was part of a dual strategy, the other aspect of which was 'to stirre up the Counties to Petition' for the same ends.[45] It would not be long, however, before examples occurred of another innovatory practice which is itself eloquent of the heightened significance of the army almost as an unofficial fourth estate of the realm. Writing a year later, on the eve of their county being convulsed by a renewal of civil war, some of the self-styled 'well affected' of Kent reminded Lord General Fairfax of how, disillusioned by parliament's neglect or rejection of their petitions, people had turned to him for assistance, buoyed up by sympathy for their aspirations expressed in the momentous army declarations of the summer of 1647.[46]

There are numerous examples of civilian petitions to the Lord General and the army to use their influence with parliament to further the petitioners' case. In June 1647 Fairfax referred four such petitions to parliament: one from 'the well affected' of Norfolk and Suffolk; another from the same of Essex; and the other two from inhabitants of Buckinghamshire and Hertfordshire. All four saw the disbandment of the army as a disastrous expedient to be avoided at all costs if a second war was to be averted and the liberties of Englishmen preserved against the designs of a Presbyterian-dominated parliament whose rejection and destruction of the petitions of the well affected is especially deplored. To these general matters the Hertfordshire petition adds its own more radical recommendations against leniency to royalist delinquents and, those two great radical touchstones, tithes and arbitrary copyhold fines.[47]

Buckinghamshire conservatives might argue with reason that the Buckinghamshire petition represented the views of only a tiny minority, unlike the earlier county petition which had requested the disbandment

44. *A Petition of divers Officers of the Army* (23 May 1647), BL., 669, f11(15); *A humble Petition of the Souldiers of the Army* (May 1647), BL., E.391(2), no pagination. See also *A Declaration of the Army* (16 May 1647) BL., E.390(26), passim. *A Perfect and True Copy of the severall Grievances of the Army* (27 May 1647), BL., E.390(3).
45. *Clarke Papers*, I, 100–1.
46. *The Groans of Kent* (May 1648), Oxford, Worcester College pamphlet collection, pp. 4–5.
47. *L.J.*, IX, 262–3, 263, 277–9; *HMC.*, 6th Rep. App. (*House of Lords Calendar 1647*), p. 183; *Parliamentary History*, XV, 483–9. The petition from Norfolk etc. should not be confused with another even more radical and specific petition of early July, which, though it deplores obstacles to petitioning, was nevertheless delivered directly to parliament. It also adds complaints against corruption in the courts, changes in the control of the London militia, which was now dominated by Holles's city allies, and emphasizes the need for the unworthy to be removed from places of trust (*The humble Petition of the peaceable and well affected Inhabitants . . . of Norfolke and Suffolke . . . with the City and County of Norwich* (2 July 1647), BL., E.396(22)).

of the army.[48] But this did not deter some 400 inhabitants of Buckinghamshire from petitioning Fairfax on 25 November asking him to refer their grievances to the House of Commons.[49] Neither this nor a further petition in the same month from freeholders and labourers in the part of the county near Windsor, nor a December petition from some Surrey farmers, can be described as radical in content. All were directed against free quarter, pressure on which issue might provide the General with useful material in the struggle to get parliament to provide arrears of pay for the soldiers.[50] The November petitions to Fairfax from inhabitants of Rutland and Hertfordshire were different: the former against tithes and abuses of impropriators, and the latter for a peace settlement along the lines envisaged in the army's own declarations.[51]

Holles and his parliamentary Presbyterian associates were predictably shocked not only by the content of many of these petitions, but also by the unconstitutional innovation of petitioning to and through the army. One pamphleteer singles out for particular disapprobation the petitioners' habitual use of the phrase 'the sense of the army . . . as if the sense of the Army were the supreme Law of the Realme' and the army the sovereign power.[52] Another deplored the encouragement given by the army to petitions from sectaries for greater toleration and other such outrageous things.[53] Colonel-General Sydenham Poynz, commander of the Northern Association army, had different reasons for his objections in that many of the soldiers under his command, who desired a closer association with the New Model Army and had outrageously kidnapped him early in July 1647, also petitioned an embarrassed Fairfax against him.[54]

48. *Two Letters written out of Lancashire and Buckinghamshire* (12 July 1647), BL., E.397(24), p. 5.
49. *C.J.*, V, 368.
50. The petition of the Buckinghamshire freeholders etc. was presented to Fairfax on 22 November 1647 and heard in parliament on 7 December along with other petitions from Middlesex and Hertfordshire. Fairfax also presented the Surrey farmers' petition to parliament on 3 December (*L.J.*, IX, 556, 564–5; *C.J.*, V, 375–6; *The humble Petition of the Farmers in the County of Surrey* (14 December 1647), BL., E.420(2), pp. 4–5).
51. *Two Petitions to the Generals Excellency* (1 November 1647), BL., E.412(18), pp. 1–3.
52. *A Religious Retreat sounded to a Religious Army* (August 1647), BL., E.404(34), pp. 11–12. For other similar expressions of disapproval, see *The Case of the Army Soberly Discussed* (3 July 1647), E.396(10), pp. 4–5; *A Word to Lieut. General Cromwell* (30 December 1647), E.421(20), pp. 5–6; *Works of darkness brought to light* (1647), BHPC., p. 14. For an eloquent non-Presbyterian objection, see Walker, *Independency*, pp. 10–11.
53. *Questions propounded to all wel-affected Citizens and Others* (1647) (Oxford, Worcester College pamphlet collection), p. 4. For a more favourable view of this practice, see *Two Declarations, the first from Newmarket* (22 June 1647), BL., E.393(31), p. 5.
54. *The humble Petition of the Souldiers of the Northern Association* (21 July 1647), BL., E.399(32), pp. 3–10. For a more detailed account of this incident, see below, pp. 390–92.

Sir William Waller, another inveterate anti–New Model former general and now an MP, alleged that some petitions to the army were 'framed in the army and were attested only by a few inconsiderable hands privately gained by the brokerage of som independent factors',[55] while the royalist newswriter *Mercurius Rusticus* refers to forged signatures to such 'Petitions for the maintenance of the Army &c. or purging the Houses'.[56]

Three very different petitions from different groups of London apprentices early in July 1647 cast interesting light on the relations between the City, the army and parliament at that difficult time.[57] One group's petition to parliament was of a characteristically conservative Presbyterian sort: strong on the need to uphold the Covenant and Anglo-Scottish amity and to put down sectaries. The other group's petitions, one to parliament and the other to the army, were completely different from this: strongly pro-army, critical of the reconstituted and anti-Independent City Militia Committee, and apprehensive of the dangers of counter-revolution and a second war which militia control by the city allies of Holles and the parliamentary Presbyterians portended.[58] At the beginning of October there was another appeal to Fairfax, this time from citizens who had been savagely molested when trying to present a petition to the currently ruling counter-revolutionary municipal authorities on 2 August at Guildhall. Having petitioned parliament fruitlessly for redress on 24 August, they now petitioned Fairfax who took up their case with parliament.[59] In November it was reported that London weavers were planning a meeting at Mile-Inn [Mile End ?] with the object of promoting a petition to the

55. Waller, *Vindication*, p. 155. For a similar charge, see *The Lawfulnesse of the Late Passages of the Army* (June 1647), BL., E.394(12), p. 8. Waller is referring specifically to petitions from Essex, Norfolk and Suffolk early in 1647.
56. *Mercurius Rusticus* (12 November 1647), BL., E.414(5), p. 6. For another denunciation by the same, see *Mercurius Rusticus* (December 1647), E.419(19), p. 6.
57. On these relations, see below, pp. 178–8.
58. For the conservative petition to parliament, see *L.J.*, IX, 330; *C.J.*, V, 243; *The Petition of the Young Men and Apprentices of London* (July 1647), BL., E.398(23) and BL., 669, f11(41). This petition was again to achieve prominence during the London counter-revolution of late July (CLRO., Jor. 40, fo. 240). For the radical petitions to the army and parliament see *The humble Petition of the Young men and Apprentices . . .* (11 July 1647), BL., E.399(2), pp. 3–6, and *The Petition of many thousands of Young Men and Apprentices . . . to Parliament* (13 July 1647), E.398(9), pp. 3–8. These petitioners were told that parliament would consider their requests in reasonable time (*C.J.*, V, 243; *L.J.*, IX, 329).
59. *L.J.*, IX, 401–2; *HMC., 6th Rep. (House of Lords Cal. 1647)*, p. 193; *Two Petitions from the City of London* (12 October 1647), BL., E.410(20), pp. 1–6. See below, pp. 138, 353. For an intervention by Fairfax in August on behalf of molested intruded parsons in Leicestershire, Northamptonshire, Essex and Hertfordshire, see *L.J.*, IX, 389, 390–1, 398; *Two Letters from his Excellency . . .* (August 1647), BL., E.402(28), pp. 1, 4; *A Proclamation by his Excellency . . .* (11 August 1647), E.401(42), pp. 1–3.

General for the redress of their grievances, which were not specified but may well relate to action taken against them on account of the practices complained of in the City petition of 8 August.[60]

This section concludes, as it began, with petitions from soldiers, but petitions which were significantly and ominously different from the simple request for redress of purely soldierly grievances in the soldiers' petition to their General in March 1647. On 18 October 1648 Fairfax intimated to parliament that a number of petitions were currently circulating among the soldiers about their arrears of pay. Rather than await their consummation, the House of Commons obliged by voting for a speedy settlement of the army's arrears. In addition Fairfax brought two other petitions to the notice of the House. The first, from the officers and soldiers of Colonel Fleetwood's regiment, was common-place enough, complaining of the need to exact free quarter on account of the failure to collect arrears of assessment. But the second, from Commissary General Ireton's regiment, was more ominous; as Bulstrode Whitelock puts it, 'a subtle Petition, and the beginning of the design against the King's Person, but not discerned till afterwards'. Amongst other things, the petition asked for justice on those responsible for both civil wars from the king downwards.[61] It is noteworthy that these proposals should have come from Ireton's regiment, for they anticipate some of the radical conclusions of the army's massive Remonstrance of the following month, of which Ireton was to be the principal architect. The contrast between the purely soldierly grievances of the soldiers' petition of March 1647 and the radical and potentially regicidal platform of this petition of October 1648 mirrors the process of the politicization of the army; a process in which its experience as a recipient of civilian petitions is an important and neglected factor.

Petitioning campaigns of 1646–7

It will come as no surprise that the most common complaint of provincial petitions over the whole of the period 1646–8 related to the weight of financial and other burdens on war-torn counties, as in the petitions from the Wiltshire committee in June 1646 against the depredations of Massey's brigade and from the Yorkshire committee in August against

---

60. *A New Declaration from Eight Regiments* . . . (25 November 1647), BL., E.416(35), p. 3. For the petition of 8 August, see above, p. 125.
61. Whitelock, *Memorials*, p. 338 (18 October 1648); *The Copie of Two Petitions* (24 October 1648), BL., E.468(32), pp. 1–6; *C.J.*, VI, 55. For other such petitions, see Whitelock, *Memorials*, pp. 341, 352, 359 (30 October, 27 November and 26 December); *Clarke Papers*, II, 59.

the burdens of Scottish occupation.[62] Such complaints did not end with the conclusion of the war and were increased with the renewal of war in 1648.

Nearer, however, to a co-ordinated petitioning campaign, as distinct from isolated *cris de cœur*, are those petitions, especially of the year or so before the end of March 1647, which related to the high Presbyterian campaign in London.[63] This element of organized campaigning is clearly apparent in the petition which was presented to the London Common Council on 9 March 1646, whipped up by the high Presbyterian divines of Sion College and, according to the Independent Thomas Juxon, subscribed by about a hundred persons, though a modern investigation has revealed only forty-five names.[64] It was designed to precipitate a further petition, from Common Council to parliament, as part of a two-pronged municipal and clerical attack from the City and the Westminster Assembly of Divines against the forthcoming parliamentary ordinance perfecting the machinery for defining the scandalous sins which merited suspension from the communion table. Initially Common Council responded as intended, and it was only at the last possible moment on 13 March that the City delegation was dissuaded from delivering its petition by the intervention of Recorder Glyn, who was also MP for Westminster, at the very door of the parliament house. For the time being the petition was shelved, but on 24 March Common Council decided to heed the advice of a parliamentary committee, which had earlier been sent down to discuss the matter with it, to abandon all further efforts. By so doing it avoided the fate of the Westminster Assembly, which, undeterred, had gone ahead with its petition, for which it was sharply reprimanded by the House of Commons on 11 April not only for committing a breach of parliamentary privilege – the ordinance had not yet passed through both Houses – but also because, 'being only called to advise, [they] did . . . prescribe . . . what they [viz. the Commons] ought to do'.[65] In the view of city high Presbyterians and their Scottish mentor, Robert Baillie, this at least

---

62. For the petition from Wiltshire, see Whitelock, *Memorials*, p. 215; Cary, *Memorials*, I, 101 and note; from Yorkshire, Bodleian, Tanner MSS., 59, fo. 473.
63. See below, p. 281. For important background, see V. Pearl, 'London puritans and Scotch fifth columnists: a mid-seventeenth century phenomenon', in A.E.J. Hollaender and W. Kellaway (eds.), *Studies in London History . . .* (1969), pp. 325–31, and 'London's Counter-revolution', in Aylmer, *Interregnum*, pp. 31–6; M. Mahoney, 'Presbyterianism in the City of London 1645–1647', *Hist.J.*, XXII (1979), 93–114.
64. For Juxon's account, see BL., Add. MSS., 25,465, fos. 63–6. For the modern correction and other details, see Mahoney, art. cit., pp. 101–8.
65. *C.J.*, IV, 506, 511, 518; BL., Add. MSS., 31,116, fos. 261–1(b); Add. MSS., 10,114 fo. 12; Add. MSS., 25,465 (Juxon's Journal), fos. 68–8(b); *Westminster Assembly Minutes*, pp. 225–6.

was an honourable defeat in a godly cause, in contrast with the City's shameful surrender.[66]

The abortive City petition of March was concerned with one central issue which seems to have been abandoned as a regrettably lost cause in the succeeding high Presbyterian petitions of 1646–7. The first of these was presented to parliament on 20 May 1646 along with a remonstrance which, as Juxon tells us, it had been the propounders' original intention to present without any accompanying petition, but to be co-ordinated with a strike against payment of Excise and other taxes. However, Common Council decided otherwise.[67] The second petition, whose subscription was accompanied by scenes of violence and the imprisonment of three citizens for soliciting hands to it, was submitted to parliament on 19 December,[68] and the third on 17 March 1647.[69] All three petitions followed the same procedural pattern as the abortive petition of March 1646. All contained a mixture of religious and secular demands, the former the contribution of high Presbyterian clerics in London. Indeed, according to the royalist Nicholas Oudart, the petition of March 1647 was actually framed in Sion College, and the same may have been true of the other petitions.[70] The control of sectarian excesses figures prominently in all of them. Among the secular items, the need to expedite arrangements for negotiations with the king looms large, while the need for the City to control its own militia appears in both the May and December petitions. Another feature of two of the petitions is irritation at interferences with the collection of debts, whether the familiar issue of 'protections' to MPs and their servants (May) or the implications of sequestration procedures in this respect (December). The May Remonstrance also demanded the abolition of the Committee for the Advance of Money at Haberdashers' Hall.

66. Baillie, *Letters*, II, 366.
67. For Juxon's account of these events, see BL., Add. MSS., 25,465, fos. 68(b)–9, 75–5(b). For the petition and Remonstrance, see *C.J.*, IV, 555–6; *L.J.*, VIII, 322–4; BL., Add. MSS., 31,116, fo. 271; Whitelock, *Memorials*, p. 212 (26 May); *Parliamentary History*, XIV, 418–25.
68. Information on the petition derived from Dr Williams's Library, MS. 24.50 (continuation of Juxon's Journal), fos. 94(b)–96(b); *C.J.*, V, 20–1, 24; BL., Add. MSS., 31,116, fos. 293(b), 294; *Parliamentary History*, XV, 235–6; Baillie, *Letters*, II, 412, 416; *Montereul Correspondence*, I, 352, 367. See also Mahoney, *Hist.J.*, art. cit., pp. 109, 111; Pearl, 'London's Counter-revolution', in Aylmer, *Interregnum*, pp. 41–3.
69. Information on this petition from CLRO., Jor. 40, fos. 207–8; Dr Williams's Library, MS. 24.50, fos. 103–3(b): *The Petition of the Lord Major [sic] and Common Councel* (17 March 1647), BL., E.381(2), pp. 3–14: *Nicholas Papers*, pp. 80–1; *Montereul Correspondence*, II, 42–3, 73.
70. *Nicholas Papers*, pp. 80–1. On the Remonstrance of May 1646, see *The Pulpit Incendiary* (4 May 1648), BL., E.438(10), p. 19; and, for a denial of Sion College's involvement, see *Sion College, What It Is and Doeth* (24 May 1648), BL., E.444(3), pp. 9–10.

None of these petitions was received enthusiastically by parliament. Indeed, the House of Commons gave serious consideration to whether both the May petition and remonstrance and the December petition were breaches of parliamentary privilege, and the value of their ultimate decisions to give proper consideration to both was in effect notably depreciated: in the case of the May petition, by the House's according the same consideration to a rival petition on 2 June, which it would normally have rejected out of hand on account of its radical Leveller features;[71] and, in that of the December petition, by the long ensuing delay, which a dispatch of 3 January from Bellièvre, the French ambassador, suggests 'peut estre à dessein de les ennuyer'. This is more than likely, especially since parliament had still not attended to the petition at the beginning of March,[72] at about the time that the last of our petitions was formulated. The strong emphasis of this last petition on the dangers of an over-inflated army being quartered so near London and of the petition reportedly circulating among the soldiers would make it the more acceptable to Holles and his parliamentary Presbyterian colleagues, many of whom would accord an equally warm welcome to the petition's concern for the strict observance of the Covenant and the suppression of heterodox religious opinions and practices. Parliament responded by indicating that it already had some of these matters under consideration and would make time for the remainder.[73]

It will have been noticed that in these later London petitions there is an element of what was shortly to become a central feature of the campaign of Holles and the parliamentary Presbyterians: the desirability of cutting the army down to size by demobilizing most of those soldiers who would not enlist for service in Ireland. This theme is also present in some other petitions and made them a useful potential weapon in Holles's armoury. Back in February 1647 Nicholas Oudart had written of such petitions being organized in the eastern counties,[74] and while those he mentions in Norfolk and Hertfordshire do not seem to have materialized, those in Suffolk and Essex certainly did. Indeed, the Essex petition, which has already been treated in another context,[75] was an anti-army petition par excellence, while that from Suffolk,

71. C.J., IV, 561; BL., Add. MSS., 31,116, fo. 272; Whitelock, Memorials, p. 213 (2 June); Pearl, 'London's Counter-revolution', in Aylmer, Interregnum, pp. 35–7; Ashton, Civil War, pp. 251–2.
72. Montereul Correspondence, I, 370. For two later royalist comments on the delay, see Bodleian, Clarendon MSS., 29, fo. 72(b); Nicholas Papers, p. 81.
73. C.J., V, 115; L.J., IX, 82; CLRO., Jor. 40, fos. 210(b)–1; BL., E.381(2), pp. 13–14; Whitelock, Memorials, p. 244 (17 March).
74. Nicholas Papers, pp. 74–5.
75. See above, pp. 43–4, 118, 118–19.

which was presented to parliament on 16 February, included a clear recommendation for the disbandment of the army, along with the need to regulate the Excise. In addition, as might be expected in a county where the influence of the pious Barnardistons was so strong, there was a model high Presbyterian platform including the establishment of a thoroughgoing Presbyterian hierarchy of assemblies and the stricter enforcement of the Covenant.[76]

Of course the March petition of the soldiers, which occasioned the disastrous and inappropriate parliamentary Declaration of Dislike,[77] helped to exacerbate conservative disapprobation of the army. Yet during the succeeding months there is scant evidence of anything resembling a petitioning campaign for disbandment as distinct from complaints about free quarter and the excesses of soldiers, as in the petition of the Devon grand jury on 1 May.[78] The one provincial exception is the Essex petition presented to parliament on 6 April and occasioning, as was shown earlier, a rebuke for the manner of its organization if not for its substance,[79] and which was anyway followed by a very radically phrased petition from the self-styled 'well-affected' of the same county urging the dangers of hasty disbandment.[80] As to London, in view of the widespread belief that the City fathers, along with the Presbyterian grandees in parliament and the Scots commissioners in London, were at the centre of the anti-army campaign,[81] it is the more surprising that it is not until one of the petitions of apprentices early in July that the disbandment of the army features in any of the London petitions of these months, and then only as one of a number of conservative demands. This petition was, it will be remembered, opposed by two other petitions from a different group of apprentices, the first to Fairfax and the army council and the second to parliament,

76. *L.J.*, IX, 18–19.
77. Compare the relatively mild rebuke administered to the almost exactly contemporaneous officer petitioners despite their complaints of the non-observance of Magna Carta and the Petition of Right. It seems likely that Holles had other uses for such officers in mind, quite distinct from their declared willingness to serve in Ireland (*The Petition of the Colonels, Lieutenant Colonells [sic], Majors and other Officers* (March 1647), BL., E.382(4), pp. 3–8; *Parliamentary History*, XV, 338–40).
78. *L.J.*, IX, 171–2. The petitioners also complained against the Excise, the abuses of sequestration, the shortage of parsons and the impoverishment of people who had faithfully served parliament.
79. *C.J.*, V, 134; Rushworth, *Historical Collections*, VI, 449; *The humble Petition of the Deputy Lieutenants, Justices of the Peace and Commons of the County of Essex* (13 March 1647), BL., 669, f10(102); [A. Warren], *A full Vindication of the Armie* (12 October 1647), BL., E.410(18), p. 23; *A New Found Stratagem* (April 1647), BHPC., pp. 3–14. See above, pp. 43–4, 118–19.
80. *L.J.*, IX, 262–3; *HMC., 6th. Report (House of Lords Cal. 1647)*, p. 183.
81. For a later statement of this view, see *The Scots Cabinett Opened* (August 1648), BL., E.456(30), pp. 4–5; also Oxford, Worcester College, Clarke MSS., 41, fo. 58.

which it reached on 13 July, beating the more conservative apprentices' petition by one day.[82]

The latter petition was to attain renewed prominence in London during the tumultuous days of late July,[83] when the existence of a counter-revolutionary petitioning campaign is hardly in doubt. According to the conservative Presbyterian MP Sir John Maynard, 'the richest citizens (especially those of the kings party)' sought to ply Common Council and, through it, parliament with a succession of such petitions.[84] But not all London petitions at this time were of this sort. When, on 23 July, parliament passed an ordinance which infuriated conservative feeling in the city by putting control of the city militia out of the hands of Holles's London allies, it might conceivably claim to be acting in response to local pressure, having received only on the previous day a petition from some officers of the trained bands in two wards of the city complaining of how worthy (viz. Independent) officers had been replaced by unsatisfactory (viz. Presbyterian) ones.[85] But such was not the prevailing sentiment in the city, which was better expressed by the so-called Petition and Solemn Engagement of the citizens, to which hands were energetically solicited by 'agitators' – it is curious how in this and in the title of the Solemn Engagement, the organizers were, perhaps deliberately, making use of terms devised in the hated New Model Army. Approved by Common Council, the Petition and Solemn Engagement was presented on 22 July to the House of Commons who gave it distinctly short shrift, ordering the City MPs, Atkins, Pennington and Venn, to convey the House's displeasure to the Lord Mayor and to tell him to keep such tumultuary petitioning under control in future.[86]

But they had not seen anything yet. On 26 July, amidst unprecedented scenes of violence, a counter-revolutionary mob burst into the parliament house, this time forcing its petition down the throats of the intimidated MPs. Parliament was forced to approve the demands that the king be brought to London to treat; that the army be ordered to keep a safe distance from London; and that the hated militia ordinance of 23 July be revoked along with the previous order of the Lower House declaring signatories of the Solemn Engagement to be guilty of high treason.[87] On 27 July Common Council heard what were in effect

82. On these and other City petitions of the previous weeks, see above, p. 137.
83. This episode is treated in greater detail below, pp. 181–5, 349–55.
84. HLRO., Braye MSS., 96, fo. 237 (photocopy of entry in John Browne's Commonplace Book in New Haven, Yale University, Beinecke Library, MS. fb, 155).
85. C.J., V, 254.
86. C.J., V, 255; *A Petition from the City of London* (July 1647), BL., E.399(35), pp. 1–6.
87. C.J., V, 258, 259; L.J., IX, 355, 356; HMC., *House of Lords MSS., Addenda 1514–1714* (1962), p. 473; Rushworth, *Historical Collections*, VI, 642, 643. The incident is treated by Dr Pearl in Aylmer, *Interregnum*, pp. 49–51, and below, pp. 182–3, 349–52.

two more petitions, one of them from 'Young Men and Apprentices' and the other from 'divers well affected Citizens', about the need to put the city into a posture of defence against the now almost inevitable onslaught of the New Model Army.[88] Over the previous week counter-revolutionary petitions had become mob diktats, forced upon a Common Council which, although it might be in broad sympathy with their aims, was probably apprehensive about the consequences of the violence which accompanied them; and then upon a terrified parliament, and, after 26 July, an increasingly incomplete one, as Independent MPs and even some moderate Presbyterian and non-party men took refuge with the army. The radical Independent Edmund Ludlow, never reluctant to identify Presbyterian with royalist aims, was exaggerating in seeing tumultuary petitioning simply as a device fostered by the royalists and encouraged by Charles I and his advisers.[89] Probably much nearer the mark is a pro-Presbyterian account which, while retrospectively playing down the violence of these incidents and insisting that 'multitudes petitioning make not a tumult', was nevertheless prepared to admit that an inflammatory role had been played by many '*Cavaliers, Malignants*, yea and Sectaries too who mixed themselves among the honest young men'.[90]

Violence also features prominently in the treatment of petitioners who were opposed to the policies pursued by those who currently held sway in the city. The detailed story of the brutal assault by reformadoes under Poynz and Massey on those citizens who were attempting to deliver a petition at Guildhall on 2 August counselling moderation and emphasizing the danger that counter-revolutionary extremism would lead to a second war is best told as a feature of the history of the London counter-revolutionary turmoil of late July and early August. This nasty incident has already been noticed in the context of petitions to the army to which the molested petitioners were to turn in October following their failure to obtain redress from parliament on 24 August.[91]

Following the army's occupation of London on 6 August, the municipality had to change its tune. The chief object of its petition in September was to offer (unconvincing) excuses for its backwardness in

88. CLRO., Jor. 40, fos. 240(b)–1; *A Remonstrance and Declaration of the Young Men and Apprentices* (31 July 1647), BL., E.400(31), pp. 1–4. The citizens' petition recommended Major General Massey as commander of the proposed city defence force.
89. *Ludlow Memoirs*, I, 160–1.
90. *The Army Anatomized* (4 December 1647), BL., E.419(6), p. 23. Italics in original.
91. *A peaceable Petition of a Very Great Number of Citizens* (2 August 1647), BL., 669, f11(58); *L.J.*, IX, 401–2; *HMC., 6th. Rep. (House of Lords Cal. 1647)*, p. 193; *Two Petitions from the City of London* (October 1647), BL., E.410(20), pp. 1–6. See above, p. 131, and below, p. 353.

collecting assessment arrears,[92] and of that of 1 December to obtain the release of the Lord Mayor, the Recorder and the three aldermen who had been imprisoned for their part in the July counter-revolution. The contention of the latter petition that the City fathers had been innocent of any involvement in or responsibility for these occurrences was unlikely to convince many.[93]

There is in fact little to be discerned in the way of a coherent pattern about the petitions of the last five months of 1647. The radical petitions from Hertfordshire, Rutland, Oxfordshire and Buckinghamshire have already been mentioned elsewhere,[94] while two Leveller petitions of November relating to the Agreement of the People were rejected with contumely.[95] The only common factor between the petitions in December from Irish gentlemen bewailing the wretched state of that kingdom,[96] from clothiers, staplers and woolmongers,[97] and from maimed soldiers in the Savoy hospital soliciting contributions towards their fuel supply,[98] is the apparently distressed condition of the petitioners.

Petitioning campaigns of 1648

During the year which began with the Vote of No Addresses and ended with Pride's Purge and the preliminary arrangements for the king's trial, the variety, complexity and sheer number of petitions – well over a hundred, not including private petitions from individuals – make orderly classification an even more difficult task than for the petitions of the previous year. However, during the spring and summer, if there is one theme which predominates and characterizes more petitions than any other, it is the request for a treaty with the king with a view to the final settlement of the kingdom. When the first of these aims had

92. CLRO., Jor. 40, fos. 255, 255(b)–6, 257; C.J., V, 298, 301; HMC., 6th. Report (House of Lords Cal. 1647), p. 195.
93. Jor. 40, fos. 263–3(b), 264; L.J., IX, 550–1; C.J., V, 374; The humble Petition of the Lord Major [sic] Aldermen and Commons (1 December 1647), BL., E.419(17), sig. y; Parliamentary History, XVI, 364–7. The petition also asked for the avoidance of free quartering in London and the disbandment of supernumerary soldiers.
94. C.J., V, 301; The Copie of Three Petitions . . . (September 1647), BL., E.407(29), pp. 1–6; Two Petitions to the Generals Excellency (November 1647), E.412(18), pp. 2–3. See above, pp. 120, 125–6n, 129–30.
95. C.J., V, 354; BL., 669, f11(98); Leveller Manifestoes, pp. 235–41.
96. The Kingdomes Weekly Intelligencer, Number 238 (7/14 December 1647), BL., E.419(24), p. 762; The Perfect Weekly Account Number 50 (8/15 December 1647), BL., E.419(28), no pagination.
97. Cal.SPD. 1645–7, p. 580.
98. For cynical royalist observations about parliament's attitude to this, see Mercurius Pragmaticus number 14 (14/21 December 1647), BL., E.421(1), no pagination.

been achieved in early autumn, the focus changed and there was a flood of petitions denouncing the treaty.

The Vote of No Addresses was of course designed to inhibit petitions for negotiations with the king by making approaches to him a treasonable matter, so it is hardly surprising that there were for the time being no petitions either against the Vote or in favour of a treaty. There were, however, petitions applauding the Vote and parliament's Declaration defending it, from Taunton in February and the well-affected of Buckinghamshire in March.[99] Indeed, with the exception of the abortive Leveller petition in Kent and London in January,[100] the petitions of the first three months of 1648 are, to say the least, hardly indicative of widespread dissent against government policies. There are a few politically neutral petitions,[101] and a few others of a mildly contentious sort.[102] There is, however, one petition which, given the advantages of hindsight, seems to foreshadow the forthcoming armed conflict. On 1 March Lord General Fairfax presented to the Speaker of the House of Commons a petition which he had received, signed by thirty-six officers serving under Major-General Rowland Laugharne in South Wales. The petitioners were protesting against their proposed disbandment and their unsatisfied arrears of pay, as well as against the aspersions on the loyalty of their commander who was rumoured to be about to defect to the insurgent Colonel Poyer in Pembroke Castle. Whether their indignation was genuine or simulated, Laugharne and his men were to be in full revolt within a fortnight.[103]

On 28 January the news-sheet *The Kingdomes Weekly Post* reported that parliament had responded favourably to a number of petitions asking for a tightening of religious controls and measures against sectaries, by speeding up the implementation of the ordinance of 19 August 1645 for the construction of Presbyterian 'classes' and the

99. *The Humble Petition and Grateful Acknowledgement of the Town of Taunton* (9 February 1648), BL., E.427(21), pp. 3–7; *The Humble Petition and Representation of the County of BUCKINGHAM* (9 March 1648), E.432(12), pp. 3–8.
100. See above, p. 127.
101. E.g. in March from the customs commissioners bewailing the likelihood of their insolvency; from ex-servants of Charles I who had faithfully served parliament asking for arrears of pay; and from sick and wounded soldiers for relief (Rushworth, *Historical Collections*, VII, 1016, 1018, 1044).
102. E.g. the petition of the Levant and East India Companies in January asking for confirmation of their privileges (*C.J.*, V, 430); the petitions from Exeter and Devon in February complaining of free quarter and the burden of taxation (Exeter, Devon R.O., Act Book of Common Council of City of Exeter no. 9, 1647–55, fo. 8; QS. box 55; Roberts, *Devon*, pp. 10–11; see above, pp. 120–21); and of the Committee of Accounts at Cornhill on 11 March complaining of the obstacles imposed on their county sub-committees and asking for the protection of the Indemnity ordinance (*C.J.*, V, 492; Rushworth, *Historical Collections*, VII, 1023; see above, p. 101n).
103. Bodleian, Tanner MSS., 58, fos. 733, 735.

election of congregational elders, something that would be warmly welcomed by high Presbyterians in London and elsewhere.[104] The London City fathers continued to attempt to secure the release of the imprisoned aldermen, though the petition on behalf of two of them in February did not improve its chances of success by associating their names with that of Sir John Maynard, whose forthcoming trial was a source of considerable embarrassment to the government.[105] The City petitions of April and May for their release were to be attended with rather more success.[106]

While there had been some fifteen petitions (other than those from individuals) between 1 January and 21 March 1648, the subsequent months down to the end of August saw at least 56, of which 36 and probably more can be broadly described as conservative in character.[107] Most important, the Essex petition of 22 March marks the beginning of what can reasonably be described as a petitioning campaign in favour of a personal treaty with the king, of which the petitions from Kent, Surrey, Sussex and the City of London are the other most important cases. Apart from the treaty, the other most significant issues featured in these petitions are the City's desire to control its own militia, its distrust of the powers of militia recruitment vested in Major-General Skippon and its ambition to absorb suburban militias (seven cases);[108] the call for stricter religious controls (five cases); and complaints about the dismissal of municipal officers (five cases of which four relate to London). Criticism of the army features in at least six petitions of which five look for relief via its disbandment. Of these, apart from the Kent, Surrey and Sussex petitions, which are treated later, there are petitions from the inhabitants of Hampshire on 14 June (not presented) and the City of London on 8 August.[109] Illustrative of a new episode in the City's

104. *The Kingdomes Weekly Post . . . Number 5* (26 January/2 February 1648), BL., E.425(5), pp. 34–5. See *An Ordinance for dividing . . . the severall Counties . . . into distinct Classical Presbyteries . . .* (29 January 1648), E.423(3); *A&O.*, I, 753–4, 1062–3.

105. *Cal.SPD. 1648–9*, pp. 16–17. On Maynard, see above, pp. 113–16.

106. CLRO., Jor. 40, fo. 269(b); Rushworth, *Historical Collections*, VII, 1100, 1124–6; *Parliamentary History*, XVII, 171–3.

107. If one were, quite reasonably, to include petitions from reformadoes for payment of arrears of pay in this category, this number would be increased to 42. For such petitions, see CLRO., Jor. 40, fo. 266(b) (a petition to the Common Council of London); *L.J.*, X, 250; *C.J.*, V, 664–5; Rushworth, *Historical Collections*, VII, 1181, 1221; *A Petition to the House of Commons . . . of one hundred [and] forty odd field officers* (22 August 1648), BL., E.461(1), pp. 1–5. On the reformadoes, see below, pp. 384–98.

108. On this, see below, p. 155.

109. *The Declaration Together with the Petition and Remonstrance of the Lords, Knights, Gentlemen, Ministers and Freeholders of the County of Hampshire* (June 1648), Codrington pamphlet coll., also BL., E.447(18), especially sig. A3. For the City's

uneasy relations with the army is its petition of 27 April, arising out of a sworn affidavit that army officers had been heard discussing a plan by the army to occupy London in the event of a Scottish invasion. The earl of Manchester, the Speaker of the Upper House, reassured the petitioners that there was no such plan (how did he know?) and that the Lords saw no reason 'why such a slight information should be any blemish or scandall to the Army'. Parliament did, however, order the army to a further distance from London, which decision was treated by Common Council as a favourable response to its petition.[110]

It is now time to turn to the petitioning campaign for a personal treaty with the king in London, a campaign which was ultimately successful, even though the treaty was to be in the Isle of Wight. In most of these petitions the request for a treaty was only one, though the most important, of the petitioners' requests, and since some of the others were of a distinctly counter-revolutionary character and the petitions were advanced while fighting in the Second Civil War was still going on, the government was surely wise to be cautious about a metropolitan venue, even though the treaty did not open until September when the worst dangers were over.

The petitioning campaign may be said to have opened on 22 March with the decision of the Essex Grand Jury at the Chelmsford assizes to draw up a petition in the name of the gentry and freeholders of the county. Apart from the very real grievances about the burden of taxes and free quarter emphasized in the petition, it is particularly notable as the first since the Vote of No Addresses to ask parliament to arrange a personal treaty with the king. The petitioners somewhat reluctantly agreed with the suggestion of the Lord Lieutenant, the earl of Warwick, that there should be a delay of seven days before delivering the petition at Westminster on the extravagantly optimistic grounds that the king and the parliament were anyway on the verge of coming to terms. According to the earl of Lanark's anonymous English correspondent, this delay added materially to Warwick's growing unpopularity in the county. The same writer estimates that by 28 April 24,000 signatures

petition, see *L.J.*, X, 424, 427; Rushworth, *Historical Collections*, VII, 1220; *Parliamentary History*, XVII, 387–91, especially 389–90. For the petitions from Kent, Surrey and Sussex, see above, pp. 46, 121–2, and below, pp. 144–53. The Hampshire petition was abortive, however.

110.   CLRO., Jor. 40, fos. 269, 272(b); *L.J.*, X, 234–5; *C.J.*, V, 546; *HMC., 7th. Rep. (House of Lords Cal. 1648)*, p. 23; Rushworth, *Historical Collections*, VII, 1070; *The true answer of the Parliament to the petition of the Lord Major [sic]* (April 1647), BHPC.; *The humble Petition of the Lord Major, Aldermen and Commons of the City of London* (April 1648), Codrington pamphlet coll., pp. 3–12: *A Declaration of the . . . Lord Mayor Aldermen and Common Councell* (April 1648), BL., E.437(2), pp. 1–3.

had been obtained; an overstatement if Sir William Hix's final figure of 20,000 is to be credited.[111]

On the previous day (27 April), alarmed by these developments, the House of Commons ordered all Essex MPs to attend the petitioners' scheduled rendezvous at Stratford Langthorne to urge on them the danger of such proceedings in 'these distracted and tumultuous Times' and the desirability of the county's making its representations to parliament through its MPs rather than by petitioning.[112] But parliament had been overtaken by events. On 28 April, at a meeting at the Talbot inn in Chelmsford, subscribed copies of the petition were collected to be delivered to Major Stephen Smith of the Essex militia who would be responsible for delivering them to the House of Commons as Sir William Hix was to be for delivery to the House of Lords. The petitioners attending the rendezvous on 4 May were urged to accompany the subscribed petition to Westminster 'if it may be with their convenience'.[113]

'The Essex peticon went to ye parliament', laconically observes a local diarist in his entry for 4 May, adding as a matter of no less interest, 'A fayre but cold season'.[114] On the same day a declaration, allegedly from the Essex Grand Jury, recommended the use of sanctions in the form of a refusal to pay taxes until the petitioners' demands had been met, as well as arrangements to protect petitioners from reprisals, and, most alarmingly, that the county should be put into a posture of defence.[115] On 17 May the Declaration was read to a horrified House of Commons which ordered its Committee of Printing to investigate who had composed and published it, and made arrangements to suppress it.[116] If one royalist newsletter, written later that summer, is to be credited, such

111. *The humble Petition and Desires of the Grand Jury at the last Assizes holden at Chelmsford* (April 1648), Codrington pamphlet and BL., E.434(22), pp. 1–6; *The humble Petition of the Grand Jury at the Assizes holden at Chelmsford* (May 1648), BL., 669, f12(20); *L.J.*, X, 243, 244; Rushworth, *Historical Collections*, VII, 1101–2; *Hamilton Papers*, I, 171, 188–9; B. Lyndon, 'Essex and the King's Cause in 1648', *Hist.J.*, XXIX (1986), 19–23. When Sir William Hix presented the petition to the House of Lords on 4 May, he specified about 20,000 signatures 'to which there would have been many more, if more time had been spent therein' (*The Answer of the Lords and Commons to the Essex petition* (4 May 1648), BL., E.438(16), p. 5).
112. *C.J.*, V, 546, 547.
113. BL., 669, f12(20).
114. Chelmsford, Essex R.O., D/DQs. 18, fo. 35 (Clopton's diary).
115. *The Ingagement and Declaration of the Grand Jury, Freeholders and other Inhabitants of . . . Essex* (4 May 1648), BL., E.433(9), no pagination; *A Method of putting the County of Essex in a posture of Defence* (May 1648), E.443(13), pp. 4–6. The proposed tax strike is reported in a letter from England to the earl of Lanark (SRO., GD 406/1/2464).
116. *C.J.*, V, 563.

arrangements sometimes went far beyond the bounds of due propriety. Put on to it, the author claims, by Lady Mildmay, the wife of the MP for Maldon, one Captain Palmer, 'a trooping Saint', and six of his men wounded and robbed the London merchant George Friar at his Essex house at Wanstead. Friar had incurred the displeasure of the Mildmays as 'a chief one that promoted the Loyall Petition . . . of the County of Essex'.[117]

Anxious to avoid giving the impression to the Scots that English differences were about to be settled by peaceful means, the earl of Lanark's English correspondent, in a letter of 9 May, contrasts the enthusiastic reception of the 2,000 Essex petitioners as they made their way through London with the cool response of the parliament.[118] But in actual fact the Speaker of the House of Lords assured Sir William Hix, who delivered the petition there, that everything possible would be done 'for settling the kingdome in a firme and lasting peace'.[119] But this was not to bear fruit until the end of the summer, and in the meantime the despised docility of the 'Essex calves' was to become a source of ridicule both to more militant petitioners elsewhere and to royalist agitators.[120] The stridently militant tone which had characterized the Essex Declaration was hushed, at least for the moment. On 5 June, however, Clopton records in his diary that there had been a meeting at Chelmsford 'to second ye former petition' with another, and that members of the county committee had been taken hostage pending parliament's giving satisfaction.[121] This event marks the preliminaries of Essex's participation in the Second Civil War.

May was, in fact, the great month for aggressively worded petitions for a personal treaty, and there is no better example of the connection between such petitions and the outbreak of the Second Civil War than the case of the Kentish petition. This originated on 11 May in an unofficial meeting of members of the grand jury of the county which had earlier refused to find true bills against persons arrested for participating in the riots in Canterbury the previous Christmas.[122] The petition was clear, concise and to the point, for all the criticism of its wording

117. *The Royall Diurnall . . . Number 5* (22/29 August 1648), BL., E.461(13), no pagination.
118. SRO., GD 406/1/2464.
119. BL., E.438(16), p. 5. For the Commons' reception of the petition, see ibid., pp. 5–6.
120. See, e.g., *HMC., 12th. Rep. App. i, pt. IX (MSS. of the Duke of Beaufort)*, p. 20; *Divers Remarkable Passages Concerning the Original and Progresse of the present great Action in Essex* (1648), Chelmsford, Essex RO., Landon pamphlet coll., pp. 14–15. See also ibid., p. 2.
121. Chelmsford, Essex RO., D/DQ. s. 18, fo. 38(b).
122. On this, see below, pp. 240–41, 359–61.

from a Norfolk participant in the subsequent Kentish troubles.[123] It asked for a personal treaty with the king, government according to old-established laws, protection of property according to the Petition of Right, the discontinuation of innovatory taxes including the Excise, and the disbandment of the army.[124] Alarmed not least by the petitioners' expression of solidarity with those in other counties who entertained similar aspirations and grievances, the Deputy Lieutenants of Kent, meeting at Maidstone on 16 May, issued a declaration forbidding the calling of meetings to subscribe the petition which they pronounced to be seditious; a charge which was indignantly repudiated by the leading petitioners who firmly disclaimed any opposition to parliament, to which, indeed, they were looking 'for a just relief of our grievances'.[125] One account, of which Roger L'Estrange claimed authorship, reckons that the declaration was subscribed by 27,373 hands, but this is almost certainly an exaggeration.[126] Subscribed copies were to be brought to Rochester on 29 May, and a rendezvous was called for the following day at Blackheath. From there the petition was to be carried *en masse* to Westminster, a prospect which, in view of the violence which had attended the delivery of the Surrey petition on 16 May,[127] must have filled the government with apprehension.

A significant step nearer to armed conflict was taken by the calling out of the trained bands to suppress petitionary gatherings, even though, according to Matthew Carter, the author of an admirable contemporary account of these events, the response in some districts was unimpressive for the good reason that the officers of the trained bands were themselves busily engaged in the business of organizing the petition which they had been ordered to suppress.[128] On 26 May the petitioners issued a manifesto declaring the reasons for their dislike of the intimidatory actions of the county committee.[129] To exacerbate matters still further,

---

123. *L'Estrange his Vindication*, sig. A2. For an admirable and less frivolous contemporary account, see Carter, *True Relation*, pp. 6–9. See also *A Letter from a Gentleman in Kent* (15 June 1648), BL., E.448(34), pp. 4–5.

124. *The humble Petition of the Knights, Gentry, Clergy and Commonalty of the County of Kent* (May 1648), BL., E.441(25), pp. 2–7; also BL., 669, f12(28): *Cal.SPD. 1648–9*, p. 63; Carter, *True Relation*, pp. 9–11.

125. Carter, *True Relation*, pp. 13–20; *A brief Narration of some Arbitrary Proceedings of the Committee chosen for the County of Kent (But acting against it)* (August 1648), BL., E.459(12), pp. 3, 9; E.448(34), pp. 5–6.

126. *A Letter Declaratorie to the Disturbers of the Peace of the County of Kent* (18 May 1648), BL., 669, f12(27). For L'Estrange's claim to the authorship of this, see *L'Estrange His Vindication*, sig. B. Professor Everitt mentions 20,000 signatures to the petition being spoken of (Everitt, *Kent*, pp. 241–2).

127. On the delivery of the Surrey petition, see below, pp. 149–52.

128. Carter, *True Relation*, pp. 20–1.

129. For the manifesto, see ibid., pp. 22–6; *The Manifest of the County of Kent* (May 1648), BL., 669, f12(34).

if one admittedly partisan account is to be believed, the two Kentish MPs to whom the presentation of the petition was entrusted and who were themselves county committeemen had abused their trust by tampering with the text of the petition so as to distort its meaning.[130]

On 21 May Philip Ware, the mayor of Rochester, where subscribed copies of the petition were due to be handed in eight days later, had written to parliament expressing his alarm at the report that the committee was planning to quarter a regiment in his city to stifle the petition and plunder the petitioners, and that one committeeman had even declared that it might be expedient to hang two petitioners in every parish.[131] Another letter written on the same day mentioned a design for the soldiers to carry off petitioners. The seizure of the magazine at Rochester by supporters of the petition as a defence against such horrific eventualities heightened tension still further and made a renewal of civil war all but inevitable.[132] Rochester was, of course, dangerously near to the naval shipyard at Chatham, and the master shipwright Peter Pett, in a letter written on 15 June, probably to the Admiralty committee, tells of how he had been under intolerable pressure during the last week of May both to sign the petition himself and to allow signatures to be canvassed in the shipyard. The line was becoming dangerously thin between allowing such action, which he steadfastly refused to do, and watching helplessly while mariners and shipwrights deserted and stores and ships were taken over by those who were fast becoming not simply petitioners but also insurgents.[133]

With peaceful petitioning now merging with violence, parliament opted for a policy of damage limitation. The earl of Thanet, 'that Ambidextrous Lord', as Roger L'Estrange describes this very early defector from the ranks of the petitioners,[134] was to be sent back to Kent to undeceive petitioners about the rumours of the grisly fate in store for them, and to undertake that, provided that they gave up the Rochester magazine, laid down their arms and retired peacefully home, parliament would hear their petition.[135] Great hopes were entertained by some

130. BL., E.459(12), p. 5.
131. Bodleian, Tanner MSS., 57, fo. 93; Cary, *Memorials*, I, 422; BL., E.459(12), pp. 4–5; *A Declaration of the severall proceedings of both Houses . . . with those in the County of Kent now in Arms* (5 June 1648), E.446(1), pp. 3–4; *An Impartiall Narration of the Management of the late Kentish Petition* (21 July 1648), E.453(37), pp. 1–2; *Cal.SPD. 1648–9*, pp. 95–6.
132. *A Letter from Rochester in Kent* (22 May 1648), BL., E.443(26), pp. 1–3.
133. *HMC., 13th. Rep. Portland MSS.*, I, 459–62; *Naval Documents*, pp. 348–51.
134. *L'Estrange his Vindication*, sig. C.
135. *C.J.*, V, 572, 572–3, 576; *L.J.*, X, 279, 280, 282, 285, 286; Rushworth, *Historical Collections*, VII, 1127; Bodleian, Bodley MSS., dep.C 168, no. 75; *Cal.SPD. 1648–9*, pp. 76, 96–7; BL., E.446(1), pp. 4–8.

moderates for the success of Thanet's mission,[136] though hardline Roundheads thought its concessions disgraceful and viewed the petition as part of a Cavalier plot 'to put all things in a flame'.[137] They need not have worried, for the failure of the mission was ensured by the petitioners' understandable unwillingness to lay down their arms and put themselves, as they saw it, at the mercy of a revengeful county committee.[138] The Kentish manifesto of 26 May and the Remonstrance which followed it affirmed their intention, in the words of the Remonstrance, 'to act the last Scene of this Tragedy with our Swords in our hands'.[139] When we next encounter them, it will be as insurgents in arms, not as petitioners.

But it is as petitioners in arms that we take our leave of them. On 29 May the House of Commons considered two letters from the Kentish petitioners, one to the Derby House Committee and the other to the Lord Mayor of London. Both declared their undeterred intention to rendezvous at Blackheath on 30 May and from there to proceed to Westminster with their petition, requesting the Lord Mayor to allow them free passage through the city.[140] That might have been acceptable to both City and parliament if the petitioners had accepted the terms offered by Thanet. But their fear of harassment by the forces of their enemies on the county committee and, as a paper found on the person of one of the insurgents captured after the battle of Maidstone on 1 June emphasized, their anxiety that they should not suffer the same fate as the Surrey petitioners a fortnight earlier, made them reluctant to lay down their arms.[141] This was doubly unfortunate in that it was anyway decided that the petition should be carried from Blackheath to Westminster only by a small delegation of ten gentlemen and ten yeomen. But in any case access was denied to them and the House of Commons referred them instead to Lord General Fairfax, whom the petitioners found awaiting them at Blackheath 'in a Warlike posture', impervious to their plea that he mediate with parliament on their behalf, 'chusing on the

---

136. See, e.g., *The Last Newes from Kent* (May 1648), BL., E.445(9), no pagination; *Newes from Kent* (25 May 1648), E.445(4), pp. 2–3.
137. *The Designes of the Rebels in Kent* (27 May 1648), BL., E.446(18), pp. 3–4.
138. *L.J.*, X, 290; BL., E.446(1), pp. 8–11.
139. *A Remonstrance Shewing the Occasion of the Arming of . . . Kent* (26 May 1648), BL., 669, f12(34), also printed in Carter, *True Relation*, pp. 29–30 and summarized in *Cal.SPD. 1648–9*, pp. 88–9. For the manifesto see BL., 669, f12(33) and Carter, *True Relation*, pp. 23–6. See also *The Declaration and Resolution of the Knights Gentry and Free-holders of . . . Kent* (29 May 1648), BL., E.445(10), pp. 1–3. L'Estrange claimed to be the author of the Remonstrance and to have obtained his Kentish colleagues' approval of it (*L'Estrange His Vindication*, sig. B2).
140. *C.J.*, V, 577.
141. *A letter from . . . Lord Fairfax* (5 June 1648), BL., E.445(40), pp. 7–8. See also *A Seasonable Caution to the Citie of London* (2 June 1648), E.445(43), especially pp. 3–4.

contrary to pursue them as Rebels'. The Second Civil War in Kent had begun.[142]

By now such petitioning had become identified with insurgency in the minds of both central and local authorities. On 9 June the county committee of Hampshire issued a warning against tumultuary gatherings, emphasizing how 'divers who have been in Armes against the Parliament . . . have vpon a specious pretence of Petitioning the Parliament . . . drawne together great multitudes . . . in a riotous and warlike manner . . . to the great danger of inflaming the Kingdome againe into a new and fatall Warre'. The committee was the more concerned in that copies of the Kent, Surrey and Sussex petitions were circulating in east Hampshire where they might serve as models to be emulated.[143] This Hampshire petition, accompanied by a fierce declaration deploring the outrageous treatment of the Kent and Surrey petitioners and threatening recourse to arms if no satisfactory answer was forthcoming, seems never to have reached parliament. It asked for the return of religion to its Elizabethan and Jacobean condition, the full restoration of the king, the disbandment of the army and payment of its arrears, and the passing of an Act of Oblivion.[144]

The Surrey petition seems to have owed its origins to both the Grand Inquest at Assizes and the Grand Jury at Quarter Sessions, along with 'divers other Knights and Gentlemen'. On 2 May parliament received notice of a warrant from the High Constable of Surrey desiring the people of Mortlake to meet with others at Leatherhead 'to join in preferring a petition to the Parliament'. The House of Lords asked the Derby House Committee to order the Surrey sheriffs and Deputy Lieutenants to take effective action to prevent the tumults and disturbances so often connected with such occasions, and, indeed, the Surrey petition, like that of Kent, was of a sort to gladden the hearts not only of conservative parliamentarians but also of erstwhile Cavaliers. The petition, which was reported to have been subscribed by more than 5,000 persons, requested a personal treaty with the king at Westminster, his re-establishment in the throne of his ancestors, the restoration of ancient and known laws, the disbandment of the army (though with its arrears of pay satisfied) and the enforcement of the ordinances regulating

142. BL., E.453(37), pp. 1–3.
143. A Declaration of the Committee for the Safety of the County of Southampton (9 June 1648), BL., 669, f12(60).
144. The Declaration Together with the Petition and Remonstrance of the Lords Knights Gentlemen Ministers and Free-holders of . . . Hampeshire (14 June 1648), BL., E.447(18), sig. A2–A3. An official petition from the Hampshire Grand Jury to Chief Baron Wylde on 5 July was concerned with the deficiencies of an ordinance regulating free quarter (Bodleian, MSS., dep. C. 175, no. 119).

free quarter in the meantime; and, finally, a stop to 'the War now beginning'. A later declaration of the petitioners admits that the petition was somewhat incautiously penned and that it certainly had not been their intention that Charles I 'should be brought in without satisfaction and security, first given to the Kingdom . . . (although many of our Countrymens affections run strongly toward the bringing in of the King . . . without any conditions) yet should it be so, the Kingdom must of necessity be miserably inslaved'.[145]

The circumstances of the Surrey petition were not quickly forgotten. After the Restoration of 1660 there was a determined attempt in the county to have Sir Richard Onslow excepted from the Act of Indemnity and Oblivion on account of his alleged threats, when sheriff in 1648, to use armed force against the petitioners.[146]

A very hostile account[147] describes the rendezvous of the petitioners on Putney Heath on Tuesday 16 May, and their march to London 'with Trumpet, Pipe and Fiddle, such instruments of musick [as] were never used by Petitioners, but more fit for morrice-dancers (which the greatest part showed them to be)'. According to this account, as they marched through London, some of the petitioners were shouting 'for God and King Charles'. In emphasizing their provocation of the soldiers guarding parliament and especially their threats to parliament itself, the author seems deliberately to be evoking memories of the previous 26 July. The onset of rain as they arrived in Westminster sent some of them scurrying for shelter in local alehouses, from which they later emerged

145. Evidence of the text and history of this petition is in *The humble Petition of divers thousands . . . in Surrey* (May 1648), BL., 669, f12(26); *C.J.*, V, 549–50; *L.J.*, X, 239; Rushworth, *Historical Collections*, VII, 1116; *Parliamentary History*, XVII, 139–40. For the later disclaimer about the conditions of the king's reestablishment, see *A Declaration of the Knights Gentlemen and Freeholders of . . . Surrey . . .* (18 May 1648), BL., E.443(8), pp. 3–4; also E.445(4). Hamilton's correspondent's statement that there were 8,000 petitioners, of whom 3,000 accompanied the petition to Westminster, is clearly an exaggeration (*Hamilton Papers*, p. 200; see also SRO., GD 406/1/2465; HMC., *11th Report, Hamilton MSS.*, p. 123).
146. Stafford, Staffordshire RO., MS. D(W) 1778/I/i/81. The document's location is curious and I am grateful to Mrs S. Corke for drawing my attention to it. The evidence about Onslow's role is contradictory and two witnesses denied his making any such threats (Surrey RO., Guildford Muniment Room, MS. 111/10/5).
147. *A true Relation of the Passages between the Surrey Petitioners and the Soldiers . . .* (17 May 1648), BL., E.443(5), pp. 1–6. My own description is based on this and other accounts in Rushworth, *Historical Collections*, VII, 1116–17; Whitelock, *Memorials*, p. 305 (entry for 16 May); *Clarke Papers*, II, 11–13; *Ludlow Memoirs*, I, 188–9; *A true Narrative of the Grounds and Manner of the late Skirmish . . .* (22 May 1648), BL., E.443(29), pp. 1–8; *The Sad and Bloody Fight at Westminster* (18 May 1648), E.443(17), pp. 1–6; *The particular relation of the skirmishing at Westminster on May 16 . . .* (18 May 1648), E.443(14), no pagination; Bodleian, Clarendon MSS., 31, fos. 83(b)–4; T. May, 'A Breviary of the History of the Parliament of England' (1650), in Maseres, *Select Tracts*, I, 114–15; *Whitelock Diary*, p. 215.

shouting 'High for King Charles, we will have an answer of our Petition . . . or we will pull the Members out of the House by the Ears'. Adorned with white and green ribbons, they made for the House of Commons, knocking down and disarming two sentries and killing a third. According to our admittedly less than impartial informant, when the remaining soldiers demanded that the murderers be handed over, the petitioners again drew their swords and attacked them. The guards would certainly have been overcome but for the arrival on the scene of a party of 500 foot-soldiers sent from Whitehall, who, according to this account, behaved with exemplary restraint, killing only four or five of the tumultuous petitioners and wounding others, two soldiers being killed and several wounded in the whole affray.

Our informant was no doubt selective in his choice of the evidence of depositions to illustrate how 'sidling and pipering Petitioners' turned into 'riotous and peace-disturbing men'. Indeed, as a subsequent Surrey declaration put it, most of the deponents were themselves 'the very actors and executioners; and therefore of small validity to prejudice us with sincere and honest men'.[148] However, there is no reason to believe that all these things were fabrications. Apart from predictable depositions from soldiers about the provocation and violence offered to them, there is one interesting deposition from a civilian who, on his way to Charing Cross, was mistaken by another London gentleman for one of the petitioners, and assured that if the petitioners would remain in town for two or three days, 'we will have many hundreds to joyn with you, God damn me, if we do not, and we will reward you well for your pains'. One soldier from Colonel Barkstead's company gave a vivid description of being assaulted in Palace Yard by petitioners shouting 'Here is one of the souldiers that would have no King', carrying him off to the river stairs before he was released by other soldiers. He identified among his assailants one Thomas Mark, a Surrey man, accompanied by one whom he thought to be a waterman.

The mention of watermen, whose royalist sympathies were notorious, and other Cavaliers among the crowd suggests a strong likelihood not only that the occasion acted as a spur to the metropolitan disaffected, but also that extremist royalist elements may have taken over a peaceful demonstration and turned it into a riot in a manner not unknown in our own times. When Clement Walker mentions persons 'purposely set on work . . . to mix with them [viz. the petitioners] and disorder them', it is not altogether clear whether he refers to royalist extremists or government *agents provocateurs*,[149] but we have it on the

148. *A Remonstrance or Declaration from the County of Surrey* (1648), Codrington pamphlet coll., p. 3.
149. Walker, *Independency*, The Epistle to the Reader, no pagination.

evidence of remarks by the petitioners themselves that from the first 'many of the Kings party joyned with us . . . but . . . they made use of that pretence of petitioning . . . to exasperate as many as they could that . . . they might the easilier accomplish their design of restoring the King to an unlimited power . . .'.[150] It may well have been such royalist extremists who were behind the plan reported by Colonel Barkstead to Fairfax to take revenge by falling upon Colonel Harrison's regiment which was quartered in Surrey.[151]

Of course, there were other versions of events which were as partial in their emphasis on the good behaviour of the petitioners as the foregoing account was on behalf of the soldiers. Clement Walker's disgust at what he saw as the brutality of the soldiers and their plundering as well as physically assaulting peaceable petitioners who were armed only with sticks is paralleled by that of the formal protest and declaration published on the petitioners' behalf on 18 May.[152] On the same day another account entitled *The Sad and Bloody Fight at Westminster* was published,[153] which, while its version of events is nearer to those favouring the soldiers than it is to those of Walker or the Surrey declaration, is certainly more balanced than either in that it eschews attaching indiscriminate blame either to the soldiers or to the petitioners. It describes the peaceful and orderly delivery of the petition to the House of Lords where it received a placatory, if somewhat temporizing, reply. If this account is to be believed, the trouble came over the delivery of the petition to the Lower House which, after adjourning for an hour, re-convened to debate it. During the debate MPs were alarmed by 'a great noyce about the staires and in the Court of Requests and the Hall and other places', and it was only with difficulty that the milling groups of petitioners were persuaded to await the House's decision. For a while they waited, 'merry with a paire of Bagpipes', but the crowd were soon again pressing on the guards, throwing up their

150. *A Declaration of the Knights, Gentlemen and Freeholders of the County of Surrey* (18 May 1648), BL., E.443(8), pp. 4–5. For another suggestive observation, see E.443(14), no pagination.
151. *Clarke Papers*, II, 12–13.
152. Walker, *Independency*, The Epistle to the Reader, no pagination; *A Remonstrance or Declaration* (1648), Codrington pamphlet collection and BL., E.445(8), pp. 3–8. See also *The just measure of a personall Treaty* (July 1648), BL., E.445(39), p. 7, and the account given in a royalist newsletter of 18 May (Bodleian, Clarendon MSS., 31, fos. 83(b)–4). A hostile account describes the petitioners as being armed with 'Swords, Rapiers, Clubs and Quarterstaves, with which they knockt down and slew our men' (BL., E.443(29), p. 6). The Surrey Remonstrance (p. 5) says that to describe the petitioners' riding switches as quarter staffs was 'to make mountains of molehills'. The charges about plundering by the soldiers are admitted by the army's apologists (E.443(29), p. 6, corrected pagination).
153. BL., E.443(17), pp. 1–6.

hats and shouting Cavalier slogans. The guards – or at least those
surviving the affray – were saved only by the arrival of reinforcements
and in the ensuing fracas there were fatal casualties on both sides as well
as many wounded.[154] The House discontinued discussing the petition
after hearing a report from the officer in charge of the guard who
delivered it, if Ludlow is to be believed, bleeding profusely from the
wounds which he had received in trying to quell the tumult.[155] However, this officer's version of the incident was not acceptable to some of
the MPs who had some sympathy with the petitioners, and the House
appointed a committee to examine the truth of the matter.[156] As a
royalist sceptic observed, 'you may be sure none but of their own side
shall . . . testify, & they being the partys, witnesses & judges, no doubt
the Surrey men will be found to have done yᵉ wrong'.[157] Finally, on 22
May, an ordinance against tumultuary petitioning passed both Houses,
and the number of persons bringing petitions to parliament was in
future to be restricted to twenty.[158]

On 20 May both Houses approved proposals presented on the
instructions of the House of Commons by the gentlemen [MPs] of
Surrey 'for allaying all Humours and Discontent in that County'. These
were that the earl of Northumberland should visit Surrey accompanied
by a number of gentlemen nominated by both Houses. The mission was
to convey parliament's condign disapproval of the disorders of 16 May
and its intention of instituting a full inquiry into the incident. However,
its message was not entirely unconciliatory in that it also stressed that
parliament recognized that these disorders 'were contrary to the Desires
and Liking of that County' and that it had no desire to hinder the
presentation of petitions 'in a due and fitting Way'. Indeed, those
petitioners who had comported themselves in such a way on 16 May
and yet had had their horses confiscated were to have them restored. As
to the petition's chief objective, parliament was indeed preoccupied
with the need for a treaty and settlement and the pursuit of such laudable aims could only be hindered by such 'tumultuous Interruptions'.[159]

When Northumberland reported on his mission on 26 May to the
House of Lords, it appeared that the Surrey petitioners were still

154. One account puts the Surrey slain at 8, with 32 wounded, with 2 watermen slain and
      others wounded, and 2 parliamentary soldiers slain, and some wounded. In addition,
      30 Surrey men were taken prisoner, which, it would seem, was when the plundering
      occurred (BL., E.443(14), no pagination).
155. *Ludlow Memoirs*, I, 189.
156. *C.J.*, V, 562.
157. Bodleian, Clarendon MSS., 31, fo. 84.
158. Rushworth, *Historical Collections*, VII, 1122: *A&O.*, I, 1139.
159. *C.J.*, V, 565, 566, 566–7; *L.J.*, X, 272.

pressing for an answer to their petition of 16 May and demanding the punishment of 'those that committed that bloody Murder and other Outrages upon the Petitioners'.[160] While this last grievance went unredressed, the petitioners at least received a formal reply to their petition from the House of Commons on 10 June. The Commons congratulated them on their recent peaceful demeanour – as distinct from that on 16 May? – and politely reminded them of the progress parliament was making towards arranging a treaty with the king and easing the burdens on the people; a development which had been seriously retarded by 'these great Insurrections and Commotions'.[161]

The Sussex petition presented on 7 June need not detain us so long, more especially as details relating to its organization and subscription have already been given elsewhere. Apart from its demand for the discontinuance of garrisons within the county, it had the same basic demands as the Kent and Surrey petitions: a treaty with the king and settlement of the kingdom; the disbandment of the army; observance of known laws; and relief from taxation.[162] The petitioners were accorded a polite reception by both Houses, especially the Lords, who promised their endeavours towards a treaty with the king as well as some relief from taxation as soon as this should prove possible. According to one unsympathetic observer, a taste of the rough treatment meted out to the Surrey petitioners would have been a more appropriate response and might have prevented the disturbances which were brewing around Horsham and Pulborough towards the end of the month 'because their Petition is not answered'.[163]

Thus the agitation over and attempted suppression of the Kent petition issued in a renewal of civil war, the Surrey petitioners were battered at Westminster, and those of Sussex got off relatively lightly despite some punitive action against a few of them. All, however, could ultimately take satisfaction from the fact that, whatever the immediate outcome, their main aim, a treaty with the king (though admittedly not in London), was eventually realized. The petitioners of the City of London could share this satisfaction, in their case without any of the

160. L.J., X, 283. See The Desires of the County of Surrey (25 May 1648), BL., E.445(4), no pagination. For the partial concession to the Surrey demand about soldiers in the shire, see above, p. 67.
161. C.J., V, 592.
162. The humble Petition of the Knights, Gentry, Clergie and Commonalty of the County of Sussex (7 June 1648), BL., 669, f12(42); L.J., X, 315–16; HMC., 7th. Report (House of Lords Calendar 1648), p. 30. On the organization of and subscription to the petition, see above, pp. 121–2.
163. C.J., V, 591; Rushworth, Historical Collections, VII, 1146; The Answer of the Lords and Commons to the Petition . . . of the County of Sussex (9 June 1648), BL., 669, f12(45); A Letter from Horsum [sic] in Sussex (June 1648), BL., 669, f12(60).

hardships inflicted on the other petitioners. Between 22 March, when the ball had been set rolling by the Essex petitioners, and the end of August, there were as many as eleven petitions from London sources for a personal treaty, though, as in the case of the county petitions, many of them coupled this with other demands. Three of these petitions were official City petitions from the Lord Mayor, aldermen and Common Council, and it is noteworthy that the first of these was not submitted until 1 June, months after the Essex petition and days after those of Surrey and Kent. This petition has already been noted as mainly significant in accompanying another petition from divers citizens making some distinctly contentious demands as well as asking for a treaty to be arranged.[164] Another private petition to Common Council and forwarded by it to parliament was made on 4 July by officers of the London trained bands, and, while this was chiefly concerned with militia matters, it also asked for a treaty with the king in London.[165]

The cautious and measured approach of the City fathers, although it was ultimately to bear fruit in the Treaty of Newport, irritated some of the hotter-spirited Londoners. As early as 3 June a paper was circulating among the freemen of the City urging them to press a more positive approach on the Lord Mayor and his colleagues whose alleged pusillanimity it strongly deplored. Along with the inevitable high Presbyterian religious proposals, the paper demanded that the king be brought up to Westminster to treat without preconditions of any sort.[166] But, in contrast with their behaviour almost a year earlier, the City fathers were now proceeding with studied moderation. In these circumstances they were even less likely to accede to a rumoured suggestion from the insurgent sailors that the City should join them in a petition for a personal treaty with Charles I.[167]

An additional source of complaint for those who bewailed what they saw as the excessive caution of the municipal authorities was the ruling obtained by the latter from parliament debarring all petitions from city sources which had not gone through Common Council. Despairing of

164.	C.J., V, 581; L.J., X, 294, 295–6: CLRO., Jor. 40, fos. 278(b)–9, 280; HMC., 7th. Report (House of Lords Cal., 1648), p. 28; Two Petitions to . . . the Lords and Commons (1 June 1648), BL., E.445(24), pp. 1–5; Parliamentary History, XVII, 194–7. See above, p. 124.
165.	CLRO., Jor. 40, fos. 283, 284, 284(b)–5; C.J., V, 624; Rushworth, Historical Collections, VII, 1176; Two Petitions Presented To . . . The Lords and Commons (4 July 1648), BL., E.451(4), pp. 1–5. The House of Lords expressed cautious approbation of the petition. The House of Commons agreed to what concerned militia matters but made no mention of a treaty.
166.	The humble Desires of the Loyall hearted, wel-affected Freemen of the City of London (3 June 1648), BL., 669, f12(39).
167.	The Reasons ye Navy gieve for their Resolution (17 June 1648), BL., E.448(3). MS. in Thomason's hand.

decisive action from that body, some citizens sought a remedy in Common Hall, whose membership comprised all the freemen of the City. But they feared a possible postponement of the annual midsummer meeting of Common Hall to prevent it from being used for this end.[168] However, in the event it did meet as usual on 24 June, when it added to its normal function of electing the next Lord Mayor and other City officials that of receiving and approving a request for an official City petition for a personal treaty. A committee was appointed by Common Hall to draft such a petition, which, after some cavilling about details, Common Council approved on 26 June. The petition was presented to and approved by both Houses of Parliament on the following day. It requested a personal treaty with the king to which the Scots should be invited to send representatives, even though the Scottish army of the Engagement was then on the verge of invading England; and the preservation of both king and parliament and the purity of religion, which, in this context, of course, meant Presbyterian religion.[169]

The last and most forthright City petition in favour of a treaty was presented to parliament on 8 August. With its additional demands for, *inter alia*, the disbandment of the army, the restoration of the rule of law and the observance of the Self Denying Ordinance, this is the nearest the City came to the more peremptory demands of the Surrey and Kent petitioners. It may be that the City governors felt that the quiescence of the City through the summer months had both sufficiently emphasized its reliability and strengthened its hand. The petition was well received in the Upper House, but had a rough passage in the Commons, where John Weaver, the radical Independent MP for Stamford, alleged that it indicated that the citizens 'were become malignant . . . and intended to desert the Parliament', while Colonel Harvey complained that the many good men who had mistakenly subscribed it had been 'forc'd by a Company of Knaves'. But others were found to speak in its favour, and the Commons answered the petitioners by emphasizing parliament's endeavours to bring about a treaty and its hopes that the king would agree to one.[170]

168. *The necessity of the speedy calling of a Common Hall . . .* (21 June 1648), BL., E.449(10), especially pp. 4–5. See also *To all the Honest, Wise and Grave Citizens of London . . .* (23 June 1648), BL., 669, f12(54).

169. CLRO., Jor. 40, fos. 281(b)–2; *A Petition presented at a Common Hall* (24 June 1648), BL., E.449(35), pp. 4–6; *L.J.*, X, 349–50; *C.J.*, V, 613–14; HMC., *7th. Report (House of Lords Calendar 1648)*, p. 33; Rushworth, *Historical Collections*, VII, 1167–8; *Parliamentary History*, XVII, 264–7.

170. *L.J.*, X, 424, 427; *C.J.*, V, 665–6; Rushworth, *Historical Collections*, VII, 1220, 1222; *The humble Petition of the Lord Major [sic], Aldermen and Commons . . .* (8 August 1648), BL., E.457(10), pp. 1–6, also E.458(7); *Parliamentary History*, XVII, 387–91, 393–5. The petition also stressed its concern for the settlement of the church according to the Covenant and the relief of Ireland.

There is insufficient space here to do more than mention in passing the other London petitions asking for a treaty along with the redress of the petitioners' own peculiar grievances. In late June there were such petitions from the commanders and mariners of shipping on the Thames and from both the Wardens and the younger brethren of Trinity House;[171] and in the last two weeks of July, from the London watermen, a body never deficient in royalist zeal, whose trade had greatly suffered since the migration of the court in 1642, and who were, as one pamphlet puts it, motivated less by optimism about the likely success of a treaty than by 'Loyalty to their wronged Soveraigne';[172] from some inhabitants of Westminster, Southwark and the suburbs, who also sought a unified metropolitan militia;[173] and, finally, from some reformadoes who were also seeking their arrears of pay.[174]

Not all of the petitions from London, as from provincial, sources at this time were of a conservative nature. At least two of those presented between the beginning of June and the end of August can be described as non-partisan,[175] while it is not easy to characterize the petition which was forwarded by Common Council to parliament on 31 August. This petition's request for the removal of 'jealousies and present distempers and obtaining a right understanding between Parliament, City, and Army and Kingdom' is too vague to admit of classification in political terms.[176] Five petitions may confidently be described as radical – or, at least radical Independent – in politics, and it is significant that none of these came down emphatically against a treaty. Indeed, the only one in which a treaty figures prominently at all, coming in mid-August from people describing themselves with the inevitable adjective 'well-affected', is even mildly supportive of the idea of a treaty in the Isle of Wight, while being conscious of the danger that parliament could be diverted from pursuit of its central war

171. *L.J.*, X, 351–2; Rushworth, *Historical Collections*, VII, 1169; *Parliamentary History*, XVII, 269–73.

172. *L.J.*, X, 385; *C.J.*, V, 639–40: Rushworth, *Historical Collections*, VII, 1196: *A Speedy Cure to Open the Eyes of the Blinde and the Eares of the Deafe Citizens* . . . (4 August 1648), BL., E.456(28), p. 8.

173. *C.J.*, V, 638–9; Rushworth, *Historical Collections*, VII, 1192–3; *A Petition . . . by the Inhabitants of the City of Westminster, the Hambletts of the Tower, the Burrough of Southwark and Parts adjacent* (17 July 1648), BL., E.453(31), pp. 3–6.

174. *HMC., 13th. Rep. App. iv, pt. i*, p. 490. The reformadoes petitioned again on 8 August in support of the City's petition of that date (Rushworth, *Historical Collections*, VII, 1220–1; *The Petition of 8000 Reduced Officers and Souldiers* (8 August 1648), BL., E.457(29), pp. 1–6).

175. Petitions of 30 June and 15 July by Common Council against the proposed imposition on coal at Newcastle (CLRO., Jor. 40, fos. 283, 287–7(b)).

176. CLRO., Jor. 40, fos. 295(b)–6; Rushworth, *Historical Collections*, VII, 1248; *Three Petitions* (31 August 1648), BL., E.461(23), pp. 1–3.

aims.[177] Whatever its reservations about the possible dangers of treating with the king, this petition certainly cannot be regarded as the opposite extreme to the enthusiastic petitions for a treaty from conservative London petitioners over these three months.

It was only when the treaty had become an established fact that the petitioning scene changes to become dominated by petitions of a diametrically opposite tendency to those which had prevailed over the past three months. Beginning with the radical petition of 11 September from some self-styled well-affected persons of London,[178] and finding further expression on 13 September in the Oxfordshire petition denouncing those who 'cry *Peace, Peace*, but seek after *Blood*',[179] and those in October from Leicestershire, Newcastle-upon-Tyne, York and Somerset,[180] the petitions which now hold the stage are those seeking to abort the treaty and demanding the bringing of delinquents to justice. Significantly, a petition signed by 309 of the inevitably well-affected of Nottinghamshire, which can be dated from internal evidence to after Pride's Purge, identifies those who had supported a treaty with adherents of the insurgents and the Scottish invaders in the Second Civil War.[181] Doubtless such an identification was made for partisan political ends and may even have been believed by those who made it. But, as a description of the temper and aspirations of those who petitioned for a renewal of negotiations with Charles I in 1648, it is a palpable oversimplification of a complex phenomenon. That the aims of some of these petitioners had points in common with those of Cavalier insurgents is clear from the foregoing account. That recourse to force of arms in the event of the failure of peaceful petitioning was also on the cards in Essex, Kent, Sussex and perhaps Surrey is no less clear. Nevertheless, the main factor which converted petitioners into active belligerents was undoubtedly the repressive response of the government, and especially

177. *The Humble Petition of divers Well-affected Citizens of London* (August 1648), BL., 669, f12(106). Thomason's notes on his copy describe some of the petitioners as Independents, Levellers and sectaries.

178. *C.J.*, VI, 18; Rushworth, *Historical Collections*, VII, 1257–8; *Leveller Manifestoes*, pp. 283–90; *Leveller Tracts*, pp. 148–55; *Parliamentary History*, XVII, 451–60. The petition is commended and parliament's attitude to it criticized in the pamphlet *Fruitfull England like to Become a Barren Wilderness* (17 October 1648), BL., E.467(36), p. 9. For royalist condemnation of it, see *Mercurius Melancholicus, Number 56* (18/25 September 1648), E.464(38), pp. 175–6; *Mercurius Elencticus, Number 45* (27 September/4 October 1648), E.465(33), no pagination.

179. Rushworth, *Historical Collections*, VII, 1261. For a royalist criticism of this petition, see BL., E.465(33), no pagination.

180. For the Leicestershire petition, *The Humble Petition of the Committee, Gentry and Ministry and other the inhabitants of the County of Leicester* (2 October 1648), BL., E.465(36), pp. 3–7. For Newcastle and York and Somerset petitions, *Parliamentary History*, XVIII, 30–2, and on the latter, see above, pp. 117–18.

181. HLRO., MP. [1648].

of its provincial agencies, to the petitioning campaigns; a factor which finds its most striking manifestation in Kent. To that extent the government played into the hands of Cavalier insurgents and inflated the numbers of those in arms against it. The case of the City of London, on the other hand, demonstrates how the main aim of the conservative petitioners of 1648 could be achieved without recourse to force. Just as it can be argued that their petitioning campaign achieved its end when the Vote of No Addresses was revoked and the Treaty of Newport set up, so did the subsequent radical petitioning campaign against that treaty also achieve its end. That it did so, however, was due to the purge of parliament by Colonel Pride rather than to the response of a free parliament to these petitions.

V

THE ARMY AND
COUNTER-REVOLUTION

... it is not the desire of the Army to make themselves Masters of the Parliament, but to make the Parliament Masters of themselves.

'Queries whether the Army ought to insist upon, their Charge against those persons they have accused' (June 1647), Oxford, Worcester College, Clarke MSS., 41, fo. 60

... all the burthens of the Land must still be laid to the charge of the Army ... because the Army must be made odious, before the People would be induced to rise, or a cleare way be made for the King.

Londons New Colours displaid (July 1648), BL., E.452(25), p. 3

Nulla fides pietasque viris qui castra sequentur.

Ardua Regni: Or XII Arduous Doubts of great Concernment to the Kingdome (25 February 1648), BL., E.429(5), p. 10

A brutal, licentious and sectarian soldiery

Complaints against the violence of soldiers to civilians do not cease with the end of the First Civil War. Such violence was often indiscriminately directed against both ex-Cavaliers and supporters of parliament alike and must be accounted an important factor in the alienation of many of the latter as well as the hardened irreconcilability of the former. The closing months of the war had seen many such incidents. Sent down to Reading on parliamentary business in March 1646, William Ball, MP for Abingdon, produced a sorry tale of violent behaviour including the murder of one loyal parliamentarian countryman by soldiers of his own side. Ball concluded that the mutual antipathy of soldiers and countrymen was such that 'we are like to heare little other then killing

& robbery if there be not a speedie supply of money for the souldierie'.[1] The disorderly conduct of Edward Massey's brigade in the West Country had earned it a particular notoriety in the closing year of the war. In June 1646 the Wiltshire county committee complained that 'none could travail nor remain in their houses with safety', and Lord General Fairfax himself found it difficult to put into effect parliament's order to disband the brigade, whose soldiers, for want of pay, resorted to indiscriminate levies and wanton plunder.[2]

During the war some country people had reacted positively to such provocation by support for the Clubmen Associations in some counties including Wiltshire, and there were also lesser examples of spirited resistance such as one mentioned by Ball in his report from Berkshire.[3] The government might argue hopefully that military disorders were inevitable, if regrettable, products of wartime conditions, and that the coming of peace would quickly put an end to them. It is one of the prime causes of the growth of disaffection and alienation which is crucial to the subject of this book that this was not to be so. Indeed, the continued violence of soldiers was the more intolerable, 'there being no visible *Enemy* to oppose them'. Such complaints were to multiply down to the outbreak of the Second Civil War in 1648, when at least a 'visible Enemy' reappeared, its forces no doubt swollen by the proliferation of such incidents.[4] Although the outrages were not always perpetrated by proper soldiers, but, like those reported by William Cope, sheriff of Oxfordshire, on 4 May 1647, rather by 'divers Persons who call themselves Soldiers, and rob and spoil the Country',[5] many of them were undoubtedly the work of authentic soldiers whose pay was heavily in arrears. Enough of these cases, especially of attacks on magistrates and county committeemen, were reported in an earlier chapter[6] to underline the point that if the magistracy was not safe from attacks, no-one could be. They were welcome grist to the mill of royalist propagandists such as the newswriter *Mercurius Elencticus*, who in early January 1648 observed that there had never been 'so many and such unheard of *Murders*, *Robberies* and *Rapes* . . . as at this present'.[7]

---

1. Bodleian, Tanner MSS., 60, fo. 491.
2. Cary, *Memorials*, I, 101–2 and note; Whitelock, *Memorials*, p. 215 (18 June). For a similar complaint on 8 July against Massey's soldiers, from Dorset, see Bodleian, Tanner MSS., 59, fo. 392.
3. Bodleian, Tanner MSS., 60, fo. 491.
4. See *The Army Anatomized* (4 December 1647), BL., E.419(6), pp. 8–9; *Mercurius Elencticus, Number 12* (5/12 January 1648), BL., E.422(25), p. 50; 'Memoirs of Denzil Lord Holles', in Maseres, *Select Tracts*, I, 232.
5. *C.J.*, V, 161–2; *L.J.*, IX, 179, 180.
6. See above, pp. 98–9.
7. *Mercurius Elencticus, Number 12* (12 January 1648), BL., E.422(25), p. 50. See also *Mercurius Elencticus, Number 6* (29 December/5 January 1647/8), E.421(6), p. 44.

Such incidents may well have multiplied with the onset of the Second Civil War. On 16 August 1648, for instance, six eye-witnesses testified to the devastation wrought by some (probably irregular) soldiers at the house of Sir Humphrey Foster at Aldermaston in Berkshire. When visited by ten or a dozen soldiers demanding quarter, Sir Humphrey politely insisted that the Lord General had specifically exempted him from quartering though he expressed his willingness to find alternative quarters both for them and for others in their regiment, regaling them with beer before they went away. But the impression that they had departed well satisfied was to be rudely contradicted by their return in much greater numbers – some sixty or eighty, the witnesses stated – when Sir Humphrey and some of his guests were at dinner. After wounding the butler, they burst into the dining-room with swords drawn and pistols cocked, and forty or so men quartered in the house overnight, departing around four o'clock in the morning, and taking with them horses and horse furniture from the stables and park and arms from the house. Three of the miscreants, a captain, a lieutenant and a corporal, were later bound over to stand trial at the assizes for a subsequent robbery in Wiltshire.[8] Indeed, no-one, however exalted, was safe from the soldiers' attentions, as witness the complaints of the earl of Leicester in September 1648, though admittedly only against the insolence, not actual violence, of the soldiers quartered at Sevenoaks near his house at Penshurst Place.[9]

It seems likely that the known cases of misdemeanours by soldiers which occasioned disciplinary action against them are no more than the merest tip of an iceberg. On 30 December 1647 Major General John Lambert, the able commander of the army in the north, established special machinery for dealing with the complaints of local inhabitants against disorderly soldiers.[10] Lambert's concern has already been remarked in connection with cases relating to quartering, which in fact form a substantial proportion of those offences punished by the Council of War meeting at Ripon, Knaresborough, York and Pontefract.[11] But there were many other cases, among them the wounding of an inhabitant of Ripon by a drunken corporal and the rescuing of an arrested outlaw and participation in a riot at Stokesdale, where a hapless magistrate was dragged from his shop and threatened with his life.

8. Bodleian, Tanner MSS., 57, fos. 199–9(b).
9. Cal.SPD. 1648–9, p. 292. The Derby House committee ordered the Kent Committee to punish the offenders.
10. A Declaration of the Northern Army (1 January 1648), Oxford, Codrington pamphlet coll., pp. 10–13; West Yorkshire Archive Service, Wakefield RO., MSS. C 469/2, no foliation.
11. See above, pp. 64–5.

Punishments varied between execution (although one corporal guilty of murder was reprieved by Lambert) to periods of imprisonment on bread and water and standing in the pillory and being whipped through the streets afterwards.[12] On 29 January 1648 Lambert reported a deteriorating situation both as to the impoverished condition of his soldiers and the volume of complaints against them, and two days afterwards he decreed that soldiers 'of deboyst or dishonest conversation' should be among those to be disbanded first.[13]

Whether plans for demobilization were likely to be any more successful early in 1648 than they had been in the spring and early summer of the previous year was indeed a question. In March 1647 Holles and his parliamentary Presbyterian associates had been confident that they were on to a good thing in terms of their own popularity in the hard-pressed country, when they planned to disband the vast bulk of that part of the army which would not engage for the Irish service. However, the behaviour even of those dutiful soldiers who did so engage was often less than exemplary, as is revealed by local complaints against soldiers in transit for Ireland in Lancashire, Somerset and Devon in March and May 1647.[14] Nevertheless, it was the disobedience and disorders of those who refused to go along with Holles's plans and resisted disbandment which excited the most unfavourable comment. Resistance to disbandment became connected in the popular mind with lawless outrages such as the case of the dissident soldiers who, clamorously resisting the persuasions of some officers about parliament's votes and declarations about disbandment, seized on the ammunition wagons and surgeons' chests and later broke into a house at Braintree stealing £500. Although they were apprehended later, they were subsequently released by the very soldiers into whose custody they had been put. In the view of one parliamentary committee all these and other disorders could have been avoided by the sending down of two months' pay for the soldiers.[15] However, there were cases of officers and soldiers who had taken the wages paid to them as a condition of their disbandment, but subsequently refused to disband and continued to exact free quarter and levy money for their maintenance.[16]

---

12. Wakefield R.O., MSS. C 469/1, 2, passim.
13. *A Proclamation Published by Major Generall Lambert* (January 1648), BL., E.424(11), pp. 1–6.
14. *Cal.SPD. 1645–7*, p. 532; *L.J.*, IX, 171, 172. The soldiers of Sir Arthur Lofthouse's regiment en route for Ireland claimed they were 'beat out of the Countie' by local countrymen around Bristol (Oxford, Worcester College, Clarke MSS., 41, fo. 32).
15. Bodleian, Tanner MSS., 58, fos. 127, 129.
16. See, for example, Fairfax's response to a complaint of the Devonshire county committee and JPs on 9 November 1647 (*The Copie of a Letter from Sir Thomas Fairfax* (November 1647), BL., E.413(12), pp. 2–6).

Even more alarming than the army's defiance over disbandment was its increasing assumption in the course of the summer of 1647 of a more or less independent political role. Manifested by such things as its seizure of the king, its Solemn Engagement of 5 June and Declaration of 14 June,[17] its attempted impeachment of eleven leading Presbyterian MPs,[18] and its willingness to receive petitions from civilians,[19] the army's new pretensions profoundly shocked conservative-minded parliamentarians.[20] Further factors heightening this alarm were the connected attributes of the allegedly lowly social composition and religious heterodoxy of a large part of the officer corps of the New Model Army.[21] Thus a lengthy anti-army pamphlet of December 1647 deplores both the alleged fact that '*the Mechanick Agitators of the Army* are . . . become Lords and Princes over us all', anticipating Denzil Holles's celebrated observation that 'The wisest of men saw it to be a great evil that Servants should ride on Horses'. In turn the pamphlet went on to deplore the evident connection between religious radicalism and social levelling as manifested in the army. Influenced by radical sectarian divines like Dell, Saltmarsh and Hugh Peter, the army had become a principal force in the pursuit of 'their *great Design of Universal Toleration* of all Opinions, *Parity and Community* of all mens estates . . . and *Liberty of Conscience in all Religions*'.[22] To the by now inveterate Presbyterian William Prynne the army had come to resemble the 'Rebellious popular Army' of Jack Cade, always a potent image of social disruption. Soldiers, and more especially their officers, observed another conservative parliamentarian, 'whereof many are risen from mean trades and estates', had no desire to revert to their pre-war 'low conditions'.[23]

No less subject to conservative disapproval than mechanic officers and agitators were mechanic preachers, a phenomenon increasingly, though by no means exclusively, associated with the army. On 26 April

---

17. The Solemn Engagement is printed in *Leveller Manifestoes*, pp. 146–51; the Declaration or Representation in *Leveller Tracts*, pp. 52–63. Neither, of course, is in any sense a Leveller document.
18. On the army and the eleven members, see below, pp. 170–77, 178.
19. On this, see above, especially pp. 128–32.
20. See, for example, *A Religious Retreat Sounded To a Religious Army* (August 1647), BL., E.404(34), especially pp. 1–4, 11–12, 17–20; *The Lawfulnesse of the Late Passages of the Army* (June 1647), E.394(12), passim.
21. For a modern account questioning how far these stereotypes were in fact true, see M.A. Kishlansky, *The Rise of the New Model Army* (Cambridge, 1979), pp. 39–46, 50, 62–6, 218–21. For a summary, see Ashton, *Civil War*, pp. 231–3.
22. *The Army Anatomized* (4 December 1647), BL., E.419(6), pp. 4, 19; 'Memoirs of Denzil Lord Holles', in Maseres, *Select Tracts*, I, 191.
23. [William Prynne], *IX Queries* (June 1647), BL., E.394(1), p. 4; Nathaniel Ward, *To the High and Honourable Parliament . . . The Humble Petitions, Serious Suggestions* (2 May 1648), BHPC., p. 24.

1645 parliament had banned preachers who had not been properly ordained, and Lord General Fairfax was commanded to take due care that this order was rigorously observed in the army. The order was renewed on 31 December 1646 in response to a City of London petition complaining of its widespread disregard, especially 'by preaching Soldiers and others who infect the Flock . . . with strange and dangerous Errors'.[24] But complaints continued.[25] Soldiers in pulpits were in fact simply the most striking manifestation of the army's growing reputation as a receptacle for sectaries of the wildest and most subversive kind; in a social, no less than a religious, sense. According to Denzil Holles, the army's most influential opponent in 1647, such persons had come to constitute a majority among the soldiers, and committed one outrage after another, including interrupting and even pulling down orthodox ministers during their sermons and getting into their pulpits themselves.[26] In essence Holles's picture is not very different from the standard royalist denunciation of 'an irreligious, bloodthirsty, plundering Army of Sectaries'.[27]

Religious heterodoxy was a frightening enough phenomenon *per se*, but its terrors were the greater to contemporary men of substance because, rightly or wrongly, they associated it with socially and politically subversive tendencies towards the levelling of estates and the threat to order and magistracy.[28] But, for a time at least in 1647, orthodox Presbyterians also entertained other, and in a sense diametrically opposite, fears about the army. These fears were given apparent substance by the army's leniency to the king after taking him from Holdenby on 4 June, more particularly in the matter of allowing him the use of his own chaplains and the Book of Common Prayer and taking a less severe view of episcopacy in the peace terms favoured by the army, the Heads of the Proposals.[29] Was there indeed a danger that the army might 'set up what God and the State have pulled downe, and pull downe what hath been set up with much paines and prayer'? Other threatening portents were that in some places where the army had been quartered the use of the Prayer Book had been restored and formerly extruded Anglican ministers reinstated:

24. BL., Add. MSS., 22,620, fos. 24, 104(b)–5; Add. MSS., 31,116, fo. 295(b); *C.J.*, V, 34–5; Rushworth, *Historical Collections*, VI, 143–4; *Parliamentary History*, XV, 222–3, 279. On the petition, see above, pp. 134–5.
25. See, e.g., *Clarke Papers*, I, 4; Nathaniel Ward, op. cit., p. 26.
26. Maseres, *Select Tracts*, I, 230–1.
27. *The Royal Diurnall . . . Number 5* (22/29 August 1648), BL., E.461(13), no pagination.
28. See, e.g., *The Army Anatomized*, p. 4; *The Petition of Right of the Freeholders and Free-men of the Kingdom of England* (8 January 1648), BL., E.422(9), p. 15; *The Earnest and passionate Petition of divers thousands . . .* (3 February 1648), E.425(10), pp. 4–5; Nathaniel Ward, op. cit., p. 25.
29. On the Heads of the Proposals, see above, pp. 24, 25–8.

This doth utterly blast the esteeme of your Army in the hearts of good men, who conclude that your way cannot be of God; surely when Hee gives the Kingdome to the Saints, hee will not suffer them to give such large toleration to erronious opinions.[30]

That such 'erronious opinions' included Anglican as well as sectarian beliefs helps to point up the fact that there was a perceived danger on the part of the parliamentary Presbyterians that the army might become a potent instrument in the revival of royalism in return for a substantial measure of that toleration of which Presbyterians so strongly disapproved. To discount this danger because it ultimately came to nought on account of Charles I's vacillation and duplicity would be resorting to hindsight. It is therefore important to give it some attention before turning to more familiar aspects of the army's challenge to the parliamentary Presbyterians.

A passing scare: the army and the revival of royalism

The familiar notion of the king's leading a counter-revolutionary force composed of army deserters, city militiamen, forces diverted from the Irish service and re-enlisted reformadoes, which will feature prominently in the last two sections of this chapter, had not been the only possible scenario in the revival of royalist aspirations in 1647. As early as Easter week a petition had been presented to the king at Holdenby by an army officer who claimed – no doubt with great exaggeration – that its contents represented the views of the army as a whole. Its purport was that the king had only to put himself in the hands of the army, and the soldiers would see to it that he was restored 'to his throne, Crowne & dignity'. The king is reported as wisely declining the invitation, refusing to take any action which might 'engage our poore people in another Warre, too much bloud hath binne shed already'. Characteristically, however, Charles seems to have been unwilling to shut this particular door irrevocably, keeping his options open by letting the soldiers know that once he had been fully restored to power, he would 'auspiciously looke upon their Loyall intentions'.[31]

In the following month of May there was widespread alarm among senior army officers at the use to which their enemies, both in and outside parliament, were putting this petition, copies of which had come into their hands; and, in particular, at the rumoured danger that

---

30. BL., E.404(34), pp. 15–16. For a similar observation, see E.419(6), pp. 11–13.
31. Bodleian, Tanner MSS., 58, fo. 46.

the army might itself become a counter-revolutionary force and the instrument of a revived royalism:

> And that the Army was no longer a new Modell but had 4,000 Cavaleers in it . . . that the King and Cavaleers have their . . . whole dependence upon this Army.[32]

Fantastic as such fears may appear in the light of our knowledge of the subsequent course of events, they persisted and were intensified following the army's abduction of the king from Holdenby on 4 June. Only two days after this event, Charles is reported to have told an astonished Fairfax, who visited him at the house of Sir John Cutts at Childesley Hall near Cambridge, as the Lord General took his leave of him, 'S^r, I have as good Interest in the Army as you, by which I plainely saw the broken reede he leand on'.[33]

As to the increasing possibility of rapport between ex-Cavalier and ex-Roundhead soldiers, Clarendon plausibly suggests that one possible issue for the meeting of minds was parliament's failure to observe meticulously some of the more generous articles of surrender which had been granted to royalist garrisons by Roundhead commanders during the First Civil War. That parliament often proceeded 'with more severity than was agreeable to justice and to the intention of the articles' could be conceived as no less derogatory to the honour of the victors than to the interests of the vanquished.[34] Certainly there is more than a grain of truth in Clarendon's suggestion that the sharp change in attitude to the king on the part of the dominant Presbyterian party in parliament which was ultimately reflected in its plans in July for him to come to London to treat may be attributable to Presbyterian apprehension 'that the army would make a firm conjunction with the king, and unite with his party, of which there was much show'.[35]

32. *A Perfect and True Copy of the Severall Grievances of the Army* (May 1647), BL., E.490(3), sig A2^v, here citing 'a person of eminence' (the earl of Pembroke?) addressing the Common Council of London. See also *Divers Papers from the Army* (15 May 1647), E.388(18), p. 6: *Nine Proposals by Way of Interrogation* (2 July 1647), E.396(8), p. 7; *Clarke Papers*, I, 24, 25–6. 4,000 is also the number of Cavaliers mentioned by Thomas Juxon, who describes the fuss about the petition as a mere fabrication of the army's enemies (Dr Williams's Library, MS. 24.50, fos. 107–7(b)). On all these allegations, see Woolrych, *Soldiers and Statesmen*, pp. 69–71.
33. West Yorkshire Archive Service, Leeds City RO., Bacon Frank MSS., BF/13/7, fo. 183.
34. Clarendon, *Rebellion*, IV, 236. As late as 5 May 1649, the House of Commons set up a committee to consider the grievances of those who had not had the articles under which they had surrendered properly observed and an act was passed for the relief of such persons in the following month (Whitelock, *Memorials*, pp. 386, 394 (sub dates 5 May, 18 June 1649)).
35. Clarendon, *Rebellion*, IV, 230.

The eloquent appeal of the royalist ex-judge David Jenkins to the army to earn the gratitude of posterity by espousing the king's cause has already been mentioned in another context.[36] During the summer of 1647 the dangers that this might happen were sharply underlined by a report reaching the House of Commons on 21 June that the current Cavalier rising in Glamorgan, whose leaders gloried at being at one with Jenkins's views, had been sparked off 'under pretence that the King and Sir Thomas Fairefaxe's Army are joined'.[37] One notorious royalist delinquent, Sir Thomas Lunsford, writing on 16 June from imprisonment in the Tower, emphasized the desirability of an alliance between king and army, urging the soldiers to take their stand on more fundamental principles than mere soldierly grievances such as pay and indemnity. For, Lunsford continued, if the army settled with parliament for anything less than the full restoration of the king, they would have no assurance – even if they got rid of their Presbyterian enemies in parliament – that the City of London would not raise another force to control the army and maintain the Presbyterian hegemony in the country.[38]

Aware of these dangers, Presbyterians sought to disabuse both the army and the king about the pretended advantages of their grotesque association. Was it really in the soldiers' interest or to their credit, asked one pamphleteer, 'that Judge Jenkins and other desperate Malignants should bee the chiefe Vindicators of your proceedings?' Nor should the king be deceived about allying with the soldiers, for 'tis notoriously known how their Principles are directly against Monarchy', and the price of their alliance would be royal support for the notoriously republican (as it was alleged) Independents in parliament, a condition which, at this point, seems to have been viewed with much greater horror by the parliamentary Presbyterians than it was by the king.[39] Such views, which were zealously put out by many Presbyterians, were not in essence different from those expressed by some royalists who argued that the army had taken the king from Holdenby 'for danger, not from danger'.[40] Presbyterian alarmists claimed to have derived their information about the army's aims from persons close to Cromwell and the radical Colonel Thomas Rainsborough. From such sources they

---

36. See above, p. 110; and D. Jenkins, *An apology for the army touching* (1647), BHPC., pp. 1–3, 8–10. For a less tactful criticism of the army for failing to restore the king to his full rights, see *Certaine Observations on that Letter written to the Two Houses from the Army* (8 July 1647), BL., E.398(10), especially pp. 1–3.
37. *C.J.*, V, 218. On the Glamorgan rising, see below, pp. 341–6.
38. *An Answer to a Letter Written from Cambridge* (16 June 1647), BL., E.397(5), pp. 1–4.
39. *Works of darkness brought to light* (1647), BHPC., especially pp. 10, 19–20.
40. *The Mistake of the Times* (July 1647), BL., E.399(18), p. 3.

learned – or so they alleged – 'that the Designe of taking the King [viz. from Holdenby] was not to joyn with him against the Parliament . . . but to bring him to Justice'.[41] Indeed, Vice-Admiral William Batten, a close ally of the parliamentary Presbyterians, was reported in the House of Lords on 16 September as saying that the army would eventually cut off the king's head.[42]

In repudiating such allegations the army grandees had to steer a very delicate course between support for the king's restoration and respect for the liberties of parliament and people. They certainly could not content themselves with emphasizing, as they did in a pamphlet of 26 June, that their endeavours 'were only for the stating of his Majesty in his Royall Rights and preservation of the peace of the Kingdome'.[43] Given Presbyterian smears about their regicidal and republican intentions, they had of necessity to stress this aim, but at the same time they had to beware of the opposite extreme. Thus their genuine concern for the interests of the king and his followers must not, as a newsletter from army headquarters at Reading on 17 July emphasized, 'prejudice the subjects liberty. Monarchy may be so settled, but not to be hurtfull as formerly.' The same source was also at great pains to stress both the limits imposed by the army on the visits to the king by ex-Cavaliers, where 'civility is connived at, but that party not comply'd with', and, above all that there was no question of the countenancing of the enlisting of ex-Cavaliers in the army.[44] Similarly, a pamphlet published in mid-August, after the army's occupation of London, firmly maintained that, while the soldiers 'never took up Armes to destroy the King' but to rescue him from the disastrous influence of his evil counsellors, they certainly had no intention of participating in a revival of militant Cavalierism.[45]

At this stage of proceedings the king, while not abandoning his double game of playing off the army and the parliament against one another, may have been far more responsive than anti-army observers suggest to the army grandees' plans for a settlement which would have involved some degree of royal rapprochement with the parliamentary Independents. According to the prejudiced and slanted later account of Cromwell's former subordinate officer and later bitter opponent, Major

41. *Some Queries propounded to the Common Councell and Citizens of London* (July 1647), BL., E.400(26), p. 3. See also *A Declaration of the Officers and Armies illegal, iniurious proceedings* (8 July 1647), E.397(8), passim and especially p. 8.
42. *L.J.*, IX, 433. Evidence of words spoken at Sandwich on 6 September. Another witness, however, stated that Batten merely said 'That he feared the Army would not deal fairly with the King or words to that Effect'.
43. *The Last Votes from the Armie* (26 June 1647), BL., E.394(10), no pagination.
44. *Clarke Papers*, I, 215–16.
45. *Vox Militaris* (August 1647), BL., E.401(24), pp. 10–11, 15.

Robert Huntingdon, Ireton had assured Charles that the army 'would purge and purge, and never leave purging the Houses, till they had made them of such a Temper as should do his Majesty's Business'.[46] It is only fair to add that what Ireton and his colleagues conceived of as the king's business in this context was the establishment of a just and secure settlement along the lines of the Heads of the Proposals. Some royalist observers, however, were expressing great optimism about the prospects for the king, despite the defeat of the counter-revolutionary coup of July and the army's occupation of London. A source close to the king at his house at Oatlands in Surrey observed that Fairfax 'useth his utmost endeavors for the speedy settling of his Dread Soveraign in his just Rights and Authority'. With the Lord General's co-operation the king would soon be back in Whitehall to establish a lasting peace.[47]

What exactly the last writer saw as Fairfax's role is uncertain. Did he see him as the propounder of peace terms which he was prepared to negotiate and revise in the king's favour? Or as something more sinister? Was the counter-revolutionary mantle to pass from the City, the reformadoes and Holles's militant Presbyterians to the Lord General and his army? On 9 August, when passing through Croydon in Surrey, Fairfax was presented with some appropriately styled 'uncertain Proposals' which invited him, as Judge Jenkins had done earlier, to fulfil his manifest destiny by bringing the king in honour and glory to London, enabling a lasting peace to be established on the only possible and viable basis: the restoring of the king to his full regal authority. For bringing this about, the Lord General would ever be honoured as 'the beginner, so the perfecter and finisher, of our Peace and Happinesse'.[48] With such wild notions in the air it is hardly surprising that in the army's fiery Remonstrance of 18 August designed to justify to a lukewarm parliament its action in occupying London and quelling counter-revolution there, its leaders were anxious to draw a sharp distinction between, on the one hand, the aim of the London counter-revolutionaries of 26 July to bring the king to London where he would serve as a rallying point for those who were prepared to countenance a second civil war as a means of achieving their ends; and, on the other, the soldiers' desire to see the king brought back to London, but 'on such Terms . . . as may render both him and the Kingdom safe, quiet and happy . . . when his

46. *Parliamentary History*, XVII, 363, 368.
47. *Two Declarations The First from the Kings Most Excellent Majesty* (15 August 1647), BL., E.402(15), no pagination. For similarly optimistic reports from royalists, see Bodleian, Clarendon MSS., 30, fos. 30, 35.
48. *Certain uncertain Proposals from Freeborn Subjects of England to his Excellency Sir Thomas Fairfax* (12 August 1647), BL., E.401(33), especially p. 2.

being there may be likely to produce . . . not greater Disturbances . . .
but . . . a Peace indeed'.[49]

Peace on the army's terms proved to be no more acceptable to the
king than it had been to the parliamentary Presbyterians. Its failure,
confirmed by Charles's flight to the Isle of Wight in November, was to
be a crucial factor in ranging the army against the king as well as
destroying royalist hopes of a more militant alliance with the army than
had ever been a really serious possibility. It may also have brought the
parliamentary Presbyterians somewhat closer to the king as they renewed that struggle with the army which had been another principal
feature of the spring and summer of 1647. To that struggle we must
now turn.

The army, the eleven members and the seven peers

The army's move to impeach eleven Presbyterian MPs in the summer
of 1647 was in the first place designed to exact retribution from those
whom it deemed especially responsible for the attempted humiliation of
the soldiers in the Declaration of Dislike of 30 March and the events
immediately following it. The denial of the right to petition for redress
of soldierly grievances was deeply resented, as indeed was what the
soldiers regarded as a wilful and malevolent misrepresentation of their
desires.[50] Secondly, once the army had responded by formulating its
own plans for a just settlement, it was painfully conscious of the
obstacles presented to their realization by the continued domination of
parliament by Denzil Holles and its other enemies of March and April.
Finally, there was genuine fear of a counter-revolutionary conspiracy, of
which the eleven members were at the centre, along with the Scottish
commissioners in London and their allies in the City government,
aiming to restore the king unconditionally (which they certainly had no
intention of doing), to bring the army to heel and to suppress sectarian
heresy. So much for the ends of counter-revolution. The means were to
be the diversion of obedient soldiers who had volunteered for Ireland
from that service to employment against the army at home; the

---

49. *Parliamentary History*, XVI, 261–3. See also *Certain new Proposals from his Excellency Sir Thomas Fairfax . . .* (August 1647), BL., E.404(26), no pagination.
50. See, e.g., *Divers Papers from the Army* (May 1647), BL., E.388(18), pp. 3–4, 8–9, 10–11; *The Declaration of the Armie . . .* (May 1647), E.390(26), pp. 3–6, 10; *A Perfect and True Copy of the Severall Grievances of the Army* (May 1647), Chelmsford: Essex R.O., Landon pamphlet coll., also BL., E.390(3), sig.A2; *A Motion from the Army* (June 1647), E.391(5), no pagination, clause I; CLRO., Jor. 40., fo. 219(b) (letter to Lord Mayor); *Parliamentary History*, XV, 471.

re-enlistment of reformadoes or disbanded soldiers; the encouragement of deserters from the New Model and the putting of the City of London Militia under the control of Holles's City allies. The reconstructed City Militia Committee along with a revived parliamentary Committee of Safety was to create and organize a counter-revolutionary force which would co-operate with a Scottish invasion. Arguments emphasizing the need for such a force if the army's aggression was to be curbed and the army brought to obedience to parliament were to be found in plenty.[51] To the army, of course, such preparations and arguments were eloquent proof of its own conspirary theory, and indeed two strongly anti-New Model ex-commanders, Sir William Waller and Edward Massey, were among the eleven members charged.[52] The army's seizure of the king at Holdenby on 4 June could plausibly be represented as a pre-emptive strike against the burgeoning conspiracy.[53]

The army's strategy in impeaching only eleven MPs is at first sight rather puzzling in that, as Professor Woolrych puts it, that number was 'too small to change the balance of parties in the House decisively, but rather large if it was seriously hoped to make the charges stick'.[54] But the strategy is surely best understood as a significant warning shot across the Presbyterian bows, to induce moderate Presbyterians to withdraw their support from the more extreme plans of Holles and his associates. It was an earnest of more to come, if the warning should not be taken. As one parliamentary Presbyterian pamphleteer put it, 'if upon a generall accusation . . . you would have them [viz. the eleven] sequestered from the House, may you not by the same rule sequester a hundred the next day after?'[55] Characteristically pressing this sort of argument to extremes,

51. See, e.g., *Questions propounded to all wel-affected* . . . (23 June 1647), BL., E.393(23), pp. 1–4; *Eight Queres* [sic] (15 June 1647), E.392(22), especially pp. 5–6; [William Prynne], *IX Queries* (June 1647), E.394(1), p. 10.

52. Colonel-General Sydenham Poynz later stated that he also had offered the services of his Northern Association army to the Speaker, though long before the end of the summer his soldiers had succeeded in getting rid of him (*The Vindication of Collonell General Points* (1648), BL., E.469(23), p. 7). On Poynz see below, pp. 390–93.

53. See Bell, *Memorials*, I, 353 (Rushworth to Lord Fairfax, 9 June); *A true impartiall Narration concerning the Armies preservation of the KING* (June 1647), BL., E.393(1), especially pp. 3–7.

54. Woolrych, *Soldiers and Statesmen*, pp. 137–8. As well as the pioneering and still valuable account in Gardiner, *Civil War*, III, especially pp. 298–9, 302–5, 322–8, 348–9, there are important modern contributions by two historians of the army: Woolrych, op. cit., especially pp. 128–9, 137–9, 141–2, 144, 158, 166, 171–4; and M.A. Kishlansky, *The Rise of the New Model Army* (Cambridge, 1979), especially pp. 243–56, 261–2.

55. *The Lawfulnesse of the late Passages of the Army* (June 1647), BL., E.394(12), p. 13. Elsewhere the author argues that any attempt to justify the army's action in terms of necessary retaliation against parliament's attempt to raise a force against it was invalid, since no such attempt was being made (ibid., p. 10). See also *Eight Queres* [sic], (15 June

William Prynne maintained that the army might as well suspend the whole House as eleven members of it.[56]

According to Sir William Waller, whose account of how the charges against the eleven were drawn up is probably more witty than accurate, Ireton and his colleagues first 'proposed the name of the party; and then they fell to pumping, what they should say against him. . . . However, they must be sure to cast dirt enough, and something would stick.'[57] The general tenor of the charges relating to an alleged counter-revolutionary conspiracy to restore the king has already been indicated. Additionally the eleven were charged with obstructions to and delays in the administration of justice and begetting scandalous misinformation about the army which they designed 'to break and pull . . . in Pieces'. The army's demands for action against the eleven were first formulated in its celebrated Representation of 14 June, appended to which is an account of the charges against them,[58] and for the first time an account of the exact identity of these 'very Conscientious, able, knoweing men', as their military ally, Colonel General Sydenham Poynz, describes them.[59]

The list of the accused was headed by Denzil Holles and Sir Philip Stapleton. Holles, of course, had been one of the five members whom Charles I had unsuccessfully tried to arrest in January 1642, as one royalist propagandist ruefully observed,[60] and the stale charges which Lord Saville had made against him and Bulstrode Whitelock two years earlier were again dragged up against him.[61] Stapleton, along with Sir

1647), E.392(22), p. 6. For an attempt to answer such arguments, see *Reasons why the House of Commons ought . . . to suspend the Members charged by the Army* (July 1647), E.396(1), pp. 8–9.

56. [W. Prynne], *IX Queries* (June 1648), BL., E.394(1), passim, especially p. 6. For a not very impressive reply to Prynne's arguments, see *An Answer to a Pamphlet . . . Intituled Nine Queries . . .* (June 1647), E.394(18), passim. In their formal answer to the charges, the eleven also make the point about the applicability of the charges to the House of Commons as a whole (*Parliamentary History*, XVI, 116–17).

57. Waller, *Vindication*, pp. 174–6.

58. *Parliamentary History*, XV, 470–5. For a good discursive account of the nature of the army's case, see Oxford, Worcester College, Clarke MSS., 41, fos. 56–61. The fullest account is in the army's Remonstrance of 18 August (*Parliamentary History*, XVI, 251–73). See also *The poore Wise-mans Admonition* (June 1647), BL., E.392(4), passim; E.396(1), passim. For the formal charges in full, see *Parliamentary History* XVI, 70–92; Bell, *Memorials*, I, 367–83. For the eleven's formal reply to the charges, which was not delivered to parliament until 19 July, see *Parliamentary History*, XVI, 116–59.

59. Poynz, *Vindication*, BL., E.469(23), p. 6.

60. [James Howell], *A Letter to the Earle of Pembrooke* (1647), BHPC., p. 6. For similar observations, see [William Prynne], *IX Queries*, BL., E.394(1), p. 6. On Holles's career, see P. Crawford, *Denzil Holles 1598–1680* (1979).

61. For Holles's own answer to these and other charges, in addition to his formal answer along with those of the other accused, see *Parliamentary History*, XVI, 116–59; *A grave and learned Speech or an Apology delivered by Denzill Holles Esq.* (20 July 1647),

John Clotworthy and John Glyn, the Recorder of London, were former middle-group politicians who had since moved sharply to the right. Clotworthy was accused of collusion with the Irish confederate rebels and of fraudulent conversion of funds which has been voted for Ireland where he had extensive interests.[62] Glyn, along with Sir William Lewis, was also charged with illicit financial practices – in the latter's case as Governor of Portsmouth during the war – and of facilitating the penetration of commissions of the peace and county committees by cavalier delinquents in their native Wales, and, in Glyn's case, in Middlesex also.[63] The two virulently anti-New Model ex-generals Edward Massey and Sir William Waller have already been encountered and will be many times again, as has the distinguished lawyer and redoubtable opponent of revolutionary illegality, Sir John Maynard.[64] Edward Harley, the Herefordshire Presbyterian, was dismissed contemptuously as 'an innocent Puny' hardly worthy of the attention of his accusers who 'have not time to kill flies'. Yet they did find time on account of the part he had played in the proceedings against the soldiers' March petition.[65] Anthony Nichols, a relation of the great John Pym, had merited Independent hostility in connection with 'recruiter' elections in Cornwall,[66] and Walter Long for his activities as Parliamentary Driver, that is, a sort of party whip for the Presbyterians in the House of Commons.[67]

The charges against the eleven were never fully pressed to a trial, although this possibility was to hang over their heads for almost another

BL., E.399(14), pp. 1–6. On Saville's original charges in 1645, see Crawford, op. cit., pp. 114–20; MacCormack, *Revolutionary Politics*, pp. 77–88; Ashton, *Civil War*, pp. 237–40.

62. Bell, *Memorials*, I, 375–7; *Parliamentary History*, XVI, 81–3. For the official reply to these charges, see ibid., pp. 134–41. He was formally absolved of these charges in September 1648 (*C.J.*, VI, 8; Rushworth, *Historical Collections*, VII, 1254).

63. On Glyn and Lewis, see Bell, *Memorials*, I, 377–80; *Parliamentary History*, XVI, 83–8; *A Letter . . . from the well-affected Party in the City* (10 July 1647), BL., E.397(19), pp. 6, 7; *A Vindication of Sir William Lewis . . .* (9 July 1647), E.397(14), pp. 3–7; *Clarke Papers*, I, 141. For their formal reply to the charges, see *Parliamentary History*, XVI, 141–50. The Accounts Committee at Cornhill had vindicated Lewis for alleged misuse of public money when Governor of Portsmouth.

64. On Massey and Waller, see below, pp. 393–7; on Maynard, above, pp. 113–16.

65. BL., E.397(19), p. 7; [A. Warren], *A full Vindication of the Armie* (12 October 1647), E.410(18), pp. 40–1; Bell, *Memorials*, I, 372–4; *Parliamentary History*, XVI, 76–7. On Harley see Jacqueline Eales, *Puritans and Roundheads: The Harleys of Brampton Bryan and the outbreak of the English Civil War* (Cambridge, 1990), pp. 14, 187–90. For the formal answer to the charges affecting Harley and others, see *Parliamentary History*, XVI, 126–30.

66. Bell, *Memorials*, I, 381; *Parliamentary History*, XVI, 89; for a denial, see *A brief Justification of some of the XI accused Members* (13 July 1647), BL., E.398(3), pp. 8–9; *Parliamentary History*, XVI, 151–3.

67. Bell, *Memorials*, I, 382–3; *Parliamentary History*, XVI, 90–1. For a denial, see BL., E.398(3), pp. 9–10; *Parliamentary History*, XVI, 153–7. Long was also accused of cowardice in the field.

year. As the Independent politician Edmund Ludlow observed,[68] the army's interests were served equally well – perhaps even better – either by their suspension, as the army had demanded on 23 June,[69] or, following the Commons' indignant refusal two days later to countenance this,[70] by their offer to withdraw made at the end of June.[71] This was not formally accepted by the House until 20 July when it gave them leave to withdraw for six months with passports to go abroad if desired.[72] To Marchamont Nedham, the chameleon political journalist who was currently adopting a pro-Independent posture, the eleven's willingness to withdraw was in itself 'Argument enough of *guilt*'. Those of a different political persuasion, however, saw it as the unfortunate consequence of an outrageous breach of parliamentary privilege.[73] To this charge made by Prynne and others the army's defenders returned the brazen reply that 'no Privilege ought to protect evil Men in doing Wrong to Particulars or Mischief to the Public'.[74]

Despite obtaining leave of absence for six months on 20 July the eleven were still attending the House at the end of the month.[75] That they were able to do so was due to momentous happenings in the meantime, and notably the counter-revolutionary assault on parliament

68. *Ludlow Memoirs*, I, 151–2. See also the view of John Rushworth in a letter to Ferdinando, Lord Fairfax that 'more than a suspension is not desired' (Bell, *Memorials*, I, 357). For a similar verdict from the opposite side of the House, see *A Declaration of the Officers and Armies illegall, iniurious proceedings* (8 July 1647), BL., E.397(8), p. 5.

69. *L.J.*, IX, 291; CLRO., Jor. 40, fo. 225(b) (letter to Lord Mayor); *The last Propositions proposed by his Excellency Sir Thomas Fairfax* (15 June 1647), BL., E.393(4), no pagination, clause II; *Three Letters from His Excellency Sir Thomas Fairfax* (June 1647), E.394(11), pp. 3–4; Cary, *Memorials*, I, 247–8, 255–6; *Parliamentary History*, XV, 473, XVI, 6, 12–13, 18, 25.

70. *C.J.*, V, 223; *The Votes of the . . . House of Commons in Vindication of the eleven Members* (June 1647), BL., 669, f 11(34); *Cal.SPD. 1645–7*, p. 597 ('Perfect Occurrences, no. 26'). One pamphlet argues that it now behoved the army to make reparations to the eleven (*Nine Proposals by way of interrogation* (July 1647), BL., E.396(8), p. 5).

71. *Parliamentary History*, XVI, 38–9; *The Petition of the Members of the House of Commons who are accused by the Army* (29 June 1647), BL., E.396(7), pp. 3–7. According to one account the eleven would have preferred to get the House to vote its adjournment (*A Letter from a Gentleman to his Father* (3 July 1647), E.396(13), pp. 3–4).

72. *C.J.*, V, 251–2; *Desires Propounded to the House of Commons* (July 1647), BL., E.399(11), pp. 5–6.

73. For Nedham's view, see [M. Nedham], *The Lawyer of Lincolnes-Inne reformed* (July 1647), BL., E.395(4), pp. 1–4. Nedham argues, rather perversely, that, far from breaking parliamentary privilege, the army's attack on the eleven was designed to preserve it. For a denial that it was analogous with the king's attempted arrest of the five members in 1642, see *Reasons why the House of Commons ought . . . to suspend the Members charged by the Army* (July 1647), E.396(1), p. 9. For the view that it was, on the contrary, a breach of privilege, see W. Prynne, *IX Queries* (June 1647), E.394(1), especially p. 6.

74. *Parliamentary History*, XVI, 6–8, 12–13; BL., E.394(11), p. 7. For similar arguments see E.396(1), pp. 3–6, 8–9.

75. *C.J.*, V, 250, 251–2, 260.

on 26 July. This precipitated the flight of the Speakers and many MPs to the army, leaving what was virtually a Presbyterian Rump which received the eleven back with open arms. However, their claim that the tumult had compelled them to resume their seats no less than it had compelled their opponents to flee hardly merits serious consideration.[76] Did they play a leading part in London's counter-revolution?[77] According to admittedly partial accounts by Fairfax and his council, the eleven had been very active in London both before and after the coup of 26 July.[78] In a declaration of 3 August explaining the reasons for the army's imminent march on London, the Lord General expressed the hope that the eleven would be handed over to him to stand trial.[79] He may in fact have been somewhat relieved when they escaped and, after avoiding attempts to intercept and bring them back, six of them landed at Calais, where Stapleton died of the plague shortly afterwards.[80] Their flight and the army's occupation of London on 6 August marked the effective conclusion of the parliamentary Presbyterian counter-revolution.

Writing from Edinburgh on 1 September, Robert Baillie blamed the miscalculations of the eleven for the failure of the parliamentary Presbyterians to consolidate their ascendancy in the summer of 1647. Their first error, he argued, was to urge the premature withdrawal of the Scottish army from England in February, believing 'that this wes [sic] the only means to gett that evill [New Model] army disbanded, [and] the King and peace settled according to our minds'. Their second was to consent to the revocation of the Declaration of Dislike of 30 March notwithstanding the army's defiance of parliament over disbandment. Next was their failure to take strong and effective action following the army's abduction of the king from Holdenby on 4 June. And finally there was their neglecting to secure the persons of the two Speakers and the leading Independent MPs, to prevent their flight to the army following the coup of 26 July.[81] No doubt it was unfair to blame the

76. *A New Remonstrance of the Eleven Impeached Members* ... (14 August 1647), BL., E.402(3), especially pp. 2–3.
77. For a judicious appraisal of the evidence, see Crawford, op. cit., pp. 156–7.
78. Notably in the army's Remonstrance of 18 August (*Parliamentary History*, XVI, 256, 260–61). See also *New Propositions from His Excellency Sir Thomas Fairfax* (18 August 1647), BL., E.404(26), sig. A2ᵛ.
79. *L.J.*, IX, 378; *Parliamentary History*, XVI, 235–6. See also *Clarke Papers*, I, 220–22.
80. See *HMC., 5th Report (Duke of Sutherland's MSS.)*, p. 173 (wrongly calendared as 31 [sic] April 1647); *Sir Philip Stapleton DEAD of the Sicknesse at CALLICE* (23 August 1647), BL., E.404(22), pp. 1–6. For the account of Vice Admiral Batten who was instrumental in allowing the members to escape under the authority of the Speaker's pass, see *Naval Documents*, pp. 364–5. For Juxon's account, see Dr Williams's Library, MSS., 24.50, fo. 119. The six members concerned were Holles, Stapleton, Waller, Long, Clotworthy and Lewis.
81. Baillie, *Letters*, III, 16–17.

eleven – as distinct from some of their more timid colleagues – for all
these things and more especially the last, since they were not in parliament on 26 July. But in any case all was now lost. The eleven were
dispersed, one of them had died and two others, Glyn and Maynard,
were in the Tower. On 8 September, the day after Glyn was disabled
from sitting in the House, the Commons also decided to impeach seven
peers for their part in the July counter-revolution. The most important
of the accused lords was Lord Willoughby of Parham, who as Lord
Lieutenant of Lincolnshire had been one of the first peers to defy
Charles I in 1642, but who had also temporarily replaced the earl of
Manchester as Speaker of the Upper House following the coup of 26
July.[82] But long delays ensued before the Commons finally presented
their charges, which was not done until the last week of the subsequent
January.[83]

Around the same time, newsletters of varying political hues were
reporting the resumption of proceedings against the surviving ten
members, of whom the main object of attention was Sir John Maynard,
as was Willoughby of the seven accused peers. However, the verdict
of the royalist newsletter *Mercurius Elencticus* that it was intended that
Maynard and Willoughby should be made 'to pay for all' probably
overstates the case.[84] On 6 February 1648 Willoughby wrote to the
Speaker of the House of Lords, complaining politely about the delays
and protesting the consistency of the principles which, he claimed, had
always animated him.[85] The earl of Lanark's royalist correspondent in
England informed the earl that English royalists would shed few tears if
Willoughby ended on the scaffold, in view of his opposition to the king
in 1642.[86] Given the ultimate outcome of the cases in June, he would

82. On Glyn and Maynard, *C.J.*, V, 295, 305. The impeachment of Glyn was ordered on
    16 September along with that of his London associate, Commissary Lionel Copley.
    On the seven lords, *C.J.*, V, 296. The six other peers were the earls of Suffolk, Lincoln
    and Middlesex, and Lords Berkeley, Hunsdon and Maynard (not to be confused with
    Sir John Maynard).
83. For these proceedings and delays and the final bringing of the charges, *C.J.*, V, 344,
    372, 374–5, 444–5. 448–50; *L.J.*, IX, 545, 546, 553; *L.J.*, X, 13–14; *HMC., 7th
    Report App. (House of Lords Cal. 1647–8)*, p. 5; *The Kingdomes Weekly Intelligencer,
    Number 238* (7/14 December 1647), BL., E.419(24), p. 762, and ibid. (for 25 January/
    1 February 1648), E.424(10), pp. 821–4; *The Perfect Weekly Account* (8/15 December
    1647), E.419(28), sig. Z2; *Mercurius Pragmaticus, Number 20* (25 January/1 February
    1648), E.424(7), no pagination; *The Kingdomes Weekly Post* (26 January/2 February
    1648), E.425(5), p. 34,
84. *Mercurius Pragmaticus, Number 20* (25 January/1 February 1648), BL., E.424(7), no
    pagination; *The Kingdomes Weekly Intelligencer* (25 January/1 February 1648),
    E.424(10), pp. 821–3, 824; *The Kingdomes Weekly Post . . . Number 5* (26 January/2
    February 1648), E.425(5), pp. 34, 36; *Mercurius Elencticus, Number 10* (26 January/2
    February 1648), E.425(7), p. 73.
85. *A Letter Sent from the Lord Willoughby of Parham* (February 1648), BL., 669, f11(124).
86. *Hamilton Papers*, p. 153.

probably have avoided this fate, but choosing not to put it to the test he jumped bail and fled to Holland.[87] In the meantime proceedings against the other six peers, the surviving ten members and some of the London aldermen went ahead painfully slowly.[88] Parliament was to have more urgent matters to attend to on the eve of the Second Civil War. Indeed, the survivors of the eleven members were allowed to resume their seats in early June, a concession which clearly presaged the dropping of all charges against them on 24 June, along with the charges against the seven lords and their London aldermanic associates in the counter-revolution of the previous July. Parliamentary unity was at a premium with a new civil war on the government's hands and even if parliament's dropping of the charges against all these various accused was not simply a response to Scottish pressure, as Robert Baillie claimed, it was certainly anxious to avoid a Scottish invasion if at all possible.[89]

'Who would have thought', inelegantly declared an anti-Presbyterian pamphleteer in July 1648, that 'the late *exiled Members* would have so soone returned to their *old Vomit*'; and in particular to agitation for a treaty with the king?[90] Significantly when that agitation was crowned with success in the autumn, among the parliamentary commissioners chosen to treat with Charles I on the Isle of Wight was Denzil Holles himself, leader of the eleven members, and the earl of Middlesex, one of the seven formerly accused peers.[91] However, the June debate in the House of Commons about the readmission of the disabled ten members had been predictably acrimonious. The case against both them and their defenders was put with vigour and venom, but in vain.[92]

It was shown earlier that some conservative Presbyterians had seen the attack on the eleven members as the first stage in an Independent army design to destroy the Presbyterian ascendancy in the House of Commons. The attack on the seven lords was, if anything, more alarming. Given the size of the membership of the Upper House, this could be plausibly represented as 'a plot . . . to destroy . . . the House of Peers, by leaving them not Members enough to sit'. For 'what assurance

87. *The Kingdomes Weekly Post, Number 8* (16/22 February 1648), BL., E.428(13), pp. 59–60. For Willoughby's own account of the reasons for his defection, see below, p. 410.
88. L.J., X, 102; HMC., *7th Report App. (House of Lords Cal. 1647–8)*, p. 13; Rushworth, *Historical Collections*, VII, 1022. On 12 April the six lords entered a formal plea of not guilty. Willoughby, of course, was now in Holland (ibid., p. 1056).
89. C.J., V, 583–4, 586, 588, 589–90; L.J., X, 303, 307, 308; Rushworth, *Historical Collections*, VII, 1156, 1164–5; *Whitelock Diary*, p. 216; Whitelock, *Memorials*, p. 306 (3 June); *Parliamentary History*, XVII, 226; *State Trials*, IV, 987–8; Baillie, *Letters*, III, 46.
90. *Londons New Colours displai'd* (July 1648), BL., E.452(21), p. 12.
91. *Parliamentary History*, XVII, 436–7.
92. Ibid., pp. 226–8.

have the few remaining unimpeached Lords . . . that their turnes and impeachments will not be next, till they be all impeached, ejected and made no House . . . ?'[93] In the view of radical Independent politicians, whether or not they entertained such plans, the army should have applied pressure to parliament in June 1648 to prevent its *volte face* in the matter of the ten surviving members, six peers and three aldermen. Its failure to do so then was to bear its own sour fruit in parliament's dissipation of the advantages gained by the army's victory in the Second Civil War in entering into futile and dangerous negotiations with the king.[94] The army, of course, had been preoccupied by other matters in June 1648, but once it regained control of events as a result of Pride's Purge on 6 December, it was determined not to repeat its mistake. On the same day as Pride's Purge the army delivered its demands to the Rump, denouncing the readmission of the ten and its intention of renewing the charges against them and all who were implicated in the coup of July 1647. Here was one object of Pride's Purge which was directed not only against the surviving ten members and six peers but against all at Westminster (and in the City) who had gone along with their policies.[95] On 12 December the House of Commons revoked its June order which had resulted in the readmission of the surviving ten members. By that time the five of them who were still around (Clotworthy, Harley, Lewis, Massey and Waller) were in custody along with forty other members. As a result of the seclusion of many others, the worst fears of the Presbyterians were now realized.[96] For the result of the army's completion of the unfinished work of 1647 was the end not simply of the Presbyterian parliamentary ascendancy but also of the monarchy and the House of Lords.

The army and the City of London

Among the more enthusiastic supporters of the policies of Denzil Holles and his Presbyterian colleagues against the army had been the municipal

---

93. *Ardua Regni* (25 February 1648), BL., E.429(5), p. 10.
94. See, e.g., *Fruitfull England like to Become a Barren Wilderness* (7 October 1648), BL., E.467(36), p. 6; also *The Scots Cabinett Opened* (4 August 1648), E.456(30), pp. 9–10.
95. The army's proposals are printed in Whitelock, *Memorials*, p. 354 (sub date 6 December); also *The Armies Impeachment* (12 December 1648), BL., E.476(6), pp. 4–5. See also *The Impeachment Demands and Proposals of the Army* . . . (December 1648), E.475(36), pp. 4–5.
96. *Parliamentary History*, XVIII, 464–71; Whitelock, *Memorials*, p. 356 (12 December). On the personnel of the imprisoned and secluded members see D. Underdown, *Pride's Purge* (Oxford, 1971), pp. 210–13. Underdown estimates that 186 MPs were secluded but not imprisoned.

government of the City of London.[97] The City's support for Holles and the militant wing of the parliamentary Presbyterians also helps to explain its backwardness in collecting and paying over its monthly assessments which were monumentally in arrears over the whole of this period, a factor of first-rate and perhaps neglected importance in considering its relations with the army. Preoccupied though the army commanders may have been during the summer of 1647 with the central issues of incipient counter-revolution dealt with in the preceding section, they still found time to complain about the City's dilatoriness in paying over its assessment arrears, emphasizing the army's patience which was 'hitherto not to be exampled, we think, in other armies'.[98] In stressing the need for parliament to arrange for payment of the soldiers' arrears of pay in its petition of 8 June, the City was hypocritically throwing stones from a glasshouse, as much the worst offender in the matter of assessment arrears.[99]

The first crisis in the army's relations with the City came to a head on 10 June 1647 when Fairfax and twelve other high-ranking officers wrote to the Lord Mayor and his colleagues informing them that the army was about to draw closer to London to press its demands for arrears of pay and an end to the recruitment of deserters and reformadoes.[100] Although on the following day parliament established its Committee of Safety which was to co-operate with the City Militia Committee in concerting measures for the defence of London,[101] the army's threat seems to have had the desired effect and the Lord Mayor's conciliatory reply to Fairfax on 12 June did much to defuse the situation.[102] The Common Council's committee sent to consult with the army council of war at St Albans, a contact which was to be maintained over the ensuing weeks, was courteously received and the army council for its part agreed not to quarter nearer than thirty miles from

97.   On the City and the army in the spring and summer of 1647, see also V. Pearl, 'London's Counter-revolution', in Aylmer, *Interregnum*, pp. 44–56; M.A. Kishlansky, op. cit., passim.
98.   *The Declaration of the Army* (16 May 1647), BL., E.390(26), p. 9.
99.   CLRO., Jor. 40, fo. 218(b); *L.J.*, IX, 251–2; *The humble Petition of the Lord Major [sic], Aldermen and Commons* (8 June 1647), BL., E.391(6), p. 2; *Parliamentary History*, XV, 420.
100.   CLRO., Jor. 40, fos. 219(b)–20; *A Letter Sent to the Right Honourable the Lord Mayor . . .* (10 June 1647), BHPC.; *Sixe Propositions . . . to the Citie of London* (June 1647), BL., E.392(17); *Parliamentary History*, XV, 431–4; Carlyle, *Cromwell*, I, 228–31.
101.   *C.J.*, V, 208, *L.J.*, IX, 258.
102.   CLRO., Jor. 40, fos. 221–1(b); Rushworth, *Historical Collections*, VI, 557–8; *Parliamentary History*, XV, 438–40. See also the petition of citizens of 17 June urging conciliation of the army (*The humble petition of divers Citizens* (June 1647), BL., 669, f11(24)).

London.[103] Moderate counsels had come to prevail in both City and army and the former had withdrawn, for the time being at least, from the extremist plans of Holles and his colleagues. The crisis had been averted.[104]

But for all the apparent easing of tension the army was no nearer to fulfilment of its demands. Reformadoes abounded in London however much the City fathers might protest that their recruitment was not their work but that of the parliamentary Committee of Safety;[105] the City Militia Committee continued to be controlled by Holles's City allies and 'unreliable' (viz. Independent) officers were forced to resign their commissions;[106] the deserters from the New Model continued to be enlisted, though on 28 June parliament was to order that no soldier should leave the army without the General's permission;[107] and while such deserters and reformadoes were paid, the serving soldiers' pay, like the City's assessments, was still lamentably in arrears, and yet, as the army was to complain on 18 July, £230,000 of these arrears had recently been paid over to the city assessment treasurers at Weavers' Hall.[108] In London both friends and foes of the army seem daily to have expected the army to occupy the capital with, so the latter predicted, the prospect of rapine and plunder.[109] Some of these gloomy prognos-

---

103. *The Treatie Between the Commissioners from the Lord Mayor . . . and Sir Thomos* [sic] *Fairfax . . .* (14 June 1647), BL., E.392(25), no pagination; Bodleian, Tanner MSS., 58, fo. 159. For a regretful account of the *détente* by one of the eleven members, see Waller, *Vindication*, pp. 149–52. On 11 June the House of Lords had ordered the army to keep at least 40 miles away from London (*L.J.*, IX, 256, 258), but it was still nearer than that on 21 June, despite the dispatch of a month's pay to it (Tanner MSS., 58, fos. 214, 222; *Parliamentary History*, XV, 501–2).
104. See the letter of 22 June from John Rushworth to Ferdinando Lord Fairfax, announcing a 'very fair' correspondency between army and City (Bell, *Memorials*, I, 358).
105. On this and other complaints, see CLRO., Jor. 40, fos. 223–3(b), 224(b)–5, 225(b)–6, 227, 228, 228(b), 229–30; *L.J.*, IX, 266, 275, 281, 287, 290–1, 299–300, 310–11, 320; *C.J.*, V, 213, 216, 217; *The Propositions of His Excellency Sir Thomas Fairfax* (27 June 1647), BL., E.394(19), pp. 1–3; *A Manifesto from Sir Thomas Fairfax . . .* (27 June 1647), E.394(15), no pagination; *Three Letters from His Excellency . . .* (June 1647), E.394(11), pp. 7–8; Oxford, Worcester College, Clarke MSS., 41, fos. 163–3(b); Cary, *Memorials*, I, 245–9; *Parliamentary History*, XV, 489–90, XVI, 14–19, 24–7, 36–7, 96; *Clarke Papers*, I, 141–2, 152.
106. See *Clarke Papers*, I, 152–6.
107. *C.J.*, V, 226; *L.J.*, IX, 303. A parliamentary ordinance of 19 June had previously indemnified deserters against punishment by the army. (*A&O.*, I, 957–8; *L.J.*, IX, 282; BL., 669, f11(27).)
108. CLRO., Jor. 40, fos. 237(b)–8; Bodleian, Tanner MSS., 58, fos. 315–15(b); *L.J.*, IX, 341; *Parliamentary History*, XVI, 360–1; *The Proposals Delivered to the Earl of Notting-ham . . .* (18 July 1647), BL., E.399(10), pp. 3–4; *New Propositions from Sir Thomas Fairfax* (July 1647), E.399(20), E.400(6), no pagination in either.
109. See, e.g., *HMC, 10th. Rep. App. IV (Captain Stewart's MSS.)*, p. 97; *A Letter written from a Person of Worth* (22 June 1647), BL., E.393(28), pp. 1–4; *Certaine seasonable Queries* (3 July 1647), E.396(17), pp. 2–3; *Eighteene Queries* (2 August 1648),

tications were, no doubt, deliberate alarmism, and although on 25 June Fairfax did his best to reassure the citizens, on the following day the army was at Uxbridge.[110] Responding perhaps to the Lord Mayor's request that it should move further from the capital and not seek to 'overthrow the fundamentall Constitution of Parliament',[111] but probably more to the promised withdrawal of the eleven members and parliament's declaration against deserters of 28 June,[112] the army moved its headquarters to Reading.[113] But Robert Baillie and other diehard Presbyterians complained that such *détente* as had occurred was the result of the City's cowardly desertion of Holles's party and the cause.[114] Moreover, on 17 July a newsletter from Reading reported a renewed likelihood that the army would again move towards London to obtain its long-desired ends: 'as in particular declaring against forreign forces [viz. the Scots] coming in, the putting reformado's [*sic*] out of the line, and suspending the 11 Members, but more especially to desire the Parliament to putt the Militia of the Citty of London into the same hands as it was before'.[115]

The need to revise the composition of the City Militia Committee, which, since a parliamentary ordinance of 4 May, had been dominated by Holles's City allies, had been a prime argument for the army to occupy London.[116] But for a mere three days following 23 July that aim seemed to have been achieved[117] and the occupation rendered

E.400(35), p. 4. *Questions Propounded to all wel-affected, wealthy Citizens* . . . (1647), Oxford, Worcester College pamph. coll., pp. 1–2. For an opposite view, seeing the possible occupation of the City as a blessing to be welcomed, see *Reasons why the House of Commons ought* . . . *to suspend the Members charged by the Army* (July 1647), BL., E.396(1), p. 11 (corrected pagination).

110. CLRO., Jor. 40, fo. 230; BL., E.394(11), pp. 6–8.
111. CLRO., Jor. 40, fos. 229–30. For a disavowal of the City's fears see *The Last Votes from the Armie* (26 June 1647), BL., E.394(10), passim.
112. *C.J.*, V, 226; *L.J.*, IX, 303.
113. *Parliamentary History*, XVI, 35–6.
114. Baillie, *Letters*, III, 9; *HMC., 5th. Report, pt.i*, p. 179; *A Letter from a Gentleman to his Father* (3 July 1647), BL., E.396(13), p. 3.
115. *Clarke Papers*, I, 214–16.
116. See Fairfax's emphasis on the importance of this matter in his letter of 19 July to the Lord Mayor, reproduced in October 1648 (*The Declaration of* . . . *the Lord Generall Fairfax* (23 October 1648), BL., E.468(28), p. 2. See also CLRO., Jor. 40, fo. 237(b).
117. The army's view of the militia issue is most clearly expressed in the Council of War's declaration of 3 August (*L.J.*, IX, 375–8; BL., E.401(2); CLRO., Jor. 40, fos. 248–50(b); *Parliamentary History*, XVI, 225–37), and in its famous Remonstrance of 18 August (ibid., pp. 251–73, and especially pp. 252–4, 256–61). For the views of its opponents, see, e.g., *Some Queries propounded to the Common Council* . . . (July 1647), BL., E.400(26), especially pp. 1, 4–12. These views are in broad agreement with the official City view in a declaration of 31 July (CLRO., Jor. 40, fos. 244(b)–6; Rushworth, *Historical Collections*, VI, 648–51). For similar arguments, see *New Presbyterian Light springing out of Independent Darknes* (July 1647), BL., E.400(24), especially pp. 3–6.

unnecessary. On that date and under pressure from the army, parliament revoked the Militia Ordinance of 4 May, thus altering the composition of the City Militia Committee.[118] There is no need to go along with the ingenious and far-fetched view held by both Holles and Clement Walker that the new Militia Ordinance of 23 July was a Machiavellian device designed to provoke disturbances in the city (which, of course, it did) and thus provide a justification for the army's occupation of London.[119] Indeed, on 25 July the parliamentary commissioners with the army expressed the view that the ordinance had in fact cut the ground from under the feet of the more militant spirits in the army and thus rendered its occupation of London less rather than more likely.[120]

Had they been in London at the time, they might have been less optimistic. On 22 July the Solemn Engagement and Petition of the citizens had demanded both the revocation of the ordinance and the bringing of the king to London to treat without conditions.[121] The immediate response of the army's Council of War was to condemn the Solemn Engage-ment as 'a businesse set on foot by the malice of some desperate minded men', which both confirmed the army's suspicions about a long-standing counter-revolutionary conspiracy and vindicated its consequent intention of moving towards London.[122]

If the army had occupied London before this time, as some of its fiercer spirits had urged,[123] it would have rendered itself wide open to the accusation that it had done so to impose its will on parliament in matters such as the eleven members and the militia, not to speak of its own narrow interests in forcing the City to cough up its assessment arrears. But, following the counter-revolutionary coup of 26 July it could plausibly represent its occupation of London as designed to restore the integrity of parliament, many of whose members, including the Speakers of both Houses, had been driven by an unruly mob of reformadoes, apprentices and others to take refuge with the army.[124] From that violence some of its own members, including Scoutmaster General Watson, had also suffered,[125] but that was incidental. It was the

118. C.J., V, 254, 255, 256–7: A&O., I, 990–91.
119. 'Memoirs of Denzil Lord Holles', in Maseres, Select Tracts, I, 273–4: Walker, Independency, pp. 12–13.
120. L.J., IX, 355–6; HMC., 6th. Rep. App. (House of Lords Cal. 1647), p. 90; Cary, Memorials, I, 315–17, 319.
121. For more detail see above, p. 137.
122. A Copy of a Paper delivered to the Commissioners of Parliament . . . (23 July 1647), BL., E.399(31), especially pp. 3–5; Parliamentary History, XVI, 168–70.
123. The Intentions of the Armie plainely discovered (31 July 1647), BL., E.400(37), p. 3, represents Col. Whalley as one such person.
124. See the letter of 27 July from John Rushworth to Ferdinando Lord Fairfax (BL., Add. MSS., 29,747, fos. 15–16).
125. For Rushworth's account, see ibid. For Juxon's account, Dr Williams's Library, MS. 24.50, fo. 115. For information in a newsletter from London, Clarke Papers, I, 218.

assault on parliament, unchecked and even perhaps encouraged by the City fathers, which provided the army with the cast-iron excuse for occupation which it had lacked before 26 July. The feeble mayoral reply to Fairfax's letter of 29 July accusing the Lord Mayor and his colleagues of culpable negligence, and even, in some cases, of positively encouraging the rioters, convinced nobody. The Lord Mayor complained that Fairfax had been misinformed about the circumstances of the tumult and that he had supplied no precise information about the identity of those who were guilty of complicity with the rioters. Thrashing around for excuses, he blamed the uncertainty about militia control consequent on the parliamentary ordinance of 23 July (which in turn had been revoked by the intimidated parliament on 26 July) for the failure to bring the disturbance promptly under control.[126]

The question of the complicity or otherwise of the Lord Mayor and his colleagues is treated more fully elsewhere,[127] though it can here be said with certainty that, at the very least, no serious attempt had been made to deter the rioters. The tumultuous events of 26 July and after were ultimately to be a source of great embarrassment both to the City authorities and to their parliamentary Presbyterian allies. However, Denzil Holles in his *Memoirs* made the best he could of it, arguing that the army had applied far more horrid force to parliament than the apprentices had done. For while the latter's outburst on 26 July had been 'a sudden tumultuary thing of young idle people, without design', the army's was part of 'a . . . deep-laid design' for revenge and national domination.[128] Holles and his more extreme colleagues were, it would seem, as obsessed by their own conspiracy theories, as were, *mutatis mutandis*, the army and their Independent allies by theirs. But while the wilder spirits prevailed for a time in London and Westminster on and after 26 July, the army's response was more disciplined and controlled in dealing with the City which, as Rushworth informed Lord Fairfax, 'will be forced to put yᵉ sword into Madd mens hands that will destroy them selves'.[129]

126. CLRO., Jor. 40, fo. 243(b); *L.J.*, IX, 359–60; Rushworth, *Historical Collections*, VI, 647; *Two Letters from His Excellency* . . . (July 1647), BL., E.400(23), pp. 2–4: *Several Orders and Votes of both Houses* . . . (July 1647), E.400(34), pp. 3–4.
127. See below, pp. 350–53.
128. Maseres, *Select Tracts*, I, 278. For similar observations, see *The Army Anatomized* (4 December 1647), BL., E.419(6), p. 20; *Vox Civitatis* (28 September 1647), E.409(10), pp. 5–6; *The Machivilian Cromwellist* (10 January 1648), E.422(12), pp. 5–7. For the argument that the Declaration of August of the MPs who fled to the army was 'more dangerous and treasonable then that Engagement of the Citizens which the subscribers thereof voted to be treasonable', see *An Engagement of the Lords and Commons that went to the Army* . . . *4 August 1647* (15 December 1647), E.419(27), especially p. 8.
129. BL., Add. MSS., 29,747, fo. 16.

The 'Madd men' in question included two of the eleven members, Major General Edward Massey and Sir William Waller. Waller was much the senior of the two, but it was Massey who was appointed as Commander in Chief by Common Council on 30 July and confirmed by parliament on the following day, while Waller was put in command of the horse on 3 August.[130] Waller was later to offer some caustic comments on the City fathers' lack of resolution in face of the crisis, when they commanded, so Waller claimed, a larger and more formidable force than Fairfax had at his disposal. Thomas Juxon's admittedly hostile account of an ill-attended rendezvous of the city defence forces provides a less impressive picture, while a royalist newsletter of 2 August remarks on the rush of trained band officers to relinquish their commissions and the almost total disinclination of the suburbs to support the defence of the city.[131]

With such inauspicious portents, there was little left for the City and the Presbyterian rump of a parliament to do but to attempt to persuade the army that its presence in London was not necessary since order had been restored and the fugitive MPs could return with impunity. The last of these attempts by parliament on 3 August, designed to dissuade the army from rendezvousing on Hounslow Heath prior to occupying London, also rebuked the army for behaving provocatively by securing the estuary blockhouse at Tilbury; by its violence to some reformadoes awaiting pay not far from Westminster; by its securing of the person of the Presbyterian MP and former parliamentary commander of Newport Pagnell, Sir Samuel Luke; by its mobilizing local trained bands without authority from parliament; and by its affronts to the Scottish commissioner, Lauderdale, at Woburn.[132] Such sentiments, accompanied by frantic attempts to organize London's defences,[133] were unlikely to persuade the army that its march on London was unnecessary. Fairfax and the Council of War rejected all such approaches, declaring on 2 August their firm intention personally to see the Speakers and the

130. CLRO., Jor. 40, fos. 244, 246(b); *C.J.*, V, 261; *L.J.*, IX, 362, 363, 371, 372.
131. For Waller's comments, see Waller, *Vindication*, pp. 188–9. For Juxon's account, see Dr Williams's Library, MS. 24.50, fo. 116. For the royalist newsletter, see Bodleian, Clarendon MSS., 30, fo. 24.
132. For attempts to stave off the army, see CLRO., Jor. 40, fos. 243, 247–7(b); HLRO., MP 30/7/1647; *L.J.*, IX, 360, 361, 372–3; Rushworth, *Historical Collections*, VI, 654; *A Declaration of the . . . Committee for the Safety and the Militia of London* (1 August 1647), BL., E.401(6), pp. 5–6, BL., 669, f11(54). On 2 August the Westminster Assembly of Divines offered its services as a mediator between army and City (*L.J.*, IX, 368; *Parliamentary History*, XVI, 204). On Lauderdale, see below, p. 318.
133. CLRO., Common Hall Book 2, fos. 83, 83(b); Jor. 40., fo. 243; *L.J.*, IX, 360–61; *C.J.*, V, 263.

fugitive peers and MPs reinstated at Westminster.[134] On 3 August the army rendezvoused on Hounslow Heath prior to its occupation of London. The Lord General, the Speaker and the other fugitive parliamentarians rode through the ranks of the soldiers, 'being a mile and a half in length putt in Battalia, every man cried out "Lords and Commons and a free Parliament", expressing their willingnesse and Resolution to lay downe their lives butt to sett the Parliament free'.[135]

This restoration of parliament's integrity was the basic justification – or as a cynic might put it, the perfect excuse – for the army's occupation of London. On 3 August Fairfax and his Council of War issued a declaration to this effect which was also the fullest and most coherent explanation to date of its actions since mid June. Its details need not detain us, for they simply adumbrate the familiar central features of the alleged counter-revolutionary conspiracy to which the army's occupation of London would give, it was hoped, the final quietus.[136] The Common Council's response was appropriately abject, conceding a safe passage through the City for the fugitive Speaker and members and their guard of honour of two or three regiments, who, it nervously requested, should be restrained 'from doeing anie offence or preiudice to this Cittie'. On the following day it yielded possession to the army of all those forts which it had enumerated within the lines of communication.[137] Southwark had already facilitated the army's access to London by refusing to let any of the City's forces over London Bridge, and the Captain Lieutenant of the Southwark trained bands, William Braine, was, in subsequent days, to become the object of both opprobrium and physical assault for his part in what royalists and other counter-revolutionaries deemed to be a gross act of treachery.[138]

134. *A Declaration from His Excellencie . . . and his Councell of Warre* (August 1647), BL., E.401(4), pp. 3–5; *Parliamentary History*, XVI, 210–12.
135. *Clarke Papers*, I, 220 (newsletter from the army).
136. CLRO., Jor. 40, fos. 248–50(b); *L.J.*, IX, 375–8; *A Declaration of his Excellency . . . and his Council of War* (3 August 1647), BL., E.401(2); *Parliamentary History*, XVI, 225–37.
137. CLRO., Jor. 40, fo. 250(b), 251, 251(b); *Two Letters* (5 August 1647), BL., E.401(7), pp. 1–3; *Articles of the Treaty . . . betwixt . . . Sir Thomas Fairfax and the Commissioners for the City* (August 1647), E.401(11), no pagination. For Thomas Juxon's vivid account of these events, see Dr Williams's Library, MS. 24.50, fos. 117(b)–18. For fears as to the likelihood of plunder by the army, see *Eighteene Queries* (2 August 1647), E.400(35), p. 4.
138. *A Paire of Spectacles for the Citie* (4 December 1647), BL., E.419(9), p. 8 (corrected pagination). See Braine's petition of 11 August (*L.J.*, IX, 383; *C.J.*, V, 271; *HMC., 6th. Rep. (House of Lords Cal. 1647)*, p. 191). See Juxon's account of the yielding of Southwark (Dr Williams's Library, MS. 24.50, fo. 117(b)). Similar insults were offered to Braine's commanding officer, Colonel John Hardwick (*HMC., 6th Rep. (House of Lords Cal. 1647)*, p. 193: HLRO., MP., 23/8/1647, fos. 27, 28).

Reflecting with relief on the city's and the kingdom's narrow escape from counter-revolutionary tyranny, thanks to the resolution of the army, the Independent Thomas Juxon nevertheless emphasizes

> that it was neuer in ye minds of the army to carie it one [*sic*] soe far; but [they] were brought to it one thing after an other . . . by the designes of y^r enemies. . . . Neuer was ye King nearer the injoyment of his desires to retourne to London vppon a Cleare board. But had it bin don we had bin all ruined. . . . And . . . if . . . at aney tyme the Compassiones of God were strongly moueing for ye Kingdome & Cittie . . . [it] was at y^s time.[139]

Juxon's elation is naturally paralleled by counter-revolutionary dejection. 'The storme is now ouer', bewailed a royalist observer on 5 August, 'and we haue put out our right eyes, hauing at length willingly parted with that which was the sole cause of the Citties rising vizt. the Militia of ye Citty'.[140] With the failure of London's counter-revolution, royalists had little choice, for the time being at least, other than to consider again what was on offer by way of peace proposals.

Juxon offers a lively description of the great multitudes – including aldermen in their gowns – going down to Westminster on 6 August for a very different purpose from that which had taken them there during the tumult of 26 July. He also remarks on the exemplary and disciplined behaviour of the soldiers escorting the formerly fugitive Speakers and members back to parliament – 'twas not heard of soe much as an apple tooke by any of them' – in contrast both to the widely propagated fears about a disorderly and plundering soldiery and to the uncontrolled behaviour of the brutal and undisciplined reformadoes who had lorded it in London over the past weeks. The unexceptionable and disciplined demeanour of the soldiers was also remarked by some observers who cannot be described as friends of the army.[141] Not by all of them, however, for as Juxon went on to observe, there were some who insisted on seeing the occasion as an insolent 'triumph' inflicted by the army on a defeated and humiliated city, while Clement Walker mentions threats by some of the soldiers to cut the throats of those who had remained in parliament after 26 July.[142] One early straw in the wind

139. Dr Williams's Library, MS. 24.50, fo. 118(b).
140. Bodleian, Clarendon MSS., 30, fo. 29.
141. See, e.g., *A Religious Retreat Sounded to a Religious Army* (27 August 1647), BL., E.404(34), pp. 2–3. For Juxon's account, Dr Williams's Library, MS. 24.50, fos. 118(b)–19(b). For an adverse comment on the false predictions of London Presbyterian ministers, see *The Pulpit Incendiary* (4 May 1648), BL., E.438(10), p. 42.
142. Walker, *Independency*, pp. 18–19. See also *The Army Anatomized* (4 December 1647), BL., E.419(6), pp. 29–30; *The Petition of Right of the Free-holders and Freemen* . . . (8 January 1648), E.422(9), p. 13.

was the refusal on 9 August of Fairfax, who had been created Constable of the Tower, to accede to the request of the City deputation at his inauguration that he continue the appointment of Colonel Francis West as Lieutenant of the Tower, a post which was in the Constable's gift. Fairfax intimated that he preferred Colonel Robert Tichborne, who was also a Londoner, but a noted Independent. West, whom the new Constable politely described as 'a worthy man', had in fact completely identified himself with the counter-revolutionary developments of the previous weeks.[143]

The City's undignified consumption of humble pie is contemptuously described in a newsletter as early as 5 August, the day before the army's full occupation of London:

> Such is the suddaine turne of affaires in the Citty that they who before threatned nothing butt ruine to the army . . . doe now begin to repent, nay are ashamed to show their heads . . . and have recalled their Declaration . . . against the Army. Happy is that Commander that laid downe his commission butt two dayes since, hoping itt will save his stake, as Col. Campfeild and others.[144]

But the army also had its problems. The situation was broadly that if it were to remain in London, in such great numbers, it might be in no position to deal with counter-revolutionary outbursts in the provinces, such as the recent disturbances in South Wales.[145] On the other hand, to move from London might make possible a recurrence of the developments of late July, especially with so many of those responsible still at large. Hence the need to act promptly against such offenders, whether the eleven members, most of whom had fled, or their city associates, the Lord Mayor and other persons, who were imprisoned to await trial for high treason, or, at the very least, in some cases, high crimes and misdemeanours.[146] For an uncomfortable fortnight the situation was rendered even more difficult by the unco-operative attitude of the House of Commons. Despite the restoration of the fugitive Independent MPs, the Presbyterians were still dominant in the Lower House, which had also to be brought to heel, since it was showing a remarkable

---

143. *Cal.SPD. 1645–7* ('Perfect Occurrences', no. 32), pp. 598–9; *L.J.*, IX, 375; *C.J.*, V, 269; *Two Speeches Made by the Speakers of both Houses* (August 1647), BL., E.401(15), pp. 3–4. For Juxon's account, see Dr Williams's Library, MS. 24.50, fo. 119.

144. *Clarke Papers*, I, 221.

145. On these disturbances, see below, pp. 341–6.

146. For a moderate plea, which, while recognizing the army's grievances about the militia in July, calls on it now to treat those who had opposed it then in a spirit of forgiveness, see William Levitt, *The Samaritans Box Newly Opened* (17 November 1647), BL., E.416(4), especially pp. 6–9, 12.

reluctance to go along with the more co-operative House of Lords in annulling the measures passed between 26 July and 6 August. It was finally to yield only on 19 August, and then only after further pressure from the Lords and from the army, the latter trenchantly expressed in its famous Remonstrance of 18 August.[147] As to the City, long before the end of the year, in late November, it was petitioning parliament for a recovery of much of what it had lost as a result of the events of July and August, including control of its own militia and the dropping of charges against the ex-Lord Mayor, delinquent aldermen and others, disingenuously protesting that they had never any knowledge of or consented to 'that late dangerous engagement' which they utterly abhorred.[148]

Another issue on which the army found reason to deplore parliament's less than wholehearted co-operation was the City's assessment arrears. On 26 August the Commons tried to negotiate with the City for a loan of £50,000 for soldiers' pay, which was to be repaid – an astonishing arrangement – by being deducted with interest from the arrears already due from it.[149] There followed on 23 September and again in October and November requests from the army council that a stiff monetary penalty should be imposed if the arrears were not paid by a stipulated date, and, moreover, that the Lord General should, if necessary, be accorded the power to collect both arrears and penalty by force. In November it was only through the intervention of parliament on its behalf and the City's promise to make a more determined effort to bring in the arrears that it was saved from having 1,000 soldiers under Colonel Hewson quartered upon it, and again on 5 December the army council remonstrated that the army's patience was not inexhaustible.[150] Nevertheless, by the spring of 1648 the City's assessments were still heavily in arrears, and a parliamentary ordinance of 24 April appointed commissioners in the wards for getting them in; again, it would seem,

147. For full details, see Ashton, *Civil War*, p. 304. The Remonstrance is printed in *Parliamentary History*, XVI, 251–73.
148. *The Perfect Weekly Account, Number 8* (30 November/8 December 1647), BL., E.419(17), sig. y–y^v.
149. *C.J.*, V, 284, 301; CLRO., Jor. 40, fos. 255, 255(b)–6, 256(b), 257–7(b); *HMC., 6th. Rep. (House of Lords Cal. 1647)*, p. 195.
150. CLRO., Jor. 40, fos. 260–60(b), 261(b), 262; *Cal.SPD. 1645–7*, p. 603; *L.J.*, IX, 539, 562; *C.J.*, V, 366; *A Letter from Sir Thomas Fairfax to the Lord Major* [sic] (19 November 1647), BL., E.416(18), pp. 3–7; *A Letter from the Lord Major, Aldermen and Common Counsel* (20 November 1647), E.417(2), also E.417(3), pp. 3–8; *A New Declaration from Eight Regiments . . .* (25 November 1647), E.416(35), pp. 1–2; *Mercurius Melancholicus, Number 13* (20/29 November 1647), E.417(17), p. 77; *Mercurius Pragmaticus, Number 11* (23/30 November 1647), E.417(20), no pagination; *An Humble Representation from His Excellencie . . .* (8 December 1647), E.419(16), pp. 20–1; Bell, *Memorials*, I, 386–8.

only with indifferent success.[151] There we must leave the matter for the moment.

On 4 February 1648 the City entertained Fairfax, his principal subordinates and some of the army's parliamentary allies to a banquet, where 'the Fife and Drum played all dinner while, and, to make up the Harmony, the Citie Trumpeters afforded great melody', the mood being marked by post-prandial mutual assurances of good affection.[152] As Colonel Overton, the Governor of Hull, remarked in a letter a week later, the army now had nothing to fear from the City, which had 'nothing left to hedge in the cuckoo, or to head their headless multitudes. The militia, Tower and army is all our own, and nothing theirs, except their wealth and voices, and that not unquestionable.'[153]

As to the militia, that potentially contentious matter was to be more or less settled in late April by a compromise, however uneasy, whereby the City was formally to regain control, but the commander of the London defence forces was to be Major-General Philip Skippon. Skippon was a pious Presbyterian in religion, but also a New Model stalwart and infantry commander, a man in whom Fairfax had complete confidence. Needless to say, royalist and ultra-conservative elements would greatly have preferred Major-General Browne, for whose appointment in place of Skippon there was further unsuccessful agitation in June. As to the Tower, Colonel Tichborne, Fairfax's nominee of the previous August, was finally replaced as Lieutenant by none other than Colonel Francis West. This might be regarded as a potential conservative victory, had it not been for Skippon's removal of most of the arms and ammunition in the Tower to Windsor Castle. Another consequence of the army's confidence in Skippon's appointment was the removal at the end of May of Colonels Barkstead's and Rich's regiments from Whitehall and the Mews, where they had long been a source of disquiet as a potential means whereby the army might intimidate parliament, even though they went no further than Southwark in order to protect London from a possible attack from the Kentish insurgents. The earl of Lanark's English correspondent had doubtless been whistling to keep Scottish spirits up by reporting on 22 February that the army had 'made no farther entry vppon the Citties priviledges who keepe their Armes and stand on theire owne Leggs'.[154] Things were no worse for

151. *A&O.*, I, 1128–31; *L.J.*, X, 229–30.
152. *The Kingdomes Weekly Post, Number 6* (2/9 February 1648), BL., E.426(13), p. 44; *The manner of . . . Sir Thomas Fairfax . . . entertainment* (February 1648), Codrington pamph. coll., pp. 4–6.
153. Bell, *Memorials*, II, 11.
154. SRO., GD 406/1/2458. It had been rumoured earlier in the month that Fairfax had persuaded Lord Mayor Warner that the London trained bands' arms should be

the City by May, but its ability to stand up to the army was not notably improved.[155]

While there had been no foundation in the optimistic rumour circulating in the Netherlands towards the end of February that half of London had been burned down as a result of fights between the soldiers and the citizens,[156] every attempt was made by royalists and others to keep the City in mind of its long-standing grievances against the army. One strongly anti-Independent and anti-army pamphlet of January 1648 which we have already had occasion to notice in other contexts hardly missed a single possible point in this matter.[157] In particular, the Scots Engagers, alarmed at the dangers of rapprochement between the City and the hated sectarian army, did their utmost to convince the citizens of the need to preserve their traditional alliance.[158] Indeed, two incidents in April did appear to offer a threat to continuing good relations between army and City. The first was a riot on 9 April. While this might have betokened deeper discontent, it had arisen out of a trivial incident following an attempt by the Puritan Independent Lord Mayor John Warner, who had succeeded the deposed royalist John Gayre in September, to repress 'Sporting, Tipling and other Disorders' on the Sabbath. The disorder began in Moorfields and spread across the City with extensive damage to property. But far from the army's role in suppressing the riots notably alienating the citizens and affording a golden opportunity for a Scottish invasion, as Lanark's correspondent had hoped it might,[159] the Lord Mayor and Common Council offered heartfelt thanks to the Lord General for the invaluable co-operation of his men with the City trained bands, and the soldiers were voted £1,000 in recompense. The danger that this minor anti-Sabbatarian tumult might have developed into something seriously political was

---

handed over to the army (*Mercurius Elencticus*, *Number 10* (26 January/22 February 1648), BL., E.425(7), p. 76, and ibid., *Number 11* (2/9 February 1648), E.426(12), p. 84).

155. For a much more detailed account of the developments in this paragraph, see I. Gentles, 'The Struggle for London in the Second Civil War', *Hist.J.*, XXVI (1983), especially pp. 291–5.

156. Rushworth, *Historical Collections*, VII, 1015.

157. *The Petition of Right of the Free-holders and Free-men . . .* (8 January 1648), BL., E.422(9), pp. 12–13. Some of the grievances here mentioned, e.g. the replacement of West by Tichborne in August, were as has been shown, repudiated during the subsequent weeks.

158. On this see *Arguments Against All Accommodation and Treaties Between the Citie of London and The Ingaged Grandees* (4 April 1648), BL., E.434(20) (also Codrington pamphlet coll.), pp. 1–6. One of the declared aims of the Scots parliament was that 'the City of *London* may enjoy its liberty and, priviledges which it had before the late encroachment of the Armies' (*A Declaration of the Parliament of Scotland* (April 1648), Codrington pamphlet coll., p. 11).

159. *Hamilton Papers*, p. 181.

emphasized by reports of the beating of drums on the river to involve the seamen and watermen '*for God and King Charles*'. Clement Walker's verdict that the army had welcomed the tumult as an excuse to stay in the vicinity of London should not be taken too seriously, though this was doubtless a consequence of it.[160]

Another occurrence in April offered a more serious threat to the improved relations between army and City. This was the affidavit sworn by one John Everard on 23 April, deposing that, while lying in bed at an inn in Windsor, he had overheard a conversation in the adjoining room between some high-ranking army officers to the effect that there was a plan for the city to be disarmed to prevent it from joining forces with the expected Scottish invaders.[161] These revelations fostered a state of alarm bordering on panic in the city. 'The Common Council were this day all in a flame', wrote one observer, 'because of confident intelligence of an intention to plunder the citty, confirmed by the draweing of the army very close and round it . . .'.[162] The matter was referred to parliament, the chains were raised again in the London streets and other defensive measures adopted. Parliament, while ordering the examination of Everard, tended to pooh-pooh the alleged army plots, and the most notable longer-term product of the scare was the appointment of Skippon to his command of the London forces. But the incident had temporarily revived something of the tense atmosphere which had prevailed in June and July of the previous year in relations between City and army.[163]

One of the main causes of resentment of many citizens – though not of the Independent Lord Mayor John Warner – against the army was

160. *L.J.*, X, 188, 190–2, 194, 195; *C.J.*, V, 528, 529; Rushworth, *Historical Collections*, VII, 1051–2, 1055–6, 1059–60; *Whitelock Diary*, pp. 211–12; Whitelock, *Memorials*, pp. 298–9 (10 April); *An Act and Declaration of the Common Council touching the late Insurrection* (11 April 1648), BL., E.435(22), pp. 3–7; *A full Narration of the late Riotous Tumult* (11 April 1648), E.435(24), pp. 1–4, 9–10; *The Rising and Routing of the Mutineers . . .* (April 1648), E.435(4), pp. 1–6. For a very partial account, as biassed as his account of the clash between the Surrey petitioners and the soldiers on 16 May, see Walker, *Independency*, preface, and pp. 55–8.
161. For the affidavit see BL., 669, f12(10); CLRO., Jor. 40, fo. 267(b); Rushworth, *Historical Collections*, VII, 1070.
162. *HMC., MSS. of the Earl of Ancaster.* p. 414 (Captain M. Foster to John Pidgeon).
163. CLRO., Jor. 40, fos. 267(b), 269, 270–1; *A Declaration of the Lord Major Aldermen and Common-Councell . . .* (25 April 1648), BL., E.437(2), pp. 1–3; *The Humble Petition of the Lord Major, Aldermen and Commons* (25 April 1648), Codrington pamphlet coll., pp. 3–12; *The true answer of the Parliament to the petition of the Lord Major* (25 April 1648), BL., E.437(2); *L.J.*, X, 234–5; *C.J.*, V, 546: Rushworth, *Historical Collections*, VII, 1072–4; *HMC., 7th. Rep. (House of Lords Cal. 1648)*, p. 23; *Hamilton Papers*, pp. 190–1. For the questioning of the appropriateness of Skippon's appointment, given his connection with the army and lack of a visible estate in the city, see *Certain Quaeries* (July 1648), BL., 669, f12(90).

removed in late May and June, when firstly Recorder Glyn and eight senior trained band officers who had been imprisoned and awaited trial for the part they had played in the London counter-revolution of July 1647 were released on 23 May and the charges against them dropped. This was followed by the release of Warner's predecessor as Lord Mayor, the deposed Alderman Sir John Gayre, along with his three aldermanic colleagues, Atkins, Langham and Bunce, on 6 June, when the charges against the ten survivors of the eleven members were also dropped. The aldermen, like Sir John Maynard, had previously refused to accept the jurisdiction of the House of Lords. In view of their role during the summer of the previous year, some eyebrows must have been raised at the request for their release being couched in terms of its being 'a Means for the better raising of Forces for the securing of the Parliament and City'. However, their day had passed and with it their ability to threaten the safety of either.[164]

But mutual suspicions survived the extraordinary *volte face* of 6 June. The old opponents of the army canvassed the need to disarm sectaries – whom, amongst others, including apprentices, Skippon had begun to recruit in alarming numbers[165] – who, it was feared, might well join forces with the army to plunder and subdue the city once the soldiers returned from their campaigns. Concessions such as the restoration of West to the Lieutenancy of the Tower and the dropping of the charges against the aldermen were, it was argued, mere sops to keep the citizens quiet for the time being and the army would show its true hand later.[166]

164. CLRO., Jor. 40, fos. 277, 279, 281; *L.J.*, X, 278, 296, 303, 307, 308; Rushworth, *Historical Collections*, VII, 1124–6, 1134; *Two Petitions to the Lords and Commons* (June 1648), BL., E.445(24), p. 5; *Parliamentary History*, XVII, 171–3, 197. For the articles which had been brought against the aldermen in April, see *L.J.*, X, 213–15, 217–19; *Parliamentary History*, XVII, 96–103. For their refusal to accept the jurisdiction of the House of Lords, *L.J.*, X, 208, 231–2; *HMC., 7th. Rep. App. (House of Lords Cal. 1648)*, p. 23; Rushworth, *Historical Collections*, VII, 1070; *The Humble Petition of the Worshipful . . . Aldermen* (April 1648), Codrington pamphlet coll., pp. 5–8.

165. For the argument that to oppose Skippon's raising of these recruits would be to play into the hands of the Cavaliers, see *A Serious Advice to all the Honest Presbyterians* (August 1648), BL., E.456(33), pp. 1–5. On the concern about Skippon's allegedly indiscriminate enlistments and his dispute with the City Militia Committee, CLRO., Jor. 40, fos. 288(b), 289–9(b), 291–1(b); HLRO., MP. 11/8/1648, 25/8/1648; *L.J.*, X, 390–1; *C.J.*, V, 671–2; Rushworth, *Historical Collections*, VII, 1199, 1207–8, 1224, 1227; *Certain Quaeries* (July 1648), BL., 669, f12(90): *The humble Petition of the Lord Major . . .* (July 1648), BL., E.453(39), pp. 1–2, 5–6; *The Letters Commissions And other Papers . . . communicated to the Common-Councel* (26 July 1648), E.456(31), pp. 5–6, and Gentles, *Hist.J.*, art. cit., pp. 295–300.

166. See *The humble Desires of the Loyall hearted wel-affected Freemen . . .* (3 June 1648), BL., 669, f12(39); *Take Warning before it is too late; or Notice to the City of London* (June 1648), BL., E.445(39), passim, esp. pp. 3–4; *The necessity of the speedy calling a Common Hall* (21 June 1648), E.449(10), p. 5; *To all those that challenge an interest in the Common Hall* (23 June 1648), BL., 669, f12(54); *The Resolutions of the Army against the King,*

In their turn the soldiers and their political allies were quick to note, as in the mid-August petition of radical Independents and Levellers, that the City's untoward zest for a treaty with the king had not been accompanied by 'the like expression of their zeal for the Reformation of Religion, Freedom of Parliament and Liberty of the Subject to be provided for in that Treaty . . . whereby they have too much gratified and strengthened the Common enemy . . .'.[167] The parliamentary decision to countenance a treaty with the king was indeed the greatest reward for the City's quiescence in the Second Civil War, but this again was hardly designed to make for good relations with the army.

The mid-August petition had also stressed the assumed connection between malignant counter-revolutionary intentions – or, at the very least, a deficiency of enthusiasm for the parliamentary cause – and footdragging over assessment arrears which had persisted through the Second Civil War. On 27 July a visiting parliamentary committee urged on Common Council the need for expedition in this matter. This or a similar incident occasioned the derision of the royalist commentator *Mercurius Elencticus*, who describes Common Council as fawning on the committee 'like so many poore Curres', and rejoiced that the decay of trade which he ascribed to insurgent successes at sea rendered their efforts fruitless. On 25 August the House of Commons, after urging the army's needs on Common Council nine days earlier without effect, required it to send up the names of assessment defaulters and negligent collectors. 'The Forces in the North [are] to have shoos and stockings provided', observed *The Moderate* for 23 August, 'but not till the City be pleased to pay their arreares'.[168]

The soldiers' frustration turned to anger in September as their valour in the Second Civil War seemed likely to be wasted by the opening of a treaty with the king of which the City had been one of the most enthusiastic advocates. While the army had been campaigning against what ought to have been the common enemy, protested a paper on 26 September purporting to express the views of the army as a whole, there had developed a movement in both City and parliament 'to set up that Party at home, which we are pulling downe abroad'. Besides seeking to

Kingdome and City (July 1648), BL., 669, f12(89); *Looke to it London threatened to be fired by Wilde-fire-zeal* . . . (July 1648), BL., E.457(27). For attempts to assuage the City's fears, see *The Resolution of the Armie Concerning the City* . . . (17 August 1648), E.459(18), p. 6: *Lieutenant Generall Cromwell His Declaration Concerning the City* . . . (August 1648), E.459(24), pp. 1–3.

167. *The Humble Petition of divers Well-affected Citizens* . . . (August 1648), BL., 669, f12(106).

168. CLRO., Jor. 40, fos. 289, 295–5(b): *C.J.*, V, 682; Rushworth, *Historical Collections*, VII, 1229; *Mercurius Elencticus, Number 46* (23/30 August 1648), BL., E.461(20), pp. 323–4; *The Moderate, Number 7* (22/29 August 1648), E.461(16), no pagination.

new model the Common Council and to get the militia into their own hands – no doubt a reflection on the restrictions on Skippon's activities – these delinquents had stirred up simple people to put their names to a petition for a personal treaty and persuaded parliament to revoke the Vote of No Addresses. The language and sentiments of this declaration have such a strong affinity with those of the radical Londoners' petition of 11 September that one is tempted to suggest common authorship, or at least, collusion with the petitioners.[169]

In a debate in the House of Commons on 4 October, it emerged that the City's assessments were in arrears to the shocking amount of £80,000, a revelation which invoked appropriate fulminations from Independent MPs, among them John Venn, himself one of the MPs for the City, and Thomas Chaloner, who emphasized the contrast between the City's ingratitude to the army and the army's patience under such delay and provocations.[170] On 18 October the City was ordered to pay its arrears by 1 November.[171] Needless to say, it failed to do so and by the end of November the army's much-lauded patience was approaching breaking point on this and other matters and Fairfax announced that it was about to march on London. On the following day he wrote to the Lord Mayor and his colleagues emphasizing the urgency of the need to raise money to pay the soldiers who would now be quartered in London, though, as far as possible, in 'greate and voyd houses'.[172] On 1 December the House of Commons ordered the City immediately to pay £40,000 of its arrears, but it was too late to stay the army's march on London, which, in any case, had far more important and momentous objectives than the collection of assessment arrears. Nevertheless, as Fairfax pointed out to the Speaker on 3 December, the House itself had ordered that the army should move to garrisons and towns, and there was nowhere 'of like conveniency . . . as this place [viz. London] . . . or so much of the assessments like to come in . . . to put them into a present condition of maintaining themselves without free quarter'.[173]

169. *The Demands, Resolutions and Intentions of the Army* (26 September 1648), BL., E.464(41), pp. 3–4. The petition of 11 September (see above, p. 157) is printed in *Parliamentary History*, XVII, 450–60.
170. *Parliamentary History*, XVIII, 21–3.
171. *C.J.*, VI, 55.
172. CLRO., Jor. 40, fos. 304(b), 305, 308; *L.J.*, X, 618; *Parliamentary History*, XVIII, 266–72. On 1 and 4 December Fairfax issued two proclamations regulating the behaviour of the soldiers to be quartered in London (*Three Proclamations by His Excellency* . . . (December 1648), BL., E.475(9), pp. 3–6; Whitelock, *Memorials*, p. 354).
173. Bodleian, Tanner MSS., 57, fos. 448, 452; CLRO., Jor. 40, fos. 305(b), 306, 306(b); *C.J.*, VI, 92; Cary, *Memorials*, II, 73–4; *A Declaration of the Proceedings in Parliament* . . . (December 1648), BL., E.475(31), pp. 4–5.

The irony in the Lord General's remarks is unmistakable and one suspects that he was enjoying the events of these early December days hugely. His next unpleasant surprise for Common Council was a demand on 6 December for 3,800 beds along with 'sufficient furniture for lodging' the soldiers in Westminster at the time of Pride's Purge. Common Council's alternative offer to raise a loan of £10,000 to be repaid out of the City's assessment arrears was frustrated by the unwillingness of the parliamentary committee for army to provide the necessary assurances to potential lenders and the bedding had to be provided.[174] But this was not the only or the least shock administered to the citizens on the day of Pride's Purge. On that same day Major General Skippon was ordered to take care to suppress any tumultuous gatherings in the city. One of his measures was to restrain City Militiamen from going to Westminster, ostensibly to provide a guard for the parliament, which of course was already being done – albeit in a very different manner – by Colonel Pride's men.[175] Again on the same day, a deputation from Common Council attended the Lord General not only about the inevitable matter of assessment arrears and lodging for the soldiers but also to check the authenticity of an alarming but all too plausible rumour that one of their sheriffs, Major-General Richard Browne, was about to be arrested by the army. The rumour proved to be well founded. Browne was taken into custody on 10 December and a deputation of aldermen sent to plead for his release offered to engage themselves for his appearance when required and 'for his Civil & quiett deportment' in the meantime.

Browne was accused of plotting with Denzil Holles and the parliamentary Presbyterian militants to invite the Scottish Engagers to invade that summer. Brought before the Council of War, he insisted that they had nothing against him save 'the honest Endeavours to preserve his Majesty and his Posterity together with the Parliament, City and Kingdom, with the Laws and Government thereof, from being rooted up by them'. He was imprisoned along with others including Waller, Massey and Commissary Copley. History appeared to be repeating itself. Browne had been the great and unrealized white hope of the City in 1648 as the others had been in 1647. There is a nice but probably apocryphal tale about Browne's arrest by none other than the notorious Cornet Joyce (now promoted to a higher rank): that Joyce predictably had answered Browne's protest with the words 'doe you thinke that I,

174. CLRO., Jor. 40, fos. 307, 307(b); *The Impeachment Demands and Proposals of the Army* (December 1648), BL., E.475(36), p. 6; *The Lord Generals Warrant sent to the City* (December 1648), E.475(39), no pagination; *A Declaration . . . concerning the supply of Bedding* (December 1648), E.479(40), pp. 6–7.
175. C.J., VI, 93, 95.

who layd hands upon a King, feare [to] apprehend you who are but his Sheriffe?'[176] He might indeed have added that it was equally unlikely that those who had so flagrantly violated the privileges of parliament in Pride's Purge would scruple at infringing the privileges of the City of London. They did not. Memories of the City's counter-revolution of July 1647; disgust at the abandonment in May and June 1648 of the charges against the aldermanic leaders of that counter-revolution; and resentment at the City's enthusiasm for the treaty in the Isle of Wight, all combined to direct the army's offensive in December 1648 as much against the City of London as against the parliamentary Presbyterians and others who had rested their hopes on negotiations with the king.

Thus the army now set out to complete the unfinished business of August 1647. Not that the City offered the same military threat as at the earlier date. There were no longer any reformadoes and army deserters to augment its defences, and a report to the Common Council on 13 December observed that the unprofessional appearance and conduct of the trained bands 'gives occasion to the souldiers belonging to the army to laugh at them'.[177] This time Fairfax was unlikely to withdraw his troops without laying his hands on at least a very substantial part of the City's assessment arrears. First he ordered the seizure of the contents of the treasuries at Weavers' and Goldsmiths' Halls in anticipation of the City's paying up. This, as he put it, again no doubt with conscious irony, would save his soldiers from being troublesome or chargeable to the City.[178] To judge by the numerous complaints about the disorderly behaviour of the soldiers which extend well into 1649, they were nothing if not troublesome; unlike their predecessors whose exemplary behaviour in August 1647 was noted earlier.[179] Their unruliness may have contributed to the solution of the problem of the City's assessment arrears, for, as a result of Fairfax's threat at the end of January 1649 to quarter soldiers on the defaulting wards, a further £40,000 was immediately forthcoming from the City.[180]

176. CLRO., Jor. 40, fos. 307, 307(b); Rep. 59, fos. 325–5(b); *The Armies Impeachment* (12 December 1648), BL., E.476(6), pp. 4, 5–6; *The Demands and Desires of the Lord Generall Fairfax* (December 1648), E.475(36), pp. 1–2, 4; *The Impeachment Demands and Proposals . . .* (December 1648), E.475(36), pp. 4–5; *The unparalleld Arrest* (1648), Oxford, Worcester College pamphlet coll., pp. 3–7; Whitelock, *Memorials*, p. 356 (12 December 1648); *Parliamentary History*, XVIII, 465–6.
177. CLRO., Jor. 40, fo. 308(b).
178. Ibid., fos. 308, 308(b); *A Letter of His Excellency to the Lord Major* (9 December 1648), BL., E.475(32), pp. 3–8, also E.475(39), no pagination; *A Declaration of the Citizens . . . to the Lord General* (12 December 1648), E.476(6), pp. 1–3; *The Demands and Desires of the Lord General Fairfax* (December 1648), E.475(36), pp. 1–3.
179. For examples, CLRO., Rep. 59, fos. 339(b), 343 (1 and 8 February 1649); Whitelock, *Memorials*, p. 357 (20 December 1648).
180. CLRO., Jor. 40, fo. 309; Rep. 59, fos. 333–3(b); Whitelock, *Memorials*, p. 361 (6 January 1649).

VI
THE REVIVAL OF ROYALISM

. . . Majesty in eclipse, like the Sun, drawes eyes that would not so much
as have looked towards it, if it had shined out, and appeared like it
selfe. . . .

> The Kings Estate at Present (5 July 1647),
> BL., E.396(19), p. 2

Now fellow-subjects . . . consider how the case stands betweene his
Majesty and you; Is not his case your owne? have ye not beene both
alike abused, gulled and oppressed? Is not he deprived of his Crowne,
and are not you deprived of your liberties and estates? Is it not plaine
that his Prerogative and your freedome must fall together? and is not a
speedy settlement the only meanes to preserve them? and is there any
probability of setling till his Majesty be setled in his Throne?

> An Allarme to the City of London by the Scotch
> Army (29 August 1648), BL., E.461(19), p. 5

The more you crush him, the sweeter savour comes from him; and
while he suffers, the Spirit of God and glory rests upon him. There is a
sweet glory sparkling in him: by suffering, though you see it not. You
do but rend away his corruptions from him: and naturally men are ready
to pity sufferers. When nothing will gaine me, affliction will. I confesse
his sufferings make me a Royalist, that never cared. . . .

> William Sedgwick, Justice upon the Armie
> Remonstrance (11 December 1648),
> BL., E.475(34), pp. 30–1

Varieties of royalism

The process of alienation from the parliamentary regime which was
the subject of earlier chapters was the prime, if negative, cause of the
revival of enthusiasm for the monarchy, and in some cases of the
beginnings of such enthusiasm among those who had previously been

either indifferent to the struggle in the First Civil War or even moderate supporters of the parliamentarian cause. If Charles I were to gain the maximum advantage from this situation it was essential for him to identify himself with the popular grievances and to equate his own with his subjects' misfortunes. As in 1641–2,[1] a main danger was his wayward and erratic temperament and propensity to swing from one attitude to its opposite: from the moderate ideas of Hyde and Falkland to the extremism of the Cavaliers around the queen. Had he at last learned from his mistakes of that time and become fully conscious of the need to display consistency of purpose and concern for the interests of his subjects beyond those of extremist Cavaliers and rabid anti-Puritans?

Towards the end of the First Civil War one becomes aware – however faintly – of the re-emergence of a theme which had characterized royalist propaganda at the time when Falkland and Hyde had had Charles's ear and which royalists like Judge Jenkins were to labour in 1647:[2] that the king's willingness to concede so much in 1641–2 had simply fed parliament's craving for more. For instance, royalist papers of January 1646 stress both the concessions made by the king and his eagerness for a settlement in sharp contrast to parliament's determination to press its military advantage to extreme conclusions.[3] But Charles was doing no more than making the best out of what he regarded as a very bad job: to emphasize the constitutional concessions which had been forced out of him in 1641 as if they had been willingly conceded. The wise advice proffered by the Scottish chancellor Loudoun in July and October 1646 about the disastrous likely consequences of Charles's unwillingness to accept the Anglo-Scottish peace terms fell on deaf ears,[4] and, as the French ambassador Bellièvre remarked in a dispatch to Brienne in October, the king's intransigence was the despair of his more sagacious advisers.[5] Others of his followers would doubtless have been satisfied with no less than a complete reversion to the *status quo ante* not 1642 but 1639; a return to the days of the Star Chamber, High Commission and non-parliamentary rule. Nor is there the slightest doubt that it was this latter position, rather than that of 1641, which was the best of all Charles's ideal, even if not practicable, worlds, as a parliamentary pamphlet of August 1647 was to argue convincingly.[6]

---

1. See Ashton, *Civil War*, especially pp. 145–8, 159–66.
2. D. Jenkins, *Lex Terrae* (1647), BHPC., especially pp. 15–16. For another later example, see *A calme Consolatory view of the sad Tempestuous affaires* (April 1647), BL., E.384(13), p. 7.
3. Bodleian, Tanner MSS., 60, fos. 373, 384–5(b).
4. For Loudoun's advice, see above, p. 12.
5. *Montereul Correspondence*, I, 297. 'Ceux qui sont affectionez à son seruice, disant qu'ils ne peuent rien faire pour luy, n'ayant eu despuis deux mois le moindre proposition de sa part qui leur donnat moyen de soustenir son parti'.
6. *Eighteen Queries* (2 August 1647), BL., E.400(35), pp. 2–6.

The tragedy of post-war royalism is that while the king recognized that in the conditions of 1646–7 this ideal was right outside the realms of practical possibility, he never convincingly and consistently modified his aims in accordance with this fact. When he might at last seem to be moving in this direction at the end of 1647, emphasizing in a letter of 6 December what a notable contribution to a settlement of the kingdom he had made 'by devesting Himself of so much power and authority, as by this last Message He hath promised to do, upon the concluding of the whole Peace', it was too late.[7] The sorry tale of evasive tactics and unreliable undertakings between his being handed over by the Scots in February and his flight to the Isle of Wight in November had dispelled any illusions that he had at last seen the error of his ways and could now be relied upon to accept and observe moderate and reasonable terms.[8]

Even if this had not been so, some of the king's most fervent followers were an obstacle to the establishment of any image of the moderate monarchy wedded to the constitutional changes of 1641. One did not have to be among the most accommodating of moderate royalists to recognize what harm Cavalier extremists, 'dammee Cavalier blades', might do to the royal cause. Edward Symmons, the author of an impeccably royalist treatise published in November 1647 who was certainly not lacking in devotion to the king and hatred of his enemies, nevertheless thanked God that he himself had been preserved 'from the mischiefs (of being beaten and pistolled) often threatened by some of the prophaner sort of our Cavalleers for my free preaching against their blasphemy and dissolutenesse, their self-seeking, lust-pleasing and King-neglecting basenesse'.[9] 'Have you not heard', asked a moderate royalist pamphleteer in August 1648, 'that a good Cause is often lost by wicked Instruments?' The same writer strongly deplored the fact that

> If a man nowadays remembers not to tithe his words with a *God-dam-mee* . . . we juge him for no right Cavallier nor the Kings friend. Or if another will not drinke till his Imagination coynes miracles to make him see stars at noone . . . we condemne him for a precise fellow, Coxcomb and a Round-head. . . . So . . . feare the most of us [to] shake hands with the very power of godlinesse itselfe, because we will not seeme to be like our Adversaries. . . .

---

7. *His Majesties Most Gracious Message to His Two Houses of Parliament* (December 1647), BL., E.419(11), pp. 3–7; *The Kingdomes Weekly Interlligencer Number 238* (7/14 December 1647), E.419(24), pp. 761–2.
8. For a detailed account of the negotiations over these months, see above, pp. 15–30.
9. Edward Symmons, *A Vindication of King Charles* (November 1647), BL., E.414(16), Preface, no pagination.

Writing while the Second Civil War was still raging, the author regretfully concluded that

> if we turne our rage upon God, and dart defiances at Heaven, from our frequent swearing and accustomed prophanation, All the service we can doe our Prince . . . will bee . . . [to] weigh him downe with our sins in a few dayes, much more then our swords will be able to raise him againe in a few yeares.[10]

> *The King and's people long since had been one*
> *Had not such tos-pots sworne him out on's throne*

was the verdict of one anti-royalist news-sheet that autumn, dwelling on the behaviour of Cavalier prisoners in Peterhouse, where was 'such a crew of matchlesse monsters of that generation . . . daily skirmishing with sacke and whores and discharging oathes and blasphemies'.[11] The picture might be overdone but the stereotype was only too familiar.

Riotous behaviour, unrestrained lust and violence when that lust was thwarted feature prominently in an incident complained of in a petition from fourteen of the shopkeepers of the New Exchange in the Strand to the House of Lords on 3 February 1648. The occasion was one of a number of violent incidents in which arrogant and overbearing Cavaliers had run amok in the area with the minimum of interference from local constables. Several of the offenders had already been sued to outlawry, but since they seem to have been able to rely on the co-operation of the sheriffs and their officers, this did not deter them. On this occasion the earl of Anglesey and some cavalier companions attempted to force their lascivious attentions on a maiden in one of the shops, 'with French complements and . . . the Maiden's modest blushes put her to a retreat, which caused some of the neighbour shop keepers to desire the Royalists to bee civil, for which he [*sic*] got some sword-blows over his neck & shoulders & [was] in danger to lose his life'. The Cavaliers had departed with swords drawn and pistols cocked, swearing 'Damme, they would kill all that should . . . resist them', and threatening to return with the same object in view. Apparently no attempt had been made either by the Westminster constables or the guards in the Strand to restrain their outrageous behaviour.[12]

Naturally a propensity for drinking deeply, especially at appropriately royal occasions, did not preclude – indeed, it might encourage – a

---

10. *Englands Dust and Ashes Raked up* (16 August 1648), BL., E.459(10), pp. 94–7.
11. *Mercurius Anti-Mercurius Number 2* (26 September/2 October 1648), BL., E.465(11), pp. 3–4.
12. *L.J.*, X, 18–19; *The Kingdomes Weekly Account . . . Number 5* (2/9 February 1648), BL., E.426(14), pp. 33–4.

willingness to disrupt the celebrations of the opposing party. Such an occasion was the celebration in Salisbury on 22 September 1646 of the day of thanksgiving ordained by parliament for victory in the war. On this occasion celebratory bonfires in the city were wantonly destroyed by a number of Cavaliers in search of a fight. One of them, a certain John Beckham, previously overhearing a discussion about the arrangements for providing the bonfires, had pronounced 'that he was a Cavaleire & soe would Liue and dye, And . . . that they were Rebelles. And speakinge alsoe aboute makinge a Bon fier and ioyninge theire moneyes to buy faggottes . . . Beckham asked what against the Kinge[?]'. When destroying the bonfires, Beckham and two companions attacked the celebrants with staves calling them rogues, and it seems surprising that there was no effective resistance to them.[13] Such incidents seem to have increased in both number and ferocity as disillusionment with the post-war regime gathered pace. One particularly nasty incident took place in the Strand in December 1647 and is recounted gleefully by the royalist newswriter *Mercurius Melancholicus*. Passing a portrait of the king displayed outside a limner's shop, an over-zealous Puritan knocked out the eyes. The limner naturally demanded recompense, and the offender refusing was set on by the crowd drawn there by the incident. The crowd took it upon itself to 'doe exemplary justice on him, carrying him to the Muse [viz. Mews], and therein rebaptized him in the horse poole, slit his nose, tore in pieces his clothes . . . and so dismist him with as much life in him as might make him sensible of a hanging'.[14]

Men swollen by arrogant pride, boiling over with resentment at their humiliations attendant upon military defeat, were not slow to attempt to turn even the most minor unrest or disturbance to their advantage. An official newsletter of February 1648 tells of such a one, who was apprehended in Southwark for being in London without leave contrary to parliamentary ordinance and sent to the Gatehouse. Having been 'high in his cups' he had asked those around him, 'if you saw a tumult in the street, would you goe out with your sword, and give the word for God and King Charles? Besides many other such like speeches.'[15] We have already had occasion to note the Cavalier propensity to turn demonstrations into tumults in the case of the disturbances in London in July 1647 and the presentation of the Surrey petition in May 1648.[16] The mob which sacked the Excise House at Worcester in January 1648 were shouting 'downe with the Committee, and for God and King

13. BL., Add. MSS., 22,084, fo. 6.
14. *Mercurius Melancholicus* (11/19 December 1647), BL., E.420(4), p. 94.
15. *The Kingdomes Weekly Post Number 7* (9/15 February 1648), BL., E.427(11), p. 49.
16. See above, pp. 150–51.

Charles', influenced, so a local Roundhead claimed, by 'a pestilent booke' called *Loyalty speakes truth* which was circulating in that city, and all part of a deeply laid royalist design.[17] Excise was certainly a sufficiently detested tax for the Cavaliers to be happy to claim some of the credit for associating with disturbances against it. On 15 January 1647 two sub-Commissioners of Excise in Yorkshire complained to their superiors in London about

> the Evill Carraige of one Mr Marwood . . . who came into the [Excise] office [at Leeds] accompanied with diuerse other Cauvaleirs . . . & then in an vnseemly behauiour & threatning speeches against our proceedings to ye ill example of ye Countrey people present, Snatches the Ordnance from vs, cast it with fury vnder his feete, vttring vnciuill speeches against ye Parliament, as modesty will not permitt to mention, offered to drawe his sword against some of vs that were then there, but being prevented, he fell vpon our cheife Clarke and tore his flesh, [and] afterward mett with him abroad & beate him with his Cane . . . Swearing that if euer he mett him againe, he would be the death of him. Wee thought good to acquaint you with what desperate Men we have to deale with.[18]

It was not only with their political enemies that Cavaliers showed a propensity to pick quarrels. Readiness to take quick offence at real or imagined slights or insults combined with undisciplined behaviour and often with over-indulgence in strong drink meant that fierce disputes and duels between those who should have been comrades were always on the cards, even among those engaged in desperate campaigns in the Second Civil War. Following a duel between two Cavalier officers at Pontefract Castle, which had recently been successfully taken by royalist insurgents, duelling was prohibited to the garrison on pain of death by an order of 7 October 1648; one of the duellists was imprisoned – had the other been killed? – and a high-ranking officer, Colonel Ashton, who had played some part in the arrangement of the duel, was confined to his chamber.[19] Indeed, recourse to duelling extended to the highest. In late October, in exile in France, Prince Rupert seems to have gone out of his way to provoke a duel with the senior royalist councillor Lord Culpepper. According to a letter to Speaker Lenthall from Walter Strickland, parliament's agent at the Hague, 'one of the Prince's great creatures, Sir Robert Welsh, a papist, struck my Lord Colepepper; which men think was by Prince Rupert's instigation', and indeed on 22

17. *A Letter to a Member of the House of Commons* (February 1648), BL., E.425(20), pp. 3–6.
18. Bodleian, Tanner MSS., 59, fo. 663.
19. West Yorkshire Archive Service, Leeds City R.O., Bacon Frank MSS., BF/3, p. 86.

November it was reported that a challenge had passed between Rupert and Culpepper.[20]

One of the ways in which roistering Cavaliers made themselves a nuisance to the general public was by forcing people to drink the king's health. A certain Captain Musgrave, a reformado officer who was to end up in Newgate prison, had been, according to a formal deposition given in September 1647, very prominent in the counter-revolutionary mob which assaulted parliament on 26 July 1647. The witness stated that Musgrave had uttered numerous murderous sentiments about some of the MPs whom he reviled as 'Traytors; put them out, hang their gutts about the necks & many such like words'. According to another informant, 'Captain Musgrave having calld for Beare began to drink the Kings health and desired . . . this Informant to pledge the same, which he refusing, there was a cry taken vpp, there are Spies amongst vs'.[21] The incident clearly illustrates how willingness to drink the king's health became both a royalist shibboleth and a mark of disloyalty to parliament. As the royalist *Mercurius Elencticus* would put it, 'It is the prime *Marke* of their [viz. the Roundheads'] *fidelity* to the *Kingdome* to speake *Treason* against his *Majesty*, but an Infallible *Symptome* of *Malignancy* in us but to *Drinke* the Kings *Health*'.[22] On 8 December 1647 Francis Palfreman, the owner of the Three Cranes tavern near the Savoy, and Edward Sacker deposed before the House of Lords that about nine persons, among them the Cavalier Colonel Wiltshire and one Pope, coming out from a cookshop by the Savoy during the night, called for wine from the tavern and then proceeded to force passers-by to drink the king's health. The House ordered that two JPs examine the offenders and report their findings to it.[23] Nor did parliament's victory in the Second Civil War succeed in putting an end to the practice. On 17 November 1648 the Derby House Committee ordered City militia officers to take measures against the continuing practice on public holidays of forcing people to drink the king's health at bonfires in the city which provided both the occasion for the assembling of malignants and a potential focus for counter-revolutionary insurrection and tumult.[24]

In the meantime, however, the habit spread even to the army itself. In April 1647 some of Fairfax's soldiers in Norfolk beat up a

---

20. *Naval Documents*, p. 391; Whitelock, *Memorials*, p. 351 (entry for 22 November 1648).
21. HLRO., MP., 25/9/1647, fos. 21–2.
22. *Mercurius Elencticus Number 10* (26 January/2 February 1648), BL., E.425(7), pp. 70–71. On 20 May 1646 the Westminster Assembly had resolved that drinking of healths ought to be added to the enumeration of scandalous sins (*Westminster Assembly Minutes*, p. 234).
23. *L.J.*, IX, 566.
24. *Cal.SPD. 1648–9*, p. 327.

Presbyterian constable and others for refusing to drink the king's health.[25] A news-sheet reported in early January 1648 that a soldier was whipped naked three times around the turnpike at Oxford for drinking the king's health 'in a deboyst manner'.[26] Finally, if the earl of Lanark's ever-hopeful English correspondent's report is to be credited in his dispatch of 18 April 1648, the troops of Colonel Thorney's regiment of horse, moving reluctantly from Lincoln to Leicester under orders, demanded to be disbanded with two months' arrears of pay paid to them. After getting drunk, they told Thorney that if he would not drink the king's health with them, he was no colonel to them.[27]

The outrageous behaviour of the wilder Cavaliers could not but tarnish the whole royalist image in some degree at least and militate against the easy gaining of recruits from less strongly committed sources. Incidents such as some of those which have been recounted here helped to foster the terrifying image of Cavalier violence and rapine which had exercised the popular imagination at least since the publication of Goodwin's *Anti-Cavalierism* in 1643. This in turn was held up as a disincentive to entering into a treaty with the king, which, some represented, would be as certain to result in the triumph of rampant Cavalierism as a royalist victory in the Second Civil War would have done. Thus the citizens of London were warned by one radical pamphleteer that 'if you desire to see your Wives and Daughters ravished before your faces, and your Childrens brains dasht against the stones by blood thirsty Cavaliers', all that was needed was to follow the prescription of the 'headstrong Aldermen and Common-Councel-men, in their hasty pursuance of a personall Treaty with the King'.[28]

However, while all such Cavaliers were obviously royalists, by no means all royalists were wild, violent and feckless Cavaliers. Nevertheless, there can be no doubt that the reputation of royalism as a whole did suffer in the popular estimation from being tarred with the Cavalier brush. Just as acts of royalist extremism during the first half of 1642 had imposed limits on the returning tide of loyalty to the king and away from Pym and his followers, so did they have a similar effect in 1647–8. There would be many who would regretfully agree with the view of a pro-army pamphleteer early in 1648 that while Charles himself bore some responsibility for the sorry state of his kingdom, the chief obstacle to a settlement lay in his followers: 'those Incendiaries which have been Actors of this Designe against the Kingdom, those he calls friends,

25. Woolrych, *Soldiers and Statesmen*, p. 69. On royalist sentiments among soldiers in Norfolk, see ibid., pp. 69–70.
26. *The Kingdomes Weekly Intelligencer* (4/11 January 1648), BL., E.422(18), p. 800.
27. *Hamilton Papers*, p. 185.
28. *The Voice of Conscience to All well meaning Citizens* (July 1648), BL., 669, f12(83).

which the Parliament calls Delinquents. . . . He hath wrapt up his interest too much with theirs.'[29] But it will now be appropriate to turn from those considerations which were stemming the flow of returning sympathy for the royalist cause to those which, apart from negative factors such as disenchantment with the parliamentary regime, were pulling in the opposite direction.

Popular sympathy for the king

While the behaviour of unregenerate Cavaliers might militate against the unquestioning adherence to the idea of a revived monarchy of all who were experiencing a sense of alienation against the parliamentary regime, there was unquestionably a groundswell of enthusiasm for the king from the time of his being handed over by the Scots in February 1647. Moreover, while the restoration of the king's authority was increasingly represented as necessary to the safeguarding of the freedoms threatened by the parliamentary regime, this did not preclude a revived reverence for the mystical and quasi-divine attributes of monarchy. In a letter of 18 February 1647 to the exiled Sir Edward Nicholas, the royalist Nicholas Oudart mentions the multitudes who were already flocking to Holdenby to be touched for the king's evil, despite the parliamentary order of 9 February forbidding them to do so.[30] The phenomenon was a cause of alarm to the parliamentary commissioners at Holdenby who on 20 April wrote to Speaker Lenthall emphasizing that, despite all their efforts, 'Diseased people doe resort hether and their numbers doe daylie encrease, whoe remaine day and night at the gates with importunity, clamor and curses, of whome diuers have gott admittance'.[31] The commissioners asked to know parliament's pleasure on the matter, but the demand for the exercise of the royal healing power was unassuageable, and continued after Charles's departure from Holdenby. At Caversham in July 'he touched abundantly for the king's evil & cured many', besides liberally granting audiences and offering his hand to kiss, apparently determined to be gracious to all around him, in contrast to the frigid royal image which he had presented in earlier and better times.[32] As to the king's evil, there were some surprising recipients of the royal touch. The diary of Captain Adam Eyre, a Yorkshire officer in the parliamentary army, contains an intriguing

29. *Englands Condition Considered and Bewailed* (18 January 1648), BL., E.423(6), pp. 14–15.
30. *Nicholas Papers*, 75; *L.J.*, IX, 6.
31. Bodleian, Tanner MSS., 58, fo. 74.
32. *A Joyfull Message For all Loyall Subjects* . . . (July 1647), BL., E.398(15), no pagination.

entry dated 22 September 1647, the day on which he and his wife arrived back home following a business visit to London. On the trip the apparently scrofulous Mrs Eyre had managed an interesting diversion, when she 'procured a touch from the King for the evil'. Such an incident could easily be a source of embarrassment to the captain if knowledge of it got around, and indeed later diary entries in December and January 1647–8 suggest that relations between the Eyres may have been less than harmonious.[33]

Extolling in early August the 'brave blades', who he hoped would shortly be employed in defence of London's July counter-revolution, the parliamentary Presbyterian Sir John Maynard also marvelled how 'The K[ing] by his Wisdome since he was taken by Cornett Joyce hath gayned vpon all men of the best quallity both in Citty & Countrey'.[34] It was indeed following the army's seizure of the king on 4 June and during his subsequent journeys with an army escort that some of the most enthusiastic demonstrations occurred. As Charles, accompanied by two regiments, drew near to Cambridge on his way to Newmarket, the inhabitants decked their windows and streets with green boughs and rose bushes and strewed the ground with rushes and herbs. However, they were to be disappointed, for, perhaps fearing turbulent undergraduate demonstrations of royalist enthusiasm, the king's Progress – for it was beginning to resemble that – was diverted from Cambridge, despite Charles's reported wish 'that no Scholler be debar'd from kissing of his hand'. In the nearby village of Trumpington, through which he did pass, the streets were decked with cut boughs and celebratory bonfires erected.[35]

Similarly when Charles left Royston accompanied by Colonel Whalley and two regiments of horse, the Hertfordshire country people flocked to see him. Bells were rung in the villages through which he passed, the people throwing up their hats and shouting huzzah. At Baldock the rector in full canonicals saluted the king, 'May God bless your Majesty', toasting him with the parish communion cup. His most notable reception of all was probably at St Albans, from which he went on to Hatfield House, though the political behaviour of its owner, the earl of Salisbury, can hardly have met with his approval.[36] In general

33. West Yorkshire Archive Service, Wakefield R.O., Diary of Captain Adam Eyre, fos. 21–1(b). The later entries are not foliated.
34. HLRO., Braye MSS., 96 (photocopy of John Browne's Commonplace Book in Beinecke Library, University of Yale, Osborne MSS., Fb. 155), fos. 238–9.
35. *An Extract of certain Papers of Intelligence from Cambridge* (June 1647), BL., E.393(15), pp. 1–2; *Papers from the Army* (June 1647), E.392(14), no pagination; *His Majesties Propositions* (June 1647), E.392(12), no pagination; Kingston, *Hertfordshire*, p. 66.
36. Kingston, *Hertfordshire*, pp. 71–2.

the enthusiasm of the crowds at seeing their king would seem to a good royalist cleric like Edward Symmons an apt illustration of his argument that, if left to themselves, the people would quickly rally to the king, since 'they know him to be so full of grace and goodnesse'. This alone explained what Symmons denounced as his enemies' dastardly and desperate attempts to blacken him with slander and calumny.[37]

Like the Cambridge undergraduates, the London apprentices were denied the sight of their king, though during the high summer of 1647, culminating in the resolutions of the Presbyterian 'rump' parliament following London's counter-revolution of 26 July, the pressure for the king to be brought to London to treat unconditionally was intense. On 11 June an apprentice fly-sheet was scattered up and down the streets of London calling on people to 'vote, Fight, Cast up our Cappes and crie Vive le Roy to the late drop of Blood'. For 'Tempora mutantur et nos mutamur in illis'.[38] Perhaps times had not changed quite as much as they hoped, and the king was not to return to London until he came to face trial and execution eighteen months later. In the meantime, sold by the Scots, deprived of the company of his wife and children, shifted from place to place by the army since 4 June but not allowed to approach his capital, Charles was forcefully represented as deserving of his subjects' compassion.[39]

In the summer of 1647 there circulated in verse a contemplation of the king's manifold misfortunes:[40] his virtual imprisonment – 'which', as another pamphlet put it, 'if it bee a *Plague* to a *private* man must needs be an *Hell* to a *King*';[41] deprivation of the company of his wife and family; the threat even to his very life; his subjects' ingratitude for the reforms which he had so willingly conceded; and other trials which he suffered. The piece was written on the model, but without any hint of the genius, of George Herbert's *The Sacrifice*, in which of course it is Christ who is the sufferer. The miserable versification of the piece does not seem to have been detrimental to its circulation or impact on the reader, and the analogy between Charles and Christ was all too soon to become part of the royalist stock-in-trade.

37. Symmons, *A Vindication of King Charles*, pp. 248–9.
38. BL., E.392(7). See also the more conservative of the two apprentices' petitions, that of 8 July (BL., 669, f11(41), and above, pp. 131, 136–7) and their declaration of 31 July (*A Remonstrance and Declaration of the Young Men and Apprentices* (31 July 1647), BL., E.400(31), p. 4).
39. For royalists making much of these matters, see, e.g., James Howell, *A letter to the earle of Pembrooke* (1647), BHPC., especially pp. 9–10; *The Remonstrance of the Inhabitants of the three Isles . . .* (27 November 1647), BL., E.417(5), pp. 3–7.
40. *His Majesties Complaint occasioned by his late sufferings* (June 1647), BL., E.393(38).
41. *The case of the King stated* (1647), BHPC., p. 8.

The hand of God was indeed visible everywhere, no less to the upright royalist – as distinct from the Cavalier blade – than to his Puritan opponents. An example is Edward Symmons, who ascribed it to the workings of Providence that he had not published his lengthy *A Vindication of King Charles* two years earlier, for 'peoples hearts were not then so capable to receive a *Vindication* of their Soveraigne . . . as now they are even forced to be, by that illustrious eminency of his *graces*, which hath beamed forth in his dark condition, even to the conviction and admiration of all reasonable creatures'.[42] If Sir John Berkley is to be believed, even Oliver Cromwell himself was moved by the king's condition. In his Memoirs Berkley tells how, when he met Cromwell at Reading in July 1647, Oliver told him 'that he had lately seen the tenderest sight that ever his eyes beheld, which was the interview between the King and his Children, and wept plentifully at the remembrance of it'.[43] If Cromwell could be thus moved by the king's condition, how much more could be expected from royalist sympathizers or even from non-partisan observers! As Symmons was to exhort them, 'Tis true, He is in a low condition at the present but must our Allegeance therefore be at so low an ebbe, as to suffer him with silence to be blasphemed?'[44]

At Hampton Court where the king moved in August, it was reported on 26 August that many flocked there in ever-increasing numbers, 'ten, sixteen and twenty Coaches in a day. And we perceive the comming of divers Malignants hither.'[45] Writing on 29 August, however, Colonel Whalley, who was in charge of security at Hampton Court, mentions 'great resort of all sorts of people to him [Charles], but not so many Cavaliers as is reported; it is confessed, no Gentleman is debarred the liberty of kissing the King's hand, yet no stranger stayes long'.[46] According to one newsletter, among the throng of visitors to Hampton Court one September day was a woman who, exclaiming that '*We all come to serve the King, but what is it that we give him?*' removed a ring from her finger as a personal gift for him. Charles exploited the situation adroitly, returning the ring with his thanks and the message that 'had she brought him a Kettle for his Kitchin, or something for the Chimney, his Chamber or some other furniture, he would readily have accepted it,

42.   Symmons, *A Vindication of King Charles*, Preface, no pagination.
43.   Maseres, *Select Tracts*, I, 365.
44.   Symmons, op. cit., Preface, no pagination.
45.   *The Copy of a Letter from his Majesties Court* . . . (August 1647), BL., E.404(36), p. 5.
46.   *A Letter Sent from Col. Whalley* (31 August 1647), BL., E.405(4), p. 5. The courtier John Ashburnham was denied access for a time on refusing to give his parole that the king would not leave Hampton Court (Ashburnham, *Narrative*, II, 100–101).

for his condition was such that he wanted Houshold stuffe to begin the world againe'.[47]

Increasingly it became the concern of royalist propagandists not simply to arouse compassion for the king's captive condition but also to identify his plight with that of his people as a whole, robbed of their liberty as he was of his,[48] as well as being, as it was complained after the king absconded from Hampton Court in November, forced by threats to his life, to fly to the Isle of Wight. So much, protested a remonstrance in November purporting to come from the inhabitants of that island along with those of Guernsey and Jersey, for the parliament's declared intentions of making the king great and glorious! 'But behold his greatnesse and glory when he is forc'd to flie for his life . . . to so remote [a] place of his Dominion for shelter and refuge.'[49] Elaborating on this theme in what was to become a royalist commonplace which was much later to find its most familiar and anything but commonplace expression in Andrew Marvell's *Horatian Ode*, the royalist newswriter *Mercurius Pragmaticus* in December argued that it had been a deliberate stratagem of government to alarm the king into escape from Hampton Court. The object was 'as well to secure him out of the reach of the *Scots*, as to haue him out of the *eye* of the *People*'.[50] Yet, of course, it was in the Isle of Wight that Charles was to agree to the Engagement with the Scots, while, as to the people, they continued to pay court to him, though obviously he was geographically less accessible than he had been at Hampton Court. An account from Cowes dated 24 November tells of the eagerness of many of the gentry of the island to gain admittance to the king and kiss his hand.[51]

Nevertheless, security arrangements and constraints on the king were tighter than at Hampton Court. On 17 November *The Perfect Weekly Account* reported that the House of Lords was currently debating some instructions sent by the Commons to Colonel Hammond, the Governor of the Isle of Wight, to the effect that none who had borne arms against parliament and no foreigner should be allowed access to the king without parliamentary sanction. On 19 November Hammond wrote to the Speaker of the Upper House detailing the measures which he had

47. BL., Add. MSS., 46,375, fo. 98 (*The Kingdomes Weekly Intelligencer, number 227*) (14/21 September 1647).
48. For a splendid example, see *The Case of the King Stated* (1647), BHPC., especially pp. 8, 19, 20–1. For a later example, see *Great Britans* [*sic*] *Vote; or God save King Charles* (27 March 1648), Codrington pamphlet coll., p. 6.
49. BL., E.417(5), especially pp. 4–5.
50. *Mercurius Pragmaticus, Number 22* (7/14 December 1647), BL., E.419(22), no pagination.
51. *A Declaration and Message from the Kings Majesties Court in the Isle of Wight . . .* (November 1647), BL., E.417(7), p. 2.

taken in this respect with regard to control of the vessels coming from the mainland. He was, however, unhappy about parliament's orders to him to arrest Ashburnham, Legge and Berkley, the king's close advisers. He emphasized that it would be impossible to put this order into effect without keeping the king close prisoner, for Charles had pronounced that he must share their fate since he, not they, bore the ultimate responsibility for the flight from Hampton Court. Hammond instead preferred to accept the parole of the three royalists that they would stay on the island and stressed that if they were imprisoned, the king would anyway have no-one of appropriate rank to serve him, which would redound very much to the Governor's dishonour. He won his point and the three were not imprisoned.[52]

On 6 January 1648 parliamentary authority was given to Colonel Hammond and Sir William Constable to remove all from attendance on the king whom they suspected to be – hypocritical phrase! – 'prejudicial to the Safety and Security of the King's Person' even when such appointments had had parliamentary approval.[53] When Charles demanded to know the reason for this sudden change and how it could be reconciled with Hammond's honour, the Governor replied that the king was not ignorant of the reasons for this restraint; his acting by other counsels than were compatible with the good of the realm. He went on to say that he had no doubt that if the king wished to get away from the Isle of Wight, Ashburnham and the others would afford him all the assistance he needed.[54] In the following month restrictions on those with access to the duke of York were also tightened and the earl of Northumberland, who had charge of the duke and the king's other children, was ordered to see them observed. The duke was taken to task for corresponding by letter with his father, and admitted his fault, undertaking 'never to engage myself any more in such Businesses'.[55]

Sympathetic accounts of the rigours and humiliation of the king's confinement at Carisbrooke were, no doubt, grossly overdone. Nevertheless, they probably succeeded in increasing sympathy for his plight among moderate persons as well as inspiring futile attempts, such as that of Captain Burley, to rescue him.[56] At least the official news-sheets seem to have been anxious to dispel such rumours and reports about the stringency of the king's confinement, as well they might in view of

52. *L.J.*, IX, 538; *The Perfect Weekly Account* (17/23 November 1647), BL., E.416(27), no pagination; *The Last Newes from the Isle of Wight* (November 1647), E.417(10), pp. 4–8; *Mercurius Elencticus Number 4* (19/26 November 1647), E.417(9), p. 31; E.417(7), p. 4.
53. *L.J.*, IX, 642; *HMC.*, *7th. Report Appendix (House of Lords Cal. 1647–8)*, p. 2.
54. *Cal.SPD. 1648–9*, pp. 2–3.
55. *L.J.*, X, 77; *C.J.*, V, 470.
56. On Captain Burley's failed coup, see below, pp. 361–2.

the fact that those participating in the violent Christmas tumult at Canterbury cited the treatment of the king as one of their principal concerns.[57] Thus *The Kingdomes Weekly Intelligencer*'s report for 10 January 1648 was at great pains to emphasize 'that his Majesty is not under that restraint as many here beleive, but taketh the aire and rideth abroad at his pleasure'. However, its readers might draw different conclusions from its assertion that the guards accompanying the king on such occasions were there simply 'to secure his person'.[58] The royalist *Mercurius Pragmaticus*, moreover, was sceptical about whether 'he [Charles] shall have libertie to walke at all, unlesse Mr Hammond's worship be pleased to give him leave'.[59] Indeed, as *Mercurius Elencticus* was to report later, Hammond's request for a modification of his instructions so as to allow the king greater liberty to walk abroad had been disallowed by the Speaker as an inappropriate subject for debate in the House. In consequence, 'His Majesty is still *pinn'd* up in a *narrow Roome*, where he is not permitted to do the *necessities* of *Nature*, with out *Eyes* upon Him, and deprived all *Society* of his *Friends* and all the Outward comforts whatsoever . . . things never yet denyed to the veryest Rogues in Newgate'.[60] In a later number the same royalist newswriter complained that the king was not only restrained as to what visitors should be allowed to see him and the conditions in which he could receive them, but that the size of his household had been reduced to thirty. Indeed, the radical Independent Sir Robert Wroth had argued in parliament that if Charles were brought speedily to trial, that expense too would be reduced: an economy which was not adopted, continued the writer, only because 'they dare not exercise *all* their *cruelty* at once upon His *Person*; it must be done by *Degrees*'.[61] Later in the year during the Second Civil War the misfortunes of the royal captive were to become a prominent element of the manifestoes and pamphlets of royalist insurgents,[62] as well as of

---

57. *The Declaration of many thousands of the city of Canterbury* . . . (5 January 1648), BL., E.421(23), pp. 4–5. On the Canterbury tumult, see above, pp. 96–7, and below, pp. 240–41, 359–61.
58. BL., E.422(18), p. 800.
59. *Mercurius Pragmaticus Number 17* (4/11 January 1648), BL., E.422(17), no pagination.
60. *Mercurius Elencticus Number 10* (26 January/2 February 1648), BL., E.425(7), p. 72. For another comparison between the king's condition and that of 'the veriest Rogues in the Gaole', see *Mercurius Pragmaticus Number 4* (27 January/3 February 1648), E.425(12), p. 28. For another complaint about the king's plight, see *Mercurius Bellicus no. 4* (14/20 February 1648), E.428(4), defective pagination.
61. *Mercurius Elencticus Number 11* (2/9 February 1648), BL., E.426(12), p. 80.
62. See, e.g., *The Declaration of Col. Poyer and Col. Powell* (10 April 1648), Codrington pamphlet coll., also BL., E.435(9), especially p. 3; *The Remonstrance and Declaration of the Knights Esquires Gentlemen and Freeholders in Colchester* (6 July 1648), Oxford, Worcester College pamphlet coll., also BL., E.451(11), p. 4; *A Speedy Cure to Open the Eyes of the Blinde and the Eares of the Deafe Citizens of London* (4 August 1648), BL., E.456(28), especially pp. 5–6.

petitions for a treaty with the king, such as the Hampshire petition of June 1648.[63]

Parallel with such attempts to make the most out of the privations of the captive king went an increasing emphasis on the time which he spent at his religious devotions and in spiritual contemplation with the aid of Anglican divines such as Dr Sheldon and Dr Hammond, the former a future Archbishop of Canterbury and the latter a relation of the king's gaoler. The image presented dwelt on Charles's spiritual, even Christlike, qualities and was of course to find its most celebrated expression in the *Eikon Basilike* after his death. It will not be enough for the king to be crucified, argued a royalist newswriter more than a year before Charles's execution. His murderers will also cast lots for his vesture.[64]

At the same time royalist propagandists did their utmost to exploit the allegedly outrageous treatment of the king over the four bills in December 1647, and following his rejection of these, the parliamentary Vote of No Addresses at the beginning of January. 'Me thinks', urged one of them, 'the heart of every true *English man* should bleed at it.'[65] Another, while bewailing this sorry state of affairs, emphasized that it was but temporary, and that 'his sacred *Majesty* shall arise (like the *Sun*) in *Glory* and be freed from those thick *Clouds* and Foggy *vapours* that so long have interposed betwixt him and his *Loyall* Subjects'.[66] Separated from his beloved and vilely abused queen by rebels who aimed at the total destruction of monarchy, Charles, emphasized a royalist pamphlet published at the end of December 1647, had suffered more than any other prince, but his spirit remained invincible.[67]

So absurdly overdone were to be the arguments and charges of parliament's Declaration on the Vote of No Addresses and the army's declaration in support of the Vote[68] that they were most likely to invoke sheer incredulity from all except the most committed of radical parliamentary Independents. At this point the moderately penned royal answer to the parliamentary Declaration on the Vote beginning with

63. *The Declaration Together with the Petition and Remonstrance of . . . the County of Hampeshire* (14 June 1648), Codrington pamphlet coll., also BL., E.447(18), sig. A3ᵛ. On this abortive petition, see above, p. 148.
64. *Mercurius Pragmaticus Number 17* (4/11 January 1648), BL., E.422(17), no pagination. For an even earlier comparison of the king's sufferings with those of Christ, see Symmons, op. cit., pp. 42–4, 51–2, 55–6, 82–3, 241–51.
65. *Mercurius Pragmaticus Number 29* (28 December/4 January 1647/8), BL., E.421(29), no pagination. For these developments, see above, pp. 36–40.
66. *Mercurius Elencticus Number 6* (29 December/5 January 1647/8), BL., E.421(6), pp. 43–4.
67. *A New Creed Consisting of XII Articles . . .* (30 December 1647), BL., E.421(18), p. 4.
68. On the Declaration and the king's reply, see above, pp. 39–40.

the carefully calculated emphasis on the king's forced isolation from his subjects was likely to have a much wider appeal to an audience far beyond the ranks of extreme Cavaliers. For the Vote of No Addresses had done no less than to disenable the king from exercising his prime functions of protecting his subjects and, as such, betokened the virtual relinquishment of his sovereignty. When this was gone, what was left?

> Patience hath noe merit for subjects towardes their King, being their bounden duty, but where fidelitie is shipwrackt no Reverence can be expected and subjects that reign and triumph over their king, whom they use as a Captiue, pretend Patience to let him live, but his invincible Magnanimitie and Patience amongst the Barbarous Injuries he daylie suffers must one day cast shame on their faces and Horror on their Consciences for their faithlesse and Cruell dealing with him.[69]

Parliament's drastic and extremist moves at the beginning of 1648 probably had the effect of making an increasing number of people anxious that that day would come sooner rather than later.

For it was not just Cavaliers who were aggrieved, and even outraged, by the apparent marginalization of the king by the Vote of No Addresses. In this present chapter much use has been made of royalist propaganda material such as news-sheets and pamphlets. It would, however, be dangerous to assume that their sentiments were shared by a great many outside the narrow circles of the Cavalier faithful to whom such opinions were meat and drink. The extremism, violence, frequent coarseness and spite of newswriters such as *Mercurius Pragmaticus*, *Mercurius Elencticus* and *Mercurius Bellicus* automatically excluded them from exerting much influence on moderate people, and they were for the most part preaching to the converted. By contrast, the studied moderation of the royal reply to the Declaration on the Vote of No Addresses was calculated to appeal to a wider audience. For the events at the beginning of 1648 had made it necessary for moderate and conservative people, as well as Cavalier extremists, to ponder the implications for them of an England without a king. Would considerations of order, hierarchy and obedience survive in a society from which kingship, the keystone of the arch of order, had disappeared? Even if it did not disappear, how much of regal authority – and, through it, all other authority – could survive the buffetings and humiliations to which Charles had been subjected since 1646, and which now appeared to be

---

69. 'Considerations upon occasion of the Late Declaration of the Army' (1 February 1648), Bodleian, Bodley MSS., dep. C 168, no. 43 (Nalson MSS., N.XV, 43), especially pp. 100–1. For another attack on the Declaration on the Vote of No Addresses, see *Mercurius Bellicus* no. 4 (14/20 February 1648), BL., E.428(4), pp. 1–2.

mounting to a new climax? To remove monarchy or to reduce the king's authority to that of a Venetian doge, as Charles himself had scornfully characterized parliament's Nineteen Propositions of June 1642,[70] was to put the whole hierarchical structure of society to the hazard by attacking its most potent symbol. Watching the social certainties of their world apparently disintegrating before their very eyes, it was surely natural for fearful conservatives, by no means all of whom were old-style royalists, to ponder how far these things had been the consequence of the original act of disobedience in 1642, and whether they were now to be accelerated by those of January 1648. In the exploitation of the fear of anarchy lay one of the most formidable weapons in the royalist armoury, and some of the more perspicacious of the parliamentary radicals were well aware of this fact; as witness a radical pamphlet in October 1647, counselling its readers to 'beware that yee be not frighted by the word ANARCHY unto a love of Monarchy which is but the gilded name for *Tyranny*'.[71]

The pamphlet's warning was timely, given the increasing inclination to look upon what was seen as the government's 'subversion of our Fundamental Laws, Customary Immunities and Municipal Priviledges deriv'd to us . . . by our proper Birth-rights' as connected with the decline of royal power.[72] A royalist newswriter such as *Mercurius Pragmaticus* may have been catering mainly, as has been argued above, for a limited Cavalier public, but when he urged in January 1648 that the imprisonment of the king and the abolition of first fruits and tenths were 'a faire *Introduction* to the intended Parity', he was playing on fears which were by no means confined to Cavaliers.[73] When a conservative Presbyterian MP (almost certainly Sir John Maynard) launched an attack in the House of Commons in late January on some anti-monarchical and anti-House of Lords utterances by the radical Independent MP, Henry Marten, he described Marten's views as being 'all for parity and Anarchy and I conceiue his end is to bring all to confusion that hee may bee chosen as one of the Tribunes of the People or a John of Leiden'.[74] The thrust of this parliamentary Presbyterian's argument is virtually indistinguishable from that of *Mercurius Pragmaticus*, or from that of another royalist newswriter, *Mercurius Melancholicus*. Referring in the

---

70. *His Majesties Answer to the XIX Propositions* (June 1642), BHPC., p. 17. There are many references here to the social disruption consequent upon the diminution of royal power.
71. *A Call to All the Souldiers of the Armie* (29 October 1647), BL., E.412(10), p. 6.
72. *The Remonstrance of the Northern Associations* (15 November 1647), BL., E.414(12), p. 5 and passim.
73. *Mercurius Pragmaticus Number 17* (4/11 January 1648), BL., E.422(17), no pagination.
74. 'A Spech [*sic*] in answer to Mr Martyn' (January 1648), BL., E.422(32) (in Thomason's hand). On Maynard, see above, pp. 113–16.

following month to the planned impeachment of the seven peers as the probable prelude to the end of the House of Lords and perhaps of the peerage in general, *Melancholicus* observed that 'They that have throwne his Majestie out of his Throne are now levelling at Nobility'.[75]

That the nobility owed its position to the king was an inescapable fact which in the last resort made parliamentarian peers such as Viscount Saye and Sele and the earl of Warwick blanch at the prospect of an end to monarchy and Charles himself was prepared to make the most of this. Just as he had worked – though unsuccessfully – on Essex's scruples in 1642, so was he to attempt to put Lord Admiral Warwick to shame in a letter of 22 September 1648, rebuking him for insulting the prince's insurgent fleet; an act of gross impropriety in 'a Person of Honour . . . (whose own Condition so absolutely depends upon the Preservation of the Regal Power)'.[76] As to Saye and Sele, it was surely his realization that monarchy itself, and with it the whole social hierarchy, was at stake if the negotiations on the Isle of Wight in the autumn of 1648 were not crowned with success, which impelled him to join with his former Presbyterian opponents in a desperate but unavailing attempt to reach a final settlement with the king. *Mutatis mutandis*, such considerations probably influenced a vast number of politically conscious people of moderate views, however repelled they may have been by that Cavalier extremism which had so recently issued in a second civil war.

As early as May 1647 a somewhat over-optimistic royalist correspondent had suggested that, as a result of the king's observed constancy to his principles and parliament's irresolution and worse, Charles 'acquires great numbers to his side, in soe much as tis conceaved that there may be shortly a greater revoult than ever'.[77] Even if many of those who were increasingly drawn towards the king were not prepared to fight for him in a second war, the growth of their sympathy for Charles which has been a main theme of this chapter was obviously a matter of deep concern to the parliamentary government. Hardly less a matter of concern was the fear that royalists were creeping back into positions of trust and authority in the realm to which we now turn our attention.

Royalist infiltration of office

Moved by the widespread fear that parliament having won the war was in danger of losing the peace, some London apprentices of a politically

75. *Mercurius Melancholicus* (12/19 February 1648), BL., E.437(23), p. 148.
76. L.J., X, 522.
77. Bodleian, Clarendon MSS., 29, fos. 219–19(b).

Independent disposition petitioned on 1 March 1647 that the king's former followers should be formally debarred both from holding any office or exercising the vote in national and local affairs.[78] On 10 June, beginning at the top with parliament itself, it was ordained that no-one who had borne arms against parliament, acted by Commission of Array or voluntarily aided the royalist cause in any way, however indirectly, should sit in the House of Commons. The army's Remonstrance of the 21st of that month went further, demanding that the disablement of such persons should be permanent.[79] Further categories to be disabled were added on 9 July, including any who had sued for pardons from the king for having supported parliament in the war.[80]

The fact that legislation about local and other offices had to wait until September may have something to do with parliamentary preoccupation with the dispute between the army and the eleven members as well as with parliamentary Presbyterian tenderness for the local influence of royalists in some regions, as was shown earlier by reference to Glyn's and Lewis's activities in Wales and elsewhere.[81] If this is true, it seems likely that the eclipse of the eleven members, the general discomfiture of the parliamentary Presbyterians and the defeat of London's counter-revolution in August cleared the scene for further action. When this finally came it was at least far-reaching. A parliamentary ordinance of 9 September 1647 attended comprehensively to the problem, prohibiting any who had been sequestered or who had served in arms against parliament from occupying local, municipal or county office.[82] On 21 September the army council at Putney recommended going further, extending the period of disablement to five years with the right to grant exemption from it being confined to parliament. It also proposed that such royalist delinquents should lose the franchise in both local and parliamentary terms.[83] This was done in a further parliamentary ordinance of 4 October which also, somewhat incongruously, vested in the parliamentary Indemnity Committee, which had been established in the previous May, power to examine such cases and discharge such

78. *The Petition of divers young Men and Apprentices of the City of London.* This petition of 1 March was also reproduced and forwarded along with the apprentices' petition of 13 July (*The Petition of many thousands of Young Men and Apprentices* (13 July 1647), BL., E.398(9), pp. 6–8).

79. *C.J.*, V, 205; *Cal.SPD. 1645–7*, p. 560; *A Remonstrance of the Representations of the Army* (June 1647), BL., E.393(17), no pagination.

80. *C.J.*, V, 233, 238. On 5 July there was a majority of 31 against the motion for the ordinance being put. The ordinance passed in a modified form on 9 July.

81. On the army and the eleven members, see above, pp. 170–78. On the activities of Glyn and Lewis, see above, p. 173.

82. *A&O.*, I, 1009; *C.J.*, V, 292; *L.J.*, IX, 430.

83. *The Intentions of the Armie Concerning the Kings Majesty* (September 1647), BL., E.408(16), pp. 4–5.

delinquents from office and disenfranchise them.[84] The scope of the ordinance extended from the meanest office such as parish constable[85] to prestigious offices such as mayors, sheriffs, JPs and Deputy Lieutenants. 'So fearefull are the *Houses* of themselves', commented a royalist news-writer, 'if men that love *Kings* and *Justice* should ever be in *Authority* again.'[86]

There can be no doubt that the ordinances were widely evaded. The Grand Inquest at the Somerset assizes at Chard on 27 March 1648 presented 'that notwithstanding divers ordinances to the contrary, Delinquents and men of ill affection to the Parliament are chosen and still retain offices of judicature and trust'.[87] On 22 September 1648 the fact that many Cavaliers had slipped through the net devised by the ordinances of a year or so earlier was made clear by the order of the House of Commons that all JPs, Deputy Lieutenants, committeemen and military commanders who had engaged in the recent tumults – the Second Civil War was now virtually over – should immediately be dismissed.[88]

In the matter of municipal offices, the House of Commons on 27 September 1647 had ordered a letter to local authorities to be drawn up informing them of the ordinance of 9 September against the election of ex-Cavaliers.[89] In many cases, of course, the legislation had already been anticipated by wholesale local reconstruction, more particularly in municipalities which had been in royalist hands until the closing months of the war. In Chester an ordinance of 1 October 1646 had dismissed the royalist mayor, aldermen, common councilmen and other munici-pal officers, and the new parliamentarian mayor, William Edwards, had been given power to make appointments to those positions which had hitherto been occupied by royalists.[90] In Worcester, which had fallen to parliament even later, it seems that four ex-royalists were still serving on the governing body of the city during the summer of 1647 and had even

84. *A&O.*, I, 1023–5; *An Ordinance . . . for disabling Delinquents . . .* (4 October 1647), BL., E.410(3), pp. 3–8.
85. For an example of its application to a very minor office, that of Steward of the Courts Leet and Baron of the manor of Leeds, see PRO., SP. 24/1, fos. 67(b), 98.
86. *Mercurius Pragmaticus number 14* (14/21 December 1647), BL., E.421(1), sig. O2ᵛ.
87. *HMC., 13th. Report, Appendix Portland MSS.*, I, 448. Serjeant Wylde reported back to the Commons in the following month after having ridden the western circuit (*C.J.*, V, 534; Whitelock, *Memorials*, p. 300 (18 April)).
88. Rushworth, *Historical Collections*, VII, 1270.
89. Bodleian, Tanner MSS., 58, fo. 539.
90. *Cal.SPD. 1645–7*, pp. 474–5. For full details, see A.M. Johnson, 'Politics in Chester during the Civil Wars and the Interregnum', in P. Clark and P. Slack (eds.), *Crisis and Order in English Towns* (1976), pp. 215–16. However, a report of 3 July 1647 revealed that there were still ex-royalist soldiers and officers serving in the Chester garrison (Bodleian, Tanner MSS., 58, fo. 325).

succeeded in securing the election of one of their number, George Heminge, as the next mayor. However, on receiving a certificate to this effect from the Worcestershire county committee, the House of Commons ordered on 4 September that the election should be null and void and that the existing incumbent should remain in office until further notice. Nevertheless, Heminge and nine other sequestered or sequestrable delinquents were still sitting in the Worcester Chamber and Common Council as late as June 1648.[91] In Oxford, the former royalist headquarters in the Civil War, well-affected citizens complained to the Indemnity Committee in November 1647 that the ex-royalist George Bangor was continuing to occupy the post of town clerk in defiance of the recent ordinance.[92] The mayor and two of the four ex-Cavalier aldermen of Wigan in Lancashire, whose case came before the Indemnity Committee in December 1647, proved even more difficult to dislodge. Although the five were formally disabled again by an order of 12 February 1648, three of them, including the mayor, while formally acquiescing, continued to exercise office as if nothing had happened, and their dismissal had to be reconfirmed and they subjected to large fines of £70 and £50 on 20 June. By that time Lancashire was preparing to meet a new royalist insurrection and a Scottish invasion, from which the disabled aldermen might perhaps entertain hopes of reinstatement.[93] The same is true, perhaps to an even greater degree, of Carlisle, where six ex-Cavalier aldermen and seven commoncouncilmen seem, for a time at least, to have ignored the ordinances disabling them, and the four of them who persisted still further, despite orders from the Indemnity Committee to relinquish their positions, were fined sums of £30 and £20 in February 1648. Two of these were to be in arms against parliament during the Second Civil War.[94]

Such cases were by no means confined to former royalist strongholds. In his diary entry for 21 December 1646, the London Independent Thomas Juxon records the election to Common Council of 'severall knowne Mallignants' largely as a result of Presbyterian efforts to keep out Independents at all costs.[95] It will be recalled that the Lord Mayor, Sir John Gayre, and three London aldermen were imprisoned for months and threatened with impeachment for their part in London's counter-revolution of July 1647. Originally Presbyterians, they had by that time become barely distinguishable from royalists. The same might be said of

91. HLRO., MP., 4/9/1647; C.J., V, 292, 297; L.J., IX, 430; PRO., SP. 24/3, fos. 7(b), 118(b).
92. PRO., SP. 24/1, fos. 81(b), 98(b), 104(b).
93. SP. 24/1, fos. 103(b), 162–2(b); SP. 24/2, fos. 115, 176–6(b).
94. SP. 24/1, fos. 119–19(b), 161–2.
95. London, Dr Williams's Library, MS. 24.50, fo. 97(b).

John Utting, the mayor of Norwich in 1648. The Norwich riots of 24 April were precipitated by an attempt of Utting's enemies to have him carried off in custody to answer charges against him in parliament. One of these charges was that he had countenanced the election of a royalist, Roger Mingay, to the aldermanry.[96] There were tumults in Maidstone in 1647 over the election of a mayor. Not only was the successful candidate, Thomas Brooke, 'a person disaffected to the Parliament', but two of the voters were technically disqualified for royalist delinquency. On 3 November the House of Commons referred the matter to the Indemnity Committee which declared Brooke to have been improperly elected, and he had to relinquish office to the runner-up as well as to suffer disenfranchisement along with the two delinquent voters.[97]

As a final example, as many as eleven of the municipal governors of Stamford in south Lincolnshire had opposed the parliament during the war, as appeared from an information laid by some of the 'well-affected' of that town before the Indemnity Committee in February 1648. Some of them resigned, and others were formally disabled, though one proved particularly recalcitrant and was not forced out until May.[98] It was important, stressed Luke Robinson, MP for Scarborough, in a letter to the bailiffs of that borough in March 1647, months before the ordinances of September and October had clearly laid down the criteria for disqualification from office, that they should take the utmost care to exclude from their number, not only returning malignants, but also any who were simply 'not very well affected'.[99]

Similar considerations applied to rural magistracy. A pamphlet published in July 1648, seeking to express the views of those Kentish gentlemen who had stayed loyal to parliament during the Second Civil War, emphasized the fact that 'those that have been notorious enemies to the Parliament' had been serving as Deputy Lieutenants, JPs, committeemen and in other places of trust. It was by such means, the author argued, that 'the well affected party is most of all opposed, vexed, and grieved in all parts of the Kingdom, and that in a way of revenge for assisting the Parliament in the late Wars'.[100] One such 'way of revenge' will form the subject of the final section of this chapter.

There was obviously a much greater eagerness of royalists to serve on the Commissions of the Peace, the traditional and time-honoured organs of local administration and government, than on newfangled

96. On the London aldermen, see above, pp. 187, 192. On Utting and the Norwich riots, see below, pp. 369–75.
97. PRO., SP. 24/1, fos. 66(b)–7, 73–3(b); C.J., V, 349, 350.
98. SP. 24/1, fos. 147(b)–8; SP. 24/2, fo. 116.
99. Northallerton, North Yorkshire RO., MIC 1320/1158. I am indebted to the kindness of Mr M.Y. Ashworth in drawing my attention to this reference.
100. The Groans of Kent (July 1648), BL., E.453(4), pp. 3–4.

and politically suspect bodies such as the county committees. Much was made in an earlier chapter about royalist sneers that the disabling of ex-Cavaliers from being JPs would inevitably fill the Commission of the Peace with bumpkins.[101] Making a different point, another royalist newswriter, writing after the Second Civil War, remarked that if indeed Cavaliers were inappropriate persons to serve as JPs, this was simply because 'they have much honesty, too much in-sight, in the Mystery of our New Government'.[102] Inappropriate or not, there were numbers of them to be found on the bench at Quarter Sessions. Thus the former royalist activist Charles Steynings was nominated to the first post-war Commission of the Peace in Somerset in July 1646, while another such Cavalier, Sir John Pole, was acting as a JP in Devon in the summer of 1646, even though he was around this time fined £1,000 for his delinquency in fighting against parliament in the war.[103]

After September and October 1647 such appointments were, of course, in contravention of parliamentary ordinances. But the ordinances were sometimes disregarded, and some cases were marginal and by no means straightforward. Sir Richard Samwell had sat on the Northamptonshire Commissions of the Peace since the end of the Civil War and was still sitting apparently unaffected by the ordinances of September and October 1647, when he was accused on 15 September 1648 before the Indemnity Committee, not of having borne arms against parliament, but of frequently manifesting his disaffection to it and refusing to execute its orders. Sensing perhaps that the case was not so straightforward as might appear at first sight, the Indemnity Committee gave Samwell until 15 December to produce evidence to disprove these accusations which had their origins in an information from some so-called 'well affected' ministers and other inhabitants of the county. No decision had been reached in the case by the end of the year.[104]

Infiltration by royalists was, of course, a bigger problem in some regions than in others. One does not normally think of Hertfordshire as a militantly royalist county, even though, largely through the agency of Lord Capel, it was to provide many recruits for the royalist insurgents in Essex in the Second Civil War. A petition heard in parliament on 18 June 1647 from some knights, gentry and freeholders of the county complained of malignants and 'neuters' being preferred to places of trust and profit, such as governors of towns and forts, JPs, Excise commissioners and members of Accounts sub-committees. But in addition

---

101. *Mercurius Pragmaticus number 22* (7/14 December 1648), BL., E.419(22), sig. N2–N2ᵛ. See above, p. 104.
102. *Mercurius Elencticus number 44* (20/27 September 1648), BL., E.464(46), pp. 355–6.
103. Underdown, *Somerset*, p. 140; Roberts, *Devon*, p. 14.
104. PRO., SP. 24/3, fos. 78, 133(b).

the petitioners were indignant that whole counties such as Devon and Cornwall and indeed the whole Principality of Wales which had been consistently hostile to parliament during the war had the right to elect MPs, whereas they should rather have been disenfranchised at least 'until such Time as it shall appear that their former Enmity and Rancour be laid aside'.[105]

It was earlier observed in another context how the Welsh Presbyterian MPs, John Glyn and Sir William Lewis, had connived at and even encouraged the penetration of the Commission of the Peace by malignants, especially in Denbighshire, Caernarvonshire and Brecknockshire, and, in Glyn's case, in Middlesex too.[106] Similar charges applied to the manning of many of the Welsh county committees, though less so than to the Commissions of the Peace, with which one more readily associates royalists. 'Yet', as the historian of the Welsh committees remarks, 'little as they [viz. the royalists] might be trusted, parliament had to use them, if its committee was to have any weight', the most striking example of royalist penetration being the committee of Carmarthenshire.[107] In Wales, then, it was the shortage of persons of even remotely prestigious status which explains such recruitment from ex-Cavalier sources. The same may well be true of other remote parts such as the Lake District. On 14 February 1648 information was heard by the Indemnity Committee to the effect that Sir Wilfred Lawson, who had fought against parliament in the First Civil War and was to do so again in the Second, was acting both as a Deputy Lieutenant and a member of the county committee of Cumberland.[108]

But such developments, though doubtless more plentiful in such out-of-the-way parts, were certainly not peculiar to them. It was not just against Archer, Lister and their Independent and sectarian allies on the Lincolnshire county committee that Colonel King had thundered from the chair in his celebrated address to the Grand Jury at the assizes at Folkingham on 5 October 1646. He had also denounced the nomination of 'notorious Delinquents' to the committee, even if it is true that the main thrust of his offensive was against low-born radicals such as John Archer.[109] Similarly, on 22 July 1646, Colonel Thomas Bulstrode

105. L.J., IX, 277–8.
106. Bell, Memorials, I, 378–9, 380; Parliamentary History, XVI, 85–6, 88. For a contesting of these charges, see ibid., pp. 143–4, 148–50; A brief Justification of some of the XI accused Members (13 July 1647), BL., E.398(3), pp. 7–8. See above, p. 173.
107. A.H. Dodd, Studies in Stuart Wales (Cardiff, 1971), pp. 132–3.
108. P.R.O., SP. 24/1, fo. 169(b).
109. Edward King, A discovery of the arbitrary, tyrannicall and illegal actions (1647), BHPC., p. 10. On King's attack on the committee, see C. Holmes, Seventeenth Century Lincolnshire (Lincoln, 1980), pp. 188–93, 199, and his 'Colonel King and Lincolnshire Politics 1642–46', Hist.J., XVI (1973), especially pp. 475–9.

provided information about the composition and behaviour of the Buckinghamshire committee which was designed seriously to alarm Speaker Lenthall. While one part of that committee consisted of good men zealous for the parliamentary cause, there was also 'a party that seldom appears at the committee, but when some personal or private respect does draw them thither'. On such occasions they sought both to oppose the efficient conduct of parliamentary business and 'to gratify notorious malignants'. Bulstrode singled out Thomas Terill for particular mention as such a committeeman whose actions had helped materially to weaken parliamentary strength in the county. This he had done by diverting the county treasury to other uses than the efficient prosecution of the war; by hindering the collection of the monthly assessment; by advocating the premature disbandment of Bulstrode's soldiers; and by using his influence to the utmost on behalf of scandalous and malignant parsons. While such committeemen were not technically royalists, their behaviour, while unquestionably self-interested, was hardly less in the royalist interest.[110]

On 4 November 1647 parliament heard a petition from some ex-Cavaliers who had formerly compounded on terms laid down in the surrender articles of Exeter, which parliament itself had approved on 6 May 1646. Among them were five barristers and five attorneys who had been disabled from practising in public courts and from occupying chambers or commons in Inns of Court since the ordinances against employment of delinquents extended to many of the professions. But the Exeter articles had specifically allowed to those comprehended within them the right to exercise their trades and professions.[111] That exception from the operation of parliamentary ordinances had to be made in such cases was a source of disquiet to many parliamentarians and annoyance at the commanders who had granted such surrender terms in the first place. But as in the other cases which have been considered in this section, exceptions to such ordinances were by no means unknown even in cases where individuals could not invoke the protection of Surrender Articles. The records of the Indemnity Committee yield a number of such cases: among them, an ex-royalist attorney practising in the town court of Derby and three others, one of whom was practising as an attorney and the others acting as officials of courts in Somerset.[112] While the number of such extant cases is certainly insufficient to justify the widely expressed fears of many persons who

110. Cary, *Memorials*, I, 128–30. The role of 'scandalous and malignant parsons' is dealt with in the next chapter, pp. 246–6.
111. HLRO., MP., 4/11/1647; *L.J.*, IX, 511. On the significance of Surrender Articles, see above, p. 166.
112. PRO., SP. 24/1, fo. 145; SP. 24/2, fos. 65, 167(b).

were sued by former Cavaliers that the courts were dominated by such persons, it could be that they were the merest tip of an iceberg.

Royalist litigation thwarted

The relevance of the theme of the preceding section to the growing fears of soldiers and civilians that unless some protection was afforded to them, they might become the victims of revenge suits brought before partial courts by ex-Cavaliers was underlined in a pamphlet of August 1647. This made an eloquent contrast between, on the one hand, the broken promises to, and mounting arrears of pay of, the soldiers, and, on the other, the scandal of 'Cavaliers admitted to sit in Parliament-Committees, made Sherifs, Mayors, Justices of the Peace, by meanes whereof our arrears and rewards for our faithfull and painfull service . . . were like to paid to all of us (as they were to some) by imprisonments, troubles, perplexities and the gallows'.[113] By this time, of course, parliament had created its Indemnity Committee in response to the situation. It had admittedly not gone all the way to satisfy the demand expressed in the army's Remonstrance of 21 June, 'That no malignants or others may be admitted to prosecute those who have acted for the Parliament . . . in any sort whatsoever'.[114] Nevertheless, the Indemnity Committee was at least given the power to suspend or discharge such suits once they had been brought. Moreover, this power was clearly associated with the committee's additional function of disabling ex-Cavalier attorneys and other legal functionaries who were still practising in the courts in defiance of parliamentary ordinances to the contrary, and by whose means, as the Grand Inquest at the Somerset assizes as late as 27 March 1648 put it, 'frivolous and vexatious actions are brought and violently prosecuted against the well affected party'.[115] In addition, not only were some judges in such cases suspect of having royalist sympathies, but there were also grave suspicions about the partiality of some of the juries impanelled. On 5 September 1648 the House of Commons expressed serious concern that in many counties (Surrey, Sussex, Kent and Essex were specifically mentioned) malignants had

---

113. *Vox Militaris* (August 1647), BL., E.401(24), pp. 9–10. These fears also bulk large among the grievances of the soldiers of Colonel Rich's regiment expressed in a paper of May 1647 (*Divers Papers from the Army* (May 1647), BL., E.388(18), p. 8). They also lie behind the emphasis on the need for indemnity in the soldiers' famous petition of March 1647 which was so roughly treated by parliament (Cary, *Memorials*, I, 85; Bodleian, Tanner MSS., 58, fo. 13).
114. *A Remonstrance of the Representations of the Army* (June 1647), BL., E.393(17), no pagination.
115. *HMC., 13th. Report Appendix, Portland MSS.* (1891), I, 448; *C.J.*, V, 534.

been preferred above others as jurors, with obvious dangers to the well-affected accused.[116] The list might appropriately have included Somerset, for in June the attention of the Speakers of both Houses had been drawn to the case of a parliamentary trooper who had been condemned and hanged in that county for having slain a Cavalier officer. The jury in this case, it was alleged, 'would have condemned all those that act for the parliament', an assertion which must have sent shivers down the spines of the well-affected.[117]

For both soldiers and civilians who had technically violated the law under orders and in the exigencies of war the dangers were very real indeed. On 4 March 1647 the Suffolk county committee reported to the Speaker that 'many well affected persons for the Parliament haue now seuerall actions layd vpon them (for taking away of horses, armes & leavying assessmentes . . .) from seuerall persons conceived to be ill affected'. This was the main, but by no means the only, cause for disquiet. In addition, 'many tenantes of Papistes & delinquentes are sued & molested by ther landlordes now returned, vpon pretence of breaches of Covenantes', not to speak of malignant excluded parsons resorting to other parishes or even returning to their own, a development which will be treated in the chapter which follows.[118] On 18 June a petition from some gentlemen and freeholders of Hertfordshire complained of how a certain Cardwell, 'a Man of notorious Lewd Life & Conversation, and withal a most desperate Malignant', had caused three soldiers to be arrested and charged for acts done under orders during the war. Fortunately for them, their colonel appeared on their behalf in court, and if he had not been prepared to become bound for them to appear at the next sessions, they would certainly have been remanded to Hertford gaol. In the event, thanks, it was claimed, to the presence of two or three honest men on the Grand Jury, no true bill was found against the soldiers. The petition is at pains to underline their good fortune in this, emphasizing that there was 'but little Favour or Mercy to be had for Parliamentary Soldiers by the Justices of our County'.[119]

The variety of such suits was very great and has been analysed in detail elsewhere.[120] Most of them have in common the fact that they related to acts done under orders in time of war mainly by soldiers, but

116. C.J., VI, 6; Rushworth, Historical Collections, VII, 1252. The House ordered that all insurgents in the Second Civil War should be disabled from jury service for ever and from election to municipal office. But this touched only the fringes of the problem.
117. HMC., 13th. Report Appendix, Portland MSS., I, 457.
118. Bodleian, Tanner MSS., 59, fo. 792.
119. L.J., IX, 278.
120. See R. Ashton, 'The Problem of Indemnity, 1647–1648', in Politics and People, pp. 117–40.

also by civilians: for example, by constables for actions such as the confiscation of the plate of a malignant parson in Dedham in Essex at the beginning of the First Civil War and the allegedly wrongful arrest and imprisonment of Cavaliers in Mevagissey in Cornwall.[121] Both soldiers and civilians, but especially the former, were prosecuted for acts such as the requisitioning of horses and arms and their confiscation from Cavaliers under orders and, in the case of soldiers, as legitimate prize in battle.[122] The defendants in these suits included not only the original takers of the horses and other property but also those who had ultimately purchased them.[123] There was also a number of prosecutions for trespass, burglary, breaking and entering and the like charges, brought by householders – normally, one would suspect, of Cavalier sympathies – against soldiers or ex-soldiers who had entered their houses in pursuit of fugitive Cavaliers. Such suits were normally, but not quite invariably, discharged by the Indemnity Committee which frequently also awarded damages to the defendants.[124] One ex-soldier was sued for burglary in May 1648 by the allegedly disaffected householder with whom he had been quartered, but was rescued by the Indemnity Committee which discharged the suit on 30 November, awarding £20 damages to the defendant.[125] Captain Anthony Beckwith was both sued for battery and outlawed for having wounded a Cavalier, who had attacked him in Beverley, 'vtteringe ill language against the Parliament'. Beckwith appealed to the Indemnity Committee which discharged both the

121. PRO., SP. 24/2, fo. 80(b) (Sherman et al. v. Smith); SP. 24/2, fos. 4(b), 116(b), 122 (Cocke v. Oliver). In this and succeeding references the names of the petitioners (viz. defendants) are given first in accordance with the practice in the Indemnity Committee Order Books.

122. Examples are in SP. 24/1, fos. 155(b), 164, 168 (Avoke et al. v. Crosse et al.); ibid., fo. 165 (Stockdale v. Ewen); SP. 24/2, fos. 15(b), 110(b)–11, 120(b) (Boulton v. Allen); ibid., fo. 132, SP. 24/3, fos. 19(b)–20, 79–9(b) (Lea v. Grundy); SP. 24/2, fo. 136 (Gouldes v. Moore); ibid., fo. 156 (Goddard v. Haulyn); SP. 24/3, fos. 5(b), 112, 131(b) (Meeson v. Whittall); ibid., fo. 72(b) (Arnold et al. v. Ginger); SP. 24/2, fos. 28, 74(b), 112(b) (Goodriche v. Wood); SP. 24/1, fos. 68(b), 91(b), 99, 112, 167(b) (Gwynn v. Pritchard); SP. 24/2, fo. 151(b) (Clarke v. Browne); SP. 24/1, fo. 174, SP. 24/2, fo. 32(b) (Browne v. Purdue et al.).

123. Examples are in SP. 24/1, fo. 155 (Honywood v. Walgrave); ibid., fos. 155, 190, SP. 24/2, fos. 85(b)–86 (Drake v. Donckley); SP. 24/1, fo. 175(b), SP. 24/3, fo. 8 (Falkener and Harrison v. Heywood); SP. 24/1, fo. 118(b), 139, 180(b)–1, 192, SP. 24/2, fo. 106(b) (Balston v. Simondes); SP. 24/2, fos. 20, 68, 75(b) (Wright v. Harrison); SP. 24/1, fo. 185 (Greene v. Burlton); SP. 24/2, fos. 45, 104(b), 160(b), 166 (Watkins v. Wollams); ibid., fos. 62(b), 120(b)–1 (Cheney v. Morgan); SP. 24/1, fo. 194, SP. 24/2, fos. 58, 71(b), 129 (Dolphin v. Palmer); SP. 24/2, fos. 24(b), 42, 73(b), 88, 132–2(b) (Monckton v. Hemminges).

124. Examples are in SP. 24/1, fo. 179(b) (Brigges v. Smith); SP. 24/2, fos. 1(b), 98, SP. 24/3, fos. 72, 75(b) (Price v. Longwell); SP. 24/2, fo. 44(b), SP. 24/3, fos. 88, 147(b)–8 (Mills v. Willmott).

125. SP. 24/2, fos. 118(b)–19, 175–5(b); SP. 24/3, fos. 162–2(b).

outlawry and the prosecution on the grounds that he had been maliciously prosecuted for acting in self-defence and that his life would indeed have been in danger if his troopers had not come to his rescue in time.[126]

Civilians who had been the victims of Cavalier predatory action or of sequestration by royalists during the war were obviously better placed in their search for redress than were their royalist equivalents who had suffered similar damage from the parliamentary side. But they were not always successful. The contrast between the treatment of Robert Trippett, who recovered a house taken from him during the war, and James and John Linley, who recouped themselves for £300 worth of corn and goods confiscated by the earl of Newcastle's sequestrators, is illuminating. Both were sued for trespass and battery, but the Indemnity Committee responded to the Linleys' appeal to it, but not to Trippett's. Although reasons are not given other than that Trippett's case did not fall within the Indemnity Committee's terms of reference, the crucial difference would seem to be that, while both parties had acted to regain rightful possession of property confiscated by royalists, the Linleys' action had been sanctioned by the county committee, while Trippett had taken the law into his own hands. So in the one case, the suit was discharged and the Linleys were awarded very generous damages of £70, while in the other, for once, Cavalier litigation was allowed to proceed.[127]

Many suits for false arrest, wrongful imprisonment and assault and battery were brought against officers and soldiers for acts done during and after the First Civil War, and the Indemnity Committee was normally prepared to intervene on behalf of the accused, among whom were the former Treasurer, Provost Marshal and commander of the parliamentary garrison of Brecon in South Wales.[128] Civilian constables were among the other defendants prosecuted, but the most bizarre and striking case was the suit brought by the ex-Cavalier Edward Preddon against Henry Simball in 1648. Simball had been keeper of Peterhouse prison in London in which many Cavalier prisoners of war, including Preddon, had been confined. Preddon had escaped from the gaol but, with astonishing nerve, returned to taunt and threaten Simball, who was provoked to attack him, providing thereby the occasion for Preddon

126. SP. 24/2, fos. 105(b), 175(b)–6; SP. 24/3, fos. 35–5(b).
127. SP. 24/2, fos. 104(b), 119(b), SP. 24/3, fo. 14 (Trippett v. Burrowes); SP. 24/2, fos. 143(b), 148, SP. 24/3, fos. 91, 128(b), 145, 149 (Linley v. Kerisforth et al.).
128. SP. 24/1, fo. 160(b), SP. 24/2, fos. 97(b), 118–18(b), SP. 24/3, fos. 6–6(b), 63 (Pritchard et al. v. Bowen et al.); SP. 24/2, fo. 86(b), SP. 24/3, fos. 11, 153 (Gwynn v. Search). For a similar suit against an ex-soldier and civilians, see SP. 24/2, fos. 80(b)–1, SP. 24/3, fos. 9, 68(b)–9 (Goddard v. Griffith).

to sue him for assault and battery. Not surprisingly, the Indemnity Committee ordered that the suit be discharged and, following the failure of Preddon to appear before it, ordered that he be brought up in custody.[129]

Another type of suit which illustrates the sheer effrontery of Cavalier litigants, as well perhaps as their confidence about the likelihood of verdicts in their favour in the courts, at least if it had not been for the intervention of the Indemnity Committee on behalf of the defendants, are cases on bonds which had been extracted by royalist soldiers during the war from persons who had been at their mercy; whether from prisoners of war, as a condition of their release – one such person maintained that he had entered into such a bond only as an alternative to being hanged if he did not[130] – or from civilians as a *pis aller* to being pillaged, or as a condition of repossessing goods or property which had already been looted.[131] Such bonds were sometimes assigned – often no doubt at a discount – to others in discharge of obligations. This happened, for instance, to a bond which had been extracted by a Cavalier captor of Richard Donnald, an inhabitant of Stamford, who had been imprisoned for neglecting to pay and collect a tax levied by the wartime royalist garrison at Newark. The condition of the bond was to pay £100 to a Newark vintner, whose wares had no doubt been in great demand by the Cavalier garrison, but by November 1648 it had come into the hands of a London grocer to whom it had presumably been assigned. In any case the whole business had long before come within the cognizance of the Indemnity Committee.[132]

To the ex-soldiers and civilian supporters who had fought and worked for the parliamentary cause and now found themselves prosecuted at law for acts done under superior command and in the interests of the war effort, the multitude of such suits, the optimism of the royalist plaintiffs, and the verdicts which were frequently reached in the courts against the defendants were all too clear evidence that the Cavaliers were climbing back into the saddle again. To the royalists, on the other hand, thwarted so often in such suits by the intervention of the Indemnity Committee and its frequent reversal of verdicts reached in their favour in the courts, the situation provided yet another example

129. SP. 24/1, fos. 34, 131(b), 134(b); SP. 24/2, fo. 42(b).
130. SP. 24/2, fo. 175 (Packer v. Barkeley). For another example of a bond extorted from a prisoner in wartime being sued by a Cavalier, see SP. 24/1, fo. 191(b), SP. 24/2, fos. 13, 24 (Middleton v. Ward). For the case of a mortgage (as well as cash) being extorted and sued at a later date, see SP. 24/3, fo. 136(b) (Raymond v. Butcher).
131. SP. 24/2, fo. 106 (Mott v. Fowke); SP. 24/2, fos. 142(b), SP. 24/3, fos. 34–4(b), 104(b)–5 (Greenewood v. Crosse).
132. SP. 24/1, fo. 156; SP. 24/2, fos. 7(b)–8, 35; SP. 24/3, fos. 118, 128.

of the regime's disregard for due legal process. Moreover, royalists had the additional grievance which came from contrasting their own helplessness in the face of legal suits brought against them with the protection afforded to their enemies by the Indemnity Committee. It might indeed seem to the disgruntled Cavalier that there was one law for the victors and another for the vanquished. Here was yet another factor exacerbating the temper and grievances of the vanquished which was to contribute to the many causes which ultimately issued in the renewal of civil war. No doubt the most extreme royalists would never have been satisfied. But that the situation worried others, including some of those who were contemplating returning to England from abroad, is beautifully illustrated by a letter from the royalist exile Francis Harding to Speaker Lenthall on 19 February 1648. Carefully considering the pros and cons of returning to England, Harding's frank letter raised considerations of great relevance to formerly highly placed royalists: 'such as haue had the Chardge of Government of Townes or other ffortifications in his Majestys seruice, vppon the surrenders of which there hath beene assurance giuen . . . by Artickeles . . . that they should not bee prest to othes, not to bee molested for hostile Actes, [have] ffree Lyberty to Compound for their Estates, And to enjoy them vnmolested . . . which haue beene soe farr from beeinge obserued that ther is noe fayth kept with them therin'. Unlike their former enemies who could claim the protection of the Indemnity Committee, they were helpless and, having compounded at high rates, were 'in a far worse Capassetie then they were formerly, beeing Left . . . in those parts wher they had Commaund to bee prossecuted by Lawe for what was Acted by them in the Warrs, euery man beinge at liberty to Rate his owne Losses at his owne Estimation, some pretending them selues damnefied 500^{li} that wear neuer worth 50^{li}'. In such circumstances compounding was but 'a Snare to bring them to a farther misserie'. All that such moderate men now desired, Harding concluded, was 'that wee be not Inioyned to performe Impossibylleties, in layinge on us what wee ar not able to performe'. Freed from this and from the obligation to take the Covenant, they would cheerfully return and compound.[133] But in the aftermath of civil wars such opportunities for reconciliation rarely prevail.

133. Bodleian, Tanner MSS., 58, fo. 709.

VII

THE SURVIVAL OF
ANGLICANISM

Let the Petitions and complaints of the honest and well-affected party . . . judge, whether the case stands with them now, as it did severall years after this Parliament began, when one or two honest men in a Parish could be able to cast out their scandalous Minister by their addresse to the Parliament notwithstanding the power and opposition of manie great men, and now twenty honest men cannot put out a loose Minister, nay hardly keep out those from re-entrance which were first cast out by the Parliament. . . .

> Vox Militaris, Or an Apologeticall Narration Concerning the Officers and Souldiers of the Armie (August 1647), BL., E.401(24), p. 14

Further . . . I beheld . . . Divines of unreproveable life and Doctrine chased from their Churches, beaten and dragged to prisons, haled before Committees, and there charged with blasphemie by fellowes of no reputation, religion nor honesty, whose Arch-priest and Witnesse was a fleshly brother, bold, lusty robustious Cobler . . . to the . . . deep scandall of these reverend men.

> England Dust and Ashes raked up (16 August 1648), Preface 'To thee Reader', BL., E.459(10), not paginated

Prayer Book versus Directory of Worship

While the use of the term Anglicanism is technically an anachronism in a seventeenth-century context, it is a convenient shorthand term for describing that non-Puritan Protestantism which had as its basis the reverence for episcopacy and, more especially, for the Book of Common Prayer. For while horror at the proliferation of sectaries and at toleration of their heterodox beliefs and practices, including lay preaching and the more ribald forms of iconoclasm, was something which Anglicans and Presbyterians had in common, there were other matters in which there was a great gulf fixed between them: notably the Anglican reverence for Christmas, episcopacy and the Book of

Common Prayer, and dislike of strict sabbatarianism. One should be extremely cautious about adding a taste for ritualism to this list; for while, as Dr Green has conclusively demonstrated, it was a Puritan strategy to tar all parsons using the Book of Common Prayer with a Laudian ritualist brush, this was more often than not an attempt to blacken both them and their 'massbook' by association; only one step removed from the frequent accusations of drunkenness, swearing and cursing, womanizing and neglect of parochial duties: charges which were sometimes true and sometimes not.[1] An eloquent example where it is not always easy to dissociate truth from fiction was the case of Richard Laytonhouse, the rector of Desford, whose case came before the Leicestershire county committee in June 1646. Laytonhouse had on many occasions neglected to use the Presbyterian Directory of Worship as recently prescribed by parliament and used instead of the Book of Common Prayer. To go with this, he had neglected observance of monthly Fast Days, profaned the Sabbath and spoken against the Covenant. With these faults went disgraceful demeanour and behaviour. He neglected study, preferring to work on his glebe, was a curser and swearer as well as 'a common fighter and quareller', and sexually incontinent, having reputedly fathered two bastards. To round this off he had even been indicted for burglary. With such a reputation it was not surprising to find that he had also allegedly preached against the parliament.[2] Another Prayer Book parson, Thomas Aylesbury, rector of Kingston Deverill in Wiltshire, was charged with concluding a wartime sermon, on a Friday Fast Day of all times, by expressing the opinion that the rebellion against Charles I was worse than that of Absalom against Saul.[3] Royalism was in fact a far more common Anglican characteristic than ritualism. As a general observation, it would in fact be unwise to go beyond the statement that Anglicans were the proponents of the maintenance of a measure of ceremony and decent order in worship.

Of that order the Book of Common Prayer was then, as it is now, the perfect expression. On 10 February 1647 the Scottish Lord Chancellor, the earl of Loudoun, expressed formal regret 'that the service book [is] still retained in some places of England . . . and the Directory verie much slighted and by some avowedly written against'.[4] Indeed, in some places the parliament's ordinance of 1646 enjoining the use of the

---

1. I.M. Green, 'The persecution of "scandalous" and "malignant" parish clergy during the English Civil War', *Eng. Hist. Rev.*, XCIV (1979), 507–31, especially 519–20. See also J. Spurr, *The Restoration Church of England 1646–1689* (1991), p. 7.
2. Bodleian, MSS. J. Walker, c. 11, fo. 74. For similar examples of the association of the Prayer Book with ritualism and a variety of vices, see ibid., fos. 19–20, 26–7, 65, 81.
3. BL., Add. MSS., 22,084, fo. 8.
4. Bodleian, Tanner MSS., 59, fo. 736(b).

Presbyterian Directory of Worship seems to have been more or less a dead letter from the beginning. Nathaniel Gill, rector of what is to this day the very out of the way parish of Burgh-next-Aylsham in Norfolk, though officially sequestered, continued to officiate occasionally in the parish church administering the sacraments according to the Prayer Book, 'sicut meus est mos', at least down to 1648. So did the arch-Laudian divine, Henry Hammond, even though subject to what amounted to house arrest in his Bedfordshire parish of Clapham.[5] As late as January 1648, when the Dorset county committee intervened against the offending parson, the Prayer Book was still being used in the parish church at Gillingham.[6] Other parsons carried on as long as they could, only submitting to the use of the hated Directory when under extreme pressure and returning to the Prayer Book at every conceivable opportunity. Philip Oldfield, the rector of Lasham in Hampshire, a man who 'hath expressed great malignancie against the parliament' and had once caused the articles of the Hampshire clubmen to be published in the parish, was, nevertheless, not sequestered from his benefice until 24 July 1647. Among his many offences were that he 'hath laid aside the directorie . . . & retorned vnto . . . the use of the Comon prayer booke abolished by Ordynance of parliament'.[7] On other occasions, extruded parsons sometimes returned to their livings, finding their way into church and parsonage house and reintroducing the use of the Prayer Book to the great joy of many of the parishioners.[8] Occasionally, as in the London parishes of St Alphage Cripplegate and St Benet Sherehogg in October, parsons from outside were invited to officiate on an occasional basis and used the Prayer Book, it presumably being their willingness to do so which afforded the reason for their being invited.[9]

Sometimes the use of the Prayer Book was forced upon reluctant and intimidated intruded parsons. On the day after Christmas Day 1646, when he had been humiliated by his parishioners over his attempt

5. On Gill, see PRO., SP. 24/2, fo. 8(b); and Ketton-Cremer, Norfolk, pp. 250–2; Walker Revised, p. 268. On Hammond, see J.W. Packer, The Transformation of Anglicanism 1643–1660 (Manchester,1969), p. 12; Spurr, op. cit., pp. 9–12.
6. Mayo, Dorset, pp. 318–19.
7. BL., Add. MSS., 15,671, fo. 159(b); Walker Revised, p. 188.
8. Examples of such cases between August and October 1647 are: in Shepperton, Middlesex (BL., Add. MSS., 15,671, fo. 172(b)); in Soham, Cambridgeshire (ibid., fos. 208–8(b)); in Ramsey, Huntingdonshire (ibid., fo. 239); and in several Cambridgeshire parishes (HMC., 6th. Report Appendix (House of Lords Cal. 1647), pp. 218–19). Sometimes the parson who intruded and used the Prayer Book was not the originally extruded parson. This happened at Kelshall in Hertfordshire in August and at Buckland in Gloucestershire in September (BL., Add. MSS., 15,671, fos. 164(b), 217(b)).On reintrusion in general, see below, pp. 257–62.
9. BL., Add. MSS., 15,671, fos. 226, 240(b), 262. See below, p. 263.

to enforce parliament's anti-Christmas ordinances, Matthew Clarke, the intruded parson of Stretham in the Isle of Ely, had an even more unpleasant experience. As he detailed in his petition presented to parliament on 6 January 1647, some of his parishioners who, contrary to orthodox Presbyterian practice, had 'sung a dead Corpse to the Church Gate', had pulled him out of a neighbour's house and threatened to bury him alive if he did not conduct a burial service for the dead woman, using the Book of Common Prayer. Clarke and others also testified that an attempt had been made to break into the parsonage house 'to the endangering of his life, the frightening of his Wife great with Child and Family, and affronting him in his Ministry, Obstruction of Reformation, Contempt of Ordinance and Dishonour of Parliament'. The ringleader seems to have been one Humphrey Lawrance, a disorderly alehouse keeper who had also pronounced that the parson 'kept a Bawdy-house and he was a Rogue: and that the Parliament put in none but Rogues'. The Directory of Worship, the officially approved form of worship and that which was certainly favoured by Clarke over the Common Prayer Book, was described by another of his molesters, rather oddly, as 'an old Thing out of Date and not to be used', while another said that Clarke was the only person in the Isle of Ely who used it, which seems most unlikely. The two ringleaders were committed to gaol by the House of Lords. It must in all fairness be admitted that after the event a number of other parishioners had testified in favour of the parson and against his assailants, and notably, against the parish constable who had spoken not a word for the keeping of the king's peace, but instead had threatened 'that if anie would take the woman out of the grave, he would be one of those should helpe to bury . . . Clarke in it'.[10]

If in some cases the use of the Prayer Book was enforced on reluctant parsons by violence, in others efforts to prevent its use were met with violence. In November 1647 the royalist newswriter *Mercurius Elencticus* reported gleefully on how soldiers attempting to interrupt a Prayer Book service at Newark were driven off by 'the Resolute and Religious Dames of the Towne . . . (*manibus tantum expansis*)'.[11] Indeed, the use of the Prayer Book was still ordained by statute in distinct contradiction to the technically less authoritative ordinance enjoining the use of the Directory of Worship. On 26 October 1646, in response to complaints that suits were being brought in Buckinghamshire against godly ministers for not using the Prayer Book as enjoined by statute, it is not

10. HLRO., MP., 7/1/1646–7, fos. 69–70; *L.J.*, VIII, 651, 693; *HMC., 6th. Report Appendix (House of Lords Cal. 1646–7)*, p. 152. On the events of Christmas Day, see below, p. 239.
11. *Mercurius Elencticus . . . no. 3* (12/19 November 1647), BL., E.416(13), p. 21.

surprising to find the House of Commons ordering that an ordinance should be drawn up to repeal the statute in question, as well as to disable malignant parsons from preaching.[12] But nothing seems to have been done and in any case it was constitutionally impossible for a statute to be repealed by an ordinance. Hence such suits continued to be brought, if less frequently. Once indeed the Indemnity Committee had been established in the summer of 1647, there was protection available for defendants in such suits. As late as November 1648 five Cambridgeshire parsons were indicted at Quarter Sessions for refusing to administer the sacraments according to the Book of Common Prayer and using the Directory instead and the Indemnity Committee appears to have experienced some difficulty in getting the chief justice of sessions, the Clerk of the Peace and a member of the jury to appear before it to answer the complaints of the parsons in question about the indictment.[13] Although the Indemnity Committee's intervention on behalf of an alderman of Ripon in the summer of 1648 was in restraint of a charge of assault and battery against him and not against the application of the statute enjoining the use of the Prayer Book, the case is nevertheless of interest in this context since it arose as a result of the alderman's forceful intervention against the burial of a child which was being conducted by a delinquent parson using the Prayer Book and not the Directory.[14]

The Prayer Book in fact was to find some incongruous defenders. A newsletter of 26 July 1647 reporting some of the happenings in London's counter-revolution told of an ex-soldier who had, when serving in the parliamentary army, torn up copies of the Prayer Book with his own hands, but had since repented and said that he would rather have his hand cut off than do so again.[15] But the army to which he had once belonged appears also to have had second thoughts about the Prayer Book, if its toleration of its use in royal circles and elsewhere, which so alarmed the Presbyterians, is anything to go by.[16] Most startling of all, there were even Presbyterians who in certain circumstances favoured its use over that of the Directory. According to Mercurius Pragmaticus, no less a person than Stephen Marshall himself used the Prayer Book for his daughter's wedding, 'which being objected to him, he had the Impudence to make answere that he gave her a

12. Whitelock, Memorials, p. 230 (26 October 1646).
13. PRO., SP. 24/3, fos. 118(b), 118(b)–19, 152(b), 163.
14. PRO., SP. 24/2, fos. 99(b), 171(b); SP. 24/3. fos. 42–2(b).
15. Clarke Papers, I, 218.
16. A Religious Retreat Sounded To a Religious Army (August 1647), BL., E.404(34), pp. 15–16; A WORD to Mr Peters and two WORDS for the Parliament and Kingdom (9 November 1647), BL., E.413(7), p. 9; Works of darkness brought to light (1647), BHPC., pp. 6, 16. See above, p. 164.

good *portion*, and to avoide future broiles, made use of the *Common-Prayer*, that the Marriage might stand good in *Law*'.[17]

As the value of the Prayer Book became increasingly appreciated more or less in proportion as its use was officially inhibited, it was the Puritan establishment, the denouncers of Laudian innovation in the 1630s, which now incurred the odium of innovation. Another source of revulsion from Puritanism for many people was Puritan sabbatarianism, or at least its rigid and unrelenting applications, coupled with the additional innovations of Days of Fasting and Humiliation and the prohibition of the celebration of Christmas, and it is to such considerations that we now turn.

Sabbath-breaking and Christmas observance

As in the matter of the Directory of Worship, every attempt was made to discredit parsons who were lax in seeing to the strict observance of the Sabbath and who encouraged Sunday afternoon games in the spirit of the early Stuart Declarations of Sports. In the strict Puritan view, of course, Sabbath-breaking was a serious, not a minor, sin and those who committed it were persons who might indeed be expected to indulge in a wide variety of vicious practices, of which an addiction to ceremony and ritual was all of a piece with sexual incontinence, drunkenness and consorting with bad and often seditious company. The charges brought against John Hubbock, the rector of Nailstone who was sequestered by the Leicestershire committee in March 1646, are a good case in point. Hubbock's encouragement of football, shovel board and quoits on Sundays was coupled with habitual drunkenness and sexual misconduct – he was accused not only of being a whoremaster and himself sleeping with harlots, but even of cheating one of them by paying her 3d. instead of a groat for her services. To these personal offences were added denunciations of parliament and the publicly expressed hope that the Scots would denounce the Covenant and come to the king's assistance, a hope which, early in 1646, was, of course, also entertained by Charles I himself.[18] Even more colourful charges were brought against Thomas Bird, vicar of Somerby in the same county, in the following month. Another frequent profaner of the Sabbath, on which day he was often drunk and on one particularly notorious occasion had urinated into a pot of milk boiling on the fire, Bird also was accused of having forced

17. *Mercurius Pragmaticus no. 29* (28 December/4 January 1647–8), BL., E.421(29), sig. Q3. For another comment on the same incident, see Walker, *Independency*, pp. 52–3.
18. Bodleian, MSS. J. Walker, c. 11, fos. 63–4; *Walker Revised*, p. 238.

1. James, first duke of Hamilton by Daniel Mytens. This is generally reckoned to be Mytens's masterpiece; a much earlier portrait than that painted by Van Dyck around 1640.

2. William earl of Lanark and second duke of Hamilton. Lanark succeeded to the dukedom following the execution of his brother, the first duke, in March 1649.

3. William earl of Lanark and second duke of Hamilton with John earl and later first duke of Lauderdale. There are two versions of this double portrait said to have been painted in Holland by Cornelius Johnson in 1649. This version is in the collection of the duke of Hamilton and Brandon at Lennoxlove and the other was formerly at Ham House, the English residence of the Lauderdales, and is now in the Victoria and Albert Museum. Interestingly, the original consists of two pieces joined down the middle with the right hand portion dated 1649.

4. The Devon Petition of 22 February 1648. Copies of this petition were circulated to parishes for subscription, but it was never presented to parliament.

5. The death of Dr (Colonel) Michael Hudson. Hudson had accompanied the king in his flight from Oxford which culminated in Charles's giving himself up to the Scots at Southwell in May 1646. The illustration depicts Hudson's ghastly end more than two years later in June 1648. Following a not very successful attempt to raise forces for the king in these parts, Hudson and his followers were cornered at Woodcroft House in Northamptonshire. Hudson retreated, fighting, to the top of the house. There his tenuous and desperate hold on the roof was disengaged by the simple means of slicing his fingers with a sword blow, and he fell into the lake from which he was dragged before being finally dispatched.

6. Major-General Edward Massey. A mercenary officer whose services had been offered to and rejected by the king, Massey became the hero of the successful parliamentary defence of Gloucester in 1643. One of the eleven Presbyterian members attacked by the army in 1647, he was secluded and imprisoned at Pride's Purge.

7. Major-General Sir William Waller. Popularly dubbed 'William the Conqueror' by his Roundhead admirers, at least before his defeat by the royalists at Roundway Down in 1643. One of the eleven members attacked by the army in 1647, he was purged and imprisoned by Pride in December 1648.

8. Charles I in captivity. A print from one of many royalist broadsides in 1648 which obviously overdoes the severity of the king's confinement at Carisbrooke.

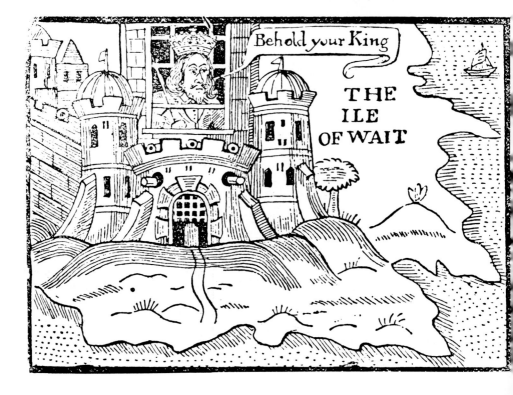

9. Murrough O'Brien, first viscount Inchiquin. President of Munster and a close ally of the English parliamentary Presbyterians, Inchiquin defected to the king early in 1648, allying himself both with Lord Taafe, leader of the Irish confederate Catholics, and with the marquis of Ormond, Charles I's Lord Deputy of Ireland.

10. Henry Rich first earl of Holland. An earlier portrait of Holland from what was for him the far happier time of his eminence as courtly luminary and favourite of the queen.

11 (right) and 12.   Duke of Buckingham and earl of Peterborough. Buckingham and Peterborough were Holland's allies in the short-lived and mismanaged rising of July 1648, who, unlike Holland and Buckingham's brother Lord Francis Villiers, escaped with their lives. Like Holland, but more permanently, Peterborough had earlier defected to the king at Oxford in 1643. The insignia of the Garter in the portrait of Buckingham dates it at 1649 at the earliest, and the costume suggests sometime soon after this date. In this respect, this fine portrait is in marked contrast to the Restoration fop portrayed in J. M. Wright's better known and later portrait of 1669.

13. Vice-Admiral William Batten. Obviously a post-Restoration portrait of Batten who, as Surveyor of the Navy, inspired Pepy's dislike and contempt. A seasoned parliamentarian naval commander, Batten defected to the insurgent fleet in August 1648.

14. John first Baron Byron. Dobson's portrait clearly reveals the wound sustained by Byron at a skirmish with some Roundhead troops at Burford in January 1643. His Second Civil War strategy in North Wales and the West Midlands aroused extravagant but unrealized royalist and Scottish Engager expectations.

15. Sir Marmaduke Langdale. Commander of the northern horse at Naseby and elsewhere, in the First War, Langdale was badly let down by Hamilton and the Scots Engagers in the Second.

16. Arthur Lord Capel and his family. The gardens displayed in the rear of Johnson's portrait are probably of Little Hadham, Capel's seat in Hertfordshire, from where he left in 1648 to join the insurgents in Essex.

17. Sir Charles Lucas. Lucas probably sat for Dobson in 1645 at Oxford following his appointment as Lieutenant-General in the royalist army. A modern copy is in the Moot Hall at Colchester. Lucas's seat was just outside that town following the capitulation of which he was shot along with Sir George Lisle.

his unwelcome sexual attentions on a woman in childbed, later claiming in his defence that he had visited her only to make arrangements for her to be churched. The latter ceremony was, in any case, deplored by Puritans as redolent of the grosser forms of Laudian ritualism – of which Bird was also accused, having erected a stone altar in the church. Most bizarre of all, however, was his practice of going hunting in his surplice, which on one occasion he tore when leaping over a gate and the parish had to replace with another, Bird declaring that he would keep the torn one for hunting in. If we add to these scandals, his marrying a couple without banns or licence and having 'a piper plaie before him from the alehouse at twelve a clocke at night', scaring the villagers out of their sleep, we have virtually all the ingredients appropriate to the discrediting of a Sabbath-breaking Anglican parson by associating him with a variety of scandalous sins.[19]

The interval between the two civil wars abounds with complaints about the disregarding of the ordinances enjoining strict observance of the Sabbath and with proposals for stricter enforcement. For example, such complaints were a feature of the proceedings at both the Dorset assizes at Dorchester on 13 August 1646 and the Wiltshire assizes at Salisbury on 15 March 1647,[20] as well as of a petition of godly London citizens heard by the Court of Aldermen on 11 November 1647 which prompted both an appeal to parliament for stiffened legislation and orders to city constables and other officers for more rigorous searches for violators of the Sabbath.[21] Sins were in fact compounded and enormities rendered the more enormous for being committed on a Sunday. When a Westminster JP complained to parliament on 7 February 1648 about the gross misbehaviour of some of the boys of Westminster School who had assaulted a young girl of about fifteen in the cloisters of the abbey, it is a question whether the fact that the incident took place on a Sunday was not in his eyes a greater offence than the outrage *per se*.[22] Moreover, working was no less reprehensible than lechery and frivolity on such days. On 11 September 1646 the

---

19. MSS. J. Walker, c. 11, fos. 19–20(b); *Walker Revised*, pp. 231–2. On the apparent antithesis between piping and proper religious observance, see C. Hill, *Society and Puritanism in Pre-Revolutionary England* (1964), pp. 191–2. For other similar cases from Leicestershire, see MSS. J. Walker, c. 10, fos. 26–7, 32–3(b), 65, 74; from Gloucestershire, BL., Add. MSS., 15,671, fo. 217(b); and from Lancashire, MSS. J. Walker, c. 10, fos. 53(b)–4, 61, 62(b), 64(b)–7: W.A. Shaw (ed.), *Minutes of the Bury Presbyterian Classis* (Chetham Soc., new ser., XXXVI (1890), pt. i), 48–51, 77–8, 82–5, 87–8, 91, 102, 104–5.
20. *Western Assize Orders*, pp. 238–9, 249–50.
21. CLRO., Rep. 59, fo. 35(b); *The Perfect Weekly Account . . . no.* 47 (17/23 November 1647), BL., E.416(27), no pagination.
22. *HMC., 7th. Report Appendix (House of Lords Cal. 1647–8)*, p. 8; *L.J.*, X, 32.

Assembly of Great Yarmouth ordained that the boom in the haven be closed on Sundays to prevent fishermen sailing on the Sabbath, and the town authorities were no less strict about other forms of Sabbath violation.[23]

On 31 March 1648 a greatly stiffened ordinance for Sabbath observance such as the London petitioners had demanded the previous November received its second reading in the House of Commons and was committed,[24] while the matter remained a prominent feature of parliamentary peace proposals to the king right down to the time of the Treaty of Newport in the autumn of 1648.[25] In June 1648, at the height of the Second Civil War, violation of the Sabbath was still a major concern of parliament, further prompted by a petition from the Presbyterian provincial assembly of London.[26] On 8 August John Warner, the Lord Mayor of London, who had had much frustrating experience of the difficulty of enforcing observance of the Lord's Day and Fast Days in London, issued a proclamation deploring their neglect as well as the prevalence of 'the odious sin of Drunkennesse and prophane swearing and cursing'. The proclamation endeavoured to stiffen enforcement of the sabbatarian regulations. Sunday buying and selling, travelling on business, labouring, opening of taverns, alehouses and other such establishments were to be put down vigorously and constables and churchwardens were to make regular searches for violators and to make note of their names.[27]

The neglect and unpopularity of regimented Sabbath observance extended also, *mutatis mutandis*, to Fast Days. In a number of the cases where parsons were accused of anti-sabbatarian activities these, not surprisingly, were coupled with failure to observe Fast Days.[28] But there are some cases where the latter offence does not seem to have accompanied the former, as well as vice versa. This is true, for example, of the charges brought against Thomas Rowson, parson of Hoby in

---

23. NNRO., Great Yarmouth Assembly Book 1642–1662, fo. 91(b). For other sabbatarian restrictions in Yarmouth in October 1647 and October 1648, see ibid., fos. 112(b), 133.

24. *C.J.*, V, 522; Rushworth, *Historical Collections*, VII, 1045; Whitelock, *Memorials*, p. 297 (31 March 1648). The proposed ordinance, however, seems to have got no further than this.

25. See, e.g., Gardiner, *Constitutional Documents*, p. 293; BL., E.390(4), pp. 4–5; *His Majesties Propositions for a safe and well grounded Peace* ... (June 1647), E.392(12), no pagination; *Parliamentary History*, XVIII, 4, 137; Bodleian, Rawlinson MSS., A114, fos. 26, 36; *HMC., MSS. of the Earl of Ancaster*, pp. 415–17; Whitelock, *Memorials*, p. 335 (2 October 1648).

26. *C.J.*, V, 612; *L.J.*, X, 352–3.

27. *A Proclamation by the Lord Mayor of London for the strict observance of Sunday* (8 August 1648), BL., 669, f12(104). The opening hours of drinking establishments were limited on other days also.

28. This is true, for example, of the case of Richard Laytonhouse cited above, p. 230.

Leicestershire, on 28 April 1646,[29] and against another Leicestershire parson, George Rogers, who like many anti-sabbatarian clergymen was also accused of often being 'much overtaken with drinke'. Rogers's defence against the charges on 13 December 1646 offers a graphic illustration of the scope afforded by such regulations for the exercise of inquisitorial procedures and perhaps also the venting of personal spite by enemies some of whom were still withholding tithes from him, and 'sett the souldiers vpon mee, crying out that I was a malignant'. In addition, he suffered from eavesdroppers 'at the windowes of mine house . . . when I was alone with family at rest and quiett'.[30]

Obviously, sabbatarian regulations offered a promising field for Cavalier propagandists, since offenders against such regulations and those, who if not actually offending, nevertheless found them irksome were to be found well outside the ranks of old-style Cavaliers. Indeed, they extended to some of the soldiers of the New Model Army itself. One Presbyterian and anti-army pamphlet of December 1647 complained about the Cavalier-like behaviour of many soldiers, who, as well as fighting and playing games on Fast Days and Sundays, emulated the behaviour of their former enemies in such matters as swearing blasphemous oaths such as 'dammee', 'God's wounds' and the like. Another urged the need to curb the soldiers' propensity 'to prophane the Lords daies, by their ordinary marching and travailing, when there is neither hast nor need'.[31] Would the Lord of Hosts favour armies which chose to campaign on a Sunday, one is tempted to ask, but such authors, and especially the first, were seeking to blacken the army in the eyes of their readers, and while there is no smoke without fire, it would obviously be wrong to see such misbehaviour as typical of the army as a whole, still less of its officer class. By way of corrective, it is interesting to find a petition of 12 July 1649 from officers who had engaged for service in Ireland, recommending an uncompromisingly radical programme including the abolition of tithes, the simplification of legal procedures and the release of prisoners for debt, also demanding that 'all Drunkenness, profane Swearing, Vncleanness, Abuses of the Lords Day &c. may be restrained, not tolerated'.[32] Indeed, it will be recalled that it was the New Model soldiers who had helped the London trained bands to put down the anti-sabbatarian riots in early April 1648.[33]

29.   Bodleian, MSS. J. Walker, c. 11, fos. 34–4(b).
30.   Ibid., fos. 78–8(b).
31.   *The Army Anatomized* (4 December 1647), BL., E.419(6), p. 6; [Nathaniel Ward], *To the High and Honourable Parliament. The humble Petitions, serious Suggestions* (2 May 1648), BHPC., p. 26.
32.   Whitelock, *Memorials*, p. 398 (12 July 1649).
33.   See above, p. 190.

These last were probably the most serious of all anti-sabbatarian disturbances, over these years. Lord Mayor Warner was in fact responding to the complaints of divers godly Citizens about playing games and drinking on the Sabbath, when, on 9 April, he sent out watchmen and other officers to seek out such violators of the Lord's Day. Finding in Moorfields 'divers loose fellows . . . playing at Cat, drinking and other disorders' at the time of the Sunday sermon, they attempted to restrain and detain them, but without success. When the trained bands were called in, the area around Moorfields and Finsbury was in turmoil. The dissident young men, now transformed into rioters, seized a piece of ordnance and, on the following day, broke into the magazine at Leadenhall. Some of them broke through into Fleet Street and the Strand, where, according to one observer, they were 'encouraged by divers Malignants'. There were shouts of 'Now for King Charles' and drums were beaten on the river to arouse the notoriously pro-Cavalier Thames watermen, and perhaps the seamen too, to rise, 'for God and King Charles'. Following the dispersing of the rioters and the arrest of some of the ringleaders, Common Council on 11 April asked parliament to set aside a day of thanksgiving for the City's deliverance from 'a horrid and detestable act'. Bulstrode Whitelock, whose normally laconic *Memorials* provide an unusually detailed account of these tumultuous events, expressed the view 'that this insurrection . . . (if it had not been so soon . . . nipped in bud) might have proved of most dangerous consequence . . . and have occasioned a new War'. He may have been exaggerating, but it is none the less important not to underestimate the currents of popular irritation and anger which could be aroused by the tactless and unimaginative application of restrictions which some considered to be irksome in any case.[34]

But one should also beware of going to the other extreme. It has been argued by Christopher Hill that strict Sunday observance was less unpopular than is often assumed,[35] and indeed the Jacobean and Caroline Declarations of Sports had aroused fierce opposition which certainly cannot be dismissed by seeing it as the work of a minority of Puritan zealots and fanatics. The Puritan inhibiting of the celebration of Christmas may well have been more unpopular than Puritan sab-

---

34.   This account is based on *L.J.*, X, 188, 190–2, 194, 195; *C.J.*, V, 528, 529; Rushworth, *Historical Collections*, VII, 1051–2, 1055–6; Whitelock, *Memorials*, pp. 298–9 (10 April 1648); *Clarke Papers*, II, 3–4; CLRO., Jor. 40, fo. 267; *An Act and Declaration of the Common Council of the City of London touching the late Insurrection* (11 April 1648), BL., E.435(22), pp. 3–7; *A full Narration of the late Riotous Tumult* (11 April 1648), E.435(24), pp. 1–4, 9–10; *The Rising and Routing of the Mutineers . . .* (April 1648), E.435(4), pp. 1–6. There is a very partial account in Walker, *Independency*, Preface and pp. 55–8.
35.   C. Hill, *Society and Puritanism in Pre-Revolutionary England*, pp. 145–218.

batarianism, at least when the latter did not assume too inquisitorial a character. One thoughtful royalist, not altogether unfairly, saw the Puritan anti-Christmas campaign as part of a systematic programme of '*suppression and demolition of all Monuments of Christianity*' and cited as an example the destruction of the Glastonbury thorn 'that it might no longer Preach vnto men the Birth day of their Saviour' – viz. by flowering at Christmas.[36] But Puritans were certainly not alone in deploring the survival of what many Protestants regarded as such un-wanted relics of a popish past which any thoroughgoing Reformation would have extirpated. However, the Puritan attempt to enforce the parliamentary ordinance prohibiting the celebration of Christmas at all was a different matter and aroused widespread indignation. The attempts of mayors and other municipal officers to put the ordinance into effect at Christmas 1647 produced serious disturbances, notably in Canterbury, Ipswich and London. Nor were such disturbances confined to towns. Before the Christmas period in 1646 Matthew Clarke, whom we have already encountered as the intruded parson of Stretham in the Isle of Ely who got into trouble with his parishioners over his refusal to use the Prayer Book,[37] had impressed upon his parishioners that Christmas Day was no holiday but just another day. In protest on Christmas Day some of them brought into church – their choice is curious – not a malignant parson, but a soldier, to preach. In the afternoon service they found Clarke at his reading desk in the church and threatened that if he did not preach a sermon, they would pull him down and set up the soldier again to preach in his stead. Clarke had to yield 'for Quietness-sake', as he put it in his petition to parliament on 6 January 1647.[38]

On 24 December 1647 the House of Commons noted disapprov-ingly that some Londoners who had dutifully obeyed parliamentary ordinances not to observe holy days and Christmas and to open their shops on such days had suffered affronts and abuse. Accordingly the Militia Committees of London and Westminster were ordered to take precautions against disturbances of the peace on the following day 'by any Malignants or others' and to see to it that all malignant parsons who had supported the enemy in the Civil War should be put out of London.[39] In the event the militiamen's zeal may have been excessive, for in the ensuing disturbances one young man died in Newgate prison to which he had been dragged having been wounded by the trained

36.   Edward Symmons, *A Vindication of King Charles* (November 1647), pp. 75–6.
37.   See above, pp. 231–2.
38.   HLRO., MP., 7/1/1646–7, fos. 69–70; *L.J.*, VIII, 651, 693; *HMC., 6th. Report Appendix (House of Lords Cal. 1646–7)*, p. 152.
39.   *C.J.*, V, 403.

bands on Christmas Day. In consequence a royalist commentator describes Lord Mayor Warner, who took his duty in repressing Christmas festivities at least as seriously as enforcing Sabbath observance, as deserving of a '*hempen-Ruffe* instead of a *Golden Chaine*, for certainly the *Iudges* (though never so corrupt) cannot produce one *Worme-eaten* Statute to pronounce the *Young-man* worthy of *Death* for gazing only upon *Rosemary* and *Bayes* . . . *Emblems* of the *Growth* and *Beauty* of *Christ* and his Church'.[40] The Lord Mayor's repressive actions were, however, to find one striking defence in a Roundhead broadsheet emphasizing the duties of obedience and the need for order in terms which would not have been inappropriate in a royalist propagandist pamphlet of the early 1640s.[41]

At his examination before a committee at Westminster one of the churchwardens of St Margaret's Westminster offered an interesting explanation of the decision to have a service and sermon on Christmas Day above all others and contrary to parliamentary ordinance. He related how it had been decided at a parish meeting that since – despite the statute – the people would not go to work on that day, a sermon would contribute to drawing them to church rather than – pious hope! – to alehouses and taverns. This was all very well and not especially convincing, and in any case did not excuse the parishioners' choice of an ex-royalist preacher for the occasion when St Margaret's was decked with rosemary and bays and the *Nunc Dimittis* set by the parish clerk to be sung 'at the desire of severall eminent persons then present at Church'.[42]

The most serious pro-Christmas disturbances took place at Canterbury which, as a strongly partisan and pro-royalist account was to put it in the following June, could without exaggeration be described as 'the immediate cause of these last troubles [viz. the Second Civil War] in *Kent*'.[43] For that reason detailed treatment of these riots has been left to a later chapter in the context of disturbances, some of which prefigure and others – like those at Canterbury – lead on to the renewal of civil war in 1648.[44] The mayoral precepts enforcing a parliamentary anti-Christmas ordinance prohibited both religious services and the closing

---

40. *Mercurius Elencticus Number 12* (5/12 January 1648), BL., E.422(25), p. 46. For a similar satirical attack on Warner's pulling down of Christmas decorations at the conduit in Cornhill, see *Mercurius Pragmaticus number 29* (28 December/4 January 1647/8), E.421(29), sig. Q^v.
41. *A Word in season: or A Check to Disobedience* . . . (13 January 1648), BL., E.422(26), pp. 3–8.
42. *The Kingdomes Weekly Post* . . . (29 December/5 January 1647–8), BL., E.422(1), p. 2.
43. *A Letter from a Gentleman in Kent* (15 June 1648), BL., E.448(34), especially pp. 2–5. For the unashamedly royalist manifesto of the aims of the Canterbury insurgents, see *The Declaration of the City of Canterbury or County of Kent* (5 January 1648), E.421(23), pp. 3–7.
44. See below, pp. 359–61.

of shops on Christmas Day and both were disobeyed, the latter in particular leading to widespread looting. In a combination of festive spirit, with the rioters helping themselves to free drink at the expense of the magistrate, and brutal violence, the mob got out of hand and a riot bade fair to become an insurrection. This cannot be said of the Christmas riots at Ipswich, where the ringleaders were all safely locked up by 27 December and casualties seem to have been fewer, even though they did include a man named Christmas 'whose name seemed to blow up the coales of his zeale to the observation of the day'.[45] As to ultimate consequences, unlike Kent, east Suffolk was relatively untroubled during the Second Civil War.

Revulsion from sectarian excesses

Writing on February 1647 from Kendal to his patron Lord Wharton in London, the Presbyterian parson, Henry Massy, complained of the proliferation of sectaries in the Lake District as elsewhere, for which he blamed the absence of a strictly enforced religious settlement. Liberty of conscience and toleration of heterodox opinion were, in his view, 'destructive both to pietie and politie' and if granted in religion, there was no reason why they should not apply to politics and other matters. Concede toleration in the greater matter, and it must be conceded in the lesser.[46] Londoners of course were no strangers to the phenomenon remarked by Massy. In July 1647 some apprentices of London petitioned that, inter alia, 'the Government of the Church may be speedily setled, Conventicles (the Seminaries of Separation) supprest, and a toleration of licentious libertie . . . declared against', and there was a spate of treatises, the most celebrated and vituperative of which is Thomas Edwards's Gangraena, to the same effect.[47] As to the socially and politically subversive connotations of sectarianism stressed in Massy's

---

45. BL., E.422(1), p. 1. See also *The Kingdomes Weekly Intelligencer number 241* (27 December/4 January 1647–8), E.421(30), pp. 786–7.
46. Bodleian, Rawlinson Letters 52, fo. 32.
47. For the petition, see CLRO., Jor. 40, fo. 240; BL., 669, f 11(41). For examples of treatises to this effect, see T. Edwards, *Gangraena* (1646), passim; *Vox Civitatis* (28 September 1647), BL., E.409(10), pp. 2–3; *Hinc Illae Lacrimae* (23 December 1647), E.421(6), pp. 12 (corrected pagination), 20, 23; *The Army Anatomized* (4 December 1647), E.419(6), pp. 4, 15, 31; *A New Magna Charta* (17 February 1648), E.427(15), p. 1. As Edwards emphasized in another tract of 1647, sectaries and heretics had throughout history pleaded for toleration 'whilst weak and few . . . yet when they have come to grow strong and to have power in their hands . . . they have been the greatest tyrants and persecutors' (T. Edwards, *The Casting Down of the last and strongest hold of Satan* . . . (1647), cited by J.W. Packer, *The Transformation of Anglicanism* (Manchester, 1969), p. 145).

letter, these also were emphasized in a cogently argued Presbyterian pamphlet of 1647, which deplored, *inter alia*, 'the endeavours of the Sectaries to overthrow and alter the very foundamentals of the government of the Kingdom'. They offered a threat to the House of Lords by arguing that peers should not sit in parliament unless elected to it, and indeed to monarchy itself through sectarian opinion that 'the King for his mis-government must lose his life'.[48] The petition of some orthodox (presumably Presbyterian) ministers of the county of Rutland to parliament on 15 May 1648 complained about the activities of Samuel Oates, a local Anabaptist preacher, not only because he reviled the clergy as '*Scribes and Pharisies, Antichrist's Prelates, Persequutors of the Truth &c.*', but also for 'outfacing Magistracy, yea, uttering most seditious and treasonable Speeches against Monarchy itself '.[49]

A Presbyterian pamphlet of July 1647 waxed indignant about the army's alleged recruitment not only of Irishmen and ex-Cavalier soldiers but also of Anabaptists and other sectaries 'who . . . intend . . . some Anarchical destructive designe . . . to ruin Parliament, Monarchy, and all kind of Government'.[50] Others of a similar disposition associated sectaries with the Leveller notions of Lilburne and Overton who stormed against all authority and dominion, while still others argued that they favoured not only political democracy but also the parity of property and estates.[51] In these fears Presbyterians and royalists were at one. Sir Marmaduke Langdale, the commander of the royalist insurgents in the north during the Second Civil War, wrote on 8 August 1648 to Sir Charles Lucas, one of the royalist commanders in besieged Colchester, expressing, with the aid of colourful metaphor, the view that 'nothing had so much infected the affections of the people as the seditious doctrine of sundry Sectaries and Non-Conformists in these parts [viz. Westmorland] who bestowed of their oyle in laying *adulterate colours* upon the face of Rebellion'.[52]

---

48. *Works of darkness brought to Light* (1647), BHPC., pp. 8–10. For similar observations, see *Some Queries propounded to the Common Councell and Citizens of London* (30 July 1647), BL., E.400(26), pp. 2–3, 11; *Hinc Illae Lacrimae*, p. 11 (corrected pagination); *The Petition of Right of the Free-holders and Free-men . . .* (8 January 1648), E.422(9), p. 15; *Great Britans [sic] Vote . . .* (27 March 1648), Codrington pamphlet coll., p. 6; *A Declaration and Brotherly Exhortation of the General Assembly of the Church of Scotland* (August 1647), BL., E.407(24), esp. pp. 4–5; *L.J.*, X, 242. For another eloquent Scottish condemnation of the evils of toleration, see the papers of the Scottish commissioners of 18 December 1647 objecting to the four bills (*Parliamentary History*, XVI, 449–53, 455–7).
49. *L.J.*, X, 259.
50. *IX Proposals by way of Interrogation* (July 1647), BL., E.396(8), pp. 7–8.
51. E.g. *Hinc Illae Lacrimae*, p. 2; *The Army Anatomized* (4 December 1647), BL., E.419(6), p. 4; *A Paire of Spectacles for the City* (4 December 1647), E.419(9), pp. 5–6.
52. *A Letter from Sir Marmaduke Langdale* (August 1648), BL., E.457(20), p. 4.

Many Anglican worshippers had disapproved of the extremes of Laudian ritualism and the cult of reverencing altars and church monuments, but both they and the Presbyterians were horrified by the worst excesses of sectarian iconoclasm which extended far beyond the ravages of a William Dowsing in Suffolk; or of Colonel Venn, MP for London, described by *Mercurius Pragmaticus* as 'that wicked Philistian which spared not the *Ashes* of the *dead* and persecuted the Saints in *Church windowes* and robb'd us of much of the glory of our *Nation* by defacing those famous *Monuments* at Windsor'; or of the parliamentary Visitors of Oxford University who were authorized by a parliamentary ordinance of 27 May 1648 'to take away and to destroy all such Pictures, Relics, Crucifixes and Images . . . judged by them to be superstitious or idolatrous'.[53] The inhabitants of Scarborough in September 1648 were no doubt justified in fearing that the pews and seats in their church would be defaced by parliamentary soldiers.[54] But this was nothing to what soldiers were capable of, fired either with sectarian zeal or with the mindless vandalism which characterizes so many men under arms in any age. A Presbyterian pamphlet of December 1647 recounts with horror how some soldiers had dared 'to bring a *Horse* into a *Church*, to piss into the *Font*, and with that pisse . . . to baptise the horse in the Font, to signe it with the signe of the crosse, to have Godfathers and Godmothers for it, and to name it *Baal-Esaw*'.[55] Whether the soldiers were sectarian zealots or simply blaspheming vandals, incidents like this were welcome grist to the mill of royalist as well as Presbyterian antisectarian publicists.[56]

From well before the end of the First Civil War there had been abundant complaints about the proliferation of sectarian congregations, especially in London.[57] But not only did heterodox preachers abound.

53. On Dowsing, see R. Loder (ed.), *The Journal of William Dowsing of Stratford . . . (1643–4)* (Woodbridge, 1786), passim. On Venn, see *Mercurius Pragmaticus number 11* (23/30 November 1647), BL., E.417(20), sig. L2. For the iconoclastic instructions to the Oxford visitors, see *A&O.*, I, 1143.
54. Northallerton, North Yorkshire RO., Scarborough Corporation Minute Book, 1621–1649, fo. 163(b). I owe this reference to the kindness of Mr M.Y. Ashworth.
55. *Hinc Illae Lacrimae*, p. 10 (corrected pagination).
56. See, e.g., James Howell, *A letter to the Earle of Pembrooke* (1647), BHPC., pp. 8–9; Edward Symmons, *A Vindication of King Charles* (November 1647), BL., E.414(16), pp. 74, 81.
57. See, e.g., the Remonstrance of the Lord Mayor, Aldermen and Common Council of 20 May 1646 (BL., Add. MSS., 31, 116, fo. 271; Whitelock, *Memorials*, p. 212 (26 May 1646)); the City petitions of 19 December 1646 (*Parliamentary History*, XV, 228–9) and of 17 March 1647 (*To the Parliament: The Petition of the Lord Mayor and Common Council* (17 March 1647), BL., E.381(2), pp. 4–5). For a fuller discussion of these, see above, pp. 134–5.

It was not unknown for them to be found officially administering the cure of souls in parish churches. On 13 June 1646 the Committee for Plundered Ministers heard a petition from an Essex parson, William Michael, who had been sequestered from the rectory of Chickney on what turned out to be a mere technicality. Michael complained that the sequestrators of the parish had appointed two men to succeed him at least temporarily, one of whom was an Anabaptist and the other of unspecified denomination but certainly a layman, both of whom were corrupting the parishioners 'with erroneous doctrine'. The committee restored Michael to his living and discharged his sequestration, though the record does not state whether any action was taken against the sequestrators who had perpetrated this outrage.[58]

The case highlights three connected points for consideration: the appointment of sectaries to livings; the use of unordained lay preachers; and the spread of heterodox doctrine as a consequence. The growth of the influence of sectaries was a matter of alarm to both royalists and Presbyterians, even though *Mercurius Rusticus* was to argue that the former sometimes colluded with sectaries to remove godly intruded parsons and incite parishioners not to pay tithes to them.[59] When the Presbyterian magistrate Colonel King gave his celebrated charge to the Folkingham sessions in Lincolnshire in October 1646, he made a point of asking the Grand Jury to present 'all Papists, Anabaptists, Brownists, Separatists, Antinomians and Hereticks, who take upon them to creep into houses and lead captive silly women laden with sinnes'.[60] The undoubted horror of conservative-minded people, both Presbyterians and royalists, at the phenomenon of unordained ignoramuses preaching the word has already received attention in another context, that of soldiers in the pulpit.[61] Of course not all, or even most, lay preachers were soldiers and the activities of those who were not were hardly less alarming than those of the ones who were. The parliamentary declaration of 31 December 1646 forbidding preaching by unordained persons therefore met with wide approval from both Presbyterians and Anglicans even if it did also arouse misgivings in some rather surprising places on account of some of its unforeseen consequences. For instance, on the very day that the declaration passed in the Lower House, the earl of Leicester mused, somewhat extravagantly, in his

58. BL., Add. MSS., 15,670, fo. 105(b).
59. *Mercurius Rusticus* (12 November 1647), BL., E.414(5), p. 1.
60. Edward King, *A discovery of the arbitrary, tyrannical and illegal actions* (1647), BHPC., p. 16. See also King's charge to the Grand Jury at Sleaford on 11 January 1647 (Bodleian, Tanner MSS., 59, fo. 668(b)).
61. See above, p. 163–4.

Journal that both husbands in the privacy of family devotions and parliament men in employing Scripture to reinforce their cases in speeches in parliament might be deemed to fall within the prohibited category.[62] Our third point, the erroneous doctrine which was propounded when unlettered and unordained preachers abounded, was, to an age of piety if also one of religious intolerance, perhaps the most alarming danger of all, and a proposed ordinance in September 1646 laid down severe penalties, including the death penalty, for those refusing to abjure denial of doctrines such as the Trinity and both the divinity and humanity of Christ.[63]

The prospect of sectarian 'saints' ruling the earth horrified both Presbyterians and royalists and seemed to be prefigured by the ever-increasing influence of sectaries who, as a city Presbyterian pamphlet of September 1647 put it, 'screw'd themselves into places of trust and profit in Martiall and Civill affaires'.[64] The growth of conservative alarm and even of counter-revolutionary sentiment in late 1647 and 1648 owes much to such fears and the feeling that events were moving rapidly in a direction which was as repellent to Presbyterians as it was to royalists. The next chapter will explore the extent to which these two basically conservative forces were able to find common ground in the face of this common danger. But first we must turn to developments in which there was little or no common ground between them: the fight back of extruded Anglican parsons and of the religion, if not of Laud, at least of Hooker, Whitgift and the Elizabethan settlement. We have already observed its strength over the issue of the Book of Common Prayer. It is now time to turn to its other manifestations.

62. *Sydney Papers*, p. 2. For the declaration, see BL., Add. MSS., 22,620, fos. 164(b)–5; Add. MSS., 31,116, fo. 295(b); *C.J.*, V, 34–5.
63. *An Ordinance presented to the Honourable House of Commons* (10 September 1646), BL., 669, f 9(50). Among the other prohibited views were denial of the resurrection and the ascension as well as of the validity of infant baptism and the divine authority of Scripture and the sanctity of the Sabbath. Also condemned were belief in purgatory, mortalism, worship through pictures and images and the view 'that all men shall be saved [and] that a man by nature hath free will to turn to God'. The last of these beliefs was held by many non-Puritan Protestants. For other denunciations of heretical doctrines, see, e.g., *Vox Civitatis* (28 September 1647), BL., E.409(10), p. 5; *A Paire of Spectacles for the Citie* (4 December 1647), E.419(9), p. 6; and, of course, T. Edwards, *Gangraena*, passim.
64. *Vox Civitatis*, p. 2. See also *A New Magna Charta* (17 February 1648), BL., E.427(15), pp. 3–4. On the growth of sectarian influence in parliament, see Walker, *Independency*, pp. 69–70, an admittedly exaggerated view, but one which expresses real apprehensions.

Anglican resistance: i. denial of entry and withholding of tithes

On 7 February 1646 the parliamentary commissioners with the army which was investing the royalist stronghold of Newark wrote to the Speaker of the House of Commons informing him of the very great difficulties which were currently being experienced by the county committee of Lincolnshire which had 'no power to remove ye malignant Ministers there nor yet to settle any good ones in such places as are voyd'. The letter cited as an example of the former a certain Dr Hurst, 'one of ye first in Lincolnshire that stirred up the Gentlemen & Country people against you. Hee hath bin constantly with the Enemy in Newarke endeavouring to do all the Micheife he could possibly.' The commissioners suggested an appropriate replacement for Hurst, who had publicly characterized four notable Roundheads including Fairfax and Cromwell as the four horns of the beast. They also expressed confidence that the county 'may in short time be replenished with godly and able Ministers'.[65] They seem to have been unduly optimistic about the ease of this undertaking. In England in general it still had not been completed two years after the end of the war, and, indeed, even during the Commonwealth 'malignant divines' who had hitherto survived the hostile attentions of county committees and the Committee for Plundered Ministers still remained to be dealt with, as a glance at the pages of Dr Matthews's invaluable study reveals.[66]

In addition, there was the problem presented by returning royalist ministers at and after the end of the war. On 8 September the Northumberland committee wrote to George and Robert Fenwick, the first of whom was MP for Morpeth along with his brother John. The letter bewails the return of 'malignant' royalist parsons, 'ready to blow the trumpett to a new commotion in these parts after the departure of the Scots Army'. The reappearance in full canonicals of Geldard Alvey, the former high-church vicar of Newcastle, after a long spell in gaol in Norwich and Great Yarmouth, provoked a violent demonstration in church which is vividly described by John Fenwick. Fenwick's devoutly Puritan wife seems to have egged on like-minded members of the congregation

> who fed upon the Vicars new dressing (the Surplice and Service-booke) which set the malignant superstitious people in such a fire, as men and women fell upon my wife like wilde beasts, tore her cloaths and gave her

---

65. Bodleian, Tanner MSS., 60, fos. 420–20(b). Hurst was extruded before the end of 1646, though he later gave trouble over the tithes of his former benefice (BL., Add. MSS., 15,671, fo. 150; *Walker Revised*, pp. 252–3).
66. *Walker Revised*, passim.

at least an hundred blowes and had slaine her if the Maior had not stept out of his pue to rescue her . . . such was the peoples madnesse after their Idols.[67]

There seemed in fact to be a real danger that Northumberland, which was to have a high number of Anglican reintrusions (see Table 1 on p. 266, below), might easily slide back into its entrenched royalism of before the invasion of 1644 and that the return of parsons such as Alvey would contribute materially to this development. On 9 March 1647 the Committee for Plundered Ministers extracted a reluctant undertaking from Alvey that he would cease to intrude and exercise the ministerial office in the benefices of Newcastle and Eglington from which he had been sequestered during the war until such time as the sequestration should be lifted, which was a most unlikely contingency anyway.[68]

While such dangers might be more apparent in remote and formerly royalist areas such as Northumberland, they were by no means peculiar to them. On 4 March 1647 the Suffolk committee warned the Speaker about the numbers of malignant ministers returning to that county.[69] Later that year, on 18 October, Dr Thomas Hill, the Master of Trinity College, Cambridge, alerted the earl of Manchester to the dangers of delinquent dons returning to resume their Fellowships as well as of virtual malignants already in place, such as the newly elected proctors, Cowdrey and Moore. The majority of Fellows in some colleges, includ-ing his own, were 'professed malignants', who sought 'to work the University into its former model'. Such Fellows used the Prayer Book, extolled episcopacy and denounced Heads of Houses who had been intruded by parliamentary authority as usurpers and thieves.[70]

The sequestration of a 'scandalous and malignant' minister and the administration of his living by sequestrators until such time as a suc-cessor approved by the Westminster Assembly was appointed by the Committee for Plundered Ministers by no means always meant that the parish had seen the last of its former incumbent. It was quite common for the officially extruded minister, sometimes with his wife's help and on more than one occasion acting entirely through the agency of his wife,[71] to deny entry to the intruded parson, the sequestrators or

---

67. Bodleian, Tanner MSS., 59, fo. 528; J. Fenwick, *Christ Ruling in the Midst of His Enemies*, cited by R. Howell, *Newcastle Upon Tyne and the Puritan Revolution* (Oxford, 1967), p. 142; Walker, *Sufferings*, p. 184; *Walker Revised*, p. 288.
68. Bodleian, Bodley MSS., 324, fo. 180.
69. Tanner MSS., 59, fo. 792. The committee also warned against returning royalist gentlemen who had taken neither the Covenant nor the Negative Oath.
70. *HMC., 6th. Report Appendix (House of Lords Cal. 1647)*, p. 202.
71. E.g. at Rede, Suffolk, in 1646 (Bodleian, Bodley MSS., 324, fo. 22(b)); at Calbourne, Isle of Wight, in 1647 (BL., Add. MSS., 15,671, fo. 183; *Walker Revised*, pp. 190–1); and in Bath, Somerset, in 1646 (J. Wroughton, *The Civil War in Bath and North Somerset (1642–1650)* (Bath, 1973), pp. 116–17).

both. In this he sometimes also could count on the co-operation of his churchwardens.[72] On occasion what seems to have amounted to a faction among the parishioners – and the number of sympathizers may have been much larger – took his cause into their own hands. That James Potter, the rector of Binfield in Berkshire, was not sequestered until 13 July 1647 seems a trifle surprising since he had frequently 'expressed great malignancie to the parliament', on one occasion declaring that those who had died fighting for parliament against the king had no hope of salvation. Incriminating this might be, but it does not seem to have cost him the sympathy of some of his parishioners, for on 10 October the Committee for Plundered Ministers heard the complaint of the sequestrators against nine parishioners, four of whom were women, who had continued to keep the church door locked both against them and any visiting parson whom they might appoint to take services there. Potter, on whose behalf the nine parishioners were clearly acting, was still occupying the parsonage house. He chose to ignore an order from the committee and stayed put until on 16 October it ordered him to be brought up in custody to answer for his contumacy.[73]

Many of the cases of tenacious Anglican parsons who offered what amounted to more than a show of resistance to their deprivation, and are numbered under the heading 'Entry denied' in the table at the end of the chapter, had acquired a reputation for delinquency through their sermons, churchmanship or allegedly scandalous life. Many were unrepentant royalists like James Potter at Binfield. Another such was Edward Salter, the pluralist rector of both Great Chesterton in Rutland and St John's in Stamford, Lincolnshire. Although officially sequestered from his Stamford rectory in January 1645, Salter had still not yielded possession of it to the sequestrators as late as July 1647, when he was again ordered to do so. During the war he had served with the royalist garrison at nearby Burghley House as well as at Belvoir Castle, and his wife, the sister of a royalist captain, had acquired a reputation as a particularly fervent royalist.[74]

Some of the extruded parsons managed, rather surprisingly, to find livings elsewhere, but even then entry was sometimes denied to their

---

72. E.g. during the summer and autumn of 1647 at East Horsley in Surrey (BL., Add. MSS., 15,671, fos. 180, 197(b), 224); in Maidstone and Sandwich in Kent (ibid., fo. 175; HLRO., MP., 12/10/1647, 23/10/1647, 4/11/1647; L.J., IX, 477, 491, 511; HMC., 7th. Report Appendix (House of Lords Cal. 1647–8), p. 7); and at Calverleigh in Devon (Western Assize Orders, pp. 265–6).
73. BL., Add. MSS., 15,671, fos. 147(b), 230(b), 243; Walker Revised, pp. 70–1.
74. BL., Add. MSS., 15,671, fos. 95, 175; Walker, Sufferings, p. 366; Walker Revised, p. 256. Other Lincolnshire examples of entry being denied to sequestrators are Morton Hay Bourne (BL., Add. MSS., 15,671, fos. 41, 140, 140(b)); Colsterworth (ibid., fo. 35); and Market Deeping (ibid., fos. 80–80(b), 187(b)).

intruded replacements. Robert Turney, the extruded rector of Spring-field in Essex, succeeded in finding another benefice, but his wife con-tinued to occupy the Springfield parsonage house and to deny entry to the intruded parson.[75] Perhaps she was hedging her bets, for an extruded parson who found a living elsewhere was still vulnerable, as is shown by the case of John Kidbye. Kidbye had been extruded from the vicarage of Kirby-le-Soken in Essex back in September 1643 for uttering what were regarded as dangerously anti-parliamentarian sentiments. How-ever, he found a living at Shenfield in the same county to which he was presented by the House of Lords, responding to the parishioners' appeal that he had been sequestered from his former living without having been given a fair hearing. But it was not long before he was in trouble at Shenfield too, when the living was sequestered from him to Henry Goodeere on 2 March 1647. Unlike Kidbye's former intruded successor at Kirby-le-Soken, however, Goodeere had to contend both with Kidbye's continued occupation of the parsonage house and his ordering the parishioners not to pay tithes to the intruder, who had still not obtained possession on 18 August, when the Committee for Plundered Ministers ordered Kidbye to be brought up in custody.[76]

Nor did parliament's victory in the Second Civil War prevent continued attempts to keep parliamentary intruders out of the livings to which they had been presented under the auspices of the Committee for Plundered Ministers. On 28 November 1648 George Warde, the intruded vicar of Yalding in Kent, petitioned the House of Lords that he was being denied occupation of his glebe by William Brooke on the grounds that Warde 'came not in by the Kings power, therfor he may try his right, or words to that effect'. The petitioner prayed that Brooke should be ordered to yield him possession of the glebe, or answer for it to the House, which took order to this effect.[77]

The Committee for Plundered Ministers was, given its terms of reference, not unjust in its treatment of extruded parsons. It took pains to force often reluctant intruders to pay the fifth part of the income of the benefice to the dependants of the extruded in cases where it was deemed that the latters' residual resources were insufficient to provide for them. In addition it frequently allowed the extruded parson and his wife a reasonable time – sometimes as long as three months – before they had to leave the parsonage house,[78] a concession which was

75. Ibid., fo. 206; Bodleian, Bodley MSS., 323, fo. 101; *Walker Revised*, pp. 165–6.
76. BL., Add. MSS., 15,671, fo. 176; Walker, *Sufferings*, p. 419; *Walker Revised*, p. 157.
77. HLRO., MP., 28/11/1648; *L.J.*, X, 612.
78. As at Tempsford in Bedfordshire during the summer of 1647 (BL., Add. MSS., 15,671, fos. 112(b), 145; *Walker Revised*, p. 65).

sometimes abused and entry denied to the intruder even after the period of grace had expired.[79]

The cases cited here are only a very few examples of those whose number appears in Table 1 at the end of the chapter (pp. 265–6). But such cases of denial of entry do not always constitute the sum total of the extruded parsons' resistance, and are sometimes simply the first stage in a process. In September 1646 William Harwood (or Herwood) had appealed unsuccessfully against sequestration from the rectory of Monks Risborough in Buckinghamshire, but he obstinately refused to yield possession of the parsonage house and produce of the glebe to Michael Anderson, the intruded minister, and was committed to prison by the Committee for Plundered Ministers in March 1647. He was released in the following month on giving his bond to yield the parsonage house quietly to Anderson. But once released, he refused to comply and was in gaol again at the end of May. His subsequent relinquishment of the rectory heralded a change of strategy rather than an acceptance of defeat, for in July he was again called before the Committee, this time for urging his ex-parishioners to withhold their tithes from Anderson. In support of his action he urged a royal proclamation from Oxford in 1643 backed up by an alleged recent declaration by Lord General Fairfax against the payments of tithes to intruded ministers, of which more will be said later. In addition, he instituted a lawsuit for riotous behaviour against those parishioners who had assisted in Anderson's induction, though this suit was discharged by order of the Indemnity Committee on 29 October.[80] The case thus neatly illustrates three important strategies of Anglican resistance, but before moving to the second of these, tithe-withholding, the connection between this and denial of entry needs emphasis. For the latter was normally accompanied by the former,[81] and was sometimes coupled with the sequestered parson's refusal to hand over the tithe book without which the intruded parson lacked the necessary information of what was due to him from his parishioners.[82]

---

79. As at Bebington in Cheshire in July 1647, where entry was being denied by some parishioners to the intruded minister, even though the sequestered parson had died in June (BL., Add. MSS., 15,671, fos. 100, 100(b); *Walker Revised*, p. 92).

80. Bodleian, Bodley MSS., 324, fos. 70, 170, 210(b), 239; BL., Add. MSS., 15,671, fos. 39–9(b), 125(b), 178(b)–9, 218(b); P.R.O., SP. 24/1, fos. 62(b)–3; *Walker Revised*, p. 74.

81. As, for example, at Radwinter in Essex and Newington in Buckinghamshire in January 1646 (BL., Add. MSS., 15,670, fos. 6(b), 7(b)); and at Stoke Climsland in Cornwall in October 1646 (*HMC., 6th. Report (House of Lords Cal. 1646)*, p. 137; *L.J.*, VIII 531).

82. As at Sturminster Newton Castle in Dorset at the end of 1646 and beginning of 1647 (Mayo, *Dorset*, pp. 99–100; *Walker Revised*, p. 137); and at Minster in Kent, where the intruded parson was the notorious iconoclast Richard Culmer. For information on

Until quite recently discussion of the problem of tithe-withholding was almost invariably couched in terms of the conscientious scruples of sectaries and others who abhorred paying for the maintenance of ministers of an established church from which they completely dissociated themselves. But the work of Dr John Morrill in particular has taught us to see such cases as a mere drop in the ocean when set beside the phenomenon of the withholding of tithes from intruded Puritan ministers often at the behest of the Anglican parsons whom they replaced.[83] That said, it is of course still important not to overlook the quite different cases such as that of John Stubbings, the vicar of Ambrosden in Oxfordshire, who, fortunate not to have been sequestered himself, none the less suffered because 'the Phanatical People would pay him no Tythes'.[84] Nor should it be forgotten that withholding of tithes need not be based on ideological grounds or religious preferences as distinct from a reluctance to pay taxes of any sort.[85] Here, though, we are concerned with the sort of case to which Dr Morrill has drawn attention, examples of which are very numerous. However, there may well have been occasions when such considerations simply offered a handy excuse for not paying tithes which might have been withheld in any circumstances. Even in those cases where the evidence in terms of statements by the withholder gives little indication of his motives, the accompanying circumstances sometimes give such an indication. Such were cases where the tithes are not only withheld from the intruded parson but paid to his extruded predecessor instead, and cases where the latter reintruded and previously withheld tithes are paid up during his reintrusion.[86] As the case of the complaint of the Wiltshire committee on 28 June 1647 against the denial of tithes to godly

Culmer and his case, see Bodleian, Bodley MSS., 323, fo. 157; Bodley MSS., 324, fos. 102(b), 109(b); BL., Add. MSS., 15,670, fos. 105(b), 106(b), 107(b); Add. MSS., 15,671, fos. 83(b)–4, 98(b), 137(b), 139(b), 179, 186, 191(b), 216(b); Walker, *Sufferings*, p. 219; *Walker Revised*, p. 213; Everitt, *Kent*, pp. 53, 59, 60, 85–6, 117, 127, 202–4, 225–6, 233.

83.   J.S. Morrill, 'The Church in England 1642–9', in idem (ed.), *Reactions to the English Civil War 1642–1649* (1982), especially pp. 110–11.

84.   *Walker Revised*, p. 300. For obvious reasons no such cases are included in the figures for tithe-withholding at the end of the chapter, pp. 265–6.

85.   As perhaps in the case of Nicholas Townley esquire of Littleton in Middlesex who pronounced in November 1646 that 'he would rather die in the field then pay any tythes', but gave no reason why. However, Townley later sued the intruded minister and a serjeant-at-arms for wrongful arrest on the order of the Committee for Plundered Ministers for non-payment (Bodleian, Bodley MSS., 324, fos. 35, 95(b), 230(b); PRO., SP. 24/1, fos. 75, 83(b), 97(b), 126).

86.   To avoid double counting, in cases where withholding of tithes to intruders is combined with the reintrusion of sequestered parsons, the figures in Table 1 on p. 266 are included under the latter heading (viz. *reintrusion*). To that extent the table understates the number of cases of tithe withholding.

intruded ministers suggests, such reintrusion and payment of previously denied tithes were normally connected:

> But . . . these scandelous Ministeres formerly outed for theire Delinquency doe take boldnes to make Comotions in the Country . . . [and] come with theire Assistantes and take vp Tythes in theire owne persons, driue out honest Ministeres . . . and bring the Comon prayer Booke againe into the Churches.[87]

Such reintrusion was in a word indivisible and included both occupancy of the church and taking possession of the tithes. No less shocking to the Wiltshire committee was the connivance of local JPs at these goings-on.

If, as in Wiltshire, help for the hard-pressed intruded parsons was not forthcoming from the JPs, they could perhaps turn to more sympathetic authorities. The county committee was often more receptive, though, as the Wiltshire case suggests, not always in a position to translate sympathy into effective supportive action. There was also the army. In September 1647 it was reported that intruded ministers in north Yorkshire were endeavouring – unsuccessfully it would seem – to persuade Major General Lambert to afford them assistance in the collection of their tithes, which were being withheld, though whether by ordinary tithe-defaulters or conscientious objectors on behalf of extruded parsons is not clear.[88] Indeed, in some circumstances soliciting help from soldiers might be distinctly counter-productive. On hearing in April 1648 complaints about tithe-withholding from the intruded parson Dr Arthur Wingham, whose parish is not specified in the record, some JPs issued instructions to local soldiers and others to distrain forcibly on the property of the withholders. This elicited a vigorous response from the withholders, which not only took the form of a lawsuit and the arrest of the distrainers but also their being beaten up, and Wingham's stable being broken into to recover the distrained cattle, as well as the committing of 'seuerall other outrages'.[89]

Just as entry into a sequestered living was sometimes denied to the sequestrators as well as to the intruded parson, so is this also true of tithe payments. Given his active involvement in the implementation of the royal Commission of Array in 1642 as well as his reputation for Laudian innovation in the 1630s, it is surprising to find that Francis Holyoake, the aged rector of Southam in Warwickshire – he was seventy in 1647 – was not sequestered from that living until April 1647. His spirit unbowed, he was already in trouble by August for forbidding

---

87. Bodleian, Tanner MSS., 58, fo. 283.
88. *A Fight in the North At the Dales in Richmondshire* (September 1647), BL., E.407(45), no pagination.
89. PRO., SP. 24/2, fo. 46(b).

his parishioners to pay tithes to sequestrators rather than to himself.[90] Sequestrators may in fact have been in a stronger position in respect of forcing tithe payments than were many intruding parsons, some of whom had to wait an inordinately long time before being able to lay their hands on the tithes withheld from them, as Richard Culmer, the unpopular Puritan parson of Minster in Thanet and Gervase Kiddall the intruded minister at Swaby in Lincolnshire discovered to their cost.[91] In August 1647 such parsons experienced a further, if temporary, setback from a curious development which has already been noted in passing. This was the use made by some extruded parsons of what they claimed to be a declaration by no less a person than Lord General Fairfax in support of a royal wartime proclamation of 1643 forbidding the payment of tithes to ministers who had been intruded into livings by parliamentary authority. A number of extruded parsons seized on the opportunity presented by the genuine but ineffective proclamation and the spurious declaration, among them Dr Thomas Cookson, an ex-Cavalier and notorious preacher of sedition against parliament. Cookson personally went from house to house in his former parish of Marston Moretaine in Bedfordshire forbidding the parishioners to pay tithes to the intruded parson, and citing the proclamation and fake declaration as his authority.[92] But the most remarkable of such cases was that of the petition of four intruded parsons with livings in Northamptonshire, Leicestershire, Hertfordshire and Essex, which was heard in parliament on 20 August 1647 against their molestation by the extruded ministers of these livings who cited Charles I and Fairfax as their authority for helping themselves to tithes, as well as, in some cases, reintruding themselves. The petition which made the greatest stir was that of Edmund Spinks, the intruded parson at Castor in Northamptonshire, and this was because his extruded competitor for the tithes and benefice was Dr William Towers, the bishop of Peterborough, who

90. BL., Add. MSS., 15,671, fo. 181. On Holyoake, see Walker, *Sufferings*, p. 276; *Walker Revised*, pp. 363–4; Hughes, *Warwickshire*, pp. 67, 68–9, 80, 148, 325. For other examples of tithes being withheld from sequestrators on behalf of extruded parsons, see Add. MSS., 15,671, fo. 157 (in Histon, Cambridgeshire); ibid., fos. 6, 120 (in Wardsley, Huntingdonshire); and ibid., fos. 119, 175–5(b), 184(b), 252 (in both Cranford and Kessingland in Suffolk).
91. For the reference to Culmer, see above, p. 250, note 82. For Kiddall, see BL., Add. MSS., 15,670, fo. 102; Add. MSS., 15,671, fos. 109(b)–10; *Walker Revised*, p. 258. Culmer's attempts to secure his tithes lasted through most of 1646 and had still not been settled by September 1647. Kiddall petitioned the Committee for Plundered Ministers for help on 6 June 1646 and had still not been satisfied in early July 1647.
92. BL., Add. MSS., 15,671, fo. 182; *Walker Revised*, p. 64. Cookson had also been the parson of Millbrook in the same county. One victim of similar tactics around the same time was John Ley, the celebrated Puritan controversialist and member of the Westminister Assembly, in respect of the tithes of the parish of Astbury in Cheshire (Add. MSS., 15,671, fo. 182(b)).

had held the living *in commendam*. The bishop got his servant John Parvoe publicly to read the proclamation and false declaration in Castor church, for which offence the House of Lords forced Parvoe to recant publicly in the same place and at the same time to acknowledge that the rightful recipient of the tithes was Spinks and not the bishop.[93]

Fairfax's alleged declaration was a passing wonder which contributed to some disorder but only for a time. What it had served to emphasize was the ultimate threat to parishioners who paid their tithes to intruders that, even if they were not brought to account for some time, that time would come. This point was strongly made by Henry Gilbert, the extruded rector of Clifton in Staffordshire, a cleric with an active royalist past. In September 1647 the House of Lords heard how Gilbert had written to his former parishioners warning them that if they paid tithes to the intruded parson, they should 'be careful to tie him unto such Conditions and upon so good Bail, that, when the Laws shall once again recover their Force, you may come to no Damage . . . nor I may be moved to use such Extremities against you which the Law . . . (I doubt not) will one Day afford me'.[94] Similarly, in the following month a petition from William Howe, the sorely harassed intruded minister of Gedney in Lincolnshire, complained that, on being warned – not by the extruded parson but by one of their own number – that if they paid tithes to Howe they would have to pay them to another later, many of his parishioners had withheld their tithes from him. Chief among their number was 'one Mordecay Williamson a notorious Delinquent who hath beene in Arms against the Parliament', and had contumaciously refused to appear before the local JPs when summoned by them.[95] In another case, the parish of Taplow in Buckinghamshire, it was a church-warden who in the summer of 1647 took the lead in encouraging at least two of the parishioners to withhold their tithes from the intruded parson.[96] But the most common instigator of tithe-withholding was the extruded parson,[97] who sometimes also tried to divert the payment of tithes to himself.[98]

93. HLRO., MP., 17/9/1647, fos. 37–37(b); *HMC., 6th. Report Appendix (House of Lords Cal. 1647)*, pp. 195–6; *L.J.*, IX, 389, 390–1, 435; *Walker Revised*, p. 13.
94. *L.J.*, IX, 449; *HMC., 6th. Report Appendix (House of Lords Cal. 1647)*, p. 197; Walker, *Sufferings*, p. 255; *Walker Revised*, pp. 322–3.
95. HLRO., MP., 28/10/1647.
96. BL., Add. MSS., 15,671, fos. 179(b), 191.
97. Examples in 1647 are: in Sevenoaks, Kent (Bodleian, Bodley MSS., 324, fo. 198; BL., Add. MSS., 15,671, fo. 183); in Hallingbury, Essex, where the extruded parson also reintruded (Add. MSS., 15,671, fos. 19, 129(b), 169(b), 227(b)); in Swaby, Lincoln-shire (Add. MSS., 15,670, fo. 102; Add. MSS., 15,671, fos. 109(b), 110); and in Collingbourne Kingston in Wiltshire (Add. MSS., 15,671, fo. 116).
98. Examples in the summer of 1647 are: in Chiddingfield, Surrey (BL., Add. MSS., 15,671, fos. 98, 243(b)); in Cliddesden and in Baghurst, Hampshire (ibid., fos. 113(b)–14, 126(b), 185, 192(b), 205); in Cransford and in Euston, Suffolk (ibid., fos. 100, 119,

Despite the fact that from the summer of 1647 the circumstances could hardly have been less propitious for litigation by extruded parsons and their allies among their former parishioners on account of the application of the Indemnity Ordinances, there are a number of examples of such litigation. Many of these usually unsuccessful litigants were parishioners suing against the intruders' right to receive the tithes or against distraint of their property carried out as a consequence of their withholding of tithes.[99]

Even at the best of times such litigation was expensive, and, because of the activities of the Indemnity Committee, this was the worst of times for such litigants. Just as instances of tithe-withholding were most difficult to deal with when the withholder was a locally powerful and influential person, such as the lord of the manor at Euston in Suffolk or a titled person (a knight) at Blaby in Leicestershire,[100] so was it normally only such powerful and wealthy people who could bear the great costs of litigation, especially given its likely failure. Deprived of their parochial income, few extruded parsons were in a position to do so, and, in the cases of those who were, circumstances were usually untypical. This is true of the tithe suits which were brought by two academics, Dr Henry Stringer, the Warden of New College and Professor of Greek at Oxford, who had been deprived of his Buckinghamshire rectories of Waddesdon and Hardwick, and Dr Cheney Rowe, the extruded rector of Orwell in Cambridgeshire, who was Vice-Master of Trinity College, Cambridge. Both were former royalists, and Rowe indeed had been prominent in the collection of plate in Cambridge for the royal cause in the early days of the war. Both brought suits for tithes against the intruding parsons in their former livings. Stringer may have encouraged the tithe-withholders in Hardwick to resist arrest, 'some of them being rescued & the serieants deputies beaten & abused'. Rowe, however, was more successful in his lawsuit, surviving the initial hostility of the Indemnity Committee,

147, 184(b)); in Sandon, Essex (ibid., fos. 119(b), 188(b)); in Hardwick, in Swaffham Prior and in Cheveley, Cambridgeshire (ibid., fos. 152(b), 155(b)–6; 164(b), 173–3(b), 191); in Walford, Warwickshire (ibid., fo. 154).

99. Examples are: PRO., SP. 24/1, fos. 109(b), 122(b), 123 (Viney v. Prior); ibid., fo. 174 (Goodriche v. Robertes); SP. 24/2, fo. 166(b); SP. 24/3, fos. 28, 40(b)–1, 130(b)–1 (Baseley v. Dennis); SP. 24/3, fos. 37, 80(b), 81(b) (White et al. v. Edwards). In the last case both the intruded parson and the tithe collector were sued. For cases of suits against intruded parsons for distraining cattle and other property and attempted recovery of this by means of writs of *replevin*, SP. 24/3, fos. 123, 134, 152(b) (Rogers v. Ashbye); SP. 24/3, fo. 131 (Hubbert v. Warner et al.). In the last case a verdict against the intruded, and in favour of the sequestered, parson had been reached in the Hundred Court before the case came before the Indemnity Committee on 18 November 1648.

100. For Euston, BL., Add. MSS., 15,671, fos. 100, 147. For Blaby, ibid., fos. 21(b), 48(b), 49(b)–50.

against which he won an appeal and was even restored to his benefice and his sequestration discharged in August 1648.[101]

The defendants in such suits were a mixed bunch, including, of course, as in the last cases, intruding parsons, but also sequestrators[102] and those who farmed tithes from them;[103] as well as parish constables and those assisting them in distraining on tithe-withholders' property and summoning them to appear before magistrates.[104] In at least one case, during the autumn of 1648, an unfortunate purchaser of cattle which had been sold following distraint was sued by the former owner.[105] The fact that such suits usually fell foul of the Indemnity Committee did not deter the plaintiffs, who themselves included tithe payers as well as extruded parsons, though it is arguable that there would have been many more such prosecutions if it had not been for this committee's activities. This may also help to explain the fact that, far from being a surrogate for violence, litigation was sometimes accompanied by violence. This, for instance, occurred in an unnamed parish early in 1648, when some tithe-withholders sued certain soldiers and other persons who, acting under orders from local JPs, had distrained on their cattle. Not content, however, to await the verdict of the courts, and perhaps fearing that any such verdict would be frustrated by the Indemnity Committee, some of the parishioners broke into the intruded parson's barn, from which they retrieved the distrained cattle,

101.   On Stringer, ibid., fos. 93, 108(b), 128(b), 131, 139(b), 155, 162, 253(b); PRO., SP. 24/1, fos. 44(b)–5; Walker, *Sufferings*, pp. 15, 97, 127; *Walker Revised*, p. 76. On Rowe, SP. 24/1, fos. 127, 136(b), 152, 161; SP. 24/2, fo. 3; Walker, *Sufferings*, pp. 160, 339; *Walker Revised*, p. 86.
102.   E.g. SP. 24/2, fos. 2, 45, 94(b), 100; SP. 24/3, fos. 146–6(b) (Bennett et al. v. Guines et al.); SP. 24/2, fo. 164; SP. 24/3, fo. 3(b) (Watson v. Atkinson); SP. 24/2, fos. 135(b)–6 (Hesledon v. Ainsworth); SP. 24/1, fo. 141; SP. 24/2, fos. 5(b)–6, 8(b), 16(b); SP. 24/3, fo. 139(b). This last was a case involving six extruded Norfolk parsons, including Nathaniel Gill, whose other activities have received notice above (see p. 231). The suit was brought against a sequestrator of the parish of Swanton Abbott.
103.   E.g. SP. 24/1, fo. 149; SP. 24/2, fos. 146(b)–7, 159 (Jackson et al. v. Doddinge); SP. 24/1, fo. 188(b) (Sugg et al. v. Wrench).
104.   E.g. SP. 24/2, fos. 29, 59–9(b), 94(b)–5 (Richardson v. Warner); SP. 24/3, fos. 74, 94(b), 118 (Freny v. Dunmore); SP. 24/3, fos. 77(b), 90–90(b), 127, 132(b)–3 (Jackman v. Sandham); SP. 24/3, fos. 77(b)–8, 85 (Wade v. Blicke). The last three cases all came before the Indemnity Committee in September 1648. It ordered two suits to be discharged and deferred judgment on the third. In the case of Hart v. Samwell relating to the distraint of cattle for unpaid tithes in the parish of Kislingbury in Northamptonshire, one of the distrainers, Thomas Perkins, languished in irons for some five weeks in Northampton gaol, having been remanded in custody until the next assizes. He was released by order of the Indemnity Committee (SP. 24/2, fo. 174(b); SP. 24/3, fos. 21(b)–2(b), 38–8(b)). For a similar case, see SP. 24/3, fo. 150(b) (Mason et al. v. White).
105.   SP. 24/3, fo. 151(b).

administering a severe beating to the distrainers in the process. The latter appealed on 20 April to the Indemnity Committee to discharge the suit against them, and it is surprising to find that, even in November, the Committee had still not reached a decision on what seems to be a relatively straightforward case.[106] Nor was violence restricted to tithe cases. In most of the issues where the loyalties of parishioners were divided between the extruded and the intruded parsons, violence was never far from the surface, and sometimes erupted, leading in at least two cases to charges of manslaughter: of a woman in Shipley in Sussex, a consequence of resistance to a demonstration in church against the intruded parson; and of a child who died after being hit by the shutter of a window which was being forced by parishioners who were pursuing a ringleader of the disturbances in the parish against the intruded minister of North Kilverton in Leicestershire in 1647.[107] Violence was also all too frequently a feature of the circumstances attending the reintrusion of previously sequestered parsons, which is the main subject of the concluding section of this chapter.

Anglican resistance: ii. reintrusion and patronage

The litigation about tithes which formed the greater part of the lawsuits brought against intruded parsons was sometimes the prelude to the physical reintrusion of Anglican parsons into parishes from which they had been extruded; but sometimes occurred more or less simultaneously with it.[108] Many of the suits, though not always on tithes, illustrate the opposition not only to the persons and churchmanship of intruded ministers but also to their political sympathies. An interesting case is that of Paul Amirant, the intruded minister of East Dereham in Norfolk, who in November 1647 complained to the Indemnity Committee that he was being molested and indeed prosecuted at law by some of 'the disaffected party' in the parish for having extolled parliamentary victories in the war in a sermon given on an official parliamentary Day of Thanksgiving. Royalists in the parish naturally took exception as these

---

106. SP. 24/2, fos. 46(b), 75(b); SP. 24/3, fo. 111 (Wingham v. Colston et al.).
107. On Shipley, SP. 24/1, fo. 148. The case came before the Indemnity Committee on 3 February 1648. The fifteen plaintiffs, eight of whom were women, were ordered to appear before the committee on 17 February, and their failure to do so suggests that they may have dropped their case. On North Kilworth, SP. 24/3, fos. 19, 28(b)–9. The Indemnity Committee ordered this case to be discharged. The child had in fact died months after the injury.
108. As at Walpole St Andrew in Norfolk at the beginning of 1647 (Bodleian, Bodley MSS., 324, fos. 126(b), 182–2(b); Walker Revised, p. 272); and Walkern in Hertfordshire in June 1647 (BL., Add. MSS., 15,671, fos. 73, 253; L.J., IX, 389, 390).

victories had, after all, been won against the king, and they brought charges against Amirant 'vnder a false pretence of speakinge words against the Kinge'. But the Indemnity Committee came to his rescue on 21 December, discharging the suit against him and ordering Norfolk MPs to accord him their protection in future.[109] Perhaps if they had not, Amirant himself might have been the victim of an Anglican reintrusion as many other Puritan ministers were (see Table 1 at end of chapter, p. 266).

It is hardly surprising that some of the parsons who attempted to reintrude themselves into the livings from which they had been extruded had earlier attempted to deny entry to church or parsonage house or both to the intruding ministers approved by the Committee for Plundered Ministers, though there is certainly no complete correlation between the two.[110] As in the case of denial of entry, the wives of the reintruders often played a notable role in the occupation and retention of the parsonage houses. In July 1647 one of them, Mrs Beardsall, the wife of the reintruding parson at Arkesden in Essex, protested that 'she will first loose her life' rather than yield up the parsonage house, while in June 1648 Richard Atkinson, who had temporarily reintruded at Kessingland in Suffolk during the previous year, brought a suit for assault against a sequestrator, who claimed that he had done no more than attempt to restrain Mrs Atkinson from breaking up his cart.[111] The frequent association of reintrusion with tithe denial has already been emphasized as has the petition of 20 August 1647 by four intruded parsons some of whom had suffered from both.[112] Three days after that petition had been heard in parliament, an ordinance was passed 'for keeping in godly Ministers placed in Livings by Authority of Parliament'. The ordinance required local magistrates to apprehend reintruding 'malignant' ministers, who were made liable to one month's imprisonment, and to see that their intruded successors

109. PRO., SP. 24/1, fos. 84(b), 113, 116(b).
110. E.g. Edward Moringe, a royalist, at Cliddesden, Hampshire, in 1647, where he had in the previous year resisted extrusion (Bodleian, Bodley MSS., 324, fo. 201; BL., Add. MSS., 15,671, fos. 113(b)–14; *Walker Revised*, p. 188); and Stephen Nettles who had denied entry to the intruded minister at Lexden in Essex in 1645 and reintruded himself in 1647. Nettles had been charged with womanizing, frequenting taverns and neglecting to present the Covenant to his parishioners. He was later to serve with the royalists in Colchester in the Second Civil War (BL., Add. MSS., 15,671, fos. 162, 171(b)–2; Walker, *Sufferings*, p. 318; *Walker Revised*, p. 159).
111. On Beardsall, see BL., Add. MSS., 15,671, fos. 129(b)–30, 154(b), 168; *Walker Revised*, pp. 145–6. On Atkinson, see Add. MSS., 15,671, fos. 175–5(b), 252; PRO., SP. 24/2, fo. 164; SP. 24/3, fo. 3(b); *Walker Revised*, p. 326. For another pertinacious reintruding wife, Mrs Clark, in Ashton-super-Trent, Derbyshire, see Add. MSS., 15,671, fo. 259; *Walker Revised*, p. 105.
112. On the petition, see above, pp. 253–4.

were peacefully settled in their livings, employing, if necessary, the local trained bands to secure these ends.[113]

Reintrusion was likely to be achieved the more easily and peaceably after a living fell vacant through the death or translation of the intruder or his temporary absence. One victim of the latter circumstance and former proponent of a *cause célèbre* of the 1630s was the one-time prebendary of Durham, Peter Smart, whose Puritan scruples had been outraged in the 1630s by John Cosin's ritualistic innovations in the cathedral.[114] The extruded parson, Thomas Gowen, whom Smart had replaced in the Hampshire rectory of Bishopstoke, was many years later to embrace the Catholic faith, but it was in his high Anglican personification that he took advantage of Smart's temporary absence in the autumn 1647 to reintrude both himself and the Book of Common Prayer, at least for a time.[115]

Even in such cases where an extruded parson exploited the effective absence of an intruder to reintrude himself, he would scarcely have been able to succeed, even temporarily, without the active co-operation of a significant number of parishioners, and often, though not always, of the churchwardens.[116] It almost goes without saying that, except in the sort of cases cited above when the intruder was absent, an element of violence was of the essence of the act of reintrusion, especially where the parish was riven by factions supporting the contending parties. There were, however, different degrees of violence, and three examples must suffice to illustrate cases of reintrusion where violence bulked large. One of the intruded divines whose petition was heard in parliament on 20 August 1647[117] was Thomas Jenkins, whose petition presents a graphic picture of a violent reintrusion in the parish of North Kilworth, Leicestershire, by the formerly extruded parson Samuel

---

113. *A&O.*, I, 999–1000; *L.J.*, IX, 400; *An Ordinance for Keeping in godly Ministers* (23 August 1647), BL., E.404(27), pp. 5–8.

114. On this, see Ashton, *Civil War*, p. 28.

115. BL., Add. MSS., 15,671, fo. 239; Walker, *Sufferings*, pp. 77, 254; *Walker Revised*, p. 183. A similar case of reintrusion during the intruded minister's absence is that of James Chibbald at the London benefice of St Nicholas Cole Abbey early in 1647. Chibbald was ordered to leave on 16 April (Bodleian, Bodley MSS., 324, fos. 217–17(b), 237; *Walker Revised*, p. 44).

116. Examples of parishioners actively co-operating with reintruding parsons during the summer of 1647 are in Wistow, Huntingdonshire, where there had previously been opposition to paying tithes (BL., Add. MSS., 15,671, fo. 180(b); Bodleian, Bodley MSS., 324, fos. 194(b)–5(b), 212; *Walker Revised*, p. 206); in Lexden, Essex (Add. MSS., 15,671, fos. 162, 171(b)–2); in Ashurst, Sussex (ibid., fos. 91(b), 118, 128; *Walker Revised*, p. 356); in Corringham, Essex (Add. MSS., 15,671, fos. 151, 173–3(b), 194(b), 214(b)); in Girton, Cambridgeshire (ibid., fo. 171; *Walker Revised*, p. 83); and probably at Church Langton, Leicestershire (Add. MSS., 15,671, fos. 130, 170; *Walker Revised*, p. 232).

117. On the petition, see above, pp. 253–4.

Cotton, who a year earlier, in August 1646, had been seen armed with a long knife attempting to escape arrest by an under-marshal in Leicester. The picture of a militant pro-Cavalier parson is confirmed by Jenkins's encounter with Cotton on 10 August 1647 when the latter

> came into the Field, and struck me . . . and carried away the Profits of the Glebe; and after endeavoured to take a Fork, saying 'That I deserved to have it thrust into my Guts' and said 'The next Time he met me he would sacrifice me'. And on the next day . . . the said *Sam. Cotton*, with such as have been in Arms against the Parliament, and some of the Inhabitants, violently seized on my House, shamefully abused my Wife by dragging up and down and kicking of her though with Child, cast out and spoiled a great Part of my Goods, and possessed the rest, discharged against those who came by Order for my Assistance, disarmed them and now do keep the House and Church by Force of Arms, in Contempt of Orders of Parliament. And he said also 'That he would shortly make me and a Hundred such Rogues as I am to fly . . .'. And some of the rich Men of the Town did . . . force me to go towards the Head Quarters, as a close Prisoner, without any . . . Warrant from the Parliament or his Excellency.

Needless to say, this last deficiency had not prevented Cotton from citing Fairfax's alleged declaration as his authority, which in turn cut no ice with the House of Lords which ordered Jenkins's reinstatement.[118]

The disturbances at Soham in Cambridgeshire in the summer of 1647 were even more spectacular. Roger Exeter (or Hechstetter) had been sequestered from the living by the earl of Manchester's commission back in April 1644 for being addicted to ritual and ceremony, as well as to the ale-house and disaffected company, and refusing to take the Covenant or to press it on his parishioners. He had been replaced by 'a godlie and orthodox divine', John Fenton, who, as far as can be seen, enjoyed the living without major incident for three years, until, in July 1647, he clashed with five tithe-withholders, in a failed attempt to arrest whom the deputy of the Sergeant-at-arms was violently assaulted and threatened with death. Still worse was to follow, for on 8 August some seventeen parishioners, led by two gentlemen, one of whom had been a prominent tithe-withholder, shut Fenton out of the church and brought back Exeter and another sequestered parson to officiate there using the Book of Common Prayer, one of the parishioners citing Fairfax's fake declaration and the royal proclamation of 1643 as the authority for what they did. Two days later Fenton was violently thrown out of the parsonage house, his possessions hurled outside after

118.   *L.J.*, IX, 389, 390–1; Walker, *Sufferings*, p. 221; *Walker Revised*, pp. 233–4.

him, and those attempting to come to his rescue severely beaten. The hapless parson's complaints to authority availed him nothing, for the delinquents appeared before the JPs armed 'with swordes, Clubbs & staves to iustifie their insolent practices'. Having then forcibly reoccupied the parsonage house, Exeter was apparently still there on 12 October when Fairfax was asked to send a detachment to evict him, reinstate Fenton, and apprehend the parishioners responsible for the disorders.[119]

At Fisherton Anger in Wiltshire – or Angry Fisherton as it was appropriately misnamed in a contemporary pamphlet – soldiers were sent in August 1647 to interrupt the services and arrest the extruded parson Richard Kent, who had taken over the parish church and was there 'officiating with their Masse Book' (viz. the Book of Common Prayer). According to this account the soldiers found the church packed with Cavaliers who hurled stones and brickbats at them and they were forced to withdraw. Following this minor triumph, the Cavaliers turned their attention to the aged parson who had been put in by parliament to replace the sequestered Kent, but had now been shut out of the church. They broke into the parsonage house, wounded him in the head and threw his aged wife downstairs, 'making themselves merry with what they found in his house'. These things, the account concludes, 'are like to bring this Kingdome into a sad condition, except some speedy course be taken for the timely preventing thereof'.[120] The emphasis is not overdone and a number of other cases of violent reintrusion could be cited, did space permit.[121]

It was, of course, violence on a vastly greater scale which was responsible for the reintrusion of formerly sequestered Anglican and royalist parsons in the areas which fell under the control of the royalist insurgents in the Second Civil War. In Westmorland in May 1648, as one godly complainant puts it, the returning malignant parsons 'advance the Book of Common Prayer, erect and use the condemned ceremonies . . . of cringing, bowing &c., & resolve to cut off the Parliament and their Adherents'. Similarly when Colonel Morrice achieved his astonishing coup and took Pontefract Castle for the king in June, he

---

119. BL., Add. MSS., 15,671, fos. 110(b), 162(b), 173(b), 208–8(b), 241–1(b); Walker, *Sufferings*, p. 236; *Walker Revised*, p. 81.
120. *True Intelligence from the West* (24 August 1647), BL., E.404(14), pp. 1–6; *Walker Revised*, p. 375.
121. E.g. at Potton, Bedfordshire, in August 1647 (BL., Add. MSS., 15,671, fos. 191(b)– 2, 229(b), 248; *Walker Revised*, p. 66); at Offord Darcy, Huntingdonshire, in July 1647 (Add. MSS., 15,671, fos. 91, 122(b)–3, 220–20(b); Walker, *Sufferings*, p. 231; *Walker Revised*, pp. 234–5, under Leicestershire); Weston Longueville and Calveston (1647), and Didlington (1648), all in Norfolk (Add. MSS., 15,671, fo. 247; PRO., SP. 24/3, fo. 79(b); *Walker Revised*, pp. 263–4); and at Andover, Hampshire, in July 1647 (Add. MSS., 15,671, fos. 111(b), 146(b), 240(b); Walker, *Sufferings*, p. 225; *Walker Revised*, pp. 180–81).

quickly replaced the parliamentary-approved minister there by the royalist Charles Dallison, though this was not strictly a matter of reintrusion. Finally, while there is little or no evidence of reintrusion in royalist-occupied Anglesey in 1648, this was probably because it was not necessary, since, as one contemporary complained, the royalist gentry and their supporters among the parish clergy, had still been firmly entrenched after the parliamentary victory in the First, and even after Anglesey fell to the parliament in the Second, Civil War.[122]

While reintrusion was the most important manifestation of the resuscitation of Anglicanism, it is only one of many. Some benefices were invaded by Anglican parsons who had no previous connection with them, like Paul Knell, who had been chaplain to a royal regiment of cuirassiers and who in July 1647 intruded himself into the church of St Dunstan in Canterbury, denouncing Roundheads as 'Rebles and Traytors';[123] and William Wake, 'one of the most noted old Royalists', who took advantage of the vacancy of the living of Bryanston in Dorset in the spring of 1648 to act as 'pretended . . . Pastor to a gathered Church of large Extent, consisting all of Cavaliers, some dwelling as far as *Exeter*', naturally using the Prayer Book and administering sacraments in the old manner. On two occasions Wake and his confederates were arrested by order of the Dorset committee, but 'both times were rescued by the rude Multitude, Men and Women with Clubs and Staves, and with the Assistance of one Major Kendall a Cavalier'. He was carried to Blandford in triumph and the officers arresting him given a good beating and threatened with hanging. Once again Fairfax was asked to send a detachment to deal with the trouble and on 6 April the vacancy at Bryanston was filled by the appointment of William Browne, 'an able and orthodox divine'.[124]

The word of true Anglicanism could also be propagated by issuing invitations to appropriately 'disaffected' clergymen to take occasional services. This was done at a number of London and Westminster parishes, including St Michael Royal in June and St Clement Dane in July 1647 and at least two Inns of Court in 1648;[125] and in a church in

122. On Westmorland, *Propositions from Westmorland* (May 1648), BL., E.446(29), pp. 4–5. On Pontefract, West Yorkshire Archive Service, Leeds City R.O., Bacon Frank Papers, BF. 13, fo. 155 ('Some Account of Coll. Morrice'). On Anglesey, Aberystwyth, National Library of Wales, Llanfair and Brynodol MSS., P505.
123. BL., Add. MSS., 15,671, fo. 135(b); *Walker Revised*, p. 221.
124. Rushworth, *Historical Collections*, VII, 1037–8; Whitelock, *Memorials*, p. 297 (25 March 1648); Mayo, *Dorset*, pp. 370–1; Walker, *Sufferings*, p. 393; *Walker Revised*, p. 138. Wake's son was to become Archbishop of Canterbury in the reign of George I.
125. BL., Add. MSS., 15,671, fos. 76(b), 144(b)–5. The Inns of Court involved were Grays Inn in the spring and the Temple in the autumn of 1648 (Whitelock, *Memorials*, pp. 300 (17 April), 346 (16 November)).

Bath where in the summer of 1648 Dr Jones, 'a great plunderer and late Chaplain of the King's army', was invited by a local Cavalier to conduct services, drew large and sympathetic congregations and was protected on his way to and from church by an armed Cavalier escort.[126] Among the charges which were brought against Mayor Utting of Norwich in April 1648 which prompted the House of Commons to order his arrest, which in turn sparked off serious rioting in Norwich, were that he had encouraged the employment of sequestered and malignant parsons as occasional preachers in that city.[127] But the most usual offenders who were brought to book for such actions by the authorities were not high civic officials such as Utting, but the local churchwardens who were clearly taking great risks in issuing such invitations, as in the metropolitan parishes of St Giles Cripplegate in May, and St Alphage and St Bennet Sherehogge in October 1647, and St Martin's Westminster in January 1648.[128]

The extrusion of 'malignant' parsons and their replacement by 'godly' ministers by agencies such as the earl of Manchester's commission of 1644 and the Committee for Plundered Ministers clearly involved interference with the rights of lay and other patrons. Where the latter had been themselves sequestered, there was no great problem, even if the legality of the action was disputable. For instance, the claim of an extruded parson such as Hugh Hawswell, a prebendary of Winchester and Fellow of All Souls, that he had been properly presented to the rectory of Cheriton in Hampshire by the bishop of Winchester cut no ice with the Committee for Plundered Ministers.[129] But this rule did not always apply. The House of Lords in particular showed great solicitude for the rights of its order in these matters. The patron of the rectory of Kenilworth in Warwickshire was the earl of Monmouth, who had supported the king during the war, and, when the living fell vacant in December 1646, exercised his patronage on behalf of William Morris. Not surprisingly the result was a storm in the parish since Morris had been extruded from a Kentish living in July 1644 for scandalous behaviour which included swearing, drunkenness and drinking Prince Rupert's health on a parliamentary Fast Day in an ale-

126.   J. Wroughton, *The Civil War in Bath and North Somerset*, p. 114.
127.   *C.J.*, VI, 294. On the disturbances at Norwich, see below, pp. 369–75.
128.   BL., Add. MSS., 15,671, fos. 43(b), 226, 234, 240(b), 262; *Mercurius Pragmaticus Number 1* (13 January 1648), E.422(31), pp. 5–6.
129.   BL., Add. MSS., 15,671, fo. 207(b); Walker, *Sufferings*, p. 184; *Walker Revised*, p. 184. Hawswell's case was the stronger for his never having been found guilty of any sort of delinquency. Other cases in 1647 based on the presentation by delinquent patrons were in the parishes of Newton and Weybread in Suffolk (Add. MSS., 15,671, fo. 188; Bodleian, Tanner MSS., 137, fo. 114); and Abberton in Essex (Bodleian, Bodley MSS., 324, fo. 131, 210; BL., Add. MSS., 15,671, fos. 12, 74, 210, 226–7).

house whose landlady he had also kissed. Morris's new and outraged parishioners at Kenilworth petitioned that he was no fit minister for them, enclosing a certificate from the county committee to the same effect. The petition rolled out all the familiar charges about bad behaviour and a liking for the company of those who had been in arms against parliament, and added to these Morris's neglect of Fast Days and theological unsoundness – he had affirmed 'that Abraham was justified by workes'. But, strong as their case appeared, their efforts were unavailing. The House of Lords had already ordered the county committee on 1 May 1647 to see to it that Morris should be quietly settled in the living and its subsequent receipt of the petition did not alter its decision.[130]

The patron of the rectory of Plumbland in Cumberland, Joseph Parker, was inhibited from exercising the right of presentation as a convicted recusant and had entrusted presentation to Richard Skelton. But Skelton had himself borne arms against parliament in the war, and when, following the resignation of the incumbent, Launcelot Fisher, in December 1647, he presented Joseph Nicholson, who had been a not very adequate assistant curate in the parish, there was an outcry from many parishioners, not only about Skelton's royalist past but also about an alleged 'Simoniacall Contract' between Fisher and Nicholson. The rival candidate favoured by the protesters and the Cumberland committee was one Garwen (Gavin?) Egglesfield, a godly parson as was shown by his being approved by the Westminster Assembly. But, as at Kenilworth, the House of Lords chose to back the patron's presentation of Nicholson, who arrived in the parish accompanied by Fisher, the high constable and 'strangers with swords, Pistolls & other weapons'. The church door was broken in and the church left open to all comers including gypsies who endangered the fabric by lighting fires. In the following month of January 1648, the already bizarre picture was completed by the astonishing disclosure that Egglesfield, the godly and conformable parson favoured by the dissentient parishioners and the county committee, had himself been in arms against parliament when a scholar of Queen's College, Oxford, during the civil war. The choice therefore lay between a parson, presented by an ex-Cavalier acting as the trustee of a Catholic recusant, and another ex-Cavalier, even if a reformed one. On 25 February the House of Lords came down in favour of Nicholson, no doubt on similar grounds to those which had prompted their decision at Kenilworth.[131]

130. HLRO., MP., 20/5/1647; L.J., IX, 170, 229; HMC., 6th. Report Appendix (House of Lords Cal. 1647), pp. 179–80; Walker Revised, pp. 222–3.
131. HLRO., MP., 10/12/1647, 20/1/1647–8; L.J., IX, 474, X, 78; HMC., 6th. Report Appendix (House of Lords Cal. 1646–7), pp. 214–15; HMC., 7th. Report Appendix (House of Lords Cal. 1647–8), p. 4; Walker, Sufferings, p. 316; Walker Revised, p. 103.

The last two cases are extreme instances of patrons who were out of sympathy both with Puritan Protestantism and the government at Westminster. But, even without this identification between patronage and Cavalierism, the notion of patronage *per se* did not fit very happily with the Puritan ethos, however much some Puritan magnates may have exploited it for godly purposes. The incompatibility is illustrated by a petition of 12 October 1648 from seventy-two parishioners of Middleton in Lancashire. Objecting to the secrecy with which the patron, William Ashton, was surrounding his right to present to the vacant living, the petitioners feared that his preferred nominee would be 'an Irishman and, some say, a cavalier'; or, at the very least, someone without any proper calling. The dispute, which lingered on well into 1649, provides an apt illustration of the incompatibility of the notions of lay patronage and presbyterial election.[132] However, as will appear from the chapter which follows, this issue was only one of a number of obstacles to a settlement which would be acceptable both to the king and to the Presbyterians. It may be true that those for whom Presbyterianism was little more than a convenient party label with a minimum of reference to religious convictions were drawing closer to Charles I from the summer of 1647 onwards. But the gap between Presbyterians, in the religious sense of the term, and the king, whose devotion to Anglican ecclesiastical organization and forms of worship was unwavering, was as great as it had ever been.

Table 1: Action by or in favour of extruded parsons in 1647

The figures in the following table are derived chiefly (though not exclusively) from the Order Books of the Committee for Plundered Ministers (BL., Add. MSS., 15,670 and especially 15,671). The heading 'Entry denied' denotes refusal to admit a minister appointed by this body or by other parliamentary agencies. 'Reintrusion' denotes the return of ministers to officiate in the benefices from which they had been officially extruded. 'Intrusion' here denotes the unofficial intrusion of ministers hitherto unconnected with these benefices to the detriment of those ministers who had been 'intruded' by the above authorities. Virtually all cases of reintrusion also involved the appropriation of tithes so, to avoid double counting, only those cases where tithe-withholding is not accompanied by reintrusion are included under the heading 'Tithes denied' and then only when it is clear that tithes are withheld because of disapproval of the officially intruded minister or on behalf of an extruded minister. The unit is the parish. The figures are minimum figures. London is not included.

132. Bodleian, MSS. J. Walker, c. 10, fos. 61(b)–62, 64, 66, 67.

Table 1: *Continued*

County	Entry denied	Tithes denied	Reintrusion	Intrusion
Bedfordshire	nil	1	3	nil
Berkshire	2	nil	nil	nil
Buckinghamshire	2	5	2	nil
Cambridgeshire	nil	6	6	nil
Cheshire	nil	2	3	nil
Cornwall	nil	nil	1	nil
Cumberland	nil	1	nil	1[†]
Derbyshire	nil	nil	1	nil
Devon	2	nil	nil	nil
Dorset	2	5	1	nil
Durham	1[*]	nil	nil	nil
Essex	2	14	9	nil
Gloucestershire	1	2	nil	1
Hampshire	1	3	5	nil
Herefordshire	nil	nil	nil	nil
Hertfordshire	nil	2	1	1
Huntingdonshire	nil	1	4	nil
Kent	5	12	4	2
Lancashire	1	nil	nil	nil
Leicestershire	5	2	4	nil
Lincolnshire	4	5	1	nil
Middlesex	nil	4	2	nil
Norfolk	1	nil	3	2
Northamptonshire	3	nil	2	nil
Northumberland	nil	nil	5	nil
Nottinghamshire	2	nil	nil	nil
Oxfordshire	1	1	nil	nil
Rutland	nil	nil	nil	nil
Shropshire	nil	nil	nil	nil
Somerset	3	nil	nil	nil
Staffordshire	2	nil	nil	nil
Suffolk	4	5	1	1
Surrey	1	6	nil	nil
Sussex	2	1	2	nil
Warwickshire	3	2	nil	1
Westmorland	nil	nil	nil	nil
Wiltshire	nil	1	2	nil
Worcestershire	nil	nil	nil	nil
Yorkshire	1	1	2	nil

[†] Not a delinquent.
[*] But not on behalf of an extruded minister.

VIII

PRESBYTERIANS AND ROYALISTS

... For those who make thee belive that any alterations can make the Covenant passable can stop at nothing ... whosoever gives thee that advyce is ether foole or knave; for this damned Covenant is the product of Rebellion and breathes nothing but Treason.

Charles I to Henrietta Maria, 19 December 1646,
Clarendon SP., II, 313

... all their Brethren of the *presbyterie* are in the same *predicament* with *Cavaliers* which is a brave reward for all their *Loanes* and *Thanksgivings*.

Mercurius Pragmaticus Number 14 (14/21 December 1647),
BL., E.421(1), sig. Q2^v

Episcopacy was the roote of the former war. Presbyterianism you will find to be the roote of the succeeding. The lamb and the dragon cannot be reconciled. ...

Thomas Margetts to William Clarke, York,
8 April 1648, *Clarke Papers*, II, 2

Fluctuating Presbyterian fortunes to August 1647

It used to be customary to interpret the parliamentary conflicts between Presbyterians and Independents along largely confessional lines. While it was clear that the Independents also took up a politically more radical, and the Presbyterians a politically conservative, stance, this was seen as all of a piece with their religious beliefs. The work of Professor David Underdown and other historians has done away with these comfortable certainties, though not every historian of the period has gone along with all of their findings.[1] But unless one does so, it is not easy to come to

---

1. See D. Underdown, *Pride's Purge* (Oxford, 1971), especially pp. 45–75; idem, 'The Independents Reconsidered', *JBS.*, III (1964), 57–84, and 'The Independents Again', *JBS.*, VIII (1968), 83–93, and 'The Presbyterian Independents Exorcised; a Brief

terms with the existence of religious Presbyterians who were Independents in politics or Presbyterians in politics who were Erastian or episcopalian in religion. For example, Denzil Holles, the leader of the parliamentary Presbyterians, was of far too Erastian a turn of mind for his religious views to meet with the approval of the high Presbyterian divines of Sion House and the Westminster Assembly. Clarendon describes Holles as 'the frankest amongst them in owning his animosity and indignation against all the Independent party, and was no otherwise affected to the Presbyterians than as they constituted a party upon which he depended to oppose the other'.[2] In the best of all possible worlds, he would probably have opted for *iure humano* episcopacy. In the real world, however, the natural conservatism of such people, the old 'peace party' connections of most of them, and the need to pursue their aims in close alliance with the Scottish covenanters, once the latter had become disillusioned by their original alliance with the 'war party', made support for religious Presbyterian causes a logical product of their political circumstances. To those of them who were Presbyterians in religion as well as in politics the identification, of course, presented no difficulty, while to those political Independents of a Presbyterian religious persuasion, it was other than religious considerations which kept them opposed to the parliamentary Presbyterians.

But, it might be asked, did not the religious orientation of the parliamentary Presbyterians militate against their becoming allied with that other great conservative force, the king and the Cavaliers? Holles himself had, of course, been one of the five members whom the king had sought to arrest in January 1642. But that was a long time ago, and more recently he had been accused of colluding with the royalists at Oxford in the autumn of 1644 over devising an appropriate royal reply to parliament's preliminary overtures about the peace negotiations which were to take place at Uxbridge the following January. Although parliament had rejected these allegations made by the turncoat Lord

---

Comment', *P&P.*, 47 (1970), 128–30; V. Pearl, 'Oliver St John and the "middle-group" in the Long Parliament, August 1643–May 1644', *Eng. Hist. Rev.*, LXXXI (1966), esp. pp. 490–2, and eadem, 'The "Royal Independents" in the English Civil War', *TRHS.*, 5th ser., XVIII (1968), 69–96. For sharply differing views, see G. Yule, *The Independents in the English Civil War* (Cambridge, 1958), passim and esp. pp. 35–41; idem, 'Independents and Revolutionaries', *JBS.*, VII (1968), 11–32, and 'Presbyterians and Independents. Some Comments', *P&P.*, 47 (1970), 130–3; S. Foster, 'The Presbyterian Independents Exorcised. A Ghost Story for Historians', *P&P.*, 44 (1969), 52–75. For criticism of this article by a number of historians and for Dr Foster's rejoinder to them, see *P&P.*, 47 (1970), 116–46. For an earlier pioneering article on this subject, see J.H. Hexter, 'The Problem of the Presbyterian Independents', reprinted in his *Reappraisals in History* (1963), pp. 163–84.

2. Clarendon, *Rebellion*, III, 497. For a useful modern study of Holles, see P. Crawford, *Denzil Holles 1598–1680. A Study of his political career* (1979).

Saville in the summer of 1645, on 6 May 1646 Holles's political opponent, the radical Independent MP Henry Marten, was to attempt to resuscitate them, producing in the House of Commons a letter from Saville concerning Holles's alleged correspondence with Lord Digby and other royalist leaders. The allegations were disregarded and a parliamentary diarist dismisses them with the observation that 'because ye Lord Saville was . . . heretofore Convicted of falsehood ye house gave little Creditt to it'.[3] But that they could be made at all was a sure indication of the change in Holles's position vis-à-vis the king since 1642. Nor was he the only MP against whom such charges were made. His name had been associated with that of the political 'Presbyterian' Bulstrode Whitelock in Saville's charges of 1645, while on 7 August 1646 the House of Commons ordered £500 damages to be paid to Sir Richard Onslow, MP for Surrey, whom we have already encountered in respect of his decidedly unroyalist behaviour in connection with the Surrey petitioners in May 1648. The damages were to be paid by George Withers, the author of a pamphlet alleging that Onslow had sent money to the king at Oxford during the war.[4]

There are both positive and negative indicators in respect of the likelihood of a rapprochement between the parliamentary Presbyterians and Charles I. Positively, there was the natural leaning of the most socially and politically conservative of the parliamentary groups towards the king as the keystone of the arch of order that they wished at all costs to preserve, even if they would not countenance a return to the *status quo ante* 1641. As was seen in the last chapter, this found one important expression in the shared distaste of king and Presbyterians for sectarian excesses.[5] This distaste was compounded out of social as well as religious considerations. As Hyde put it in a letter from Jersey to Lord Jermyn on 8 January 1647, many were drawn both to the English Presbyterians and to the Scots 'out of an opinion that they are freinds to Monarchy and Order, and out of horror of ye odious Parity which they ridiculously conceaue ye Independents would bring in'; not least because of their toleration of sectaries. Hyde took a different view. The Independent leaders, like their Presbyterian opponents, were mostly men of substance, and as such no less opposed than they to anti-monarchical and egalitarian views which 'would shake their owne Property and euery part of their condicion which made Life pleasant to them . . .'.[6] There were, however, others who saw fit to emphasize the socially subversive

---

3. BL., Add. MSS., 31,116, fo. 268(b). On Saville's charge in 1645, see MacCormack, *Revolutionary Politics*, pp. 68–91; Ashton, *Civil War*, pp. 237–41.
4. *C.J.*, IV, 639–40. On Onslow and the Surrey petition, see above, p. 149.
5. See above, pp. 241–5.
6. Bodleian, Clarendon MSS., 29, fos. 52–2(b).

connotations of Presbyterianism as well as of Independency and sectarianism. In their objections on 1 June 1647 to the coming visitation of the
University commanded by parliamentary ordinance with the object of
enforcing adhesion to the Covenant and the establishment of Presbyterian discipline, the Masters, scholars and other members of Oxford
University pointed to an element in classical Presbyterian discipline
which appeared to give the lie to the notion of religious Presbyterians
as staunch upholders of the established order. This was 'the leaving of so
much power in so many persons [viz. congregational elders] . . . many
of them of meane quality, for the keeping back of thousands of
well-meaning Christians from the benefit and comfort of the blessed
Sacrament'.[7] Another weakness in the Presbyterian claim to be a bul-
wark against anarchy and upholder of the social order was stressed in a
reply of the English parliament on 4 January 1648 to a declaration of the
kingdom of Scotland which had castigated the attacks on the king's
authority by English sectaries and their Independent allies. The English
reply was to the effect that Presbyterians in glass houses had no occasion
to cast stones. Had not the Presbyterian parsons in London 'done what
they could to stir up the people in the late tumult [viz. on 26 July 1647]
and force upon the Parliament'?[8]

The last point, however, cut both ways, for while tumults were to be
deplored and their instigators condemned, it needed to be remembered
that one object of the tumult of 26 July 1647 was to bring the king to
London and to restore his rightful authority. On balance, it seems likely
that Hyde's measured and considered statement about the spurious
nature of the alleged difference between the social standing and attitudes
of parliamentary Presbyterians and Independents found less credence
than Denzil Holles's celebrated distinction between Presbyterian 'gentlemen who had estates which required their looking-after' and those
of 'the violent party', the Independents, 'whose only employment
was . . . to drudge and carry-on their Masters work, having thereby a
greatness far above the sphere they had formerly moved in'. Their
master, in Holles's view, was, of course, Cromwell, and he made much
of Oliver's derogatory and incautiously expressed remarks about the
peerage. As to 'the mercenary Army raised by the Parliament', which
the parliamentary Presbyterians would unsuccessfully seek to disband

---

7. *Reasons why the University of Oxford cannot submit to the Covenant* (1 June 1647), BL.,
    E.391(15), pp. 32–3.
8. *An Answer To . . . The Declaration of the Kingdome of Scotland* (4 January 1648), BL.,
    E.421(32), p. 11. For similar charges see *The Pulpit Incendiary* (4 May 1648), E.438(10),
    pp. 9–10, 13, 19, 33–4, 37. For Presbyterian denials of such charges, see *The Pulpit
    Incendiary Anatomized* (13 May 1648), E. 442(5), pp. 6–7; [C.B.], *Sion College, What It
    Is and Doeth* (24 May 1648), E.444(3), pp. 22–3.

during the spring and summer of 1647, 'most of the Colonels and officers [were] mean tradesmen, Brewers, Taylors, Goldsmiths, Shoemakers and the like; a notable dunghill, if one would rake into it, to find-out their several pedigrees'.[9]

It has already been emphasized that not by any stretch of the imagination could Denzil Holles be described as a high Presbyterian in his religious views. Nevertheless, his views about the low social origins of sectaries, Independents and army officers were shared by many high Presbyterian divines, one of whose opponents cites, for example, the statement by the distinguished Presbyterian minister, Edmund Calamy, in a sermon at St Michael's Cornhill in London, that 'WE LIVE NOW IN RISING TIMES, WHEREIN MEN RAISED UP FROM THE DUNGHILL DOE GOVERN THE KINGDOME ALMOST'.[10]

On the negative side, and affording significant obstacles to Presbyterian rapprochement with the king, was Charles's refusal to accept the Covenant and his reverence for episcopacy and the Prayer Book. This posed serious problems for Presbyterians, including parliamentary Presbyterians of an Erastian turn of mind such as Holles, who though not wedded to Presbyterian ecclesiastical polity for its own sake, were obliged to do more than pay lip service to it on account of the importance of retaining two main and indispensable sources of Presbyterian support, the Scots and the City of London. There is, it is true, some oversimplification in the observation in the London Independent Thomas Juxon's Journal entry for 18 February 1646 that 'The Scots, the [Westminster] assembly, city, lords, Stapletons [Presbyterian] party and the malignants, their interests all meet in one'.[11] For it needs to be remembered that the religious considerations which brought the City and the Scots together, and therefore strongly influenced the parliamentary Presbyterians who needed to keep both these elements sweet, were precisely those things which made Presbyterian rapport with king and Cavaliers the more difficult.

The City's Presbyterian interest is considered in detail in the next section of this, and the Scots in the next, chapter. However, in the present context it is convenient to recall some of the factors making for alliance between the Scots and the English Presbyterians once the Scots had become thoroughly disillusioned at the failure of their original alliance with the parliamentary opponents of the Presbyterians to yield

9. 'Memorial of Denzil Lord Holles' (1699), in Maseres, *Select Tracts*, I, 201, 214, 276–7. The traditional stereotype has been challenged by M.A. Kishlansky, *The Rise of the New Model Army* (Cambridge, 1979), especially pp. 41–50, 63–4, 74–5, 218–19.
10. *The Pulpit Incendiary*, pp. 6–7.
11. BL., Add. MSS., 25,465, fo. 60.

significant fruit.[12] The Scots' determination to pursue these ends via negotiations with the king – unlikely though these were to succeed on account of their religious demands – in turn brought them closer to the old parliamentary peace group with a resulting change of nomenclature whereby the latter, plus some recruits from the conservative wing of the old middle-group, had become known as Presbyterians. Another point of contact, however temporary and abortive, was the association of the Presbyterian leaders, Holles and Stapleton and the earl of Essex, with the Scottish commissioners in London in the projected impeachment of Oliver Cromwell in December 1645.[13]

The following year was to see a variety of manifestations of closer rapprochement between the Scots and the parliamentary Presbyterians including, if the names of tellers in House of Commons motions are anything to go by, Presbyterian support for a number of motions which favoured Scottish interests.[14] The London Independent Thomas Juxon observed in his Journal entry for 14 February 1646 that 'the Scots are cried up more than ever and the covenant pressed, the godly party in the house [viz. the Independents] represented . . . as men that would have no piece [sic], government, nor no kingly power and would . . . disunite the two kingdoms'. It was, Juxon regretted, not only bad and interested men who opposed the Independents, but also some men of conscience who mistakenly saw them as conspiring to inhibit the likelihood of a lasting peace settlement.[15] Denzil Holles, a politician whom Juxon would certainly have regarded as one of the former, portrays the Scottish rapprochement with the Presbyterians as, in part at least, the product of an Independent plot to deprive the Scottish army of funds and increase its unpopularity by forcing it to have recourse to free quarter.[16] It was primarily a mutual desire for peace which was respon-

12. For an account of some of the reasons for Scottish disenchantment with the war party given by the Scottish Commissioners in London on 15 October 1645, see BL., Add. MSS., 37,978, fos. 29–30(b).

13. Whitelock, *Memorials*, pp. 111–13 (December 1645).

14. E.g. on 13 November 1645 on the removal of Scottish forces from English garrison towns (*C.J.*, IV, 341; BL., Add. MSS., 31,116, fo. 242(b)); on 30 June 1646 about whether details of the preamble and alterations to the peace propositions should be communicated to the Scottish Commissioners (*C.J.*, IV, 593); on the second reading on 14 August of a proposed resolution to punish the authors and printers of scandalous papers against the Scots (*C.J.*, IV, 644); on 27 August and 5 September to pay to the Scots an additional sum over and above the £200,000 already voted by parliament. Here the Presbyterians were responding to a complaint of 18 August from the Scottish Commissioners (BL., Add. MSS., 31,116, fo. 281; Add. MSS., 10,114, fos. 17(b)–18; *C.J.*, IV, 655–6, 663).

15. BL., Add. MSS., 25,465, fo. 58(b).

16. 'Memorial of Denzil Lord Holles', in Maseres, *Select Tracts*, I, 216–30. For an opposing interpretation which sees the Scots and parliamentary Presbyterians as scheming to make the New Model Army unpopular and bring about its disbandment as the chief obstacle to their plan to restore the king on their own terms, see *The Scots Cabinett Opened* (4 August 1648), BL., E.456(30), esp. pp. 4–6.

sible for the situation whereby, as Holles's colleague Bulstrode Whitelock puts it, 'the *Presbyterian* Party here sought, as far as modestly they could, to support the interest of their Brethren of *Scotland*', though Whitelock neglects to point out that this very support would, largely for religious reasons, make it more difficult to reach the desired agreement with the king.[17]

Catholic observers such as the queen herself and Bellièvre, the French ambassador in London, were impatient with the king's losing the opportunity to align himself with the Presbyterians and at his scruples about the need to preserve episcopacy.[18] Pressure for the king to accept the Newcastle Propositions also came from his friends in Scotland who were certainly not noted for great Covenanting zeal. According to a dispatch from Montereul, the French ambassador in Scotland, to Mazarin on 23 July, the duke of Hamilton was strongly urging the necessity of the king's agreeing to the Propositions, in the hope that his consent would cause him to be brought to London, where his friends, whose morale would receive an enormous boost from his presence there, would all rally to his support.[19] But the king's assent to the Propositions was taken as the *sine qua non* of any such improvement in his prospects. In a letter to Hamilton from Newcastle on 8 August, Sir Robert Murray mentions the report of Cheisley, the Scottish commissioners' secretary, to the effect that none of the English friends of the Scots – presumably he refers to the parliamentary Presbyterians – dared to speak out in his defence, 'lest they be thought accessory to the refusall of the propositions', and subsequent letters in November speak of the progressive discouragement of the Presbyterians and decline of their influence in parliament.[20]

In a dispatch of 13 September Bellièvre confided his opinion to Brienne that 'si cette fois le Roy d'Angleterre refuse de signer les propositions, il perd ici tous les Presbitériens et, par conséquent les Ecossois . . . et donne aux Indépendans [*sic*] tout aduantage qu'ilz peuuent souhaiter'.[21] As was shown in the first chapter, Charles was always aware of the Independent option which was to become vitally important in the summer of 1647.[22] Its advantages and disadvantages for him were in fact the opposite of those prescribed by the Presbyterians. Rumoured to be anti-monarchical and, even if not, certainly less

17. Whitelock, *Memorials*, pp. 212–13 (30 May 1646).
18. On Bellièvre's impatience expressed in his dispatches to Brienne, see *Montereul Correspondence*, I, 257, 262, 284–5.
19. Ibid., I, 231–5.
20. *Hamilton Papers*, pp. 106–7, 120, 126.
21. *Montereul Correspondence*, I, 257.
22. See above, pp. 13–14, 20, 24, 33.

attractive to Charles in political terms than the Presbyterians, the Independents also were suspect on account of their tenderness to sectarian extremists. On the other hand, they were thought to be far more indulgent to the king's desire to retain some form of episcopacy, provided this was coupled with toleration for tender consciences. In his Journal entry for 27 April 1646, while the war was still on, Juxon had remarked how the parliamentary factions were already competing for the support of the king and that, notwithstanding their allegedly anti-monarchical stance, the Independents 'will admit of a moderate episcopacy. This the King does infinitely desire . . . beleiving that if he have the bishops again, he shall work out the rest and them too.'[23] Towards the end of 1646 the Scottish Presbyterian Robert Baillie was seriously worried. At the beginning of the year he had been concerned because 'we see no appearance that the King, for all his desperate condition, is minded to yield what both Kingdoms hes concluded to have'. At the end of it, while he was no more satisfied on this point, he had the additional worry that Charles was being drawn towards the Independents 'for the undoeing of Scotland and the Presbyterian partie here' [viz. in London].[24] On 20 December Bellièvre reported to Brienne that the Independents were boasting that Charles was paying court to them, and that it was even said that one of them had gone to France for discussions with the queen.[25]

If religious considerations created formidable barriers to an understanding of Presbyterians with the king, there was at least scope in other areas, among them in attitudes to Charles's defeated followers which ranged from toleration to positive sympathy. One interesting sideline which points the difference between Presbyterians and Independents in this respect relates to the arrangements for the funeral of the most eminent of all the wartime Presbyterian leaders, the earl of Essex. Essex's brother-in-law, the royalist marquis of Hertford, had been designated as chief mourner, but on 17 October 1646 the House of Commons divided over a procedural motion to put the question that neither Hertford nor any other active supporter of the king during the war should be allowed to attend the funeral. That motion was, however, lost by 48 votes to 36, with the Independents Sir William Armine and Dennis Bond acting as tellers in favour and the Presbyterians Stapleton and Whitelock against.[26] No less telling was a motion which was won resoundingly on 19 December by 168 votes to 92, with the

23. BL., Add. MSS., 25,465, fos. 70–70(b).
24. Baillie, *Letters*, II, 338, 412.
25. *Montereul Correspondence*, I, 352–3.
26. *C.J.*, IV, 697; BL., Add. MSS., 10,114, fo. 21(b); Add. MSS., 31,116, fo. 286(b).

Presbyterians Holles and Waller acting as tellers in favour, that £500 should be allowed out of the sequestrated estate of the royalist grandee, the marquis of Worcester, towards the expenses of his funeral.[27] From here might be but a short step, as enemies of the Presbyterians pointed out, for those who displayed such indulgence to royalist delinquents, to denounce parliamentary proceedings against them as 'punishing men for *keeping Covenant*'. Such indulgence would aid the Presbyterians not at all, as one of their later critics warned them, for 'if the Cavaleerish partie get the day . . . they have their bands and chains and fetters already prepared for your hands and feet'.[28]

Despite Bellièvre's irritation at the king's scruples about the Covenant which inhibited any alliance between him and the Presbyterians, it was also his view that it was crucially important to the royal interest to maintain factional balance at Westminster so that neither political faction should ever preponderate, and, above all, that they should not join forces.[29] In a letter written in March 1647 the French ambassador mentions a scheme being considered by Sir Philip Warwick and the royal council in exile in France for embroiling the Presbyterians and Independents in conflict and affording an opportunity for the king to take whichever side suited him best in the resulting circumstances.[30] In an undated memorial of 1646 relating to their mission to France to consult the queen about the possibility of the Prince of Wales going to Jersey, the royalist Lords Capel and Culpepper emphasized that the chief hope of restoring the king lay in the exploitation of the current rife divisions between Presbyterians and Independents at Westminster.[31] However, as to Jersey, a significant incident was to occur in May 1647 in respect of royalists, Independents and Presbyterians. On 6 May the House of Lords drew up a plan for an expeditionary force against Jersey under command of Colonel Rainsborough. Rainsborough was an Independent, and even though he had not yet acquired the notoriety which was later to come through his association with Levellers in the army, the idea of a force going to Jersey under an Independent commander was as unwelcome to the parliamentary Presbyterians as it was to the king. A paper drawn up for the attention of the House of Lords suggested that a more suitable commander of the expedition would be a certain Colonel Aldrich who had the double advantage of being both a French-speaker and a Presbyterian. Alternatively, it would be better to request

27. *C.J.*, V, 20; BL., Add. MSS., 31,116, fo. 293(b).
28. *The Pulpit Incendiary* (4 May 1648), pp. 33, 40.
29. For Bellièvre's many statements to this effect, see, e.g., *Montereul Correspondence*, I, 445–6, II, 52–3, 164, 170–1, 172, 197. Much the same view was held by Montereul, the French ambassador in Edinburgh (ibid., II, 172, 214–15).
30. Ibid., II, 73.
31. *HMC., 12th. Report, part ix. MSS. of the Duke of Beaufort* (1891), pp. 17–18.

the king to require the royalist governor Carteret to surrender Jersey to parliament rather than to have it overrun by Independents who would 'spoile the isle by their preaching and Overthrow the Gouernement and the true Religion'.[32] Not all royalists, however, favoured the Presbyterians over the Independents as the lesser of two evils. Writing from unhappy exile in Paris on 19 January 1647, the impoverished courtier Endymion Porter pronounced that 'if the Independants would but alter their opinions a little, and saye they would have a king, I would goe to them presently and kiss their feete . . . but a pox uppon the presbiterians . . . they wil not fall owt till it bee to late to doo our master good, or to save our nation from a generall ruin'.[33]

In a letter written on 14 February, two days before the king's arrival at Holdenby, Bellièvre, who seems to have laboured under the mistaken belief that the king would be virtually in the hands of the Independents at Holdenby, also gave some consideration to the pros and cons of a royal rapprochement with the Independents, which, of course, was not to become a serious possibility until the army had abducted the king on 4 June. The French ambassador seems also to have been intriguing to detach members of the Upper House from support for the Scots (and therefore for the English Presbyterians also) with its fundamental disadvantage that it betokened terms for a settlement to which the king would never agree. Compared with this the Independents might appear to offer a less rigid alternative despite their allegedly anti-monarchical views. In March Bellièvre wrote again, once more lamenting Charles's indecisiveness and failure to side with either party: 'Ne faisant rien, il hazarde tout'.[34] In particular, what Charles risked was the danger of a complete Presbyterian hegemony with that party able to work its will with the minimum of reference to the royal interest. For, with the unpopular Scots army departed and plans afoot to disband the New Model, the Presbyterian ascendancy seemed assured, and on 30 March George Gillespie wrote from London that 'the Independent party is for the present sunk vnder water in the Parlament and runne downe'.[35]

The main features of the alleged Presbyterian counter-revolutionary plot during the spring and summer of 1647 have been dealt with in an earlier chapter dealing with the army's attempt to impeach the eleven Presbyterian MPs for their part in it.[36] How far was the restoration of the king central to this design? According to one able anti-Presbyterian pamphleteer, Amon Wilbee, the Presbyterians were certainly not acting

32. HLRO., MP., 6/5/1647; L.J., IX, 180.
33. Nicholas Papers, p. 72.
34. Montereul Correspondence, I. 445–9, II. 52–3.
35. Baillie, Letters, II, 512 (Appendix LXVI, no. 12).
36. See above, pp. 170–78.

disinterestedly on the king's behalf, but pursuing their own advantage while keeping him a virtual prisoner in humiliating conditions at Holdenby. Like their Scottish allies, they had conveniently ignored 'that part of the Covenant which concernes his Majesties person and authority', and were concentrating on 'that part . . . which concernes the [Presbyterian] reformation of Religion in the three Kingdomes'.[37]

Of course, Wilbee's treatise is a party political pamphlet which conveniently understates the Erastian element in the religious settlement of 1645–6, which had the full support of Holles and many other parliamentary Presbyterians, however much it might fall lamentably short of the requirements of the high Presbyterian clerics of Sion College or the General Assembly of the Scottish kirk. The resulting delicate balance is admirably illustrated by the twin facts of Holles's support for the celebrated – in high Presbyterian terms notorious – measure creating secular machinery for dealing with scandalous sinners, but not for the resolution of 11 April 1646 condemning the Westminster Assembly's petition against the ordinance.[38] But the defects of Wilbee's analysis do not alter the fact that he was making some shrewd political points. In the present context, there are interesting affinities between his pamphlet and that of a contemporary royalist observer, which in turn provide support for the view that, in some respects at least, the Independents were nearer to the royalist position than were the Presbyterians. Ignoring, like Wilbee, the Erastian elements in the religious settlement of 1645–6, our anonymous royalist author criticizes the Presbyterians for rushing headlong into the establishment of a religious settlement on the Scottish model. This was both anathema to the king and would quickly become far more unpopular than the worst sort of episcopacy.[39]

It is, of course, hardly surprising that, following the abduction of the king from Holdenby on 4 June, the parliamentary Presbyterians should be concerned to rescue him from the army's clutches. But it was the Presbyterian determination to regain control of the king rather than their disinterested support for the royal interest which lies behind their unsuccessful motion of 8 June in the House of Commons for the king to come to his Surrey residence at Oatlands and the successful (but

---

37. A. Wilbee, *Plain Truth Without Feare or Flattery* (1647), Oxford, Worcester College pamphlet coll. The passage which follows is mainly derived from the argument on pp. 3–8. It is clear from internal evidence that the pamphlet was written before the army's abduction of the king on 4 June.
38. *C.J.*, IV, 428, 506; BL., Add. MSS., 10,114, fo. 12; Add. MSS., 31,116, fos. 21–1(b). See Ashton, *Civil War*, pp. 242–6. Much the best treatment of the issue of the legislation on scandalous sins and exclusion from taking Communion is by W. Lamont, *Godly Rule: Politics and Religion 1603–1660* (1969), pp. 118–28.
39. *A true account and character of the times* (August 1647), BL., E.401(13), pp. 3–4.

ineffectual) one of 15 June that Fairfax should deliver him up to such persons as parliament would appoint.[40] But is this qualification about Presbyterian support for the king applicable in quite the same measure in considering the temporary transformation wrought by the counter-revolutionary coup of 26 July in London and Westminster, as a result of which parliament virtually became a Presbyterian Rump? On 31 July the House of Lords, condemning the army's seizure of the king, declared that Charles should be invited to London to treat about a settlement 'with Honour, Freedom and Safety'. On 2 August the House of Commons concurred with the Lords' votes and also invited the Scottish commissioners to make their own addresses to the king 'for a safe and well grounded Peace'. The procedural motion that this question be put was carried by 73 votes to 32, with the Presbyterians Stapleton and Herbert acting as tellers in favour, and the actual question was then carried without a division.[41]

Of course, if the view of Wilbee and other Independents, as well as of some royalists, that the Presbyterians sought simply to dominate, not to restore, the king, is correct, Charles was right not to respond to the invitation. But, according to Bellièvre writing on 5 August on the eve of the army's occupation of London and the effective end of Presbyterian hegemony, Charles had missed a great opportunity through his own indecision: 'Il a perdu depuis dix jours l'occasion de se restablir'. This he might presumably have done by espousing either the cause of the City or that of the army, but his natural irresolution prevented him from doing either. A dispatch from Montereul, Bellièvre's counterpart in Scotland, to Mazarin on 3 August offers a different and more far-sighted view, stressing that the apparent Presbyterian triumph in the coup of 26 July might all too easily and suddenly be reversed, as indeed was to happen three days later when the army occupied London and restored the Speakers and the Independent MPs who had fled to it.[42] At least one royalist commentator in early August would probably have agreed with him. The king ought not to favour any party but one 'which cometh honest to his principles' and the temporarily dominant Presbyterian party in London 'have too much of the Presbytery to be true to the Prerogative'.[43] Indeed, even after the army took over on 6 August, there were those who continued optimistically to maintain that the king's great hope lay in exploiting factional rivalry. A royalist newsletter of 12 August voiced the opinion that 'the Antipathy of [the] two great factions, the instability of their Condition without ye kings

40.   C.J., V, 203, 210–11, 212.
41.   L.J., IX, 362, 366, 368; C.J., V, 262, 264; BL., 669, f11(55).
42.   Montereul Correspondence, II, 214–15, 218–20.
43.   A true account and character of the times, p. 7.

Concurrence and earnest expectation of ye whole Kingdome will without any doubt in a short time force a full Complyance with ye Kings desire'.[44] But it is arguable that it was this very eagerness to obtain the maximum benefit by playing off one party against the other which was to cause Charles to miss the opportunity of rapprochement with the army and the Independents in the subsequent weeks, just as he had earlier missed that of rapprochement with the Presbyterians.

There, for the moment, our narrative ends. During the previous analysis great importance was attached to the support afforded by the Scots and the City of London to the parliamentary Presbyterians. The Scottish factor will be dealt with in detail in the next chapter, and it will now be necessary to look more closely at that other Presbyterian stronghold, the City of London.

A bastion of Presbyterianism: the City of London to August 1647

Over these months London, the 'chief foundation' of English Presbyterianism, as Clement Walker described it,[45] presents the supreme example of a city where Presbyterianism was in complete ascendancy, at least so far as municipal government was concerned, though there were prominent elements of Independent opposition here too. Of no other substantial municipality is this true to quite the same degree. For example, in Norwich, the second city of England, factional strengths were far more equal. On 2 September 1646 the mayor, sheriffs and common councilmen of Norwich issued a declaration against 'a scandalous [Independent] pamphlet lately sett forth stiled vox populi or the peoples crye against the Clergy', and in particular that it did 'very falcely and scandalouslye impeach & asperse the Ministers of this Citty'. The declaration called for the arrest and punishment of those responsible for the pamphlet, and there was in fact something of a pamphlet war between Independent and Presbyterian factions.[46] An historian of seventeenth-century Norwich sees the high water mark of local Presbyterianism as being reached towards the end of the year, when, on 5 December, the Norwich Assembly appointed a committee to nominate congregational elders and organize Presbyterian classes, as had in fact been ordered by a letter from Speaker Lenthall as long ago as 25 September 1645. However, no further progress seems to have been

44. Bodleian, Clarendon MSS., 30, fo. 35.
45. 'The Mysterie of the Two Juntoes . . .', in Maseres, *Select Tracts*, I, 345.
46. NNRO., Norwich Assembly Book 1642–1668, fo. 45. On this controversy, see Evans, *Norwich*, pp. 158–65.

made in 1647, and if there was a Presbyterian ascendancy of sorts in the city, it was a precariously balanced one with neither faction enjoying anything like monopoly of civic office. Presbyterian civic worthies were often intimately associated with local royalists, as was to be especially demonstrated early in 1648, when the Presbyterian mayor John Utting was instrumental in the appointment of an ex-Cavalier alderman and of Anglican divines to preach in the cathedral and city churches. Opposition to his actions was to set off a chain of events which ultimately issued in the ferocious Norwich tumults of 24 April 1648, in which royalist elements were prominent in his support. The suppression of the riots ushered in a period of clear Independent ascendancy in the city.[47]

The connection, emphasized by the Independent Thomas Juxon, between the Scots and the London Presbyterians and the important role of the Scottish divine Robert Baillie and of Sion College, the nerve centre of religious high Presbyterianism, have received attention in a brilliant article by Dr Valerie Pearl.[48] The relations, also noted by Juxon, between these forces and royalism is, however, none too easy to pin down. The high Presbyterian London churchmen saw themselves as the guardians of what they regarded as true Protestant order and discipline against sectarian excesses, and were later to argue that their opponents sought to lay them low and make them odious, so that 'the furious bloody Sectaries might be provoked to Assassinate them as they walke in the streets'.[49] But, for what it is worth, these same opponents were at pains to emphasize the tenderness of high Presbyterian preachers in London for the king and the prerogative and their carping criticism of both parliament and the army. 'Could *Oxford Aulicus* or *Pragmaticus* himself ever do more than [they] to lay all our evills at the Parliaments doores . . . ?'[50]

The close relations between the City and the Scots are, in the nature of things, more abundantly documented, and it is of course important to emphasize that what held them together was their mutual desire for a peace settlement with the king, although not, as it turned out, on terms which were acceptable to him, at least as far as religious matters were concerned. Referring, in a letter to Scotland on 15 January 1646, to

47. On Norwich over these years, see ibid., pp. 155–82. On the Norwich riots, see below, pp. 369–75.
48. V. Pearl, 'London Puritans and Scotch Fifth Columnists: a Mid-Seventeenth-century Phenomenon', in A.E.J. Hollaender and W. Kellaway (eds.), *Studies in London History* (1969), pp. 317–31. See also Pearl, 'London's Counter-revolution', in Aylmer, *Interregnum*, pp. 29–56. For Juxon's observation, BL., Add. MSS., 25,465, fo. 60.
49. *The Pulpit Incendiary Anatomized* . . . (13 May 1648), BL., E.442(5), pp. 8–11. See also [C.B.], *Sion College, What It Is and Doeth* (24 May 1648), BL., E.444(3), especially pp. 5–7.
50. *The Pulpit Incendiary* (4 May 1648), BL., E.438(10), pp. 3–6. See also ibid., pp. 11–12, 14–16, 33–4, 41–3, 54, 61–2.

parliament's discouraging reception of petitions from the Westminster Assembly, the city ministers and the City of London itself, for a godly ecclesiastical settlement on high Presbyterian lines, Robert Baillie pronounced that 'our last refuge is to God, and, under him, to the City' which had that day petitioned for a campaign to suppress all sectaries in London. 'No doubt', Baillie continued, 'if they be constant, they will obtain all their desires; for all know the Parliament here cannot subsist without London; so whatsomever they desyre in earnest . . . it must be granted'.[51] On 11 February Juxon reports in his Journal a visit from the Scottish commissioners to the Common Council of London, bringing a letter from the Scottish parliament thanking the City warmly for its expression of love and its endeavours towards settling the church according to the Covenant. The Commissioners assured the City that, despite pernicious rumours to the contrary, 'they [the Scots] should always be firm to their covenant and to live and die with them in the full prosecution of that'. A week later Juxon told how the official City response assuring the Scots that it was 'resolved to stand to their covenant in the Scotch sense' was carried to the House of Commons for its approval, but the House's consideration of it was deferred.[52]

As was shown in an earlier chapter, Robert Baillie was chagrined at the City's betrayal of his faith in it and its failure to go all the way in March 1646 in support of the opposition of the Westminster Assembly and the Scottish commissioners in England to the ordinance on scandalous sins. 'Our great hope on earth, the City of London, has played nipshott', he observed ruefully on 31 March.[53] For all that, the City was again active in petitioning for high Presbyterian causes in May and December.[54] Certainly the City's Remonstrance of May was meat and drink to the Scots and it is interesting to find this being backed up by a petition drawn up by the Presbyterians of Norwich which, however, came to nothing as it provoked a counter-petition from the local Independents, so that the two virtually cancelled each other out and neither was presented to parliament.[55] Similarly the London petition and remonstrance of December 1646 left little to be desired even by the most fervent of Scottish covenanters with its complaints against army

---

51. Baillie, *Letters*, II, 336–7.
52. BL., Add. MSS., 25,465, fos. 56(b), 59–9(b). The first incident is also mentioned in Baillie, *Letters*, II, 352–3, and Meikle, *Correspondence*, p. 161. The slavish adherence to an inflexible Scottish interpretation of the Covenant is one of the things for which the Presbyterian ministers associated with Sion College were attacked by their opponents (see, e.g., *The Pulpit Incendiary*, especially pp. 24–38, 61–2).
53. On this see Baillie, *Letters*, II, 360–1, 362, 363, 365, 366; *Westminister Assembly Minutes*, pp. 225–6; and above, pp. 133–4.
54. See above, pp. 134–5.
55. Evans, *Norwich*, pp. 158–9.

officers who had not taken the Covenant, the inundation of heresy and the unchecked excesses of sectaries and denunciation of those seeking to divide the two realms.[56] Thus, despite some disappointments, the relations between the City and the Scots had held firm and at the end of the year the disapproving Thomas Juxon wrote in his Journal that 'what was desired by ye Scottes, ye Cittie would solicite for y^m in Remonstrances and Petitions and what the Cittie desired, the Scotts would not faile to seaconde'.[57]

In a letter written on 2 October Robert Baillie had expressed surprise and disappointment at the failure of Alderman John Langham to be elected Lord Mayor and at how 'by the cunning of some, Gayre is the man, a greater malignant than sectarie'.[58] The choice was significant. Notwithstanding his pre-Civil War reputation as a staunch opponent of arbitrary royal government and one of four aldermen who, in 1640, had been imprisoned for refusing to assess the inhabitants of his ward towards a loan from the City to the king, Sir John Gayre was by now a royalist in all but name. Nevertheless, to the London Independent Thomas Juxon he was the lesser of two evils; 'a man Competently wise . . . but not ouer well affected to ye Parliament'. Langham, on the other hand, was the favoured candidate of the Scots and of London high Presbyterians, 'a most violent man (like an English Mastiff whatsoeuer you sett him vppon can hardly pull off)'; a choleric and self-willed Presbyterian of the most unaccommodating sort.[59] It will be remembered that both Gayre and Langham were to be among those who were singled out to be impeached by the army for their part in the counter-revolutionary disturbances in London in late July 1647 and that following a long imprisonment awaiting trial, they were to be released in May 1648 as a gesture of conciliation towards the City.[60] Both were ultimately to be discharged from the aldermanry and permanently disabled in April 1649.[61]

Ultimately Baillie was to overcome his initial disappointment at the failure to elect Langham and presumably became reconciled to the view

56. *Parliamentary History*, XV, 221–35, especially p. 232. For Scottish approval, see Baillie, *Letters*, II, 412, 416; *Rec.CGA. 1646–8*, p. 161.
57. Dr Williams's Library, MS. 24.50, fo. 96(b).
58. Baillie, *Letters*, II, 400.
59. For Juxon's view, Dr Williams's Library, MS. 24.50, fos. 91–1(b). For a more hostile view by another Independent, A. Wilbee, *Plain Truth Without Feare or Flattery* (1647), Oxford, Worcester College pamphlet coll., p. 10. On both Gayre and Langham, see V. Pearl, *London and the Outbreak of the Puritan Revolution* (1961), pp. 301–2, 321–3; Pearl, 'London Puritans . . .', in Hollaender and Kellaway, op. cit., pp. 321, 328–9; Pearl, 'London's Counter-revolution', in Aylmer, *Interregnum*, pp. 38, 55; R. Ashton, *The Crown and the Money Market 1603–1640* (Oxford, 1960), p. 181.
60. See above, pp. 187, 191–2, 218.
61. *C.J.*, VI, 181. Langham was rehabilitated at the Restoration. Gayre died in 1649.

that a crypto-royalist Lord Mayor and the prominence of similar persons in city magisterial circles need not be a disaster for the Scottish and high Presbyterian interest. At least he informed Robert Blair in a letter of 3 November that leading City fathers and Presbyterian ministers had assured him that while 'they will be ready to spend the last drop of their blood in his Majestie's service' this would be conditional upon his accepting the Newcastle Propositions, and that even if he did accept these but refused to give his consent to the Covenant being enshrined in an act of parliament, 'the hearts of the Citie he would never get while he lived'.[62] Of course, Charles was under pressure from the queen, Bellièvre and others to make some such concessions, and in December Jermyn and Culpepper wrote urging on him that 'the Scots upon that encouragement may yet joyne with the Pres[byterians] and City of London in appearing for your interestes'.[63]

Nevertheless, Baillie's initial misgivings about the City's preference for Gayre over Langham were not altogether ill-founded, for the new Lord Mayor was just the sort of 'Presbyterian' of whom the French ambassador was to express high hopes early in 1647 following the Presbyterian successes in the Common Council election of December 1646; 'Presbyterians' who would not be insistent on rigidly high Presbyterian religious terms of settlement with the king, provided that they got what they wanted in the matter of royal acceptance of the existing religious settlement and confirmation of the City's privileges and customs. What was vitally important, in Bellièvre's view, was to wean the City from dependence on the Scots who held it fast in matters unacceptable to the king, since Bellièvre's own attempts to persuade Charles to agree to such terms had been so patently unsuccessful. Thus on 2 January 1647 he informed Brienne that the recently presented petition from the City to parliament 'parle fort peu du Roy . . . et ce qu'elle en dit est entièrement rapporté au conuenant [sic]'.[64] Herein, despite the importance of a Lord Mayor and other aldermen with royalist sympathies, lay the chief obstacle to the City's being won for royalism, and Baillie probably had stronger grounds for optimism than had Bellièvre. On 26 January Baillie wrote to William Spang expressing thankfulness for what had actually been achieved by way of Presbyterian reformation in England, even if some of the more Erastian elements in the religious settlement gave grounds for disquiet.[65] His hopes about the City's continued support would no doubt be strengthened by the news retailed in one of Bellièvre's dispatches in March, that it was now

62. Baillie, *Letters*, II, 408.
63. *Clarendon SP.*, II, 312.
64. *Montereul Correspondence*, I, 367.
65. Baillie, *Letters*, III, 1–3.

preparing a petition that the king should be strongly urged to take the Covenant and should not be allowed to approach London until he had done so; a sad blow to the hopes which Charles also entertained of the City.[66]

The months of the struggles between the army and a Presbyterian-dominated parliament in the spring and summer of 1647 were to see an even more pronounced Presbyterian ascendancy in the City. After the parliamentary ordinance of 4 May whose effect was to put the London Militia Committee back into the hands of Holles's Presbyterian allies in the City, there seems to have been a fairly systematic purge of existing militia officers of a different persuasion. An admittedly partisan Independent paper drawn up early in July gives some sense of the peculiar flavour of this purge. Early in May, presumably shortly after the Ordinance of 4 May, one militia commander, Lieutenant Colonel Petit, was, according to his own account, called before the London Militia Committee with the Presbyterian Alderman Gibbs in the chair, and told that a condition of his continuing to serve was 'that hee . . . take notice hee must fight against all mallignants, sects and sectaries and all Godly persons that shall come to oppose the Citty'. The Lieutenant Colonel answered that he thought all members of the committee professed godliness and that he would not engage against any godly man; an embarrassing reply which prompted one committeeman to explain 'that their meaning was that if any out of pretence of Godlynesse should come to oppose them, that hee should fight against such, or words to this effect'. During June there were further and more audacious changes. A number of militia officers, including a lieutenant colonel and a captain, were dismissed on grounds of their Independency, the Militia Committee having declared that 'they would have none of that judgment in comand [sic]'. Fourteen members of the Tower Hamlets Militia Committee, 'honest, active men for the Parliament', were put out and replaced by four 'disaffected men that never lent penny unto the publique but what they were forced unto'. Divers other officers 'of approved fidelitie and trust' were dismissed, and replaced by malignants, who presumably were ex-Cavaliers. Another disreputable recruit was a captain who had deserted from the New Model Army, probably in response to the invitation from the parliamentary Committee of Safety and perhaps, despite its disclaimers, the London Militia Com-

66. *Montereul Correspondence*, II, 73. A petition is also mentioned in a letter of 4 March from the royalist Nicholas Oudart to Sir Edward Nicholas in France. The writer describes the petition as being framed at Sion College by the London Presbyterian divines and sent to Common Council asking for a petition to parliament to be drawn up 'that y[e] [Newcastle] Proposicions might be presd, religion and the covenant settled universally in the kingdom [and] the King not sufferd to come nearer London for feare of tumults, &c' (*Nicholas Papers*, pp. 80–1). See above, p. 134.

mittee.[67] Clement Walker's account of a counter-revolutionary design for what he called 'a new-modelled Army under Presbyterian Commanders' seems to be no exaggeration of what was going on through the medium of these two committees during these summer months.[68]

During the eleven days of London's counter-revolution which began with the coup of 26 July, Presbyterians and royalists joined in demanding that the king be brought to London or to one of his nearby houses to treat without prior conditions. London Presbyterian parsons were later hard put to it to disprove the charges of Hugh Peter and others that they had egged on the rioters to intimidate the parliament to issue such an invitation to the king as well as to revoke the newly passed Militia Ordinance, just as Peter had earlier blamed them for agitating for the disbandment of the New Model Army.[69] That the Presbyterian City authorities had been, at the very least, negligent in failing to put down the tumult on 26 July, or, at worst, had actively encouraged the rioters, is reflected in the charges to be brought against the deposed Lord Mayor, Sir John Gayre, and others of his aldermanic colleagues who were to be committed to the Tower following the army's occupation of London on 6 August.[70] Similarly that the accusations against the London Presbyterian ministers of stirring up seditious tumults received the stamp of parliamentary approval is shown, for example, in the reply of parliamentary commissioners on 4 January 1648 to a declaration of the Scottish parliament.[71] Indeed, the anti-Presbyterian author of *The Pulpit Incendiary* was later to argue that the ministers had some indirect responsibility for the city riots of 9 and 10 April 1648.[72] However, from here onwards it will be appropriate for London manifestations of religious and political Presbyterianism to be treated in the context of general developments over the remainder of our period.

Presbyterianism in eclipse, August 1647–June 1648

The collapse of the London counter-revolution and the removal of the eleven members from the parliamentary scene through imprisonment,

---

67. *Clarke Papers*, I, 152–6.
68. C. Walker, 'The Mysterie of the two Juntoes . . .', in Maseres, *Select Tracts*, I, 346.
69. For details of these developments, see above, pp. 137–8. For accusations against London Presbyterian parsons, see 'A Word for the Army by Hugh Peters [sic]', *Harleian Miscellany*, VI (1810), 67; *The Pulpit Incendiary*, pp. 9–10, 13, 19–20, 33–4, 37. For denial of such charges, see *The Pulpit Incendiary Anatomized*, pp. 6–7; [C.B.], *Sion College, What It Is and Doeth*, pp. 22–3; *A Word to Mr. Peters and two Words for the Parliament and Kingdom* (9 November 1647), BL., E.413(7), esp. pp. 5, 19–23.
70. See above, p. 187.
71. *An Answer To . . . The Declaration of the Kingdome of Scotland* (4 January 1648), BL., E.421(32), p. 11.
72. *The Pulpit Incendiary*, pp. 37, 42–3.

exile, and, in Stapleton's case, death, marked the end of what had threatened to be a revival of Presbyterian fortunes. As far as the hopes of negotiations with the king were concerned, it was now the army's – or, according to Dr Adamson, the Independent grandees' – Heads of the Proposals which, for some weeks at least, held the field rather than parliament's Hampton Court (or Newcastle) Propositions. Following the king's flight from Hampton Court, there is a further shift in a more radical direction which was certainly not favoured by conservative Presbyterian elements any more than it was by royalists. Such was the failure to respond to the king's approaches from the Isle of Wight, the presentation of the Four Bills in December, and, following the royal rejection of these, the Vote of No Addresses and the strongly anti-monarchical Declaration on that Vote.[73] Of course the Presbyterians were not completely cowed and quiescent during this time. In the House of Commons, for example, it is interesting to note that following the king's flight from Hampton Court in November, there was a division on the motion that anyone harbouring or concealing the royal fugitive should be proceeded against as a traitor. The motion passed by 61 votes to 50, but, despite the fact that the Presbyterians had been robbed of eleven of their leading MPs, two Presbyterians acted as tellers against the motion, and it is perhaps worth noting that the presence of the missing eleven would have made it a tied vote. Although Stapleton, of course, was now dead, the point is not entirely academic since the procedural motion that the question be put had passed by only ten votes.[74] Nor could Presbyterian preachers be kept quiet, especially in London, and complaints against them for stirring up trouble continued. Some of them made much of the king's unhappy fate as prisoner of the army — 'As for instance *Mr. Wall of Michaels Cornhill London*, [who] frequently in his prayers for the King, bewails his being driven like a *Partridge* from mountain to hill, and his sad condition under *restraint*'.[75]

However, the initiative over the months following the collapse of the July counter-revolution undoubtedly lay with the parliamentary Independents and the army. Replying on 4 January 1648 to Scottish objections to parliament's failure to disband the New Model, 'an Army to inslave the King and Subject', the English Parliamentary Commissioners retorted that the Presbyterian religious settlement would not last five minutes if it were not for the army. This was because '*England* in general loves Episcopacy better [than], and Popery as well as, Presbytery; for in times of Episcopacy they had all things in plenty and

73. On all these developments, see above, pp. 33–40.
74. *C.J.*, V, 358.
75. *The Pulpit Incendiary*, p. 14.

good fellowship to boot: who shall expect to enjoy Bishops lands in lieu of the money you had, if no Army?'[76]

During the summer of 1647 many English Presbyterians had hoped that their hegemony might be reinforced by Scottish intervention, and, in particular, through a Scottish invasion to rescue the king from the army. Were there any grounds for hope for a restoration of the Presbyterian fortunes by similar means in 1648? A difficulty here was that it was the Scottish Engagers rather than the Scottish kirk which supported invasion and while some leaders of the Engagers – the earl of Lauderdale is the outstanding example – were themselves devoted covenanters, for others talk of the Covenant and religion was little more than a convenient cloak to obscure the fact that their main aim was the restoration of the king and power for themselves. Moreover, by no means all English parliamentary Presbyterians favoured the establishment of a Scottish-type ecclesiastical polity in England, although most historians have given insufficient credit to Scottish flexibility in such matters.[77] Some Presbyterians may have felt vulnerable to Independent criticisms of the Scots for undue interference in English affairs 'as if our Kingdom and theirs were not distinct, governed by distinct Lawes'.[78]

Another particularly delicate area where charges of interference in English affairs were levelled against the Scots related to their solicitude for their Presbyterian brethren in the City of London. In the Additional Instructions to the English Commissioners in Scotland on 7 March 1648, the commissioners were ordered to complain that the Scottish commissioners in England 'have from time to time made Applications to the City of *London* in their Common Council, without the Leave of the Houses . . . as if the said City had been a free State'.[79] But this does not appear to have deterred the Scots, whose parliament in April declared as one of its aims that 'the City of *London* may enjoy the liberty and priviledges which it had before the late encroachment of the Armie' (viz. presumably before 6 August 1647).[80] It may well be that this declaration influenced the English parliament to adopt a more accommodating attitude to the City during the ensuing weeks.[81] There was, of

---

76. BL., E.421(32), pp. 16–17. For similar arguments, see *The Pulpit Incendiary*, p. 43; *The Scots beaten with their own weapons* (1648), BHPC., p. 5.

77. On this, see Stevenson, *Revolution and Counter-Revolution*, pp. 120–1. Telling examples of Scottish flexibility are a letter of 17 September 1646 from the Scottish Commissioners in London and the reply of the Commissioners of the General Assembly of the Scottish Church on 23 September (*Rec.CGA. 1646–8*, pp. 57–9, 74–5). See also the Commissioners' paper of 21 January 1647 (ibid., pp. 182–6)).

78. *The Scots beaten with their own weapons*, pp. 1, 3.

79. *C.J.*, V, 483; *HMC., 7th Report Appendix (House of Lords Cal. 1647–8)*, p. 13.

80. *A Declaration of the Parliament of Scotland* (April 1647), Codrington, pamphlet coll., p. 11; *Rec.CGA. 1646–8*, p. 468.

81. On this, see above, pp. 191–2; below, pp. 291–2.

course, nothing novel about this Scottish solicitude for the City, but the declaration was particularly significant in the context of the spring of 1648 when the Scottish Engagers were counting on support from the City for their forthcoming invasion; this notwithstanding the warning of Lanark's English correspondent that the English Presbyterians 'ever were and wilbee enemies to monarchy'.[82]

In the event the City was prepared to go some way to oblige the Scots, though not, as it turned out, to the extent of taking up arms in support of the invading army of the Engagement. However, that was all in the future and what its attitude would be in the event of such an invasion was still a matter for conjecture. Early in March a promising sign, according to the view of Lanark's correspondent, had been the failure of an underhand attempt to persuade the City to petition for peace negotiations with the king, because the citizens did not wish to offend the Scots.[83] Is the writer suggesting that the City was anxious to do nothing to impede the planned Scottish invasion? In any case, when such a London petition was made, it was not until two months later, on 29 May, and even then it was not an official City petition at all. Indeed, if Thomason's description is correct, the circumstances appear to betoken the realization of the great nightmare of Bellièvre and Montereul, in that 'the Presbiterian[s] & Independant[s] did Compose and agree in this petion [sic]'. If this is true, the Independent petitioners probably belonged to the moderate wing of the party which itself was now in danger of splitting disastrously over the very issue of treating with Charles I. Chief among the petitioners' desires were parliamentary confirmation of the ancient constitution with King and both Houses of Parliament; the preservation of religion according to the Covenant; the satisfaction of the just demands of the Scots, which did not necessarily mean yielding to all the demands of the Engagers; prompt attention to national grievances, and more particularly to cases currently depending before parliamentary committees; and the settlement of the militia in what the petitioners would regard as safe hands. Attention to these matters, the petitioners argued, would have the effect of stopping the mouths of all but the irreconcilable calumniators of parliament. Even more important, it would remove the case for all but royalist risings in support of a Scottish invasion by cutting the very ground from beneath the Engagers' feet.[84]

One of the petitioners' aims had already been achieved a month

82. *Hamilton Papers*, p. 175. In a later letter of 2 May, however, the correspondent was more hopeful about the City's constancy despite the possible danger of reconciliation between Presbyterians and Independents there (ibid., p. 195).
83. SRO., GD/406/1/2227.
84. *The humble Petition of divers Citizens* (29 May 1648), BL., 669, f12(38).

earlier on 28 April with the vote that the fundamental constitution by King, Lords and Commons should not be altered. This was backed not only, as might be expected, by parliamentary Presbyterians, but also by a number of Independents, including, we are told, William Pierrepoint and Sir Henry Vane. Pierrepoint's support is not surprising in view of his middle-group past, but the attitude of the far more radical Vane is. On the same day the resolution that any MP might propound any motion for the settlement of the kingdom was carried without a division; a procedural motion that the question be put having previously been won by 146 votes to 101, with the Presbyterians Sir Henry Cholmeley and Lord Cranborne acting as tellers in favour and the radical Independents Sir Michael Livesay and Sir William Masham as tellers against.[85]

The developments described above have clearly demonstrated the possibility of co-operation between parliamentary Presbyterians and Independents faced by the prospect of a Scottish invasion and a renewal of civil war at home. Such co-operation was not confined to Westminster. A letter in June tells of Presbyterians and Independents combining in Northamptonshire – and probably in Leicestershire and Rutland too – to raise forces to combat the now apparently inevitable Scottish invasion.[86]

The Presbyterians and the Second Civil War

It is not necessary to make allowance for the Cavalier bias of the earl of Lanark's English correspondent to recognize the force of his contention in a letter of 10 April 1648 that the Scottish Engagers would find a far more reliable source of support for their invasion in the English royalists than in the English Presbyterians.[87] Among the most significant reasons for this were to be the hostility of the General Assembly of the Scottish church to an invasion and the more lenient attitude of the English

85. *C.J.*, V, 547; Rushworth, *Historical Collections*, VII, 1074; *Hamilton Papers*, p. 191. For another case of Vane voting with 'the malignant partie' against 'the honest partie', see *Clarke Papers*, II, 17. This was on 24 May, presumably on the motion favouring negotiations with the king once the outstanding issues of religion and militia control had been settled (*C.J.*, V, 572). On this there was a large majority of 169 votes to 86, which suggests that some Independents probably voted along with the Presbyterians. On Pierrepont's political views, see D. Underdown, *Pride's Purge* (Oxford, 1971), pp. 63, 64–5, 71–2, 95–6; V. Pearl, *TRHS.*, art. cit., pp. 85–7. On Vane, see V. Rowe, *Sir Henry Vane the Younger* (1970), passim.
86. *A letter . . . concerninge the affaires in Leicester, Rutland and Northamptonshire* (June 1648), BL., E.449(24), pp. 5–6.
87. *Hamilton Papers*, p. 180.

parliament to the survivors of the eleven Presbyterian members and the London aldermen for complicity in the counter-revolution of July 1647.[88]

But before this supreme test of Presbyterian intentions there occurred other, if less significant, developments across the Irish Sea. These appeared to betoken some sympathy on the part of English parliamentary Presbyterians with the case of Lord Inchiquin, who, from having been both President of Munster and commander of the parliamentary forces in that province against the confederate Catholic insurgents, now deserted that cause and declared the intention of collaborating with his former enemies. On 13 April 1648 the House of Lords considered a letter of 5 April from a parliamentary sea commander, Captain Crowther, written on board ship in Kinsale harbour and giving details of Inchiquin's defection, and of how 'for the managing of this Design, he had Correspondence with the King, the *Scotts*, and generally all the Presbyterian Party, who were agreed with the King'.[89] In a later Protestation of 6 May, publicizing the reasons for what the parliament regarded as his treachery, Inchiquin listed the damage done to the English parliamentary cause by the Independent hegemony and, not least, 'how they privately and publikely endeavor to take off all the Presbiterian party both in that and in this Kingdome from their Command as men not fit to be trusted because faithfull not factious and for no other reason'.[90] The need to dispel suspicions about Presbyterian collusion with Inchiquin points to the significance of the fact that the tellers in favour of a motion in the House of Commons on 13 April to concur with the Upper House in its action in sending Inchiquin's son to the Tower as a hostage were the Presbyterian MPs Sir Thomas Dacres and Sir Walter Erle. In a sparsely attended House the motion passed only by 37 votes to 33, which prompts conjecture about the political affiliations (if any) of those voting against it.[91]

At home, however, the voting on two motions in the House of Commons seemed – if the identity of the tellers is anything to go by – to indicate less than wholehearted Presbyterian support for two measures to secure the kingdom against insurrection and invasion. On 21 April the Presbyterians Erle and Dacres were again tellers in favour of an amendment which would have attenuated the force of a motion to disarm delinquents, proposing that actual adherence to insurgent forces should replace mere suspicion of the likelihood of such adherence

88. On the opposition of the kirk, see below, pp. 326–31, 335–6. On parliament, the eleven members and the London aldermen, see above, pp. 191–2.
89. *L.J.*, X, 189.
90. *The Lord Inchiquin's Protestation on Sexto Maii 1648* (14 June 1648), BL., E.447(13), p. 3. On Inchiquin, see below, pp. 400–402.
91. *C.J.*, V, 529.

as the criterion for disarming. The amendment was narrowly defeated by 74 votes to 71, the tellers against it being the Independents Sir John Danvers and Sir Henry Mildmay. Similarly on 5 May there was a Presbyterian attempt to weaken the force of a motion to put the seven northern counties into a posture of defence by an amendment which would make the resolution permissive rather than compulsory. After the failure of the amendment by the substantial majority of 127 votes to 76, the original substantive motion passed without a division. For our purposes it is significant that the Presbyterians Sir John Curzon and Giles Green acted as tellers for, and the Independents Sir Peter Wentworth and Sir William Brereton against, the amendment.[92]

Reference was made earlier to the opposition of the General Assembly of the Scottish kirk to the policies of the Engagers as a factor influencing the attitude of the English Presbyterians to the possibility of a Scottish invasion. In April Lanark's English correspondent had mentioned Argyll's dispatching of the eminent English Presbyterian divine Stephen Marshall from Scotland with a mission to try to secure some agreement between the Presbyterians and Independents and to deter the former from co-operating with the Scottish Engagers in the event of an invasion. Similarly, on 27 May the same correspondent wrote warning Lanark about the dangers presented by efforts of his opponents, the earl of Argyll and the anti-Engagement party in Scotland, to convince the English Presbyterians, through letters to the earl of Manchester and others, that the Engagers were hand in glove with the king and the English Cavaliers 'and of party to destroy Covenant, Presbytery, and Parliament of England . . .'. Such attempts, he continued, had come near to convincing the Presbyterians whose consequent disinclination to co-operate with a Scottish invasion had been further strengthened by the parliamentary vote three days earlier for a personal treaty with Charles I once the issues of religion and control of the militia had been satisfactorily settled.[93]

Thus the view that English Presbyterian sympathies in the Second Civil War were firmly with the Scottish invaders[94] is belied by their quiescence in the struggle for which they were to reap their ultimate reward later that summer. Indeed, the royalist commander in the north, Sir Marmaduke Langdale, was surely right to warn the duke of Hamilton, the commander of the Scottish army of the Engagement, not

92. C.J., V, 539, 551.
93. Hamilton Papers, pp. 177, 202–3; C.J., V, 572.
94. See, e.g., T. May, 'A Breviary of the History of the Parliament of England' (1650), in Maseres, Select Tracts, I, 113, 122, 125–6. For the emphatically anti-Engager sentiments of one London Presbyterian, see P.S. Seaver, Wallington's World (1985), pp. 172, 178.

to take the English royalists for granted in his concern to win over the Presbyterians.[95] Langdale is here referring principally to the Presbyterians in the north of England. As to the Presbyterians of London, it has already been shown that they had positive reasons of their own for backing parliament against the Engagers.[96] Parliament's new-found leniency towards the imprisoned Lord Mayor and Presbyterian aldermen and the survivors of the eleven Presbyterian members, its concessions to the City, its declaration in favour of a monarchical constitution and its visible move away from the rigorous extremism of the Vote of No Addresses were all elements in a well-conceived and highly successful plan to spike the Engagers' guns.[97]

Writing on 25 August to his patron Lord Wharton in London, Francis Higginson, parson of Kirkby Stephen in Westmorland, told of how he had stayed in his benefice until Scottish and Cavalier intimidation and plundering had made things intolerable, though he also mentions earlier attempts by the Scots Engagers to woo local Presbyterians for their support.[98] Indeed, on 10 August the duke of Hamilton had been at pains to reassure fugitive Presbyterian parsons that they had nothing to fear from the Scottish Engagers who were themselves Presbyterians and sought not just to restore the king but also to create the conditions for a proper Presbyterian ecclesiastical settlement in England. A response from ten such ministers of Lancashire who had left their county livings for fear of molestation by Scots and Cavaliers has survived. These divines affirmed that while they shared Hamilton's eagerness both for the restoration of the king and a Presbyterian settlement, they also had no doubt about the devotion of the English parliament to these laudable aims.[99] If there is any truth at all in the account given in a letter of 8 August from two parliamentarian fugitives at Lancaster to the county committee at Manchester, the ten had been well advised to leave their cures. The letter tells a sorry tale of Scottish plundering and other outrages, which were apparently indiscriminate rather than selective in that they were directed against both local Cavaliers and local Presbyterians, against whom in particular, however, 'They rail without measure . . . and profess the destruction of so many as they can get'.[100]

---

95. *Propositions of Sir Marmaduke Langdale to Duke Hamilton* (June 1648), BL., E.451(30), no pagination; *The Declaration and Propositions of Major General Langdale . . .* (Edinburgh, 7 July 1648), E.452(31), pp. 1–2.
96. See above, pp. 191–2.
97. CLRO., Jor. 40, fos. 269(b)–70; *C.J.*, V, 565; *L.J.*, X, 266; *Parliamentary History*, XVII, 147–9.
98. Bodleian, Carte MSS., 103, fos. 167–7(b).
99. *The Copy of a Letter From Duke Hamilton . . .* (10 August 1648), BL., E.460(38), pp. 3–7; Ormerod, *Tracts*, pp. 252–3.
100. *Severall Letters of Complaint from the Northern parts* (August 1648), BL., E.459(7), pp. 3–4. See also Ormerod, *Tracts*, pp. 254–5.

In London as in the north the Presbyterian brethren held firm against any temptation to join the Scots or the nearby Cavalier insurgents in Kent, Surrey or Colchester, though there are references to the recruiting of [Presbyterian?] apprentices to help the beleaguered royalists in Colchester. In general, like their brethren in the north and indeed like Argyll and the anti-Engager kirk party in Scotland, London Presbyterians displayed their awareness of, as one anti-Scottish pamphlet puts it, 'how inconsistent the King's interest was to the Covenant and Presbyteriall government'.[101] As a statement in August emanating from the House of Commons puts it, it was the king who was the main obstacle to a Presbyterian settlement, as witness his determination to uphold epsicopacy which he was to maintain to the end of his days.[102] But while the London Presbyterians were to stand by parliament in 1648 as they had not done in July 1647, it would be rash to assume that their support was enthusiastic and without ambivalence. Indeed, there were many who still profoundly mistrusted them[103] and looked for a repetition of the events of a year earlier, only now in a situation of far greater danger, with the added perils of a Scottish invasion and a renewal of Civil War. At least one northern Cavalier entertained hopes for support for the royalist cause from the London trained bands.[104] Was it not true, asked one radical pamphleteer, that the officers of the city trained bands 'did demand of their Soldiers whether they would engage for the King and a personal Treaty'? Not surprising then that the London Presbyterians were agitating and indeed petitioning for the amalgamation of the metropolitan militias which would then be under their control; to the extreme danger of parliament if the events of 1647 were anything to go by. Was not the malignant Presbyterian influence also apparent in a city petition to parliament in which the petitioners 'call the Scots their *Brethren* whom the Parliament have declared to be *enimies?*' Was London again about to be convulsed by apprentice tumults in favour of an unconditional treaty with the king, to the approval of both Presbyterians and Cavaliers?[105] That it was not was partly due to the tight grip kept on metropolitan security by that pious

101. *The Scots Cabinett Opened* (4 August 1648), BL., E.456(30), pp. 11–12.
102. *The Parliaments Proposalls to the Kingdom of Scotland* (August 1648), BL., E.458(16), especially pp. 5–6. Although this was designed chiefly for Scottish consumption, the point would not be lost on English Presbyterians.
103. See, e.g., *The Moderate: Number 7* (22/29 August 1648), BL., E.461(16), sig. G^v; T. May, 'A Breviary . . .', in Maseres, *Select Tracts*, I, 125–6.
104. Rushworth, *Historical Collections*, VII, 1197.
105. *Designes Vnmasqued; or the Several Reasons of the Three Militias of Westminster, Hamblets of the Tower and Burrough of Southwark against the Pretended Union with the Militia of London* (31 August 1648), BL., E.462(12), especially pp. 10–12. For petitions concerning militia amalgamation, see above, pp. 124, 141, 156.

Presbyterian Major General Philip Skippon, but partly also to Presbyterian Londoners' ability to learn from their mistakes of a year earlier.

Quiescence rewarded and hopes unfulfilled

It was because the Presbyterians kept their hands clean in the Second Civil War that their request for renewed negotiations with the king bore fruit. The City had petitioned for such a treaty and for a Presbyterian religious settlement on 27 June[106] and in the debate in the House of Commons on 3 July which resulted in a vote for a treaty provided the king agreed to three prior conditions, the arguments of radical Independents such as Scot, Harvey, Vane and Mildmay may well have been counter-productive. In Scot's ferocious words, there was no case 'for a Peace with so perfidious and implacable a Prince'. At any rate they did not deter the parliamentary Presbyterians from urging the necessity of a treaty and for it to be held in London rather than, as some suggested, at Holdenby or in the Isle of Wight where Charles might be too much in the power of the army. Speaking emphatically along these lines was, amongst others, that crashing Presbyterian bore, Sir Simonds D'Ewes, who urged that in the circumstances parliament had little choice but to trust the king.[107] On 22 July a procedural motion to put the question that a treaty with the king should be debated on the following Monday was passed by 48 votes to 35 and the question itself then passed without a division. The two tellers for the procedural motion were the Norfolk Presbyterian Sir John Potts and John Bulkeley, a former middle-grouper and Independent and one of those whose support for negotiations with the king was a sign of the disastrous split in the Independent ranks which has been so brilliantly depicted by Professor Underdown. One of the tellers against the motion was the pious Presbyterian William Purefoy, but Purefoy's Presbyterianism was confined to religious matters and in politics he was a radical Independent.[108] By contrast the parliamentary Presbyterians' tenderness for the king was demonstrated in the debate of 2 August on the personnel of a committee of both Houses which was to deliver a message to the king informing him of parliament's resolutions in favour of a treaty. On this occasion the

---

106. *L.J.*, X, 349–50; *C.J.*, V, 613–14; *HMC., 7th. Report (House of Lords Cal. 1648)*, p. 33.

107. *Parliamentary History*, XVII, 276–9; *C.J.*, V, 622; Rushworth, *Historical Collections*, VII, 1174. The three conditions were the settling of Presbyterian government for three years, the settling of the militia in parliament's hands, and the revoking of wartime declarations against parliament. The conditions were later abandoned.

108. *C.J.*, V, 644. On the Independent split, see D. Underdown, *Pride's Purge*, pp. 76–105.

Presbyterian MP for Colchester, Sir Harbottle Grimston, took exception to the Independents' candidate, Sir John Harrington, MP for Rutland and a former servant of the king, who had, however, previously distinguished himself by seconding a motion for Charles's impeachment, and in consequence 'could be no welcome Messenger to his Majesty'.[109] That a further London petition of 8 August again in favour of a treaty came from people of a decidedly Presbyterian disposition is suggested by their additional concern with the incompleteness of the religious settlement and the increase of 'Blasphemy, Heresy, Schism and Prophaneness'.[110]

The decision to negotiate with the king was a triumph for the Presbyterians. Yet only nine of the fifteen commissioners appointed by parliament to treat with the king at Newport in the Isle of Wight were Presbyterians, including the formerly proscribed Denzil Holles and John Glyn, who had been restored to their parliamentary seats along with other survivors of the eleven members. Five of the remaining commissioners were moderate Independents, such as William Pierrepoint, John Bulkeley and Lord Saye and Sele, whose support for negotiations had produced the split in the Independent ranks. Their appreciation of the frighteningly radical alternatives to negotiation which were ultimately to be implemented in December and January after the negotiations had been brutally aborted by the army persuaded them to co-operate with their former Presbyterian opponents. The motives of the other commissioner, the radical Independent Sir Henry Vane, have always been a matter of mystery and conjecture.[111]

It is important not to yield, as some historians seem to have done, to the promptings of hindsight and to regard the Treaty of Newport as doomed from the outset.[112] On the contrary, it was fear that it might well succeed which prompted the army grandees to abort the proceedings. As Charles I was at pains to emphasize in a paper of 9 October, he had made numerous substantial concessions,[113] mostly, but not entirely, on civil issues, and indeed they were such as might have sufficed in

109. *Parliamentary History*, XVII, 357.
110. *L.J.*, X, 424, 427; Rushworth, *Historical Collections*, VII, 1220; *The Humble Petition of the Lord Major [sic] Aldermen and Commons . . .* (8 August 1648), BL., E.457(10), pp. 1–5; *Parliamentary History*, XVII, 387–91. The Commons' reply emphasized both that an ordinance had been passed for settling Presbyterian church government and that the House had resolved on a personal treaty with the king in the Isle of Wight (ibid., p. 393).
111. See Ashton, *Civil War*, pp. 334–5. On Vane, see V.A. Rowe, *Sir Henry Vane the Younger*, pp. 107–11.
112. See, e.g., MacCormack, *Revolutionary Politics*, p. 286.
113. Bodleian, Rawlinson MSS., A114, fos. 35(b)–6(b); *Parliamentary History*, XVIII, 42–6. See also his letter of 9 November to the earl of Loudoun (BL., Add. MSS., 15,750, fo. 37).

circumstances other than those of total defeat in two wars. On civil matters he had yielded much, but the sticking point came on religion. For 'Presbyterian Independents' like Edmund Prideaux and William Purefoy, Charles's determination to rescue as much as he could of episcopacy from the ruins would simply confirm their conviction that there was no contradiction between their religious (Presbyterian) and political (Independent) convictions. On the other hand, for men such as Sir Simonds D'Ewes and John Swynfen, who were Presbyterians in both senses, the contradiction must have been both real and agonizing, while political Presbyterians such as Denzil Holles probably experienced considerable irritation at circumstances in which the religious scruples of both king and parliament were standing in the way of a desperately needed settlement. The voice of dispassionate reason sounds most clearly perhaps in an admirable letter of 6 November from the moderate Independent and former middle-grouper John Crewe to his Presbyterian colleague at Westminster, John Swynfen. Crewe, who was himself one of the parliamentary commissioners at Newport, stressed the very real danger that parliamentary rigidity on religious terms might redound to the discredit of Presbyterianism and breed future enmity to it if such rigidity were seen to inhibit a settlement with the king. Too much attention, Crewe continued, was being paid to episcopal lands, both by the king and by self-interested parliamentarians. Would it not be sensible for the lands, at the end of the proposed ninety-nine years of lease, to be resumed and used to augment the value of small ecclesiastical benefices, thus providing powerful – and godly – reasons why episcopacy should not be restored?[114]

On the other hand, it might be asked, what was the difference between the king's current concession of a trial period of three years for a Presbyterian religious settlement and the terms of his Engagement with the Scots in December 1647? The Scottish invasion had been crushed, but was Charles to be rewarded by being granted the same terms which he had agreed with the Engagers? Had Preston and Colchester been fought in vain? A moderate parliamentarian like Crewe might deplore parliament's rigidity over the religious terms of a settlement, but it is hardly surprising that by the time of Crewe's letter early in November, the king had been informed of parliament's total dissatisfaction with his answers to its propositions 'in regard the King hath reather framed a new Proposition then consented to that presented to him'. He had consented to a Presbyterian settlement only for a trial period of three years and had not precluded the possibility of his creating bishops during that period nor of the restoration of episcopacy

114. *Cal.SPD. 1648–9*, p. 319.

after it had ended. He had given no satisfaction as to the permanent alienation of episcopal lands nor against the use of Catholic services in the Queen's Household or for the use of the Directory of Worship in his own.[115] On 20 November parliament reiterated its total dissatisfaction with the king's replies, to which he responded by stating that he had conceded as much as he could and would go no further.[116]

After the parliamentary commissioners had taken what proved to be their final leave of the king on 27 November, there took place three crucial divisions in the House of Commons. On the face of it the fact that the tellers for the procedural motion of 4 December to put the question that the king's last reply to parliament's propositions at Newport was satisfactory were the radical Independents Edmund Ludlow and Nicholas Love is surprising until it is realized that the object of the question was to wreck the prospect of further negotiations, since nobody, Presbyterian or Independent, considered Charles's replies as they stood to be satisfactory. The procedural motion was heavily lost by 144 votes to 93 and the question was not tabled. On the other hand, the substantive motion on the same day that the army's removal of the king from the Isle of Wight had been done 'without the Knowledge or Consent of the House' was passed without a division, the words 'or Consent' having been added as a result of an amendment which had been carried by 136 votes to 102, with the Presbyterians Sir Robert Pye and Sir Samuel Luke acting as tellers in favour, and the Independents Ashe and Chalonor against. Finally came the momentous motion of the following day carried without a division that the king's replies at Newport were 'a Ground . . . to proceed upon for the Settlement of the Peace of the kingdom'. The procedural motion that this question be put had previously been passed by 129 votes to 83, the Presbyterians Lord Cranborne and Sir Ralph Assheton acting as tellers in favour. It was to be the last gesture of the parliamentary Presbyterians, for this was the resolution which finally precipitated Pride's Purge.[117]

While the work of Professor Underdown has conclusively demonstrated that the old view that Pride's Purge was a purge of Presbyterian MPs by the Independents and the army is an oversimplification and that it was rather a purging of those who supported negotiations with the king, there can be no doubt that among such persons Presbyterians were the most prominent, and even more strongly represented among those

115. Bodleian, Rawlinson MSS., A114, fos. 49–50. For the king's denial of such intentions, see ibid., fos. 53–3(b).
116. Ibid., fos. 58(b)–60(b); *Parliamentary History*, XVIII, 244–8, 251. On the king's position on episcopacy, see, e.g., Rawlinson MSS., A114, fos. 32–4(b); BL., Add. MSS., 32,093, fo. 249; *His Majesties Paper . . . Touching Episcopacy* (9 October 1648), BL., E.466(6), p. 2.
117. *C.J.*, VI, 93.

who were not only secluded but also imprisoned.[118] By Christmas Day, however, sixteen of the latter had been released. Of the remaining eighteen, four (Lewis, Swynfen, Birch and Green) are described by the royalist observer John Lawrans as 'prudentiall men' likely to yield to terms in return for regaining their freedom. Of the others, Lawrans specifies two groups of irreconcilables of whom the most dangerous were confined separately as 'the pillars of the scottish interest'. These were Sir John Clotworthy, Sir William Waller, Edward Massey, Richard Browne and Lionel Copley, the last four of whom had also been deeply involved in London's counter-revolution in July 1647. Hardly less instransigent were William Prynne, Edward Stephens, Thomas Geven and Clement Walker, the last of whom, though a non-party man whose *The Mysterie of the Two Juntoes* wished a plague on both Presbyterians and Independents, was in reality far more hostile to the latter. The remaining five (Strode, Leigh, Wheeler and the Harleys father and son) are mysteriously described by Lawrans as 'middle men', and he makes no mention of Denzil Holles, who seems to have made himself scarce and was nowhere to be found.[119]

According to Lawrans the outlook was worse for the Presbyterian leaders than it was for the king, for the radical Independents and the army leaders simply saw the purge as enabling them to come to a settlement with the king, carrying on much from where they had left off at the time of the Heads of the Proposals but now unencumbered by Presbyterian and other opposition. Once parliament had been dissolved, there would be room in its successor for royalists though none for Presbyterians. The king would also have an admittedly meagre 'share of government in ye same equipage (perhaps) as the D[uke] of Venice?' The chief significance of his coming trial would be simply 'a meanes to give him oportunity [*sic*] to cleare himself from the scandalls & aspersions first charged vpon him by ye Presbiterians'. Once his name had been cleared, the way would be open for an Independent approach to him for a settlement and the only doubt was whether or not Charles would go along with this.[120]

In retrospect this looks like absurdly overoptimistic moonshine, the fantasies of a royalist who was whistling to keep his spirits up. Indeed,

118. D. Underdown, *Pride's Purge*, pp. 143–72, 208–56.
119. Bodleian, Clarendon MSS., 34, fo. 17. On Holles, see P. Crawford, *Denzil Holles*, p. 177. Lawrans does not specify which of the two younger Harleys this refers to. Underdown calculates that only sixteen MPs remained imprisoned on 26 December (*Pride's Purge*, p. 168 note), but his list does not include the two Harleys, neither of whom was released until after the execution of the king (J. Eales, *Puritans and Roundheads. The Harleys of Brampton Bryan and the outbreak of the English Civil War* (Cambridge, 1990), pp. 192–3).
120. Clarendon MSS., 34, fos. 17–17(b).

in another letter of 29 December, Lawrans admitted that his own optimism was not shared by many of the king's friends.[121] But before dismissing it completely, it is perhaps as well to recall that Oliver Cromwell was currently making another approach to Charles I via the earl of Denbigh and that some hope of a compromise was still in the air even if this would leave the king shorn of most of his authority; a mere duke of Venice, as Lawrans put it. Our royalist observer was at least right in his assumption that the crucial question was whether Charles would go along with such an approach. In the event he would not, and this finally sealed his fate.

A call from the House of Commons on 1 January 1649 for the well-affected to ready themselves in arms 'lest the Presbyterians . . . do joyn with their Brother Malignants to raise new troubles'[122] would probably not have occasioned great alarm. For as the events of the Second Civil War had demonstrated, royalists and Presbyterians were not natural allies, for all their shared concerns about the need for ordered government and dislike of sectarian excesses. Indeed, according to one royalist paper produced soon after the execution of the king, the Presbyterians were no less guilty of regicide than were the Independents who had straightforwardly, if perniciously, attacked the king 'as ye sole cause of so much bloodshead [sic]'. But he 'had bin murthered a long time before by ye Presbyterians' in depriving him of his authority, liberty, company of wife and children and attendance of his servants;

> & in a word of all those comforts wch might make life valued . . . So y^t there was nothing left for ye Independents to doe, but to put an end to those Calamities, vnto which this miserable man, this *vir dolorum* . . . had bin so accursedly plunged by ye Presbyterians.[123]

This is surely flying too far in the opposite direction from the statement of 1 January associating Presbyterians with likely royalist plots. If Charles's death was indeed a consequence of Presbyterian (no less than of Independent) acts, it was assuredly an unintended consequence.

121. Ibid., fo. 18(b).
122. Whitelock, *Memorials*, p. 360 (1 January).
123. 'On ye Kings death', Bodleian, MSS. Add. C132, fos. 27–7(b).

IX

PRESBYTERIANS AND ENGAGERS

The *Parliament* of *Scotland* is wholly *Presbyterian*, and would be Loyall if the Clergy would suffer them. They have now the third time sent an Army into *England*. The first was for themselves. The second for the Parliament here. And the third for the KING. Their first expedition was with Honour and Successe; Their second with Successe and Profit; Their third, neither with Successe, Honour, nor Profit. . . .

Certaine Considerations Touching the Present Factions In the KINGS Dominions (6 October 1648), BL., E.466(3), p. 6

The parting of allies

On 5 May 1646 the Scottish Commissioners in England reported from the small Nottinghamshire city of Southwell an event which, they claimed, 'haueing overtaken vs vnexpectedly hath filled vs with amazement and made vs like men that dreame'. The event was the arrival of Charles I in their midst at a time when the Scottish army was besieging the nearby royalist stronghold of Newark.[1] But, as a very sceptical anti-Scottish commentator was to put it much later, 'the dreame was soone over and they awakt'.[2] Expressing confidence in the king's declared intention to satisfy the just and reasonable demands of both nations, the Scottish commissioners with the army assured their English parliamentary counterparts that the Scottish army would do nothing that was contrary to the Solemn League and Covenant 'or weaken the vnion & Confidence betwixt the Nations'. The English commissioners promptly informed Speaker Lenthall that they had extracted an undertaking that the king would not be moved away and had made arrangements for a meeting between the two sets of commissioners.[3] This meeting took place on the same night in the meadows between Farnton and Kelham,

1. Bodleian, Tanner MSS., 59, fo. 117; *Cal.SPD. 1645–7*, p. 433.
2. *The Scots Cabinett Opened* (4 August 1648), BL., E.456(30), p. 3.
3. Surrey R.O., Guildford Muniment Room, 111/10/4.

when the English commissioners received further assurances even though they were denied access to the king.[4] It is not unreasonable to doubt, as others did at the time,[5] whether the Scots were quite so astonished as they claimed to be at the king's appearance in their midst. In a letter of 23 April Robert Baillie had reported a rumour 'that the King resolves to goe to the Scots army, knowing their compassionate hearts and love to the King, if he would doe his duetie'. In a later letter of 26 June, however, Baillie seems more conscious of the dangers threatened than of the opportunities presented, by Charles's coming to the Scots. In it he cites a letter from the king to the marquis of Ormond in Ireland confiding to him 'his designe to go to the Scotts army . . . to work them to his designes, since the Parliament were resolute to ruine him'.[6] Whatever the king's intentions, his presence with the Scots was shortly to become a major disruptive element in Anglo-Scottish relations, adding to the numerous other long-standing causes of discord which combined to bring the two nations to the brink of war in 1646 and over that brink in 1648.

Religion was one source of contention. Both the Scottish kirk and nation, declared the Scottish Lord Chancellor, the earl of Loudoun, had been 'scandalized and grieved in the matter of Religion'. Admittedly the use of the Presbyterian Directory of Worship had been ordained, but the Book of Common Prayer was still in use in many places in England. The establishment of classical presbyteries was painfully slow, delaying that religious unity between the two nations which the Scots saw as the prime aim of the Solemn League and Covenant of 1643. Sectaries were tolerated rather than put down and heresy and blasphemy abounded. There was even a danger that Scotland itself would be infected.[7]

The air of superiority and overweening authority which emanates from some Scottish pronouncements bewailing the inadequacy of the

4. Bodleian, Carte MSS., 80, fos. 429, 431.
5. See, e.g., Henry Marten, *A corrector of the answerer to the speech out of doores* (Edinburgh, 1646), BHPC., pp. 4–5, 9. For a reiteration of denial of prior knowledge by the Scottish Commissioners, see Carte MSS., 80, fos. 488–8(b).
6. Baillie, *Letters*, II, 365, 374–5. The king's letter to Ormond had come into the possession of General Monroe, the Scottish commander in Ireland, who transmitted it to the Committee of Both Kingdoms.
7. For Loudoun's declaration, Bodleian MSS., 59, fos. 736–7. For similar complaints, BL., Add. MSS., 38,847, fos. 9(b), 35; *L.J.*, VIII, 461–2; Rushworth, *Historical Collections*, VI, 236–7, 253–5; Baillie, *Letters*, II, 336–7, 341, 357, 360. Examples of continuing complaints in 1647–8 are *A Declaration of the Representation of the Kirke of Scotland* (25 July 1647), BL., E.400(12), pp. 2–3; *A Declaration and Remonstrance of the present engagement of the Kingdome of Scotland* (17 August 1647), E.402(14), pp. 6–7; *A Declaration and Brotherly Exhortation of the Church of Scotland . . .* (20 August 1647), E.407(24), pp. 1–14; *A Declaration or Remonstrance from the Kingdome of Scotland* (31 January 1648), E.424(5), pp. 1–5; *Rec.CGA. 1646–8*, pp. 289–96.

English religious settlement of 1645–6 must have been a source of extreme irritation to many of the Englishmen to whom they were addressed. But while this is a factor contributing to the estrangement of the two nations, it is important not to overstress it. As the Scottish commissioners in London advised the Commissioners of the General Assembly of the Scottish Church in a letter of 17 September 1646, while the many obstacles to complete Presbyterian uniformity in England were to be regretted, it was also important to bear in mind what had been achieved in England. In their response the Commissioners of the General Assembly paid generous tribute to English progress 'in making so many mountaines plaines, and crooked things straight and laying so fair a foundation for a more perfect building', and emphasizing that the current lack of religious uniformity must not be allowed either to jeopardize Anglo-Scottish unity or to delay the departure of the Scottish army from England.[8] A further statement on 19 December, besides concurring on these points, also anticipated important future differences by deploring current interpretations of the Solemn League and Covenant which emphasized the clause about the preservation of royal authority and soft-pedalled, or even ignored, the rest.[9] That there was much room for disappointment for Scottish Presbyterian evangelists, faced by what they regarded as the deficiencies of the English religious settlement of 1645–6 and the obstacles in the way of further improvement, is beyond dispute. But the leaders of the Scottish kirk are not always given sufficient credit for sympathetic appreciation of the difficulties facing their English brethren and the need to make allowance for the tender consciences of dissidents in matters of ecclesiastical organization, as distinct from fundamental doctrinal issues.

However, the Scots had a multitude of other grounds for complaint. Not the least of these was a spate of anti-Scottish pamphlets criticizing the inactivity of the Scottish army in England.[10] During June 1646 there were reports by the Scottish commissioners in England of 'odious calumnies' spread abroad to the effect that the Scottish parliament had no intention of moving its army from England 'till every farthing that is due . . . be paid', and that the Scots were dragging their feet about the peace propositions to be presented to the king; indeed, that they were enemies to peace, desiring nothing but 'to continue their army in this kingdome for their owne gayne'. Fortunately this particular crisis passed and, on 27 June, the commissioners were able to report general agreement with the English about the propositions, except on a few minor

8. *Rec.CGA. 1646–8*, pp. 57–9, 74–5.
9. Ibid., pp. 148–53; *A Solemne and Seasonable Warning . . .* (December 1646), BL., E.419(34), pp. 1–6.
10. In reference to such complaints, see Baillie, *Letters*, II, 343.

points which could be easily settled.[11] However, the flow of anti-Scottish publications continued and there were further Scottish complaints through the summer and autumn of 1646.[12]

Calumnies of a different but no less damaging sort were spread by Charles I's two Cavalier attendants, Dr Michael Hudson and John Ashburnham, who had accompanied him from Oxford to Southwell and had been subsequently imprisoned by the Scots. Both later escaped and Ashburnham's experience made him violently anti-Scottish to the end of his days. Both now offered support to the prevailing suspicions that the Scots 'had drawne the King to our army by fair promises; and when we had gotten him, we did use him roughlie as a prisoner'.[13]

Around the same time in April and May 1646 there were two notable occasions for fierce Anglo-Scottish dispute. The first arose from the decision of the Scottish commissioners to print and publish the papers which they had presented to the English parliament detailing Scottish objections to parliament's peace propositions. The publication of the papers before parliament had time to give them proper consideration infuriated MPs who voted on 13 April that the papers should be publicly burnt by the common hangman. Even though this was modified a week later, reserving this humiliating fate for the preface rather than the papers themselves, this was hardly less offensive to the Scots, whose commissioners had received no formal intimation of either decision.[14] They had further serious grounds for complaint early in May, when two of their messengers were detained, the first in London and the second near Newark, en route for Scotland, their letters opened and scrutinized, and their secretary, John Cheisley, subjected to rigorous examination by the English authorities. The Scottish commissioners were unconvinced by the English explanation of the detention of the first messenger and incredulous at the English commissioners' denial of knowledge of the second case.[15] But there was to be a recurrence of

11. Meikle, *Correspondence*, pp. 193–4, 196. For earlier reports about anti-Scottish calumnies, see Baillie, *Letters*, II, 341, 352–3. On debates and delays about the Propositions, Meikle, *Correspondence*, pp. 175, 191; *C.J.*, IV, 545; BL., Add. MSS., 31,116, fo. 296(b); Add. MSS., 10,114, fo. 15(b).

12. BL., Add. MSS., 38,847, fo. 35; Bodleian, Carte MSS., 80, fos. 488–9; *L.J.*, VIII, 461–2; *Some papers given in by the commissioners* (Edinburgh, 1646), BHPC., pp. 16–17; Whitelock, *Memorials*, p. 230 (31 October).

13. Baillie, *Letters*, II, 375. Ashburnham's allegations made in France may have helped to prompt Mazarin's letter to Sir Robert Murray in June 1646 complaining about the Scottish treatment of the king (*Montereul Correspondence*, II, Appendix, 582–3). For Ashburnham's own account of these incidents, see Ashburnham, *Narrative*, II, 72–87.

14. *C.J.*, IV, 507, 517; Rushworth, *Historical Collections*, VI, 253–7; Whitelock, *Memorials*, pp. 206–7 (14 April), 207 (21 April); Meikle, *Correspondence*, pp. 173–4, 174, 176; Baillie, *Letters*, II, 366–7.

15. Bodleian, Tanner MSS., 59, fos. 160, 177, 189–9(b); Carte MSS., 80, fos. 433, 437–8(b); Meikle, *Correspondence*, pp. 180–1, 185.

such incidents in 1647.[16] Somewhat different but no less irritating was the seizure of a printed 'separate' of Lord Chancellor Loudoun's speeches made in October on another matter of Anglo-Scottish discord which will be dealt with later, the problem of whether one or both nations had the right to dispose of the person of the king.[17]

Almost from the time of Scottish entry into the First Civil War, it had been a legitimate Scottish grievance that the English parliament was not living up to its obligation to make appropriate payments to its Scottish allies according to the terms of the treaty of 1643. By the closing months of the war and in those following its end many Scottish soldiers were in a desperate condition, those in Yorkshire being described by the Scottish commissioners in November 1645 as lacking stockings and shoes.[18] Although the English parliament did authorize some payments, the complaints of the Scottish commissioners grew in both frequency and urgency, not failing to make the point that the English soldiers were paid far more promptly than the Scottish.[19] English replies range between the conciliatory and the positively insulting. On 14 February 1646 parliament ordered £15,000 monthly (out of the £30,000 due according to treaty) to be paid to the Scottish army before Newark, stipulating, however, that none of this should go to the supernumerary Scottish cavalry, whose numbers should be reduced to those stipulated in the Anglo-Scottish treaty. The answer of the English commissioners at Lincoln on 15 April to a further Scottish complaint was more brusque and peremptory. Ignoring the Scottish commissioners' protests to the contrary, the supernumerary horse were described as 'vseless in the seruice against Newark and haue neuer done any duty', adding darkly that 'what they haue done we shall leaue for another time'.[20]

The Scottish commissioners' letters of complaint display a commendable appreciation of the fact that their soldiers were not the only sufferers and that, as a consequence of the English parliament's failure to pay them what was due to them, many country folk suffered grievous hardships from free quartering. On the other side it is cheering to find a letter from the county committee of Nottinghamshire to the Scottish

16. Another Scottish messenger was intercepted at Stilton in June 1647 (Bodleian, Tanner MSS., 58, fos. 290, 345; *L.J.*, IX, 302; *HMC., 6th Report Appendix (House of Lords Cal. 1647)*, p. 184. In August Cheisley himself was temporarily detained (Tanner MSS., 58, fos. 468, 504–4(b); *L.J.*, IX, 387; *HMC., 6th Report* . . . , p. 192).
17. *Some papers given in by the commissioners* (1646), BHPC., p. 17; Meikle, *Correspondence*, p. 223. On the controversy over the disposal of the king, see below, pp. 311–13.
18. BL., Add. MSS., 37,978, fo. 34.
19. E.g., Bodleian, Tanner MSS., 59, fos. 71, 394; Tanner MSS., 60, fo. 411; Carte MSS., 80, fos. 389, 411, 413, 441–1(b); Meikle, *Correspondence*, pp. 156, 175, 193. For a similar complaint about the supply of the Scottish army in Ireland, see the letter of 13 November 1646 from Cheisley printed in *Rec.CGA. 1646–8*, pp. 577–9.
20. Tanner MSS., 60, fo. 443; Carte MSS., 80, fo. 405. For other English complaints about supernumerary horse, see ibid., fos. 393, 405–5(b).

commander, the earl of Leven, on 3 February 1646, which is a model of politeness and sympathetic understanding.[21] On 17 February, however, the Scottish commissioners wrote to Lieutenant General Leslie mentioning an abundance of complaints about the behaviour of Scottish soldiers in Yorkshire and asking the General to take decisive remedial action. They also enjoined him to make clear to his soldiers the condign punishment they were to expect if they offered any injury to country people's goods or persons, as well as to announce in the localities where his soldiers were quartered that complaints would be heard and swiftly and justly dealt with by the Scottish military authorities, an order which Leslie seems promptly to have put into effect.[22] But, as Sir George Vane had observed as long ago as December 1644 in a letter to his father from Durham: 'The truth is the soldiers are our masters and do what they list'.[23] Among the complaints of the Yorkshire committee and of others against Scottish quartering practices in the summer of 1646 were wholesale destruction of meadows, wasting of corn, payment (when indeed it was made) for horse and other meat at niggardly rates, resale at a profit of provisions exacted by way of free quarter, and soldiers demanding extravagant fare from their hosts.[24] Plain food was not good enough for them, complained Thomas Smallwood of the Scottish soldiers quartered in Cleveland in May 1646. 'They will not eat either salt beef, or milk or butter, nor drink any small beer, but force the poor men to buy them mutton, lamb and chickens, and ale in abundance.' There were similar complaints to the Yorkshire MPs in May, and from the Yorkshire county committee in June.[25] Nevertheless, it is difficult not to sympathize with the case put by the Scottish commissioners on 11 July emphasizing that if the Scottish soldiers 'knew of any other way to keepe themselves from disbanding or starving but by taking quarter when no money is provided for them, they would most heartily embrace it'. In any case once the money due to them was paid, the Scots would be happy to allow deductions for quartering debts, despite the disparity between the pay of English and Scottish soldiers.[26]

21. Tanner MSS., 60, fo. 402.
22. Meikle, *Correspondence*, pp. 160–1; *Parliamentary History*, XIV, 272. For a later example, Tanner MSS., 59, fo. 394.
23. *Cal.SPD. 1644–5*, p. 174. For similar complaints from Newcastle in November 1644, ibid., pp. 120–1; from Westmorland in the spring of 1645, ibid., pp. 413–14; from Yorkshire in October 1645 and the first half of 1646, Tanner MSS., 59, fos. 195–5(b), 216–16(b), 266, 351–1(b), 366–6(b); Tanner MSS., 60, fos. 556–6(b); Carte MSS., 80, fos. 470(b)–1; Cary, *Memorials*, I, 66–71; *Parliamentary History*, XIV, 85–9; from Northumberland and Durham in July 1646, Tanner MSS., 59, fos. 225, 387–7(b).
24. Carte MSS., 80, fos. 470(b)–1; Cary, *Memorials*, I., 69.
25. Cary, *Memorials*, I, 68–71; Carte MSS., 80, fo. 471.
26. Carte MSS., 80, fos. 394–6(b). See also the Scottish army's Remonstrance of June 1646 (ibid., fos. 443–6). Scottish soldiers besieging Newark were paid only $1\frac{1}{2}$d a day

How efficacious was the machinery for dealing with local complaints? On 6 May 1646 the Nottinghamshire county committee, no longer so tolerant of Scottish quartering practices as it had been in February, reported to the parliamentary committee with the army that Nottinghamshire countrymen 'neither dare complayne nor confesse their greivances'. On 10 April the English parliamentary commissioners similarly complained to the Scottish commissioners of the overawing of local people by the Scottish soldiers quartered on them, which may have prompted the Scottish commissioners to suggest a week later that the forces stationed in places from which complaints were coming might be removed elsewhere in order that 'the Inhabitants may without fear bring in their Complaints'.[27]

But the miseries suffered by the inhabitants of the northern counties extended far beyond being impoverished by Scottish free quartering. To their complaints in May 1646 on this score of quartering malpractices in Yorkshire and Cleveland, some of which have already been noted, Thomas Smallwood and Emmanuel Issacher added a number of violent outrages perpetrated by Scottish soldiers. According to Issacher, 'such are the villanies, outrages, plunderings, strippings, beatings, woundings, besides some rapes and murders, as flesh and blood till now did never endure the like nor free-born Englishmen ever pass by without satisfaction'. Smallwood's account of the outrages in Cleveland was even more explicit. Here Scottish soldiers robbed travellers on the highway so that no-one dared to visit the fairs or markets. They stole horses, and beat the householders, both male and female, with whom they were quartered. The only case, to Smallwood's knowledge, of justice being done on offenders was that of a soldier being shot for killing his landlord in cold blood.[28] 'Cleveland', wrote another observer on 24 May, 'has long lain a-bleeding . . . but alas, it has now even received its death wound'. Five Scottish cavalry regiments were quartered there and were 'as unruly and merciless as . . . Mahometan Tymareots in Candie: there is no safety for any man that has been in parliamentary employment . . . to come amongst them; for they unhorse all such, and rob them too and . . . tell them that it is not fit that a base roundhead should either ride or have money in his purse'.[29] The language suggests that some of these outrages may have been committed by former Cavalier soldiers who had entered the Scottish service; another cause, as will be seen later, of strained relations between the two realms.[30] Be this as it may,

---

and their English counterparts 8d a day and 12d every third day. The pay of both was heavily in arrears.
27. Tanner MSS., 59, fo. 133; Carte MSS., 80, fos. 401, 409.
28. Cary, *Memorials*, I, 66–71.
29. Ibid., I, 64–5.
30. See below, pp. 310–11.

such incidents contributed powerfully to anti-Scottish feeling, especially in the north, and were recalled with trepidation when the Scots again invaded – this time, on the other side – two years later.

In June complaints were heard in the House of Commons from northern county committees 'of many foule & horrible Outrages Committed there by ye Scottish Army . . . by ravishing of women, Burning & hanging up . . . both men & women till they did declare where their Monny was Or . . . gave them what they would have'.[31] Among the most horrible crimes alleged against Scottish soldiers in the north and mentioned in a letter of 2 June from the Scottish commissioners as particularly angering English MPs were the cutting off of a man's hand for endeavouring to rescue his goods from plunder, the beating out of another's brains and the murder of a defenceless woman.[32] In a Remonstrance of 24 November the Commissioners of the General Assembly of the Scottish church felt bound not only to sing the praises of those Scottish soldiers 'who . . . walk . . . as souldiers of Jesus Christ', but also to denounce those of them who 'walk lowsly and disorderly, ryotously spending what they violentlie spoile, and making the lives of the commons bitter . . . by their insolencies and oppressions'.[33] To judge by the above complaints, exaggerated though some of them may have been, they were putting it very mildly.

Shocking though the above outrages might seem, it was events in the small Yorkshire town of Tickhill which acquired a nationwide notoriety during 1646. Even though the cases in this 'poore town . . . by the inhabitantes given up for lost'[34] were certainly no more, and probably less, horrendous than those in Cleveland and a number of other parts, what particularly aroused English ire were the allegedly partial judgements of a Scottish military tribunal in the cases coming before it. Of seven Tickhill cases which came before the Council of War of Colonel Frazer's regiment at Laughton in Yorkshire on 21 April, three were of soldiers charged with rape, all of whom were acquitted. One of them, William Frazier, was declared not guilty in deed if not in intention, and the woman herself expressed the view that he had already been punished enough. Andrew Frazier was technically not guilty of rape, but had persuaded the girl's father to allow his daughter to lie with him and claimed that 'the woman her selfe was willing to it'. His offence, however, was judged to be sufficiently serious for him to be sentenced to hang by the hands for two hours every day except Sunday until his regiment left Tickhill. Accused of raping widow Crompton's daughter

31. BL., Add. MSS., 31,116, fos. 272(b)–3.
32. Meikle, *Correspondence*, p. 189; *HMC., 13th. Report Appendix Portland MSS.*, I, 365.
33. *Rec.CGA. 1646–8*, p. 121.
34. Bodleian, Tanner MSS., 60, fo. 415.

in Tickhill, John Frazier was acquitted of rape but punished for his lesser offences.

> He denies hee ever knew her carnally, but shee being sitting in a chair and markeing some sport with her, and that both of them kissed one another, and that hee had some intention to haue had carnall dealing with her, and that hee was between her leggs, confesses the woman refused . . . vnlesse hee made her promise of marriage, to which hee answered that hee could not grant and that hee promised to give her contentment some other way, but for any carnall copulation denied it.

Three soldiers were acquitted of assaulting male inhabitants of Tickhill and the only offender to suffer the supreme penalty was one Robert Maxwell who was found guilty of robbery with violence. On 4 May the English parliamentary commissioners complained about the alleged partiality, procedure and membership of the tribunal or Council of War, all the members of which were officers in Colonel Frazer's regiment, as well as about its failure to deal with 'Offenders of greater quality'.[35]

As one English pamphleteer admitted, the English failure to pay the Scots according to agreement was an extenuating factor when considering the excesses of free quartering but this hardly extended to rapes, murders and other crimes.[36] That such incidents heightened the danger of clashes between the Scots and the complaining northerners is hardly surprising, though the latter were at an obvious disadvantage faced by a well-armed and well-trained soldiery. On 11 May the Yorkshire county committee warned the government that 'wee doe not see how tis possible to prevent tumoultuous riseings and mischeivous effectes' in the county.[37] On 24 October the Scottish commissions wrote to the Speaker of the House of Lords, gravely worried at rumours in the north of country people designing 'to surprise and injure our Forces, as they lie dispersed in their severall quarters'.[38] Earlier than this, the much-enduring inhabitants of Tickhill had not been entirely passive in the face of Scottish provocation. So at least it would seem from a petition two years later in July 1648, from a Scottish officer, Major David Melvin, for £110. 15s. damages which had been promised him in 1646 by the English parliamentary commissioners with the army before Newark. This was in respect of losses including four horses, horse furniture and weapons, which he had suffered at Tickhill, along

35. Bodleian, Carte MSS., 80, fos. 415–17, 423–3(b).
36. [Edward Bowles], *Manifest Truths* (December 1646), BHPC., pp. 40–1.
37. Tanner MSS., 59, fos. 218–18(b).
38. *Some papers given in by the commissioners* . . . (Edinburgh, 1646), BHPC., pp. 14–15. The commissioners hoped that northern county committees would take this in hand rather than Scottish soldiers having to take action.

with 'the barbarous and vnchristian vsage' of him by some of the local inhabitants. Having been assaulted by one group with pitchforks and halberts and left lying in his own blood, he was then attacked by another, robbed of his clothes and forced to walk on foot to Pontefract 'which well nigh putt a period to your petitioners daies'.[39]

However, it was not only from outraged civilians that the admittedly impoverished Scottish soldiers had to fear violence. During the summer and autumn of 1646 there was an almost constant threat of clashes between English and Scottish armed forces in the north over rival claims on quartering.[40] The Scottish forces, and indeed the local countrymen, had to contend with competition for quarter from local Yorkshire cavalry and units both of the New Model Army and of the army of the Northern Association.[41] The Presbyterian leader Denzil Holles was full of praise for the tact and restraint shown by the commander of the latter force, another political Presbyterian, Colonel-General Sydenham Poynz. The pressure put on the Scots by the New Model Army was, on the other hand, in Holles's view, part of a design by his political opponents to bring about conflict between the two nations.[42]

Serious though these dangers were, disputes over quartering were only one reason for possible clashes between the armies. On 28 April the Scottish commissioners reported to the Committee of Estates at Edinburgh their alarm at the news that 'the care of reducing Newarke as well as Oxford is recommended to Sir Thomas Fairfax'. This would create a very real danger that the Scottish army would be uncomfortably sandwiched between Fairfax's forces to the south and the army of the Northern Association to the north. According to later dispatches from the commissioners on 12 May and 2 June, it was also being urged in English government circles that an additional pretext for Fairfax's proposed move northwards was the need to put down the disorders of Scottish soldiers in the northern counties.[43] As late as September 1646 Robert Baillie was referring gloomily in a letter to William Murray to

---

39. HLRO., MP., 25/7/1648.
40. See the fear expressed by the Scottish commissioners at Newcastle on 28 May (Tanner MSS., 59, fo. 254; see also Carte MSS., 80, fos. 441–1(b)).
41. On competition from Yorkshire troops, Tanner MSS., 59, fos. 185, 195–5(b), 216–16(b); from the New Model, *Some papers given in by the commissioners* (Edinburgh, 1646), BHPC., pp. 14–15, 17; from the Northern Association army, Tanner MSS., 59, fos. 243–3(b), 266, 320, 334–4(b), 571.
42. Maseres, *Select Tracts*, I, 225–6. For an example of Poynz's discretion and restraint, see his letter to Speaker Lenthall of 23 October (Tanner MSS., 59, fo. 571). Holles's Scottish associate Robert Baillie shared his conspiracy interpretation of quartering clashes, but seems inclined to ascribe a somewhat different role to Poynz (Baillie, *Letters*, II, 375).
43. Meikle, *Correspondence*, pp. 178–9, 183–4, 189–90.

the very real dangers of an outbreak of war between the two kingdoms, with disastrous consequences for all except those English malcontents who wished nothing better than to embroil the two kingdoms in conflict as part of a radical design to extirpate monarchy altogether.[44] It was probably with some relief that the Scottish commissioners reported to Edinburgh on 27 October that the English parliament had decided both that Fairfax's forces should not march further north and that some money should be made available to meet the needs of the Scottish army.[45]

The recruitment of ex-Cavalier soldiers in the Scottish army, especially after the surrender of Newark in May 1646, was doubtless an especially disruptive factor in the clashes between Scottish and English soldiers, as well as heightening the fear that the Scottish army might be used to further royalist ends once Charles had surrendered himself to the Scots. There were indeed ex-Cavalier soldiers in the Scottish army even before Charles's arrival at Southwell and the fall of Newark. On 7 April a letter from the Scottish commissioners mentions complaints that such Cavaliers were influential in causing soldiers to be billeted on well-affected householders while malignants got off scot-free,[46] and on 10 April the English parliamentary commissioners complained of the plundering and violent acts of ex-Cavalier soldiers sheltered by the Scottish army, 'and that many of them publiquely declare their Hatred to our Cause, and theyr desire to serue the Enemy'.[47] On 17 April the Scottish commissioners provided a list of fifty-seven such persons, including many ex-royalist officers of different ranks from colonel downwards and three former governors of royalist garrisons.[48]

On 13 May, following a demand from the English parliamentary commissioners two days earlier, the earl of Leven ordered that no officers under his command should have any dealings with anyone who had formerly served against the English parliament and that all such persons already with his army should be discharged forthwith.[49] There is abundant testimony to the role played by such 'roaring soldiers . . . formerly belonging to Newark and other garrisons of the kings' in encouraging Scottish soldiers 'to committ fearfull outrages' as well as

44. Baillie, *Letters*, II, 395–6.
45. BL., Add. MSS., 37,978, fos. 127–7(b); Meikle, *Correspondence*, p. 224. See also *The Answer of the Commons . . . To the Scots Commissioners Papers* (hereafter cited as *The Answer*) (4 December 1646), BHPC., pp. 47–8.
46. Meikle, *Correspondence*, p. 173.
47. Bodleian, Carte MSS., 80, fo. 397. Some of the outrages in Cleveland mentioned above (p. 306) were certainly the work of ex-Cavaliers in Colonel Vandruske's regiment.
48. Ibid., fos. 407, 421–1(b). Compare Baillie's assertion on 24 April that there was no shelter in the Scottish army for ex-royalist soldiers or even for the king himself, unless they were prepared to take the Covenant (Baillie, *Letters*, II, 368).
49. Bodleian, Tanner MSS., 59, fo. 184; Carte MSS., 80, fo. 439. For a letter on behalf of the Scottish Commissioners on this matter, see Tanner MSS., 59, fo. 198.

inciting them against parliament.[50] However, in a letter to the Speaker of the House of Commons on 11 July, the Scottish commissioners protested that effective action had been taken to expel not only ex-royalists but also reformadoes from their army.[51] In general the English parliament was probably hardly less justified in its alarm about renegade Cavaliers sheltering in the Scottish army in 1646 than it was to be two years later by the protection which the Engager-dominated Scottish parliament was to accord to royalist refugees in Scotland.

A major issue which probably contributed more than any other to bringing the two nations to the brink of war was the dispute about the right to decide on the disposal of the king. On 6 May the House of Commons voted that this should rest solely with the English parliament and that Charles should be handed over by the Scots and be confined in Warwick Castle, although the force of this resolution was weakened by the Lords' unwillingness to go along with it. A week later the Commons agreed to put their case at a conference between the Houses, urging that for the king to remain in the hands of what was described as a mercenary Scottish army in England in the pay of the English parliament was not only dishonourable to England but also dangerous, especially since so many ex-Cavaliers were serving with the Scottish army. When in England the king should be disposed of solely by the English parliament.[52]

To do the Scottish case justice, it needs to be appreciated that, unlike the English parliamentarians, the Scots were not claiming an exclusive right to dispose of the king. What they desired was that decisions on this should be taken jointly by both nations on account both of the obligations of the Solemn League and Covenant and treaty of alliance and of the fact that Charles was king of Scotland as well as of England. The English case, resting mainly on Charles's current presence on English soil, was rejected by the Scots on the grounds that 'allegeance hath no limitation of place' and that it was unacceptable for the realm where the king currently happened to be to inhibit him from exercising his kingly office in respect of the realm from which he was absent.[53] While recognizing the legitimate Scottish interest in Charles as their king, the English insisted on the fundamental difference between that interest when the king was in Scotland and when he was in England.[54] The

50. E.g., Tanner MSS., 59, fos. 266, 366–6(b); HMC., 13th Report Appendix Portland MSS., I, 365; Cary, Memorials, I, 82–3; Meikle, Correspondence, p. 189.
51. Tanner MSS., 59, fos. 394(b)–5.
52. C.J., IV, 541, 543; BL., Add. MSS., 31,116, fos. 268(b), 269–9(b); Whitelock, Memorials, p. 209 (6 May); Montereul Correspondence, II, Appendix, 580–1 (letter from Sir Robert Murray to M. du Bosc).
53. Some papers given in by the commissioners . . . (October 1646), BHPC., pp. 7–9; The Answer, pp. 40–2.
54. The Answer, pp. 6–9, 20–3.

radical Independent MP, Thomas Chaloner, developed an ingenious theoretical argument in defence of this position. Echoing the familiar notion of the king's two bodies, Chaloner maintained that the kingly office must be distinguished from the person of the king; that 'Persona sequitur locum; and his Person must be disposed of by the Supreame power of that Countrey wheresoever he shall happen to abide'. English people, he concluded, would have thought it very strange that they could not dispose of the king's person without Scottish consent, though, needless to say, he omitted to mention that many English people would be shocked by the very idea that anyone, English or Scottish, might dispose of the king's person.[55]

The Scottish case was expounded ably and succinctly along the lines outlined above in three speeches made before a committee of both Houses in the Painted Chamber by the Scottish Chancellor Loudoun between 1 and 10 October.[56] The need for a joint Anglo-Scottish decision was firmly argued. As to what could be done with the king, Loudoun was adamant about the undesirability of his going to Scotland, where 'the bloody, barbarous Irish, banded with a wicked crew of Malignants, possessed the mountains and never conquered part of that Kingdome'. It would surely be far better and, as Loudoun argued with astonishing optimism, far more likely to produce royal co-operation over the Newcastle Propositions if Charles were to be received in London 'with freedome, honour and safety'. In propounding this solution, the Scottish Chancellor specifically rejected the stock English objection that the only people likely to profit from it would be English malignant royalists who would exploit the opportunities it presented for tumults and disturbances. Needless to say, he was also scathing about the English contention that the Scottish covenanting army was a mercenary force in English pay and as such not responsible only to the Scottish parliament.[57] Loudoun concluded the last of his three addresses on 10 October by emphasizing that just as the Scots had not fawned on the king at the height of his power, so were they now sensible of the need to preserve his honour when his fortunes were at a low ebb. Most of his arguments were reiterated in a paper from the Scottish commissioners on 20 October,[58] which also stressed that the disposal of the king by only one of the two nations would be contrary to the Solemn League

55. Thomas Chaloner, *An Answer to the Scotch Papers* (1646), BHPC., pp. 2–8. For scepticism about the likelihood of such an Anglo-Scottish joint decision, see Henry Marten, *A corrector of the answerer . . .* (Edinburgh, 1646), BHPC., p. 7. On the king's two bodies, see Ashton, *Civil War*, pp. 184–5.

56. *Several speeches spoken by John Campbell earl of Loudoun* (Edinburgh, 1646), BHPC., pp. 21–8.

57. On this point, see also *Some papers given in . . .* , pp. 6–7; *The Answer*, pp. 34–5.

58. *Some papers given in . . .* , pp. 1–14.

and Covenant. The point was sound enough, but it touched English susceptibilities on the raw. Many Englishmen were irritated beyond measure by the use of the Covenant to justify Scottish interference in what were regarded as autonomously English affairs. If all matters covered by the Solemn League and Covenant were bound to be settled by the will of both nations, argued one English paper, the Scots would be given an unacceptably large say in an unacceptably wide variety of English affairs. The English would not think of making such demands on the Scots; nor should they on the English.[59]

A shrewd point was made in addition to the above arguments, in the enormous paper issued by the House of Commons on 28 November, the day on which it resolved that Scotland should have no say in the disposal of the king.[60] Were not Scottish arguments against unilateral disposal of the king applicable to their own actions in receiving Charles at Southwell and in marching away with him without proper consultation with the English parliament?[61] It was a widely held belief among English Independents that the king had come to the Scots as part of a prearranged plan.[62] The Scots had been more than a trifle disingenuous both in their feigned surprise at the king's first coming to them and in their transparent pretext for subsequently moving north with him.[63] In any case, his coming and leaving with them of his own free will, as the Scots claimed, was hardly an argument for him to be permitted to go wherever he wished, since both were part of 'a designe on his part against the good of both Kingdomes'.[64] The lengthy paper concluded, not without irony, that only when each nation enjoyed its peculiar rights untramelled would Anglo-Scottish unity be 'strong and . . . lasting'.[65] By the end of 1646 it was neither.

The dispute about the disposal of the king, as one royalist pamphlet later put it, 'as if he were a Child, a Ward, or an Ideot',[66] threatened not only the total disintegration of the Anglo-Scottish alliance, but even war between the former allies. Although this latter outcome was avoided, the dispute, along with other issues of contention between the kingdoms, is of considerable importance in considering the seeds of the later Scottish Engagement with the king. But it is also important to consider these developments against the background of 1646 and not to read back too much of 1648 into them. Scotland was not yet ready for the

59. *The Answer*, pp. 10–16, 43–6.
60. Ibid., passim; *C.J.*, IV, 729, 730.
61. *The Answer*, pp. 56–7, 60–2.
62. See Marten, *A corrector of the answerer* . . . pp. 4, 9.
63. *The Answer*, pp. 47–54.
64. *The Answer*, pp. 61–2.
65. Ibid., p. 66.
66. *Lex Talionis or a Declamation Against Mr Challener* (5 July 1647), BL., E.396(20), pp. 2–3.

Engagement nor were English royalists ready to link their cause with the Scots. In a letter of 26 January 1647 Robert Baillie argued that Charles I's chief error and that which had contributed most to his undoing was his expectation that the Scots would 'espouse his quarrell'. If the king had only made significant concessions, perhaps even short of taking the Covenant himself, but at least allowing it to be incorporated in statutes in both his kingdoms, things might have been different; 'certainly', in Baillie's view at least, 'Scotland had been for him as one man'.[67] As to the royalists, many of them saw Charles's action in putting himself into dependence on the Scots as a disastrous mistake. The opinion of the exiled courtier Endymion Porter expressed in a letter to Secretary Nicholas on 19 January 1647 flatly contradicts that of Baillie. Porter averred that it would have made no difference whatever concessions the king might have made to the Scots, for 'they would have doon like Scotts had hee doon all the unworthie acts they could have desierd of him'.[68] This view is shared in a sharply critical observation by Edward Hyde, who also believed that Charles had made a terrible mistake in throwing himself on the mercy of the Scots.

> . . . For I would rather he should have stayed in Oxford, and after the defending of it to the last biscuit, been taken prisoner with his honest retinue about him, and then relied upon his own virtue in imprisonment than to have thrown himself into the arms of the Scots, who held them not fairly open. . . . I thought it an unkingly thing to ask relief of those who had done all the mischief. . . .[69]

Royalist suspicions about the Scots went beyond high Presbyterian covenanters, and extended to the Hamilton brothers, the duke of Hamilton and the earl of Lanark who, it was later alleged, had added double dealing with the king at Newcastle to their deceits during the First Civil War which had earned Hamilton years of imprisonment in Pendennis Castle.[70]

Charles's own reward for his gross miscalculations was to be told by the Scottish commissioners on 14 January 1647 that the Scots would find it impossible to assist him to regain his authority in England if he refused to accept the Newcastle Propositions and that to come to Scotland without doing this would be dangerous both to him and what was left of Anglo-Scottish unity. If he did come without making this concession, it would be necessary to put a guard on his person, 'to

---

67. Baillie, *Letters*, III, 4.
68. *Nicholas Papers*, p. 71.
69. *Clarendon SP.*, II, 338–9.
70. Oxford, Worcester College pamphlet collection, *Digitus Dei Or Gods Justice upon Treachery and Treason* (1649), pp. 15–16; *The manifold Practices and Attempts of the Hamiltons* (23 May 1648), pp. 21–2.

preserve you in safety and your kingdom in peace'.[71] Indeed, they had already increased his guard at Newcastle as a precaution against his escaping.[72] However, the king's failure to set the English and the Scots at each other's throats ought not to be regarded as indicating that the Scottish decision to hand him over in return for part at least of what was due to them from the English parliament was the product of an amicable agreement between allies. There was much acrimonious haggling over the amount of money which was actually owed to the Scots. Following original estimates by the Scottish commissioners in August 1646 that the net sums due, including deductions for quartering debts, varied between about £1,300,000 and £1,245,000,[73] there followed a process of hard and realistic bargaining which did nothing to improve Anglo-Scottish relations. Certainly the first English offer of £100,000 down and a further £100,000 on the departure of the Scottish army was derisory; as niggardly as the original Scottish estimates had been overinflated. The Scots countered with a demand for £600,000 of which half was to be a down payment. Ultimately they accepted an offer of £400,000, payable in instalments, a sum which the Scottish commissioners had previously decided would be the least they would accept.[74] But there was still scope for further misunderstanding and the Scots were particularly worried by the English insistence that the garrison towns occupied by the Scottish army were not 'cautionary towns' and should not therefore be held by them until the agreed payments had been made.[75] Mutual distrust about the proper observance of terms may also have been reflected and formulated in arrangements on 19 and 24 December for exchange of hostages as pledges that each nation would fulfil its part of the bargain.[76] The resolution of the House of Commons on Christmas Eve thanking the Scottish commissioners for their services was no doubt prompted more by relief than by anything else;[77] a relief

71. Burnet, *Lives of the Hamiltons*, pp. 394–5. On 16 January there was a declaration of the kingdom of Scotland that, in the event of the king's refusing to accept the Propositions, every effort should be made to strengthen Anglo-Scottish accord and to offer further assurances against a separate peace being made (Bodleian, Carte MSS., 80, fo. 527). See also the Scottish parliament's letter of intent of the same date (ibid., fos. 531–2).

72. *Montereul Correspondence*, I, 378, 381. For an abortive plan in late December and early January for Charles to escape from Newcastle in a Dutch vessel, see F. Peck (ed.), *Desiderata Curiosa* (1735), II, 31–3.

73. BL., Add. MSS., 31,116, fo. 281; Add. MSS., 10,114, fo. 17; *C.J.*, IV, 655–6; Bodleian, Carte MSS., 80, fos. 490–1, 492–3; Meikle, *Correspondence*, pp. 204–6, 208–12. The total included the enormous sum of £60,000 for interest chargeable for payments not made at the contracted time.

74. *C.J.*, IV, 659, 663; BL., Add. MSS., 31,116, fo. 282(b); Add. MSS., 10,114, fos. 17(b)–18; Meikle, *Correspondence*, pp. 208–9.

75. Meikle, *Correspondence*, pp. 210–12, 214.

76. *L.J.*, VIII, 618–19, 641–2; *C.J.*, V, 36–8; *Cal.SPD. 1645–7*, p. 499.

77. *C.J.*, V, 27–8; BL., Add. MSS., 31,116, fo. 294(b).

which was shared by the staunch parliamentary Presbyterian allies of the Scots since they were all too aware of what their association with them was costing them in general popularity.

The origins of the Engagement

It will be recalled that the main obstacle to the achievement by the Scots of their essential war aims was Charles's antipathy to the Presbyterian religion. This made him impervious to the persuasions of widely different personages, including the queen, the French ambassadors in London and Edinburgh, the Scottish earls of Loudoun, Traquair and Lanark, the Scottish commissioners in England and the aged moderator of the General Assembly of the Scottish Church, Alexander Henderson.[78] But it did not inhibit him, desperate as his condition was in 1646, from trying to win over the Scots, despite his belief that, as he put it in letters to Lords Jermyn and Culpepper and Jack Ashburnham in August, 'no engagement will serve them but such as I shall never be able to retyre from'; and more especially the establishment of a religion which he regarded as inimical to monarchy.[79] There was as yet no clear antici-pation of the readiness of the Engagers to espouse the royal cause in return for a minimum of concessions; not even for the abolition of episcopacy in England. As Baillie put it rhetorically in a letter of 18 August 1646: 'Will that plumm please Scotland so weell as to make them joyne with the Malignants against England?' – as indeed they were to do in 1648. No, as Baillie reaffirmed in November, the king's position was desperate 'through his unexampled obstinacie. Againe, I tell yow . . . the Covenant is his safety; nothing less will doe it.'[80] For Charles, of course, this price was too high, and he held on until December 1647 when the main concessions were made not by him but by the Scottish Engagers. But far from ranging the Scottish nation behind him, the Engagement split that nation asunder.

From the middle of 1646 both Bellièvre and Montereul were search-ing for a possible nucleus for a royalist party in Scotland, a successor to

78. For the efforts of the queen and the French ambassadors, see above, pp. 10–11, 273, 283; also *Montereul Correspondence*, I, 221–2, 333–5, 358–63. For the requests of the Scottish commissioners in June 1646, ibid., I, 209–10. For the offer from the Scottish army in the same month, Bodleian, Carte MSS., 80, fos. 447, 448. For the persuasions of the Scottish earls, *Montereul Correspondence*, I, 222, 400; Burnet, *Lives of the Hamiltons*, pp. 386–8, 392–3. For Henderson's conversations with Charles at New-castle in June, Bodleian, Clarendon MSS., 28, fos. 78–80, 82–3.
79. *Clarendon SP.*, II, 242–4, 247–8. For a similar point by Bellièvre in a dispatch of 20 September, see *Montereul Correspondence*, I, 263–4.
80. Baillie, *Letters*, II, 389, 410.

the vanquished Montrosians[81] and, as such, quite distinct from both the Hamiltonian and Argyll factions. However, the main stumbling-block remained the king's refusal to accept the Covenant and the permanent establishment of a Presbyterian ecclesiastical polity in England.[82] Charles, however, probably recognized much better than the two French diplomats did that his chief hope lay with the duke of Hamilton and his brother the earl of Lanark, and in October he took some trouble to dissuade Hamilton from leaving the country and to assure him, through Sir Robert Murray, of his unwillingness to credit scandalous reports about Hamiltonian ambitions and disloyalty.[83] Nevertheless, the limits of Hamiltonian acquiescence at this time were demonstrated in a letter of 8 December in which Lanark endeavoured to persuade the king that to yield over the Covenant and other religious issues was essential to his interest. However, even given such concessions, which Charles was not in any case prepared to make, the predicted Scottish response would amount to less than the armed intervention which he was seeking, and was later to obtain from the Engagers at a much lower price.[84] At this juncture therefore the same religious obstacles which prevented the Scottish covenanters from falling in with the king's desires prevailed also with the Hamiltons, even if for reasons of state rather than of religious conviction. Such objections were also decisive in preventing anything coming from the offer which Bellièvre claimed to have negotiated at the beginning of 1647 with a number of officers in the Scottish army, including some governors of fortresses, to place their forces and fortresses at the king's disposal in return for a royal promise to establish Presbyterianism permanently in England.[85]

For a brief spell between mid-February and early June 1647 Scottish worries about the king seemed to be over with Charles in the safe hands of their English Presbyterian associates at Holdenby. That Scottish horror at Cornet Joyce's abduction of the king on 4 June was not less than that of the English Presbyterians is clear from a formal Remonstrance by the Scottish commissioners and an address by the earl of Lauderdale to a committee of both Houses in the Painted Chamber on 7 June, which stressed that the Scots would, if necessary, be prepared to engage in joint action with the English parliament to rescue the king from the army;[86] more especially since another Scottish nobleman, the

81. For suggestions by Bellièvre that Charles should take refuge in the highlands, where he would be safe, at least for the winter, see *Montereul Correspondence*, I, 290, 362.
82. See, e.g., *Montereul Correspondence*, I, 287–90, 294, 359–60.
83. Burnet, *Lives of the Hamiltons*, pp. 372–3, 374–6; *Hamilton Papers*, p. 119.
84. Burnet, *Lives of the Hamiltons*, pp. 386–8.
85. *Montereul Correspondence*, I, 382–3, 392.
86. *Parliamentary History*, XV, 401–6. For other expressions of Scottish disapproval, see Cary, *Memorials*, I, 232–3; Bell, *Memorials*, I, 354; and (later) the Scottish commission-

earl of Dunfermline, had disclosed on the king's authority that Charles had been removed unwillingly from Holdenby.[87]

While Clarendon was perhaps a trifle premature in seeing in the angry Scottish response to the abduction of the king the origins of the later Engagement,[88] the incident certainly cannot be left out of account in any consideration of factors creating the atmosphere and mood which made the Engagement possible. It was, moreover, ultimately to play a crucial part in the ideology of the Engagers, as witness a declaration of the Scottish Committee of Estates on 21 July 1648 which indignantly recalled the events in which 'a party . . . commanded by a Taylor, a Cornet of theirs, one *Joyce*, violently seized upon the Person of the King'.[89] Scottish uneasiness was compounded when the king clearly appeared to prefer residing with the army to being in parliament's care at Holdenby[90] and matters were made worse by an incident on 31 July, when the earl of Lauderdale, one of the Scottish commissioners in England, was denied access to the king at Woburn. Lauderdale was peremptorily ordered by the soldiers there to get up from his bed in his lodgings and be gone.[91]

These events occurred during the brief counter-revolutionary ascendancy in London after 26 July, when circumstances could hardly have been more propitious for a Scottish invasion. Before the incident at Woburn Lauderdale had succeeded in meeting the king at Latimers and, as Bellièvre reported on 29 July, had obtained from him assurances which would strengthen the case for Scottish intervention.[92] The Scots were also in close accord with the aims of the London counter-revolutionaries. For example, the petition from young men and apprentices on the eve of the coup of 26 July contained a number of demands which were meat and drink to the Scottish covenanters: among them, the upholding of the Solemn League and Covenant; the suppression of sectarian conventicles and an end to indiscriminate religious toleration; the disbandment of the New Model Army; and, not

ers' letter of 5 November (*A Letter from the Scots Commissioners* (20 December 1647), BL., E.420(5), pp. 1–3).

87. *A true Copy of his Maiesties Message . . .* (8 June 1647), BL., E.391(8).
88. Clarendon, *Rebellion*, IV, 256.
89. *A Declaration of the Committee of Estates . . .* (21 July 1648), BL., E.453(32), p. 5. For an earlier denunciation, see *A Declaration and Remonstrance . . . of the Kingdome of Scotland* (17 August 1647), E.402(14), title page and pp. 4–5.
90. See Charles's correspondence with Lanark on this subject (Burnet, *Lives of the Hamiltons*, pp. 402–4). For an unusual Scottish view that Charles was far better off with the army, see *HMC., Mar and Kellie MSS.*, I, 204–5.
91. *L.J.*, IX, 367–8; *C.J.*, V, 263; *Parliamentary History*, XVI, 201–3; *HMC., 6th Report (House of Lords Cal. 1647)*, p. 191; *A Letter from the Commissioners of Scotland . . .* (11 August 1647), BL., E.400(33), pp. 1–8; *The Votes of both Houses in Answer to . . . the Scots Commissioners* (1 August 1647), E.401(6), pp. 1–6.
92. *Montereul Correspondence*, II, 210.

least, the punishment of all who were guilty of 'dividing the King from his people or one of his Kingdomes from another'.[93]

The alternative to a Scottish invasion, as Montereul coolly and judiciously pointed out in a dispatch to Mazarin on 3 August, was for the Scots to sit still and quietly reap the benefits arising from the existence of a truncated English parliament which viewed the Scots with favour. In any case, Montereul had always been sceptical about the Scottish ability and will to mount an effective invasion even in these unusually favourable circumstances. He was also well aware of the danger of a reversal of fortunes in London, which was in fact to occur only three days later.[94] Of course, for the Scots to sit still was the last thing that some royalist militants desired, being convinced that the king's main hope rested in Scottish military intervention on his behalf. As one of them observed, despite the differences between them, the fortunes of king and Scots were indissolubly linked. The king had no chance of recovering his power without Scottish aid, which it was in the Scottish interest to accord to him. For had it not been the object of the English army and its Independent allies 'utterly to banish all *Scotch* Interest out of *England*', in which campaign the crushing of the parliamentary Presbyterians had been a vital element? The army and the Independents were anti-monarchical, and the Scots ought never to forget that, by that very Covenant which they were so zealous to maintain, they were also bound to safeguard the king's person and authority. Moreover, the Scots should reflect that the surest and most honourable way of laying their hands on the arrears due to them was from a king whom they had been instrumental in restoring.[95] But this was so much Cavalier wishful thinking. Nearer to reality was Montereul's report, in a dispatch of 31 August, of a conversation with the earl of Argyll who insisted that the Scots ought not to intervene to re-establish Charles's power without receiving satisfaction from him as to their religious demands 'ce qu'il desesperoit qu'il fît jamais'. If only the king would make these concessions, Argyll assured the French ambassador that he would be willing to place an army of 10,000 foot and 6,000 horse at his disposal.[96]

Despite bellicose sermons from many Scottish ministers, both the Scottish Committee of Estates and the Commissioners of the General Assembly of the kirk were in broad agreement about the need for caution concerning intervention in England, in sharp contrast to the situation which was to prevail in the following year. Declarations

93. CLRO., Jor. 40, fo. 240.
94. *Montereul Correspondence*, II, 206–7, 213.
95. *The case of the king stated* (1647), BHPC., pp. 16–18.
96. *Montereul Correspondence*, II, 244–5.

from each body issued in mid-August appear to betoken a mutual accord and the kirk's declaration was as vehement in its denunciation of the Independent Heads of the Proposals as was the parliamentary declaration in denouncing sectarian excesses, mechanic preachers and the heretical and republican proclivities of the New Model Army which was holding Charles captive. If no redress was obtained, concluded the parliamentary declaration, they would be justified in making 'such provisions of Armes and other Military forces as may serve our Religion, our King, Kingdome and Parliament'.[97] But a Scottish invasion was even less likely now that the New Model Army was occupying London, having successfully suppressed the Presbyterian counter-revolution there; and, not least, given the king's unwillingness – in contrast to his attitude a few months later – to countenance such intervention.[98] There was some alarm early in September about the menacing presence of the Scottish army under David Leslie on the borders, but the dangers of a Scottish invasion were more apparent than real.[99]

Towards the end of August the Scottish Committee of Estates decided to send the earls of Lanark and Loudoun to test the king's reaction to what seem to have been tentative peace proposals more favourable to the royal interest than anything which had been suggested earlier. What seems to have upset this promising move was, if Montereul's account is to be credited, the intervention of Argyll who objected that such proposals would endanger Scottish relations with the English parliament, whereupon the instructions to Loudoun and Lanark were modified in a way which would certainly make them less attractive to the king. Other reasons for the delay were difficulties over obtaining passports for the earls from the English which would allow them to visit the king at other places than Oatlands, from where he had in any case now departed, and (possibly) the fact that the Scots had received no apologies for the army's outrageous treatment of Lauderdale at Woburn in July and no assurance that similar indignities would not be heaped upon Lanark and Loudoun.[100] Ultimately Lanark was able to leave for England on 29 September and Loudoun followed a few days later, after what must have been considered an adequate

97. *A Declaration and Remonstrance . . . of the Kingdome of Scotland* (17 August 1647), BL., E.402(14), pp. 3–8; *A Declaration and Brotherly Exhortation of the General Assembly* (20 August 1647), E.407(24), especially pp. 8–9.
98. On this, see *A Letter from an honourable Gentleman in the Court . . .* (23 August 1647), BL., E.404(8), pp. 2–4.
99. *A Declaration of the Scottish Armie* (September 1647), BL., E.406(22), no pagination.
100. *Montereul Correspondence*, II, 236–9, 250–1; Burnet, *Lives of the Hamiltons*, pp. 409–10. In the meantime the Hamiltons sent a Mr Leslie to reassure the king of Scottish support (ibid., pp. 406–7).

explanation of the Woburn incident by Fairfax and Colonel Whalley on 17 September.[101]

In the opposing attitudes to the mission of Lanark and Loudoun we see some anticipation of the later struggle over the Engagement with Loudoun differing from his brother Argyll as he was later to do for a time in his association with the Engagers. Another anticipation of this struggle was a highly significant Remonstrance from the Commissioners of the General Assembly of the Church to the Committee of Estates on 13 October. The Remonstrance bewails the proposal (which was favoured by the Hamiltons but bitterly opposed by Argyll) to disband the covenanting army and replace it by a quite different force 'which may be prejudiciall and destructive to this Cause and Covenant'. This was coupled with a warning to the Committee of Estates against associating itself with any other design which might be inimical to the ends of the Covenant.[102] The lines of battle which were to characterize Scottish politics during 1648 were already in process of formation.

On 22 October Lanark and Loudoun accompanied by Lauderdale met the king at Hampton Court and assured him that the Scots would be prepared to intervene in England on his behalf if only he would give them satisfaction in the matter of religion. The marquis of Ormond, the king's Lord Deputy of Ireland, whom the Scots consulted on Charles's suggestion and who had only recently handed over Dublin to the forces of the English parliament, suggested that the inauguration of a vigorous royalist offensive in Ireland might usefully be timed to coincide with a Scottish invasion of England on the king's behalf. The Scottish envoys at Hampton Court later suggested to Charles that he should contrive affairs so as to return with them to Scotland. However, they emphasized that if he did, nothing could be done on his behalf without significant concessions on religion which, cognizant as he was of the more attractive terms of the Independents' Heads of the Proposals, he was unwilling to make.[103] The Scottish commissioners were among the last visitors the king had at Hampton Court before absconding to the Isle of Wight and it will be remembered that flight to the Scots, as in May 1646, was indeed one of the options to which Charles gave serious consideration but this time turned down.[104]

In the context of the negotiations with Ormond, it is worth mentioning that disputes over the control and payment of Scottish forces in

101. *Montereul Correspondence*, II, 272–3: *An Answer from … Sir Thomas Fairfax to . . . the kingdome of Scotland* (September 1647), BL., E.407(46), pp. 1–5.
102. *Rec.CGA. 1646–8*, pp. 314–18.
103. On these developments, see Stevenson, *Revolution and Counter-Revolution*, p. 94. On the Heads of the Proposals, see above, pp. 24–8.
104. See above, pp. 27–8; *A More full Relation of his Majesties departure from Hampton Court . . .* (22 November 1647), BL., E.416(23), p. 6.

Ireland had been yet another long-standing and hitherto unmentioned factor in the deterioration of Anglo-Scottish relations. On 13 March 1647 the English parliamentary Committee for Irish Affairs resolved that England could no longer support the Scottish army in Ireland and notice should be given it to disband.[105] Eleven days earlier Montereul had informed Mazarin that the English were demanding that the Scots hand over Belfast to them. Belfast was a fortified town of great strategic significance and it was doubtful if a Scottish army could be kept on in Ulster without it. Early in the following month Montereul reported that he had learnt from Argyll that the English proposed to pay no more to the Scots than the cost of the transportation of their army home, and that the Scots, for their part, were resolved to stay in Ireland, including Belfast, at least until a beginning was made in the payment of the £800,000 due to their army there from the English parliament.[106] As it happened, with renewed activity from the Irish confederate forces later in the year, Scottish withdrawal from any part of Ireland was not a practical proposition. Moreover, during the second half of 1647, following the quelling of the July counter-revolution in London by the army, there was much unease among Scottish commanders in Ireland about the likely neglect by an Independent-dominated parliament and army of the provisions of the Solemn League and Covenant relating to the establishment of Presbyterianism in Ireland. This apprehension manifested itself especially in Munster where, on 30 August, Major-General Robert Sterling, the Scottish commander under Lord Inchiquin, resolved along with his subordinate commanders to make an armed stand for the Covenant against the sectarian English army. Sterling sent details of his plans to the Scottish generals in Leinster and Ulster, to General Leven in Scotland and to the Scottish parliament, but some of his letters were intercepted en route. Inchiquin was commanded from England to send over Sterling in custody, but his sympathies were almost certainly more with the Scots than with the Independent-controlled English parliament.[107] Indeed, following

---

105. *C.J.*, V, 113; *HMC., 6th. Report App. (House of Lords Cal. 1646–7)*, pp. 163–4. This brief section on Ireland was written before reading the brilliant essay by J.S.A. Adamson on the 'British' significance of Irish affairs which will appear in J. Ohlmeyer (ed.), *From Independence to Occupation; Ireland 1640–1660* to be published by Cambridge University Press. I am deeply indebted to Dr Adamson for making the typescript of this remarkable essay available to me even though it was too late to make use of it here.

106. *Montereul Correspondence*, II, 38, 39; *HMC., Ormonde MSS.*, II, 60. For a demand for payment by the Scottish commissioners, see Bodleian, Tanner MSS., 58, fo. 649. See also Cheisley's letter of 13 November 1646 (*Rec.CGA. 1646–8*, Appendix III, 577–9).

107. *HMC., 13th Report App. Portland MSS.*, I, 434–5; *A Great Plot Against The Parliament of England And The Army* (September 1647), BL. E.408(10), no pagination.

Inchiquin's own defection and agreement with some of the Irish confederates early in 1648, the Scottish Engagers were to attempt in June to recruit his support for their own designs.[108]

Although the Irish scene was more than a mere sideshow, the main Scottish attention was directed at home and not England. The king's flight from Hampton Court on 11 November was a crucially important event in the developments which led to the Engagement at the end of the year. On 17 November the Scottish commissioners in London complained of being left completely in the dark by the English parliament about the circumstances of Charles's departure. Nevertheless, having perused a copy of the letter which he left behind at Hampton Court, they had concluded that he had had 'just cause to look to his owne safety and preservation' in view of the threat to his life. The English parliament was left in no doubt that Scotland was deeply concerned about the king's safety, and duty bound to endeavour its utmost to prevent his ruin and to see him brought in honour and safety to London to negotiate a final settlement with his parliaments.[109]

In a dispatch of 16 November Montereul reports the rumour that the evicted Presbyterian MPs and former parliamentary military commanders, Sir William Waller and Edward Massey, had endeavoured to persuade the earl of Argyll to use his influence to bring about a Scottish invasion of England, and that Argyll had replied that the Scots would not fail to invade as soon as there was good reason for them to do so, but the time was not yet come.[110] Nor was such disinclination to proceed immediately to precipitate military action confined to the likes of Argyll. Even Lauderdale and other future Engagers were still reluctant to commit themselves to an invasion without obtaining the assurances about religious reformation which they had sought when they visited Charles at Hampton Court in October and November. However, was it not possible that the king's flight and the failure of the army to respond to his proposals from the Isle of Wight might dispose him to make the required concessions to the Scots? Certainly, he was now of necessity very conscious of the possible advantages of the Scottish option, even though he told Lanark in a letter of 19 November that 'change of place hath not altered my mind from what it was when you last saw me'.[111] If he would go some way to meet the Scottish requirements, and if the English parliament were to refuse to countenance that

108. *HMC., 13th. Report App. Portland MSS.*, I, 469–70.
109. *A Letter from the Scots Commissioners . . .* (19 November 1647), BL., E.416(10), pp. 3–4. For letters earlier in November demanding a treaty with the king, see *The Transactions between his Majesty the Parliament of England the Estates of Scotland and the Army . . .* (20 December 1647), BL. E.420(5), pp. 1–4.
110. *Montereul Correspondence*, II, 320.
111. Burnet, *Lives of the Hamiltons*, p. 413.

personal treaty which the Scottish commissioners, in the name of their parliament, were again to demand on 23 November,[112] anything might be possible; even that Scottish military intervention which Charles had vainly sought back in 1646.

The English parliament's rejection on 27 November of the Scottish demand for a personal treaty along lines agreed by both parliament, as at Uxbridge in 1645, and its choosing to proceed via the Four Bills provide the immediate background to the Scottish Engagement with the king at Christmas.[113] Parliament's refusal on 15 December to give the Scottish commissioners a sight of the bills before they were transmitted to the king[114] produced a number of strongly worded Scottish protests, including an enormous paper delivered on 17 December.[115] Apart from the Scottish objection to the initial mode of procedure by bills rather than by personal treaty, the fact that religious considerations appeared nowhere in the Four Bills was particularly alarming. This surely was to allow scope for what were, from the Scottish standpoint, unacceptable concessions to be made to the king, perhaps even including the return of moderate episcopacy; or, at the other extreme, the establishment, not of a strict Presbyterian ecclesiastical polity according to the Solemn League and Covenant, but of 'a meer Shadow of Presbyterian Government, an external Form of Discipline without Life or Power', leading to toleration of 'a vast Deformity or Multiformity of Heresies and Sects'.[116] Herein lies the very heart of the Scottish kirk's fears about English intentions.

To the long catalogue of Scottish complaints, the English parliament replied that it had in no way violated the Anglo-Scottish treaty of alliance and that the business of sending the Four Bills to the king would admit of no further delays. This in turn produced a mercifully short answer from the Scottish commissioners on 20 December, addressed to the Speaker of the House of Lords, and regretting, more, it would seem, in sorrow than in anger, 'that so little Regard hath been had to our Desires as not to take them into Consideration' before transmitting the Four Bills to the king.[117] On that same day Bellièvre reported the departure of the English parliamentary commissioners to the Isle of

112. Tanner MSS., 58, fo. 593.
113. HLRO., MP., 27/11/1647; C.J., V, 368. On the Four Bills, see above, pp. 35–9.
114. C.J., V, 385, 386.
115. L.J., IX, 582–4. The paper is printed in *Parliamentary History*, XVI, 430–73. See also *A Declaration of the Lords and Commons Concerning the Papers of the Scots Commissioners* (13 March 1648), BHPC., pp. 81–3.
116. The Scottish religious objections are elaborated in *Parliamentary History*, XVI, 443–57. Similar objections were put to the king after his rejection of the Four Bills (*Cal.SPD. 1645–7*, pp. 582–3).
117. *Parliamentary History*, XVI, 471–3. The Four Bills are printed in Gardiner, *Constitutional Documents*, pp. 335–47.

Wight, noting in the same dispatch that the Scottish earls of Loudoun, Lanark and Lauderdale were to leave on the same day for the same destination where they would meet up with the earl of Traquair, the Scottish Treasurer. It is the conjuncture of these two circumstances which helps to explain the otherwise rather surprising concessions made by the Scottish commissioners in their Engagement with the king in contrast to their insistence in their October meetings with the king at Hampton Court that no active Scottish help for him would be forthcoming unless he accepted the Scottish demands about religion. If the terms of the Engagement had not been kept secret for some time, they would certainly have met with the disapproval of the Scottish parliament as well as of the kirk. Indeed, the former had to be manipulated very carefully before finally accepting them, while the opposition of the latter was to remain implacable. There is much to be said for Dr Stevenson's argument that Charles may have deceived the Scottish commissioners into agreeing these terms by deliberately giving the impression that he was seriously considering giving his consent to the Four Bills.[118] It is, moreover, arguable that Charles used the Four Bills to extract maximum concessions from the Scots, while using the Scottish commissioners' objections to the bills as an excuse to the English parliament for his not accepting them.[119] Against this view, one should perhaps set Clarendon's interesting, if by no means unbiassed, verdict that Charles was deceived by the Scottish commissioners into accepting terms which were contrary to his interests.[120]

What were these terms and in what sense do they represent a substantial Scottish concession? First and foremost, far from agreeing to the permanent establishment of Presbyterianism in England, Charles consented only to an interim establishment for three years. The permanent settlement to follow this trial period was to be concluded via negotiations between the king, the parliament and the Westminster Assembly of Divines, with Charles nominating twenty additional members to the last body. During the three years the king and his household were to be free to worship as they pleased, though sectaries – a category which was significantly made to include religious Independents – were not to be allowed that privilege. Charles was to confirm the Covenant without being obliged to take it himself. In return for these things, the Scots undertook to press for a personal treaty to settle English and

118. Stevenson, *Revolution and Counter-Revolution*, pp. 96–7. The Engagement is printed in Gardiner, *Constitutional Documents*, pp. 347–53.
119. See the king's letter of 28 December to the Speaker of the House of Lords (*Cal.SPD. 1645–7*, p. 583).
120. Clarendon, *Rebellion*, IV, 292–303. Montereul also took the view that the king's interest took second place to those of the Scottish Engagers (*Montereul Correspondence*, II, 364–5).

Scottish affairs, and if the English parliament should refuse to go along with this, the Scots were, if necessary, to enforce it by invading.

At some time, probably towards the end of January 1648, Charles sent a formal message to his Scottish subjects, emphasizing, with an air of injured innocence, that he did not wish to provoke them to interfere in the affairs of their neighbour kingdom, but simply to inform them of his sufferings and justify his proceedings vis-à-vis the English parliament. The response was a formal Scottish resolution to assist the king and his loyal English subjects 'against the disloyal party and wicked Incendiaries that are now about his Majesties person'.[121] But this was not to go unchallenged.

The struggle over the Engagement

The main theme of Scottish history over the ensuing months was the struggle between the Engagers led by the Hamiltons, who achieved a significant ascendancy in the parliament early in 1648, and their opponents whose main lay champion was the marquis of Argyll, and whose main institutional focal point was in the General Assembly of the Kirk. For while these anti-Engagers saw the Engagement as a violation of the Covenant, the Engagers sought to emphasize that theirs was the true interpretation of the Covenant and to win over both Scottish and English religious Presbyterians. While it may be difficult to see Engagers such as the Hamiltons as motivated by religious considerations, there were other Engagers, of whom Lauderdale is a good example, who were both pious sons of the kirk and regretted what they regarded as the mistaken attitude of the Commissioners of the General Assembly to the Engagement.

It is arguable that the Engagers' attempts to placate an implacable kirk induced a debilitating ambivalence which put in hazard the enthusiastic co-operation of English Cavaliers and episcopalians. On the other hand it did nothing to gain compensating assurances of support from the English Presbyterians, who were far more likely to pay heed to the arguments of the Commissioners of the General Assembly and the tireless persuasions of Argyll about the rectitude of the kirk and the self-seeking aims of the Engagers.[122] The Engagers' fruitless attempts to placate the kirk were probably the most important factor in delaying efficient Scottish mobilization and the invasion which inhabitants of

---

121. *His Majesties most gracious message to his great councell of Scotland* (1648), BHPC., pp. 2–6.
122. On Presbyterian loyalty to the English parliament, see above, pp. 291–4. For examples of Argyll's efforts to persuade them, see *Hamilton Papers*, pp. 177, 202–3.

northern England were awaiting with trepidation in the spring and early summer of 1648.[123] By contrast, of course, the attitude of English Cavaliers was characterized by growing impatience rather than apprehension, for in the meantime the fate of royalist insurgents in the north, in Wales and in Kent and Essex was being jeopardized by Sottish delays.[124] Not that all English royalists relished the prospect of military co-operation with the Scottish Engagers. Hyde's misgivings were sincere and profound though of little practical significance.[125] But even that indefatigable urger of prompt Scottish intervention, the English correspondent of the earl of Lanark, while emphasizing in a letter of 18 April 'ane excellent disposition in the whole Kingdome to receaue you [viz. the Scots]', also pressed the point that if the English royalists found that they could manage without Scottish aid, they might well 'be readyer to exclud you then to receaue your assistance'.[126] Writing from St Germains to Lanark on 18 April Mungo Murray spoke of many Cavaliers in France who would prefer the king to perish rather than that the Scots should be his rescuers,[127] while on 9 July Sir William Bellenden reported similar attitudes prevailing among the exiled Cavaliers at Amsterdam who were overcome with joy at news of the risings in Kent and Essex (though the former was by then virtually quelled), not least because 'the Kings busines was now to be doin without the assistance of the Scotes, and that the Princes person was not to be trostid to . . . that perfideus mercenarie nation'.[128] Many royalists also had misgivings about Hamilton's appointment as commander-in-chief of the Scottish invading army, given his reputation for deceit which had caused his imprisonment by Charles in Pendennis Castle during the First Civil War and his reported ambition to obtain the Scottish crown for himself. Rejoicing at the failure of Argyll and the kirk to wreck the Engagement, one pamphleteer notes the snag that 'the report of Duke *Hamilton* being made Generall is like water to our wine and afflicts us with fears'.[129] It was reported from York on 5 May that the northern royalist commanders Sir Marmaduke Langdale, Sir Thomas Glemham and Sir

123. See, e.g., letters from York in March and April and from Lancaster in May (Rushworth, *Historical Collections*, VII, 1047, 1123; *Clarke Papers*, II, 1).
124. E.g., letters from Lanark's unnamed English correspondent (SRO., GD/406/1/ 2209; *Hamilton Papers*, pp. 162, 164, 169–71, 177–8, 181, 182–3, 188–9); from Lord Byron, the newly appointed royalist commander in Lancashire, Cheshire, Shropshire and North Wales (ibid., pp. 167–8); and from James Fenne on 21 June (ibid., p. 218).
125. See Clarendon, *Rebellion*, IV, especially pp. 295–303.
126. *Hamilton Papers*, p. 194.
127. Ibid., p. 186. The editor misreads 'Scotes' as 'notes' (cf. *HMC., 11th. Report Appendix 6*, p. 121).
128. *Hamilton Papers*, pp. 228–9.
129. *The manifold Practices and Attempts of the Hamiltons* (23 May 1648), Oxford, Worcester College pamphlet coll., pp. 3–4.

Philip Musgrave were very aggrieved against the Scots and, in particular, Hamilton, presumably for their delays in invading.[130] Yet on 14 June a letter from Edinburgh reported that the army of the Engagement would still not be fully mobilized for another month.[131]

Letters in late March from Lanark and Lauderdale sought to explain to the king the difficulties under which they had laboured since their return from the Isle of Wight in December.[132] Needless to say, the chief difficulties came from the kirk. Lanark's royalist correspondent in England was constant in his urging the need for prompt Scottish intervention but was no less conscious of the uneasiness of the English Presbyterians and sensed that 'Hamilton can doe nothing without Argyll'.[133] But Argyll was busily employed in persuading the English Presbyterians that the Engagers were no sincere covenanters, and Hamilton had to do not only without him but also without Argyll's brother, Chancellor Loudoun, who had been a party to the original Engagement but now deserted that cause.[134]

In retrospect perhaps the time and trouble taken by the Engager-dominated Scottish parliament in trying to bring the kirk round to its point of view seems a particularly futile exercise and one foredoomed to failure. The precise terms of the Engagement had not been divulged for some time and a letter on 27 March from Robert Baillie provides eloquent testimony of the shock administered to a godly Scottish Presbyterian on learning the shameful truth.[135] To such people the king's declaration to his Scottish subjects from Carisbrooke on 23 March, like the Engagement itself, was more significant for what it omitted than for what it promised.[136] Sectaries were condemned, but not Erastians – was not the English church of which Charles had been head conceived along Erastian lines? No-one, least of all the king, was to be obliged to take the Covenant; and there were no guarantees for the permanent establishment of Presbyterianism in England. The Engagement had not advanced but rather betrayed the Presbyterian cause.

The first major blow in the kirk's battle against the Engagement was delivered on 1 March, the day before what was to be an Engager-

---

130. *The Declaration of Sir Thomas Glenham* [*sic*] *Sir Marmaduke Langdale and Sir Philip Musgrave* (May 1648), BL., E.446(29), p. 3. Langdale and Musgrave wrote on 11 and 14 June emphasizing Langdale's need for Scottish help in a desperate situation near Carlisle (*Hamilton Papers*, pp. 210–11, 213).
131. Rushworth, *Historical Collections*, VII, 1157.
132. Burnet, *Lives of the Hamiltons*, pp. 430–1.
133. *Hamilton Papers*, p. 173.
134. Burnet, *Lives of the Hamiltons*, p. 434; Baillie, *Letters*, III, 38.
135. Ibid., III, 32–4.
136. *His Majesties Declaration . . . to His Native and Loyall Subjects of Scotland* (23 March 1648), BL., E.433(17), pp. 1–5.

dominated parliament was due to meet,[137] and it occupied the forefront of parliament's attention when it did meet. This was a forthright declaration against the Engagement, and was followed, as Montereul observes in a dispatch of 14 March, by a spate of sermons by ministers preaching not just against the Engagement but also against the king.[138] The furious denunciation of the Engagement by the great mass of the ministers of the kirk did not, however, quite succeed in drowning the voice of dissident pro-Engagement ministers. According to Baillie, the Engagers 'had laboured . . . to make a partie among the ministers to oppose us', and he mentions five such persons in particular, of whom one, William Colville, had objected that it was a minister's duty to support the unconditional restoration of the king, whatever Charles might have done previously to merit distrust.[139] But it was another of Baillie's dissidents, Andrew Ramsay, who excited the special disapprobation of the Commissioners of the General Assembly. Ramsay had, like the others, not only refused to read the Declaration in church, but when summoned before the Commissioners to answer for his fault, he came accompanied by 'a promiscuous multitude . . . in a great number, in a very tumultuous way to our meeting'. Ominously their behaviour was countenanced by some Members of the Scottish Parliament.[140] Indeed, if it had not been for the existence of such dissident ministers the army of the Engagement would have gone without chaplains, and, even as it was, it was woefully short of good Presbyterian ministers to fill this role. On 26 September, long after that army had suffered ignominious defeat in England, the Commissioners of the General Assembly summoned before them seven such ministers to answer for the offence of going with the invading army to England where they reputedly still were; and another ten who had also performed ministerial duties with the army, but were now in Scotland. Some of these were certainly out of reach, however, serving with the returning Engagers in Scotland under Lanark and George Monroe.[141]

Following the Declaration of 1 March the Commissioners of the General Assembly produced Eight Propositions on 22 March in answer to parliament's request that it should reconsider the case for the

137. On the Engager majority in parliament, see Baillie, *Letters*, III, 35. The Engagers were even more dominant on the newly created parliamentary Committee of Danger (*Montereul Correspondence*, II, 422).

138. *Montereul Correspondence*, II, 423. For the Declaration of 1 March, see *Rec.CGA. 1646–8*, pp. 372–82. On parliamentary disapproval of it, see Baillie, *Letters*, III, 36–7.

139. Ibid., III, 34–5, 41.

140. *Rec.CGA. 1646–8*, pp. 423, 424, 427–8, 446; Rushworth, *Historical Collections*, VII, 1040. Ramsay was also at fault for having expressed in a sermon the view that Presbyterianism, like episcopacy, was *iure humano* (*Rec.CGA. 1646–8*, p. 540).

141. *Rec.CGA. 1648–9*, pp. 73–4; also p. 97.

Engagement before condemning it out of hand. The Propositions reiterated the now familiar case against the Engagement and war with England in association with papists, prelatists and other malignants. The king's so-called concessions on religion were declared to be totally inadequate and the plan to reinstate him without first securing adequate safeguards that he would fulfil the ends of the Covenant was inadmissible. The commissioners questioned whether the soldiers of the invading army would be men who had given proof of their integrity in the cause of the Covenant and demanded a say in the formulation of any oath which should be administered to them such as they had had in the formulation of the Solemn League and Covenant in 1643.[142] This implicit contrast between the Engagement and covenanting armies was significant. A letter of 12 April mentions the organization of a petition among officers of the latter against war with England.[143] Indeed, the loyalty of old covenanting officers to the present parliament was very doubtful. A letter of 29 April from Edinburgh ascribes to Argyll the intention, in the event of an invasion of England by the army of the Engagement, 'to follow with another Army in the Rear of them'.[144] While nothing came of this, there are a number of cases of notabilities such as Lord Ross refusing colonelcies in the new army and of others refusing to serve on shire Committees of War.[145]

The Declaration of 1 March and the Eight Propositions were the most complete statements to date of the case against the Engagement, though there were to be many subsequent papers and notably a lengthy and somewhat prolix *Representation* by the Commissioners of the General Assembly on 28 April, which maintained, *inter alia*, that to restore the king to full power without first obtaining from him security for the fulfilment of the ends of the Covenant was the equivalent of placing the king's restoration above that of Jesus Christ.[146] Parliament's answer to the Eight Propositions on 27 March had been a mixture of conciliation, evasion and outright prevarication and was treated with hardly veiled contempt in the Commissioners' reply two days later. Far from violating Anglo-Scottish unity, parliament maintained unconvincingly that the

---

142. *Rec.CGA. 1646–8*, pp. 429–31; *Eight Propositions* (22 March 1648), Codrington pamphlet coll., pp. 2–5. On the drafting of the Propositions, see Baillie, *Letters*, III, 39–40. The Propositions are reproduced and discussed in Rushworth, *Historical Collections*, VII, 1047–9.
143. *The Demands and Proposals of the Parliament of Scotland* (April 1648), BL., E.436(6), p. 5; *The Declaration and Propositions of Lord General Leven* (April 1648), E.436(12), p. 5.
144. BL., E.438(17), p. 4.
145. Stevenson, *Government*, pp. 64, 66–7, 69–70.
146. For the *Representation*, see *Rec.CGA. 1646–8*, pp. 489–512, especially pp. 499–500; BL., E.461(2), pp. 33–55, especially pp. 43–4. The point was forcefully reiterated in a declaration of 5 May (*Rec.CGA. 1646–8*, p. 525) and in the reply to parliament on 15 August, two days before the battle of Preston (*Rec.CGA. 1648–9*, pp. 20–2).

Engagement would strengthen such unity. It also undertook that if papists and malignants rose when the Scottish army was in England, it would ruthlessly put them down, whereas it was common knowledge that it was the intention of the Engagers to join forces with them.[147]

Of course, the kirk was subjected to parliamentary accusations of meddling outside its proper sphere, and it was in answer to such a charge made on 11 May that it produced a *Vindication* of its proceedings which is a classic statement of the two-kingdom theory that would not have shamed Andrew Melville. The *Vindication* argued that it was not the kirk but parliament which had trespassed, by including religious matters in its declaration, 'without the knowledge and consent . . . of the Kirk', and by reinterpreting the Covenant in a novel and unacceptable way. By contrast, the kirk's insistence on the religious qualities appropriate to office-holders and military commanders was no usurpation of parliament's functions and distinct from the actual business of choosing them. Indeed, it was sinful to choose such officers if they did not have these qualities. To the parliamentary charge of encouraging disobedience to the law, the Kirk Commissioners replied that it was their duty to do this when such laws contravened the law of God: 'it be no Treason to obey God rather than man'. The thin end of the wedge implications of this argument will be all too familiar to students of high Presbyterian – or, for that matter, papistical – apologetics, and the *Vindication* concluded by contrasting the opponents of the Engagement, who had always been godly and well-affected persons, with its supporters, many of whom had been disaffected to the godly cause from the beginning.[148]

Compared with such uncompromising and forthright statements, parliamentary declarations give the impression almost of falling over backwards in trying to satisfy the kirk's objections; as, for example, in a Declaration of 12 June, which regretted that its proceedings had been misunderstood by the many petitioners against the Engagement and maintained that it put a higher priority on the religious ends of the Covenant than on the reinstatement of the king. Only those who had themselves taken the Covenant would be employed in the army of the Engagement which, moreover, would not associate with any who would not engage themselves to these pious ends. The declaration may not have gone far to satisfy the objections of the petitioners to whom it

147. For parliament's answer, see *Rec.CGA. 1646–8*, pp. 416–20, 522–3. For the Kirk Commissioners' response, see ibid., pp. 420–3; *A Declaration of the Commissioners of the General Assembly* (26 August 1648), BL., E.461(2), pp. 16–19.

148. 'The humble Vindication of the Commissioners of the General Assembly' (Edinburgh, 6 June 1648), printed in *A Declaration of the Commissioners of the General Assembly* (26 August 1648), BL., E.461(2), pp. 56–65 (corrected pagination) and in *Rec.CGA. 1646–8*, pp. 547–56.

was addressed, but it may have done something to still the doubts of those Engagers who were also pious Presbyterians.[149]

Despite the Scottish parliament's protestations to the contrary, the Engagers from the first associated both with English Cavaliers and with reformadoes from the English army such as Captain Wogan, who brought a troop of soldiers with him to Scotland.[150] In a dispatch of 15 February Montereul reported the daily arrival of Cavalier fugitives in Scotland, including such notabilities as Sir Marmaduke Langdale, Sir Thomas Glemham and Sir Charles Lucas. In a further dispatch of 8 March he reported that some of these were being passed off as fugitive English Presbyterians fleeing from Independent persecution at home.[151] This subterfuge was perhaps the more necessary in view of the kirk's insistence that Cavalier 'enemies to the Cause and Covenant' should not be encouraged but vigorously opposed.[152] But whether it deceived any, in view of the celebrity and notoriety of many of the fugitives, is very doubtful. As an English pamphlet was to put it much later, 'it were strange a Leopard should change his spots or a Black Moor . . . his hue, that Langdale, Glemham, Goring, Lucas, Louborough [sic] should be Covenanters'.[153] Malignants of all sorts were flooding into Scotland, reported a letter from Edinburgh on 14 March, and another on 5 April described the streets of the Scottish capital as swarming with English fugitives, among them the northern Cavaliers, Sir Philip Musgrave and Sir Thomas Glemham.[154] Among those whose extradition the English parliament requested, along with Musgrave, Glemham and the renegade Wogan, was the Catholic Colonel George Wray, a Northumberland Cavalier, who had fought for the king in the first war and was to play a notable part in the capture of Berwick in the second. But the Scottish parliament chose either to ignore or, at best, to take a very legalistic line on the matter of extradition, refusing to extradite any save 'such only of the *English* Nation who have incensed the King of *Scotland* against

149. *A Declaration of the Parliament . . . to the Synods and Presbyteries* (27 June 1648), BL. E.499(46), pp. 3–5.
150. On Wogan, see below, pp. 415–16.
151. *Montereul Correspondence*, II, 398, 419.
152. *Eight Propositions* (22 March 1648), Codrington pamphlet coll., p. 3; *Rec.CGA. 1646–8*, p. 404. This was confirmed by the Scottish parliament, if only for the sake of appearances (*A Declaration of the Parliament of Scotland* (April 1648), Codrington pamphlet coll., p. 12; Rushworth, *Historical Collections*, VII, 1067–9). For a further statement by the kirk to this effect on 10 June, see *A Declaration of the General Assembly* (26 August 1648), BL., E.461(2), p. 67 (corrected pagination); *Rec.CGA. 1646–8*, p. 564. For approving comments on an earlier resolution against malignants in arms, see Baillie, *Letters*, III, 34, 39, 42, 43.
153. *A Looking-Glass for the Well-Affected in the City of London* (23 August 1648), BL., E.460(26), p. 8. Three of those named had certainly taken refuge in Edinburgh earlier in the year.
154. Rushworth, *Historical Collections*, VII, 1032, 1052; *Packets of Letters from Scotland . . .* (17 April 1648), Codrington pamphlet coll., p. 2.

the Kingdom of England', an answer which infuriated the English parliament.[155]

Although the Scottish parliament strove to maintain the illusion that the capture of Berwick and Carlisle at the end of April had been independent Cavalier enterprises which had nothing to do with Scotland, few were deceived, and, of course, it was the more difficult to keep up the pretence after these towns were handed over by their captors to the Scots in the first week of July.[156] The intervening period must have seemed an agonizingly long time to the beleaguered Cavaliers in the two towns, and on 11 May a letter from Newcastle refers to their impatience 'that the Scots appear not for them before this'.[157] In the meantime there were of course complaints from the English parliament about Scottish connivance at the capture of the two towns and Scottish shipping of arms and ordinance to the Cavaliers in Berwick.[158] The Scottish replies were evasive to the point of deceitfulness. On 8 July the Committee of Estates, with breathtaking mendacity, contrasted, for the benefit of the English parliamentary commissioners in Scotland, the English parliament's failure to deliver adequate and prompt replies to Scottish official communications, with the frankness and promptness of Scottish answers to English questions relating to Berwick and Carlisle, omitting, of course, to mention how misleading, evasive and even mendacious such answers had been.[159] On that same day the army of the Engagement at last invaded England. A Scottish letter of the previous month had predicted that 'the Cavalleering party about Berwick and Carlisle . . . will bee all one' with the Scottish army of the Engagement once it invades.[160] Well, not completely perhaps. Back in April Sir Philip Musgrave had reportedly informed his Scottish friends 'that the Cavaleers would nott joyne in a body with . . . the Scotts . . . butt are

155. L.J., X, 208–9, 223–4, 225–8; C.J., V, 541–3, 544; Rushworth, Historical Collections, VII, 1056, 1064, 1066, 1067, 1106; Packets of Letters from Scotland . . . (17 April 1648), pp. 1–2; HMC., 13th Report App. Portland MSS., I, 451.

156. See the letter from six Northumberland cavaliers, of whom the most important was Colonel Charles Brandling of Alnwick, supporting the mayor of Berwick's concern about the coming occupation (SRO., GD/406/1/2356). On Brandling, see Cal.CC., II, 1401–2; Newman, Royalist Officers, p. 40. On the same day Langdale was requested to facilitate the handing over of both towns (SRO., GD/406/1/2354).

157. Rushworth, Historical Collections, VII, 1114.

158. E.g., PRO., SP. 21/9, fo. 66; L.J., X, 244, 250, 266, 284–5; C.J., V, 551; Rushworth, Historical Collections, VII, 1105; Parliamentary History, XVII, 146–7, 260–1.

159. Bodleian, MSS., dep. C173 (Nalson coll., vol. 20, no. 42). For an example of one such reply on 10 May, see L.J., X, 265–6. For a denunciation on 15 August by the Kirk Commissioners of the parliament's evasiveness over Berwick and Carlisle, see Rec.CGA. 1648–9, pp. 23–4.

160. A Letter from a good hand out of Scotland (June 1648), BL., E.499(24), pp. 1–2.

confident to have opportunity . . . to make a body of their own partie to carry on their owne designe'.[161] Indeed, it is arguable that the failure of the Cavaliers and the Engagers to co-ordinate strategy and tactics was to be responsible for the isolation of Langdale and the separate and crushing defeats of both him and Hamilton near Preston in August.

Previous to this there had always been some possibility that the Engagers' guns might be spiked by a pre-emptive strike from England. As early as April this seems to have been under consideration in some influential quarters in England,[162] while, once Berwick and Carlisle were in the hands of the Cavaliers from the end of April, there was an obvious temptation to strike at their Scottish backers. Even if such a move fell short of full-scale invasion, the moving of a strong force up to the borders might exert a salutary and deterrent effect on Scottish aggressive intentions, argued a friendly letter from Edinburgh on 28 June.[163] At the beginning of that month, when announcing the prospective move of Fairfax and a strong force to the north – he was at that time campaigning in Kent – the English parliamentary commissioners disclaimed any aggressive intentions against Scotland. While they were careful to emphasize that the sole object of the move was to suppress Cavalier malignants, and especially those who had taken over Berwick and Carlisle, a subsequent letter a few days later made it clear that they were well aware that both of these garrisons were being supplied from Scotland. Similarly, but more disingenuously, the Scottish parliament on 7 June described the army of the Engagement as having been mobilized simply for the defence of Scotland.[164]

Perhaps attack was deemed to be the best mode of defence. On 8 July the Scots invaded an England which was still in the throes of civil war, even though the revolts in Kent and South Wales had by then been put down. On 14 July the House of Commons issued a declaration denouncing the Scots as enemies to the kingdom and any who aided them as traitors and rebels, although the Upper House, with some dissentient voices, refused to accept the declaration as it stood.[165] It seems unlikely that, even if the Scottish Engagers had invaded at a more propitious time and had been able to rely on the active assistance of the English Presbyterians and the City of London,[166] not to speak of

161. *Clarke Papers*, II, 2–3.
162. Bodleian, Tanner MSS., 57, fo. 80.
163. *Scotlands sad Complaint* (June 1648), Oxford, Worcester College pamphlet coll., p. 4. See also *Two Letters out of Scotland* (June 1648), BL., E.449(24), p. 3.
164. *Parliamentary History*, XVII, 233-6, 251–2.
165. Rushworth, *Historical Collections*, VII, 1189–90; Whitelock, *Memorials*, p. 316 (14 July); *Parliamentary History*, XVII, 309.
166. On Independent doubts about the reliability of these elements, see, e.g., *Londons New Colours displaid* (July 1648), BL., E.452(21), p. 9; T. May, 'A Breviary of the History of the Parliament', in Maseres, *Select Tracts*, I, 122.

the now vanquished insurgents in Kent and Wales, their invasion would have had much chance of success. The fact that it also took place when Scotland itself was bitterly divided over the Engagement was a sure recipe for disaster.

The kirk triumphant

The division was further emphasized after the invasion by a number of other declarations of the Commissioners of the General Assembly denouncing the Engagement.[167] Once Hamilton had been defeated, opposition to the Engagement again took a violent form in the west as it had done earlier in the year. On 28 August the Commissioners reported 'some stirring of the well affected people of the West' in opposition to further levies in prosecution of the Engagement.[168] The western dissidents were soon advancing on Edinburgh, causing the Committee of Estates to leave the capital and take refuge with the remnants of the army of the Engagement. Three influential Engagers, Lanark, Crawford-Lindsay and Glencairn, appealed to the Kirk Commissioners to use their influence to restore peace.[169] But the Engagers, who had got no change out of the kirk in the time of their predominance, could hardly expect much in the time of their humiliating defeat in England. The Kirk Commissioners' reply was self-righteous almost to the point of smugness, regretting that the letter of the three noblemen had expressed no word of regret or repentance for the disasters which their policies and neglect of God's counsel had brought upon Scotland. It also pointedly remarked that the declared intention of the three Engagers of avoiding intestine troubles was inconsistent with their real aim 'to persew your late sinfull Engagement' in Scotland. Their only acceptable response would be true repentance and a laying down of their arms.[170] A further denunciation of the Engagers followed in a paper from the Commissioners to the Committee of Estates on 8 September, and, on the following day, in A Short Declaration to the whole Kirk and Kingdom.[171]

167. Notably on 25, 28, and especially 31 July (A Declaration of the General Assembly . . . (1 August 1648), BL., E.458(30), pp. 3–5, 7–27 (corrected pagination)).
168. Rec.CGA. 1648–9, p. 34. For a more detailed account of events in Scotland, see Stevenson, Revolution and Counter-Revolution, pp. 115–22.
169. Rec.CGA. 1648–9, pp. 36–7.
170. Ibid., pp. 41–3.
171. For the paper, see ibid., pp. 38–41. For the Declaration, see ibid., pp. 44–7; BL., E.468(8), pp. 11–14. Later in September the danger of continued activity by the Engagers was stressed by the Scottish Commissioners to England sent by the Committee of Estates which was now controlled by the anti-Engagement party (Burnet, Lives of the Hamiltons, pp. 478–80).

But, far from being chastened either by their disastrous defeat in England or by the renewed rebukes of the kirk, the Engagers, under the leadership of Lanark, Crawford-Lindsay and George Monroe, continued to insist on the consonance of the aims of the Engagement with those of the Covenant. Not surprisingly therefore the Commissioners of the General Assembly continued to denounce them.[172] On 6 October the Commissioners both excommunicated those Engagers still in arms and issued a Solemn Acknowledgment of public sins and especially the breach of the Covenant.[173] A long declaration issued on 9 October, the day before all armed forces of both sides were due to be disbanded according to the terms of the treaty of Stirling of 27 September, recounted the history of the Engagement and roundly condemned those who had continued in arms for it.[174] For all that, the terms of the treaty of Stirling were in some respects surprisingly lenient to the Engagers.[175] This may be ascribed partly to the fact that the remnants of their army had proved themselves still to be a force seriously to be reckoned with. More important, however, was the fact that Cromwell's army was now entering Scotland, and that this was a force as much feared by the kirk on account of its Independent and sectarian character as by the Engagers who had suffered such a crushing defeat at its hands in England. Cromwell's pretext for invading Scotland to protect England against the imagined danger of another invasion might be effectively removed if the Engagers could, at least for the time being, be barred from political office and influence by a treaty which at the same time secured them from loss of life and estate. Even when it became clear that the invasion could not be reversed, its worst consequences might be averted as a result of the ending of the Engager threat. With this in mind the General Assembly had resolved on 20 September to send Argyll and other representatives to the English army to request 'that the whole Armye may not come, but such a partie as give least offence to this Kirk'.[176]

In a declaration on 19 October from the kingdom of Scotland to its friends in the City of London, the Scots looked forward to the calling of a free Scottish parliament from which all Engagers would be excluded; and, in England, like their Presbyterian allies in London, to the king's restitution, not to arbitrary power, but to the exercise of lawful

---

172. Rec.CGA, 1648–9, pp. 47–51, 60–1, 64–9.
173. Ibid., pp. 78–89.
174. Ibid., pp. 89–96.
175. None were to suffer loss of life or estate, although they were not to exercise state office, at least before parliament next met in January 1649 (Stevenson, Revolution and Counter-Revolution, pp. 118–19).
176. Rec.CGA. 1648–9, p. 64.

authority 'as soon as He shall give security for settling *Religion*' and satisfaction in other matters necessary to peace.[177]

This, of course, was not to happen and a letter of 6 January 1649 delivered a bitter denunciation of Pride's Purge and its seclusion and imprisonment of the Scots' parliamentary Presbyterian allies and the forced withdrawal of others from the parliament.[178] Even more horrifying were the other consequences of the Purge: the institution of proceedings against the king for his life; the impending destruction of the monarchical constitution; the confirmation of a pernicious toleration of heterodox religious sects; and the frustration of the aims of the Covenant. The English reply was an unashamed justification of Pride's Purge as, *inter alia*, the necessary seclusion and imprisonment of MPs who had aided the invasion by the army of the Engagement. This was, of course, a grossly unfair imputation in view of the quiescence of the English Presbyterians during the Second Civil War. Pride's Purge was also defended for excluding those MPs who had wished to close with the king at Newport and thereby betrayed the religious ideals for which the Scottish kirk stood. Thus the excluded MPs were portrayed as the enemies of the kirk on two counts: for their alleged support of the Engagers and for their alleged willingness to make concessions to the king over vital religious issues. In answer to the Scottish objections about religious toleration came the unashamed contention that the English parliament found no warrant 'to persecute all that do not worship God in the same manner that we do'. Scottish allegations that the purged English parliament was hostile to the ends of the Solemn League and Covenant were vigorously denied and countered with the charge that it was the Scots who had broken the Covenant by their invasion and by countenancing and refusing to extradite malignant refugees.[179] The Scots were chided for their assumption that there could be no other interpretation of the words 'the example of the best reformed Churches' in the Solemn League and Covenant than to equate them with their own ecclesiastical system. And did the passage in that Covenant about safeguarding Charles's person and authority retain any validity when he himself had been responsible for initiating another civil war with the assistance of the Scots?[180]

The visiting of the sins of the Engagers upon their Scottish enemies was, of course, less than fair. Unlike the Engagers, their opponents were not prepared to restore the king at almost any price, and they were no

177. *A Message sent from the Kingdom of Scotland to the Citizens of London* (19 October 1648), BL., E.468(16), pp. 1–3.
178. *A Declaration of the Parliament of England in Answer to . . . the Commissioners of Scotland,* Codrington pamphlet coll., especially pp. 10–19.
179. Ibid., pp. 20–4.
180. Ibid., pp. 24–32.

COUNTER-REVOLUTION

less dissatisfied than the English parliamentarians about the king's religious concessions in the treaty of Newport and determined not to advocate his full restitution until he gave satisfaction. This did not prevent them from protesting on 22 January against the king's trial. But when the English answer came, it presented them with a *fait accompli*: that parliament had 'proceeded . . . against that Man of blood' and was shortly to proceed against other 'capitall Enemies of our Peace'.[181] Amongst the latter was the arch-Engager, the duke of Hamilton, who – perhaps to ease Scottish susceptibilities – was tried in February and executed on 9 March under his English title of earl of Cambridge.[182]

Ibid., pp. 33–7.
182. On the trial and execution of Hamilton, *C.J.*, VI, 128, 131, 136, 152, 160; Whitelock, *Memorials*, pp. 371 (1, 2, 3, 5 February), 374–5 (10 February), 375–6 (13 February), 377 (19 February), 377(b) (22 February), 378 (26 February), 378(b) (3, 6 March), 379 (8, 9, March); Oxford, Worcester College, Clarke MSS., 70, fos. 8–12; *State Trials*, IV, 1156–92, 1239; Burnet, *Lives of the Hamiltons*, pp. 504–9.

X

PREMONITORY PLOTS AND OUTBURSTS

We likewise fear . . . that a new warre will be setled in stead of an old Peace; And our lost dispirited Island imbarque in a second Adventure on a Sea of Blood . . .

> *Certain uncertain Proposals from Free-born Subjects of England . . .*
> *to his Excellency Sir Thomas Fairfax . . . presented Aug. 9 1647*
> *at Croydon in Surrey* (12 August 1647), BL., E.401(33), p. 3

Rumours of war 1646–7

On 28 November 1646 Charles I wrote to his queen from Newcastle telling her that Michael Hudson, the companion of his journey from Oxford to Southwell in April and May, had informed him 'that most of the eastern, western and southern countries [*sic*] are resolved to rise in arms, and declare for me, with putting a great body of men into the field, and possessing all the important places'. Through such means he hoped that he would soon be restored to his rightful power. On the following day the French ambassador Bellièvre wrote to Brienne confirming Charles's opinion, while confiding his own view that any such design was ill-advised without the participation of the Scots, whom the king, as was shown in the last chapter, had as yet done nothing to satisfy.[1] Bellièvre was right. In mid-January 1647 he expressed the view that a supposed letter to the king from a gentleman in Wales who had formerly held a command under him and now pronounced that by New Year's Day (25 March?) Charles would have a large army at his disposal and that half the country would have declared for him was in fact a device of the parliamentary Independents to bring discredit on the king and stem the returning tide of loyalty to him. Others again thought it the work of Hudson, harmonizing with those royal imaginings which so often deterred Charles from practicable, but to him

---

1. *Charles I in 1646*, pp. 77–8; *Montereul Correspondence*, I, 342–3.

unwelcome, courses of action such as the making of concessions to the Scots.[2]

For all these false alarms, the dangers of the renewal of war accompanied by a Scottish invasion, this time on the side of the king, loomed very large indeed in people's consciousness in the spring and summer of 1647. It will be recalled that the army represented its abduction of Charles from Holdenby on 4 June as a pre-emptive strike to prevent such a war and invasion, and this was not simply a transparent excuse to justify its outrageous action.[3] The army, wrote one officer, had every reason to suspect 'a new design . . . for the involving this Kingdome in a new Warre', which was strongly backed by elements in parliament and the City of London.[4] Both were deeply involved in the attempted creation of a counter-revolutionary force of which some account will be given in the next chapter.[5] Needless to say, those at whom such charges were levelled viewed these allegedly counter-revolutionary measures as entirely defensive against the renewed danger of civil war resulting not from their own actions but from those of the army.[6] How was it possible, asked one pamphleteer, to restrain a disobedient army other than by force of arms?[7]

It is important not to allow hindsight and our knowledge that ultimately there was no civil war and no Scottish invasion in 1647 to blind us to the significance of the apprehensions of that time. 'A little delay', as Fairfax warned the Lord Mayor on 25 June, 'will indanger the putting the Kingdom into Blood . . . if it is fit to be considered that in Wales (besides vnderhand workinges in your Citie) and other places, men are raised and that in noe small numbers'.[8] With Fairfax's warning in mind, it will be appropriate to begin our account of the counter-revolutionary disturbances of 1647–8, some of which were to anticipate and others to prepare the way for those of the Second Civil War, with developments in Wales and the Welsh Marches.

2. *Montereul Correspondence*, I, 389–90.
3. *Parliamentary History*, XV, 417; *Papers of the Desires of the Souldiers* . . . (9 June 1647), BL., E.392(5), no pagination; *A true impartiall Narration concerning the Armies preservation of the King* (17 June 1647), E.393(1), pp. 3–4, 6–7, 12; *A Copy of that Letter . . . printed July 12 written out of Lancashire* (July 1647), E.398(7), pp. 3–4; Bell, *Memorials*, I, 353.
4. *A Letter sent from an Officer in the Army* (June 1647), BL., E.392(17), sig. A3–A3ᵛ. Other examples are *A Letter from the Army* (June 1647), E.392(6), pp. 3–4; [M. Nedham], *The Lawyer of Lincolnes-Inne Reformed* (July 1647), E.395(4), passim; *A Vindication of His Majestie and the Armie* (July 1647), E.396(5), pp. 5–6.
5. See below, pp. 379–84.
6. E.g., *The Happy Union* (June 1647), BL., E.393(28), pp. 3–5; *Eight Queries* (15 June 1647), E.392(22), p. 5; [W. Prynne], *Nine Proposals by Way of Interrogation* (July 1647), E.396(8), p. 9.
7. *Questions propounded to all wel-afected* [sic] (23 June 1647), BL., E.393(23), p. 1.
8. CLRO., Jor. 40, fo. 230.

Wales and the Marches

That both north and south Wales, and especially the latter, were to be important centres of royalist insurgency in the Second Civil War is hardly surprising in view of the importance of the Principality as a royalist recruiting ground in the First Civil War. During the summer of 1647 when, as we have seen, a second war was hourly expected, there was a rising in Glamorganshire which looked like being a serious threat to political stability in the region but which was in the event fairly easily quelled. Earlier that year in January there had been a momentary scare about the possibility of an invasion of Anglesey from Ireland, following the shipwreck of a vessel at Holyhead bound for Liverpool and bearing two high-ranking Irish confederate officers who were carrying incriminating correspondence with them.[9] But the expected invasion from Ireland, like that from Scotland and like the expected risings in the English provinces, did not materialize. Apart from the coup of 26 July in London, which was much the most important counter-revolutionary occurrence of the summer of 1647, the Glamorgan rising of the previous month was the most notable threat to the government, but had been quelled by the end of the month, before the dangerously rising political temperature in London had reached boiling-point.

While royalist insurgency in Wales was to be very widespread in the Second Civil War in 1648, in the previous summer it was virtually confined to one county. Moreover, while many of those who were involved in the Glamorgan rising of June 1647 had fought for the king in the first war and were to fight for him again in the second, the most prominent of those Welshmen who had been active parliamentarians in the first war but were to change sides in the second showed no signs of their later disaffection in June 1647. Such men were Major-General Rowland Laugharne and Colonels John Poyer and Rice Powell. Laugharne, who had been the most important single commander in the ultimate conquest of South Wales by parliament in the First Civil War, remained steadfast during the summer of 1647, displaying none of that resentment and hostility which were to characterize his attitude a few months later. In a letter to Speaker Lenthall from Carmarthen on 17 June he described the leaders of the Glamorgan revolt as prominent royalists who had fought for the king in the First Civil War, or 'ancient Malignants of a deep stain' as he put it in a letter to Fairfax written on the same day. He offered the opinion that their relapse into rebellion had been aided by undue parliamentary leniency towards them, a verdict which he was to share with some members of the parliamentary

9.   Bodleian, Tanner MSS., 59, fos. 640, 642, 643, 677.

committee at Usk expressed in a letter to the Speaker on 19 June.[10] Laugharne was to earn Fairfax's thanks and admiration for his promptness in moving to suppress the rising.[11] The Lord General's gratitude was no doubt the greater on account of his embarrassment at the Glamorgan delinquents' bizarre claim that their insurgency had been inspired by events following the army's abduction of the king at Holdenby on 4 June, and the soldiers' apparent rapprochement with Charles which was to culminate in the presentation of the Heads of the Proposals in July. Further, the Glamorgan dissidents outrageously claimed to Laugharne and others that they were acting on behalf of the king and the Lord General jointly.[12] As the local committee at Usk explained, they seem to have viewed the army's seizure of the king and the opportunities which it afforded for an alternative settlement to the Newcastle Propositions as an ideal occasion to assert their long-repressed royalism to good effect by cashing in on the respect in which the army was held in South Wales and belabouring those unpopular instruments of parliamentary tyranny, the county committees.[13] However, echoing Colonel King's famous complaint against the Lincolnshire committee,[14] the Welsh dissidents were at pains to explain that it was not against the powers which local committees legitimately derived from parliament that they were complaining, but rather against their shocking abuse of that power. More particularly, they alleged that the committees had sustained their power simply by 'making all men of considerable estates Delinquent, after an arbitrary and Illegal manner, bringing others out of other Countryes, meerely out of faction to out-vote the rest of the Gentlemen'. In turn, those complaining at the committees' actions or trying to secure their accountability for the vast sums passing through their hands were effectively silenced by being declared delinquents. By such means the way was opened for a multitude of arbitrary actions and exactions contrary to parliamentary ordinances and for the self-enrichment of committeemen and their associates out of the proceeds of sequestration and through such malpractices as taking bribes as the price of their not declaring perfectly innocent persons delinquents. Religious grievances against the committee also figure prominently and especially the imprisonment of some parsons and the sequestration of the livings of, or curtailment of the payment of tithes to, 'all the ablest and sufficientest Divines in the

10. Tanner MSS., 58, fo. 218; *A full Relation of the whole Proceedings of the late Rising and Commotion in Wales* (1647), BL., E.396(9), pp. 3–4, 8.
11. BL., E.396(9), pp. 12, 14–15; Phillips, *Wales*, II, 339–40.
12. *C.J.*, V, 218; BL., E.396(9), pp. 5, 8, 11; *A Letter from the Committee at Usk* (19 July 1647), E.394(5), pp. 2–3; Phillips, *Wales*, II, 337–8, 341–2.
13. BL., E.394(5), p. 3; Phillips, *Wales*, II, 341–2.
14. On King, see above, pp. 92–3.

County'. Finally, there was the matter of the arbitrary imprisonment of some of the principal county gentry, which had sparked off the original protest and insurgency.[15]

Provoked, as they claimed, by the intentions of the committee at Usk 'to make captiue seuerall gentlemen heere of fortune and integritie', some of the fellows of the intended victims sent out warrants on 13 June requiring high constables to arrange for a general muster at Cowbridge. Within two days they had mustered a force which varied, according to different estimates, between 1,500 and 2,300 and had seized the magazine at Cowbridge.[16] They next moved to Llandaff, from where they summoned Major-General Laugharne at Carmarthen and Colonel Prichard, the Governor of Cardiff, to embrace their cause. They took pains to emphasize that they had nothing against either of these parliamentarian commanders, that their animus was entirely directed against the local committee, and that they were at one with the imagined aims of the king and Fairfax. Neither Fairfax nor the two Welsh commanders were convinced. Laugharne prepared to move eastwards to crush them, and the message sent to Prichard at Cardiff on 16 June met with a frosty response. The parliamentary Governor of Cardiff pointedly questioned the authority on which the insurgents claimed the right to muster armed forces and by which his own control of the parliamentary garrison at Cardiff was in effect being threatened. The insurgents replied by reiterating that their primary aim was 'the disburdening of this afflicted county and the vindication of our rights and liberties'. Prichard, they claimed, would be guilty of any blood that would be shed if he resisted their approach. But this did not stop him from doing so.[17]

According to Laugharne's own account in a letter of 21 June from Cardiff, which he succeeded in relieving without undue difficulty, the approach of his forces had precipitated wholesale desertion from the ranks of the insurgents, as a result of which 'the chief Actors . . . to the number of Fifty, all well mounted, are fled the Countrey'.[18] Factors contributing to this happy outcome for the government were not only the firmness of both Laugharne and Prichard in the face of a very nasty situation, but Fairfax's offer that those laying down their arms would be free from molestation.[19] Thus ended a revolt which, as one of its opponents claimed, had threatened to put the whole of South Wales in

15. *The Heads of the present Greevances of the County of Glamorgan* (1 July 1647), BL., E.396(3), pp. 1–6; Bodleian, Tanner MSS., 58, fos. 230–30(b).
16. Tanner MSS., 58, fos. 173, 218; BL., E.396(9), pp. 6–7, 11, 13; Phillips, *Wales*, II, 336–7.
17. Tanner MSS., 58, fos. 173, 175, 176, 177, 230–30(b); *A Declaration of the Proceedings . . . in Glamorganshire . . .* (June 1647), BL., E.394(5), pp. 4–6.
18. BL., E.396(9), p. 13; Phillips, *Wales*, II, 340. Many had apparently fled to Brecknockshire.
19. Cary, *Memorials*, I, 250–51.

flames, but which in reality, apart from one unsuccessful appeal from the insurgents to the inhabitants of Monmouthshire, had never looked like spreading beyond the county of Glamorgan where it was contained and crushed without much difficulty.

As to the identification of the insurgents, the difficulty which applies in every region of finding useful information to put flesh on the bones of persons named in depositions, at least below the ranks of the élite gentry, is enormously accentuated in a Welsh context where Joneses, Thomases, Powells and Pritchards – to mention but a few common Welsh surnames – abound, often without details of Christian names or places of abode. Significant details are available about only very few even of the thirty-three ringleaders whose names appear in contemporary accounts of the rising or as signatories of letters to Major-General Laugharne or Colonel Prichard. The most prominent of all these were four members of the fiercely royalist Stradling family, whose main seat was at St Donat's in Glamorgan. All but one of the four, Major Edward Stradling, were royalist commanders of considerable experience. Sir Henry Stradling had been Governor of Carlisle citadel from 1642 to 1645 and thereafter a cavalry commander under Sir Thomas Glemham until being captured at Rowton Heath near Chester. Lieutenant-Colonel Thomas Stradling had served in the family regiment under his two brothers, one of whom, Lieutenant-Colonel John Stradling, had succeeded to the command of the regiment on the death of his father, Sir Edward, in 1643 and had been actively engaged in the campaigns of 1643–4. Allowed to compound in 1646, he nevertheless took part, along with the other three Stradlings, both in the Glamorgan rising of June 1647 and in the Second Civil War in the following year.[20]

Another surname which proliferates among the dissident Glamorgan gentry of June 1647 is that of Basset, though the precise relationship between the five participating Bassets (Richard, William, Theodore, Henry and Thomas, the last-named apparently a clergyman) is obscure, and none of them seem to have played any part in the Second Civil War in 1648. Of the five the only one to achieve real prominence was the sometime Governor of Cardiff, the Glamorganshire gentleman, Sir Richard Basset of Beaupree. Sir Richard had been a Commissioner of Array for Glamorgan in 1642 and High Sheriff for the King in the following year. His appointment as Governor of Cardiff Castle in place of the Englishman Sir Timothy Tyrell in July 1645 seems to have been made as a sop to Welsh complaints, coming not least from the clubmen of the region. Be this as it may, his popularity was short-lived on

20. Newman, *Royalist Officers*, pp. 359–61. Oddly enough, the Stradlings were related to the radical Independent Edmund Ludlow (*Ludlow Memoirs*, I, 200 and note).

account of his strict adherence to his duty to the king in the matter of the provision of men and money for the royalist cause. In September, however, he surrendered Cardiff Castle with all the arms and ammunition to a combination of parliamentary forces and local clubmen, against whom he seems to have offered hardly more than token resistance. Although he compounded in the following year, he was in the forefront of the dissident Glamorgan gentry in the rising of June 1647, which however marks the end of his active resistance on the king's behalf, for, like the other Bassets, he was to play no part in the Second Civil War.[21]

Even more speculative, given the common occurrence of the surname in Wales, is the likelihood of any family connection between the five Thomases (Sir Edward, Lewis, Robert and Thomas) whose names recur in connection with the disturbances of June 1647. Only about the first two of these is there any significant information. Lewis Thomas was involved in the insurrections of both 1647 and 1648 and was to be condemned to death by court martial following his capture, holding the rank of Lieutenant-Colonel, at St Fagans in the Second Civil War. Sir Edward, although one of the most important of the Glamorgan gentlemen in the rising of June 1647, appears to have remained quiescent in the following year. Neither seems to have been in the very forefront of South Welsh royalism during the first war.[22]

Of the other gentlemen, whose names recur in the records dealing with the rising of June 1647, two stand out: Sir Charles Kemeys (alternatively spelt Kemys, Kemes and Kemish) and Sir Thomas Nott. Kemeys was the son and heir of the baronet Sir Nicholas Kemeys of Cefn Mably in Glamorganshire, who was killed during the Second Civil War, in which Sir Charles was also to fight, having, unlike his father, previously been actively involved in the rising of June 1647. Always in the forefront of South Welsh royalism, Charles had been a Commissioner of Array for Glamorgan and Monmouthshire in 1642. Holding the rank of captain, he had been captured at Highnam in March 1643. Exchanged soon afterwards, he was knighted by the king at Oxford on 13 June. In February 1646 he had played an important role as an intermediary between the South Welsh royalists and the royalist-sympathizing neutrals under Edward Carne, while in June of the following year he was one of the most prominent of the gentlemen

21. Bodleian, Tanner MSS., 58, fo. 218; Cal.CC., II, 1130–1; Cal.CAM., II, 663; A Letter from the Committee at Usk (19 July 1647), BL., E.394(5), p. 1; Phillips, Wales, I, 307–8, 316–17, 319, 348, 388, II, 286, 336, 339, 341, 342–3, 347; Newman, Royalist Officers, pp. 18–19.
22. Tanner MSS., 58, fos. 173, 175, 176, 177, 218, 218(b); BL., E.394(5), p. 1; Rushworth, Historical Collections, VII, 1128; Phillips, Wales, I, 338, 405–6, II, 341; Newman, Royalist Officers, p. 369. There can be no certain identification of the Lewis Thomas mentioned by Dr Newman with this case.

involved in the Glamorgan rising.[23] Unlike the others, who were local gentlemen with interests rooted for generations in the South Wales countryside, Sir Thomas Nott's main landed interests lay outside the Principality. The son of a London merchant, Nott had married spectacularly into the West Country gentry and was a landowner in Worcestershire and Middlesex as well as in South Wales. He had served as a colonel or lieutenant-colonel in the first war and while there are some indications that he was also to be involved in the second war, there can be no doubt that, for all his extra-Welsh interests, he was among the most prominent of the Glamorgan insurgents in June 1647.[24]

If the committee at Usk is to be believed, however, there was one other contriver of the disturbances in June 1647 who was a person of far greater distinction than any of the above participants. In claiming in their letter of 19 June that the rising had been 'contrived by Jenkins and other Delinquents in the Tower', the committee was striving to implicate the celebrated royalist judge, who was one of the most eminent Welshmen alive.[25] Jenkins's reputation as a strictly constitutional royalist and unyielding opponent of what he regarded as parliamentary illegality has been considered earlier in this book.[26] That he would have approved of his countrymen's resistance in 1647, as again in 1648, is hardly in doubt, though he himself was no Cavalier extremist. But, apart from inspiring by example, he was powerless to play any active part, since he was in prison during both the Glamorgan rising of June 1647 and the Second Civil War in 1648.

The summer of 1647 also saw troubles in the Marcher counties. In May, General Edward Massey, the hero of the defence of Gloucester in 1643 but one who was soon to be commander of the counter-revolutionary forces in London in late July and early August, had again been sent by parliament to Gloucester and from there to secure Monmouth against possible insurrections in that border shire.[27] A later document which can be dated from internal evidence at some time before the army's occupation of London on 6 August indicates grave disquiet in Shrewsbury and the adjoining countryside occasioned by the ever-increasing insolence of local Cavaliers. Many of the well-affected of this once firmly royalist town had become increasingly conscious of the need for measures to protect themselves 'against the Common

23. Tanner MSS., 58, fo. 218(b); Phillips, *Wales*, I, 388, II, 339; Newman, *Royalist Officers*, pp. 213–14.
24. Tanner MSS., 58, fo. 218; BL., E.394(5), p. 1; Phillips, *Wales*, I, 388, II, 336, 339, 341, 342, 343; Newman, *Royalist Officers*, p. 276.
25. BL., E.394(5), p. 1; Phillips, *Wales*, II, 341. A similar charge was made in a letter of 21 June from Bussy Mansell, Colonel Prichard and others (Tanner MSS., 58, fo. 218).
26. See above, pp. 109–13.
27. *Clarke Papers*, I, 93.

enemy that was as full of bloody rage and malice against vs as ever'. The county committee was prevailed upon to commission some trustworthy local gentlemen as captains and arrangements were made for townsmen to do regular guard duty, though they were backward in carrying this out, as was the Governor in responding to requests to supply arms and ammunition from the castle. Thus Shrewsbury remained vulnerable both to Cavalier subversion from within and Cavalier attack from without.[28]

It was especially from Wales that the danger to Shrewsbury had been apprehended and in fact all the Marcher towns were felt to be vulnerable from this quarter. On 5 January 1648 a letter from Hereford reported incursions from Wales which got to within about twenty miles from Hereford, when the invaders attacked and were beaten off by the soldiers of Colonel Horton's regiment.[29] Although the incident was certainly less than the 'great Rising' described in the letter, within a week, on 12 January, came news of what was to prove to be the origins of the Second Civil War in South Wales. This was Colonel John Poyer's refusal to obey Fairfax's order to surrender Pembroke Castle to the Lord General's nominee, Colonel Fleming, his imprisonment of the mayor of Pembroke and his predecessor, plundering of local inhabitants and the rapid growth of the numbers of Poyer's adherents in the castle from thirty-six to around two hundred.[30] Before the end of April many other parts of South Wales were in arms for the king. Hugh Games and others were garrisoning Brecon and the town was swarming with 'Malignant Gentlemen [who] wore Blew Ribbonds in their hats with the motto I long to see His Majestie: CR'. Laugharne was in revolt and Colonel Powell, soon to join Poyer in Pembroke, was raising an insurgent force at Carmarthen. For the time being the Welsh insurgents were thriving on rumours that the New Model Army in London had been cut off by the Cavaliers, that bishops had been re-established and the Book of Common Prayer restored.[31] With such developments, as with the disturbances in Herefordshire, Shropshire and Worcestershire in the summer, we move out of the sphere of this chapter and into that of the Second Civil War proper.

On 24 January two letters read in the House of Commons created something of a stir. One related to the arrangements for the disbandment of supernumerary forces in Gloucestershire, Herefordshire and Worcestershire, while the other gave details about a planned revolt of

28. Aberystwyth, National Library of Wales, Aston Hall MSS., 2586.
29. *A Relation of Captain Ingrams Addresse* (January 1648), BL., E.422(6), p. 6.
30. *Heads of the Chiefe Passages in Parliament Number 2* (12/19 January 1648), BL., E.423(11), pp. 10–12.
31. *A Great Fight in Wales* (29 April 1648), BL., E.438(2), pp. 1–6.

these forces organized by some eighty supernumerary officers meeting at Broadway in the Worcestershire Cotswolds. In the act of resisting disbandment the plotters sought to take Hartlebury Castle, which they hoped would be betrayed to them by its governor, Colonel Turton, and then to proceed to take Gloucester itself. In addition there was talk of surprising Hereford, Ludlow and even Shrewsbury as well as the possibility of joining forces with Major-General Laugharne from Wales, whose own resistance to forced disbandment would soon impel him into open revolt anyway. The plotters also had hopes of receiving aid in money from the discontented Londoners. For a time the supernumerary soldiers under Colonel Morgan in Gloucester managed to take over that city, refusing entry to Sir William Constable's regiment sent down to Gloucester by Fairfax to nip the design in the bud, but by 29 January Constable was safely ensconced in Gloucester and the danger was over.[32] Nevertheless, the incident caused some alarm, even if it was described by a royalist newswriter as a design to capture 'Castles in the Aire' which afforded a convenient pretext for a tightening of parliamentary controls and tyranny.[33] It is not surprising that during the Second Civil War the Derby House Committee felt it necessary to write to the committee at Gloucester on 27 July to know whether the city would be secure if Constable's regiment was removed from it for service elsewhere, and what measures they proposed for its safety in the event of this happening.[34]

The Excise riots in Worcester in late January 1648 have been mentioned earlier in another context, but in this one it is worth repeating that the rioters went to work on the Excise House there with shouts of 'downe with the Committee, and for God and King Charles'. A contemporary account of the incident stated that 'this businesse was plotted by some prime ones, and divers Souldiers that had beene Cavaliers . . . mightily incouraged them'.[35] The writer also warned of dangers in the neighbouring county of Herefordshire, and it was indeed there that the main rising in the Marcher counties in the Second Civil War occurred, led by the old Cavalier, Sir Henry Lingen.[36]

32. *Two Letters read in the House of Commons* (January 1648), BL., E.423(20), pp. 1–6; BL., Stowe MSS., 189, fos. 39(b)–40; *The Kingdomes Weekly Intelligencer* (25 January/1 February 1648), E.424(10), pp. 819–20.
33. *Mercurius Pragmaticus Number 4* (27 January/3 February 1648), BL., E.425(12), pp. 28–9.
34. *Cal.SPD. 1648–9*, p. 217.
35. *A Letter to a Member of the House of Commons* (February 1648), BL., E.425(20), pp. 3–6. See also *The Kingdomes Weekly Post Number 6* (2/9 February 1648), E.426(13), pp. 47–8 (corrected pagination). See above, pp. 79, 97–8, 201–2.
36. For Lingen's and other risings in the Marcher counties during the Second Civil War, see below, pp. 449–50, 460.

Metropolitan disturbances

The counter-revolutionary disturbances in London in July 1647, which were the gravest of all the threats to the government in that year, have already received attention in the contexts of London petitioning activity and of the dispute between the City and the army.[37] But unlike the Glamorgan rising, the London tumults were no anticipation of involvement in the much greater turmoil of the Second Civil War in the following year, when Londoners, however disgruntled, remained quiescent.

With the dispute between the army and the parliament and the fear of a Scottish invasion, supported by the army's enemies in parliament and the City, the tension rose spectacularly following the army's abduction of the king from Holdenby on 4 June. An ordinance of 10 July granted power for three months to the London Militia Committee to make thorough searches in the metropolitan area for popish recusants, ex-Cavaliers and others disaffected to parliament, an ambiguous phrase which might conceivably be held to include the army high command. Whether the body to which these powers were granted was fit to exercise them and whether it was more likely to join forces with counter-revolutionary elements in London were indeed questions which preoccupied many, not least the army grandees.[38] Certainly Cavaliers figured prominently in the tumult of 26 July. Thomas Juxon tells how a proposal that all ex-royalists in London should be forcibly disarmed, which was made at the height of the July counter-revolution, met with objections that 'they should then loose [sic] a great parte of there friendes'. He also surmises, perhaps fancifully, that the Cavaliers in London were planning to set free all royalist prisoners there and declare the duke of York their general.[39] A later account which, unlike Juxon's, is not suspect because of strongly pro-Independent and pro-army sympathies, was at pains to emphasize that the main participants in the notorious tumultuary assault on parliament on 26 July were 'Malignants [and] disbanded Souldiers not Apprentices'.[40]

On the other hand, the account of the incident by Sir William Waller, who was to be put in charge of the cavalry in the force for the defence of London, emphasizes the orderly way in which the petition

37. See above, pp. 137–8, 182–4; also V. Pearl, 'London's Counter-revolution', in Aylmer, *Interregnum*, especially pp. 44–56.
38. *A&O.*, I, 987–9; *L.J.*, IX, 325–6; *An Ordinance to enable the Committee of the Militia of London to make Searches* (10 July 1647), BL., E.397(22), especially pp. 1–2, 5–6.
39. Dr Williams's Library, MS. 24.50, fo. 115.
40. *The Case of the Impeached Lords Commons and Citizens Truely Stated* (22 January 1648), BL., E.423(16), pp. 7–8. See also *The Army Anatomized* (4 December 1647), E.419(6), p. 23.

for the rescinding of the new Militia Ordinance of 23 July was presented by the sheriffs and Common Council representatives, and that the violence only came later 'as the dregs ever stay last', forcing the Speaker to resume the Chair and preventing MPs from leaving until the House had voted to bring the king to London.[41] Be this as it may, and Waller's bias is as strong as that of Juxon, though in the opposite direction, it is beyond dispute that many Cavaliers participated in the tumult on 26 July. The role of one such 'malignant', the colourful, loud-mouthed and violent Captain Musgrave, has already been remarked elsewhere,[42] and the same depositions before the parliamentary investigators in September which describe Musgrave's behaviour also tell of another rioter, one John Utting, who urged on the others with shouts of 'a King, a King'.[43]

While only the scale, as distinct from the fact, of Cavalier participation in the tumult of 26 July is in question, the role of the king himself is a less straightforward matter. His denunciation of the counter-revolutionary violence and emphatic denial to Fairfax that he was in any way responsible for it[44] was the more necessary in view of the fact that the army clearly believed that he was deeply implicated in it, as Cromwell and Ireton made clear at a meeting with John Ashburnham in August.[45] Nevertheless, there can be little doubt that, true though his vigorous disclaimers of responsibility might be, Charles would have welcomed a successful conclusion to the counter-revolutionary episode, while taking care to distance himself from it as long as the outcome was uncertain.

What of the complicity or otherwise of the City fathers? Of the tumultuous mob on 26 July, Sir William Waller observes, perhaps disingenuously, 'What these people were, or by whom instigated and sett on . . . God knoweth I know not'.[46] But others at least thought they knew. Writing to the Lord General's father on 27 July, John Rushworth remarked that though 'this giddy-headed multitude' on the previous day was 'not yet countenanced openly with persons of estate', he had no doubt that the rulers of the City would have to account for their behaviour. Even if it is not easy to establish proof of positive promptings

---

41. Waller, *Vindication*, pp. 183–4. Parliament had condemned the Solemn Engagement on 24 July as 'tending to the imbroiling the Kingdom in a new Warre' (*L.J.*, IX, 354; BL., 669, f11(49)). It had to eat its words two days later. On the Solemn Engagement, see above, p. 182.
42. See above, p. 203.
43. HLRO., MP., 25/9/1647, fo. 21.
44. *Clarendon SP.*, II, 373; *The Kings Majesties Declaration . . .* (August 1647), BL., E.401(23), pp. 1–4 (corrected pagination); *Parliamentary History*, XVI, 205. For another royal denial of responsibility, see *The Kings . . . Most Gracious Message* (August 1647), E.401(19), no pagination.
45. Ashburnham, *Narrative*, II, 93–4.
46. Waller, *Vindication*, pp. 183–4.

of the rioters by City notabilities, in negative terms the City authorities were unquestionably gravely at fault for their inaction in the face of tumult. Rushworth observed that 'the militia stirred not, and the Lord Mayor would not. The Sheriffs came in person with some forty halberdiers which was all the militia of the City that appeared for the Parliament.'[47] Moreover, according to Speaker Lenthall, who had fled to the army after the invasion of parliament on 26 July, despite the Lord Mayor's assurances to the contrary, no adequate measures had subsequently been taken by the municipal authorities to prevent a recurrence of disturbances.[48] In a letter of 29 July to the Lord Mayor, aldermen and Common Council, Fairfax not only roundly blamed them for negligence in not acting against the riot three days earlier, but went further, averring that 'I am assured from Eye and Ear Witnesses that divers of the Common Council gave great Encouragement to it'.[49] Among those who agreed was the earl of Leicester, who had no doubt that the City fathers' guilt extended beyond interested negligence to positive complicity. While the apprentices, malignants and reformadoes were browbeating parliament to revoke the Militia Ordinance of 23 July and invite the king to London, Leicester tells us that

> At the same time came some of the Aldermen the Sherriffes, and a great part of the Common Counsell to . . . Parliament . . . which shews that the said multitude came thither upon the excitation of the Common Counsell, for as soone as they had theyr desires, they dismissed the multitude and sent them away to theyr homes.[50]

Leicester's account and verdict are corroborated by pro-Independents and army sources of which Juxon's diary is the most notable. In addition Juxon tells of violence in the days before the tumult of 26 July in his account of how, when the new Militia Committee which was the product of the ordinance of 23 July met at Guildhall, its members were assaulted by some young men and threatened that 'if they Caught them there againe, they would hange their gutts about their eares. And never left them till they had Compeld them to rise, and, as they went, followed with ill Language'. According to this account, when the aldermen and Common Councilmen brought the petition for the rescinding of the Militia Ordinance of 23 July to parliament only to be told that this could not be done, 'they tould th'Apprentizes & others

47. Bell, *Memorials*, I, 380–3.
48. *Parliamentary History*, XVI, 197–9; HLRO., MP., 30/7/1647. For a later denial of this charge, see *The Case of the Impeached Lords Commons and Citizens . . .* (22 January 1648), BL., E.423(16), p. 8.
49. CLRO., Jor. 40, fo. 243(b); *L.J.*, IX, 360; Rushworth, *Historical Collections*, VI, 647; *Two Letters from Sir Thomas Fairfax* (July 1647), BL., E.400(23), pp. 1–2.
50. *Sydney Papers*, pp. 25–6.

whoe were there in great Numbers That they had don what they could; and that now it rested in them to play their Partes'. Those parts were, of course, the violent intimidation of parliament, with, if Juxon is to be credited, the apprentices mingling and voting with MPs in the House. He also describes how Alderman Bunce stood in the Palace Yard with some Common Councilmen directing operations. Parliament sent to the Lord Mayor asking him to send down a force of trained bands, but it was only when parliament had yielded to intimidation and passed the necessary resolutions that he complied, as well as sending some who were *personae gratae* with the rioters to quieten them and tell them to go home. Like Leicester, Juxon regards it as highly significant that they complied.[51] As late as December Fairfax and the army Council expressed strong disapproval of the tendency even of Lord Mayor Gayre's Independent successor and his colleagues to treat the events of 26 July and after 'as if in those Things there had not been so much Fault'.[52]

What can be established with certainty from the official City record is that when Common Council had been informed on 26 July of the tumultuous gathering of apprentices, reformadoes and others at the door of the House of Commons, it ordered some Common Councilmen to go down to Westminster 'and vse their best indeavour by all gentle wayes and meanes . . . to appease the said multitude and to free the said house from danger'.[53] A straightforward reading of these words in the Common Council Journal, for what they are worth, suggests, if anything, civic acquiescence rather than positive incitement, though much depends on the precise meaning one attaches to the word 'appease'. It is, of course, arguable that the idea of using apprentices and reformadoes as surrogates to intimidate parliament had much to commend it to the sympathetic but cautious City governors. For whether they were instigators or simply sympathetic bystanders, the end-product of the tumult of 26 July was very much to the liking of the Lord Mayor Gayre and many of his aldermanic colleagues: the restoration of the *status quo ante* 23 July in the matter of militia control; the temporary restoration of the eleven members; and the invitation to the king to come to London for a personal treaty. That this much is true is

51. Dr Williams's Library, MS., 24.50, fos. 112(b)–13(b). For a similar emphasis see the pro-army newsletter of 26 July (*Clarke Papers*, I, 217–18).
52. *L.J.*, IX, 562; *An Humble Representation from Sir Thomas Fairfax* . . . (December 1647), BL., E.419(16), pp. 21–2. In view of the Lord Mayor's earlier condemnation of 'that dangerous Ingagement', the charge is perhaps less than fair (CLRO., Jor. 40, fos. 263–3(b); *L.J.*, IX, 550–1; *Parliamentary History*, XVI, 366; *The Humble Petition of the Lord Major* [*sic*] (December 1647), E.419(1), pp. 3–4).
53. CLRO., Jor. 40, fo. 240(b).

testified by the City's own Declaration of 31 July and its acceptance of a counter-revolutionary petition from apprentices and others.[54]

Not every petition was so favourably received at Guildhall, however. In an earlier chapter mention was made of petitioners seeking help from Fairfax for redress for the outrageous treatment meted out to them when trying to present a petition to the Lord Mayor, aldermen and Common Council on 2 August.[55] The petitioners described themselves as 'citizens of worth and quality', but their petition was decidedly unwelcome to those City supporters of Holles who were supreme in London and who were accused by the petitioners of plotting to embroil the City in a second war.[56] Nevertheless, the brutal violence let loose on the petitioners was all too symptomatic of the atmosphere of counter-revolutionary terror which had gripped London over the whole of the previous week. We have already had occasion to note how the petitioners failed on 24 August to obtain redress from parliament and ultimately turned to Fairfax to help them, though that was not until October. Their own account of the events of 2 August may be overdrawn, but there is no reason to doubt its general authenticity. There had originally been twenty-eight petitioners on that day but there were only twenty-six signatories of the unsuccessful petition to parliament on 24 August, two petitioners having been killed in the accompanying fracas of the earlier date. On that occasion the petitioners, proceeding 'unarmed in a peaceable Manner', were not only abused and struck by the Lord Mayor and others, but set upon by two sets of armed reformadoes under Poynz and Massey outside the Guildhall and in Bassishaw Street, with two resulting fatalities and many more of the 'Independent Dogs and Rogues', as their assailants described them, wounded. Despite this disgraceful assault, Poynz and Massey went unpunished, flaunting themselves on horseback up and down the streets.[57]

No doubt it was not simply political Independents and friends of the army like Thomas Juxon who noted the contrast between, on the one hand, the discipline and good order of the army's entry into London on 6 August and its orderly behaviour afterwards,[58] and, on the other, the disorderly violence of ill-disciplined reformadoes, of which the affair of the petitioners on 2 August is an extreme, but by no means a unique,

54. Ibid., fos. 240(b)–2, 244(b)–6; Rushworth, *Historical Collections*, VI, 648–51; *A declaration of the lord maior* . . . (1647), BL., E.400(29), especially pp. 6–9.
55. See above, pp. 131, 138.
56. *A peaceable Petition of a Very Great Number of Citizens* . . . (August 1647), BL., 669, f11(58).
57. *L.J.*, IX, 401–2; *HMC.*, *6th. Report (House of Lords Cal. 1647)*, p. 193; *Two Petitions from the City of London* (October 1647), BL., E.410(20), pp. 1–6; For Juxon's account of the clash on 2 August, see Dr Williams's Library, MS. 24.50, fos. 117–17(b). For a very different account, see below, pp. 392–3.
58. See above, p. 186.

example. This observed contrast is surely a factor to be invoked in explaining why there was no recurrence of the events of July 1647 during the Second Civil War.

When the charges against the former Lord Mayor Sir John Gayre, his aldermanic colleagues Adams, Bunce and Langham and other citizens and reformado officers such as Poynz, Colonel Dalbier (who was later killed fighting for the king in the Second Civil War), Colonel James Middup and Captain Robert Massey were finally approved in April 1648, they consisted in the main of their involvement in a long conspiracy together with the eleven members, culminating in their active role in the coup of 26 July and the raising of a counter-revolutionary force in London to engage in a second war and cooperate with a Scottish invasion.[59] A doubly significant figure in this alleged conspiracy was John Glyn, who, as one of the eleven members and as Recorder of London, combined in his person the parliamentary and city dimensions of this alleged conspiracy. On 3 February 1648 the radical Independent MPs, John Lisle and Thomas Scot, brought up in a conference between the Houses incriminating information relating to Glyn's behaviour during and after the coup of 26 July, which was to result in his losing his Recordership, having already, as one of the eleven members, been suspended from sitting in the House as MP for Westminster. Lisle and Scot sought to establish beyond reasonable doubt that Glyn had been a key figure in the July counter-revolution. He lived near to the parliament house in Westminster, and had been observed in Westminster Hall at the time of the tumult on 26 July, making no attempt to restrain the rioters. During the ten days of counter-revolutionary ascendancy following the coup, Glyn had been present at more meetings of the newly reestablished Militia Committee than he had attended during the whole of the previous six months, and had been associated with all the major acts both of that committee and of Common Council, as for instance the appointment of Edward Massey as Commander-in-chief of the forces defending London. If he had not himself 'absolutely approved' of the Solemn Engagement of the citizens, he had at the very least 'much extenuated and condoned it'. This, of course, is the testimony of Glyn's bitter political opponents, but there is every reason to believe that his attitude to the counter-revolutionary turn of events in July was at the very least one of cautious condonation and, not improbably, of positive and enthusiastic approval.[60]

Others had found themselves caught up in events without necessarily playing an active part in them. Of course, it could be argued that, like

59. *L.J.*, X, 201–3, 213–15, 217–19; *Parliamentary History*, XVII, 96–103. On the counter-revolutionary force and the reformadoes, see below, pp. 379–99.
60. *L.J.*, X, 16–18.

the Speakers of both Houses, they might have demonstrated their disapproval by fleeing to the army, but this required a degree of positive commitment which many, and probably most, did not possess either way. An interesting case in point is the earl of Pembroke, who on 20 August made a formal statement to the effect that in his view the House of Lords had acted under force between 26 July and 6 August, and therefore its proceedings over this period were void. In the circumstances of late August it was indeed easy, not to say advantageous, to make such a statement, and there is no record of Pembroke's expressing such reservations in the last week of July or the first week of August. However, on 14 September he made a further statement emphasizing that he had attended parliament strictly under orders, and that 'the Committee for the Safety being revived, the Guards and City and Works very strictly and strongly watched . . . I could not leave the City'. Thereafter, under constant threat from the apprentices and others, he had had no choice – was this true? – but to comply with parliament's actions, opposing, so far as he could – how far was that, one wonders? – all votes against the public interest.[61]

There we must leave London's counter-revolution of July and early August 1647. In the event, it will be recalled that the legal proceedings against the aldermen were dropped in May 1648 and the survivors of the eleven members restored to their seats as part of what appears to have been a deliberate programme of appeasement to secure the City's quiescence in the Second Civil War.[62] Helped by Skippon's firm control of metropolitan security, that policy was successful. That there was need for such measures is perhaps demonstrated by recurrent, if minor, disturbances in the meantime.

London experienced its share of Christmas disturbances in 1647, when Lord Mayor Warner attempted personally to dismantle the holly and ivy with which the conduit in Cornhill had been decorated in honour of Christmas but in defiance of parliamentary and municipal command. Like the far more serious disturbances in Canterbury, the protest had been accompanied by a Prayer Book service, when parliament had ordained that there should be no service of any kind, let alone one using the Prayer Book.[63] Potentially more serious was the design mentioned in a newsletter of 13 December 'to raise a new Army on the suddaine to surprize the Parliament and Tower'. The principal plotters were said to be Lord Cleveland and Sir Marmaduke Langdale and recruiting was said to be proceeding in and around London by some

61. L.J., IX, 433.
62. See above, pp. 177, 191–2.
63. Mercurius Pragmaticus number 29 (28 December/4 January 1647/8), BL., E.421(29), no pagination; ibid., number 1 (13 January 1648), E.422(31), p. 4; Heads of Chiefe Passages in Parliament Number 32 (12/19 January 1648), E.423(11), p. 10.

forty colonels and other royalist officers. The report that some 1,800 horse and many foot had been enlisted is almost certainly an exaggeration. Colonel Michael Hudson, who, like Langdale, was to play a notable part in the Second Civil War, in which he met a horrible end (see plate 5), was said to be planning a visit to royalists imprisoned in the Tower to confer about strategy which included a planned escape of the king from the Isle of Wight.[64] On 14 January the House of Commons was informed that Cleveland and Sir Lewis Dyve were planning to escape to lead the conspiracy, at which there was further stiffening of measures against Cavaliers and Catholics and reinforcements sent from the New Model Army to Westminster.[65] Dyve did in fact make a spectacular escape from the King's Bench prison to which he had been removed 'there in [to] rot in Prison for Debt', after having spent two years in the Tower.[66] But Cleveland stayed put in the Tower and the projected conspiracy proved to be a very damp squib.

On 15 January a major was sent to Newgate prison for endeavouring to enlist forces for the king in London.[67] On 27 January another ex-royalist officer, Lieutenant-Colonel Burgis, was committed to the Gatehouse for raising troops in London, which he protested he was doing under commission from the Spanish ambassador, for service in the Low Countries, although the government no doubt feared that they might be put to other uses nearer home, and from 29 February no-one was allowed to raise such levies for foreign service except by licence of the Derby House Committee.[68] That committee was kept on its toes throughout January with Cavaliers striving to derive the utmost advan-

64. *The Perfect Weekly Account Number 650* (8/15 December 1647), BL., E.419(28), no pagination. This is probably the alleged conspiracy seen by Bellièvre as affording a pretext for expelling ex-Cavaliers and Catholics from London (*Montereul Correspondence*, II, 355). For these measures, see *L.J.*, IX, 584; *An Ordinance for the putting out . . . all Delinquents Papists and others* (17 December 1647), E.419(30), pp. 1–4; *The Moderate Intelligencer Number 144* (16/23 December 1647), E.421(7), no pagination. Ex-royalists who had compounded or taken the Negative Oath were exempt.
65. *C.J.*, V, 432. For a royalist comment, see *Mercurius Pragmaticus number 18* (11/18 January 1648), BL., E.423(1), no pagination. One newswriter mentions a Cavalier plot to murder MPs and their friends (E.423(11), p. 14 (corrected pagination)). Actually Cleveland had honoured his four months' parole and returned to the Tower on 13 January (*HMC., 7th. Report Appendix (House of Lords Cal. 1647–8)*, p. 3).
66. For Dyve's own account of his escape, see H.G. Tibbutt (ed.), *The Life and Letters of Sir Lewis Dyve 1599–1669*, Bedfordshire Record Society, XVII (1948), 83–90.
67. BL., E.423(11), p. 13 (corrected pagination). Notwithstanding the discrepancy in rank, this may well have been the Colonel Yorke who was sent to Newgate for this offence, and who, a newsletter tells us, had sold wine at the Mitre in Bishopsgate where, no doubt, many loyal toasts were drunk (*The Kingdomes Weekly Intelligencer Number 243* (11/18 January 1648), E.423(7), p. 808). For other cases of ex-officers engaged in recruiting, see *The Kingdomes Weekly Account . . . Number 5* (2/9 February 1648), E.426(14), p. 34.
68. *C.J.*, V, 450, 473; *L.J.*, X, 4, 8–9, 81; *HMC., 7th. Report Appendix (House of Lords Cal. 1647–8)*, p. 16; HLRO., MP., 7/2/1648. Burgis had acted along with other officers.

tage out of issues such as the cost of living, the decay of trade and the unpopularity of the regiments in Whitehall and the Mews,[69] and by the successive reports of plots to take over London or to bring the king there.[70] On 14 February the Committee warned the London Militia Committee about the likelihood of trouble on Shrove Tuesday, a traditional day of apprentice turbulence,[71] while on 21 March the discovery of yet another plot to surprise the Tower was reported.[72]

There was much concern about the dangers to order in London in April and May, not without reason since South Wales was ablaze and serious trouble brewing in the Home Counties and especially in Kent. The April violence arising out of Lord Mayor Warner's officious attempts to repress apprentice games on the Sabbath has already been mentioned in another context, where emphasis was laid on the royalist slogans of the rioters.[73] In a deposition made before magistrates in mid-May one William Paradine disclosed details of what looked like a more dangerous conspiracy. According to Paradine, on the night of 1 May some thirty conspirators including Cavaliers, apprentices and gentlemen from the Inns of Court had gathered in an upper room at the Sign of the Three Tuns in Newgate 'to consult together to finde out a way to raise horse and foote, For God and King and City'. Individual conspirators were told to enlist men in the city and to deliver their names at the Sign of the Queen's Head in Lombard Street, and it was said that some 1,500 persons had already been enlisted. The plan was to obtain control of the gates of the city and all the horses the conspirators could lay their hands on. An ex-officer in the royalist army, Major Pilkington, treated the conspirators to an account of the general aims of the design which were to restore the king and the true Protestant religion and to see to the security of the City, presumably vis-à-vis the New Model Army. When one of his audience asked about sources of arms and ammunition, Pilkington replied, 'I hope there is none heere soe poore butt are able to buy two or 3 shotts apiece, for . . . when once the Gates are secur'd, wee will nott want for amunition'.[74]

Hearing from the Derby House Committee of what seems to have been this same conspiracy, parliament ordered the London militia to be in special readiness to cope with it and keepers of prisons were told to keep a special watch on malignants in their custody.[75] On 24 May the

69. See the letter of 25 January from William Clarke to Lieutenant-Colonel Reade (BL., Stowe MSS., 189, fo. 39).
70. *Cal.SPD. 1648–9*, pp. 8, 9, 10–11; *A Letter from the Major [sic] . . . of . . . Rochester . . .* (January 1648), BL., E.423(17), p. 5.
71. PRO., SP. 21/9, fo. 20.
72. Rushworth, *Historical Collections*, VII, 1035; Whitelock, *Memorials*, p. 296 (21 March).
73. See above, pp. 190–91, 238.
74. *Clarke Papers*, II, 5–6.
75. *C.J.*, V, 563, 566. During July the conveying of royalist prisoners to Peterhouse prison occasioned attempts to rescue them and it was ordered on 14 July that no more

Lord Mayor ordered the aldermen to take special measures against the danger of potential insurgents in their wards. Rumour had it that many thousands had been enlisted under the command of ex-Cavalier officers, and that it was planned to join forces with disaffected elements in the Home Counties who would then advance on London Bridge and co-operate in the seizure of the Tower. The official description of the conspiracy is not without its cloak-and-dagger aspect. The plotters swore an oath of association which bound them to the strictest secrecy. Pistols, daggers and other arms and ammunition were purchased and there was even mention of a meeting of Irish papists where 'several daggers were laid upon the Altar, and by the Priest demanded if they were sharp, and by him were sprinkled with holy water'.[76] On 26 May the Derby House Committee informed parliament that it had told the Lord General to take measures against insurrections in the Home Counties since rendezvous had been called by the Kent, Surrey and Essex insurgents dangerously close to London, at Blackheath, Putney Heath and Wanstead respectively.[77] As this last reference makes clear, we are now into the period of the height of the Second Civil War, but while the summer of 1648 was to see risings in the Home Counties, Wales and the provinces and an invasion from Scotland, which had not occurred in 1647, there was to be no repetition of the London counter-revolution of July 1647, even though apprehension of such a rising persisted for some weeks. As late as 16 August the writer of a letter to Fairfax believed that matters in London were coming to a head: 'The Citties [en]listing goes on this day more violent than ever before. . . . Thinges are high, the designe will bee speedily putt in execution, if not prevented by a blow att Colchester or the North.'[78] The blow in the north came on the very next day with Cromwell's shattering defeat of the Scots at Preston, while Colchester had surrendered by the end of the month. However, it is far too easy, employing hindsight, to play down the prevalent fear of another counter-revolution in London, though this time against the far more dangerous background of a renewal of civil war and a Scottish invasion. Chastened by their experiences of July and August 1647, the Londoners kept their heads and Philip Skippon his grip on the city, which gained by its quiescence in 1648 what it had so signally failed to achieve by its violence in 1647: that treaty with the king which had appeared to be

prisoners of quality should be brought to London (*Cal.SPD. 1648–9*, pp. 187–8; *L.J.*, X, 382; Rushworth, *Historical Collections*, VII, 1189).

76. *A Proclamation of the Lord Major* [*sic*] (24 May 1648), BL., E.445(9), no pagination; BL., 669, f12(32).
77. *L.J.*, X, 283–4; *Cal.SPD. 1648–9*, pp. 79–80, 82.
78. *Clarke Papers*, II, 30.

ruled out by the Vote of No Addresses at the beginning of the year. Patience had indeed been rewarded.

The south of England and the West Country

Kent, which had been successfully held for parliament during the First Civil War, despite experiencing a royalist uprising in 1643 and another less serious one in 1645,[79] was to experience what was, along with the Essex revolt which was belatedly connected with it, the most severe of all the royalist uprisings in the Second Civil War. At the end of the first war the local authorities showed themselves to be very conscious of the need to keep a careful watch on the survivors of the revolts of 1643 and 1645 and on Cavaliers returning home from other parts of the country.[80] The first serious trouble in Kent, however, did not come until Christmas 1647 when the tumults at Canterbury, which were the most violent of any of the Christmas disturbances in that year, triggered off a succession of events which led inexorably to the Kentish uprising in May 1648.[81] The connection operated via what the royalist *Mercurius Elencticus* considered to be the main significance of the incident, which was the excuse it gave the authorities for repression.[82] This in turn gave rise to the Kent petition of May and, following the county committee's measures against the petitioners, the renewal of civil war in Kent.[83] For although the immediate occasion of the disturbances was the official attempt to prevent celebration of Christmas, they quickly became what the Kent committee, with perhaps pardonable exaggeration, described as 'a high Insurrection' of a royalist and anti-parliamentarian character; the fruition, as the committee informed the Speaker in a letter of 21 January, of long maturing counter-revolutionary plotting. Even the game of football played in the streets may have been part of a deliberate design to attract into the city the multitudes who came in from the surrounding countryside. The Kent committee's unavailing plea that normal judicial process was an inappropriate way of dealing with offenders since no Kentish Grand Jury would find a true bill against them, was borne out by events, and is in itself an

---

79. On these, see Everitt, *Kent*, pp. 187–200, 212–18.
80. On the measures at Maidstone between April and September 1646, see I.J. Churchill (ed.), 'A Seventeenth Century Miscellany', *Kent Archaeological Society Record Publications*, XVII (1900), 138–9.
81. For a more detailed account of the Canterbury Christmas disturbances, see Everitt, *Kent*, pp. 231–40.
82. *Mercurius Elencticus* number 6 (29 December/5 January 1647/8), BL., E.421(6), pp. 47–8.
83. On these events, see above, pp. 144–8.

apt reflection on its own responsibility for the disastrous course of subsequent events.[84]

The occasion of the Canterbury Christmas riots was the mayor's order that the shops should be kept open 'on the Saturday called Christmas day, [and] that there should be no observance of that abolish'd Feast'.[85] The prohibition also extended to religious commemoration of Christmas. 'That which we so much desired that day', states one account, 'was but a Sermon . . . but that day (because it was Christs birthday) we must have none: that which is good all the year long, yet is this day superstitious.'[86] In obedience to the mayoral (and parliamentary) command some shopkeepers opened their doors – only about twelve of them if one account is to be believed – but some obstinately remained closed in observance of Christmas. The situation gave rise to violent disturbances. Many of those shops which had opened were looted, the goods on display were scattered up and down the streets, and the shopkeepers assaulted. The mayor, himself an Excise official and none the less unpopular for that, strove to restore order but to no avail. The rioters 'to confirme that they broake the Peace . . . breake [sic] his head' while he was attempting to rescue the sheriff, who received an even more severe beating, from the attention of the rioters. The protest quickly became a virulently anti-Puritan and pro-royalist demonstration. The mayor and his colleagues were escorted home 'with the *Strappado* and *Kickado*, where they made them kepe open *Butteries* as well as Shops', setting up holly bushes at their doors, and providing free drink for all comers.[87]

But this was only the beginning. By the Monday after Christmas Day the rioters had been joined by dissidents from the villages around and there were now above a thousand of them according to one contemporary estimate, many of them crying '*For God, King Charles and Kent*'. The city magazine was seized as well as weapons and munitions in the town hall. Courts of Guard were mounted in four places and everyone going into and out of the city was scrutinized carefully. What had begun

84. Bodleian, Tanner MSS., 58, fos. 653, 672–4 (letters from the Kent Committee to Speaker Lenthall on 5 and 21 January 1648).
85. Apart from the source mentioned in note 84, this account is based upon contemporary descriptions by writers of differing sympathies, viz. *The Kingdomes Weekly Intelligencer number 241* (27 December/4 January 1647/8), BL., E.421(30), pp. 785–6; *The Perfect Weekly Account number 1* (28 December/5 January 1647/8), E.421(33), sig. Aᵛ; *Mercurius Pragmaticus number 29* (28 December/4 January 1647/8), E.421(29), sig. Qᵛ–Q2ᵛ; ibid., *number 1* (13 January 1648), E.422(31), pp. 4–5; *Mercurius Elencticus Number 6* (29 December/6 January 1647/8), E.421(6), pp. 47–8; *Canterbury Christmas . . .* (1 January 1648), E.421(22), pp. 1–4; *The Declaration of the City of Canterbury or County of Kent* (5 January 1648), E.421(23), pp. 3–7. The last of these papers lays particularly strong emphasis on royalist elements in the tumults.
86. BL., E.421(23), p. 6.
87. BL., E.421(29), sig. Q2.

as a disorganized riot was developing into a more formidable challenge to the government. As one account puts it, the rioters were now 'in a Military (and not in a drinking) posture'. On 30 December the House of Commons referred the Canterbury troubles to a committee with power to examine witnesses and make arrests.[88] This they did in considerable numbers when the rebels rather surprisingly yielded without a fight to the onslaught of the Kentish trained bands early in January.

Thus ended the most violent of the Christmas disturbances of 1647, though its consequences were more far-reaching. Commenting in greater tranquillity more than a fortnight after these events, the royalist *Mercurius Pragmaticus* took heart from the episode as suggesting that 'the reigne of these domineering traytors is almost come to a period'. In the same newsletter he bewailed the failure of the Cavalier Captain Burley's futile attempt to raise a force in the Isle of Wight to rescue the king.[89] Burley seems to have brought others with him into the island and joined with local Cavaliers, causing drums to be beaten and inviting more to join him in the enterprise. However, he was soon to be immured in one of the dungeons of Carisbrooke Castle, from which place he had vainly sought to rescue his king.[90] Although it was reported early in January that he was to be tried by commission of martial law,[91] he stood trial in Winchester under a commission of Oyer and Terminer and was executed there in January. The alleged injustice of Burley's trial, presided over by the Roundhead 'Bloodsucker' Serjeant Wylde, and his steadfast end in the face of the horrible penalties of treason, confessing himself 'a sinner but not a Traytor', made useful Cavalier propaganda material. He protested on the scaffold that he had no design, as his accusers alleged, to plunge the country into a second war, but only 'to free his Majesty from bondage', and that, given the opportunity, he would do the same again.[92]

Burley's reported intention had been to carry the king to Jersey, which was in royalist hands. There were fears in February and March for the safety of neighbouring Guernsey which was rather precariously held for parliament but was threatened by royalist preparations to capture it from bases in Jersey and on the French mainland. There were

88. BL., E.421(30), p. 789; *The Kingdomes Weekly Post* (29 December/5 January 1647/8), E.422(1), p. 4.
89. BL., E.422(31), pp. 4–5.
90. BL., E.421(33), no pagination (entry for 3 January); E.422(1), pp. 4–5.
91. BL., E.421(33), no pagination; E.422(1), p. 5.
92. For royalist accounts of Burley's end, see *Mercurius Elencticus Number 10* (26 January/2 February 1648), BL., E.425(7), pp. 74–5; *Mercurius Pragmaticus Number 4* (27 January/3 February 1648), E.425(12), p. 30. For other accounts, see *A Designe by Captaine Barley* [sic] *and others* (January 1648), E.421(24), pp. 1–5; *Captaine Barley* [sic] *his Speech At the Place of Execution* (February 1648), E.425(20), pp. 1–3; *The Kingdomes Weekly Post Number 6* (2/9 February 1648), E.426(13), p. 46.

reports of Irish soldiers coming to Jersey en route, or so they claimed, to join Prince Rupert to serve the Emperor; and of the Prince of Wales's intention to join the royalists in Jersey who already had five men-of-war at their disposal to prey on English shipping for which the excellent harbour in Guernsey would make useful additional anchorage. But nothing came of these fears.[93]

Back in Hampshire, the grisly fate of the unfortunate Captain Burley does not seem completely to have deterred Cavalier militancy. On 20 and 25 January the Derby House Committee warned Colonel Hammond at Carisbrooke that there had been frequent and highly suspicious resorting of Cavaliers to Netley Abbey, inconveniently close to the Isle of Wight, and that messages from them and others were regularly being passed to the king through the medium of the woman who carried his laundry.[94] Much later, on 2 May, 300 soldiers were quartered in Winchester as a precaution against the surprising of the castle by some of the unusually large numbers of cavaliers reported in these parts,[95] one of whom, the ubiquitous Jack Ashburnham, was shortly to be apprehended in Hampshire, and confined in Windsor Castle.[96]

During the First Civil War, and especially following the victorious campaign of Rupert and Hopton in 1643, the West Country, except for a few odd parliamentarian strongholds such as Plymouth and Taunton, had been predominantly royalist country. It is therefore not surprising that, in the years between the two civil wars, the royalists held out high hopes for these parts, although in the event these were sorely disappointed. In April 1648 there were notable gatherings of Cavaliers in Bristol and Bath, those in the latter place focussing around Anglican church services and local bull-baitings.[97] Both the forbidden religious services and the bull-baitings, like race-meetings in this and other parts of the country,[98] occasioned some alarm on account of their potential for subversive activity. The intimate and complex relationship between royalism, games and revels in the West Country has recently been

93. Bodleian, Tanner MSS., 59, fos. 699, 702–2(b), 733, 794, 820.
94. *Cal.SPD. 1648–9*, pp. 6, 9.
95. Ibid., p. 57.
96. *C.J.*, V, 566.
97. On Bristol, see 'The Copy of a letter from Bristoll' sub *The Designes of the Lord Inchequin* . . . (April 1648), Codrington pamphlet coll., pp. 3–4; Rushworth, *Historical Collections*, VII, 1097; For the voting of money on 10 May for the better defence of Bristol, ibid., p. 1109. On Bath, see J. Wroughton, *The Civil War in Bath and North Somerset 1642–1650* (Bath, 1973), pp. 114–15. On 23 May Colonel Alexander Popham, MP for Bath, was sent down to Somerset to secure the peace of the county and to raise a troop of horse to suppress 'malignant, tumultuous and riotous Meetings'. Sir John Horner was also asked to use his best endeavours to this end in Somerset (*C.J.*, V, 569–70).
98. On race-meetings and the designs of northern Cavaliers on Berwick, see below, p. 366.

emphasized in the work of Professor Underdown.[99] On 8 September 1646 the Devonshire Quarter Sessions took order for the suppression of the revels which had been arranged at Cheriton Fitzpatrick and elsewhere, noting that the disorders flowing from 'excessive drinking, quarrelling and other disorderly Carriadges on such occasions' were especially dangerous 'in these times of trouble and soe great Contagion'.[100] On 28 March 1648 the earl of Lanark's royalist correspondent wrote hopefully of a gathering arranged for the following Monday for a hurling match between participants from Devon and Cornwall. This, he explained, was 'a sport they haue with a ball', adding, however, that 'tis thought they haue an other designe for they, but especially theire neighbour countye Dorsettshire, are very much discontented'.[101]

Reporting to Fairfax in May 1648 about his difficulties with the municipal authorities of Exeter about billeting,[102] Sir Hardress Waller was at pains to stress the unreliability, with few exceptions, of the county committeemen of Devon and Cornwall, 'who either do not appear to act or else seen [sic] to insinuate with the Cavaliers', and on 19 June report was heard in the House of Commons of Waller's successful crushing of royalist-inspired tumults in Devon and Cornwall.[103] But, despite government fears that such tumults might merge into active participation in the Second Civil War, as happened in Kent, the high royalist expectations from the West Country were disappointed.

The north of England and the Border

On 25 September 1646 the Committee of the Northern Association wrote to Speaker Lenthall requesting that money be made available out of the composition fines paid by delinquents 'for the suppressinge of malignantes wherewith these Northerne partes are much infested'.[104] Three days later the parson Henry Massy wrote from Kendal to his patron Lord Wharton in London expressing his alarm at the frequent gatherings of disbanded soldiers from former royalist garrisons and local Cavaliers whose 'pride & lofty carriages exceedes former tymes' and who 'insult vs much (if not more) than ever'. Massy gave voice to the fears of many local people that, once the Scots had departed, such subversives would pose a very serious threat to the peace of these parts,

99. D. Underdown, *Revel, Riot and Rebellion . . . 1603–1660* (Oxford, 1985), passim.
100. Exeter, Devon R.O., QS. Order Book 1640–51, no foliation (8 September 1646).
101. *Hamilton Papers*, p. 171. For royalist disturbances over religion in Dorset, see above, p. 262.
102. On this incident, see above, pp. 66–7.
103. *L.J.*, X, 269; Rushworth, *Historical Collections*, VII, 1156.
104. Bodleian, Tanner MSS., 59, fo. 550.

and, sure enough, on 8 February 1647, with the Scots departed, he again warned against 'home-based enemies in our country' and that 'our chavaliers [sic] hold vp there heads & seeme to have greate hopes'.[105]

Massy himself was to be a victim of the violent attentions of such people in an incident in August 1647 which has already been mentioned in the context of local opposition to county committees.[106] On 11 August some 400 royalists who had gathered on the previous day arrived in Kendal and some of them burst into the chamber where the county committee was meeting. They dragged the mayor and the committeemen to the house of a local Cavalier, one Peter Sheppard, with 'many Menaces and Threats . . . declaring themselves . . . to be the opposite to any Parliamentary Power'. They seized the local magazine, caused drums to be beaten in the town to attract recruits who 'stood for GOD and the King', and imprisoned the local parliamentarian parson, Mr Massy. When the committee demanded to know their authority for acting thus, they replied by neatly adapting Cornet Joyce's famous answer to the same question when put by the king at Holdenby in June: that 'Their Swords were their Commissions'. It was not until 29 February 1648 that the House of Lords was in a position to order the arrest of seven of the main offenders, including Anthony Knipe, Miles Holbeach, Leonard Ayrey of Fairbank Westmorland and Reginald Harrison.[107] Other principal participants besides Sheppard, who may have been the Captain Peter Sheppard who was to be taken prisoner at Appleby in October 1648 fighting for the king in the Second Civil War,[108] were Christopher Gilpin of Kentmer Hall near Kendal, who, like Anthony Knipe, was later to act as an insurgent royalist commissioner for the barony of Kendal in the Second Civil War,[109] and Captain Huddleston, a member of a very prominent local royalist and Catholic recusant family.

On 30 October 1647 the Committee for Compounding in London warned the Cumberland county committee about the role of local delinquents in fomenting tumults in several northern counties. It gave the names of forty-three royalist delinquents including seven members of the Musgrave family, one of whom, Sir Philip Musgrave, was to be second only to Sir Marmaduke Langdale as a royalist commander in the north in the Second Civil War. Some of the forty-three had failed to

105. Bodleian, Rawlinson Letters, 52, nos. 26, 32. See also no. 34.
106. See above, p. 97.
107. *L.J.*, X, 79. This account of the events of 11 August 1647 is based on the long description given to the House of Lords on 11 February 1648 (ibid., X, 42–3) and on Massy's account in a letter of 1 November 1647 (Rawlinson Letters, 52, no. 36). For another letter by Massy, see ibid., no. 40).
108. Ormerod, *Tracts*, p. 276.
109. PRO., SP. 23/171, fo. 121.

prosecute their compositions while others were lamentably behind in payment of their composition fines, and orders were given for outright sequestration of the landed and other property of the offenders. However, sequestration – unlike compounding – was administered locally, and the Committee for Compounding expressed its strong disapproval of the common local practice of letting such sequestered lands at undervalues to the very delinquents who had forfeited them, arguing that the latter were naturally 'careless of compounding, expecting a new turn' – viz. of events.[110] Besides Sir Philip Musgrave, at least ten others of the forty-three named delinquents, eleven of whom were also Catholic recusants, can be demonstrated to have actively participated as royalist insurgents in the Second Civil War.[111]

On 7 May 1647 a list had been drawn up of twenty-one coalowners in Northumberland and County Durham who were royalist delinquents, papists, or both. Of these, seventeen were specified as being in arms for the king, some of them, and notably Sir Richard Tempest of Stella, among the most notable and wealthy royalists in the north-east. The paper recommended that their pits should be sequestered and sold for the benefit of the state.[112] A letter from the north on 22 November told apprehensively of fears 'that some ill-affected persons should raise or bring in forces against the Parliament', but that there had been mass meetings of inhabitants determined to resist such risings or a Scottish invasion.[113] In the same month, however, a hopeful royalist newsletter reported how the citizens of York had been summoned by Lord Fairfax to declare whether they would side with king or parliament in the event of a Scottish invasion, and had answered 'that the Scots intended the preservation and enthroaning of his Maiesty, which the Parliament made no appearance of, and therefore should the *Scottish* Army march, they were resolved to stand upon their guard'.[114]

Mention was made in the last chapter of the collusion of northern Cavaliers such as Musgrave and Langdale with the Scottish Engagers and the direct co-operation of the latter with the Cavaliers' taking of Berwick and Carlisle in April 1648.[115] Early in February Lanark,

110. *Cal.CC.*, I, 71–2.
111. John Aglionby, John Carpe, Captain Hugh James, William Wilson, Sir William Huddleston, John Senhouse, Sir William Carleton, Sir Thomas Dacres, William Musgrave and Major Thomas Salkeld. Evidence of their involvement is in Bodleian, Tanner MSS., 57, fo. 206; Rushworth, *Historical Collections*, VII, 1177; *Cal.CC.*, III, 1703, 1704; Ormerod, *Tracts*, p. 275; *Another Letter from the North* (8 September 1648), BL., E.463(2), p. 6.
112. HLRO., MP., 7/5/1647; *L.J.*, IX, 182. A committee of nine peers was appointed on 13 May to inquire into these cases (*L.J.*, IX, 189).
113. *A Declaration of the Northern Counties* (26 November 1647), BL., E.417(10), p. 8.
114. *Mercurius Melancholicus* (13/20 November 1647), BL., E.416(17), p. 7.
115. See above, pp. 332–4.

Loudoun and Lauderdale wrote to the king informing him that Langdale had come to Scotland, 'and our first care will be to secure Berwick and Carlisle'.[116] On 12 March the English parliamentary commissioners in Scotland wrote warning the Mayor of Berwick 'of the late meetings of many Greater Delinquentes in the North of England', one of whose principal aims was to surprise Berwick which by the terms of the Anglo-Scottish treaty was not to be fortified or garrisoned.[117] A letter from Edinburgh on 14 March told of how the mayor and burgesses of Berwick had prohibited a race-meeting planned for the previous Tuesday (8 March), conceiving it to be a royalist subterfuge to capture the town.[118]

That there was genuine fear that a Scottish invasion would be accompanied or preceded by large-scale Cavalier risings in the north was to be confirmed by the fall of Berwick and Carlisle at the end of April. Noting the co-operation between Scottish Engagers and English Cavaliers, an English observer in Edinburgh in a letter of 11 April had no doubt that the latter would be able to raise great numbers of adherents in the north of England, 'the whole Northern quarter being nothing els but a masse of Malignancy'.[119] A newsletter from Berwick on 12 April reported that although Sir Arthur Haselrig was keeping a vigilant eye on the malignants of Newcastle, 'in these parts the Malignants that a long time since have been glad to keep silence begin to talk high againe, as if they were possest with some great hope'. Indeed, some stewards of local courts had charged juries to present, fine and otherwise punish all who had fought for parliament against the king, while at a manorial court in Cumberland the Cavalier Sir Richard Graham had charged his tenants to be ready to rise when he had occasion to call on them. In the same county it was reported that 'the Cavaliers are so bold as to incourage the peopl [sic], saying fight for King Charles and . . . you shall speedily be imployed'.[120]

Needless to say, the fall of Berwick and Carlisle at the end of the month was the occasion of great Cavalier euphoria in these parts and, according to one account, their numbers were growing so that the supporters of parliament were greatly outnumbered. Northern Cavaliers' spirits were high and 'they cry out in every place "hay for King Charles againe" and, satirically, "what will become of the saintes

116. Burnet, Lives of the Hamiltons, p. 427.
117. Bodleian, Tanner MSS., 59, fos. 748, 803; C.J., V, 505; Rushworth, Historical Collections, VII, 1031.
118. L.J., X, 127–9; Rushworth, Historical Collections, VII, 1032–3.
119. The Copy of a letter . . . from a knowing Gentleman . . . (April 1648), BL., 669, f12(3).
120. Declaratory Letters from the Kingdom of Scotland (April 1648), BL., E.436(12), p. 4; Packets of Letters from Scotland Berwick Newcastle and York (April 1648), Codrington pamphlet coll., p. 5.

now?" ' The writer was convinced that leniency to northern Cavaliers 'hath whetted this knife to cutt our owne throtes'. On 6 May there had been a royalist rendezvous in the Lake District at which Sir Robert and Sir Thomas Strickland had made speeches encouraging insurgency. A list of participants had been taken by one Harrison, the Clerk of the Peace for Westmorland, who was later apprehended with the list in his pocket, affording the Roundheads useful information about the principal participants in the intended rising. In York there was fear that the city was about to fall to the Cavaliers, and local royalists mistook a troop of parliamentary horse arriving from Derbyshire for their own, and shouted 'Glenham [sic] was come, Glenham was come'. The letter concludes that it was generally believed that if it had not been for that troop's timely arrival, the local Cavaliers would have risen and York would have been theirs.[121] The greatest of all dangers to the parliamentary hold in the north came in July with the Scottish invasion. However, a mixture of inept Scottish generalship, lack of strategic coordination between Engagers and Cavaliers, the failure of the northerners to rise in the expected numbers for the king, and the enormously superior strategic and tactical skills of Cromwell and Lambert and campaigning experience of the New Model Army, combined not only to save the north from being completely overrun but also to provide the most spectacular of all Roundhead victories in the Second Civil War.

The east of England

If any region merits the description of the parliamentarian heartland during the First Civil War, it is surely the Eastern Association. Nevertheless, it is important to bear in mind that the region had its notable Cavaliers also. For instance, Norfolk had reared not only the doughty parliamentarian infantry commander Philip Skippon, but also the royalist general Sir Jacob Astley of Melton Constable as well as civilian Cavaliers such as Roger L'Estrange who was to play a notable part in the Second Civil War in Kent. From Suffolk came the Cavalier ministerial family of the Jermyns as well as Sir Thomas Glemham, the royalist commander in campaigns in both civil wars. From Hertfordshire hailed the royalist stalwart, Lord Capel, a key figure in both civil wars, who was to end his days on the scaffold early in 1649 for his role in the Second Civil War. Capel also had estates in Essex, the most solidly parliamentarian county in England during the first war, but also the home of Sir Charles Lucas, who fought stoutly for the king in both wars

121. *Clarke Papers*, II, 8–10; Rushworth, *Historical Collections*, VII, 1113.

and alongside Capel at Colchester and, like him, was to be executed, though more summarily, for his part in that campaign.[122] This is to mention but a few of the best-known cases. As Professor Everitt observes in his admirable work on civil war Suffolk, there was a number of East Anglian towns, of which Bury St Edmunds, Aldeburgh, Lowestoft, Cambridge, King's Lynn and Crowland are examples, where there were powerful royalist factions, while, of course, during the spring and summer of 1648 there were royalist risings in Suffolk and Cambridgeshire at Bury St Edmunds, Newmarket, Stowmarket and Linton; at Chelmsford, Colchester and elsewhere in Essex; and at Norwich and Thetford in Norfolk.[123] While all the above risings, except those in Essex, were mere sideshows to the main fields of operations in the Second Civil War, it needs to be borne in mind that, if all of these disturbances had not been rapidly quelled, they might have developed into major revolts making significant links with royalist insurgency elsewhere.

While there were some notable disturbances such as the Norwich Excise riots in December and January 1646–7,[124] there was in 1646–7 little hint of the major part which the region was to play in the renewal of civil war in 1648, and, most notable of all, in the Essex rising and capture of Colchester. On 4 March 1647 the Suffolk county committee wrote to Speaker Lenthall expressing their apprehension at the undue influence of substantial landowners returning to the county 'who are esteemed not to be well affected', having taken neither the Negative Oath nor the Covenant.[125] On 5 August, the day before the army occupied London, the earl of Warwick, the Lord Lieutenant of Essex, informed Fairfax that he had been unavoidably delayed in meeting him during the period of London's counter-revolution, on account of the time taken by consultations with his Deputy Lieutenants about the measures to be taken against royalist malignants and soldiers coming into southern Essex in great numbers with a consequent danger of disturbance in those parts of the county near to the metropolis.[126] Also believed to be connected in some way with London's counter-revolution was an abortive plot around the same time to take over the Isle of Ely,[127] and, though in the east Midlands rather than the old Eastern Association county, some minor disturbances in Leicestershire. The place worst affected was Market Harborough, where on market day on 3 August there was an affray between self-styled partisans of Poynz and Massey,

---

122. For L'Estrange, see above, pp. 144–5. For Glemham, see above, pp. 327–8, and below, p. 450. For Capel, see below, pp. 455, 466. For Lucas, see below, pp. 454, 464.
123. Everitt, *Suffolk*, pp. 13–14.
124. On the Norwich Excise riots, see above, pp. 76–7.
125. Bodleian, Tanner MSS., 59, fo. 792.
126. *Clarke Papers*, I, 222–3.
127. Oxford, Worcester College, Clarke MSS., 41, fo. 163(b).

on the one hand, and of Fairfax, on the other. The disturbance started in the Crown inn and how far our informant is reading London alignments into a fight between local bully-boys is uncertain. Two or three of the participants were killed in the encounter and more wounded.[128]

Things may have been relatively quiet in 1646–7 but the same was not true of 1648, which saw a large number of disturbances of varying degrees of seriousness, although the only one of them in the eastern counties which developed into a major feature of the Second Civil War was in Essex. Nevertheless, this should not blind us to the considerable contemporary impact of the other disturbances, and perhaps most of all, of those in Norwich in April which it needed a substantial input of troops from outside to crush during a dramatic and bloody day whose events were for a long time to be engraved deeply into the consciousness of local people. While the Norwich anti-Excise disturbances at the end of 1646 and beginning of 1647 had had one single cause, the causes of the riot of 24 April 1648 were more numerous and complex, even though the Excise House was again to suffer its share of the rioters' attention. The immediate prelude to the disturbances was the presentation of a petition to the House of Commons on 18 April by certain prominent citizens of Norwich against their mayor John Utting, whom the House ordered to be brought up to Westminster in the custody of a pursuivant or messenger to answer charges that he had countenanced the election of a royalist delinquent alderman and the voting of delinquents in municipal elections. Utting was also accused of employing sequestered and malignant parsons to preach in churches in Norwich, including the cathedral.[129]

Once the messenger had arrived in Norwich and had formally acquainted the mayor with his mission, Utting and his close associate Alderman John Tooley responded by initiating a counter-petition testifying to Utting's exemplary conduct of his mayoral office, as well as, if some accounts are to be believed, requesting that he be not removed from Norwich.[130] For the next thirty-six hours or so, the counter-petition, which was made official at a dubiously quorate meeting of the Court of Aldermen summoned by the mayor for the Saturday morning of 22 April,[131] circulated around the city amid scenes of great

128. *A Great Fight at Market Harborough* (6 August 1647), BL., E.402(2), no pagination. The text wrongly dates the affray as 10 August instead of 3 August.
129. *C.J.*, V, 534–5. No copy of the petition has survived.
130. In the passages which follow great use is made of the remarkable set of depositions made by witnesses and accused during the months following the riots (NNRO., Norwich Municipal Records, 12(c)(i)). One deposition is to the effect that the counter-petition was 'to keep Mr Mayor at home' (ibid., dep. 112); another that it testified to his conduct of his mayoralty (ibid., dep. 156). As in the case of the petition of 18 April against Utting, no copy of the counter-petition has survived.
131. Not surprisingly, most of Utting's opponents among the aldermen seem to have refused to attend this meeting.

excitement.[132] Early in the morning of Monday 24 April, when the messenger was due to take the mayor off to Westminster, a crowd estimated at upward of a thousand people had gathered in and around the market-place. Some were doubtless there to sign or lend support to the counter-petition, while some, from the beginning, may have assembled with more violent intent. However, in the view of one of mayor Utting's aldermanic opponents, the petitioners and the subsequent rioters were 'both birds of the same feather'.[133] Given its source, this statement is obviously suspect, though there was clearly some overlap between the two elements. Some at least of the petitioners in Norwich market-place on that Monday morning were prepared to use force to prevent their mayor from being carried off if their petition failed to achieve that end. To this purpose the door of the mayor's house had been guarded overnight by what one account describes as 'severall Malignants in Armes'.[134] There is some evidence that Utting himself made unsuccessful efforts to prevent the demonstration on his behalf from merging into riot and tumult.[135] Certainly where he failed, it was unlikely that others would succeed: neither in the attempt to call out the trained bands; nor in the contemporary equivalent of reading the Riot Act, when a proclamation from sheriffs and JPs was read ordering the crowd to disperse on pain of death.[136] The messenger, whom Alderman Christopher Barret, the deputy mayor and Utting's deadly enemy, had endeavoured to persuade to leave Norwich quietly without the mayor, departed, but not of his own volition, being hustled out of the city by the mob.[137]

Although the immediate end of the petitioners had now been achieved, though by violent rather than peaceful means, the crowd did not stop there but carried on in the same violent vein. There was much looting, especially of the houses of prominent local figures identified either with the regime at Westminster or hostility to the mayor.[138] The two principal victims were a sheriff, Captain Thomas Ashwell, and a former mayor, Alderman Adrian Parmenter. Ashwell's unpopularity rested on his radical Independency, his position as an ex-New Model officer, and, above all, his role as one of the most prominent of those who had brought the petition of 18 March against the mayor. His house was ransacked for food, beer and especially arms and ammunition with

132. On the circulation of the counter-petition, see above, pp. 122–3.
133. Bodleian, Tanner MSS., 57, fo. 35.
134. *A true relation of the late great Mutiny in Norwich* (April 1648), BL., E.438(6), p. 2.
135. NNRO., Norwich Municipal Records, 12(c)(i), deps. 58, 60, 66, 95(a), 146.
136. Ibid., dep. 24. The Riot Act, of course, was not passed until 1715.
137. For evidence about his dismissal, see ibid., deps. 6, 18, 24, 61, 176.
138. BL., E.438(6), pp. 2–3. Evidence of looting of houses other than those of Ashwell and Parmenter is in NNRO., 12(c)(i), deps. 101, 171.

which it was plentifully stocked.[139] Parmenter, who was also a sub-commissioner for Excise and whose house seems also to have served as Excise Office and had attracted the attentions of the anti-Excise rioters in December 1646, was again the victim of looting. Some of the rioters, and notably a dyer named William True, who was later to be hanged for his part in the disturbances, took particular delight in laying their hands on Excise money which True boasted he would use 'to pay his souldgers'.[140]

The rioters' attention now turned to the Committee House, seat of the hated county committee, which, if one deponent is to be believed,[141] was done in a further search for arms at the suggestion of the fiery saddler, Henry Goward, another who was to be executed for his part in the tumult. The Committee House also yielded a variety of forms of domestic loot. Wandering through it, some of them with lanterns and even naked lights, the rioters helped themselves to what they found.[142] As well as weapons and domestic loot, casks of gunpowder were opened and their contents liberally strewn over floors and stairs, in which circumstances the mighty explosion which gave the whole incident its local name, the Great Blow, was all but inevitable. Some forty of the rioters perished in the explosion, 'wretches executed by their owne handes and not dying the ordinary death of men, but behold, here armes and there legges scattered every where, some token of Gods Justice on these wretches and mercy to his poore people'. At least 120 others were wounded and property damaged to an estimated order of £20,000, not counting damage to nearby churches.[143]

Despite the rioters' determination to seal off Norwich from the outside world by control of the city gates and walls, a message was somehow or other conveyed to the detachment of Colonel Fleetwood's regiment which was currently taking up quarters at East Dereham, about fifteen miles to the west. The New Model troops forced an entry into Norwich at about 4 p.m., but it was another four hours before the tumult was brought under control.[144] On 26 April the Norwich

---

139. On Ashwell, see Evans, *Norwich*, pp. 118 note, 169–70, 178–9; Ketton–Cremer, *Norfolk*, pp. 333–4, 335–6. On the disturbances at his house and threats of violence against him, NNRO., 12(c)(i), deps. 6, 8, 23–4, 48, 50–2, 58, 76, 79, 95, 95(a), 102–4, 112, 127, 149, 161, 169, 185, 210–11, 219, 222–6, 230, 235, 247–50, 253, 256, 259, 267–8, 270. Although known locally as Captain Ashwell, he had apparently reached the rank of major in the army.
140. Ibid., deps. 8, 23, 40, 116, 203–4, 252, 264, 271.
141. Ibid., dep. 9.
142. For evidence on the looting of the Committee House, see ibid., deps. 7, 9, 22–3, 54–5, 88, 110, 121, 128–9, 143, 189–90, 205, 212, 216, 218, 236, 265–6.
143. Rushworth, *Historical Collections*, VII, 1072; BL., E.438(6), p. 3; *A Letter from Norwich* (27 April 1648), E.437(12). Also a woman in a nearby street was killed by debris (NNRO., 12(c)(i), dep. 269).
144. For evidence of clashes between rioters and troopers, see ibid., deps. 114, 121, 228.

Assembly ordered that the following Thursday should be a Day of Thanksgiving for the city's deliverance. As had been done after the quelling of the London 'tipcat' riots earlier in the month, a gratuity of £200 was voted for the troops who had put down the riots and £50 for the healing of wounded soldiers and replacement of lost horses. Six troops of horse were to remain in Norwich for the time being to ensure the safety of the city from recurrence of the disorders. The election of the delinquent alderman Roger Mingay, which had provided the main element in the case against mayor Utting, was annulled as contrary to both parliamentary ordinance and local custom, since he had not yet served as sheriff. It is noteworthy that as many as eight commoners (out of twenty-eight) and four aldermen (out of thirteen) still voted that Mingay's election be confirmed.[145]

It is astonishing to find that Mayor Utting and his ally Alderman Tooley had to wait until 9 October 1649 before parliament, after long delays, passed judgment on them. Utting had been suspended from the mayoralty following the riot, though Tooley, oddly enough, had played a notable part as one of the examining magistrates interrogating suspects and witnesses. Parliament declared both to be 'Grand Delinquents'. Again rather surprisingly, the fine it imposed on Tooley (£1,000) was double that on Utting, who, however, was imprisoned for a year and Tooley only for six months.[146] The rioters themselves did not have to wait so long before being brought to judgment, though there was none of that precipitancy and near panic which had characterized the response of the Kent county committee to the Canterbury Christmas riots. A commission of Oyer and Terminer was obtained and the accused brought to trial in Norwich Guildhall in December 1648. Fifteen of the 108 accused were then acquitted, though two of them were sent to the House of Correction until they could find adequate sureties for future good behaviour. Eight of the accused were sentenced to death for murder and hanged alongside two witches outside the castle in the following month. Seven of the rioters were probably saved from the same fate only by their ability to read the neck-verse, and were imprisoned for a year. Two others, one of them a woman, were convicted of petty larceny and sentenced to be whipped, while another twenty-six were fined £30 and were to remain in prison until paying up.[147]

145. NNRO., Norwich Assembly Book 1642–1668, fos. 62, 62(b), 64(b). For the parliamentary ordinance in question, see above, p. 216. The Assembly's resolutions were all revoked at the Restoration.
146. For full parliamentary proceedings, see C.J., VI, 188, 295, 304.
147. For full details see F. Bateman and W. Rye (eds.), The History of the Bethel Hospital at Norwich (Norwich, 1906), Appendix I, pp. 105–8. This is a reliable account, unlike the editors' calendar of depositions which abounds in inaccuracies and omits much significant detail.

However, there can be little doubt that some of the principal offenders escaped scot-free in contrast to their social inferiors.[148] Among the former was a mysterious and almost ubiquitous gentleman in black who appears in several depositions and was almost certainly Mr Thomas Palgrave, a respectable merchant of White Lion Lane, who had nevertheless been active in standing rounds of drinks to petitioners in the course of which he discharged his pistol three times in one hostelry and was not averse to inciting those in his company to acts of violence. Less generous in the matter of standing drinks, but a key figure in pressurizing others to keep the city gates locked and an eloquent advocate of strong action to keep the mayor in Norwich, was Christopher Bransby, who was also associated with a Dr Brooke who had recommended the petitioners in his company to bear arms as their right.[149] All of these were as much involved in the troubles as many of those who were condemned in December but no charges were brought against them. In a letter to Speaker Lenthall on 4 May 1648 Christopher Barret, Utting's bitter opponent and currently the acting mayor, hinted darkly that 'time will evince [that] there was a greater plott in itt . . . then wee are yett aware of '.[150] Barret, of course, had a personal axe to grind, but the information relating to the activity of socially respectable figures such as Palgrave, Brooke and Bransby raises the question of whether there were not others anxious to encourage popular disturbances for political ends, risking the danger of unleashing the unruly multitude in a destructive orgy whose end none could confidently foresee. In one of the earliest depositions, Nicholas Dawes stated on 28 April that he had heard that there were committeemen who had said to the people: 'Doe you the worke; as for us we have estates to loose; you have none, & we will assist you'.[151] Incredible though the imputation may be in literal terms, it is none the less conceivably suggestive of what may have been going through the minds of Utting and his allies.

What evidence do the Norwich disturbances provide of the violent emergence of genuinely royalist sentiments such as had inspired many of the Canterbury rioters the previous Christmas? The earl of Lanark's English correspondent, while rejoicing in this tumult, saw it as the work of local Presbyterians who 'would not suffer their Major [sic] to be

---

148. Hardly any of the convicted or accused were freemen of Norwich despite the quite wide franchise in Norwich. This conclusion has been reached by comparing the names in the depositions with the lists of freemen in P. Millican (ed.), *The Register of the Freemen of Norwich 1548–1713* (Norwich, 1934), passim.
149. Depositions relating to the man in black, including Palgrave's own, are in NNRO., 12(c)(i), deps. 93, 112, 170, 176, 194, 197, 227; to Bransby and Brooke, dep. 273. Brooke's advice related to the wearing of swords in self-defence.
150. Bodleian, Tanner MSS., 57, fo. 35.
151. NNRO., 12(c)(i), dep. 36.

caried away to London'; an emphasis designed no doubt to appeal to Scottish Presbyterian sentiments, especially given difficulties which the Scottish Engagers were currently experiencing from the kirk.[152] Certainly it was a gross oversimplification to see the Norwich rioters as acting mainly in the Presbyterian interest, even in the limited sense in which this might have been true of some of their London counterparts in July 1647. The depositions provide some interesting evidence of royalist sentiments among the rioters and petitioners, some of whom asserted that they were 'watchmen for the King and Mr Maior' and others to be acting 'For God and King Charles'.[153] One deponent mentions a man standing outside a church 'to take hands to see who would be for the king', an interesting interpretation of the counter-petition on behalf of mayor Utting,[154] and there are examples of vehement royalist sentiments and threats of violence against persons who thought otherwise or who had abused the king in the past.[155] But on the whole, anti-Roundhead, and especially anti-Independent, sentiments were much more in evidence than straightforwardly royalist ones,[156] though two depositions against the saddler Henry Goward, who was later to be executed, that he had urged rioters 'to . . . blow up the Committee House upon the Roundheads', have too much of an *ex post facto* ring about them to be credible.[157]

But the fact that the Committee House was blown up by accident rather than design in no way detracts from its significance as a potent symbol of the power of the existing regime, both locally and nationally. Seen from the viewpoint of the central government, the danger of the Norwich disturbances was that the identification of that government with the attempt to carry off the mayor enormously increased popular discontent against it which might extend far beyond these mere parochial matters. The opinion of one observer that if it had not been for the timely arrival of the troopers on that day, 'it will have proved a far greater Rebellion than *Poyers*' (viz. in South Wales), and that 'men worth many thousand pounds in the City would be with them by the morning and . . . helpe promised them from the Countrey' is doubtless an exaggeration.[158] However, the processes whereby local disturbances can be transformed into major revolutions often turn on such things as this, and both the government and Utting's enemies at Norwich had

152. *Hamilton Papers*, p. 193.
153. NNRO., 12(c)(i), deps. 112, 170, 273.
154. Ibid., dep. 171. The deponent was a mill-beater, Edward Gray, who was subsequently executed.
155. Ibid., deps. 135, 138, 147, 239.
156. E.g., ibid., deps. 10, 44, 46, 54, 57, 83, 112(a), 151–2, 162, 169, 278.
157. Ibid., deps. 140–1.
158. BL., E.438(6), p. 5.

every reason to be thankful for the intervention of Colonel Fleetwood's troopers.

The dangers emphasized above of igniting Cavalier feeling in the surrounding countryside, as at Canterbury during Christmas 1647, were further underlined by the frustration of a royalist design in the west of Norfolk in May. Major Thomas Loveday, an officer in King's Lynn, related how he had been approached by one Edward Elsden of Swaffham, the market-town about fifteen miles east of King's Lynn, with a proposition to associate himself with the plans of local royalists to rise for the king. Wishing to penetrate and uncover the design, Loveday pretended to go along with Elsden who promised him a commission from the king and the Prince of Wales and suggested a meeting with some local Cavaliers at an inn in Downham Market a few days later. However, when they arrived at the appointed rendezvous, the Cavaliers were not there and nowhere to be found in the town. Elsden then volunteered to seek out the Cavaliers, most of whom lived locally, but they would do no more than send a captain to conduct Loveday to a house to meet them. Loveday's account of what followed, whether true, false or simply embellished by a vivid imagination, has all the ingredients of high melodrama. It took him half an hour to reach the house in question which was situated in a dark wood and reached along obscure paths. When he arrived and met the other conspirators, all but one of whom, a Mr Ralph Skipwith, were unknown to him, the details of the conspiracy were disclosed. All the available horses in the county were to be seized on the day, which was to be decided later, when Loveday would declare for the king at King's Lynn, bringing over some at least of the garrison with him, and 200 horse were to be sent to his aid there. At this point an awkward situation arose when 'an old rogue, a captain of the King's party' proposed that the conspirators should swear a solemn oath, but a temporary respite was afforded by the difficulty of finding a bible on which to swear, 'for I think there were very few in the House'. Confronted by the dreadful alternative of either perjuring himself or being discovered, Loveday, whose account of this is somewhat implausible, claimed to have extricated himself by persuading the conspirators to settle for entering into mutual obligations, 'and so . . . I was quit of there damnable oath'. The articles entered into were to engage with lives and fortunes to restore the king against all who opposed them. Loveday was assured that on his securing the garrison at Lynn, the king's party would flock to him in sufficient numbers for him to take over the town and surrounding marshland and to take the field offensively. However, far from doing this, on the day following the above meeting near Downham Market, he caused all the conspirators to be arrested and imprisoned, except for two of them who had gone out into the county to rally Cavalier forces and were missed by Loveday's troopers.[159]

Although there were in June reports of widespread disaffection in the Fens around Ely, Wisbech, March and Whittlesey and disturbances in Cambridge, as well as a rising in Linton which is best considered as a minor episode in the Second Civil War,[160] the nearest equivalent to the so-called 'Great Blow' at Norwich was the riot at Bury St Edmunds beginning on Friday 12 May. There was what a contemporary account describes as 'a great combustion in the town about setting up of a May-pole, which grew to that height that by Satterday sixe or seven hundred men were gotten into Armes'. As at Norwich, shouts of *'for God and King Charles'* were heard, and in addition attacks were made on soldiers, and supporters of parliament were forced to leave.[161] The Derby House Committee requested Sir Thomas Barnardiston and Sir William Playters, MPs for Bury and Orford respectively, to go to Bury to attempt to calm the tumult, at the same time taking care that some forces should be available in the neighbourhood to give assistance if this proved necessary. The two were empowered to offer an indemnity to the rioters, but only if they agreed to lay down their arms and restore the magazine which they had seized. In the event of failure they were to send for such of Colonel Whalley's cavalry as were near at hand and to suppress the rising by force. The Derby House Committee clearly feared, as their letter of 13 May to Fairfax reveals, that the riots would prove a centre for all local disaffected persons if not quickly nipped in the bud.[162] There is indeed evidence of warrants being sent out on 14 May by Sir Marmaduke Langdale, the future royalist commander in the north, to a local constable to send twenty horse to Bury with arms and men to assist in its defence against parliament. However, Barnardiston and Playters reported from Bury on 15 May that with the assistance of troops from New Model regiments and local trained bands they had gained possession of the town without much bloodshed, though two townsmen had been killed in an attempted sally. But the government's fears that the disturbance would ignite resistance elsewhere were apparently justified. Drums had been beaten at Thetford in south Norfolk and there had been similar attempts to make trouble at Stowmarket.

159. *A True Relation of a Dangerous Plot Against the Well-affected party of the Town of Lynn* (22 May 1648), BL., E.443(27), pp. 1–6.
160. On the disaffection in the Fens, see the letter of Colonel Valentine Walton to the Derby House Committee on 21 June (*HMC., 13th. Report Appendix Portland MSS.*, I, 464). On Cambridge, the letter of the local committee on 12 June (*C.J.*, V, 594). On Linton, see below, p. 433.
161. *An exact relation of the late rising at Bury* (18 May 1648), BL., E.443(9), no pagination; *Another Victory obtained by Col. Whalley* (May 1648), E.443(30), no pagination; Rushworth, *Historical Collections*, VII, 1119.
162. *Cal.SPD. 1648–9*, pp. 65, 65–6, 66–7, 67; *C.J.*, V, 558; *L.J.*, X, 268.

Moreover, as the two MPs confessed, 'We cannot yet discover the Bottom of this Design'.[163]

According to Everitt the Bury disturbances 'woke no effective response in Suffolk',[164] and, by comparison with the Kentish reaction to the Christmas rising at Canterbury, he is probably right. Nevertheless, the depositions taken at Bury in August, November and December reveal that there had been attempts to rouse local villagers to go to Bury 'to take up armes for the kinge'.[165] Among the principal activists at Bury were Oliver and John Bridgeman of Exning and Newmarket respectively. The former was alleged by one deponent on 22 December to have abused parliament as 'a company of banckrupts that had spent their estates in horseracing and whoring, and now they sate to cheat the Kingdome'.[166] And among others taken later at Bury, according to the diary of Barnardiston's steward, was an insurgent from much further afield: Sir Thomas Peyton, 'a cheife man in yᵉ Kentish rebellion'.[167] In a letter of 18 May from Windsor, Fairfax stressed the need for exemplary punishment of the chief offenders and the need for a substantial garrison to be stationed in Bury to prevent further outbreaks. Unable, however, to spare any troops of his own, he suggested that the need might be met by raising 'a particular Force . . . out of the Well-affected of those Parts'.[168]

But there were some alarming local developments even after the Bury disturbances had been suppressed, which were to culminate in the next month in the minor rising at Linton. On 31 May Sir Thomas Barnardiston wrote from his home at Kedington to warn the government about meetings of the disaffected at Newmarket 'under Pretence of Horse-racing'. Rusbrooke Hall near Bury, the seat of the notable malignant family and courtiers in exile, the Jermyns, was becoming a regular rendezvous for such Cavalier malcontents, and, with so many of the ringleaders of the Bury riots still at large, there were obvious dangers here. Moreover, Fairfax feared that many of the local horse and foot which were currently being levied for defence of the county, were disaffected and that the local defence forces needed to be remodelled. Barnardiston heard from John Clark in a letter of 30 May that the duke of Buckingham, who was soon to be one of three aristocratic leaders of a separate rising in the Second Civil War, had visited Rusbrooke Hall on the previous day, when there had been a great feast. Moreover, three

163.   L.J., X, 268–9.
164.   Everitt, Suffolk, p. 15.
165.   Ibid., pp. 96–8, 102–4.
166.   Ibid., p. 103.
167.   Chelmsford, Essex R.O., D/DQs., 18, fo. 39 (Clopton's diary); C.J., V, 592. Clopton mistakenly refers to him as Sir John Peyton.
168.   L.J., X, 267.

of the ringleaders of the Bury riots were currently in Newmarket and he feared greatly for the safety of that town.[169]

Barnardiston responded promptly and effectively, for his steward records in his diary for 1 June that he sent three men over to New-market where they took seven or eight of the Bury delinquents, and, on 6 June, that Barnardiston himself rode to Bury for discussion about the fate of the rioters there held prisoner. But, far more significant in terms of a major threat, Clopton reports in the same entry that many were in arms in Essex and had made contact with Lord Goring and some of the Kentish insurgents at Bow bridge.[170] Ever since the beginning of the agitation about the Essex petition,[171] there had been ominous rumblings of discontent in that county. It is not known whether the people assembling earlier in 'riotus & tumultious arraie' in Colchester, which was later to be the most important royalist stronghold in eastern England during the Second Civil War, were in any way connected with local Cavaliers or even inspired by royalist sentiments. In any case, the Colchester committee had taken no chances and ordered the trained bands to take measures against possible disturbances on May Day,[172] while on 3 May Colonel Whalley and Sir Thomas Honeywood were ordered by the House of Commons to suppress a tumult raised by malignants in Colchester.[173] On the following day the Colchester com-mittee emphasized the need for an effective watch to be kept on the town's defences 'in these troublesome & tumultuous tymes'. It was not long before these defences would be put to a far stiffer test.[174]

169. *L.J.*, X, 301–2; Bodleian, Tanner MSS., 57, fo. 123.
170. Chelmsford, Essex RO., D/DQs., 18, fos. 38, 38(b).
171. On this, see above, pp. 142–4.
172. BL., Stowe MSS., 842 (Colchester Papers), fo. 14.
173. *C.J.*, V, 550; Rushworth, *Historical Collections*, VII, 1101.
174. BL., Stowe MSS., 842, fo. 14(b).

XI
REFORMADOES AND TURNCOATS

And . . . wee doe further declare That under that generall notion of *Reformadoes*, we have undergone no little detriment both in Reputation and Fidelity . . . our ambition being onely with patience to attend our Pay . . . much lesse entertain . . . any thing that might . . . embroyle us in a new, but farre more fatalle Warre. . . .

The *Reformadoes Remonstrance* (6 August 1647),
BL., E.402(33), pp. 3–4

And verily there may be thought some dislike in the very primary law of nature of such tergiversation and inconstancy; since we scarce find . . . a deserter of a trust or party he once adhered to, to be prosperous, or in any eminent estimation with those to whom he resorts, though in the change there may appear evident arguments of reason and justice. . . .

Clarendon, *Rebellion*, IV, 248

The creation of a counter-revolutionary force in 1647

During the summer of 1647, and especially following the army's abduction of the king from Holdenby on 4 June, Denzil Holles and his parliamentary Presbyterian colleagues sought to create a force to counterpoise and, if necessary, combat the disobedient New Model Army. The existence of such a design has been forcefully argued by Valerie Pearl and others. Her thesis has been sharply questioned by Mark Kishlansky, who points to the reformadoes as a disorganized mob rather than a disciplined force and plays down the importance of deserters from the New Model Army.[1] But to question the adequacy of such a force is not to disprove the design to create one, whose main

1. V. Pearl, 'London's Counter-revolution', in Aylmer, *Interregnum*, pp. 44–51; M.A. Kishlansky, *The Rise of the New Model Army* (Cambridge, 1979), p. 341 note.

elements were noted in an earlier chapter.[2] It will now be necessary to fill out the details of that preliminary sketch.

The recruitment of reformadoes or disbanded soldiers from other armies than the New Model was the element which attracted most attention at the time and is dealt with in the section which follows. But not all of the men enlisted in London, and more especially those who were enlisted privately, not directly by the parliamentary Committee of Safety or the City Militia Committee, were reformadoes in the normal sense of that term. When examined by the House of Commons on 8 July, one Cornet Arundell admitted that he could not be certain how many of the approximately 2,000 men whom he had recruited over the previous week were genuine ex-soldiers. Significantly, he also admitted that he was acting without the authority of parliament or the City, and mentioned two other persons similarly engaged in recruitment at Broken Cross and Charing Cross.[3]

However, probably at least as great a menace to the soldiers of the New Model Army, more especially since they were a disciplined fighting force and not an unruly mob, was presented by those of their former comrades who had volunteered for service in Ireland.[4] That the parliamentary Presbyterian leaders had other uses in mind for these forces was to become a firm conviction of many soldiers which finds notable expression in the army's famous Representation of 14 June.[5] Around the end of June or beginning of July, Lord General Fairfax was petitioned by a certain Mr William Harrison, a gentleman who had earlier served under his command. The petitioner relates how he had encountered seven gentlemen and their servants at an inn at Stow on the Wold, who had so much money with them that 'they could not put their hands into their pockets to pay for a quart of wine, but they pulled forth handfulls of gold'. Suspecting their story that they were en route for Worcester to raise (or pay?) forces for Ireland, Harrison concluded that their real purpose was 'a designe to rayse Forces against his Excellencies Army'. He hastened to army headquarters at Uxbridge to acquaint Fairfax with his findings, but, unable to contact the Lord General personally, he petitioned him, asking for permission to take action against the delinquents in Worcestershire.[6] Apropos of the incident it is pertinent to recall that seven of the eleven Presbyterian MPs accused by the army had to answer specific charges relating to bringing troops

2. See above, pp. 170–71, 180.
3. *C.J.*, V, 237.
4. For some observations about the careerist, as distinct from the political, motives of the volunteers, see Woolrych, *Soldiers and Statesmen*, p. 135.
5. *Parliamentary History*, XV, 456–7; *Leveller Tracts*, p. 53.
6. *The Humble Petition or Representation of Mr. William Harrison Gentleman* (3 July 1647), BL., E.396(12), especially pp. 5–7.

supposedly bound for Ireland from Worcestershire to Reading. The accused members replied on 19 July that this was not done in order to augment the counter-revolutionary strength in the Home Counties, but to pay the soldiers and avoid the danger of carrying the money to Worcester when it would have had to pass near to detachments of New Model soldiers who were not above helping themselves to the funds designed for their pay, as they had done on other occasions.[7]

On 14 June the parliamentary commissioners with the army warned the Speaker of the House of Lords that Fairfax had informed them of the army's disquiet concerning the enlistment of great numbers of horsemen in London and that the soldiers were disinclined to lie quiet while such preparations were being made against them. If this was being done simply to prevent tumults, then surely 'the Trained Bands were sufficient . . . to preserve . . . Peace'.[8] However, not only was the trained bands' capacity to do this dubious, but, under the control of the Militia Committee as this was constituted after 4 May, they were in any case more likely to encourage than to suppress tumults when these were directed against the army. Indeed, the trained bands represent a further element of the planned counter-revolutionary force, though probably not a very serious threat, despite the army's anxiety to reconstitute the London Militia Committee.[9] The occasion of the calling out of the trained bands early in June excited the derision of one admittedly pro-army newsletter which reported that 'not 10 men of some Companies appeared, and of many Companies none at all but the Officers; nay, the very boyes in the streets jeered the drummers as they went about their charge . . .'.[10]

Among the other apprehensions of the army reported by the parliamentary commissioners on 14 June was one matter which must have been particularly galling to the soldiers: the enticing of their comrades to desert and come to London to swell the counter-revolutionary force there on the promise of receiving indemnity for their desertion and their full arrears of pay which was denied to those who remained in service. Legislation to this effect had been in preparation on 11 June and was consummated by an ordinance eight days later.[11] Following a succession of protests from the army, parliament went some way towards meeting its objections on 28 June with the resolution that no officer or soldier might depart without specific leave from the General,

7. *Parliamentary History*, XVI, 133–4. For a later pamphlet ridiculing this explanation, see *A full Vindication of the Army* (12 October 1647), BL., E.410(18), p. 43.
8. *L.J.*, IX, 266.
9. On this, see above, pp. 181–2.
10. *Clarke Papers*, I, 132–3.
11. *L.J.*, IX, 252, 259; *Parliamentary History*, XV, 430; *A&O.*, I, 957–8; BL., 669, f(11), 27.

though this, of course, did not affect those who had already left the colours.[12]

Parliament's invitation to soldiers to desert might seem at first sight as shocking to the modern observer as it did at the time to army commanders and their Independent allies in parliament. But in the view of the dominant Presbyterian faction in parliament, the deserters, though disobeying their commanders, were acting in obedience to the superior authority of parliament. As such, however loudly those commanders might protest, the deserters were entitled both to indemnity and to preferential treatment in the matter of their arrears of pay.[13] Indeed, the first draft of the parliamentary ordinance giving indemnity to such deserters, which was admittedly modified later in the House of Commons, significantly identifies the 'obedience' of deserters with that of those who 'refused to enter into that solemne Engagement with the fforces vnder . . . Sir Thomas ffairefax . . . in opposition to the Parliamentes direccions'.[14]

As might be expected, deserters, fearing the impermanence of undertakings about arrears of pay and indemnity, were among the chief denouncers of the army. One of them, a captain, had reportedly told a militia ensign 'that if hee would not fight against the Army, hee should be noe officer of his'.[15] Certainly such persons were unlikely to respond with anything but defiance to the message in a pamphlet in early July appealing to deserters to return to their units.[16] By the beginning of July, however, there is some indication that the City at least may have changed its tune in the matter of the recruitment of deserters as well as of other auxiliary forces, asking parliament for the metropolitan lines of communication to be closed to persons coming to London to enlist. As to deserters specifically, it requested that when these had been paid as promised, they should be disposed of as parliament should see fit.[17]

Of course, once the coup of 26 July had taken place, the City authorities had perforce to be less choosy, assuming, that is, that their earlier diffidence had been more than a mere matter of form. On 30 July the parliamentary Committee of Safety ordered reformado officers and

12. *C.J.*, V, 226; *L.J.*, IX, 303; Bodleian, Tanner MSS., 58, fo. 292. For the army's protests, see *Parliamentary History*, XV, 474, XVI, 13–14, 16, 18; *Cal.SPD. 1646–7*, pp. 590–1 (*Kingdomes Weekly Intelligencer*).
13. See, e.g., *Works of Darkness brought to Light* (1647), BHPC., pp. 14–15; *Nine Proposals by Way of Interrogation* (July 1647), BL., E.396(8), pp. 5–6; *Questions Propounded to all wel-affected Citizens* (1647), Oxford, Worcester College pamphlet collection, p. 4.
14. Compare the final ordinance (*A&O.*, I, 957–8; *L.J.*, IX, 282; BL., 669, f11(27)) with the earlier draft in Bodleian, Tanner MSS., 58, fo. 234.
15. *Clarke Papers*, I, 154.
16. *A Vindication of the Armies Proceedings* (2 July 1647), BL., E.395(6), p. 6.
17. *The Humble Petition of the Lord Major* [*sic*] . . . (2 July 1647), BL., E.396(15), p. 4; *L.J.*, IX, 310.

soldiers to assemble in St James's Fields so as to 'put them in a condition for present service in a Regimentall way'.[18] On the same day apprentices and journeymen were ordered to be ready 'vpon beate of the drum to appeare in Compleate Armes for the defence . . . of this Cittie, as they will answeare the Contrarie at their vtmost perill'.[19] On 1 August, with a New Model Army advance on London imminent, parliament gave power to the London Militia Committee and its own Committee of Safety to fine those who resisted the requisitioning of their horses and to punish those who neglected to join their units when summoned by beat of drum. It also allowed the enlistment of mariners and detachments en route for Ireland or to be disbanded.[20] Months later, in November, a certain William Williamson, who had been involved in the requisitioning of horses at this time, petitioned the Common Council that he had been arrested at the suit of persons whose horses he had requisitioned and who were now claiming about £1,400 from him on this account and threatening to sue him if he did not give satisfaction. He had also been unable to obtain repayment of the disbursements he had himself made for this service since the parliamentary ordinance on which he had based his commission had since been annulled.[21]

According to the charges which were brought against Lord Mayor Gayre and his aldermanic colleagues in the following April, there had been at least ten thousand men under arms in late July and early August 1647.[22] Sir William Waller's own account suggests even greater numbers. There were, he tells us, eighteen regiments of foot, some of them 1,800 and 2,000 strong and only one of them smaller. In addition, there were between four and five thousand horse, mounted by reformado officers and gentlemen of quality. By contrast, Waller insisted, Fairfax had not even half the number of foot, only half of whom had been in any way serviceably armed, and though his horse were numerous they were 'almost in as ill equipage as his foot'. Waller's picture is clearly designed to set off his verdict that the city had been betrayed by the pusillanimity of the Lord Mayor and his colleagues and is almost certainly overdone. It needs to be set against the Independent Thomas Juxon's description of the miserable turnout in defence of the city.[23] While the latter account may be no less overstated in the opposite

18. *Severall Orders and Votes of both Houses* . . . (30 July 1647), BL., E.400(34).
19. CLRO., Common Hall Book 2, fo. 83.
20. *C.J.*, V, 263; *L.J.*, IX, 366.
21. CLRO., Jor. 40, fo. 262(b). Obviously Williamson would be unlikely to obtain assistance from the Indemnity Committee in such a matter.
22. *L.J.*, X, 215; *Parliamentary History*, XVII, 102.
23. Waller, *Vindication*, pp. 188–9. For a similar picture of betrayal, see *The Declaration of Generall Massey and Colonell Generall Poyntz* (9 August 1647), BL., E.401(12), especially pp. 1–2, 4. Juxon's account is in his Journal in Dr Williams's Library, MS. 24. 50, fos. 116–6(b). See above, p. 184.

direction, it is undeniable that by 6 August the formidable counter-revolutionary force conjured up in Waller's prose had vanished from sight – 'in a moment slunke away and not to be found'.[24]

The problem of the reformadoes

In October 1646 divers officers who had served under the earl of Essex and Sir William Waller presented a petition to the House of Commons representing the hardships which they had suffered through wounds, imprisonment by royalists, wasting away of their resources and loss of their trades. They expressed the desire to be taken into military service again and to receive the arrears of pay due to them, or at least as much of them as possible.[25] Indeed, not the least of the reasons for the mutual antipathy between the reformadoes and soldiers of the New Model Army is that they represented competing forces for strictly limited sources of pay, which were, in both cases, heavily in arrears. Another was, of course, the deep resentment of disbanded officers and men against the prestigious and spectacularly victorious New Model Army.

By June 1647 the reformado problem had taken a more serious turn. A petition in mid-June signed by fourteen reformadoes had as its background the alarmingly increased number of reformadoes in London clamouring for pay. The petitioners complained of endeavours to render them odious as the possible fomentors of a new civil war. Hence had proceeded the ordinance to ban them from London, the execution of which would have the effect of confirming this unjustified reputation and reducing them to the status of vagabonds; an unmerited fate for men who had 'spent their Patrimony, lost their imployments and some their limbes' in parliament's service. They requested payment of part of their arrears, security on the public faith for the rest and permission to continue to solicit in London and those counties where arrears of pay were still due to them. Some of them were foreign soldiers of fortune, while others came from counties far distant from London, but all were heavily indebted and impoverished through having to wait so long for satisfaction. On 14 June the House of Lords promised to commend their petition to the Lower House, while in the meantime asking the petitioners to take care to prevent 'Tumults by the coming down of the Officers and Soldiers'.[26]

24. The phrase is Juxon's (ibid., fo. 118(b)).
25. *Cal.SPD. 1645–7*, p. 485. Referring to a later reformado petition in March 1647, Juxon observes that the petitioners were prepared to serve even in the New Model Army (Dr Williams's Library, MS. 24.50, fo. 103(b)).
26. HLRO., MP/14/6/1647; *L.J.*, IX, 265.

The warning was as timely as it was ineffective. Bitter experience was to teach that reformado requests for permission to attend in pursuit of their arrears connoted something very different from respectful attendance until authority saw fit to meet their demands. As early as 30 January the Lord Mayor had ordered special precautions including the keeping of a double watch because 'there are daylie a greate concourse of loose people and vnknowne Souldiers within this Cittie'.[27] But this was a mere trickle compared with the flood which was to follow in the summer. An admittedly biassed newsletter of 14 June told of the furore created by about a thousand reformado officers clamouring for their arrears with such aggressiveness that parliament had to send for reinforcements to the militiamen guarding the Houses and to attempt to placate the reformadoes by promising them payment of whatever was due to them after their accounts had been audited on the following Thursday. But this did not avail to prevent what another newsletter describes as 'the greatest tumults and insolencies raised upon the House of Commons that ever any yet heard of '. Some MPs, and notably Sir Henry Vane the younger, were threatened with being cut in pieces, others were vilely abused and the whole House was virtually blocked up by crowds of reformadoes clamouring for pay. The parliamentary Presbyterian leaders Holles and Stapleton went down to the Court of Requests to attempt to appease the reformadoes with promises of an additional £10,000 over and above what had formerly been granted. This appears to have quietened the clamour, but only for a time, and the whole incident was in fact a by no means minor anticipation of what was to happen on 26 July.[28]

The above accounts hint at what the army's charges against the eleven members were categorically to assert: the involvement of the Presbyterian leaders in encouraging such reformado disorders. Indeed, the army's Independent ally Edmund Ludlow saw such encouragement as deliberately designed to secure 'that being furnished with money, they might . . . stand by their patrons in whatsoever design they had to carry on'.[29] London had acted as a magnet, drawing to itself far more reformadoes than parliament had authorized payment for. These sought both to intimidate parliament into making additional grants and to

27. CLRO., Common Hall Book 2, fo. 42.
28. *Clarke Papers*, I, 134–6.
29. For the formal charge against the eleven, see *Parliamentary History*, XV, 472. For Ludlow's charge, see *Ludlow Memoirs*, I, 147. See also *The Last Votes from the Armie* (June 1647), BL., E.394(10), no pagination; *Cal.SPD. 1645–7*, p. 591 (*The Kingdomes Weekly Intelligencer*). On 25 June Fairfax wrote to the Lord Mayor complaining that honest (viz. Independent) MPs were being 'awed by the concourse of Reformado officers and others' (*Three Letters from . . . Sir Thomas Fairfax* (June 1647), E.394(11), pp. 7–8).

emphasize their value as the nucleus of a counter-revolutionary force against the army, though, as Kishlansky observes, their tumultuous behaviour suggests the reverse of a disciplined force.[30] On 17 June the London Common Council expressed alarm at 'the greate distempers and tumultuous Assemblie of Souldiers and other disaffected persons', and resolved to move parliament that all reformadoes who had not received satisfaction as to their arrears should be ordered to remove to their counties of origin and there receive such satisfaction as parliament should ordain for them.[31] However, on 19 June, by a wafer-thin majority, the House of Commons decided that those reformadoes enlisted either by the parliamentary Committee of Safety or the London Militia Committee should not be disbanded, and, indeed, a further list of twenty-six reformado officers in and about London who had not yet been enlisted was provided.[32] A revealing letter from Fairfax to the Lord Mayor on 21 June suggests that the latter's letter to him two days earlier and submitted for parliamentary approval before being dispatched had been deliberately held up by warmongers in the Commons. The letter in question had disclaimed City responsibility for the recruitment of reformadoes.[33]

Not surprisingly, reformadoes continued to be enlisted.[34] As one pro-army pamphlet put it at the time, it was all very well for the City authorities publicly to urge the expulsion of the reformadoes from London, but 'for what end they were kept there any man may Judge'.[35] Ignoring the clear implications of this charge, a virulently anti-army pamphlet early in July stressed not only the injustice of inhibiting reformadoes from attending to request payment of what was due to them – the author would not have been so solicitous about arrears due to New Model soldiers – but also the fact that many of the reformadoes were themselves Londoners who had business to conduct in the capital quite apart from their quest for their arrears of pay. To expel such persons would be 'to banish them from the place of their habitations' and to deny them the liberty of free subjects, which

30. M. Kishlansky, The Rise of the New Model Army, p. 341 note. See above, p. 379.
31. CLRO., Jor. 40, fo. 224; Bodleian, Tanner MSS., 58, fo. 196; Parliamentary History, XV, 491. This message was conveyed to parliament on the next day, 18 June (C.J., V, 216). On the same day Common Council received a petition against the enlisting of extraordinary forces against the army (The humble Petition of divers Citizens . . . (June 1647), BL. 669, f11(24)).
32. C.J., V, 217. In actual fact the House, by a majority of two votes, decided that the motion that they be disbanded should not be put.
33. CLRO., Jor. 40, fos. 224(b)–5, 225(b)–6; L.J., IX, 281, 291; Parliamentary History, XV, 489–90, XVI, 24–7.
34. See the army's protest in its second Remonstrance of 23 June (Parliamentary History, XVI, 4–19, especially pp. 16–19).
35. Oxford, Worcester College, Clarke MSS., 41, fo. 60.

was not in the power of either City or parliament to do and would certainly provoke tumultuous disorder.[36]

On 25 June the halls of the Salters', Vintners' and Haberdashers' companies were set aside for payment of the reformadoes and the House of Lords appointed three of its number to prepare an ordinance appointing a day by which the reformadoes must be gone.[37] But the payment operation was badly botched and chaos and violence erupted when payment was denied to those reformadoes whose accounts had still not been audited. As a pro-army newsletter gleefully relates, the Lord Mayor's remedy of calling out the trained bands to quell the disorders was totally ineffective since not one in twenty of the bandsmen responded to the call, and the enraged reformadoes threatened to burn down the citizens' houses.[38] On 29 June the Commons gave a first reading to an ordinance, which was ultimately passed on 9 July, prohibiting tumultuous assemblies of officers and soldiers in Westminster and London and ordering all reformadoes except those who could prove the necessity of their being in the metropolis to be gone by 15 July.[39] While the loopholes in this legislation are obvious enough, it is nevertheless likely that if it had been strictly observed, much subsequent trouble would have been avoided.

There had been further reformado infringements of parliamentary privilege on 1 July when MPs were accosted by reformado officers who, according to Juxon's account, addressed them 'verey vncivilley', telling them they would not be allowed to stir from the parliament house until they had voted them their arrears of pay. Two days later parliament received yet another reformado petition, this time from men who complained that they had not received the pay which parliament had authorized the previous month. The petitioners protested that their estates were exhausted. To the past experience of some of them of imprisonment by Cavaliers was now added that of imprisonment for debt as a consequence of parliament's neglect to pay what was due to them.[40] Over the next few months their position, if anything, worsened.[41]

On the day before the reformadoes' petition was presented, the Lord

36. *Nine Proposals by way of Interrogation* (July 1647), BL., E.396(8), pp. 5–6. Another pamphlet of 21 July saw the dispersing of the reformadoes as a crucial feature of the army's bid for supremacy (*The Totall and Finall Demands made by . . . the Agitators and Army* (21 July 1647), E.399(9), p. 7).
37. CLRO., Jor. 40, fo. 229; *L.J.*, IX, 293. The earl of Stamford entered his dissent to this resolution. See also ibid., p. 298.
38. *Clarke Papers*, I, 141–2.
39. *C.J.*, V, 227; *L.J.*, IX, 322, 322–3; *Cal.SPD. 1645–7*, p. 565.
40. Dr Williams's Library, MS. 24.50, fo. 109(b); HLRO., MP., 3/7/1647.
41. See, e.g., *The Humble Remonstrance of the Reduced Officers* (1648), Codrington pamphlet coll., p. 5.

Mayor, Aldermen and Common Council also petitioned parliament asking for measures to deal with the whole problem of the massed auxiliary forces in London. As to the reformadoes in particular, the City Fathers stressed the need for determined action to force them back to their places of habitation. Recognizing, however, that some of them might have legitimate reasons for staying, the City recommended the creation of a committee to determine such cases.[42] On 16 July the Lords recommended to the Commons that special care should be taken to pay the reformadoes their arrears for which they had again petitioned, but, needless to say, the Lower House took exception to the Lords' intrusion into their prerogative on money matters. As to the reformado petitioners, they were informed that it was impossible at the present time to grant their request, and that there was nothing for it but for them to obey the ordinance of 9 July and leave London, after which parliament would take their desires into consideration with all convenient speed.[43] But they, or most of them at least, chose to stay put.

After the counter-revolutionary coup of 26 July the City authorities continued to insist, as, for instance, in their letter of 2 August to Fairfax, that it was not by their command but by parliamentary ordinance and presumably therefore through the parliamentary Committee of Safety that reformadoes were recruited and kept on.[44] While, as has already been shown, a good deal of the recruitment of reformadoes had been done by private initiative as well as through the Committee of Safety, the role of the London Militia Committee was again to be highlighted by the army in its Remonstrance of 18 August.[45] In the meantime, as London's counter-revolution moved towards its crisis at the beginning of August and officers of the trained bands began to shed their commissions in alarmed apprehension of the approach of the army, a royalist newsletter described the strength of the residual force defending London as residing in 'high Presbyterians and Reformados countenanced only by y[e] name of Parliament'.[46]

Even before the army's occupation of London on 6 August, the hunt for the most prominent reformadoes was on. Everyone in fact knew that

42. *The Humble Petition of the Lord Major [sic] Aldermen and Commons* . . . (July 1647), BL., E.396(15), p. 3; *L.J.*, IX, 310. This task was given not to a new committee but to the City Militia Committee. For continued complaints from the army about the reformado presence in London, see *L.J.*, IX, 320; *Parliamentary History*, XVI, 96, 98–9; Bell, *Memorials*, I, 365–6; *The Armies new Propositions* (July 1647), BL., E.398(15), no pagination; *A Copy of a Letter from the Generall Councell of Warre* (July 1647), E.399(31), p. 4; Rushworth, *Historical Collections*, VI, 636.
43. *L.J.*, IX, 334; *C.J.*, V, 248, 249.
44. CLRO., Jor. 40, fo. 247.
45. *Parliamentary History*, XVI, 256.
46. Bodleian, Clarendon MSS., 30, fo. 24.

London was about to capitulate. 'Our freinds in London', relates one pro-army newsletter of 5 August, 'all yesterday went about to gett the well-affected apprentices together to seize uppon as many of the most active Reformadoes as they could light uppon'.[47] On the next day all reformadoes were ordered out of the lines of communication by 10 August and were not to come within twenty miles thereafter.[48] In addition some notorious reformadoes were arrested, among them a certain Lieutenant Rooksby who was said to have been responsible for betraying the garrison of Jamestown in Connaught to the Irish confederate rebels two years earlier.[49] The presence of such a person in the counter-revolutionary ranks obviously had good propaganda value. It is perhaps significant that, despite reformado insistence on always having fought stoutly for the parliamentarian cause, among those who were publicly to bewail their lot and the parliament's ingratitude to them was the royalist newswriter *Mercurius Melancholicus*.[50] It may indeed have been fears that here lay an obvious source of recruitment for the royalist cause in the Second Civil War that prompted favourable response to successive reformado petitions in the spring and summer of 1648 when such disorderly gatherings had an even more dangerous potential than had been the case a year earlier.[51] In responding to the last of three August petitions which came on 22 August from 1,900 officers, of whom 140 were field officers, parliament ordered that they should receive the same generous treatment as earlier reformado petitioners – 'but where's the money?' pertinently observed one newsletter.[52] In view of the role of the reformadoes in London in the previous year, it was perhaps appropriate that, in September, the House

47. *Clarke Papers*, I, 221–2.
48. *Cal.SPD. 1645–7*, p. 598 (*Perfect Occurrences Number 32*); *Parliamentary History*, XVI, 240. An ordinance to this effect did not pass the Commons until 11 August (*C.J.*, V, 272). The reformadoes' case at this time is put in *The Reformadoes Remonstrance* (6 August 1647), BL., E.402(33), pp. 1–5.
49. Rooksby's petition from prison explaining his conduct in Ireland was heard in the House of Lords on 21 September and a letter from Ormond on his behalf was read. On 12 November his bail was discharged and the case against him virtually dismissed (*L.J.*, IX, 442, 519; *HMC., 6th Report (House of Lords Cal. 1647)*, p. 209).
50. *Mercurius Melancholicus . . . number 13* (20/29 November 1647), BL., E.417(17), p. 78.
51. There was a reformado petition to the Common Council of London in early April (CLRO., Jor. 40, fo. 266(b)); and to parliament in May (Rushworth, *Historical Collections*, VII, 1109); and in late July, when aggressive intentions and the likelihood of violence were rumoured (ibid., pp. 1203, 1220–1; *HMC., 7th Report (House of Lords Cal. 1648)*, p. 36; *HMC., 13th Report Appendix Portland MSS.*, I, 490). There were three reformado petitions in August (*L.J.*, X, 424, 426–7; *C.J.*, V, 664–5; *The Petition of 8000 Reduced Officers and Souldiers* (8 August 1648), BL., E.457(29), pp. 1–3; *A Petition to the House of Commons* (22 August 1648), E.461(1), pp. 1–3). For an ordinance of 20 July to determine reformado arrears, see *A&O.*, I, 1170–4. For orders for payment of reduced officers in August, see *L.J.*, X, 423.
52. BL., E.461(1), pp. 1–5; *The Moderate Number 7* (22/29 August 1648), E.461(16), sig. G2ᵛ.

of Commons chose to raise a loan of £100,000 from the City towards the cost.[53]

Some prominent reformadoes

Among the notable parliamentary commanders in the First Civil War who had led armies other than the New Model and who played a leading part in the organization of the forces raised to defend London in late July and early August 1647 were Colonel-General Sydenham Poynz and Major-General Sir William Waller, former commanders of the armies of the Northern Association and South-eastern Association respectively. Another was the hero of the defence of Gloucester in 1643, Major-General Edward Massey. The attitudes of all three had been profoundly affected by the events of 1645–6 and more especially by the foundation of the New Model Army under the command of Sir Thomas Fairfax. Naturally hostile to the New Model, they were able to give this hostility a respectable face by seeing themselves as the obedient executants of a legitimate parliamentary determination to bring a disobedient army to book; or, alternatively, as defenders of parliament and the realm against the military despotism threatened by the army. They were emphatically not turncoats to royalism.

We have already encountered Colonel-General Poynz in the context of the firmness and restraint which he displayed in disputes with the Scots over billeting in 1646, his conduct of affairs winning the admiration of the Presbyterian leaders Holles and Stapleton.[54] In the summer of 1647 he was engaged in disputes of a different sort. Late in June he complained to Speaker Lenthall and to Fairfax that agitators from the New Model Army had come north and were fostering disobedience and subversive notions among his own Northern Association soldiers. Poynz informed Fairfax that he had given orders that they should be apprehended as indeed he had been instructed to do by parliament.[55] Not the least of his grievances, as he informed Commissary Lionel Copley in a letter of 29 June, was that the malcontents in his army, egged on by agitators from the New Model, were proposing to present their grievances to Fairfax, as the latter's own soldiers had done earlier in their celebrated March petition. 'And why to Sir Thomas? they all knowing these forces are a distinct Army and not under the command of Sir Thomas and that his Excellencie does utterly renounce their

53. C.J., VI, 7.
54. See above, p. 309. On Poynz's earlier and overseas career, see A.T.S. Godrick (ed.), The Relation of Sydenham Poyntz 1624–1636, Camden Soc., 3rd. series, XIV (1908).
55. Bodleian, Tanner MSS., 58, fos. 272, 275, 277, 278; Clarke Papers, I, 142–4; The Vindication of Collonell Generall Points (1648), BL., E.469(23), pp. 7–8, 9.

actions, as my Quarter Master informes mee.' In this, however, he seems to have been wrongly informed. Stickler though Fairfax normally was for military discipline, his lack of support for Poynz in his predicament is perhaps not surprising if there is anything in Bellièvre's report in a letter to Brienne on 24 June that Poynz had orders to move against the New Model if Fairfax did not comply with parliament's order to bring the king to Richmond Palace. In any case Fairfax was not unsympathetic in his response to newly elected agitators of the Northern Association regiments.[56]

They needed no further encouragement, and on the morning of 8 July a party of Poynz's own soldiers invaded headquarters at York and carried him off ignominiously to Pontefract; according to his wife's account, 'used somewhat contrary to the quality of a gentleman . . . carried away in his slippers, not suffered to express any conjugal comfort or courtesy to me, his wife, at his departing'.[57] Those responsible for his abduction resolved to write to Fairfax to solicit his support for Poynz's prosecution and his replacement by a more responsible commander, 'considering what dangerous consequent effects . . . might flow from such a corrupt member as he . . .'.[58] The situation was now becoming somewhat embarrassing for Fairfax, who, when Poynz was brought before him under guard at Reading, ordered his immediate release. Poynz himself tendered his resignation from his command in a letter to the Speaker of the House of Commons which also complained bitterly about his treatment.[59] From now onwards he too was, to all intents and purposes, a reformado, even if a self-discharged one.

The matter which had sparked off his soldiers' last move against Poynz had been, if their own account is to be believed, his replacement of Fairfax's relation, Lieutenant-Colonel Fairfax, by Poynz's partisan, the Lord Mayor of York, as governor of the garrison at Clifford's Tower in York, thereby strengthening the following not only of himself but also of Sir Philip Stapleton, the Yorkshire Presbyterian MP and one of the eleven members who were about to be impeached by the New Model Army. But it is important to distinguish between the occasion and the root causes of the action against Poynz on 8 July. These lay in his reaction to the events of which he had complained during the previous month, and, more particularly, the alleged corruption of his

56. *Clarke Papers*, I, 144–7; *Montereul Correspondence*, II, 176.
57. Cary, *Memorials*, I, 300–1. For Poynz's own account, see *The Vindication of Collonell Generall Points*, pp. 10–15. For his abductors' version, see *The humble Remonstrance of the Souldiers of the Northern Association* (July 1647), BL., E.399(32), pp. 7–8.
58. *The humble Petition of the Souldiery of the Northern Association* (July 1647), ibid., pp. 3–5.
59. Bodleian, Tanner MSS., 58, fo. 367; Cary, *Memorials*, I, 298–9. The Speaker ordered the restitution of the goods stolen from Poynz at the time of his abduction.

soldiers by peripatetic agitators from the New Model. The point of their stressing the Clifford's Tower business was that it was seen as part and parcel of a counter-revolutionary design to engage the kingdom in a new war; all of a piece with Poynz's order to put the Northern Association forces in readiness at Selby, Tadcaster, Ferry Bridge and other places, in close correspondence with Stapleton and his associates. Consonant with this was Poynz's continual denigration of the New Model Army and its Lord General, his recruiting of a reformado company which 'refused any engagement save against the Army'; and his declared intention 'to draw up his army to quell the rebellious Army of Sir Thomas Fairfax'. He had committed officers who had publicly praised the New Model and had hanged one soldier without having recourse to a Council of War. Papers condemning the New Model Army's actions had been read at the head of every troop and posted up in market-places. This picture of Poynz's counter-revolutionary preparation is perhaps overdone, but it is not unreasonable to wonder what his reaction would have been if the north of England had experienced the Scottish invasion which so many feared in the summer of 1647.[60]

On being released by Fairfax, Poynz made his way to London where he was just in time to take part in the July counter-revolution in close association with the other eminent reformadoes Massey and Waller.[61] In a joint declaration of 9 August Poynz and Massey were to give vent to their bitterness at being, in their view – as also in Waller's – left in the lurch by the City authorities' capitulation to the army three days earlier. They departed from London in disgust.[62] Deploring though it did Poynz's escape from just retribution, an army newsletter of 5 August, on the eve of the army's triumphant entry into London, nevertheless bears out his, Massey's and Waller's verdict that their City allies had feet of clay.[63] However, as well as their embittered New Model and Independent enemies,[64] some Londoners had good reason to abominate the two ex-generals and their reformado followers. The tale of the brutal treatment of the petitioners outside and near Guildhall on 2 August has been

---

60. This paragraph is based on *Clarke Papers*, I, 163–9; Cary, *Memorials*, I, 293, 298–301; BL., E.399(32), pp. 3–10. See also J.S. Morrill, 'Mutiny and Discontent in English Provincial Armies 1645–1647', *P&P.*, 56 (1972), 66, 70–1.

61. Some details of their involvement are given in the charges brought against the former Lord Mayor and others in 1648 (*L.J.*, X, 13, 201–2, 214–15, 217–19; *Parliamentary History*, XVII, 96–8). See also *Ludlow Memoirs*, I, 162–3.

62. *The Declaration of Generall Massey and Colonell Generall Poyntz* (9 August 1647), BL., E.401(12), pp. 3–4. For Waller's similar verdict, see above, pp. 184, 383.

63. *Clarke Papers*, I, 221.

64. For their denunciations, including a likening of Poynz and his associates to the Hothams and Carew, the renegades of 1643, see *The Arraignment and Impeachment of Major Generall Massie, Sir William Waller, Col. Poyntz* . . . (23 August 1647), BL., E.404(6), p. 5. See also *A Speedy Hue and Crie: After Generall Massie, Col. Poyntz* . . . *and other new modelled Reformadoes* (10 August 1647), E.401(20), passim.

told elsewhere.[65] But in fairness it ought perhaps to be emphasized that there is another version of events, and in particular, of Poynz's role in them. In a Presbyterian pamphlet published in the following December Poynz appears as the much-provoked hero of the occasion, and his alleged victims as

> a most rude rabble of Anabaptists and such *like seditious Sectaries* and *Schismaticks*, [who] under pretence of *presentinge a Petition* to the *Common Councel* . . . abused valiant and wel-deserving *Major-General Poyntz* . . . [and] cryed out *No Poyntz, no Poyntz*, pull'd him violently by his scarlet Cloak, asking him if he had payd for it, yea some of them . . . kicking him on his breech, yea and smiting him on his head in high scorn and contempt, insomuch that the *heroick, spirited Gentleman* . . . could no longer indure them, but that drawing his sword, other swords were also drawn, one was slain and divers others wounded. . . .[66]

The events of the summer of 1647 – carried away from York in his carpet slippers in June and pummelled and taunted in London in August cannot have done much for Poynz's self-esteem. Yet he was never again to attain the prominence which was his at and before that time. In a letter couched in depressed terms and wildly eccentric spelling from his exile in Holland to Lord Wharton in May 1648, he asked Wharton to employ his influence on his behalf, stressing that 'all thought [viz. although] I lye now vnder a darke Kloud vndesarved, I hop the tym will Com . . . that the parlement . . . will acknowledge mee for their trew and faithfull sarfant [viz. servant] as I all wayes haf bin and dou hop to Leif and dye'.[67] This plea was fruitless, but if his disappointment turned to the sort of counter-revolutionary aspirations which he had entertained during the previous summer, he achieved no prominence in the far more serious outbreaks of 1648. Lauderdale refers to him hopefully in August as the likely Major-General of an insurgent force to be raised by Lord Willoughby of Parham in Lincolnshire and East Anglia, and Walter Strickland contemptuously in October as being with the insurgent fleet in the Downs, and 'as little esteemed by them as by us'.[68] Poynz's counter-revolutionary career had peaked in 1647, and even then not very impressively.

Like Poynz, Major-General Edward Massey was a professional soldier with experience of continental warfare. The strictly professional nature of his commitment is reflected in the fact that he had offered his services

65. See above, pp. 138, 353.
66. *The Army Anatomized* (4 December 1647), BL., E.419(6), p. 24. Italics in original.
67. Bodleian, Rawlinson Letters, 52, no. 35. The letter is dated 1 May 1647 in the Bodleian catalogue, but is almost certainly attributable to 1648.
68. Lauderdale's comment is in *Hamilton Papers*, pp. 248–9; Strickland's in *Naval Documents*, pp. 391–2. On Willoughby's defection, see below, pp. 410–11.

to Charles I in the Civil War before they had been accepted by parliament. He had earlier served part of an apprenticeship in London before taking himself off to Holland. It was as the military governor of Gloucester who successfully resisted the royalist siege of that city in 1643 that Massey rose to national celebrity.[69] His successful defence of Gloucester and his campaigns in the Welsh marches and the West Country established him as a soldier to be seriously reckoned with, although his reputation was later to be sullied by his soldiers' undisciplined propensity to rapine and plunder. For all that, a conservative admirer was to rate his military achievement as at least as high as that of 'the loudest boasting *Independent* or *Sectary* in the whole *Army* (not one excepted)'. It is not difficult to guess with whom this encomiast seeks to compare him, more especially since he is also generous in his praise of Fairfax.[70]

At about the same time as Poynz was contending with the disturbances fomented among his soldiers by agitators from the New Model, Massey, who had been elected in the meantime as 'recruiter' MP for Wootton Bassett, was, if anything, in even greater trouble, as one of the eleven Presbyterian members whom the army was determined to impeach. Along with Holles, Stapleton and the others, he was charged with endeavouring to create the counter-revolutionary force which was described earlier in this chapter. More particularly he was accused of playing a central role in the design to divert the forces raised for Ireland, of which he, along with Major-General Philip Skippon, had been appointed commander, into counter-revolutionary pursuits at home. The soldiers trusted their old infantry commander, Skippon, but Massey was a completely different proposition. He was known to have been critical of the army's behaviour over disbandment, petitioning and the soldiers' arrears of pay. Additionally, in subsequent conversations with New Model officers, Sir William Waller was to become acquainted with their view, as he puts it, that Massey was looked upon as 'a profane man and unfit for a command where all the congregation was holy'.[71] This is not very surprising if there is anything in the description of him by an admittedly hostile witness as being 'something addicted to Venery and carousing', and as having acquired the habit of hard drinking from his Dutch experience.[72] Apparently Massey's 'Presbyterianism' did not extend to religious matters. But this last is a verdict of one of his

69. Newman, *Royalist Officers*, p. 248; BL., E.401(20), p. 1. The contemporary historian of the siege describes Massey as a commander of fidelity and great valour ([J. Corbet], *An Historical Relation of the Military Government of Gloucester* (1645), BHPC., p. 15).
70. BL., E.419(6), pp. 3–4. For an account hostile to Massey which nevertheless cites a similar tribute to him, see E.404(6), p. 4.
71. Waller, *Vindication*, pp. 83–5.
72. BL., E.401(20), p. 1.

opponents, and one pamphleteer from the other camp is at pains to contrast favourably his enthusiastic and efficient conduct of recruitment for Ireland with Skippon's lukewarm attitude.[73]

Massey's role in the counter-revolutionary developments of late July and early August 1647 has already received mention elsewhere.[74] The army's remonstrance of 18 August insisted that if he and his associates went unpunished, there was every reason to expect 'the like or worse attempts of violence and War' in the future.[75] On the same day a committee of both Houses set up to investigate the counter-revolutionary disturbances demanded from the City authorities a copy of the order of 30 July appointing Massey as Commander-in-Chief.[76] By that time, like Poynz, he had made his getaway, some said to Scotland, where he would doubtless find succour and sympathy from future Engagers.[77]

Although there were reports in April 1648 from a parliamentary agent in Brussels that Massey, Sir William Waller and Lord Willoughby of Parham were 'a-plotting something to the Prejudice of the Parliament' in the Low Countries along with the royalist Colonel Anselme,[78] Massey, like Poynz, played no significant part in the Second Civil War. According to his own account he was approached by both the Queen and the Prince of Wales to take on the rank of Lieutenant-General in a royalist army to invade England. He confessed to being deeply sensible of the honour, acknowledging that he would defend the English monarchy 'against any forraign enemy . . . but to engage against his Native Country, he was resolved to the contrary, saying he would never draw his sword more to involve England in bloud'.[79] He kept to his resolution, and Lauderdale's report on 19 August that great things were hoped for from a projected rising in London with Major-General Browne commanding the militia, Colonel Graves the horse and Massey the foot proved to be as illusory as his hopes of a rising in the eastern counties under Willoughby and Poynz.[80] But his military inactivity in 1648 did not save him from imprisonment at Pride's Purge.[81] Escaping at about the time of the king's execution, he, as Clarendon acidly comments, 'transported himself into Holland . . . and . . . presented

73. *The Honest Citizen* . . . (3 May 1648), BL., E.438(5), pp. 5–6. For contrary opinions that Massey and the Presbyterians had obstructed the relief of Ireland, see *Parliamentary History*, XVI, 74–81; BL., E.404(6), pp. 1–2. For a denial of these specific charges, see *Parliamentary History*, XVI, 122–3, 130–4.
74. See above, pp. 184, 354.
75. *A Declaration of the last Demands Propounded by . . . Sir Thomas Fairfax* (August 1647), BL., E.404(3), p. 2.
76. CLRO., Jor. 40, fo. 254.
77. *A Letter from an honourable Gentleman* . . . (23 August 1647), BL., E.404(8), pp. 4–5.
78. L.J., X, 193–4.
79. *The Declaration of Major Generall Massey* . . . (12 July 1648), BL., E.452(20), p. 2.
80. *Hamilton Papers*, pp. 248–9.
81. *Clarke Papers*, II, 68.

himself to the Prince with as much confidence . . . as if he had defended Colchester'.[82] Perhaps he merited a more generous encomium.

It will be recalled that despite his seniority to Massey, Sir William Waller had accepted a post subordinate to him in the counter-revolutionary force to defend London after the coup of July 1647.[83] Waller had moved a long way since 1643 when he had been the great hope of the war group in parliament who deplored the conservative politics and unimaginative strategy of Lord General Essex. The enthusiasm of his erstwhile supporters had waned in 1644 though they were still not above continuing to use him as a stick with which to beat the Lord General. His own account of his estrangement from them has the ring of truth about it, even if it does also suggest the perennial excuse of the moderate who is left behind by the course of events:

> This change was not in me, but in others: or, if in me, yet occasioned by the alteration and change of others . . . I am of opinion that all are not of the godly party that wear that badge and cognizance.[84]

Unlike Massey, Waller was not lacking in Puritan ardour, and, although a cultivated and civilized man, had been responsible for some iconoclastic excesses during the first war.[85] But what he had in common with both Massey and Poynz, and indeed Essex,[86] was a near-obsessive dislike of the New Model Army which cemented their association with the parliamentary Presbyterians. The events of the spring and summer of 1647 confirmed and deepened this connection and Waller is eloquent in his denunciation of the lack of firmness, both of the army commanders over the March petition and of the parliament which should have 'crushed the cockatrice in the egg'.[87]

Waller and Massey's careers and attitudes converge in many other respects in 1647. Waller too had been concerned with recruitment for the Irish service in 1647,[88] an experience which further widened the gulf between them both and the New Model Army. Both of them were numbered among the eleven members attacked by the army.[89] Both played a notable part in the London counter-revolution of late July and

---

82. Clarendon, *Rebellion*, IV, 467.
83. See above, p. 184.
84. Waller, *Vindication*, pp. 9–10. See also pp. 11–13.
85. For examples, see Gardiner, *Civil War*, I, 352; C.H. Firth, *Cromwell's Army* (1962 edn.), p. 328.
86. Waller was to inform D'Ewes that he and his former rival Essex had since become friends once they realized how the radicals had sought to play them off against one another (MacCormack, *Revolutionary Politics*, p. 38 note).
87. Waller, *Vindication*, pp. 50–1, 152–3.
88. See Kishlansky, *The Rise of the New Model Army*, pp. 158–9, 187–9; Woolrych, *Soldiers and Statesmen*, p. 31.
89. As MP for Andover, Waller had had to resign his army commission following the Self Denying Ordinance of 1645.

early August and both expressed disgust at being let down by the City fathers. Both were rumoured to be in Scotland in March 1648 and to have thrown in their lot with the Engagers,[90] but both went subsequently to Holland. It was later reported that Waller had played a part in the revolt of part of the fleet, but he claimed to have known nothing about it 'till it was common news and matter of discussion in every barber's shop in the Hague'.[91] Both returned to England in 1648 and supported the Newport Treaty and both were in consequence purged and imprisoned by the army in December. While Massey escaped, Waller was one of the last of the imprisoned MPs to be released from captivity, which did not happen until 1652. It was during his long imprisonment that he wrote the *Vindication* which affords so much information about his chequered and interesting career.[92]

Another victim of Pride's Purge was the Presbyterian Major-General Richard Browne who was sheriff of London at the time and whose arrest has been described in an earlier chapter.[93] Browne was an orthodox and unrelenting Presbyterian in both the religious and the political senses. Like Massey and Waller, he was charged with urging the Scots to invade in 1647 when they declined to do so, and again in 1648 when they did invade. One of his Independent enemies, the gentleman radical Edmund Ludlow, makes the most of Browne's former occupation as a London woodmonger in his sneering caricature of him in his *Memoirs*. According to Ludlow,

> . . . no sooner had the King . . . cast some slight favours upon him, giving him a pair of silk stockings with his own hand, but his low and abject original and education became so prevalent in him as to transform him into an agent and spy for the King. . . .[94]

Browne had been one of the parliamentary commissioners appointed to oversee the handing over of the king by the Scots at Newcastle in February 1647 and his subsequent transference to Holdenby House,[95] where he is reported to have rebuked Cornet Joyce for his audacious mission to abduct Charles on 4 June, saying that if only he had the strength he would have resisted Joyce's men to the death. The narrator

90. Along with two others of the eleven, Denzil Holles and Walter Long (P. Crawford, *Denzil Holles 1598–1680* (1979), pp. 173–4). For Waller's denial of any connection with the Engagers, see Waller, *Vindication*, pp. 215–18.
91. Ibid., pp. 214–15.
92. Gardiner, *Civil War*, IV, 275; D. Underdown, *Pride's Purge* (Oxford 1971), pp. 162–3; Clarendon, *Rebellion*, IV, 467; R. Zaller (ed.), *Biographical Dictionary of English Radicals in the Seventeenth Century* (Brighton, 1984), III, 280–81.
93. See above, pp. 195–6.
94. *Ludlow Memoirs*, I, 139. For a reference to Browne's activities as a timber merchant in the 1630s, see *Whitelock Diary*, p. 118 and note.
95. Clarendon, *Rebellion*, IV, 213.

laconically observes, however, that Joyce 'knew well enough that he had not strength and therefore he spake so boldly'.[96] But the ground had been laid for a measure of mutual understanding and sympathy between Charles and Browne, which is not, of course, the same as to say that the latter had become an out-and-out royalist. A letter from Wycombe on 9 July reports him as being in high favour with the king, while early in the following month, at the height of London's counter-revolution, the Presbyterian politician Sir John Maynard observed that Browne was doing the king important service in the city, and that ' 'twere well if the King tooke notice of him for it'.[97] If Browne's political opponent, the Independent Thomas Juxon, is to be believed, one of these services was to convey to the City authorities the king's exhortation to stand stoutly in defence against the army, which, if true, makes nonsense of Charles's later dissociation of himself from counter-revolutionary developments in London.[98]

It will be recalled that in the summer of 1648 Browne was the favoured candidate of the more conservative elements in the city for the post of commander of the metropolitan militias; 'a Citizen bred, and one that loveth the City heartily . . . and . . . loveth Government and order'.[99] The choice of Skippon rather than Browne was probably a crucial factor in securing the City's quiescence during the Second Civil War,[100] though it is by no means certain that Browne would have favoured City intervention on the side either of the Scottish Engagers or the English insurgents. Lauderdale's report of 19 August, two days after the defeat of the Scots at Preston, that the City had appointed Browne to command its militia, has already been mentioned and was in fact a characteristic piece of Scottish wishful thinking.[101] The only office to which he had in fact been appointed was that of sheriff of London on 24 June.[102]

96. *A true impartiall Narration concerning the Armies Preservation of the King* (17 June 1647), BL., E.393(1), pp. 4–5, 9–10.
97. *New Papers from the Armie* (July 1647), BL., E.398(1), no pagination; HLRO., Braye MSS., 96 (photocopy of John Browne's Commonplace Book in Beinecke Library, Yale University, Osborne MSS.), fo. 237.
98. Dr Williams's Library, MS. 24.50, fo. 115. For the king's protestation to this effect, see above, p. 350.
99. *The Honest Citizen* . . . (3 May 1648), BL., E.449(35), p. 5. See above, p. 189.
100. Skippon's role is strongly argued and perhaps a trifle overstressed by I. Gentles, 'The Struggle for London in the Second Civil War', *Hist. J.*, XXVI (1983), 277–305.
101. *Hamilton Papers*, p. 247. See above, p. 395.
102. *A Petition presented at a Common Hall* . . . (26 June 1648), BL., E.449(35). The election was confirmed in parliament on 6 July (Rushworth, *Historical Collections*, VII, 1179; Whitelock, *Memorials*, p. 313 (6 July)). On 6 July Browne was also appointed to a City committee to treat with a parliamentary committee about the maintaining of order in the event of the king's coming to London (CLRO., Jor. 40, fo. 284(b)).

An Independent pamphlet of early July sees Browne, 'the Presbyterian Courtier', as the likeliest leader of a counter-revolutionary force in London should Presbyterian demands for the army to release the king to attend a personal treaty in London be refused.[103] But Browne, like the City itself, kept his hands clean during the Second Civil War. Indeed, on 1 December, almost on the eve of Pride's Purge, he made what was described as a conciliatory speech in parliament undertaking to do his utmost 'to keepe a right understanding between his Excellency, the City and Army'.[104] But this was not sufficient to prevent his arrest and imprisonment at Pride's Purge. To have supported the treaty of Newport as a conservative parliamentarian was hardly less reprehensible than to have been an unregenerate Cavalier or one of the Second Civil War renegades to whom our attention now turns.[105]

Changing sides

In a letter to the earl of Lanark on 10 March 1648, Lord Byron, the newly designated royalist commander-in-chief in North Wales, Shropshire, Cheshire and Lancashire, relates how he had been diligently engaged in soliciting the aid of 'some eminent persons formerly of the adverse party'. Byron was confident that when the time came for a Scottish invasion – hopefully sooner rather than later – 'the greatest part of Lancashire, Cheshire and North Wales will declare for the King'. He also mentioned designs for the surprising of Nottingham Castle and Oxford, presumably with the aid of such defectors.[106] More explicit as to pertinent details, assuming that it is genuine and not a fake, is a declaration of 20 July 1648 from the Prince of Wales and sent by him to Sir Marmaduke Langdale, promising payment of their arrears to defecting parliamentary soldiers, just as Denzil Holles and the militant parliamentary Presbyterians had done during the summer of 1647. The declaration also stressed the need to make every effort to bring over the Presbyterians to the royalist cause.[107] Another declaration by the Lord Deputy of Ireland, the earl of Ormond, on 6 October 1648 after the

---

103. *Londons New Colours displai'd* (July 1648), BL., E.452(21), pp. 9–10.
104. *A Declaration of the Proceedings in Parliament concerning the King* (1 December 1648), BL., E.475(31), p. 4.
105. Browne was accused not only of bringing in the Scots, but of supporting the earl of Holland's rebellion (*The Impeachment Demands and Proposals of the Army concerning Major General Brown* (December 1648), BL., E.475(36), especially p. 4). The charge was brought up again in April 1649 (*C.J.*, VI, 181; Whitelock, *Memorials*, p. 382(b) (9 April)).
106. *Hamilton Papers*, pp. 166–7.
107. *The Declaration of his Highnesse the Prince of Wales* (July 1648), Chelmsford, Essex RO., Landon coll. (also BL., E.454(8)), especially pp. 4–5.

Second Civil War was virtually over, was similarly angled partly at the Presbyterians and claimed to recognize no distinction between former parliamentarians and former royalists, both of whom 'now . . . engaged in this cause shall be reflected upon with equal favour and regard', past allegiance notwithstanding.[108]

What deterrents did parliament employ to set against royalist inducements to potential turncoats? Some of the defectors treated in the subsequent pages, of whom Lord Holland, Colonel Poyer and Colonel Morrice are examples, suffered the supreme penalty for their disloyalty. On 8 June 1648 the House of Commons ordered one of its committees to inquire into those Kent and Essex insurgents who 'having formerly served the Parliament, are now run into Rebellion' and required Fairfax to try them by martial law. On 21 July trial by martial law of those who had formerly served parliament but had gone over to the insurgents was extended to the whole country, and on 22 August *The Moderate* reported that anyone who had taken the Negative Oath or the Covenant and had afterwards borne arms against the parliament should die without mercy.[109] However, the heinousness of defection is earlier reflected in the different fates ordained for those taken prisoner at St Fagan's on 8 May. The ordinary Welsh 'Country-People', many of whom had been lightly armed with clubs and similar weapons, were set free on undertaking not to rise again. The common soldiers were to be shipped to the West Indies and the officers to be tried according to the law of the land. But those who had formerly been in arms for parliament were to be tried summarily by court martial and some of them, as a letter of 21 May from Wales reported, had already been executed.[110]

No defection to the royalist insurgents in 1648 was of greater moment than that of Lord Inchiquin in Ireland. Inchiquin was President of Munster and his defection was designed to put that province at the disposal of the royalists. His motives were mixed. Frustrated ambition was certainly one of them, for his aim of subjugating the whole province, nominally to parliament but in effect to himself, had been inhibited by inadequate funds and supplies. This he was increasingly disposed to ascribe to the growing ascendancy of the parliamentary Independents at Westminster from the latter part of 1647. Despite the passing of a formal vote of thanks to him by both Houses on 1 December 1647 coupled with a gratuity of £1,000,[111] parliament had in his view inadequately recognized his signal services in Ireland, where his military successes had been achieved often with ruthlessness and

108. *HMC., MSS. of the Marquis of Ormonde*, II, 81–3.
109. *C.J.*, V, 589, 642; Rushworth, *Historical Collections*, VII, 1198–9; *The Moderate* (22/ 29 August 1648), BL., E.461(16), sig. G2.
110. Rushworth, *Historical Collections*, VII, 1131–2.
111. *L.J.*, IX, 551; *HMC., 6th Report (House of Lords Cal. 1647–8)*, p. 213.

great brutality.[112] Nevertheless, fulsome Presbyterian praise for 'the Renowned Lord *Inchequen* was by no means lacking.[113] Gardiner may well be correct in his perceptive suggestion that Inchiquin probably had far more in common with the great royalist warlords of Munster than with either his parliamentary Presbyterian supporters, or, still less, with parliamentary commanders elsewhere in Ireland such as the New Model Independent Colonel Michael Jones,[114] and it was these, along with the king's deputy in Ireland, the earl of Ormond, whom he was ultimately to make his allies.[115]

Although Inchiquin's defection from parliament was reported in late February 1648, it did not in fact take place until 3 April, although Montereul had reported from Edinburgh in March that he had offered to bring 6,000 men over to Scotland if the Scots were prepared to take positive action to aid the king.[116] At a Council of War on 6 May Inchiquin issued a Protestation denouncing some officers of his own army whom he accused of being in league with his Independent enemies in England.[117] Although later in the same month he was to shock Protestant opinion by his agreement with the Supreme Council of the Irish confederate Catholics – or perhaps because he anticipated such objections – he reaffirmed his adherence to the Covenant and the Protestant religion as well as his determination to restore both the king to his rights and parliament to its freedom and privileges; the very things in fact which he claimed the Independent ascendancy at Westminster was seriously jeopardizing. The Protestation concluded by declaring that any in Munster who refused to join with him in pursuit of these aims would be treated as an enemy to the Protestant party in Ireland, a conclusion which accorded ill with his subsequent agreement with the Irish confederate Catholics on 22 May. A week after this he received Ormond in Munster as arranged, and, in Clarendon's words, 'all the province of Munster (in which there are many excellent ports) became immediately and entirely under the king's obedience'. Perhaps this overstates the case, startling though these events and their consequences had been. For it needs to be emphasized that there was nothing like unanimity among the Irish

---

112. For examples, see Gardiner, *Civil War*, IV, 106–7; also J.H. Ohlmeyer, *Civil War and Restoration in the three Stuart Kingdoms* (Cambridge, 1993), pp. 198–9.
113. *A Word to Mr Peters and two Words to the Parliament and Kingdom* (9 November 1647), BL., E.413(7), pp. 35–6.
114. Gardiner, *Civil War*, IV, 110.
115. On Inchiquin's relations with Ormond prior to his defection, see Clarendon, *Rebellion*, IV, 290–1.
116. SRO., GD 406/1/2458; Gardiner, *Civil War*, IV, 110–11; *Montereul Correspondence*, II, 432, 437.
117. *The Lord Inchiquin's Protestation Sexto Maii 1648* (14 June 1648), BL., E.447(13), pp. 1–5.

confederate Catholics in their attitude to the 'Inchiquin truce' and the subsequent alliance with the royalist Lord Deputy Ormond. The truce was roundly denounced by the papal nuncio Rinuccini who excommunicated those who adhered to it. While the Supreme Council of the Catholic confederates refused to be intimidated by Rinuccini's anathemas, there were many, among them the marquis of Antrim and the confederate general Owen Roe O'Neill, who refused to go along with the Inchiquin truce and Ormond's use of it as a means of restoring royalist fortunes in Ireland.[118]

For all that, the combined effect of Inchiquin's defection and that of a substantial part of the parliamentary fleet to the royalists in 1648 was to widen enormously the strategic options open to the insurgents in the Second Civil War. While that war offers no other such spectacular examples of defection as Inchiquin's betrayal of a whole province, there were, as Byron had predicted, a number of significant cases of parliamentarian officers betraying their trust and attempting to hand over strong places in their charge to the insurgents. Our first such case, that of Lieutenant-Colonel Henry Lilburne, the brother of the celebrated Leveller, is a sorry tale of disastrous miscalculation and failure. Lilburne had formerly been governor of Tynemouth Castle which commanded the mouth of the Tyne and therefore the entry to Newcastle by sea. However, he had been replaced by Sir Arthur Haselrig under whom he now served as Deputy Governor, and it is not unlikely that it was this demotion, rather than any distinct political commitment, which was the main cause of his defection on 9 August 1648, which seems to have come as a complete surprise to Haselrig. Having sent away most of the officers of the guard on various assignments, Lilburne pulled up the drawbridge of the castle, released the royalist prisoners, and threatened to pistol every soldier who was not for him and the king, actually running one such soldier through with his sword. He sent messengers to Shields and other nearby places soliciting seamen and others to join his now insurgent garrison and some of them responded to the invitation. But his triumph was short-lived, and on the next day, aided partly by some soldiers and their captain who had escaped from Lilburne's clutches, Haselrig stormed the castle and Lilburne was killed in the process. Haselrig's prompt and decisive action prevented what could have been a very dangerous and embarrassing situation, not simply in terms of its strategic implications with the Scots army of the Engagement already in England, but also for the reason that, as one local observer emphasized, 'if the trafique for coales between London and Newcastle should be stopt, you in the Southerne parts would be sensible

118. Clarendon, *Rebellion*, IV, 422–3; Ohlmeyer, *Civil War and Restoration*, pp. 210–17.

of it'.[119] The argument of one royalist commentator that the whole business was no genuine royalist reverse but had been staged by the Independent Haselrig as a way of getting rid of his Presbyterian deputy, and that, following the storming of the castle, he 'then raysed the report of *Lilburnes* revolting for the King, to colour his own murthers', is as ingenious as it is unconvincing.[120]

In the same month as Lilburne's short-lived defection at Tynemouth, Captain Sir Matthew Boynton, the parliamentary governor of Scarborough Castle, emulated the success of his predecessor Sir Hugh Cholmeley in 1643 in putting the castle at the disposal of the royalist cause. Unlike Lilburne's case, his resistance lasted for months rather than hours. Like both Cholmeley and Lilburne, Boynton had been a trusted and esteemed officer of parliament, and indeed had made an unsuccessful attempt in 1647 to convince Poynz of the error of his ways in opposing the New Model Army.[121] By July 1648, however, Boynton's defection was daily expected, and a determined effort was made to dissuade him by William Dobson, the mayor of Hull, and some local Roundheads. On 31 July Boynton responded to Dobson's offer to use his good offices to obtain payment of the arrears due to the governor and his garrison, by expressing polite surprise that he should be thought to be actuated by such mercenary motives as distinct from the 'high and noble resolution' by which he was really moved.[122] The two delegates who were then sent to Scarborough to treat with Boynton offer a very different view in their report of 3 August to Speaker Lenthall. They reported that Boynton had admitted that if the offer to settle arrears had been made two months earlier, before his approach to the Lord General on the matter had been rebuffed, the present crisis might not have arisen. The report also highlights Boynton's touchiness about what was described as 'the many base wayes used to dispossesse him of his Command'. Although the meeting ended indecisively, two factors in particular may have influenced him to respond negatively to these approaches. One was the arrival of two ships with provisions and stores from royalists in Whitby and King's Lynn, and the other his prior commitment to the Prince of Wales to betray the castle for a reward of £3,000.[123]

119. Rushworth, *Historical Collections*, VII, 1126–7; *Parliamentary History*, XVII, 410; *Sir Arthur Hesilrige's Letter . . . concerning the Revolt and Recovery of Tinmouth Castle* (10 August 1648), BL., E.458(26), pp. 3–7; *A Terrible and Bloudy Fight at Tinmouth Castle* (10 August 1648), E.459(4), pp. 1–5; PRO., SP. 19/140, 187, 190–6; *Cal.CAM.*, III, 1234; Welford, *Durham and Northumberland*, pp. 114–15.
120. *Mercurius Aulicus . . . Number 4* (21/28 August 1648), BL., E.461(5), p. 32.
121. *The Vindication of Collonell General Points* (1648), BL., E.469(23), p. 7.
122. Bodleian, Tanner MSS., 57, fos. 157, 158.
123. On these events and the report of the delegates from Hull, ibid., fos. 167, 169–70. On the undertaking to the Prince of Wales, see Rushworth, *Historical Collections*, VII, 1218–19.

There followed a long siege with numerous sallies by the garrison, which had been joined by other defectors, renegades from the parliamentary service among them.[124] At the beginning of the siege Boynton held both castle and town, and the townsmen were called upon to contribute in money, provisions and men. By the second week of September the municipality was complaining about Boynton's exactions and protesting the inability of the inhabitants to pay and more.[125] By that time things were looking bad for Boynton, whose garrison was said to have dwindled to about eighty foot and twenty horse, and a determined attempt to raise the siege had been repulsed.[126] A newssheet of 6 September forecasted a quick surrender, reminding Boynton of the fate of Lucas and Lisle at newly surrendered Colchester.[127] But prospects improved with the arrival of substantial reinforcements by sea in mid-September. Among the newcomers were Welsh, Scottish and Walloon soldiers, some of whom had been wounded at the fierce affray at Deal Castle in Kent and who quickly acquired a local reputation for violence and destruction of some of the houses in the town. However, the townspeople's ordeal was soon to be over. A letter from York on 15 September reported both that the town had fallen and that some of the Walloons, whom the soldiers had taken for Irishmen, had been put to the sword.[128] The inhabitants of Scarborough were thus saved from further exactions by Boynton and there are no further complaints in the municipal records on this score. Boynton himself continued to roar defiance from the castle, proclaiming, according to one royalist account, 'that rather than yield, he will bury his bones under the walls'.[129] Indeed, he held out until 28 December when the castle was yielded on terms whose generosity was described by Colonel Bethel, the officer commanding the siege, as having been necessitated by the

124. *A Great and Bloody Fight at Scarborough Castle* . . . (11 August 1648), BL., E.458(16), pp. 1–2; *Bloody Newes from the North* (17 August 1648), E.460(10), pp. 4–6. Among these renegades were Colonel Charles Fairfax of the New Model, a former volunteer for the Irish service; Captain Wilkins, a former subordinate of Poynz; and Captain Buck, who had served under Colonel Bethel who now commanded the besieging force.

125. Northallerton, North Yorkshire R.O., Scarborough Corporation Minute Book 1621–1649, fos. 162–2(b), 163(b). I am greatly indebted to Mr M.Y. Ashworth for making these references available to me. The burdens included the raising of a company of eighty soldiers and an assessment of £20 a week. In addition Boynton raised a loan of £40 from 45 inhabitants.

126. Rushworth, *Historical Collections*, VII, 1250–1; *Bloudy Newes from Wales* (1 September 1648), BL., E.462(9), p. 3.

127. *The Perfect Weekly Account Number 26* (6/13 September 1648), BL., E.463(5), no pagination.

128. *Packets of Letters from Scotland and the North of England* (20 September 1648), BL., E.464(20), pp. 1–2; *A Letter from Newcastle* (14 September 1648), E.464(9), p. 3; Rushworth, *Historical Collections*, VII, 1265.

129. *Mercurius Pragmaticus Number 26* (19/26 September 1648), BL., E.464(45), no pagination.

danger that it might again be relieved by some of the ships of the Prince of Wales.[130]

Like Boynton and Lilburne, Captain John Morrice was involved in the subversion of a parliamentary stronghold from within, though not in the capacity of governor or deputy governor. Having served in Ireland until 1642,[131] Morrice had attained the rank of Lieutenant-Colonel in the royalist army by 1644 when, probably frustrated of further promotion, he defected to parliament. But here too he was disappointed, especially after the foundation of the New Model Army. His merciless ridicule of the military saints together with what Clarendon describes as a 'life of great license' would certainly not recommend him to the godly and upright men of the New Model. The story of his second switching of allegiance in 1648 is one of the most intriguing and bizarre episodes in either of the civil wars, for which, however, one needs no more complex explanation than that of the frustrated careerism of a professional soldier. But a second defection also called for a spectacular atonement for the first, in order, as Clarendon puts it, to 'wipe off that blemish by a service that would redeem him'. Clarendon, who admired Morrice's ingenuity, daring and panache, tells with relish how he insinuated himself into the favour of the parliamentary governor of Pontefract Castle, and hints at something stronger than friendship in his observation that the latter 'loved him above all men and delighted so much in his company that he got him to be with him sometimes a week or more at a time . . . when they always lay together in one bed'. Morrice skilfully exploited his advantage to persuade the governor to make crucial personnel changes to facilitate the coup which he was planning and which, after some false starts, was successfully executed on 3 June to the horrified amazement of the deluded governor. A fortnight later, Morrice, who had been joined in the meantime by Cavaliers from Yorkshire, Lincolnshire and Nottinghamshire, appointed a council of war of eight officers with himself as president.[132] For a time he went from strength to strength and royalist possession of Pontefract Castle could have been of crucial importance in view of the rising in the north and the Scottish invasion in July. The end of both dangers allowed the government to devote more attention to the reduction of Pontefract, and Colonel Rainsborough, the celebrated Leveller sympathizer and rejected Vice-Admiral, was put in charge of operations.[133] But on 29 October Morrice engineered a daring sally from the castle as far as

130. *C.J.*, VI, 105; *L.J.*, X, 639–40.
131. Details of Morrice's career in Ireland, beginning with his youthful service as the earl of Strafford's page, are in West Yorkshire Archive Service, Leeds City RO., Bacon Frank MSS., BF 13, fo. 146.
132. Ibid., BF 3, fo. 85. For some of the military dispositions and orders of the Council on 20 July, see ibid., fos. 85–6.
133. For Rainsborough's earlier difficulties as Vice-Admiral, see below, p. 412–13.

Doncaster in hope of taking Rainsborough hostage and, so Clarendon suggests, exchanging him for Sir Marmaduke Langdale, then a prisoner in Nottingham Castle. Although this plan was frustrated when Rainsborough was killed resisting capture, his death was the occasion of royalist rejoicing and applause for Morrice's daring and initiative. Cromwell, now returned from Scotland, took over the siege for a time and on 19 November informed Speaker Lenthall that the castle was well provisioned and its defences formidable, and that it might hold out for a further year.[134] It did, in fact, hold out until March 1649.

Major-General Lambert's terms for surrender on 19 March were not ungenerous except for six named persons, of whom one was Morrice, who had earlier offered to surrender on absurdly unrealistic terms. With a few others he succeeded in making his getaway following one last sortie before the castle was surrendered. He was apprehended early in April at Lancaster and tried and executed at York in August. Defiant to the last, he took objection to the jurors at his trial and more especially to the foreman, an old enemy of his, as well as to being denied trial by court martial as befitted a soldier, and to being put in irons after sentence had been passed. He went bravely to his death, offering on the scaffold a spirited defence of his actions.[135]

Morrice also achieved distinction of a sort as one of a number of defectors who changed sides more than once. Another was the Scottish professional soldier, Major-General Sir John Urry (or Hurry), who changed sides on at least two further occasions following his original defection from parliament to the king in 1643. Urry ended his days by being beheaded in 1650 following his support for the last and fatal venture of his former enemy Montrose. Another multiple defector was Lieutenant-Colonel Robert Brandling, one of a prominent Northumberland family from Alnwick and, in the opinion of that pillar of Cavalier consistency, Sir Marmaduke Langdale, 'a very knave'. Having defected from king to parliament in 1644, Brandling changed sides again in 1648 when he was one of those responsible for the fall of Berwick and its later being handed over to the Scots.[136]

Of all multiple defectors, pride of place, and not simply in social

134. Carlyle, *Cromwell*, I, 330–2.
135. In addition to the references in notes 131–4, this account of Morrice's exploits is based on Clarendon, *Rebellion*, IV, 396–407; *State Trials*, IV, 1249–70; P.R.O., SP. 23/14/201, 23/101/671, 23/237/234; Newman, *Royalist Officers*, p. 265; and especially on Leeds City R.O., Bacon Frank MSS., BF 3, fos. 80–9, 148–55, BF 7, fos. 1–8, BF 13, fo. 146.
136. On Urry, whose rank of major-general was obtained in parliament's service before 1644, see Newman, *Royalist Officers*, pp. 383–4; Stevenson, *Revolution and Counter-Revolution*, pp. 27–9, 32, 83, 161, 164; R. Williams, *Montrose: Cavalier in Mourning* (1975), passim. On Brandling, *Cal. CAM.*, III, 1351; *HMC., 13th Report Appendix Portland MSS.*, I, 487; Newman *Royalist Officers*, pp. 40–41, 'Catholic Royalists of Northern England 1642–1645', *Northern History*, XV (1979), 91.

terms, should probably be accorded to Henry Rich, earl of Holland. Brother of the Lord Admiral Warwick and a former favourite of the queen, Holland had once been a courtier *par excellence* – 'none', in Clarendon's view, 'was equal to him in that function and mystery'. Proficiency in this sphere was, however, no guarantee of fitness for military command and his appointment as commander of the horse in the First Bishops' War in 1638 elicited Sir Philip Warwick's derisory comment that he was 'a man fitter for a shew than a field'.[137] Early in the Civil War he had consistently favoured making concessions to reach agreement with the king,[138] and in August 1643, when parliament's fortunes had reached their nadir, he, along with the earls of Clare and Bedford, absconded to Oxford. But neither the exercise of courtly arts nor his appearance with the royal army at the siege of Gloucester and the first battle of Newbury availed to restore him to favour at court, and he returned to Westminster in October soon to be followed by the two other noble defectors. 'The silent contempt of London', Gardiner observes, 'was a welcome exchange for the scornful hostility of Oxford'.[139] But was it? The seeds of Holland's second defection in 1648 were sown by the imprisonment and sequestration which were his lot following his return to Westminster. Although the imprisonment did not last for long, it was much longer before the sequestration was taken off. Above all, he was no longer trusted nor did he occupy any place of influence in the councils of the parliament.[140] On 11 February 1647 the request of the three defecting peers of 1643 to be readmitted to parliament was considered by the House of Lords and narrowly rejected, despite personal canvassing on Holland's behalf by the earl of Northumberland, who also had contemplated defection in 1643.[141]

In addition, as in 1643 but even more so in the year of the Vote of No Addresses, Holland, as Whitelock tells us, despaired of parliament's hostility to a personal treaty, and believed that the most likely way to bring it to reason was by an armed revolt demanding the treaty which was to be one of the principal features of his own manifesto.[142] Encouraged, as Clarendon claims, by his brother Warwick who urged that 'the

---

137. Clarendon, *Rebellion*, III, 194; *Memoirs of the Reign of King Charles I by Sir Philip Warwick Knight* (Edinburgh, 1813), p. 141. See also ibid., pp. 145, 147. On Holland's courtly career, see K. Sharpe, *The Personal Rule of Charles I* (1992), pp. 164–5, 176–7, 537–8, 742–4, 806–7; B. Donogan, 'A Courtier's Progress: Greed and Consistency in the Life of the Earl of Holland', *Hist. J.*, XIX (1976), 317–53.
138. See Gardiner, *Civil War*, I, 53, 103, 145, 183–4.
139. See ibid., I, 199–202; Clarendon, *Rebellion*, III, 142–3, 146–56, 193–200, 245–6. Hyde did his utmost to persuade Charles to offer more encouragement to such defectors.
140. See Clarendon, *Rebellion*, III, 248.
141. *Sydney Papers*, pp. 6–12. For subsequent failure to get these peers readmitted, see ibid., pp. 14–15, 19–20.
142. *Whitelock Diary*, pp. 217–18; Whitelock, *Memorials*, p. 313 (5 July 1648).

Scots should not do all that work',[143] Holland joined with the royalist duke of Buckingham and his brother Lord Francis Villiers, and with the earl of Peterborough, in what was planned to be a major rising but turned out to be a very damp squib. The enterprise had the enthusiastic support of the queen and, also in France, of Holland's old courtly friend Lord Jermyn. Another courtier, Lord Culpepper, put pressure on Buckingham to accept Holland as commander-in-chief despite his inferiority of rank, as well as to agree to the profession of the aims of the Covenant, as a means of gaining support from former parliamentarians.[144] But, following a series of futile manoeuvres and a disastrous reverse in Surrey in which Lord Francis Villiers was killed, fate finally caught up with Holland at St Neots in Huntingdonshire on 10 July, where, having arrived 'so weary and shaken in his joynts . . . that he had a better will to his bed than his horse', the pathetic remains of his force were surprised by a Roundhead detachment under Colonel Scroope and he was captured. Buckingham and Peterborough escaped and fled abroad.[145]

Holland was imprisoned in Warwick Castle where he was to remain until 6 February 1649 despite his countess's vain plea that he should be brought up to his house in Kensington or some other place in or near London since he was seriously ill, though it was later to be argued, contradictorily, that he was too unwell to be brought to London to stand trial.[146] For a short time it seemed that this would not be necessary anyway, since in November the House of Lords voted his banishment along with two royalist insurgents in the Second Civil War, Lords Goring (Norwich) and Capel.[147] But Pride's Purge altered all that, and on 13 December the vote for banishment was revoked and they were

143. Clarendon, *Rebellion*, IV, 318. It may be that Clarendon overstates Warwick's encouragement. For a different view by another contemporary historian, see T. May, 'A Breviary of the History of the Parliament . . .' (1813 edn.), in Maseres, *Select Tracts*, I, 120. As to the Scots, Lanark and Lauderdale entertained great hopes for his rising and expressed deep regret at his defeat and capture (Bodleian, MS. e Mus., 203, pp. 51–2, 53–4; *Designes and Correspondence of the Present Committee of Estates* (July 1648), BL., E.459(5), pp. 11–12, 14).

144. BL., Add. MSS., 2533, fo. 458(b). Colonel Adrian Scroope, who defeated the insurgents at St Neots on 10 July, seems to have assumed that Buckingham was in command (*HMC., 13th Report Appendix Portland MSS.*, I, 478).

145. This account is based on ibid., I, 478; Clarendon, *Rebellion*, IV, 385–6; Rushworth, *Historical Collections*, VII, 1187–8; *Sydney Papers*, pp. 35–6; *A Great Victory obtained by Collonell Scroope* (12 July 1648), BL., E.452(15), pp. 1–5; *Whitelock Diary*, p. 217; Whitelock, *Memorials*, p. 315 (11 July).

146. *L.J.*, X, 436, 439, 596, 597; *C.J.*, V, 633, 676; *C.J.*, VI, 132; Rushworth, *Historical Collections*, VII, 1189, 1233; *HMC., 7th Report (House of Lords Cal. 1648)*, pp. 45, 50, 63; BL., E.467(6), p. 4; *State Trials*, IV, 1210, 1212; Whitelock, *Memorials*, pp. 372, 375 (7 and 12 February 1649).

147. *L.J.*, X, 594, 596, 613; *C.J.*, VI, 72. The Lords acquiesced in the decision on 18 November after having objected on 12 November to the breach of their privileges by the Commons.

left to stand trial.[148] Charged with treason before the special high court set up by parliament early in February 1649, Holland pleaded in vain both that he had surrendered to quarter at St Neots and that parliament had previously authorized banishment as his punishment.[149] All was to no avail and the accused were found guilty and sentenced to be beheaded. Although the Cavaliers Goring and Owen were later to be reprieved, there was no such respite for Holland despite the pleas of his wife and brother and indeed of Fairfax himself.[150] Changing sides was apparently a more serious offence than consistent and unwavering malignancy. The incongruity was noted by Holland's friend, Bulstrode Whitelock:

> Thus the Lord *Goring*, who had been no friend to the Religious Party was saved, and the Earl of *Holland*, who had been a most civil person to all, and a very great friend to the *old Puritans* . . . and protected them . . . by the same single Vote lost his life.[151]

Another multiple defector who took part in Holland's rising and was slain at St Neots was Colonel John Dalbier, 'the Dutchman to whom all causes were alike'.[152] Dalbier had served under the earl of Essex in the First Civil War, and there is abundant evidence of the important part he played in the counter-revolutionary force to defend London in the summer of 1647 and indeed of his participating in the assault on parliament on 26 July.[153] Unlike Poynz, Massey and Waller, who also served in the London defence force, Dalbier tried his hand again in 1648, possibly drawn by attachment to the Villiers brothers whose father he had served in the 1620s. As a notorious reformado defector in two successive years, he seems to have been a special object of the attention of Colonel Scroope's soldiers at St Neots, who, in Ludlow's phrase, 'to express their detestation of Dalbeir's [*sic*] treachery, hewed him in pieces'.[154]

148. *Parliamentary History*, XVIII, 472.
149. *State Trials*, IV, 1215–16; Whitelock, *Memorials*, pp. 378, 378(b) (27 February and 3 March). For the creation of the high court, *C.J.*, VI, 128, 131; *State Trials*, IV, 1208–10. The other accused were Hamilton, Goring, Capel and Sir John Owen.
150. *State Trials*, IV, 1216–17; *C.J.*, VI, 159–60; *HMC., 7th Report (House of Lords Cal. 1648–9)*, p. 71; *HMC., 13th Report Appendix Portland MSS.*, I, 512; Whitelock, *Memorials*, pp. 378(b)–9 (6, 7 and 8 March).
151. Ibid., p. 379 (8 March). The single vote was the casting vote of Speaker Lenthall in each case. In his diary for 1634/5 Whitelock characterizes Holland as 'a favourer of the Puritans' (*Whitelock Diary*, pp. 92–3. See also ibid., p. 117 note).
152. Gardiner, *Civil War*, IV, 159.
153. E.g., *C.J.*, V, 213; *L.J.*, X, 201, 214; *Parliamentary History*, XVII, 96–7; HLRO., Braye MSS., 96 (photocopy of Osborne MSS., in Beinecke Library, Yale University), fo. 238.
154. *HMC., 13th Report Appendix Portland MSS.*, I, 478; BL., E.452(15), pp. 4–5; *Ludlow Memoirs*, I, 198; Rushworth, *Historical Collections*, VII, 1192. According to this last account Dalbier died of his wounds on the next day.

One member of the House of Lords who had been persistently opposed to the readmission of Holland during the early part of 1647 had been Lord Willoughby of Parham,[155] the Lincolnshire nobleman who had been one of the first Lord Lieutenants to defy Charles I over the militia ordinance in 1642, an action for which extreme Cavaliers never forgave him.[156] Yet Willoughby was to defect from parliament in 1648. According to Dr Clive Holmes, the roots of his defection stretch back as far as 1643–4, when Willoughby had opposed the incorporation of Lincolnshire into the Eastern Association and was consequently eclipsed by the earl of Manchester and his lieutenant in Lincolnshire, Colonel Edward King. Accordingly Willoughby must have felt at best ambivalent about King's later assault on the county committee of Lincolnshire, distressingly radical though its members might be according to the standards of both of them.[157] Like Dalbier, though in a very different capacity, Willoughby had been involved in the counter-revolutionary developments of July 1647, taking over in the depleted parliament as Speaker of the House of Lords, appropriately in place of his old opponent Manchester who had fled to the army. 'Willoughby of Parham is the Glory of England', remarked the conservative Presbyterian Sir John Maynard somewhat extravagantly,[158] but his action marked him down for destruction when the army occupied London on 6 August and restored the fugitive MPs. The tale of the planned impeachment of Willoughby, along with six other peers, and his subsequent abscondence to Holland has already been told. The charge against the seven lords was, of course, to be dropped in June, though no-one could have foreseen this happening in the atmosphere of the beginning of 1648.[159] In his Declaration addressed to the Speaker of the House of Lords on 6 February, shortly before his flight, Willoughby maintained, like Waller, that his zeal for parliament had never waned, and that 'I am still upon the same foundation I ever was'.[160]

Following his flight to Holland, apart from reportedly engaging in royalist plots in the Low Countries,[161] Willoughby was later to find a new and unfamiliar role with that part of the fleet which had revolted from parliament and gone over to the Prince of Wales, a role for which

155. *Sydney Papers*, pp. 11, 14–15, 19–20.
156. See C. Holmes, *Seventeenth-Century Lincolnshire* (Lincoln, 1980), pp. 146–50; Ashton, *Civil War*, pp. 170–1.
157. Holmes, op. cit., pp. 183–5. On King and his struggle with the county committee, see ibid., pp. 188–93, and C. Holmes, 'Colonel King and Lincolnshire Politics 1642–1646', *Hist. J.*, XVI (1973), 451–84. See also above, pp. 92–3.
158. HLRO., Braye MSS., 96, fo. 238.
159. See above, pp. 176–7.
160. *A Declaration from the Lord Willoughby of Parham* (February 1648), BL., 669, f11(124), fo. 115.
161. *L.J.*, X, 193–4. See above, p. 395.

he was as inadequately fitted as he had been for military command in Lincolnshire back in 1642–3. 'I know not how he comes by that imployment, for he hath neither knowledge nor interest amongst those men' was one royalist comment.[162] To their obvious objection to serving under a landsman, the sailors added a reluctance, which was warmly applauded by old-style Cavaliers, to serving under an ex-Roundhead,[163] even if they were not to display the same reluctance to serving under their former Vice-Admiral William Batten when he too defected from parliament in August. However, persistent rumour had it that Willoughby was 'Vice-Admiral in name onely . . . and not trusted with the Secresy of Affairs'.[164] But although his appointment as Vice-Admiral might be an occasion for derision among English parliamen-tarians and indignation among royalists, it was greeted with enthusiasm by the Scottish Engagers, and notably Lauderdale who spent some time aboard the insurgent fleet in the Downs and described Willoughby as 'most honest and wholly Scots. He [is] solely engaged on our inter-ests.'[165] On 7 November a letter from the Hague reported that Willoughby and the later defector from parliament Vice-Admiral Batten had left the Prince of Wales. It would probably be more accurate to say that they had been pushed out by Prince Rupert,[166] another soldier turned naval commander. In Batten's case this was the second time in the recent past that he had to yield command to a landsman, which had been the basic cause of his defection in August 1648. Although the naval mutiny began in May, long before Batten's defection, his dismissal had been in the forefront of the sailors' grievances, which ultimately led to the defection of a significant part of the fleet to the Prince of Wales. Since these events have been the subject of a number of recent studies, a detailed account of them will not be necessary here beyond a short description of their causes and character, along with a few words about their strategic significance in the chapter which follows.[167]

162. *Hamilton Papers*, pp. 220, 221; *Naval Documents*, p. 353.
163. For illustrations of the sailors' and royalists' lack of confidence in, and dislike of, Willoughby, see *Hamilton Papers*, pp. 222–3, 229; *Naval Documents*, p. 379.
164. Evidence of Willoughby's lack of real authority is in *The Princes Commission to Capt. Green . . .* (31 July 1647), BL., E.456(31), p. 14; *Naval Documents*, pp. 376–7. In Lord Hatton's view his Vice-Admiralty was a ruse to facilitate the realization of Jermyn's ambition to be Lord Admiral (*Nicholas Papers*, pp. 96–7).
165. *Hamilton Papers*, p. 248. See also ibid., p. 246. For the Prince of Wales's undertaking to send Willoughby later with ships to the Scottish coast, see ibid., p. 243.
166. Whitelock, *Memorials*, p. 342 (7 November); *Bloudy Newes from the English Navy* (November 1648), BL., E.470(23), p. 4; *Naval Documents*, p. 392. There is some reason to believe that Rupert had done his utmost to foster the sailors' dissatisfaction with Batten (see B. Capp, *Cromwell's Navy . . . 1648–1660* (Oxford, 1989), p. 38). Warwick reported on 17 November that the duke of York had taken over the insurgent fleet (*L.J.*, X, 595).
167. See J.R. Powell, *The Navy in the English Civil War* (1962), chs. 10–12; *Naval Documents*, pp. 301–10; B. Capp, *Cromwell's Navy*, pp. 15–41; D.E. Kennedy, 'The

Batten is also important in this context because his Presbyterianism, in both religion and politics, had rendered him highly suspect to those Independents who were increasingly in control of affairs from August 1647 onwards and because his character and views point up a sharp contrast with his successor as Vice-Admiral, Colonel Thomas Rainsborough. Batten's Presbyterian affiliations had made him a willing agent in the flight of six of the eleven members to France in August which got him into trouble with the army and the Independents, and may have predisposed him, if Montereul is to be believed, to offer to declare for the Scots along with twenty-two of his ships in the event of a Scottish invasion.[168] Like Willoughby of Parham, Batten's relations with the Scots were excellent, no doubt at least partly a product of his own pious Presbyterianism. He was anti-Independent in politics as well as religion, and two witnesses, one of whom was a local JP, gave evidence at Sandwich in September 1647 that he had been heard to say that whatever it might protest at the time, the army's ultimate intention was to cut off the king's head.[169] It was undoubtedly due to intense Independent pressure that Batten resigned his commission in the same month to be replaced by Rainsborough early in October, an appointment which created a much greater stir than had Batten's resignation.[170] While Rainsborough had not yet acquired the reputation of a Leveller sympathizer, which was soon to be his following his prominence in the Putney debates at the end of October and beginning of November, he was already feared as a radical who mistrusted the Independent and army negotiations with the king over the Heads of the Proposals. But from the end of October it was especially his Leveller affiliations which were emphasized by opponents of his appointment.[171]

Much more important than the conservative seamen's objections to a landlubber as commander, especially since Rainsborough came from a naval family and had himself captained a ship before transferring to army service during the First Civil War, was their fear, almost amounting

English Naval Revolt of 1648', *Eng. Hist. Rev.*, LXXVII (1962), 247–56; R.C. Anderson, 'The Royalists at Sea in 1648', *Mariners' Mirror*, IX (1928), 34–46. And see below, pp. 438–48.

168. Dr Capp's verdict (op. cit., p. 16) that Batten's release of the six after they had been intercepted at sea was a 'blatant affront' is surely misplaced since they had the Speaker's pass to go. See *Sir Philip Stapleton Dead of the Sicknesse at Callice* (August 1647), BL., E.404(22), especially pp. 2–4; *The True Relation of Capt. William Batten* (August 1647), E.404(38), especially pp. 3–7; *Naval Documents*, pp. 285–7. On the alleged offer to the Scots, see *Montereul Correspondence*, II, 251. The unacceptable condition was that the Scots would revictual the ships when necessary.

169. *L.J.*, IX, 433; *Naval Documents*, pp. 287–8.

170. Ibid., pp. 289–90; *L.J.*, IX, 460.

171. For such objections, see, e.g., *L.J.*, IX, 606; *A New Magna Charta* (17 February 1648), BL., E.427(15), pp. 5–6. Following a conference between the Houses, it was agreed on 27 December that Rainsborough should sail with the fleet (*L.J.*, IX, 614, 615).

to phobia, about an Independent design to 'new model' the navy with the former New Model officer Rainsborough as its instrument. For, compared with the army, the navy was a very conservative force. 'The seamen', as Clarendon observed, 'are a nation by themselves . . . rude and resolute in whatsoever they resolve . . . and jealous of those tomorrow by whom they are governed this day.'[172] In June 1647 the sailors had rejected out of hand the approach of New Model agitators at around the same time as the latter were – though with much greater success – approaching the soldiers of Poynz's army.[173] There is no evidence in the fleet either of widespread sectarian beliefs or of the Leveller sympathies displayed at Putney by Rainsborough; 'a man', as a declaration of the revolted ships was to put it in July 1648, 'of most destructive principles both in religion and policy'.[174] The objections to his presumed policy have already been made clear. As to religion, the case is vividly stated by *Mercurius Pragmaticus*: that Rainsborough was no longer to be denied 'the same honour by *Sea* that the rest of the Saints injoyed by *Land*'.[175] Under him, the Declaration continued, 'we had no settled form of divine worship nor communion [and] little or no preaching on board but by illiterate and mechanic persons'. All this was taken as a clear indication of the intention to 'new model' the navy, all of a piece with 'introducing land-soldiers into every ship, to master and over-awe the seamen'. In these circumstances there was as abundant scope for sympathy for Batten, especially given the precipitate and insensitive manner of his dismissal,[176] as there was for fears about and hostility to his successor. Attempting to board his flagship in the Downs on 26 May, Rainsborough was put ashore by mutineers in circumstances even more humiliating than those of his predecessor's relinquishment of office the previous October.[177] Two days later the mutineers and the seamen from other ships which joined the mutiny issued the so-called Declaration of the Navy, expressing their abhorrence of Rainsborough and his alleged new modelling of the navy, their desire to associate themselves with the aims of the Kentish petitioners and their intention of petitioning parliament for a personal treaty with the king.[178]

---

172. Clarendon, *Rebellion*, IV, 332.
173. See *Leveller Manifestoes*, pp. 145–6.
174. The Declaration is printed in BL., 669, f12(69); also in *Naval Documents*, pp. 354–5.
175. *Mercurius Pragmaticus Number 20* (25 January/1 February 1648), BL., E.434(7), sig. V2–V2^v.
176. For Batten's own account of this in his Declaration of 21 August, see *Naval Documents*, pp. 364–5.
177. For contemporary accounts of this event, see ibid., pp. 331–2, 335–6.
178. The Declaration is printed in ibid., pp. 332–4. On the aims of the Kent petitioners, see above, pp. 144–5. On 29 June the petition of masters and mariners of Thames shipping mentions a treaty as being desired by all seamen (*L.J.*, X, 352; *Parliamentary History*, XVII, 271).

On 29 May parliament did its best to rectify this potentially disastrous situation by reappointing the earl of Warwick, who had been a victim of the Self Denying Ordinance, as Lord Admiral.[179] Had they also gone the whole way and reappointed Batten as his Vice-Admiral, as a petition from some citizens early in June suggested they should,[180] the situation might conceivably have been wholly rectified, especially given Warwick's mandate to offer indemnity to those revolted seamen who submitted to him.[181] But Batten was a highly suspect figure in government circles on account of his behaviour in 1647, his obvious resentment at what he regarded as his grossly unjust treatment and his reported intrigues with the Scots. On 23 May a royalist letter spoke of attempts to persuade him to use his influence with the sailors to bring about further defections to aid the Scots. Another possibility canvassed was his use of defecting crews to rescue Charles I from the Isle of Wight.[182] On 3 June Thomas Withering, the postmaster of Hornchurch in Essex, testified to incriminating remarks made by Batten in a Leadenhall tavern about a design to secure the defection of more ships. Following this and revelations about Batten's alleged role in the Essex rising, the net began to close in on him.[183] When summoned to appear before a parliamentary investigating committee in August, he absconded and joined the insurgent ships in the Downs accompanied by another naval defector, Captain Elias Jordan.[184] On 21 August he issued a Declaration justifying his action in terms of his unjust treatment and the humiliations which had been heaped on him and his wife and denying that he had in any sense been disloyal to parliament.[185] Here indeed was a perfect text for conservative parliamentarians driven by Independent excesses to the margin of defection to the royalist insurgents:

179.	*L.J.*, X, 290–1; *Naval Documents*, p. 336. Significantly, Warwick had been one of two members of the Upper House to record dissent on 15 March to Rainsborough's appointment to command the summer fleet. The other was Manchester (*L.J.*, X, 115). For later unjustified suspicions about Warwick's loyalty to parliament, see *Parliamentary History*, XVIII, 23; Whitelock, *Memorials*, pp. 341, 343 (2 and 14 November); *Mercurius Anti-Mercurius Number 2* (26 September/ 2 October 1648), BL., E.465(11), p. 5. Needless to say, the royalists made the most of such allegations (e.g. *Mercurius Pragmaticus Number 28* (3/10 October 1648), BL., E.466(11), no pagination). For the Prince of Wales's arrogant and unsuccessful attempt on 22 September to get Warwick to defect, see *L.J.*, X, 522–3.

180.	*L.J.*, X, 296; *Naval Documents*, p. 336. See above, p. 124.

181.	For a pamphlet condemning this attempt to detach the insurgent seamen from the Prince, see *The Sea-mens Answer* (4 October 1648), BL., E.465(27), passim. See also *The Reasons ye Navy gieue* [sic] *for their Resolution* (June 1648), E.448(3).

182.	*Hamilton Papers*, pp. 201–2, also pp. 221–2; *Naval Documents*, pp. 328–9.

183.	PRO., SP. 19/21/183, 19/22/214; *Cal. CAM.*, II, 1052–3; *Naval Documents*, pp. 343, 352.

184.	Ibid., p. 363; *HMC., 13th Report Appendix Portland MSS.*, I, 494.

185.	*Naval Documents*, pp. 364–6.

. . . I remember we fought . . . to fetch the King to his Parliament, and yet now it is made treason to offer to bring him thither; that some members were voted malignant for staying in it [presumably after 26 July 1647]; that wee took oaths to defend the Kings person and authority, and must now have a parliament settled without him; and no addresses made to him, but plots and designs to poison and destroy him; these and many other such horrible contradictions cause me to abandon these enemies of peace and to make my humble addresses to His Highness the Prince of Wales.

Nevertheless, Batten and Jordan, along with Willoughby, were to leave the Prince of Wales's service before the end of the year, and to return to England to witness events which would only have confirmed their most gloomy prognostications.

This chapter began with renegade reformadoes in the ranks of the counter-revolutionary force defending London in the summer of 1647, and it concludes with renegades in arms against parliament in 1648. One such case, that of Colonel John Dalbier, has already received mention. Another figure who created quite a stir in 1648 was Captain Edward Wogan. Wogan's defection to the Scottish Engagers, backed by a forged order of Fairfax authorizing the movement of his supernumerary troop of horse northwards from Worcestershire where they were awaiting disbandment, was the occasion of hardly less embarrassment to the Scottish parliament than the presence of Cavaliers such as Glemham and Musgrave on Scottish soil.[186] When Wogan's troops arrived in Scotland with colours flying and breathing 'Rancour against the Parliament and Army of England and how ready they should be to join against them', they found many to welcome them and a letter from Edinburgh on 14 March reported that they had received several hundred pounds – it does not say from whom – to pay for the quarters which had been assigned to them. It was also reported four days later that there were 400 English infantry in Scotland in addition to Wogan's troop of horse and that 200 foot had landed at Chester from Ireland and were making for Scotland 'by the Incitement of a Cavalier Captain who gave them Money to drink, and told them they should have Two Months Advance in *Scotland* if they would go there and Fight for the King'.[187] In the meantime the successive attempts of the English parliamentary commissioners in Scotland to get the Scottish parliament to extradite Wogan and other reformadoes and Cavaliers were unavailing,[188] and Wogan

---

186. On Wogan's defection, see *L.J.*, X, 120–1; Rushworth, *Historical Collections*, VII, 1023. See above, pp. 332–3.

187. Rushworth, *Historical Collections*, VII, 1031, 1032.

188. PRO., SP. 21/9, fos. 34–5; Bodleian, Tanner MSS., 58, fos. 777–7(b); *L.J.*, X, 114, 120, 160, 172, 202, 209, 223–4, 225–8, 266; *C.J.*, V, 541–3, 544; Rushworth,

must either have invaded with Hamilton's army or gone into England
prior to this, for he was among those captured at Appleby on 9 October,
holding the rank of colonel. But this did not keep him out of trouble,
for he was to be taken by Cromwell in Ireland in December 1649, and
it was only the need for an exchange for an English prisoner in Irish
hands which saved him from being done to death by Cromwell as a
renegade of the worst kind.[189]

Our three last defectors were Welsh and their risings constitute the
most important aspect of the Second Civil War in Wales. Unlike
Holland, Morrice or even Batten, Major-General Rowland Laugharne
and Colonels John Poyer and Rice Powell had given no major cause for
suspicion that they would prove disloyal to the parliamentary cause;
indeed, as was seen in the last chapter, parliament was particularly
indebted to Laugharne for promptly quelling the Glamorgan rising of
June 1647.[190] Of the three Powell is the least important and compared
with the others, on whom our chief attention will be concentrated, a
somewhat shadowy figure.

For all his later royalist professions, the real roots of Poyer's rising are
to be found as early as February 1647 in his petition to parliament for
repayment of the sums he had borrowed for repair and maintenance of
the castle and town of Pembroke as well as of the arrears of pay due to
himself and the garrison.[191] In February of the following year it quickly
became clear that he had no intention of handing over the castle, of
which he had been governor for the past four years, to Fairfax's
nominee, Colonel Fleming, until his demands were met (and perhaps
not even then), despite Fairfax's offer to mediate with parliament for his
arrears.[192] Ensconced in Pembroke Castle, Poyer behaved like a cross
between a warlord and a robber baron, sending out his 'Bullies', as he
called them, to plunder the surrounding countryside and more
especially the cattle of local gentlemen to whom he took exception. He
held prisoner for a time in the castle in conditions of great privation two
ministers of the gospel and two JPs, either because they had criticized

     Historical Collections, VII, 1046, 1049–50, 1056, 1064, 1066; *HMC., 7th Report (House
     of Lords Cal. 1647–8)*, p. 15; *HMC., 13th Report Appendix Portland MSS.*, I, 451;
     Packets of Letters from Scotland Berwick Newcastle and York (April 1648), Codrington
     pamphlet coll., p. 1.

189.   Ormerod, *Tracts*, p. 275; Carlyle, *Cromwell*, II, 93–4, III, Appendix, XV, 414–15.
     Carlyle misdates the letter printed in the Appendix as January 1649, whereas it should
     be 1650.

190.   See above, pp. 341–3.

191.   *L.J.*, IX, 14; *HMC., 6th Report Appendix (House of Lords Cal. 1646–7)*, p. 158.

192.   *The Kingdomes Weekly Account . . . Number 7* (16/23 February 1648), BL., E.428(16),
     p. 50. For Poyer's successive refusals to hand over the castle, see ibid., Number 2 (12/
     19 January 1648), E.423(11), pp. 10–12; *C.J.*, V, 477–8; *L.J.*, X, 89; Rushworth,
     Historical Collections, VII, 1016, 1017. For royalist delight at his defiance of 'Generall
     Tom', see *Mercurius Bellicus . . . Number 4* (14/20 February 1648), E.428(4), p. 6.

him or simply because he took exception to them.[193] One's impression from the many accounts of the man, admittedly mostly by his enemies, is of a protean character, a man of 'two Dispositions every Day'; sober in the morning and drunk in the afternoon, alternately flamboyant and withdrawn, noisy and taciturn, boastful and penitent.[194]

On 13 March Poyer issued a declaration demanding payment of his disbursements, which he reckoned at more than £1,000, and of his and his garrison's arrears of pay on the same terms as had been available to the most favoured of soldiers in parliament's service. These terms for surrender of the castle Colonel Fleming, who had come up with a force to take it over, had no authority to accept. To his negative but conciliatory answer, Poyer returned defiance, and Fleming was to find himself simultaneously attacked by Poyer's force sallying out from the castle and some of Laugharne's disbanded soldiers who were on the way to join Poyer. The result was a shattering defeat for Fleming, twenty or thirty of whose men were taken prisoner. More important, Poyer captured some pieces of heavy artillery which had been brought up to batter Pembroke Castle into submission if this proved necessary. With the news of the imminence of another revolt by groups of Laugharne's men, South Wales was now on the verge of a major insurrection, and there was 'great talk in these parts of the raising of a new Army for the King, the Royal party giving out very high speeches'.[195] Poyer began assiduously to cultivate local Cavaliers, proclaiming a new-found royalism which was the product of convenience rather than conviction. What mattered to him was his own private interests, as represented in his demand to Colonel Fleming, rather than the motives outlined in his letter sent to the Prince of Wales at the end of March along with the declaration of his and his fellow insurgent Colonel Rice Powell's intentions. Like Batten's declaration, this emphasized the gulf between declared parliamentary intentions and the reality of the rejection of true religion, the varieties of revolutionary illegality and the imprisonment of the king.[196] Doubtless the prince and the king were not deceived, but neither could afford to look gift horses in the mouth.

Major-General Rowland Laugharne was certainly the most

193. *A Declaration of Divers Gentlemen concerning Collonell [sic] Poyer* (19 April 1648), BL., E.436(7), pp. 1–6; *Heads of Chiefe Passages in Parliament Number 2* (12/19 January 1648), E.423(11), pp. 10–12.
194. See, e.g., ibid., pp. 10–12; E.436(7), pp. 1–6; Rushworth, *Historical Collections*, VII, 1053; *Another Great Fight in Wales* (May 1648), Codrington pamphlet coll., p. 6.
195. *The Declaration and Resolution of Col. Iohn Poyer* (28 March 1648), BL., E.434(11), pp. 1–6; *A Bloody Slaughter at Pembrooke-Castle* . . . (21 March 1648), E.433(5), pp. 1–3; Rushworth, *Historical Collections*, VII, 1034, 1038, 1040; *HMC., 5th Report MSS. of the Duke of Sutherland*, p. 143; Phillips, *Wales*, II, 344–5, 347–8.
196. *Colonell Powell and Col. Poyers Letter* . . . *to the Prince of Wales* (10 April 1648), Codrington pamphlet coll., passim.

distinguished parliamentary commander in South Wales, to whom parliament owed a great debt both for its victory in the region in the First Civil War and for his suppression of the Glamorgan rising in June 1647. However, long before the latter event there were those who had tried, perhaps for self-interested reasons, to cast doubts on his parliamentarian sympathies. On 19 March 1646 William Phillips, the high sheriff of Pembrokeshire, complained to Speaker Lenthall that the major-general had been a principal cause of trouble in the region both 'in respect of the grand vsurpation of the Martiall Power on ye Civill' and by the protection which he afforded to notorious royalist delinquents, some of whom he and his subordinates had forcibly released from gaol to which they had been committed by the high sheriff. As a result, the latter declared, 'there is nott scarce a royal-malignant in this County that wants [viz. lacks] his protection'.[197]

Hints of the issues which were to come to a head in 1648 can perhaps be seen in the House of Commons' vote of 8 April 1647 that 100 horse and 100 dragoons should be kept in service in South Wales under Laugharne's command. The narrow margin of three votes by which the resolution was passed could hardly be regarded as an enthusiastic vote of confidence in the major-general, who must also have been irked by the appointment of the New Model officer Colonel Okey, a radical Independent who was later to be a regicide, and a man at the very opposite pole of the political spectrum to Laugharne, in charge of the dragoons.[198] While Laugharne's services in the suppression of the Glamorgan rising in June were greatly appreciated, he was at about that time, if Juxon is to be believed, one of the non-New Model general officers whom the Presbyterian-dominated parliamentary Committee of Safety and the City Militia Committee were considering inviting to serve in the London defence force.[199] Early in the next year it was reported that the officers at Broadway who were conspiring to surprise Gloucester and perhaps other Marcher towns had hopes of help from Laugharne, who was entertaining similar grievances about the planned disbandment of supernumerary forces. At any rate, while on his way back to Wales, Laugharne was detained at Maidenhead but later gave his captors the slip.[200]

197. Bodleian, Tanner MSS., 60, fos. 578–8(b). For Laugharne's protest against such complaints, see ibid., fo. 590.
198. *C.J.*, V, 137.
199. Dr Williams's Library, MS. 24.50, fo. 110(b).
200. *Two Letters read in the House of Commons* (24 January 1648), BL., E.423(20), pp. 1–2; BL., Stowe MSS., 189, fo. 39(b); *The Kingdomes Weekly Intelligencer* . . . (25 January/1 February 1648), E.424(10), pp. 819–20; *Mercurius Elencticus Number 10* (26 January/2 February 1648), E.425(7), p. 76; *A True Relation of Disbanding the Supernumerary Forces* (28 February 1648), E.429(10), pp. 7–8; *Ludlow Memoirs*, I, 192. On the Broadway plot, see above, pp. 347–8.

On 1 March Fairfax forwarded to the Speaker a petition which he had received signed by thirty-six of Laugharne's officers and soldiers. The petition detailed the grievances which were ultimately to impel many of them to insurgency in the Second Civil War. The petitioners, who claimed to be the most heavily in arrears of any parliamentary army, resented the imputation that they planned to revolt and join with Poyer in Pembroke and the slur cast upon the honour of their major-general who had indeed obeyed parliament in ordering them to submit to disbandment.[201] For all that, it was reported on 13 March that some of Laugharne's disbanded soldiers had, as we have seen, helped Poyer to rout Fleming at Pembroke while others had taken Tenby Castle – as they claimed, for King and Parliament. The remaining soldiers professed a willingness to disband, provided – shades of the New Model in the previous year! – this was done *en masse* and not piecemeal, company by company and troop by troop.[202] But Fairfax insisted on piecemeal disbandment, and a letter of 24 March reported the defection of one company to Poyer, carrying with them forcibly the commissioners who had been engaged in disbanding them.[203] A letter of 4 April gave news of two more companies of Laugharne's horse joining Poyer, and on 7 April the Derby House Committee ordered Colonel Horton to march against the enemy in Pembrokeshire and to do his utmost to prevent Laugharne's disbanded soldiers from joining forces with Poyer. Nevertheless, the disbandment commissioners reported on 20 April that many of Laugharne's soldiers, 'after they are Disbanded and have their Money, run to Poyer'. So much for the declaration earlier in the month in which the greater part of Laugharne's forces is reported to have protested against any confederacy with Poyer![204]

The most revealing evidence relating to the immediate circumstances of Laugharne's defection are to be found in his correspondence with Colonel Horton and with commissioners appointed for disbandment of his forces.[205] All of this correspondence was conducted only a matter of days before Laugharne's defeat by Horton at St Fagans on 8 May. A letter from Laugharne on 4 May inquired abrasively of Horton what he

201. Bodleian, Tanner MSS., 58, fos. 733, 734(b)–5.
202. *A Declaration in Vindication of the Officers and Souldiers under Major Generall Laugharne* [sic] (10 March 1648), BL. E.433(5), pp. 4–6; E.434(11), pp. 1–2; Phillips, *Wales*, II, 345–6.
203. Rushworth, *Historical Collections*, VII, 1036–7, 1038–9. See also HMC., *5th Report MSS. of the Duke of Sutherland*, p. 143; Rushworth, *Historical Collections*, VII, 1050–1.
204. Oxford, Worcester College, Clarke MSS., 114, fo. 1; PRO., SP. 21/9, fo. 45; Rushworth, *Historical Collections*, VII, 1065; Whitelock, *Memorials*, p. 301 (20 April); *The Declaration and Resolution of Divers Officers and Souldiers under . . . Major General Laughorn* [sic] (April 1648), BL., E.435(26), p. 6.
205. See *A Declaration by Major-General Laugharne . . .* (8 May 1648), BL. E.442(8), pp. 4–12, on which my own account draws heavily.

and his soldiers were doing within the boundaries of his own command, and demanded that he withdraw, as well as complaining about interference with the process of disbandment. On the same day Laugharne wrote to the disbandment commissioners complaining of 'the Injuries and Affronts put upon my men, instead of receiving their Pay allowed them by the Parliament'. 'Truly', the major-general protested, 'I was confident my past Service . . . had merited much better of you'. Both Horton's and the commissioners' replies on the following day naturally rested their case on the fact that parliament had now made Fairfax supreme commander of all the armed forces, in which circumstances Laugharne's former command fell under the complete control of the Lord General. The commissioners also denied affronting the soldiers who were to be disbanded and insisted that they had faithfully observed both the letter and spirit of parliament's instructions to them. As to Horton's reply, besides asserting the legitimacy of his presence in Wales, he also stressed its objective: to put down the revolt of Poyer and others who had been declared traitors by parliament. Laugharne did not reply to Horton's letter. Such reply as he made was to come at St Fagans three days later when his forces were disastrously crushed by Horton's.[206] His reply to the commissioners on 6 May is eloquent of his wounded pride and deep sense of grievance, and perhaps an element of sheer paranoia. His and his soldiers' services had been completely forgotten, though they ought not to have expected fair treatment over pay and disbandment, 'knowing some of you have constantly designed our Ruine from the beginning'. The affronted major-general at least took comfort in the fact that 'the countrey hath a better sence of me and my abused Soldiers then you have had'.

A declaration from Colonel Horton at the end of April or beginning of May had cast Colonel Powell as the prime mover in the refusal to disband and in 'earnestly endeavouring to lay the Foundations of a new War',[207] but the defection is put in proper perspective by a dispatch to the Speaker from Colonel Thomas Wogan – who, as it was pointed out in parliament, was not to be confused with Wogan the renegade. Wogan stressed that not all of Laugharne's officers were intransigent, and he mentions four in particular who had brought their troops of horse over to Horton and fought gallantly against Laugharne at St

206. For Horton's letter announcing his victory, see ibid., pp. 7–9, 13–15; also Rushworth, *Historical Collections*, VII, 1110–11; *C.J.*, V, 556, 557; *L.J.*, X, 253. A letter from an English royalist to Scotland argued that news of Laugharne's defeat was incorrect, but confuses the major engagement with a minor one (SRO., GD/406/1/2465).

207. Rushworth, *Historical Collections*, VII, 1103–4. One commentator observes that the declaration would be lost on most of those for whom it was intended since it was not in Welsh.

Fagans.[208] As to the leader they had deserted, Laugharne found his way to Pembroke where he joined Poyer; an ill-assorted pair, there were tales of hot disputes between them and even one rumour that Laugharne had run Poyer through with his sword.[209] But, however much they disliked one another, henceforth their futures were inextricably linked. On 14 June Cromwell reported his opinion to Speaker Lenthall that Pembroke Castle could not hold out for more than another fortnight. Quite apart from the imminent starvation of the garrison if it resisted longer than that, there were serious differences among the defenders quite apart from those between the principals. The besiegers apparently heard shouts from within of 'Shall we be ruined for two or three mens pleasure. Better it were to throw them over the walls', a state of affairs not unlike what was to occur at Colchester more than two months later. It was also reported that Poyer's soldiers threatened to cut his throat if he did not surrender within four or six days. Poyer was reported to have told them that if relief did not come by the next Monday – like the Cavaliers at Colchester in August, he was sanguinely holding out the prospect of being relieved by Langdale of all people – they should believe his word no longer and could hang him. But it was not until 11 July that he surrendered the castle.[210]

On 13 August the Prince of Wales wrote to Fairfax asking on behalf of Laugharne, Poyer and Powell, now incarcerated in Nottingham Castle, that 'by your care and reasonable interposition such moderation may be vsed toward them as becomes souldgers to one another', and suggesting that if this were not to be, he would be forced to similar extremities against any parliamentary soldier falling into his hands. In his reply three days later the Lord General informed the prince that he had passed on his letter to parliament, which, he suggested, was likely to be influenced not so much by the consideration that the three had been in hostility against it 'as that they have betrayed the trust . . . reposed in them to the sad ingaging the Kingdom againe in War & Blood'.[211] The three were tried and condemned by court martial in April 1649 but were allowed to draw lots to decide on whom the death penalty should be visited. Poyer was unlucky and was shot to death in Covent Garden on 21 April.[212] The other two were surprisingly released on 7 May and

208. Bodleian, Tanner MSS., 57, fo. 62. On 20 May the House responded to Wogan's recommendation that the soldiers should have their arrears paid out of delinquents' estates by voting that they should be paid and have the same security for arrears as all supernumerary forces (C.J., V, 566; Rushworth, Historical Collections, VII, 1121).
209. Ibid., VII, 1121; Whitelock, Memorials, p. 305(b) (20 May); Phillips, Wales, I, 406.
210. Rushworth, Historical Collections, VII, 1159, 1175, 1190; Carlyle, Cromwell, I, 269–70; Ludlow Memoirs, I, 200; Phillips, Wales, I, 412–16.
211. BL., Add. MSS., 19,399, fos. 58, 60.
212. C.J., V, 670, VI, 165; Whitelock, Memorials, pp. 379(b), 382, 382(b) (12 March, 4 April, 10 April); Phillips, Wales, I, 417.

even allowed to compound for their delinquency. Money was obviously hard to come by, at least for Laugharne who found difficulty in paying his composition of £712. 7s. 6d. Astonishingly, the unpaid remains of his fine were remitted by the Lord Protector in December 1655 on the grounds of Laugharne's major services to the state before 1648; that he had given no trouble since then; and that he bore a great charge of children: a token, no doubt, of Oliver's declared policy of healing and conciliation.[213]

213. *C.J.*, VI, 204; Whitelock, *Memorials*, p. 386 (7 May); PRO., SP. 23/217, pp. 567, 569, 572–3; *Cal. CC.*, III, 2106.

XII

THE SECOND CIVIL WAR
IN PERSPECTIVE

... the former quarrel was that Englishmen might rule over one another: this to vassalise us to a foreign Nation. And their fault who have appeared in this Summer's business is certainly double to theirs who were in the first, because it is the repetition of the same offence against all the witnesses that God has borne, by making and abetting a Second War.

> Letter from Oliver Cromwell at Knottingley
> near Pontefract, 20 November 1648, to Robert
> Jenner and John Ashe in London (Carlyle,
> *Cromwell*, I, 334)

Failures of strategy and co-ordination

During the summer of 1647, while there had been serious counter-revolutionary disturbances in London, there had been no comparable risings elsewhere, other than a minor and easily quelled revolt in Glamorgan. No less important, there had been no Scottish invasion even though this had been hourly expected and indeed had formed part of the overall counter-revolutionary strategy. In the following year, by contrast, there were dangerous risings in North and South Wales, the Welsh Marcher counties, Kent, Essex and other Home Counties, and the north of England. Added to these things were a revolt of part of the navy and an invasion from Scotland, even though the latter was a long time coming, much to the annoyance of English Cavaliers. But this time, for all the confident expectations of royalist insurgents and the fears of government agencies such as the Derby House Committee, there was no rising in London. These circumstances may suggest the tentative conclusion that no counter-revolutionary rising could be successful if confined to London alone (as in 1647) or, alternatively, without the participation of London (as in 1648). This hypothesis is, however, more applicable to the counter-revolutionary failure of 1647 than to that of 1648. In the case of the latter year, it begs the question of whether the risings might have been attended with greater success if there had been a co-ordinated strategy shared by the leaders of all the different risings and if the timing of these revolts had been less haphazard than was in fact the case. The question, though counter-factual in character, is of some service in divining the reasons for the failure of the insurgents in the Second Civil War. Certainly, so far as timing is concerned, Lord Byron had outlined one essential prerequisite of success in his letter to the earl of Lanark on 10 March 1648.[1] Byron's recommendations certainly do not constitute an overall strategic view of the British military situation, but they at least stress the desirability of simultaneity of English provincial risings with one another and with the invasion of the Scottish army of the Engagement. How far this proved to be from the realities of 1648 was to be regretfully observed in an allegedly royalist account in late September, after the crisis had virtually passed. The writer sees the basic error of the insurgents as that

> First, They caused the Countreys [sic] to grow warm too early, and, in confidence of assistance from the City, to discover themselves, thinking to execute that Design by force . . . so they run out into insurrection *severally* . . . to carry it on their own way . . . whereby the hopefullest Design that ever was contrived for his Majesty . . . is destroyed.[2]

The importance of this factor is illustrated in Table 2, which shows the chronology of the most important events in different regions.

The first point which stands out from a mere glance at the table is the tardiness of the Scottish invasion in relation to events south of the border. But, as the above quotation from the royalist correspondent in the Isle of Wight makes clear, it is possible to look even at this in a different way, emphasizing not so much the delays of the Scots as the premature nature of the English and Welsh risings and the almost total lack of co-ordination between them, and even between those in the same part of the country; indeed, even within the same county. For example, in his admirable study of Kent, Professor Everitt brings out both the independence of different groups of insurgents in different parts of that county and their total ignorance of each other's plans.[3] Viewed in this perspective, insurgent campaigns in the Second Civil War appear as a series of isolated and unco-ordinated risings rather than as the execution of any unified strategic plan. In this they are as unlike (say) the royalist campaigns of 1642–3 in the First Civil War as could be.

1. *Hamilton Papers*, pp. 166–7. See above, p. 399.
2. *A Letter sent from Newport to a Gentleman in London* (September 1648), BL., E.464(29), pp. 2–3; *A Terrible Thunder-Clap from the Isle of Wight* . . . (29 September 1648), E.465(9), pp. 2–3. My italics.
3. Everitt, *Kent*, p. 251 note.

Table 2: Chronology of main events in the Second Civil War by regions

Month 1648	Scotland	Northern England	Wales	Welsh Marches & West Midlands	East Anglia & East Midlands	South-east	Navy & Overseas
February			22. Poyer refuses to yield Pembroke Castle.				
March			3. Poyer is ordered to submit. Tenby Castle falls.				
April	25. News of resolution to raise army of Engagement.	28. Berwick falls to Cavaliers. 29. Fall of Carlisle.	29. Fleming defeated.		24. Riots in Norwich.	9/10. Riots in London.	3. Inchiquin declares for king in Munster.

Table 2: *continued*

Month 1648	Scotland	Northern England	Wales	Welsh Marches & West Midlands	East Anglia & East Midlands	South-east	Navy & Overseas
May	1. Prince of Wales invited to Scotland.		8. Laugharne defeated at St Fagans. mid-May. Owen's rising in N. Wales. 25. Surrender of Chepstow Castle. 31. Surrender of Tenby Castle.		12. Riots at Bury St Edmunds.	21/22. Kent insurgents in arms.	22. Inchiquin's concordat with Irish confederate Catholics. 27. Naval mutiny against Rainsborough.
June		1. Morrice takes Pontefract Castle.	5. Owen defeated in North Wales at Y Dalar Hir.		3. News of Essex rising reaches Kent insurgents. 4. Essex insurgents seize County Committee at Chelmsford. 8. Rendezvous of Essex rebels at Brentwood.	1. Kent insurgents defeated at Maidstone. 4. City refuses passage to Kentmen. 6. Dover Castle relieved by parliament.	9. Revolted ships head for Holland.

July

8. Army of Engagement invades England.

31. Appleby Castle surrenders to Scots.

28. Boynton defects at Scorborough.

10. News of attempted betrayal of Denbigh Castle
11. Poyer surrenders at Pembroke.
14. Manifesto of Anglesey insurgents.

8. Discovery of design for risings in Marcher counties.

12. Insurgents enter Colchester.
early June: Taking of Woodcroft House in Northants.
mid-June: Rising at Linton.

29. Rising of Sussex insurgents at Horsham.

5. Holland appears in arms at Kingston.
10. Holland defeated at St Neots.
12. Walmer Castle falls to parliament.

22. Prince of Wales in Yarmouth Roads.

Table 2: *continued*

Month 1648	Scotland	Northern England	Wales	Welsh Marches & West Midlands	East Anglia & East Midlands	South-east	Navy & Overseas
August	10. Lauderdale joins fleet in Downs.	9/10. Lilburne's defection at Tynemouth Castle frustrated.		6. Failure of insurgent plot to take Stafford.			10. Lauderdale joins fleet in Downs.
	13. Scots decide on south–west route through Lancashire.	13. Langdale moves towards Preston.					14. Repulse of naval landing party before Deal.
	17. Scots defeated at Preston.	17. Langdale defeated.		17. Lingen defeated in Montgomery-shire.			
	19. Scots defeated at Winwick.						
	19. Baillie defeated at Warrington.						
	19. Hamilton plans to join Byron in North Wales or Lingen in Marches						

	Scotland / North	Northern England	Wales	Essex	Kent	Navy	Ireland & Isles
[August]	20. Cromwell moves north to deal with Monroe. 25. Hamilton surrenders at Uttoxeter.	25. Langdale captured in Nottinghamshire.		28. Colchester capitulates.	25. Surrender of Deal Castle by insurgents.		29. Naval mutiny forces prince to sail towards Thames.
September	8. Monroe retreats to Scotland.	30. Surrender of Berwick.			5. Sandown Castle surrenders to parliament.	3. Insurgent fleet returns to Holland.	
October		2. Relief of Cockermouth Castle. 9. Royalists surrender at Appleby.	2. Surrender of Beaumaris Castle.				13. Insurgents take Scilly Isles. 16. Monck takes Belfast, Carrickfergus & Coleraine. early October: Ormond lands at Cork.

That South Wales, for instance, was in revolt long before anywhere else is attributable partly at least to the fact that its insurgent leaders were disgruntled ex-parliamentary army commanders rather than royalists acting in close collaboration with other ex-Cavaliers. Nor, as was shown in the last chapter, was there any sort of co-ordination between Poyer's and Laugharne's risings, the two joining forces only after the latter's defeat at St Fagans on 8 May, and even then only reluctantly. Still less was there any co-ordination between these Welsh revolts and the royalist risings in Herefordshire and the Marcher counties and west Midlands. All of these were far smaller affairs than royalists had hoped. On 8 July a letter from the Worcestershire committee reported that the governor of Hartlebury Castle had uncovered risings planned in that county, and in Staffordshire, Shropshire and Herefordshire. The first three of these were easily foiled and one would-be insurgent who was taken prisoner revealed arrangements for a meeting to associate all four counties in a larger-scale rising for the king.[4] It was not until mid-July that Sir Henry Lingen's Herefordshire revolt was in being; two months, that is, after Laugharne had been thrashed by Horton at St Fagans and more than a week after Poyer and Laugharne, who had been bottled up in Pembroke Castle for many weeks, surrendered to parliament. Lingen had chosen to try to link up with Byron in central and north Wales, an attempt which was ended by his forces being defeated in Montgomeryshire in July.[5] No doubt linkage with the Cavalier Byron was in any case a far more attractive proposition to Lingen than association with the renegade Roundhead soldiers in South Wales, with whom many prominent Welsh royalists, and notably the earl of Carbery, found such association too distasteful a prospect to be seriously contemplated.[6] The failure of Lingen's revolt was a grave setback to the idea of a strong Cavalier force in the Marches and the West Midlands imposing a formidable barrier to Cromwell's forces marching north to encounter the Scots following the fall of Pembroke. So was the foiling of a lesser plot by a certain Colonel Stepkins to surprise Stafford early in August.[7]

Prince Charles himself was highly critical of Byron's strategy, marvelling at the opportunities which he had lost: on his failure to relieve

4. *A New Rising for the King* (8 July 1648), BL., E.452(36), pp. 1–4; Rushworth, *Historical Collections*, VII, 1185.
5. Bodleian, Tanner MSS., 57, fos. 217(b)–18; Rushworth, *Historical Collections*, VII, 1234; *A Great Victory in Herefordshire* (21 August 1648), BL., E.460(34), pp. 4–5; *The Kingdomes Weekly Intelligencer Number 274* (22/29 August 1648), E.461(14), p. 1059.
6. *A Letter containing a Perfect Relation of the Conditions of things in South Wales* (April 1648), Codrington pamphlet coll., p. 5.
7. Bodleian, Tanner MSS., 57, fos. 185–5(b); *C.J.*, V, 670; Rushworth, *Historical Collections*, VII, 1227. Stepkins was killed by the soldiers of Colonel Stone, the governor of Stafford, at an encounter three miles from the town.

Pembroke – a pretty tall order; or to seize upon border strongholds such as Shrewsbury and Chester.[8] Certainly Byron failed to achieve his main aims of barring Cromwell's route north and ultimately facilitating a junction between the Scots and insurgent forces in Wales and the Marches. In this, Shrewsbury was obviously an objective and at one time Byron seems to have come quite close to taking it. A long and informative letter of 5 August from the parliamentary governor of Shrewsbury, Colonel Mackworth, to William Pierrepoint at Westminster reveals details of a plan for two separate insurgent rendezvous in the region whose forces would coalesce and move on Shrewsbury. The plan had been revealed to Mackworth by a defector, and a force from Shrewsbury was able to surprise the insurgents at the first rendezvous and prevent them from making contact with Byron and other royalists further west at the second rendezvous at Prees Heath. The plan to take Shrewsbury had to be abandoned and Byron with about 500 horse rode off into Wales, some believed with an alternative plan to make a flanking attack on Chester. Others, more correctly, saw him as en route for Caernarvonshire and a newsletter from Chester on 5 August reported him as making for Anglesey.[9]

Byron's arrival in North Wales was obviously too late to offer any assistance to the royalist rising of Sir John Owen, who had been defeated near Aber on 5 June. Moreover, on arrival in Anglesey, his behaviour clearly demonstrated that shared royalist aims were no guarantee of co-operation. The ruling royalist magnate in the isle, Lord Bulkeley, was perhaps less unimpeachably Cavalier than Byron, having served the king in the First Civil War, but also parliament on the Commission of the Peace and Lieutenancy between the two wars. Nevertheless, although co-operation between Bulkeley and Byron was essential if the royalist aims of both were to be accomplished, Bulkeley seems to have felt threatened 'and can by no persuasions be wrought upon to hold long in Friendship with the Lord Byron', who soon departed.[10]

No less striking examples of lack of co-ordination are exhibited by the major risings in the south-east of England. Obviously the failure to pull London into the Second Civil War is crucial here. As was shown in an earlier chapter, the Kentish petitioners were denied passage

8. *A Great and Bloody Fight in Shropshire* (6 August 1648), BL., E.457(18), p. 1.
9. Ibid., pp. 1–2; Rushworth, *Historical Collections*, VII, 1219. Mackworth's account is in L.J., X, 424–5.
10. Rushworth, *Historical Collections*, VII, 1269; *The Perfect Weekly Account Number 28* (20/ 28 September 1648), BL., E.465(6), no pagination; *Clarendon SP.*, II, 418; Newman, *Royalist Officers*, pp. 47–8; N. Tucker, *North Wales in the Civil War* (Denbigh, 1958), p. 152.

through the City on their way to Westminster, and later when seeking to join their fellow insurgents in Essex; 'the City', as Ludlow aptly puts it, 'not [being] willing absolutely to espouse the Cavalier party, especially in a flying posture'.[11] Whitelock, however, sees parliament's willingness to appease the City – is he referring to the release of Gayre and the imprisoned aldermen? – as connected with fear of its likely co-operation with the Kentish men.[12] As to the other Home Counties, there were certainly tentative discussions between the Kentish petitioners and representatives from Essex and Surrey in late May at a time when the main attentions of the Kentish men were divided between the plan to march in arms to Westminster with their petition and the initiative of the earl of Thanet to persuade them to lay down their arms.[13] For all this, they were probably happy to accept the assurance that in the event of Kent rising in arms, Essex would rise also.[14] But the back of the Kent rising had already effectively been broken at Maidstone on 1 June before the Essex revolt had really got under way. Thus when the insurgents of the two counties did join forces, it was in a situation of defeat and flight, for all the grandiose plans of Goring's, Lucas's and Lisle's Cavaliers for further recruitment and refurbishment following a brief stay at Colchester before striking north to effect a juncture with Langdale; or, failing this unlikely event, with the Cavaliers of Norfolk, Suffolk and Cambridgeshire.[15] Instead, of course, the insurgents were to be bottled up permanently in Colchester.

There had earlier been some apprehensiveness in Derby House about the apparently neatly co-ordinated plan for county rendezvous on 30 May at Blackheath for Kent, Wanstead for Essex and Putney Heath for Surrey,[16] but the extent of alarm was disproportionate to the degree of effective danger. Papers found in the pockets of Kentish insurgents taken prisoner at Maidstone on 1 June emphasized the opportuneness of revolt here and now, when 'you can never have so appropriate a time to effect your desires' now that the army's affections were 'divided into severall remote parts, as *Wales, Cornwall, the North, Suffolk* &c'. The papers in question may well have been composed by the Kentish insurgents' propagandist Roger L'Estrange, who was later to protest

11. *Ludlow Memoirs*, I, 194. See above, p. 147.
12. Whitelock, *Memorials*, p. 305 (2 June).
13. On this, see above, pp. 146–7.
14. Carter, *True Relation*, p. 63. Another insurgent, Roger L'Estrange, although normally a less reliable authority than Carter, plays down the significance of the alleged coalition (*L'Estrange his Vindication*, sig. A2).
15. Rushworth, *Historical Collections*, VII, 1147; *Cal.SPD. 1648–9*, pp. 105, 118–19; Carter, *True Relation*, pp. 113–14; *A true and perfect Relation of the Condition of those Gentlemen in Colchester* (September 1648), BL., E.462(16), p. 1.
16. *L.J.*, X, 283–4; *Cal.SPD. 1648–9*, pp. 79–80; *Clarke Papers*, II, 19–20.

fiercely against the view that Kent had risen too early, arguing that Kent was already being reproached by other counties 'for sitting still so long'. On the other hand, L'Estrange, apparently unaware of the contradiction, also stresses that there was virtually no response elsewhere when Kent had already been aflame for a fortnight, and concludes that those not daring to rise now 'will (I fear) Lye still For *ever*'. Moreover, the date for the rendezvous had been fixed, and, whatever the Essex and Surrey men chose to do, further delays would rob the Kentish protest of its impetus quite apart from affording further time for the county committee to arrest the leading figures in the movement.[17]

It is, of course, all too tempting to employ time in considering the might-have-beens of History and it may not be very important or illuminating to inquire whether, for example, the rising at Horsham and thereabouts in Sussex at the end of June would have been more effective if it had occurred a month earlier when insurgency in neighbouring Kent was working up to its peak.[18] For, after all, the question could with equal validity be turned the other way round. Nevertheless, there is a certain counter-factual significance in such questions in that they underline the damage done to the insurgent fortunes by the lack of simultaneity, or even temporal proximity, of different risings and especially of those in neighbouring counties. The relatively minor risings in East Anglia afford another example. The Norwich tumult occurred in the third week of April, that at Bury St Edmunds in mid-May, while the rather pathetic Cambridgeshire and Suffolk rising at Linton was easily suppressed in mid-June. As to the much-vaunted plan for a rising in Surrey, the only development which at first had looked as if it might pose a formidable threat was the aristocratic rising of Holland, Buckingham and Peterborough which began unpromisingly at Kingston-on-Thames and concluded catastrophically at St Neots in Huntingdonshire on 10 July.[19] One of the rising's aims had been to relieve Colchester, but this would have been totally beyond the powers of the shrunken remnants of Holland's force which were surprised and routed at St Neots.[20]

17. *The Copies of severall Papers taken in the Pockets of some Prisoners . . .* (4 June 1648), BL., E.445(10), p. 8; *L'Estrange his Vindication*, sig. D3.
18. Evidence of the Sussex rising is in Rushworth, *Historical Collections*, VII, 1169; *HMC., 13th Report Appendix Portland MSS.*, I, 465; *A Letter from Horsum [sic] in Sussex* (June 1648), BL., 669, f12 (60); *The Representation of the Freeborn People within the County of Sussex* (July 1648), BL., E.451(13), pp. 3–5.
19. On Norwich and Bury, see above, pp. 369–75, 376–8. On Linton, see Everitt, *Suffolk*, pp. 94–108. On Holland's rising, see above, pp. 406–8.
20. For the hopes entertained in Colchester of relief from Holland's rising, see *HMC., 14th Report Appendix pt. ix (MSS. of James Round Esq.)*, p. 288.

It can thus be concluded that such co-operation as occurred between the different risings in the south and east came as a result of military reverses and had little or no offensive significance. Grandiose plans for the combined Kent and Essex force to march north and join forces with Langdale really belonged to the realm of fantasy. As early as 5 May the northern Cavalier commanders, Langdale, Glemham and Musgrave, had apparently already concluded that 'if the Essex and Kentish men doe not prevaile against the Army in the South, they [viz. Langdale etc.] cannot proceed with their design in the North'.[21] To the beleaguered insurgents now holed up in Colchester, Langdale's significance was to become that of the Cavalier hero rushing to their relief, and who wrote to Sir Charles Lucas on 5 August urging him to take heart from the fact that he was every day getting nearer.[22] But on the contrary, within a few days Langdale and Hamilton were to be routed around Preston and shortly after that Langdale, far from relieving Colchester, was to be incarcerated in Nottingham Castle. Apart from hourly expectation of a relief force which never came, the beleaguered insurgent garrison at Colchester continued notwithstanding to take heart from false reports of insurgent triumphs elsewhere. As one royalist pamphlet put it, Byron was active in Wales; Lambert was retreating before the Scots; while Fairfax would soon have to divert substantial forces from the siege to meet the Scots' and Langdale's advancing armies and to combat the threat of insurgency in London. All of this was again pure fantasy and how far it was believed even by the most credulous royalist partisan seems doubtful; especially towards the end of the siege, when all hopes that Langdale might come to the rescue were dashed by news of the battle of Preston and subsequent Scottish and insurgent disasters which Fairfax was careful to ensure got through to the now desperate and famished defenders of Colchester.[23]

Nevertheless, a very considerable number of parliamentary soldiers and resources were tied up in the siege of Colchester down to the end of August just as they had been in the siege of Pembroke Castle until the second week of July. Similarly, other forces which might have otherwise been employed elsewhere had to be kept under arms in the West Country under Sir Hardress Waller as a safeguard against the expected

21. The Declaration of Sir Thomas Glenham [sic] Sir Marmaduke Langdale and Sir Philip Musgrave (May 1648), BL., E.446(29), pp. 2–3.
22. A Letter from Sir Marmaduke Langdale . . . (August 1648), BL., E.457(20), especially pp. 1–3. On the continuing hopes of the Colchester insurgents of being relieved by Langdale, see Carter, True Relation, p. 154; HMC., 12th Report Appendix pt. ix (MSS. of the Duke of Beaufort), pp. 29–30.
23. Ibid. For the above optimistic account of royalist successes, see The Colchester Spie (August 1648), BL., E.459(13), no pagination.

revolt there which in fact never materialized.[24] Writing in late July in the context of the siege of Colchester, one observer described the essence of insurgent strategy as being to put the parliamentary army simultaneously under attack in as many locations as possible, so that it was formidable in none of them and must in the end succumb to the total offensive pressure. As one royalist had gleefully observed back in January, 'it will be a difficult taske . . . to *Marche* against *Iockie, secure London*, and suppresse *Tumultes* in all places at once'.[25] But, even when the point about the immobilization of large forces around Colchester, Pembroke and elsewhere is taken into account, the reality was very different from *Mercurius Elencticus's* optimistic prediction. For one thing 'Jockie' kept his English allies waiting until mid-July before invading; either that, or alternatively, they rose too early. In either case, by the time the army of the Engagement crossed the border, the danger in South Wales was over, as was the worst of that in Kent, Essex and Surrey. Moreover, as has been demonstrated, while London certainly needed to be secured for parliament, at least there was no London rising, thanks both to Skippon's vigilance and to the fact that Londoners had learnt from their experience in July and August 1647. Perhaps most important of all, the risings in England and Wales were sporadic and unco-ordinated rather than simultaneous. Quite apart from the consequence that this enabled them to be picked off separately, there was also, and not least, the greater strength, experience, military discipline and immeasurably superior generalship of the New Model Army. For

> How came 4 or 5000 in *Wales* to rout 10 or 11 or 12000? How came 2 or 300 about *Bury* in *Suffolk* to drive out of that strongly Barricaded towne 4 or 500? How came . . . 20000 in *Kent* to be . . . beaten by 3 or 4000? How came *Langdale* to refuse ingagement with *Lambert* in the North, and draw away? How were *Pomfret* forragers snapt . . . and . . . 7 or 8000 . . . driven into *Colchester* by 4 or 5000?[26]

Likewise, another admirer of the New Model Army marvelled how 'this poore despised army . . . scattered from North to South, from Wales to Dover, and from Barwick to the lands end; are used by God in handfuls to scatter the great enumerous bodies of these wicked ones'.[27]

24. See Oxford, Worcester College, Clarke MSS., 114, fo. 54(b).
25. *Sad and Dangerous Tydings from Colchester* (29 July 1648), BL., E.456(5), p. 3; *Mercurius Elencticus Number 10* (26 January/2 February 1648), E.425(7), p. 74.
26. *Colchesters Teares* (July 1648), BL., E.455(16), pp. 5–6.
27. *The Scots Cabinett Opened* (August 1648), BL., E.456(30), p. 9.

The causes of the succession of delays in the readiness of the Scottish army of the Engagement for invasion, and, more especially, the kirk's opposition to the Engagement, were dealt with in an earlier chapter, as was the anxiety which these delays occasioned among English royalists such as the earl of Lanark's anonymous English correspondent.[28] It is just possible that the outcome of the Second Civil War might have been different if the Scots had been able to invade when the hands of the New Model Army had been full in more places than Colchester; if the South Wales risings had not been over; or that in Kent had been in full flow rather than necessitating little more than tidying up; if Holland's and Buckingham's rising had not been characterized by the same military ineptitude which the former had earlier displayed in the Bishops' Wars; or if Michael Hudson had been able to recruit more insurgents in South Lincolnshire, Rutland and Northamptonshire before his revolt was easily crushed and he himself met his ghastly end at Woodcroft House in early June; or if Lingen had risen with sufficient force and early enough to divert the New Model Army's attention from South Wales. Much earlier in the year, in March, the Cavalier Lord Byron had characterized the forthcoming Scottish invasion as 'the primum mobile from whence these orbes heere must receive their motion', going on to stress that 'nothing can bee so prejudiciall to this designe as delay'.[29] But in fact delays, however much necessitated by the events in Scotland, meant that in practice the Scottish invasion was anything but a *primum mobile* for English risings, many of which had either been put down or brought well under control before a single Engager had set foot in England. Thus while Lanark's anonymous royalist correspondent sought to persuade the Scots to invade by palpably exaggerating the success achieved by insurgents in Wales and elsewhere, and urging the advisability of striking while the iron was hot, there were others who, though no less anxious for the Scots to intervene quickly, were far less sanguine about the success of English and Welsh risings. As James Fenne put it in a letter of 24 June, 'England will be lost unless the Scots army presently come in, nor otherwise can Essex or Wales hold out, whatever from sanguine men you may heare to the contrary'.[30]

In an earlier chapter dealing with Scotland and the Engagement much was said about the co-operation between the Scottish Engagers and the English Cavaliers of the north in the months before the former's invasion of England, and how the most tangible result of that co-operation had been the fall of Berwick and Carlisle to the Cavaliers as

28.   See above, pp. 326–31.
29.   *Hamilton Papers*, pp. 167–8.
30.   Ibid., p. 218.

early as April. But it was also emphasized that relations between the Engagers and the Cavaliers were by no means consistently harmonious.[31] One perhaps minor cause of difficulty was mentioned by Montereul in a dispatch towards the end of May in which he reported somewhat optimistically that Sir Marmaduke Langdale would be able to bring some 5,000 foot and 1,500 horse into the field, but that his readiness to recruit Catholics had made for some difficulties in his relations with his future Scottish allies. But Langdale and Sir Philip Musgrave may in their turn have been irritated by the fact that, while they were being harassed by Lambert's forces, the Scottish army was content to hover on the Scottish side of the border. In these circumstances such succour as it afforded to the northern Cavaliers was, as Montereul put it in a dispatch late in June, 'plustost par leur voisinage que par l'assistance qu'ils s'en peut promettre'.[32] Moreover, when the Scots did finally come in, their relations with the Cavaliers left much to be desired. On 4 August great distrust between the allies was reported, and the Scots were said to be 'putting the English upon the hardest Duty which occasioned some Quarrelling', in the course of which one soldier of each nation had been slain.[33] The mutual distrust reached its climax in Hamilton's failure to afford adequate support to Langdale around Preston and the strategic and tactical misconceptions which led to the defeat and ultimate capture of both of them.[34] Langdale and his men deserved better allies.

Writing to William Spang on 23 August when he was still ignorant of the Scottish disaster at Preston, Robert Baillie emphasized the difficulties of the English parliamentary forces held down by many and widely dispersed revolts.[35] While there is some truth in Baillie's observation that the parliamentary forces were in danger of being overstretched through undue dispersal, the greater truth that their enemies were in danger through mismanagement, strategic ineptitude and lack of co-ordination escaped him. Indeed, unknown to him, the fortnight or so before his letter had been a period of resounding triumphs for parliamentary arms, which, on 26 August, the English parliament resolved to celebrate in a Day of Thanksgiving fixed for 7 September. The keynote of these successes it saw as Haselrig's regaining of Tynemouth Castle on 11 August, following Lilburne's defection; the

31. See above, pp. 333–4.
32. *Montereul Correspondence*, II, 489–90, 512–13.
33. Rushworth, *Historical Collections*, VII, 1219.
34. For Langdale's own criticism, see *An Impartiall Relation of the Late Fight at Preston* (26 September 1648), BL., E.464(42), pp. 1–5, especially pp. 2–4; Ormerod, *Tracts*, pp. 267–70, especially pp. 268–9.
35. Baillie, *Letters*, III, 51.

routing of the royalist landing party near Deal Castle on 14 August and the subsequent taking of the castle; the victory over Lingen in Montgomeryshire by Harley and Horton on 17 August; and, above all, of course, the decisive defeat of Langdale and Hamilton and the Scots at Preston on 17–19 August.[36] And there were other triumphs too, such as those against the designs of Byron in Shropshire and Stepkins in Staffordshire. The following week was to bring news on 23 August of the capture of Langdale, who now joined Poyer and Laugharne in prison in Nottingham Castle;[37] and the week after that came the fall of Colchester itself on 28 August after a long siege which had lasted since 14 June. The fall was followed by the summary execution of Sir Charles Lucas and Sir George Lisle which was to be the occasion of so much royalist recrimination, even though perfectly in line with existing military codes of conduct.[38]

Although Sandown, Scarborough and Pontefract Castles had still to be taken, and Cockermouth Castle to be relieved,[39] the crisis of the Second Civil War had passed. There were still Scottish Engagers in the north and isolated pockets of Cavalier resistance in several places. For instance, more than three weeks after the surrender of Colchester, there was a report on 22 September of a small force of Cavalier 'Dammee Blades' plundering the well-affected of Huntingdonshire and Cambridgeshire. But, like most of the remnants of Cavalier insurgency, this was no more than a minor nuisance.[40]

The naval revolt and insurgent strategic options

The one important rising which has not yet entered into our analysis of insurgent strategy was the mutiny of part of the fleet at the end of May which received mention in the last chapter in the context of

36. C.J., V, 685; Parliamentary History, XVII, 410–12; A Particular of the several Victories and Occasions of the Day of Thanksgiving (7 September 1648), BL., E.461(8).
37. Bodleian, Tanner MSS., 57, fos. 227, 233, 235–5(b); Cary, Memorials, II, 3–5.
38. Materials for the fall of Colchester are in: Oxford, Worcester College, Clarke MSS., 114, fos. 64–4(b); Rushworth, Historical Collections, VII, 1240; A Letter sent by a Committee-man from the Earl of Norwich (25 August 1648), BL., E.461(10), pp. 4–5; The Moderate Number 7 (22/29 August 1648), E.461(16), sig. G2ᵛ–G3; A True and Exact Relation of the Taking of Colchester (August 1648), E.461(24), pp. 1–5; Carter, True Relation, pp. 173–6.
39. Cockermouth Castle in Cumbria was not relieved until 2 October. Materials relating to the siege are in: Carlisle, Cumbria R.O., D/Lec/164/1648 (Cockermouth Castle; Lord Egremont's Archive); Bodleian, Tanner MSS., 57, fo. 302; The Moderate Number 13 (2 October 1648), BL., E.467(1), sig. N3.
40. A Great Victory by the Royalists Near Huntington [sic] shire (22 September 1648), BL., E.464(34), pp. 1–2.

the defection of Willoughby of Parham and Batten.[41] There can be no doubt that the revolt of the ships, the largest of which was the flagship *Constant Reformation*,[42] notably widened the insurgents' strategic options, although here again the tale is one of missed opportunities, strategic misconceptions and lack of proper co-ordination. This is certainly true with respect to one of the foremost of these options, the affording of aid to the invasion of the Scottish Engagers. Here again Scottish delays are of crucial significance. Writing admittedly with all the advantages of hindsight, one Dr Stewart, who had spent much time with the insurgent fleet with the Prince of Wales, recounted the notable opportunities which had been lost through waiting for the Scottish invasion: 'I fear me [we?] care for nothing but help from the Scots; all others we neglected or worse'.[43] The point which Stewart was making is not that actual naval aid to the Scots diverted the insurgent fleet from other more promising strategic options, as that holding back naval resources to the end of being able to help them when they did invade had this effect. Moreover, it is difficult to see much being done in this respect directly to facilitate the Scottish invasion. On 25 July information was given to Will Murray that the Prince of Wales would do his utmost to protect Scottish merchandise and trading interests. In August Lauderdale spent some time aboard the insurgent fleet in the Downs, endeavouring to persuade the Prince to sail north and assume the command of the army of the Engagement which was shortly to crash to disaster at Preston.[44] Whether or not the insurgent fleet might have done more if the Scottish army had struck south-east through Yorkshire to make contact with the insurgents at Scarborough is at best a hypothetical question. As it was, Charles did not sail to join the Scots.

Of the other strategic options arising from the naval revolts there is little doubt that co-operation with the Kent insurgents provides by far the best example of co-ordination and co-operation both in the origins of the naval rising and in subsequent operations. As to the former, a letter from the then Vice Admiral Rainsborough to the Admiralty Committee on 24 May expressed grave concern that 'the present Distemper of this County [viz. Kent] . . . hath begot a Distemper in the Fleet which . . . will be of dangerous Consequence'.[45] He was soon to

41. See above, pp. 410–15.
42. An account of 25 July lists ten ships totalling 3,690 tons, of which the *Constant Reformation* was of 850 tons (*A Declaration of his Highnesse Prince Charles*, Codrington pamphlet coll., p. 6; *Parliamentary History*, XVII, 347). Other accounts (see below) mention eleven ships.
43. *Naval Documents*, p. 376.
44. *HMC., 11th Report Hamilton MSS.*, p. 127; *Hamilton Papers*, pp. 237–40, 244–8.
45. *L.J.*, X, 286.

be proved right. As Everitt observes, the ships in the Downs were largely manned by Kentish men and contact between them and local people ashore was close.[46] The crews had been encouraged to mutiny by the Kentish gentleman Sir Henry Palmer, a former naval officer who was well known to the sailors, and by Thomas Horsfleete of Bekesbourne and Richard and Robert Bargrave of Bridge. Matthew Carter tells of how one Major Keme, a man of many parts, who was not only a soldier but a divine and a former captain at sea, volunteered to go on board the revolted ships with a copy of the Kent petition which he persuaded the mutinous sailors to adopt. Following this success Keme was sent to Deal, where, as a former parson in the town, he had many connections, and to Walmer with a message summoning the garrisons of both castles to surrender, which they did shortly afterwards.[47]

Possession of the coastal castles and the protection which they afforded to the insurgent ships in the Downs was a vital feature of the co-ordinated operation between the Kentish and the naval insurgents, as well as affording convenient cover for a possible invasion from abroad. A letter from Colonel Barkstead to Fairfax on 29 May mentions the plans of the Kent insurgents to 'possesse themselves of all the castles and stronge holds and thereby secure landing for the Irish, French or Danes, of whose coming they fondlie flatter themselves'.[48] Indeed, this was a danger which continued to engage the government's attention long after the crushing of the principal Kent insurgent force at Maidstone on 1 June.[49] On 11 August the Derby House Committee announced that it had information about designs for a new insurrection in Kent to be joined by the malignants of Sussex, and that a rendezvous had been fixed where the Prince of Wales would meet with them.[50] A bogus Prince of Wales – 'not Prince *Charles* but a poore rascally fellow not fit for Gentleman's company' – had indeed appeared at Sandwich and deceived the local authorities in mid-May before the Kent revolt had got under way, but he had been exposed and sent to Newgate.[51] However, the government's worst fears seemed about to be realized

46.   Everitt, *Kent*, pp. 249–50; B. Capp, *Cromwell's Navy . . . 1648–1660* (Oxford 1989), p. 25.
47.   *Naval Documents*, pp. 335–6, 337–9; Carter, *True Relation*, pp. 34, 42–4, 45; *A Letter from a Gentleman in Kent* (15 June 1648), BL., E.448(34), p. 9; Everitt, *Kent*, pp. 249–50; Capp, *Cromwell's Navy*, p. 20.
48.   *Clarke Papers*, II, 22.
49.   See the letter from Sir Anthony Weldon on 4 July (Bodleian, MSS., dep. C158, no. 147).
50.   *Cal.SPD. 1648–9*, pp. 241, 246, 247.
51.   *Sad Newes out of Kent* (23 May 1648), BL., E.443(41), pp. 3–4; *A Letter from Sandwich* (21 May 1648), E.443(26), pp. 4–6; *L.J.*, X, 274–5; Rushworth, *Historical Collections*, VII, 1121; Carter, *True Relation*, pp. 35–40.

when the real prince launched two landing parties from the insurgent ships on 10 and 14 August. The first was easily defeated by Sir Michael Livesay.[52] The second contained about 750 soldiers and sailors, including Welshmen, Walloons and Dutchmen, and was reinforced by a further fifty insurgents from besieged Sandown Castle. The combined operation was commanded by Major-General Gibson, 'a mighty Scotsman', who was badly wounded in the subsequent engagement in which the invaders were routed by Colonel Rich's forces. Other notable casualties and prisoners included the Kentish gentleman, Sir John Boys, who had been the king's governor of Donnington Castle during the First Civil War. Both Gibson and Boys were later to be criticized for their part in the engagement by none other than the so-called Captain Lendall, the former bosun's mate who had engineered the original naval mutiny against Rainsborough. Lendall too was wounded, but 'had the Souldiers known him in the fight, they had not spared his life'. Colonel Rich claimed that his soldiers killed a hundred of the insurgents and that a further 350 took refuge in Sandown Castle.[53]

While the relations between the Kentish and naval insurgents do offer an unusual example of co-operation and some measure of co-ordinated insurgent strategy,[54] it is important not to exaggerate the success of these operations even in their early stages. In the first place, not every castle in the Downs fell to them. In late May the government had greatly feared that Dover Castle would be taken, and one account tells how the prospect of its being stormed made 'all *Dover* drunke with joy, a little wine and beere helping'.[55] But Dover Castle did not fall and other castles that did were retaken, some fairly quickly though others only after a prolonged period of waiting which caused the government much anxiety. Even here, it might reasonably be asked whether the revolted ships made the most of the opportunities presented by insurgent occupation of the castles, especially when the retaking of each of them progressively lessened the danger to the parliamentary regime. This point is made in Nathaniel Rich's letters to Speaker Lenthall on 12 July and 25 August emphasizing the consequences of the recapture of

52. *The Princes first Fruits* (10 August 1648), BL., E.459(23), pp. 1–2.
53. Rushworth, *Historical Collections*, VII, 1228; *Naval Documents*, p. 381; *Packets of Letters from Scotland and the North . . . and Letters from Kent* (14 August 1648), BL., E.459(2), pp. 5–6 (corrected pagination); *Colonel Rich's Letter to the House of Commons . . .* (August 1648), E.459(3), pp. 3–8; *Vindiciae Carolinae* (23 October 1648), E.468(25), pp. 3–4. Some of the insurgents who escaped later joined Boynton in Scarborough Castle. See above, p. 404.
54. On 29 July the House of Commons ordered that no Kentish insurgents who had engaged in corrupting the sailors should be permitted to compound (*C.J.*, V, 652).
55. *Newes from Kent* (25 May 1648), BL., E.448(5), pp. 12–14.

Walmer and Deal Castles respectively.[56] The retaking of the latter made prolonged presence of the revolted ships in the Downs impossible and sealed the fate of the final insurgent stronghold, Sandown Castle, which fell on 5 September. Other naval aspects of the campaign suggest that it too was a tale of missed opportunities. As one royalist sadly observed, the parliamentary fleet under Warwick had been allowed time to recover from the initial shock of the mutiny against Rainsborough and the defection of eleven ships to the Prince of Wales. The revolted ships failed to hit Warwick's ships hard and early and there were other miscalculations such as the failure to make junction with the defecting Batten in the Downs and to relieve Deal Castle through the mismanagement of the landing parties on 10 and 14 August.[57] As late as 9 September the Kent Sub-Committee for Accounts specified the names of seven Kentish gentlemen who were still 'aborde with the Prince'. Among them one is certainly identifiable as one of the Bargraves who had played such an important part in encouraging the original naval revolt in late May.[58]

In the foregoing discussion of co-operation between Kentish and naval insurgents some stress was laid on the likely significance of insurgent possession of castles in the Downs in the possible event of an invasion from the continent, and of course, the same is true, *mutatis mutandis*, of other east coast fortresses in insurgent hands such as Scarborough Castle. The possibility of aid from abroad had been pondered by royalists, both at home and in exile, long before the naval revolt,[59] which, however, brought such designs from the realm of wild speculations to that of distinct, if somewhat remote, possibility. At the beginning of July it was reported from Kent that the eleven revolted ships which were currently refitting in Holland were to be joined by fourteen Dutch vessels and fourteen regiments of Dutch soldiers in an invasion force. The report did not say whether this was to be directed at south-eastern or northern England. By 12 July, however, a setback was experienced through the reluctance of the majority of Dutch seamen and captains to engage against England. The Dutch were said to be 'sensible of the miseries of war and the happinesse of peace, and therefore . . . resolved to maintain Unity with England', that is, with

56. *HMC., 13th Report Appendix Portland MSS.*, I, 481; Bodleian, Tanner MSS., 57, fos. 235–5(b).
57. For this critique, see *Naval Documents*, pp. 377–82. On the general dangers from Kentish co-operation with the naval mutineers, see *The Sea-men undeceived* (August 1648), BL., E.459(22), p. 11.
58. BL., Add. MSS., 5,494, fo. 288.
59. An example is the design for an invasion from France in March (*The True Copy of a Letter sent from the Hague* (March 1648), BL., E.431(23), pp. 2–5).

the parliamentary government.[60] Moreover, the English ships were unlikely to be allowed by the Dutch authorities to sail until the demands of Dutch creditors for settlement of debts for victuals, beer and other supplies and services had been met. However, a newsletter of 22 July reported – incorrectly – that the Prince of Wales, and Lords Newcastle, Gerrard and Culpepper were 'floting upon the Neptune Seas towards the North of *England*', intending a landing either at Berwick or Holy Island. The report was ill informed, for when the ships did sail they made not for the north but for Yarmouth Roads.[61]

Since the prince was said to have nineteen or twenty ships and 2,000 men at his command when he appeared in Yarmouth Roads on 22 July, it must be assumed that he had received some foreign support, even if less than he had originally hoped when he had planned to sail north to make contact with Langdale and the Scots.[62] It was now believed that the plan had changed and that he was intending to go to the relief of Colchester which was only about two days march from Great Yarmouth. That Colchester was their destination was believed both by the beleaguered insurgents in Colchester and by the government which sent a force under Colonel Scroope, who had already done parliament good service against the earl of Holland at St Neots, to bar the prince's way south to Colchester. But Charles had first to win Yarmouth over, and notwithstanding widespread fears that the majority of the townspeople would favour granting him access and support, this proved not to be the case, despite a minor tumult in favour of the prince led by an alderman named Captain Johnson who eventually sailed off with the royalist ships.[63] Yarmouth was to resist further princely blandishments on 9 August, though on 6 September it was reported that some local royalist sympathizers had managed to convey a vessel laden with barrels of beef to insurgent ships anchored in Yarmouth Roads despite the attempts of a party of dragoons to prevent them.[64] Yarmouth's frigid

60. *A Declaration from the Royalists of Kent* (2 July 1648), BL., E.451(13), pp. 1–3; *The Declaration of the Hollanders Concerning their Joyning with the Royall Navie* (12 July 1648), E.453(2), pp. 1–3, 4–5.
61. *Newes from the Royall Navie* (21 July 1648), BL., E.453(41), pp. 1–2.
62. For the prince's original plan, see *The Resolution of the Prince of Wales* (2 July 1648), BL., E.451(13), pp. 1–3.
63. Rushworth, *Historical Collections*, VII, 1204–5, 1206–7; *Parliamentary History*, XVII, 338–9; *Prince Charles His Declaration* (27 July 1648), BL., E.455(7), pp. 4–5; *A Message Sent from the Prince of Wales to the Major* [sic] *of Yarmouth* (July 1648), BL., E.454(21), p. 6; *Naval Documents*, pp. 358–9; *HMC., 13th Report Appendix Portland MSS.*, I, 483. Evidence of later action against Johnson and his associates is in *HMC., 7th Report Appendix (House of Lords Cal. 1660)*, p. 113; *L.J.*, XI, 82; HLRO., MP., 3/7/1660. The last item contains a copy of the articles which were exhibited against Johnson, Israel Ingram and others before the Indemnity Committee in June 1649.
64. *Prince Charles His Letter and Declaration to . . . the town of Yarmouth* (9 August 1648), BL., E.458(23), pp. 1–5; *Newes from Yarmouth* (September 1648), E.462(22), p. 4; *The*

reception of some parliamentary soldiers who marched through the town about this time certainly did nothing to relieve the government's uneasiness about the port's security from attack. On 6 September Commissary General Ireton communicated with the bailiffs of Yarmouth, giving them the unwelcome news that he had orders from Lord General Fairfax to garrison the town if he thought it necessary; and, if not, to have the walls and forts demolished but a new fort built at the haven's mouth to secure the port against enemies at sea, who, as has been seen, had found contact with local malignants all too easy to establish. It was left to the bailiffs' choice which of these distasteful alternatives to adopt.[65]

From the early days of the siege of Colchester, the insurgents had held out hope of relief from a seaborne force.[66] 'The bottom of their confidence', wrote the Essex parliamentarian Sir Thomas Honeywood from the leaguer before Colchester, 'is from help of foreign assistance which . . . by the revolted ships and others are daily threatened'. Honeywood pointed to Harwich as a particular danger spot 'where the revolted ships may be easily fraught with disbanded soldiers'.[67] On the very eve of the surrender of Colchester at the end of August Isaac Dorislaus informed Fairfax from Holland of a design to ship over about 700 or 800 disbanded soldiers from the Low Countries in an attempt to relieve Colchester.[68] But Colchester was neither relieved nor revictualled and supplied, as, for instance, Scarborough was, and this must count as a further missed naval opportunity.

So in a sense does the case of Scarborough. The Prince of Wales was daily expected to make a landing there and indeed, Sir Matthew Boynton's resistance was effectively prolonged by the landing of a relieving force in September. Facilitated though this was by the revolted ships, it was hardly a large-scale operation, in which circumstance its total effect was simply to put off till December the ultimate surrender of Scarborough.[69] It will be recalled that William Dobson, the mayor of Hull, had done his utmost to dissuade Boynton from defecting, but this did not stop the Prince of Wales from trying to persuade Dobson to do

    Declaration and Proceedings of . . . the Prince of Wales . . . touching . . . Yarmouth (September 1648), E.462(9), pp. 1–3.

65. NNRO., Great Yarmouth Assembly Book 1642–1662, fo. 129; *Packets of Letters from Scotland and the North of England* (September 1648), BL., E.464(20), p. 6.
66. See *The Resolution of Sir Charles Lucas* (July 1648), Chelmsford, Essex RO., Landon coll., p. 2.
67. HMC., *13th Report Appendix Portland MSS.*, I, 470.
68. Oxford, Worcester College, Clarke MSS., 114, fo. 57.
69. BL., E.464(20), pp. 1–2; Bodleian, Tanner MSS., 57, fo. 256; *HMC., 13th Report . . . Portland MSS.*, I, 490–1. See above, pp. 403–5.

the same; along with Colonel Bethell, who it was widely expected would shortly be made parliamentary governor of Hull. But neither Dobson nor Bethell was cast in the same mould as the Hothams and Boynton, and there was to be no opportunity for the rebel fleet to make use of what was, next to Newcastle, the most important port north of the Humber. However, given our knowledge of the outcome, it is perhaps too easy to underestimate the danger. Certainly, in a letter from Hull to Speaker Lenthall on 28 July, Sir William Strickland saw fit to stress it as a matter of the utmost urgency.[70]

One of the most persistently canvassed options presented by the naval revolt was that the insurgent ships should descend on the Isle of Wight to rescue the king. On 27 May, the same day as the naval mutiny was to occur, the House of Commons was considering Colonel Hammond's request for a better guard at sea for the Isle of Wight,[71] and news of the mutiny was further to increase his apprehension of an attack.[72] On 19 July the mayor of Winchester also expressed alarm about the danger of the revolted ships attacking the island or even nearby Southampton, a danger which was the greater on account of the unreliability and discontents of the sailors at Portsmouth.[73] But the danger never materialized, though early in June the officers of the insurgent forces in Essex had done their best to encourage their men by fostering the rumour that 'the king is in the Ships upon the Coast of Kent'.[74]

Not too far distant from the Isle of Wight is the Dorset port of Weymouth of which came reports in late August of a royalist plot, foiled through the vigilance of Sir Hardress Waller, to take over the town and open up the port to landings from the insurgent ships.[75] It was a Weymouth mariner, William Cotton, who stumbled by accident on details of another royalist design, this time a successful one. Cotton, the master of a barque carrying Portland stone to London, had been captured at sea by an Irish man-of-war and put ashore in Normandy where he overheard a conversation about a design to take the Scilly Isles for the Prince of Wales. This was successfully accomplished in September and the Scilly Isles were to prove an extremely useful base from

70. Ibid., I, 491; Cal.SPD. 1648–9, pp. 216–77.
71. Rushworth, Historical Collections, VII, 1130.
72. See his letter to the Derby House Committee on 23 June (F. Peck (ed.), Desiderata Curiosa (1735), II, 47; see also ibid., p. 48).
73. HMC., 13th Report . . . Portland MSS., I, 485. On the 'distemper' of the sailors at Portsmouth, see also ibid., p. 489; Naval Documents, pp. 356–7, 360; A Fight at Portsmouth (28 July 1648), BL., E.456(18), p. 2; A Letter from Dover Castle (29 July 1648), E.456(2), p. 5.
74. Rushworth, Historical Collections, VII, 1143.
75. The Moderate (22/29 August 1648), BL., E.461(16), no pagination.

which to mount attacks on parliamentary and merchant shipping not only by the revolted ships, but also by Irish vessels and pirate ships operating under letters of marque from the prince.[76]

Two more strategic options arising out of the revolt of part of the fleet remain to be discussed. There are numerous different versions of what may be described as the Irish option, varying according to time, place and personal predilection.[77] Deriving his information from a parliamentary loyalist who had escaped from Lord Inchiquin's clutches, Sir Hardress Waller, in a letter of 24 June, described the intention of Inchiquin and his confederate allies to mount an attack on the West Country, landing a force in Cornwall with the aid of the revolted ships.[78] On 4 August the Devon Committee informed Speaker Lenthall that in its view the security of the whole of the West Country had been put at hazard by Fairfax's order to Waller to move his forces out of Devon. Not only was there the threat of 'intestine seditions' but also the very real danger of the prince's fleet effecting a landing in the West Country, and 'Wee heare that the Windes from Ireland are like to blow a storme upon theise Coastes'. On 7 August parliament responded to these objections by recalling the order to Waller to march out of the region.[79]

An allegedly royalist account in September outlines a different objective: 'to transport all *Inchequins* Army and as many as may be of *Taffes* to *Millford* Haven, to whom the *Welch* would soon flow in great numbers, so as the City will be able to force the Parliament to passe any thing that the King shall plausibly offer'.[80] Both the tone and content of this piece suggest a particularly unrealistic flight of Cavalier fancy, if indeed it is not a fabrication, put out by the government. Another possibility of Irish succour to the royalists in Wales, this time in Anglesey, was mentioned by the royalist newswriter *Mercurius Elencticus*, who announced early in September that Lord Byron, swearing revenge on Fairfax for the summary execution of Byron's brother-in-law, Sir Charles Lucas, at Colchester, was about to arrive in Anglesey, where he hoped to have his strength supplemented by a force from Ireland under Inchiquin. But, as has already been shown, Byron's stay in Anglesey was

---

76. Washington DC., Folger Shakespeare Library, Folger MSS., Xd. 483 (24–25); *Cal.SPD. 1648–9*, pp. 276–7, 279; *Naval Documents*, pp. 374–5.
77. On Inchiquin's defection, see also above, pp. 400–402.
78. *HMC., 13th Report . . . Portland MSS.*, I, 466.
79. Bodleian, Tanner MSS., 57, fo. 173; Rushworth, *Historical Collections*, VII, 1218, 1234.
80. *A Letter Sent from Newport to a Gentleman in London* (September 1648), BL., E.464(29), p. 5; *A Terrible Thunder-Clap from the Isle of Wyght* (September 1648), E.465(9), p. 4. Viscount Taafe was the leader of the Irish confederate Catholics with whom Inchiquin had made common cause following the latter's defection.

too short and stormy for anything to come of this, even if it was ever a serious possibility.[81]

From the Hague on 18 September serious differences of opinion at the royalist council table were reported. Prince Maurice and others were said to favour the insurgent fleet's steering for France, whereas the Scottophile Willoughby and others still opted for a northern course. The only true sailor among them, Batten, and what looks like a majority of the others favoured taking the fleet to Ireland. Those advocating this course of action emphasized that Inchiquin, who largely controlled the south along with his allies, the Catholic confederates, would be happy to co-operate with the prince, and that other persons of power and influence would welcome the help of the revolted ships against England. But, just as the sailors had earlier been unwilling to sail to Scotland, so now did the news that the Council of War intended the insurgent fleet to sail to Ireland produce a mutiny which forced the abandonment of a promising plan.[82] A juncture of English and Irish naval forces did indeed offer considerable possibilities. Irish men-of-war were already making a great nuisance of themselves in the Channel and a report from Weymouth to the Derby House Committee at the end of September warned that the Isle of Portland was in danger of being taken by them.[83] But the sailors' opposition saw to it that yet another Irish option was not taken.

Finally, and certainly not the least important, was the option of bringing pressure to bear on the City of London by threatening to prey on its overseas trade in an attempt to produce a City compliant with insurgent aims. Not only did the naval revolt mean that there were even fewer naval ships to protect shipping against pirates, some of whom were operating under letters of marque from the Prince of Wales,[84] but the revolted ships themselves constituted an additional and very considerable menace to merchant shipping. 'This desertion of the Navy', wrote Lanark's royalist correspondent on 13 June, 'is a terror to this

81. *Mercurius Elencticus Number 42* (6/13 September 1648), BL., E.463(6), p. 342. On Byron in Anglesey, see above, p. 43r.
82. *A Message from the States of Holland* (18 September 1648), BL., E.464(31), pp. 2–3; *Ioyfull News from the Royall Navy* (22 September 1648), E.464(34), pp. 3–4, 6.
83. *Naval Documents*, pp. 386–7. There was another project early in November to transport troops from Ireland to England (Bodleian, Ballard MSS., 45, sig. 2a^v). On privateering based on Irish ports, see J.H. Ohlmeyer, *Civil War and Restoration in the Three Stuart Kingdoms* (Cambridge, 1993), pp. 167–8, 190–1, 194–5, 228.
84. For instance, to the former pirate, Captain Greene. See, e.g., *Cal.SPD. 1648–9*, p. 224; *The Letters Commissions and other papers . . . communicated to the Common Councel* (31 July 1648), BL., E.456(31), pp. 7–15. For an earlier complaint on 20 March of lack of convoys to protect merchant ships against piracy, see Rushworth, *Historical Collections*, VII, 1031.

Citty, and will, I hope, doe more good uppon them then the force of any five counties conjoyned could haue donne'; and, again on 24 June, 'this Citty must goe with the fleet, and neither can nor dare doe other'.[85]

Rightly or wrongly, one correspondent reported towards the end of August that, hearing of the complaints of London merchants, the king had ordered his son to desist from detaining ships sailing to and from London. On 18 September a report from the Hague suggested that royalist councils were now also seeing that policy as counter-productive.[86] Prince Charles himself responded to this change of mood, and perhaps to his father's promptings, by writing unconvincingly to the Lord Mayor disclaiming any intention of violating the persons or goods of merchants and emphasizing that 'our only aym is to procure a subsistence for the Navy . . . that there by we may be able to protect the Ships, Vessels and Goods, and to secure the Trade, not only of the City of London, but of all . . . other subjects'.[87] This was neither an adequate response to the caution prompted by the king and royalist councillors abroad nor was it likely to cut much ice with the Londoners. The aim of obtaining financial backing from the City, as distinct from extorting it by seizing merchant ships and then allowing them to compound for their freedom, met with no response from the City. Indeed, one of its most notable and unlooked-for effects was to create disaffection among many insurgent mariners who resented rich prizes being released without any apparent benefit to any save naval commanders such as Batten and Jordan, who, they suspected, were the main beneficiaries of compounding.[88] Nor is it likely that such naval pressures would exert significant leverage on the City to agitate for renewed negotiations with the king. Long before the naval revolt the City had been among the most enthusiastic proponents of a treaty and its continued support was based on rational calculation of its best interests rather than on pressure from the revolted ships.

Insurgent war aims

Declarations and manifestoes were issued by all of the main insurgent groups in 1648, and some of these, as in the cases of Kent and Essex,

85. *Hamilton Papers*, pp. 212, 221.
86. *His Majesties Gracious Message to . . . the Prince of Wales* (25 August 1648), BL., E.461(11), pp. 1–2; *A Letter sent from the States of Holland* (18 September 1648), E.464(31), p. 2; *Ioyfull Newes from the Royall Navy* (22 September 1648), E.464(34), p. 3.
87. *Prince Charles His Letter to . . . the Lord Mayor . . .* (October 1648), BL., E.466(4), pp. 1–3; *Ioyfull Newes from the Kings Navy at Sea* (October 1648), E.466(10), pp. 4–5.
88. On this, see B. Capp, *Cromwell's Navy*, pp. 33–4.

took over the objectives of the county petitions whose presentation had been the immediate prelude to the risings. The aspirations of militant Cavaliers and of alienated parliamentarians may indeed have been worlds apart, but, if the former were to have any prospect of recruiting sizeable numbers of the latter, they obviously needed to tone down extreme Cavalier sentiments and to stress considerations such as the regime's unconstitutional excesses, inordinate cost, and shocking violations of traditional liberties. Sir Henry Lingen's Herefordshire revolt in July and August is a good case in point. Although the rising was dominated by old-style Cavaliers like Lingen himself, the insurgents' declaration of aims suggests an awareness of the danger of frightening off potential recruits from the ranks of moderate but alienated parliamentarians. It echoes the disillusionment of such people as well as the impatience and disgust of Cavaliers at the denial of opportunities 'to tast of the sweet and often promised fruit of the many Declarations of the two Houses and Armies for the settlement of the Kingdome and his Majesty in his pristine Rights . . .'. Instead, the king had been imprisoned and the queen virtually banished; the ancient and known laws violated; religion desecrated by a schismatical army which was costing the taxpayer £60,000 a month not counting the Excise, free quarter and other exactions. The declaration made the most of the unpopularity of county and other committees, their plundering of private property and the alleged intention to establish a new militia to enslave the subject under martial law. It emphasized that the insurgents aimed not only to restore the king with honour and glory, bring back the queen and free the royal children from restraint, but also to re-establish the true Protestant religion and the known laws, as well as a free parliament in contrast to that currently lording it at Westminster. Rather surprisingly, one war aim which it shared uniquely with the Scottish Engagers and which might have seemed more appropriate in a declaration coming from the City of London stressed the need to strengthen Anglo-Scottish unity. Along with the additional aims of removing illegal taxes, disbanding the army and establishing a permanent settlement of the kingdom, here was a platform that the Herefordshire insurgents felt would appeal at least as much to moderates as to Cavaliers both in Herefordshire and in neighbouring counties, drawing them into a revolt whose leaders had clearly demonstrated that 'wee squint not upon selfe-ends, but firmely fix our eyes upon the publike interest'.[89]

Lingen's short and quickly suppressed rising was preponderantly royalist and a relatively minor episode in the Second Civil War despite

---

89. *The Declaration of the Gentlemen and others now in Armes in the County of Hereford* (22 August 1648), BL., 669, f13(4); Webb, *Herefordshire*, II, 422–3.

the extravagant hopes which had been held out for it by the Scottish Engagers and English Cavaliers such as Lord Byron. But its manifesto was emphatically mainstream. The same is true, perhaps less surprisingly, of the declarations of the Welsh insurgents, Poyer and Powell in March and Laugharne in May, which display an equal concern for the rights of the king and the privileges of parliament and liberties of the people.[90] Such professions can be contrasted with the more outrightly royalist aims outlined by Sir Thomas Glemham and Sir Marmaduke Langdale for the northern insurgents acting under commission from the Prince of Wales. These confine themselves to the re-establishment of royal power, the settlement of religion and the procuring of a happy peace.[91]

It is not especially illuminating to insist that all insurgents aspired to restore the king to his just rights since this could obviously mean very different things to different people. As was argued in an earlier chapter, for a great many disillusioned parliamentarians the king had himself become the supreme symbol of that constitutionality which had been fractured by the regime at Westminster and its agencies in the counties.[92] But declarations in which the restoration of regal rights is unaccompanied by any mention of the rights of parliament and of the subject invite suspicion that the preferred option was in fact the restoration of the *status quo ante* 1640 as distinct from that before the second session of the Long Parliament. On the other hand, the best example to be found of the careful dotting and crossing of the constitutional i's and t's on the limitations on royal power is to be found in the declarations of the aims of the aristocratic revolt led by Holland, Buckingham and Peterborough; not surprisingly, in view of Holland's previous political career. These insurgents were at great pains to disclaim any intention 'to set up his Majesty in a tyrannicall power rather than . . . in his just Regall Government . . . very well consistant with the due rights and freedoms of Parliament'.[93] And for once one can readily believe them. By contrast, Byron's advocacy of the restoration of 'a free parliament' as well as of the king's rights, in his declaration to assembled insurgents at the rendezvous at Prees Heath near Shrewsbury

90. *Colonell Powell and Col. Poyers Letter to . . . the Prince of Wales and their Declaration* (March 1648), Codrington pamphlet coll., pp. 3–8; *The Declaration of Major General Laugharne [sic] . . .* (8 May 1648), BL., E.442(8), p. 3; *Colonell Powell and Col. Poyers Letters . . . to the Prince of Wales* (April 1648), E.436(14), pp. 3–8.
91. *The Commission of His Highnesse . . . to Sir Thomas Glenham [sic] and Sir Marmaduke Langdale* (2 May 1648), BL., E.441(7), p. 3. This, however, is a summary of these aims by another.
92. See above, pp. 82, 89.
93. *The Declaration of the Duke of Buckingham and the Earles of Holland and Peterborough* (5 July 1648), BL., E.451(36), p. 6; idem (6 July 1648), E.451(33), pp. 2–3; *Parliamentary History*, XVII, 290–91.

early in August, invites the question of what exactly is meant by 'free' in this context; especially since there is no mention of parliament at all in Byron's declaration in Caernarvonshire on 21 August; only of the need to uphold the fundamental law, which could mean all things to all men.[94]

No useful purpose would be served by providing further details of the citation in insurgent manifestoes of the need to restore either or both the king's rights and authority and the fundamental law and privileges of parliament. How many of the insurgents felt strongly about the last of these is, of course, quite another matter, but it was as important to their cause that they should emphasize their devotion to what they described as full and free parliaments as it was to that of their enemies to emphasize that they stood for a settlement along monarchical lines. The alternatives were for the insurgents to lay themselves open to the charge of being dyed in the wool Cavalier extremists (which of course many of them were) and for their enemies to be characterized as regicidal and republican sectaries. Oddly enough, the need to extirpate sectarian excesses does not bulk very large among declared insurgent aims, though there are abundant derogatory references to the need to disband the sectarian army. A not surprising exception is provided by the aims of the Sottish Engagers, where it is placed alongside the extirpation of popery, the establishment of a Presbyterian ecclesiastical polity and the taking of the Covenant by all. For the Scots, of course, popery extended to virtually all non-Presbyterian and non-sectarian forms of belief and worship, and its condemnation, along with that of sectarianism, was no doubt designed to appease the kirk as well as to appeal to pious Presbyterians among the Engagers. Consonant with this, the Engagers differed sharply from their English and Welsh insurgent allies in their demand for the abolition of the use of the Book of Common Prayer, which, when mentioned in other manifestoes, was usually treated with reverence and approbation, even by the drunken and rumbustious Poyer whose declaration is at pains to stress that 'the *Book* of Common Prayer is the sole comfort of the People here and their way to attain to the knowledge of the *Principles* of *Religion* and to serve God'. Such an encomium from such a person no doubt fitted beautifully the stock Puritan (and Scottish Presbyterian) picture which associated Prayer Book enthusiasts with immoral life and dissolute behaviour.[95]

Although there are some exceptions which will be specified later, it

94. *A Great and Bloody Fight in Shropshire* (6 August 1648), BL., E.457(18), p. 6; *The further Proceedings of the Lord Byron in Wales* . . . (21 August 1648), E.460(34), p. 6.
95. *Colonell Powell and Col. Poyers Letter to* . . . *the Prince of Wales with their Declaration* (March 1648), Codrington pamphlet coll., p. 8; *The Declaration of Col. Poyer and Col. Powell* (10 April 1648), Codrington pamphlet coll. (also BL., E.435(9)), pp. 4–5, 6.

is reasonable to assume that the insistence in some county petitions and insurgent manifestoes on the desirability of restoring the true Protestant religion connotes the return to the use of the Prayer Book and of 'primitive' (but not Laudian) episcopacy. Obvious cases are the abortive Hampshire petition in June which, as was emphasized in an earlier chapter, was very much the work of local Cavaliers; and the ferocious Dorset declaration of the same month, though in the event neither of those counties was to be the scene of military campaigns in the Second Civil War.[96] It is perhaps surprising that such religious aims are featured in only seven of the petitions and insurgent manifestoes and not very prominently in some of those. They do not, for instance, appear at all in the Essex petition, although the suppression of the 'pure Protestant Religion' was to be one of the grievances later specified by the insurgents in Colchester.[97]

Despite the fact that a declaration of the revolted sailors early in August specified that they aimed, *inter alia*, 'to restore our Religion unto its auncient lustre and beauty', there is no need to assume that the sailors meant by this a return to Anglican forms of worship.[98] Their much-publicized bewailing the want of proper worship in the navy under Vice-Admiral Rainsborough is more likely to have as its point of comparison the practices of Rainsborough's predecessor, the pious Presbyterian Batten. Nor is the sailors' readiness to take over the aims of the Kentish petition significant in this respect since religion does not feature in that petition.[99] When the revolted ships joined the Prince of Wales, there is no indication that the sailors were anything but happy to go along with the prince's declaration of late July which opted for a religious settlement along the lines of the King's Engagement with the Scots of 26 December 1647; that is, a Presbyterian settlement, at least for a trial period of three years.[100]

The disbandment of the army which had been such a bone of contention during the previous year also figured prominently among the aims of many insurgent groups as it had in the petitions of 1648.[101] The army, of course, took most of the blame for what was regarded as

96. *The Declaration . . . Petition and Remonstrance of the Lords Knights Gentlemen Ministers and Free-holders of Hampeshire* (June 1648), Codrington pamphlet coll. (and BL., E.447(18)), sig. A3; *The Declaration of the County of Dorset* (June 1648), E.447(26), p. 3. See above, p. 148.
97. *The Remonstrance and Declaration of the Knights Esquires Gentlemen and Freeholders in Colchester* (July 1648), Oxford, Worcester College pamphlet coll. (also BL., E.451(11)), pp. 3, 5, 7.
98. *The Declaration of the Sea Commanders and Marriners* (2 August 1648), BL., E.457(6), p. 5.
99. *Naval Documents*, pp. 333, 355.
100. *Propositions from the Prince of Wales* (29 July 1648), BL., E.456(2), p. 5.
101. See above, pp. 45, 145, 148.

excessive, and sometimes illegal, taxation, a grievance which received extensive treatment in the second chapter of this book. The need to remedy this situation, in which the Excise was reserved for special denunciation, was a feature of the demands of at least six different insurgent groups.[102] Given the importance of the role of ex-Cavaliers as leaders of such groups, it is perhaps surprising to find sequestration of royalist property cited prominently as a grievance by only one of them, which moreover was led by renegade parliamentarians rather than former Cavaliers. Poyer and Powell's inclusion of this in their declaration can surely be ascribed to their desperate but largely unavailing attempt to get the support of local Cavaliers, while their denunciation of parliament's alleged intention 'to establish *Excise, Taxes* and other *intollerable charges*' was clearly designed to appeal to a much wider public.[103] Similarly, Lingen's Herefordshire insurgents saw the ending of such taxes as one of the most beneficial products of the extirpation of arbitrary power which their hoped-for victory would achieve.[104]

As was demonstrated in the third chapter, a salient and most unpopular feature of this power was the county committees whose abolition figured among the war aims contained in several insurgent declarations and petitions.[105] Moreover, the July Remonstrance of the royalists in Colchester, who, it will be remembered, were holding Sir William Massam and other members of the Essex committee hostage, is surprisingly unique in also singling out another committee as an object of similar vituperation. This was the Derby House Committee, which is here seen as a central agency of oppression and corruption, 'wherein . . . the prime Actors are chiefe Officers of the Army, and have . . . possest themselves of the most beneficiall Offices and imployments of the Kingdome', contrary, needless to say, to the Self Denying Ordinance. Herein, argued the remonstrators, lay the chief reason why motions for a treaty and settlement with the king were rejected or intolerably delayed; 'because peace would determine [viz. end] both their power and profit'.[106]

This finally brings us to the aim which all insurgents held in common: a personal treaty with the king. A substantial part of the fourth chapter of this book was devoted to the theme of the petitioning campaigns in 1648 for the king to be brought to London to treat, and

102. These are specified above, on p. 79, note 174.
103. BL., E.435(9), p. 4.
104. BL., 669, f13(4).
105. On the county committees and the Second Civil War, see above, pp. 105–9.
106. *The Remonstrance and Declaration of . . . Colchester* (6 July 1648), Oxford, Worcester College pamphlet coll. (also BL., E.451(11)), pp. 4–5.

there is no need to cover this ground again.[107] It has also been emphasized in the present chapter that the petitions of counties such as
Kent and Essex were in effect anticipations or preliminary statements of
what were soon to be war aims. When Sir Charles Lucas, himself a local
man, sent two other Essex officers, Colonels Tuke and Maxey, into
Colchester before occupying that town, they were instructed to
emphasize 'the grounds of our engagement in pursuit of our petition',
in order to persuade the inhabitants to allow the insurgent soldiers
peaceful entrance. Indeed, according to one hostile observer, writing at
the end of July when the insurgents had already been in occupation of
Colchester for several weeks, it had been a vital part of their strategy 'To
stir up the people to petition and mutiny'.[108] And nothing stirred them
up more effectively than the demand for negotiations with the king and
a permanent settlement. Certainly in the case of the insurgents of Kent
and Essex the demand for a personal treaty with the king was not only
to be found in formal petitions and declarations of war aims but also on
the lips of the insurgent soldiers themselves. Thus the defenders of
Colchester were reported in July as calling to the New Model soldiers
over the walls 'that if they do not stir up their Masters very speedily
to a personall Treaty with the Kings Majesty, they will cudgell them
to it'.[109]

A royalist pamphlet in July had argued that in the event of parliament
refusing to sanction a personal treaty with the king, 'it is agreeable to
right reason that the people should use force and levy warre . . . to
inforce them thereunto'.[110] It is one of the ironies of the Second Civil
War and a matter of incalculable importance to the understanding of the
revolution which was to take place in December and January, that
although the insurgents fought and lost the war, parliament conceded
one of the most important of their war aims. As the quiescent and
inactive Londoners might well argue, it seemed that there had been no
need to go to war at all.

107. See above, pp. 139–56.
108. *HMC., 12th Report Appendix IX (MSS. of the Duke of Beaufort)*, p. 23; *Sad and
      Dangerous Tydings from Colchester* (July 1648), BL., E.456(5), pp. 2–3. For a similar
      view of petitions for a treaty as a Cavalier plot to get the king to London and thereby
      to stimulate unrest, see *A Letter sent from Newport to a Gentleman in London . . .*
      (September 1648), E.464(29), p. 2; *A Terrible Thunder-Clap from the Isle of Wyght . . .*
      (September 1648), E.465(9), pp. 1–2.
109. *A great and bloody Fight at Colchester* (30 July 1648), BL., E.456(11), p. 2.
110. *The just measure of a Personall Treaty* (July 1648), BL., E.451(40), especially pp. 1–6.

Insurgent recruitment and mobilization

One of the major problems facing the historian who seeks to reconstruct the planning and organization of revolts which failed is that many of these operations were necessarily clandestine, in which circumstances a disproportionate amount of the evidence which has survived emanates from the victorious party. Such evidence needs to be treated with great caution before it can be used to cast any valid light on the organization, intention and behaviour of the losers. With this important proviso, however, careful use of government records such as the proceedings of the Derby House Committee and of the Committees for Compounding and for the Advance of Money can yield information which otherwise would be entirely lacking.

We have already had occasion to observe the commissioning by the king, or the Prince of Wales on the king's behalf, of some of the major insurgent commanders such as Langdale in the north, Byron in North Wales, the Welsh Marches and Cheshire and Lancashire, and the earl of Holland in the south. In addition, the Hertfordshire nobleman, Lord Capel, was commissioned by the Prince of Wales to raise forces in Hertfordshire, Essex, Cambridgeshire, Norfolk, Suffolk and Huntingdonshire, though one knows only of his recruiting operations in Hertfordshire before he took his force to join the Essex insurgents.[111] Lesser commissions such as that of Lingen in Herefordshire and Colonel Michael Hudson in the East Midlands also came direct from the prince. According to the report of the victorious parliamentarian Colonel Thomas Wayte on 8 May, Hudson had a commission to raise twenty regiments of horse and another twenty of foot, but this in no way corresponds with the few pathetic Cavaliers who were cornered at Woodcroft House in Northamptonshire. Clearly Hudson's plan to recruit large numbers at Stamford fair and elsewhere had not been very successful.[112]

In parts of northern England, where the royalist control was tight for a time, there is some evidence of conscription for military service. There is, for instance, an order of 2 June from Langdale to four Westmorland gentlemen, Sir Thomas Sandford, John Lowther, John Dalston and Christopher Dudley, to conscript all males between the ages of sixteen and sixty, in the division of the bottom of Westmorland.[113] This is as unequivocal evidence of conscription as could be demanded. Some cases, however, are not so clear. Such was the commission issued by Langdale at Carlisle on 20 May to Captain

111. A copy of Capel's commission is in Hertford, Hertfordshire R.O., M287.
112. *L.J.*, X, 313–14; *C.J.*, V, 589.
113. Kendal, Cumbria R.O., WD/RY/HMC. 200.

William Poulden to raise a troop of horse for service around Pontefract, which was to fall to Morrice a fortnight later.[114] In other cases there is a strong likelihood of conscription even though the authorities for our information, unlike that of the Westmorland case above, are government rather than royalist sources. Writing to Speaker Lenthall on 6 July about insurgent prisoners taken in a recent engagement in Northumberland, Sir Arthur Haselrig mentions that he had discharged those of his prisoners who were 'pressed men'.[115] In the remotest part of north-western Yorkshire, it was deposed in August 1651 that George Williams of Dent, who had served Charles I in the earl of Newcastle's army in the First Civil War, had acted as high constable for the king in 1648, issuing warrants to all the hamlets in his wapentake to provide men and arms to serve under the royalist Colonel Lowther.[116] In Westmorland, a local parson deposed in December 1651 that Sir Thomas Sandford, a local collector of subsidies for the king in both civil wars, had bound over those refusing to serve the king to good behaviour. On 27 November 1648 Thomas Jon of Broodslacke deposed that at an insurgent rendezvous at Sandsforthsmore he had been told that 'yt was in vaine for him to speake in his owne behalfe to gett of [sic] from beeinge a soldier'.[117] The Lake District also provides a number of examples of men paying to avoid being conscripted – 45 shillings was the price quoted in one such case – and of others being recruited in their stead, sometimes at higher rates of pay than those paid to conscripts, even though the substitutes were sometimes manifestly unsuitable persons.[118]

There are of course many degrees and varieties of compulsion other than that of formal conscription. For instance, the tenants of great royalist landowners were obviously vulnerable to pressure put upon them to rise for the king when the occasion demanded, as was seen earlier in the case of Sir Richard Graham's tenants in Cumberland.[119] However, there are also plentiful examples of willing volunteers for the king in this part of England. For instance, by no means all of Haselrig's prisoners taken in the early July fight in Northumberland were conscripts. He also specifies 150 prisoners who had enlisted under the officers with whom they had served in the First Civil War and 'that, I believe, will never change their partie as long as they live'. In Haselrig's

---

114.   West Yorkshire Archive Service, Leeds City R.O., Bacon Frank MSS., BF 3, pp. 94–5. On Morrice and Pontefract, see above, pp. 405–6.
115.   *HMC., 13th Report . . . Portland MSS.*, I, 476.
116.   *Cal.CAM.*, III, 1185–6.
117.   PRO., SP. 23/171, pp. 107, 114.
118.   Ibid., pp. 115, 123–4.
119.   See above, p. 366.

view the appropriate fate for such irreconcilables was to be sent to the plantations.[120] One account names thirty-nine notable gentlemen among these captured insurgents: including the commander Colonel Edward Grey, the Northumberland papist and royalist veteran of Marston Moor and other battles in the first war; the local Cavalier and member of a prominent royalist family, Lieutenant Colonel John Salkield and another bearing the same surname; Sir Francis Ratcliffe and his son and two others of that name; and George Bellasis of Durham.[121]

Naturally, one can never be quite sure how far 'volunteers' were responding to intolerable pressure from their social superiors whose will it was not easy to resist. There were at least nine persons thus labelled in the regiment of Colonel John Lowther. However, the fact that six of them came from the same village, Crosby, as John Richardson, who was Lowther's cornet, suggests that there may possibly be a hidden element of compulsion here, although it is at least as likely that they may have willingly responded to enthusiastic local recruiting.[122] Among the recruiting documents for Westmorland which have survived is a list of the names of those who contributed 36 horse and 31 foot-soldiers. This almost certainly refers to the practice whereby substantial individuals made themselves responsible for recruiting, equipping and paying soldiers, while not necessarily serving themselves. In one of these cases an individual made himself responsible for as many as six cavalrymen and six foot-soldiers, while another provided and equipped four of each.[123] This sort of private enterprise recruitment was not peculiar to the north and we shall encounter numerous similar examples from many other parts of the country.

Volunteers were enrolled in great numbers at carefully chosen rendezvous, where Cavalier notabilities often made encouraging royalist speeches, as was done by members of the Strickland family at a rendezvous in May mentioned in an earlier chapter.[124] This appears to have been the rendezvous on Kendal Heath mentioned in another newsletter which tells of Sir Philip Musgrave and others urging those present to engage for the king. Proceedings there were rudely interrupted by a party of parliamentary horse which routed the Cavaliers,

120. *HMC., 13th Report . . . Portland MSS.*, I, 476–7.
121. Rushworth, *Historical Collections*, VII, 1177–8. On Grey, see Welford, *Durham and Northumberland*, pp. 215–17 and note; Newman, *Royalist Officers*, pp. 167–8. On Salkield, see ibid., p. 325.
122. PRO., SP. 23/171, p. 116.
123. Kendal, Cumbria RO., WD/RY/HMC. 200. Other examples of such provision in the north are evidenced in PRO., SP. 23/171, pp. 107, 111–12, 118 (Westmorland); *Cal.CAM.*, III, 1351 (Northumberland); ibid., III, 1416, 1417 (Yorkshire).
124. *Clarke Papers*, II, 9. See above, p. 367.

taking about 300 of them prisoner and rescuing some parliamentary sympathizers who had been brought there under duress for not answering the royalist summons to attend. Among the parliamentary trophies of this occasion were two banners bearing the motto in letters of gold 'For GOD and KING CHARLES'. The same party of horse was reported to be active in other parts of the region in obstructing malignants from attending other rendezvous.[125]

Most insurgent commissioned officers in the north had commended themselves by their social position, their Cavalier record or by having undertaken to supply men to serve under them. At least one seems to have engaged in ostentatious self-advertisement. On 13 October one Anthony Warriner of Kendal deposed that at the first insurgent muster at Tarney Bank near Kendal

> William Potter of Kendall . . . with a sword at his side . . . was very forward to profer his seruice and take vpon him Command; & did advise some soldiers to make Choise of him for a Captain, assureing them that he would be very carefull . . . for the safety of himselfe and them and made seuerall speeches setting forth his readynes to Command a foote Company.[126]

As Lambert explained in a letter to the Speaker on 20 July, his cautious retreat before the Cavaliers in the north increased their opportunities 'to recruit and grow greater every day'.[127] Sir Marmaduke Langdale's letter of 8 August to Sir Charles Lucas at Colchester, which has already been noticed earlier in another context,[128] is illuminating about the later stages of this activity. Kendal he describes as particularly favourably disposed to the insurgents who recruited many ex-royalist officers and other Cavaliers there. In the neighbouring county to the south, however, they found Lancaster, 'rather *Neutrall* then *cordially Loyall*'. Even here, however, the insurgents recruited some former high-ranking parliamentary officers – no names were given – 'who, weary of ingaging . . . in so unjust and disloyal a quarrel, become firme and fruitfull *Cavaliers*; and being persons of quality, drew others by their example to the like practice of obedience and loyalty'. But Langdale's fortunes had at that time just about reached their apogee as he now prepared to march, confident of further recruits and defectors, towards Preston.[129]

There are some, though far less abundant, references to the conscription of men by the insurgents in South Wales. Of course, the hard core

125. *A great Victory obtained in the Nort* [sic] (17 May 1648), BL., E.443(30), no pagination. Other Cumbrian rendezvous were at Tarney Bank, Sandford Moor, Cliburnhead and Kirkby Moor (P.R.O., SP. 23/171, pp. 111, 114, 116).
126. SP. 23/171, p. 122.
127. HMC., *13th Report . . . Portland MSS.*, I, 488.
128. See above, p. 434.
129. *A Letter from Sir Marmaduke Langdale* (August 1648), BL., E.457(20), pp. 4–5.

of Poyer's and Laugharne's forces was to be found in their own disgruntled soldiers who were aggrieved both at the decision to disband them and at the way of going about it. Moreover, such evidence as is available about insurgent conscription in South Wales comes entirely from their opponents for whom it had a distinct utility as propaganda and therefore must be treated with great caution. A letter from Wales on 4 April refers to Poyer's forcible recruitment of men in Pembroke town, 'who doe out of pure Fear obey him, and do make very full Appearances before him . . . with Bills, Halberts and such other Weapons as they can get'. Poyer also was reported as having pressed another hundred men to serve on the previous Sunday. Another account tells a similar story of the pressing of men by Poyer and Powell in Pembrokeshire, Carmarthenshire and Cardiganshire; 'the poor Inhabitants being compelled through Fear to appear at their Summons and pay them large Taxations besides'.[130] It has already been remarked that Poyer and Powell did not experience any notable success in recruiting former Cavalier gentry and magnates, of whom the earl of Carbery is the most notable example of their failure.[131] A letter in early April from South Wales offers the information that there were 'not many Gentleman of Note or Men of Estates . . . come in to Poyer or that give him any visible Countenance'.[132] Things may for a time have been better in Brecknockshire where Hugh Games was reported as recruiting a great number for the royalist cause.[133] Certainly the information given to Colonel Horton by William Morgan from Brecon that the gentry of that county were solidly for parliament seems unduly optimistic.[134] In Cardiganshire, Carmarthenshire and Pembrokeshire there were several cases of the government making use of ex-Cavaliers, one of them, it would seem, as a spy in the ranks of the insurgents.[135] Such cases were no doubt relatively unusual as compared with those of Cavaliers such as Major-General Stradling who rallied to the royalist cause in 1648 as in 1647;[136] or those like Carbery who this time kept their heads down.

130. Rushworth, *Historical Collections*, VII, 1050, 1065.
131. *A Letter containing a Perfect Relation of the conditions . . . of thinges in South Wales* (April 1648), Codrington pamphlet coll., p. 5. See above, p. 430.
132. Rushworth, *Historical Collections*, VII, 1051.
133. See above, p. 347.
134. Aberystwyth, National Library of Wales, Tredegar Park MSS., 105/150. This service did not save Morgan from having his house plundered by parliamentary troopers (ibid., 105/152).
135. PRO., SP. 23/126, p. 321; *Cal.CAM.*, II, 1019–21; *Cal.CC.*, III, 1835–6.
136. Stradling is the only one of the fifteen officers listed as being taken at St Fagans who can certainly be identified as having taken part in both rebellions (Rushworth, *Historical Collections*, VII, 1128; *Two Letters from Col. Horton* (8 May 1648), BL., E.442(8), p. 14). Another possible case is one Evan Price. For other participants in both risings, see above, pp. 344, 345, 346.

Of the risings in the Welsh Marches and West Midlands the most serious was that of Sir Henry Lingen in Herefordshire. The large house in that county known as Hampton Court seems to have been intended to serve as a centre for recruiting royalist malignants from all the Marcher counties, though all of the eighty common soldiers taken prisoner at Lingen's final defeat in Montgomeryshire seem to have been Herefordshire men. According to a later investigation in December 1651 Lingen seems to have gone out of his way to court the support of local Catholic gentry such as John Berrington, Bodnam Bradford, Henry Morgan and John Bowyer, all of whom were said to have encouraged their Catholic acquaintances and dependants to join the revolt notwithstanding the emphasis of the insurgents' manifesto on the Protestant religion.[137] A rising which it was hoped would link with Lingen's revolt in Herefordshire and another in Shropshire was that engineered by Colonel Dud Dudley in neighbouring Worcestershire. Dudley seems to have been about as successful in the field as he was in his much-vaunted metallurgical experiments in which he never substantiated his claim to be able to smelt iron using coal rather than charcoal. His principal associates in the abortive Worcestershire rising were the Shropshire gentleman Sir Francis Ottley and Colonel John Lane of King's Bromley in Staffordshire, formerly royalist governors of Shrewsbury and Rushdall House in Leicestershire respectively; and a Major Harcourt, who had apparently fought under Dudley in the First Civil War. Ottley, described by Byron as 'an old, doting fool', had been dismissed as royal governor of Shrewsbury in 1644. Lane had sustained ghastly wounds in the same year, but was now eager to fight again. There had been mass meetings of potential insurgents at Bromsgrove and Kidderminster, but the chance discovery of a store of gunpowder in a field near the house of another of the plotters, a parson named Broughton, led to the uncovering of the design and the arrest of the principals including Dudley.[138]

One of the main elements in the general design, of which the aborted Worcestershire rising was a part, related to Shropshire. A letter of 15

---

137. *Cal.SPD. 1648–9*, p. 246; *Cal.CAM.*, III, 1416, 1417; Bodleian, Tanner MSS., 57, fos. 217(b)–18; Rushworth, *Historical Collections*, VII, 1234; Whitelock, *Memorials*, p. 325 (21 August); *A Great Victory in Herefordshire* (21 August 1648), BL., E.460(34), pp. 1–5.

138. *A New Rising for the King* (8 July 1648), BL., E.452(36), pp. 1–4; *A Fight in Worcestershire* (12 July 1648), E.452(20), no pagination; *The Declaration of the Counties of Worcester-shire Warwick-shire Hereford-shire and Sallop . . .* (July 1648), E.452(30), no pagination. On Dudley, see Newman, *Royalist Officers*, pp. 114–15. On Ottley, see ibid., p. 280; R. Hutton, *The Royalist War Effort 1642–1646* (1984 edn.), pp. 12, 24–5, 131, 135, 159. On Lane, see Newman, *Royalist Officers*, p. 221. On Harcourt, see ibid., p. 176.

July to the Speaker from Robert Clive of Stych warned that the county was in great danger occasioned partly by the weakness of local forces and partly by extensive local recruitment of insurgents. Much seems to have been learnt of this ongoing process of recruitment by the information given by a defecting royalist to Colonel Mackworth, the parliamentary governor of Shrewsbury, which we have already observed Mackworth using to foil Byron's plans for two insurgent rendezvous in the county. If the defector's account is to be credited, royalist agents had been active in the county for several weeks, some of them under Mackworth's very nose in Shrewsbury itself. They had been assiduously canvassing the support of ex-Cavaliers, and more especially those of them who had not compounded, urging them to raise forces in readiness for the coming insurgent offensive, with Shrewsbury as a principal target. The defector revealed the names of some of the principal Cavaliers involved, among them Sir Thomas Harris who narrowly escaped arrest at the hands of Mackworth's troops, though his fanatically royalist mother-in-law was less fortunate.[139]

Professor Everitt has characterized the Kent revolt as 'the revolt of a whole countryside' and not 'of a single clique or class of the community'.[140] However much allowance one makes for the general unpopularity of Weldon and the county committee, to interpret Everitt's verdict as connoting a complete community of interest between men of widely different social degree and occupation would be to invite justified scepticism. For one thing it would involve playing down unduly the element of compulsion, not to speak of irresistibly heavy pressures on the insurgent rank and file from their social superiors such as has already been observed in some other counties. In May 1650 it was deposed against William Yappe of Snodland, who had been a violent participant in the Kent rising, that he had compelled men to serve as well as requisitioning horses from many people including one well-affected widow whom he had threatened to leave without a groat to her name. John Witharden of Milton was said to have threatened all who would not go with him to fight at Maidstone that he would tie them to horses' tails and drag them there forcibly.[141] These may perhaps have been charges brought by deponents with personal grudges against those they accused, but, even if one may discount them – and it is by no means certain that one should – there were subtler forms of pressure which might be exerted by Kentish notabilities such as Squire Hales, Sir Thomas Peyton and Sir Richard Hardres. Such pressure may also have

---

139. HMC., 13th Report . . . Portland MSS., I, 484–5; L.J., X, 424–5. See above, p. 431.
140. Everitt, Kent, pp. 240–1.
141. PRO., SP. 19/22, p. 46; Cal.CAM., III, 1229, 1310.

been present in those cases where individual gentlemen undertook to provide, pay and equip men for the service. A good Kentish example is the case of John Adye which came before the Committee for Compounding in 1651, when Anne, the wife of Stephen Meade of Newnham, deposed that on 29 May 1648 Adye sent his servant John Milborne to fetch Meade, who would be furnished with a horse, arms and ten days pay, to serve under Edward Hales who was 'then Generall of those y^t rose'. We do not know whether Meade complied, but Milborne's own deposition tells us that his master sent him, similarly furnished, to serve with an insurgent troop. Milburne later stated that his unwillingness to go was overcome when Adye told him 'That if he went not, it was at his . . . perill'. He was captured at the battle of Maidstone several days later, but released a few days after that.[142]

On 29 May Colonel Barkstead wrote to Fairfax informing him that Kentish countrymen were deserting in droves from the ranks of the insurgents, with bitter complaints against the gentlemen who had engaged them.[143] When Fairfax's troops entered Rochester, 'the women reviled . . . against Goring, Hayles and Compton who had engaged their husbands and now betraid them, cursing them for bringing in a company of strangers, Officers and soldiers that were not known to the Country [viz. County]'.[144] As to the presence of outsiders in the Kentish force, a letter from Maidstone on 2 June, the day following the battle, states that among the 1,400-odd prisoners taken, 'we find few or none to be Countrymen, but many of the King's Party and Men of Quality, some Seamen, and the rest Apprentices and Watermen from London and thereabouts'. The letter almost certainly exaggerates what may nevertheless have been a high proportion of outsiders. By contrast, however, in one list of sixty-eight persons presented on 16 March 1650 as having been involved in the Kent rising, all but one, a Londoner, came from Kent.[145]

It may well be, as the Rochester women and their husbands alleged, that many of the Kentish gentlemen who had engaged in recruiting had

142. PRO., SP. 23/158, pp. 109–10; *Cal.CC.*, IV, 2769. Evidence of other cases of individuals providing men and horses for service with the Kent insurgents is in SP. 19/14, pp. 147, 149, 150; SP. 19/21, p. 255; SP. 19/22, pp. 164, 191, 256, 262, 303; SP. 19/23, p. 4; SP. 19/129, p. 34; SP. 19/152, p. 154; *Cal.CAM.*, III, 1310.
143. *Clarke Papers*, II, 22.
144. *The Designes of the Rebels in Kent* (27 May 1648), BL., E.446(18), pp. 4–5. Ludlow stresses the disappointment of many recruits on finding the Kent forces commanded not by the local magnate Edward Hales but by an outsider, the earl of Norwich (*Ludlow Memoirs*, I, 193).
145. Rushworth, *Historical Collections*, VII, 1137; *Cal.CAM.*, III, 1211. For a detailed analysis of Kentish petitioners and insurgents which lays great stress on alienated moderates, see Everitt, *Kent*, pp. 251–3, 255–8.

deceived men into enlisting, perhaps emphasizing peaceful (though armed) petitioning as the object of their operations. At any rate, a newsletter tells of great numbers of countrymen laying down their arms and protesting 'that they will not joyne with those that have a most horrid design against the Parliament and City'.[146] Certainly in no county was the line between petitioning and militant insurgency more thinly drawn than in Kent, not least because of the repressive measures taken by Weldon and the county committee against petitioners.[147] Indeed, it is not easy to discern whether the creation of an insurgent force or the obtaining of hands to the Kent petition was the main purpose of the rendezvous called at Barnham Downs near Canterbury on 24 May. On the previous day the Kentish gentlemen who had been entrusted as commissioners ordered Colonel Robert Hammon to raise a regiment of foot whose purpose was defined as 'the more safe and speedy expedition in prefering the general Petition of this county'. Hammon seized the Canterbury magazine, beat drums in the streets and enlisted considerable numbers of men – 'more', suggests Matthew Carter, 'than ever were enlisted by one man in so short a time'. But the turnout at the rendezvous on Barnham Downs was ruined by atrocious weather, less than 600 appearing when great things had been hoped for. It was at a later and better-attended rendezvous at the same place that choice fell on Lord Goring, the earl of Norwich, as commander of the Kentish force, the duke of Richmond, who lived at Cobham, having declined the honour when it was offered to him.[148] Norwich's conduct of the subsequent campaign is vigorously defended by his Quartermaster General Matthew Carter, who indignantly repudiates the charge that the earl's reprieve from execution in 1649 was ascribable to his having let down the insurgent cause by refusing to throw in reinforcements at Maidstone. Carter's account is at great pains to emphasize that Norwich had accepted the offer of the command reluctantly, not only because of his lack of military experience but also because he hoped to act as caretaker for Richmond who might yet be persuaded.[149]

This simultaneous organization of the Kentish petition and the mobilization of an armed force to protect the petitioners from molestation by the county committee is crucial to an understanding of the origins of the Second Civil War in Kent. The link between petitioning and insurgency is eloquently epitomized in the Engagement which was part of the Kentish Remonstrance and which bound Engagers to effective opposition to all attempting to prevent the organization and

146. *The Last Newes from Kent* (May 1648), BL., E.445(9), no pagination.
147. On this, see above, pp. 145–8.
148. Carter, *True Relation*, pp. 30–2, 67–71.
149. Ibid., pp. 75–7.

presentation of the petition.[150] All this made for an extremely volatile situation in which armed petitioners could be transformed into armed insurgents in a matter of hours. Indeed one pamphlet sees armed revolt as the petitioners' aim from the outset: and the House of Commons declared on 17 July that 'the Petition was the occasion of that Rising',[151] whereas it would have been more accurate to attribute the rising to the county committee's attempts to inhibit and harass the petitioners. To Roger L'Estrange, a Cavalier from outside Kent, the ambivalence between petitioning and positive insurgency was a fundamental and debilitating defect. L'Estrange observes that he had urged that at the rendezvous at Barnham Downs it should be announed 'at the head of every Troop and Company . . . *That wee were no longer Petitioners but Souldiers . . .*' and those who disapproved should take themselves off home, provided they left their weapons behind. Such an exodus would not be inconvenient, 'for we had many Souldiers that *wanted* [viz. lacked] Armes, and many Country People that were weary of them'.[152]

Similarly in beleaguered Colchester, where there were many Kent as well as Essex insurgents, one observer was to note in July that their real strength was to be found in the core Cavaliers 'who were to be confided in [to] carry out the work, and not raw discontented countreymen who onely long for peace'.[153] In Essex, as in Kent, supporters of the county petition formed an important source of insurgent recruits.[154] A great many petitioners were among the crowds at Chelmsford addressed on more than one occasion by Sir Charles Lucas whose military prowess was not in doubt, but who had now clearly developed other skills. Like their Kentish counterparts, many of the Essex petitioners seem to have been aggrieved moderates rather than thoroughgoing Cavaliers. Some of the latter expressed doubts about their commitment to the royalist cause, arguing that 'though they engros'd our body, [they] scarce strengthened our party'. It is indeed not unlikely that some of these petitioners were among the least committed of the Essex insurgents and prominent among the thousand or so recruits who melted away at the offer of indemnity from the Essex committee.[155] But it would be very wrong to tar them all with this brush: certainly not Sir William Hix,

---

150. Ibid., pp. 29–30; *A Remonstrance Shewing the Occasion of the Arming of Kent* (May 1648), BL., 669, f12(34). See also Everitt, *Kent*, pp. 241–2.
151. BL., E.446(18), p. 3; *C.J.*, V, 637.
152. *L'Estrange His Vindication*, sig. D2.
153. *Sad and dangerous Tydings from Colchester* (29 July 1648), BL., E.456(5), p. 3.
154. On insurgent recruitment in Essex I am heavily indebted to the late B.P. Lyndon's uncompleted draft Ph.D thesis (hereafter Lyndon, Thesis), especially pp. 1–46. See also B.P. Lyndon, 'Essex and the King's Cause in 1648', *Hist. J.*, XXIX (1986), 17–39.
155. Lyndon, Thesis, p. 8.

whom we have already observed playing a leading part in the organization and presentation of the petition; or Giles Jocelyn; or William Banson of Clavering, to cite but three examples.[156] Banson indeed had impeccable royalist credentials. He had been prominent in the collection of Ship Money in the 1630s as well as in collecting signatures to the petition of 1648. He and his son were later to be accused of having 'vented very dangerous speeches against ye Parliament, the General & Army', and he was prominent at Chelmsford in getting recruits for the insurgent cause. As to the manner of his recruiting, articles exhibited against him in April 1649 contained a deposition from one Thomas Mullen, who alleged that Banson had said to him: 'hath your father three lusty sonnes & will none of them now stirr for the King?' When Mullen inquired whether Banson himself was prepared to go to fight, this provoked an angry and theatrical retort in which Banson

> swore, drawing his sword halfe out, [that] if Sir Tho. ffairfax were as neere to him as to the Deponent, hee would sheath his sword in his body as hee did into his scabard. And further said yt those that did not engage now vnder the Lord Goring & Lucas against the Parliament, we would not leave them with a groate.[157]

As in other counties, there are numerous other examples of Essex men undertaking to provide, equip and pay men to serve with the insurgent force in Colchester and elsewhere.[158]

Among those recruited by Banson were defectors from the county trained bands.[159] In a letter to Speaker Lenthall on 4 July, Sir Thomas Honeywood stated that about half of the Essex trained bandsmen had defected to the insurgents, some from his own regiment.[160] But the main group of such defectors was led by Lieutenant-Colonel Henry Farr, the commander of the earl of Warwick's regiment. Among the prisoners taken in an engagement on 13 June were bandsmen who averred that Farr had led them into the field by ordering a muster but failing to reveal his intention of revolting against parliament. On the fall of Colchester at the end of August, this was charged against Farr, who was adjudged to suffer the death penalty along with Lucas, Lisle and the

---

156. On Hix's role in furthering the petition, see above, pp. 143, 144. On his involvement in the choice of Lucas as leader and the bringing in of the insurgents from Kent, Bodleian, Tanner MSS., 57, fo. 361. On Jocelyn's part in both petitioning and recruiting, PRO., SP. 19/135, p. 97. On Banson, see below.
157. Information about Banson's activities is derived from allegations and depositions in PRO., SP. 19/129, pp. 34–9.
158. E.g. in PRO., SP. 19/21, pp. 183, 187, 191; Cal.CAM., II, 983, 1052–3, III, 1056.
159. PRO., SP. 19/129, p. 35.
160. HMC., 13th Report . . . Portland MSS., I, 473.

Italian Sir Bernard Gascoigne, but was nowhere to be found.[161] Of all counties Essex provides the most spectacular, but certainly not the only, example of defections from the county militia.[162] Nor will it surprise readers of the previous chapter that disbanded soldiers or reformadoes were quite prominent among the insurgents in both Essex and Kent. As to deserters from the New Model Army, during the third week in September two soldiers of Colonel Barkstead's regiment were sentenced to death at Yarmouth for deserting to the enemy at Colchester though one of them was subsequently reprieved.[163]

Another important source of recruits came from the volunteers raised in Hertfordshire by Lord Capel under the terms of the commission from Prince Charles.[164] On 9 June it was reported in parliament that Capel was very actively engaged 'to draw the Ignorant, Discontented and Disaffected People in that County into Rebellion'; among them Sir Thomas Fanshaw of Ware Park and Sir John Watts of Mardocks, also near Ware. On the following day another letter brought the alarming news that Lucas's and Norwich's combined forces at Chelmsford had gained a substantial accession of strength through the arrival of the cavalry brought by Capel, accompanied by 'blind Henry Hastings', the one-eyed Lord Loughborough, both of whom were experienced, though not very successful, royalist commanders of the First Civil War. The junction achieved, the combined force was preparing to strike north to make contact with Langdale. Northwards indeed they went, but they got no further than Colchester.[165]

According to a careful estimate by the late Brian Lyndon the approximate number of insurgents at the time of the beginning of the siege of Colchester in mid-June was around 5,600, with an unusually high proportion of officers to private soldiers; at the time of the capitulation of Colchester, the ratio of colonels and company officers to private soldiers was 1:255.6 and 1:105–7 respectively.[166] If government sources

161. *A True and Exact Relation of the Taking of Colchester* (August 1648), BL., E.461(24), p. 3; Lyndon, Thesis, pp. 6–8. Gascoigne was reprieved and Lucas and Lisle were shot. Farr escaped detection.
162. There is an example of a Sussex trained band captain defecting to the insurgents at Horsham in *Cal.CAM.*, III, 1233.
163. On the reformadoes, see Fairfax's letter of 27 October to Speaker Lenthall recommending that they be sent to Ireland (Bodleian, Tanner MSS., 57, fo. 391). On the deserters, see Rushworth, *Historical Collections*, VII, 1271.
164. A copy of Capel's commission is in Hertford, Hertfordshire RO., M287.
165. Rushworth, *Historical Collections*, VII, 1146, 1147; Carter, *True Relation*, p. 101; Kingston, *Hertfordshire*, p. 81. This last and normally reliable local historian mistakenly puts the point of juncture at Colchester not Chelmsford. On Capel, see R. Hutton, *The Royalist War Effort*, especially pp. 51, 59–67, 108, 122–4; Newman, *Royalist Officers*, pp. 58–9. On Loughborough, see ibid., pp. 179–80.
166. Calculations in Lyndon, Thesis, pp. 3–4. The information from which they are drawn is in lists of the defenders who surrendered (Bodleian, Fairfax MSS., 32, fo. 166; *L.J.*, X, 478).

are to be believed, all males between the ages of sixteen and sixty were conscripted in those parts of Essex which were under insurgent control. Certainly the townsmen of Colchester were subject to conscription. On 5 July the royalist Council of War in Colchester called for all adult townsmen to serve in the line under Lucas, who was, of course, a local man. That this amounted to less than total conscription seems, however, to be indicated by the fact that all who did not serve were to surrender their arms on pain of death. But not all those recruited in Colchester itself were pressed men. Some bay weavers and unemployed poor, their livelihood threatened both by economic recession and by the circumstances of the siege, enlisted voluntarily and helped to swell the size of Lucas's regiment to almost 800 men.[167]

Many enthusiastic recruits came from London to join both the Essex and the Kent risings. The City, as has been observed, kept out of the war and refused to offer passage either to the Kent petitioners bound for Westminster or later to the remnants of the defeated Kentish force seeking to join their Essex allies. But neither the City authorities nor the government were able to prevent Londoners, many of them apprentices and other youngsters, from venting their frustration at what they regarded as the City's spineless failure to aid the royalist cause, which they did by migrating in large numbers to join the rebel forces. On 30 June it was given out by the defenders of Colchester that a further 700 London apprentices bringing four pieces of ordnance had already reached Chelmsford on their way to relieve Colchester. This no doubt was a flight of insurgent fancy comparable with the rumour that Langdale was on his way to Colchester. But it nevertheless testifies to the healthy respect in which those apprentices who were already in Colchester were held by the other defenders of the town.[168] This was not, however, true of enlisted apprentices everywhere. For instance, thirty or so of the prisoners taken in the engagement with the Prince of Wales's landing party near Deal in Kent on 14 August were youths 'who cried Quarter for Gods sake, we are Apprentices of London'.[169]

Other recruits coming from London, though not all of them Londoners, included some fifty gentlemen who arranged to rendezvous at Hyde Park Corner early in June, marched all night, forced their way through a parliamentary force at Epping and joined the Essex insurgents at Brentwood on the following day.[170] There were in fact several hundred Londoners among the prisoners taken at the surrender of

167. Carter, True Relation, p. 122; Lyndon, Thesis, pp. 8–9.
168. Carter, True Relation, p. 101; Rushworth, Historical Collections, VII, 1172; HMC., 12th Report . . . (Duke of Beaufort's MSS.), p. 29; BL., E.451(8), p. 5; Lyndon, Thesis, pp. 9–10.
169. Rushworth, Historical Collections, VII, 1228.
170. Carter, True Relation, p. 102.

Colchester.[171] One can only guess at the considerations which impelled a man such as the Stepney grocer Richard Riglesworth to leave his business and join Lucas, Capel and Norwich at Colchester.[172] And other Londoners, such as the London merchant John Smith, who did not go themselves, could make their contribution by sending men to Colchester and undertaking the charge of paying and equipping them.[173] Londoners were also to be found participating in risings much further from home than the Home Counties, though obviously in lesser numbers. For instance, a report from Carmarthen on 3 May tells of the Welsh insurgent ranks being swelled by 'divers Porters, Butchers and such like rascally fellowes come hither from *London*'.[174]

Of the attempts to recruit for the king in Bristol and Bath in late April, of the abortive rising around Tavistock in late July, and of the plan in August and before to raise 800 horse and foot for a general rising in the west under the marquis of Hertford, little need be said since these risings, and especially the last, hardly got off the ground, so that the weekly purchases in London and dispatch to the West Country of riderless horses was all in vain.[175] Of the procedures whereby Cavalier recruits were raised abroad to take part in projected invasions of England or expeditions such as the attempted relief of Deal Castle in August all too little is known. On 12 July, when the eleven revolted ships were preparing to take part in such a projected invasion, a newssheet tells of a royalist recruiting campaign in Holland. Drums were beaten up in the streets of Rotterdam, where it was proclaimed that 'all Gentlemen souldiers who had a desire to serve the King of England under . . . the Lord *Hopton* should repair to the signe of the Prince of *Orange* in Broad-street'. Old Cavaliers had come in some numbers out of France to enlist in Holland, giving out that they had a design for England. But like so many other royalist designs in 1648, this came to nothing.[176]

171. Rushworth, *Historical Collections*, VII, 1249.
172. PRO., SP. 19/22, p. 63, 19/142, p. 17; *Cal.CAM.*, III, 1247. Riglesworth was informed against in July 1650.
173. PRO., SP. 21/19, p. 191; *Cal.CAM.*, II, 1061. Smith himself had Essex interests, having a residence at Low Layton.
174. *Another great fight in Wales* (May 1648), Codrington pamphlet coll., p. 5.
175. On Bristol and Bath, see Rushworth, *Historical Collections*, VII, 1097; 'The Copy of a letter from Bristoll', sub *The Designes of the Lord Inchequin [sic]* . . . (April 1648), Codrington pamphlet coll., pp. 3–4; J. Wroughton, *The Civil War in Bath and North Somerset 1642–1650* (Bath, 1973), pp. 114–15; and above, p. 362. On Devon and Tavistock (wrongly assumed by the source to be in Cornwall), *The Resolution of the Kings Subjects in Cornwall* . . . (28 July 1648), BL., E.456(18), pp. 1–2. On plans for a general rising and the purchase and dispatch of horses, Washington, DC., Folger Shakespeare Library, Folger MSS., Xd, 483(23).
176. *The Declaration of the Hollanders Concerning their joyning with the Royall Navie* (12 July 1648), BL., E.453(2), pp. 3–4.

Under insurgent rule: two case studies

Only in very few parts of the country during the Second Civil War did the insurgents succeed in establishing themselves for long enough to make any lasting impact. In one region where they did, Pembrokeshire and south-west Wales, something was said in the last chapter about the outrages which Poyer visited upon the local population.[177] In North Wales an undated petition from the self-styled 'well-affected' of Anglesey presented weeks after the surrender of the island, complained of the tyranny which had been exercised over them by Bulkeley and the Cavaliers during the previous summer. According to this complaint, vast sums of money – over £7,000 in September alone – were extorted by them, '& yᵉ same put in their owne purses', and many had been arbitrarily imprisoned rather in the manner in which Poyer had imprisoned those who displeased him. When, in August and September, the delinquents had waged a second war against parliament, they killed many of the well-affected and threatened to burn the houses of all refusing to join them and hang them at their doors. It was further cause of complaint that, despite the departure of the Bulkeleys and Byron, other delinquents were still occupying positions of power and authority in the island.[178]

The remainder of this section is devoted to what is known about life in two areas where the insurgents held sway for a longer period: the domination of the Cavaliers and Scots in the north-west; and of the beleaguered Essex and Kent royalists in Colchester.

Writing to his patron Lord Wharton in London on 25 August, the Westmorland parson Francis Higginson told of how 'Westmorland is now, Sir, made a miserable County'. The price of bread had risen more than sixfold and other foodstuffs likewise, and there was only one beast in ten left in the county due to Scottish requisitioning and plundering. Whole villages had been virtually depopulated as the inhabitants had taken refuge in the dales from the coming of the Scots and the Cavaliers. The latter had revived the use of the Prayer Book and the hated and abolished ceremonies and rituals. Before the battle of Preston on 17 August, the Cavaliers had been boastful and 'spoke of nothing but blood, death, slaughter . . . for all that have adhered to . . . the parliament'.[179] Higginson's own father had been incarcerated in Lancaster Castle. The Scots had taken some of their prisoners south with them even after their defeat at Preston. One Westmorland parson, 'after two

177. See above, pp. 416–17.
178. Aberystwyth, National Library of Wales, Llanfair and Brynodol MSS., P 505.
179. Bodleian, Carte MSS., 103, fos. 167–7(b).

nights imprisonment in the loathsome church of Preston, was sent
to wiggan', though he shortly afterwards obtained his release.[180]
Higginson's account mentions the parish of Orton as suffering particular
devastation. If a deposition brought against him in May 1651 is to be
believed, Thomas Birkbecke, the blacksmith of Orton, was one of the
chief plunderers there, as well as purchasing goods which had been
plundered by other insurgents including a cow worth £5 for which he
paid fifteen shillings, and two other beasts and a mare from the Scots.[181]

The Rev. Henry Massy tells a similar tale in another letter to Lord
Wharton on 16 September which relates how eighty of Wharton's
tenants' houses had been burnt by the enemy who had continued to
engage in plunder after their defeat at Preston. As the inhabitants of
many parts of the south-west of England had discovered late in 1645,
being exposed to the ravages of a beaten and disorderly army could be
even worse than subjection to a triumphant one. Massy's own house
had been devastated, his books and notes carried off and he valued his
personal losses at around £500. All his local friends had fled for safety
elsewhere, and he himself had found refuge as far away as Chester.[182]
When, unlike Massy, Higginson returned to his benefice at Kirkby
Lonsdale as soon as the Scots and the Cavaliers had departed, he found
that his losses were less than he had feared, though bad enough in all
conscience. For instance, the Scots had taken all the wood that they
could lay their hands on for fuel, including a bedstead which Lord
Wharton had originally given to Higginson when he had first come into
the district. As to the Lake District in general, 'this Country hath been
so far impoverished . . . that men generally think it will scarce recover
itself in 7 yeeres of Peace'.[183]

Among the refugees who fled for safety were the members of the
Lancashire county committee who left Lancaster and established themselves in the comparative safety of Manchester. Writing to that
committee in early August, two inhabitants of Lancaster paint a horrific
picture of the outrages in Westmorland and north Lancashire. All the
best sheep, cattle and horses had been driven off except for some
miserable milch kine. People had been evicted from their homes
'because Duke *Hamilton* hath told them it should be so'. Women had

---

180.   Carlisle, Cumbria R.O., D/Lec/164/1648 (Cockermouth Castle, Lord Egremont's
       Archive). I am indebted to Mr D.M. Bowcock for this reference.
181.   P.R.O., SP. 23/171, p. 125. Three other Westmorland men of the same surname are
       reported as being in arms against parliament in 1648 and a fourth as getting himself
       released from conscription by sending a substitute (ibid., pp. 113, 115).
182.   Bodleian, Rawlinson Letters, 52, no. 53. In a later letter Massy estimated his losses
       at £600 (ibid., no. 57).
183.   Ibid., no. 56.

been abominably and men barbarously used, even local Cavaliers.[184] Another account of 14 August from Preston confirms the above details but adds even more horrible outrages: among them that the Scots

> take children from their Parents, and put them to redeem them; and some have redeemed their children four times over; and when no redemption money could be had, they have killed the children. . . . They ask people if they have taken the Covenant, [and] if they answer they have, they plunder them . . . as enemies to the King; if they have not . . . they are plundered as Sectaries and Cavaliers: so that their oppressions are most insufferable.[185]

Horror stories, of course, abound in all wars and it is not always easy to distinguish between truth and propaganda fiction. The fact that the relative restraint of Higginson's account commands belief does not, however, necessarily mean that more lurid tales of the horrors of rape, murder and plunder may not at least have an element of truth, however overdone these descriptions might be. Northumberland also suffered grievously from Scottish plundering. A newsletter of 14 September from Newcastle reported that Cromwell and Lambert were hot in pursuit of Monroe and the Scots, determined, amongst other things, to recover the goods and cattle which had been plundered from local inhabitants. Report had it that Sir Thomas Fenwick had suffered damage amounting to about £2,000 from Scottish plundering, and that the sheriff of Northumberland had also lost much. Scottish depredations of sheep and cattle had been so great that there was insufficient meat to quarter a regiment in the county.[186]

Against this view of plunder, violence and disorder may be set an order of 21 August issued by Sir Philip Musgrave and the Commissioners of the Bottom of Westmorland, which gives an impression, which is no doubt somewhat exaggerated in the opposite direction, of a reasonably orderly conduct of affairs. For Cavalier power was drastically reduced but not entirely broken in the north-west immediately after the débâcle at Preston four days earlier. The order makes provision for a tax of £200 per month to be levied from the district towards the maintenance of the insurgent garrison at Appleby. Emphasis was significantly laid on assessment being made 'according to the old wonted

---

184. *Severall Letters of Complaint from the Northern parts* (2 August 1648), BL., E.459(7), pp. 3–4.

185. *Strange and Terrible Newes from Colchester and the Scottish Army* (16 August 1648), BL., E.459(24), p. 6.

186. *The Declaration of Lieutenant-Generall Cromwell* (14 September 1648), BL., E.464(9), pp. 2, 5–6; *Bloudy Newes from the North* (18 September 1648), E.464(27), pp. 4–5 (corrected pagination).

course'. The lands of those revolting against the king and those who had fled the region were to be seized and all others suspected of disaffection were to be examined. No-one was to levy volunteers without authority and there was to be no unauthorized collection of levies or composition money. The impression is one of severity towards the insurgents' enemies but certainly not one of indiscriminate Cavalier licence.[187] It was not until the relief of Cockermouth Castle on 2 October and the surrender of Musgrave and many other Cavaliers at Appleby a week later that the last remnants of insurgent rule were ended.

Some details were given in the last chapter of the privations of the inhabitants of Scarborough under the rule of the defecting governor Sir Matthew Boynton, though their lot does not seem to have notably improved after the town fell in September and the castle in December.[188] But of all insurgent strongholds, the material relating to besieged Colchester is by far the most voluminous, much of it parliamentary and royalist propaganda, in addition to the level-headed account of the man on the spot, the annalist of the Kent and Essex risings, Matthew Carter. With this last notable exception, it is probably true that the royalist accounts tended over time to become the more biassed and exaggerated if only for the reason that, as the parliamentary stranglehold tightened, exaggeration became increasingly necessary if the hopes of insurgents were not to founder completely, whereas sheer veracity sufficed to afford encouragement to their enemies. This should not, however, be taken to mean that parliamentary propagandists were never distinctly economical with the truth. Some of the stories which abounded about royalist atrocities were, when not complete fabrications, at least gross exaggerations, and need to be treated with great caution. Houses, for instance, were fired all round the town. According to Matthew Carter, this was done for the military purpose of creating clear fields of fire for the defenders, but, according to the other side, this was part of an orgy of Cavalier destruction. Some of the royalist commanders had experience of continental warfare, and it was said that they emulated the Thirty Years War practice of exacting 'fire money' from householders ranging from £14 to £40 a house. Worse, having exacted such sums, they fired the houses notwithstanding, and whole streets were said to have been reduced to ashes.[189]

187. Kendal, Cumbria R.O., WD/RY/HMC. 202; *HMC., 12th Report Appendix VII, Le Fleming MSS.*, pp. 19–20.
188. On this see an undated draft letter in Northallerton, North Yorkshire R.O., MIC/1320/1206.
189. For the conflicting views on 'firing', see Carter, *True Relation*, pp. 150–1, and *Colchesters Teares . . .* (July 1648), BL., E.455(16), pp. 9, 10–11. On 'fire money' in the First Civil War, see I. Roy, 'England turned Germany? The Aftermath of the Civil War in its European Context', *TRHS.*, 5th ser., XXVIII (1978), 136.

There were numerous reported cases of rape and other associated atrocities. One particularly notorious example of which much was made by a government propagandist related to a maidservant who, trying to protect her mistress from the lascivious attentions of the insurgent soldiers, had lighted matches tied to her fingers which were burnt to the stumps.[190] Such horror stories apart, the privations suffered by both garrison and inhabitants increased as food supplies diminished with the tightening of Fairfax's blockade. For a long time royalist news-sheets played down these shortages,[191] and indeed the discovery in the early days of the siege of large quantities of rye, salt and wine stored at the Hythe in the eastern suburbs of Colchester sustained the garrison for eleven weeks, 'and without it wee could not have subsisted five days'.[192] It was said that Fairfax's slowness in closing the besieging line around the town made possible this windfall, but, once this was done, however tardily, food shortages became chronic. One account tells of the garrison subsisting for six weeks mainly on horseflesh and, for the last three days of the siege, entirely without bread. By that time there were also only three barrels of gunpowder left.[193] It was during the second week of August, Carter tells us, that horseflesh became 'as precious to us as the choicest meats before, the soldiers in general and all officers . . . eating nothing else unless cats and dogs'. Every day stables were robbed of horses which were sold in the shambles by the pound, and soldiers tempted dogs in the streets with morsels of bread, and then knocked their brains out with their muskets. A side of dog could fetch at least six shillings.[194]

Things became even worse as the siege drew to its close. On 24 August it was reported that some of the garrison had been killed trying to get their hands on one of the enemy's horses which had been killed outside the walls. Undeterred, others came back the next day and cut off lumps of the now stinking flesh. By comparison, what the same source describes as the staple diet, puddings or pancakes made of starch, currants and sugar, appears relatively palatable. One prisoner from Colchester also mentions such pancakes, as well as the shortage of salt for preserving horsemeat, and that two carrots cost a penny as did a single parsnip.[195]

190. *Colchesters Teares* . . . , p. 10.
191. E.g. *Mercurius Aulicus number 4* (21/28 August 1648), BL., E.461(5), p. 31; *The Royall Diurnall number 5* (22/29 August 1648), E.461(13), no pagination.
192. *HMC., 12th Report . . . (Duke of Beaufort's MSS.)*, pp. 25, 26, 28; Carter, *True Relation*, pp. 114–15.
193. *A True and perfect Relation of the Condition of those Noblemen and Gentlemen in Colchester* (September 1648), BL., E.462(16), p. 5.
194. Carter, *True Relation*, pp. 147–8. For even worse conditions at the end of the siege, see ibid., pp. 159–60.
195. Rushworth, *Historical Collections*, VII, 1237; *Terrible Newes from Colchester* (24 August 1648), BL., E.460(37), pp. 4, 6; Oxford, Worcester College, Clarke MSS., 114, fo. 60(b).

Unlike royalist apologists, pro-government newsletters and other accounts say nothing about a beneficent garrison sharing its miserable food supplies with the famished inhabitants. More to their taste are horror stories such as that of a royalist officer who replied to a woman complaining that she and her child were starving: 'God dam me, That child would make a good deal of meat well boyld'.[196] This is perhaps a variant of the tale told by deserters from Colchester on 18 August, that, when women and children were clamouring at Norwich's door for bread, they were told that they must eat their children if necessary. On 17 August a woman with five children, one at her breast, beseeched the besieging soldiers at the gates to let her leave the town, but, since there were many others watching to see if she was successful, she had to be refused, hard though it was. According to the soldiers, the same woman had told them that, 'could they get but Dogs and Cats to eat, it was happy for them, but all the Dogs and Cats and most of the Horses are near eaten already'.[197]

On 22 August Norwich wrote to Fairfax desiring that the non-combatant inhabitants be allowed to leave Colchester, but since this would have the effect of prolonging insurgent resistance by reducing the demand on a by now exiguous food supply, his request was refused. On the following day Norwich sent out some 500 women

> who with much Confidence moved towards Colonel Rainsborough's Quarters; he commanded a Cannon to be shot off, but so as not to hurt them; they came on notwithstanding; he orders the firing of some Musquets . . . ; that daunts them not: he sends out some Soldiers, bids them strip some, this makes them run: but Four were stripped; the Town refuses to let them in; they stand between both. The General [viz. Fairfax] . . . tells them [viz. the insurgents] . . . they shall answer for their Blood; they regard not that.[198]

With these agonizing circumstances in mind, it is perhaps difficult to feel much regret about Rainsborough's earlier humiliation at the hands of the mutinous sailors the previous May, or even his later assassination by Morrice's soldiers at Doncaster in October; or to express relief at the reprieve which saved Norwich from execution early in the following year. The Second Civil War is no exception to the rule that the hatreds and cruelties which characterize civil wars are at least as horrifying as those in international conflicts. And while gentlemanly considerations

---

196. *Colchesters Teares . . .*, pp. 9–10.
197. Rushworth, *Historical Collections*, VII, 1232–3; Whitelock, *Memorials*, p. 325 (19 August).
198. Rushworth, *Historical Collections*, VII, 1236–7.

have prompted historians to deplore the summary executions of Sir Charles Lucas and Sir George Lisle after the fall of Colchester, it is surely at least as appropriate to bewail the misfortunes of the hapless inhabitants of that town, and especially the women and children, bullied, starved and molested in a conflict in which their own concern was at most marginal.

XIII

CONCLUSION

We . . . have . . . reviewed to the lowest stone this new raised war,
breaking out under colour of defence of his Majestie and our own
right of petitioning. And some of us have told some of the ringleaders
in this sad cause that if they . . . would give us some assurance that
his Majestie would governe (if once advanced by conquest) by
Parliamentary and not by absolute Soveraignty . . . we should . . . freely
have closed on that side.

But after to our great amazement the ringleaders of that great designe
confessed themselves uncertaine in their grounds . . . we clearly saw the
too rigid, angry and undone spirits of the Kings old Souldiers reaching
further then we professe our hopes could follow in the pursuance of the
kingdomes peace thereby. . . .

Colchesters Teares . . . Dropping from the face of a new Warr
(July 1648), BL., E.455(16), pp. 4–5

It was Dr Valerie Pearl who, in a seminal essay, characterized the
tumults in London in late July 1647 and the events of the subsequent
days as a counter-revolution which in a sense prefigured the greater
counter-revolution which was to follow, though not in London, in the
next year.[1] The term, of course, is something of an anachronism, but
even if it had been current at the time, parliamentary Presbyterians such
as Denzil Holles and Sir Philip Stapleton and their civic allies such as
Lord Mayor Gayre would have repudiated it as a characterization of
their own aims and aspirations. Rather they would have seen themselves
as the champions of parliament's original war aims of 1642. Clearly they
sought to restore the king; but to his constitutional position at the end
of 1641 not at the beginning of 1640. This position they saw as being
under threat from a disobedient and rebellious army. They discounted
the apparent moderation of the constitutional settlement favoured
by the Council of the Army that summer, choosing instead to believe
that the army's seizure of the king on 4 June betokened republican and

---

1.   V. Pearl, 'London's Counter-revolution', in Aylmer, *Interregnum*, pp. 29–56.

even regicidal intentions. In reality, however, opinion within the army began to move significantly towards such extremes only after Charles's flight from Hampton Court in the following November, and, in the case of the army commanders, not until much later still; the product of the outbreak of the Second Civil War and the subsequent treaty with the king in the Isle of Wight. In the eyes of the soldiers and their parliamentary allies that treaty appeared to be all too likely to concede to the king most of what his beaten armies had fought for in two bloody civil wars.

It is, of course, undeniable that the 'Presbyterian' counter-revolution in London in July 1647 was supported by Cavaliers many of whom were all too conspicuous among the crowds which stormed parliament on 26 July. Nevertheless, if one compares the London counter-revolutionaries of that time with those who had risen in Glamorgan in the previous month, a contrast immediately becomes apparent. The leaders of the Glamorgan rising were all Cavaliers, even if they did make a bid for wider support by claiming to be battling against the committee tyrannies which had antagonized sections of the community stretching far outside the ranks of the local royalists. Paradoxically, however, while the leadership of the English risings in the Second Civil War was overwhelmingly Cavalier, this is true of the Glamorgan rising of June 1647 but not of the far more serious revolts in South (though not in North) Wales in 1648. These, by contrast, were set off and led by ex-parliamentarian general and field officers, Major-General Rowland Laugharne and Colonels John Poyer and Rice Powell. Although these men, and especially Poyer, came to embrace Cavalier aspirations, or at least to utter Cavalier slogans, they had stood aside from the Cavalier revolt in Glamorgan in June 1647, and even, in Laugharne's case, had actually helped to suppress it. Far more striking than the fact that these parliamentary renegades were joined in 1648 by some notable Cavaliers such as Major-General Stradling is the refusal of many Welsh Cavalier grandees, and notably the earl of Carbery, to have anything to do with them. There is a very real sense in which the leaders of the insurgents in South Wales in 1648 had more in common with the London counter-revolutionaries of July 1647 than with those in Glamorgan in June 1647. This is not, of course, to claim them as parliamentary Presbyterians like the leaders of the City of London at that time; or rather, if there were parliamentary Presbyterians in 1647 with whom they might feel real affinity, it was with the likes of the anti-New Model Army generals, Sir William Waller, Edward Massey and Sydenham Poynz, who, however, unlike Laugharne, Poyer and Powell, did not rise to the counter-revolutionary bait in 1648.

These disgruntled Welsh officers ultimately came to identify their own aims with those of the royalists, just as the anti-committee insurgents in Kent came to identify theirs via the slogan 'for God, King Charles and Kent'. The risings in the Second Civil War were at best tenuous coalitions, the uneasy parties to which were, in the first place, the disgruntled ex-parliamentarian soldiers such as Laugharne, Poyer and Powell in Wales, Lieutenant-Colonel Lilburne in Northumberland and Lieutenant-Colonel Farr in Essex; secondly, moderates alienated by committee tyranny but not aspiring to return to the *status quo ante* 1641; and finally, thoroughgoing Cavaliers such as Goring (Norwich), Byron, Lucas, the Musgraves, Glemham, Lingen and Langdale. How long such a rickety alliance would have survived an insurgent victory is problematical. The quotation which stands at the head of this chapter points up some of the misgivings about the intentions of their potential Cavalier allies which were doubtless entertained by many alienated parliamentarians who wished to restore the king, but not to his powers of the 1630s. A published letter – is it genuine? – from one such Cavalier, Sir Anthony St Leger, a Kentish gentleman, to a Mr Wareham Horsemanden, one of the insurgent defenders of Colchester, in mid-August testifies to these fundamental differences. Writing from aboard one of the revolted ships in the Downs, St Leger promised that those who deserted would eventually get the punishment they deserved, along with Independents and other Roundheads. But the contempt of the true Cavalier for the aims of the moderates is brought out by his observation that: 'Had not the drunken *Dutch* and cowardly *French* deceivived [*sic*] us, we had relieved you long since, and then a figg for the Treaty'![2]

Thus while both the political and a majority of the religious Presbyterians (viz. excluding the 'Presbyterian Independents') were in the forefront of counter-revolution in 1647, at least in parliament and the City of London, the attempt of the insurgents to rally Presbyterian support in 1648 was not notably successful. It certainly did not help that the Scottish allies of the English insurgents had incurred the unequivocal hostility of the Scottish kirk which made, at best, for suspicion, and, at worst, for positive antagonism to them on the part of the English religious Presbyterians. Moreover, English Presbyterians, this time in the political as well as the religious sense of the term, were, as is emphasized above, rightly suspicious of the aims of the Cavaliers who were wooing them, as well as having learned a salutary lesson from the knocks which they had taken in 1647, an argument which applies especially to the government of the City of London. Their attitude was in essentials not dissimilar to that of the author of a pamphlet of August 1648 who deplored 'the actions of those aboard the revolted

2.   *Sir Anthonie St. Leger His Letter from Aboard the Downs* (15 August 1648), BL., E.461(3), pp. 3–4. Italics in original.

ships ... and therefore judge my selfe bound by the National Covenant ... to help to reduce them to their former obedience, whether they impede a Personall Treaty or not'. How different from the summer of 1647 when a Presbyterian's adherence to the Covenant was more likely to impel him to rise up to bring the king to London for a personal treaty with parliament and to put the disobedient army in its place! Yet our author is also at pains to stress that he was in favour of a treaty provided that it was not made to appear that parliament had been pushed into it by insurgent military action.[3] Rather than rise tumultuously as in London in July 1647, Presbyterians now chose to bide their time, which came when parliament agreed to a personal treaty in the Isle of Wight. Here at last was the opportunity to put into effect the aims of their spectacularly unsuccessful rising in London in July 1647 and to restore not the royal absolutism of the 1630s but the constitutionally restrained monarchy of 1641. These aims, of course, were ultimately to be frustrated by another illegal assault on parliament; this time not by a counter-revolutionary mob as in July 1647, but by the army in the persons of Colonel Pride and his men in December 1648.

Brutally aborted as it seemed in December 1648, these aims nevertheless resurfaced on the eve of the Restoration of 1660, only to be snuffed out once again, this time not by an illegal coup by army radicals, regicides and republicans but by the irresistible reaction which was born of the real and imagined fears and apprehensions which were aroused by such extremist elements and which swept Charles II to an unconditional restoration to the throne. As so often in English history, it was the moderates who were the losers. They had lost in 1647 from their own uncharacteristic recourse to immoderate violence to counter what they rightly regarded as the illegal behaviour of the army and its Independent allies in parliament; a counter-revolution which had brought its own Presbyterian anticipation of Pride's Purge on and after 26 July, with the important difference that it was the future purgers who were here purged. In the spring and summer of 1648 by refusing to go along with the royalist risings in Wales and the provinces and the invasion of the Scottish Engagers, the moderates got their all too temporary reward in the revocation of the Vote of No Addresses and the decision to treat with the king in the Isle of Wight. By so doing, however, they courted the wrath of a victorious army by favouring negotiations with the king whom the soldiers had come to regard as the man of blood who had plunged England into a second civil war. As David Underdown has shown, it was the moderates of all political persuasions who were the

3. *The Sea-men undeceived* ... (August 1648), BL., E.459(22), pp. 1–2.

victims of Pride's Purge along with the king and the Cavaliers. In 1660 they lost again in their attempt to revive the aspirations of 1642 and 1647–8 against the tide of Cavalier enthusiasm. The true successors of the parliamentary moderates of these years are perhaps the initiators of the Glorious Revolution of 1688.

INDEX

Adams, Alderman Thomas, 354
Admiralty, Committee of, 146, 439
Adye, John, 462
Agreement of the People (1647), 139
Aldeburgh, Suffolk, 368
Alvey, Rev. Geldard, 246–7
Amsterdam, 329
Anabaptists, see sectaries
Anglesey
    Beaumaris Castle taken, 429; Byron
    in, 431, 446–7, 469; Cavalier tyranny
    in, 469; commission of peace and
    lieutenancy of, 431; insurgent
    manifesto in, 427; petition from, 108,
    469; possible invasion from Ireland,
    341, 446–7; revolt in, 52, 108;
    royalist predominance in, 262
Anglesey, earl of, see Villiers, Charles
Anglicans and Anglicanism
    anachronism of the term, 229; and
    Prayer Book, 229–30, 259, 260, 460;
    and ritualism, 230 235, 243; and
    Sabbath observance, 234–5; attitude
    to lay preaching, 229; chaplains of
    king, 16, 19, 164, 212; confiscation
    of plate of, 225; denounce rebellion
    against king, 230; deny entry to
    intruders, 247–50, 258, 265, 266;
    deny tithes to intruders, 105, 237,
    244, 249, 250–57, 258, 265, 266;
    difficulty in replacing, 246; extruded,
    96, 229, 245, 247–56; hope Scots
    will aid king, 234; horrified at
    iconoclasm, 243; hostile to sectaries,
    229, 243; insurgents revive
    ceremonies, 469; expelled from
    London, 239; intrusion of, 265, 266;
    patronage and, 263–5; preach against
    parliament, 230, 234, 253; reintrusion
    of, 164, 224, 229, 247, 251–2, 253,
    257–62, 265, 266; return after first

war, 246–7; revival of, 5; royalism of,
230; scandalous behaviour of some
of, 229, 230, 234–5, 237, 258n,
263–4; shared views with and
differences from Presbyterians,
229–30, 243, 244, 245, 265; take
church services, 262–3, 280, 369;
violence against intruders, 257,
259–62.
Anselme, Colonel, 395
Antrim, marquis of, see MacDonnell,
    Randal
Appleby, Westmorland, 364, 416, 427,
    429, 471–2
Argyll, earl and marquis of, see Campbell,
    Archibald
Arundell, Cornet, 380
armies, parliamentary
    action against tithe withholders, 252;
    cost and unpopularity of, 43–8, 49;
    disbandment of, 44–5, 54–5, 160,
    161, 222, 347–8, 418–20; excise and
    soldiers of, 75–6; ex-royalist soldiers
    serving in, 60, 62, 99, 348; free
    quarter and, 57–70; Massey's brigade,
    132, 160n; mutinies in, 98–9;
    outrages by soldiers of, 44, 90, 117,
    132, 160 & n; pay in arrears, 98, 99,
    160, 419, 421n; payment of arrears
    to defectors, 399; violence against
    magistrates by soldiers of,
    98–9; see also New Model Army;
    Northern Association, army of
Ashburnham, John
    anti-Scottish views of, 303 & n;
    apprehended in Hampshire, 362; bad
    advice to king, 20, 24, 25, 33;
    complaints about grandees' intimacy
    with, 28–9; criticism of, 27n,
    33 & n; deplores Scots' treatment of
    king, 303; exchanged as a prisoner,

differences of with kirk over Engagement, 328–33; protects and refuses to extradite English fugitives, 332–3, 337, 415; protests against Pride's Purge and king's trial, 337, 338; Sterling informs about his Irish plans, 322;

[Scotland continued]

peace mission of Lanark and Loudoun, 319–20; petition praising Anglo-Scottish amity, 131; petition favouring Scottish presence at treaty, 155; plan to co-ordinate Scottish and Irish offensives in 1648, 321; possible invasion of in 1647, 18, 25, 27–8, 36, 38, 110n, 171, 181, 195, 317, 349, 354; precautions against king's escape from Newcastle, 315; prince invited to, 426, 439, 443; prince promises to protect trading interests of, 439; proposed royal approval of Anglo-Scottish treaties, 38; reaction of to king's abscondence, 323; ready to rescue king from army, 317; religious differences of with England, 301–2; revolted ships and, 411, 428, 439, 447; rising of covenanters in west, 335; settlement of English debt to, 15, 272n, 305, 315; shire committees of war in, 330; war aims of, 316, 451; Wogan's defection to, 332, 415–16; unwilling to resort to armed intervention for king in 646–7, 317, 319–20, 323

Scroope, Colonel Adrian, 408 & n, 409, 443

Second Civil War

additional levies during, 51–2; and Cavalier extremism, 215; and county committees, 97, 105–9, 453; army's victories against odds in, 435; causes of, 1–6; conscription by insurgents in, 455–7, 459; expectations of in 1647, 169, 339–40, 341; failure of insurgent co-ordination in, 423–38; feared dangers of insurgent victory in, 204; free quarter during, 68–70; greater guilt of insurgents in, 423; insurgent demands about taxation in, 452–3; insurgent recruitment in, 220, 454–68; insurgent manifestoes in, 448–50; revolt of Holland, Buckingham and Peterborough in, 107, 400n, 406–8, 427, 433, 436, 443; royalists the hard insurgent core

in, 464; Scottish delays prejudice insurgent opportunities in, 327; supporters of treaty tarred with insurgency brush in, 157; uneasy insurgent coalitions in, 478; victory in at risk through treaty, 41, 178; war aims of insurgents in, 107–8, 448–54; *see also* Ireland; New Model Army; royalists; Scotland; Wales; *and county and place names*

sectaries

alleged role of in counter-revolutionary disturbances, 138; and Levellers, 242; and regicide, 242, 451; call to disarm, 192; charge to present at Lincolnshire sessions, 93, 221, 244; City petition against, 192; complaints against Anabaptists, 242, 243–4; congregations in London, 243; demand toleration, 130; denounced by Scots, 270, 301, 320, 324, 337; excesses of, 1–2, 134, 241–5, 269, 280, 320; iconoclasm of, 243; in army, 164, 242; Independent petitioners represented as, 393; in Lake District, 241; in London, 241–2; lay preaching and, 163–4, 244, 320; not to have freedom of worship, 325; object to tithes, 251; officiate in parish churches, 243–4; ordinance tightening controls on, 140; petitions against, 131, 134, 318; Presbyterian and Anglican dislike of, 96, 135, 140, 229, 241–5, 269; proliferate because of toleration, 241; qualify for office by taking Covenant, 96; radical petitions and, 130, 157n; recruited by Skippon, 192; social and political subversion and, 163, 164, 241–2; suppression of planned, 135, 170; term of abuse applied to parliamentarians, 451

sequestration and compounding

abuses of, 136; compounders may stay in London, 356n; compounding to finance action against insurgents, 363; contribution to funeral expense, 274–5; decentralization of, 48, 108; denial of tithes to sequestrators, 52–3, 253n; Holland sequestrated, 407; no compounding for corrupters of revolted sailors, 441; or 'malignant' parsons, 247–50; Powell and Laugharne allowed to compound, 421–2; royalist coalowners